ACCA
COST AND
MANAGEMENT
ACCOUNTING II

STUDY AND REVISION MANUAL

T. Lucey, M Soc Sc, FCMA, FCCA, J Dip MA

Terry Lucey has been an accountant and consultant in industry and has had over twenty years examining and teaching experience at all levels of professional studies and for diploma and degree courses in business studies. He was previously Head of Department of Business Studies at the Polytechnic, Wolverhampton and is now a consultant and publisher.

Amongst his other published works are:

Investment appraisal — Evaluating Risk and Uncertainty , Accounting and Computer Systems (co-author), Quantitative Techniques, Management Information Systems and Costing.

DP PUBLICATIONS LTD.
Grand Union Industrial Estate — Unit 6
Abbey Road
London NW10 7UL
1988

ACKNOWLEGEMENTS

The author would like to express thanks to the Chartered Association of Certified Accountants for permission to reproduce past examination questions, examiners' reports, syllabus guides and commentaries.

Terminology

An important part of the study of any technical subject is to gain familiarity with the technical terminology used. The Association recommend that students studying for the Cost and Management Accounting II examination become familiar with appropriate definitions from the *Terminology of Management Accounting* published by the Chartered Institute of Management Accountants (CIMA). Accordingly, this manual uses appropriate definitions reproduced from the *Terminology* by kind permission of CIMA.

A CIP catalogue record for this book is available from the British Library

ISBN 1 870941 07 1

Copyright T Lucey © 1988

Printed by The Guernsey Press Co Ltd
Braye Road, Vale,
Guernsey, Channel Islands

STUDY AND REVISION MANUAL

Preface

AIMS OF THE MANUAL

1.   This manual is designed to provide full coverage of the ACCA Cost and Management Accounting II syllabus and contains, *within the one volume*, all the material necessary for both *study* and *revision purposes*. The student who conscientiously works through the whole book, either by self study or as part of a course, will gain a thorough understanding of the theory and practice of management accounting and will be in an excellent position to achieve a first time pass in Paper 2.4, Cost and Management Accounting II.

LAYOUT AND SCOPE OF THE MANUAL

2.   The manual is divided into three main sections as outlined below.

SECTION 1

Main contents
ACCA Paper 2.4 Cost and Management Accounting II, Syllabus, Study Guide and Commentary

SECTION 2

Main Contents:
This is the STUDY section of the manual, the core of the whole book, and consists of:
- study hints
- self contained chapters with numbered paragraphs, practical examples, diagrams, tables
- end of chapter summaries
- self review questions cross references to appropriate paragraphs
- past ACCA examination questions (with answers)
- selection of questions (without answers)

SECTION 3

Main Contents:
The REVISION section of the manual consisting of:
- Revision and examination technique hints
- Examiner's Reports
- Revision check list of essential knowledge by topic area
- Summaries of essential formulae
- Special revision questions with commentary and step-by-step answers
- Examination practice (2 mock examination papers using selected past ACCA questions, with commentary and answers).

ACCA question analysis for the 10 most recent examinations inside back cover

HOW TO USE THE MANUAL EFFECTIVELY

3.   After gaining an initial familiarity with Section 1 of the manual, students are recommended to get into the habit of making continual references to the syllabuses and question analysis so that they become fully aware of ACCA requirements.

The study hints, which are at the beginning of the STUDY section of the manual, should be absorbed before commencing the detailed reading of the various chapters. The chapters should be studied in sequence because they have been arranged so that there is a progressive accumulation of knowledge and any given chapter either includes all the necessary principles or draws upon previous chapters. Each chapter is followed by *self review* questions which you should attempt to answer *unaided* then check your answer with the text. In addition each chapter has a number of past ACCA examination questions. *Always* make an attempt at the examination question before reading the solutions, which are at the back of the section. This is considered an essential part of the learning process which greatly assists genuine understanding.

When the STUDY section has been thoroughly assimilated, Section 3 of the manual can be used as the basis of a planned, thorough revision programme. Within a topic area, the check lists of essential information and concepts should be thought of as the *minimum* necessary for examination success. Do not simply read through the check list and assume you know the item or principle involved. If the check list says you should be able to define, say, opportunity cost - *write your definition down* - and subsequent check this in the study section.

Do not skip any part of your study or revision programme.

SPECIAL NOTES FOR LECTURERS

4.   When the manual is used as a course text, lecturers require a selection of exercises and examination questions *without answers* which can be used for class and home work or for assignments. Accordingly, a selection of exercises and examination questions, over and above those provided for the student analysed by topic, is given at the end of the manual. So that lecturers can demonstrate different viewpoints and approaches the questions have been drawn from a variety of professional bodies, including; ACCA, CIMA, AAT etc. A separate answer guide is available free to lecturers who adopt the manual as a course text.

CONTENTS

SECTION 1

ACCA PAPER 2.4

Cost and Management Accounting II
Syllabus and Study Guide
Syllabus Commentary

ACCA Syllabus

PAPER 2.4 COST AND MANAGEMENT ACCOUNTING II

Content

Section 1 Accounting for products and services

Cost accumulation vs responsibility accounting implications; absorption, marginal and opportunity cost approaches; selling price valuation bases.

Section 2 Budgets and Budgetary Control

Short and long term budgeting. Budget preparation (including cash budgets).

Critical appraisal of budgeting.
Quantitative applications.

Section 3 Standard Costing

Variance analysis: sales and cost variances including input mix variances; flexible budgeting and cost centre variances; planning and operational variances; short and long term standards; standard process costs. Critical appraisal of standard costing.

Section 4 Information for Decision Making

Contribution of management accounting to decision making. cost concepts and measurement of costs for decision making in wide range of situations including pricing.

Use of discounting techniques, probabilities, indices for price and performance level changes.

Section 5 Performance Evaluation and Control

Measurement of divisional performance: monetary and non-monetary measures; critical appraisal of performance measures; inter divisional comparisons. Transfer pricing: cost and selling price based methods; with or without external markets; limited intermediate product situations; decision making and motivational implications.

ACCA Study Guide

PAPER 2.4 COST AND MANAGEMENT ACCOUNTING II

Objectives of the Syllabus

The objectives of the syllabus are to ensure a student has the ability to prepare and analyse accounting data and is able to:

- apply it in a range of planning, control and decision making situations;
- assess its relevance, strengths and weaknesses;
- consider how its use may be amended to accommodate change.

Format and standard of the examination paper

Students will be required to answer 5 or 6 questions out of 7 or 8. Compulsory questions will not be set. The examination paper will test the skills of comprehension, application, analysis and evaluation. The standard of the examination papers will range between that set in the second and third year examinations of a three year UK honours degree course. Students will be assumed to have a thorough understanding of the content of the Level 1 Paper Cost and Management Accounting I, the Economics Paper, 1.3, and of the statistical and financial mathematics studied in Paper 1.5 Business Mathematics and Information Technology. Students who have received exemption from any of these Papers should read the relevant Study Guide(s) to ensure they are familiar with the coverage and approach required. Students are advised to study Paper 2.6 Quantitative Analysis before or at the same time as Paper 2.4

Content	Knowledge Level
Section 1 Accounting for Products and Services	
Cost accumulation versus responsibility accounting implications in the context of job, process and service cost situations.	B
Absorption, marginal and opportunity cost approaches to job cost accumulation.	B

Relevance of cost and selling price valuation bases in process costing for management reporting and control.   B

Problem in relation to common costs, joint products and by-products. Charging of service costs using a range of bases from selling price to nil charge.   B

Section 2 Budgets and Budgetary Control
Short and long term budgeting.   F

Advanced master and subsidiary budget preparation (including cash budgets).   F

Critical appraisal of budgeting systems:
(a) Budget formulation: F
- use of flexible budgets;
- incremental vs zero base budgets;
- single measure or probabilistic approach;
- periodic or continuous.

(b) Behavioural influences: B
- management style: hierarchial vs democratic;
- personal vs corporate aspirations;
- competition for scarce resources;
- budgets as a bargaining process; budgetary slack;
- attainment level.

(c) Budgeting as a multi-purpose activity: F
- use in planning;
- co-ordination;
- control;
- feedback;
- responsibility accounting;
- motivation.

(d) Quantitative applications in budgeting: B
- uses in sales forecasting;
- setting purchases and production batch quantities;
- choice of sales/production mix;
- learning curve theory.

Section 3 Standard Costing
Variance analysis: F
- cost variances including input mix variances;
- sales variances including product mix variances;
- use of weighted average vs individual standards as the base for mix variance calculations (see Horngren: Cost Accounting - A Managerial Emphasis);
- flexible budgeting and cost centre variances;
- planning and operational variances.

Use of short or long term standards.   F

Use of marginal and absorption cost approaches.   F

Standard preparation and variance calculations in process costs.   F

Significance, inter-relationship and analysis of causes of variances.   F

Trend, materiality and controllability of variances.   F

Behavioural implications of standard costing.   B

Section 4 Information for Decision Making

The contribution of management accounting to decision making.   F

Cost concepts and measurement of costs for decision making; as used in decision making
situations such as: F

(a) – adoption of new products;
     – product mix;
     – methods of manufacture;
     – discontinuing product lines;
     – make or buy;
     – sell or further process;
     – shutdown and temporary closure;

(b) – price output decisions;
     – target pricing;
     – special orders;
     – new products;
     – pricing in practice;
     – inflation and price change considerations;
     – demand considerations, elasticity and change.

Section 5 Performance Evaluation and Control

Measurement of divisional performance: F
– use of monetary and non-monetary measures;
– cost, profit, return on investment, residual income;
– physical quantities, percentages, ratios, indices;
– critical appraisal of performance measures in relation to centre and
   managerial performance;
– inter divisional comparisons.

Transfer pricing: F
– cost based and selling price based approaches;
– with or without external markets;
– where limited intermediate product availability exists: optimisation of corporate
   profit; use of shadow prices.

Decision making and motivational implications of the application of various approaches
to transfer pricing.   F

General notes

Questions may incorporate:

(i)   The use of discounting techniques to allow for the time value of cash flows. Tax considerations will not be
included.

(ii) The use of probabilities to allow for uncertainty.

(iii) The use of indices to allow for the impact of changes in the price or performance levels applicable.

(iv) Consideration of non-quantifiable factors relevant in reaching a decision.

(v)   Appraisal of the environment in which the Management Accountant functions and in which specific management
accounting techniques are utilised; contingency theory as applied to management accounting.

The three knowledge levels used are:

–   I   **Introductory**
        Basic understanding of principles, concepts, theories and techniques.

–   B   **Broad**
        Application of principles, concepts, theories and techniques in the solution of straightforward problems.

- **F Full**
  Identification and solution of more complex problems through the selection and application of principles, concepts theories and techniques.

ACCA General comments

'The first paper which will be set by the new Examiner will be sat in December 1987.

Paper 2.4 will build on the knowledge acquired in Paper 1.2 and it will assume that Level 1 knowledge has been retained. Because this area is constantly changing, the paper will test students' ability not only to apply techniques with which they are conversant but also to assess their relevance, their strengths and weaknesses, and to evaluate alternative approaches to the solution of problems using different techniques.

Question in Paper 2.4 to not make specific reference to information technology - the use of spreadsheets or data bases - as these are to be examined in Paper 2.7, Information Systems in Development and Operations.

Students will not be expected to manipulate quantitative techniques for their own sake but any such techniques previously learnt in Level 1 or, indeed, in Paper 2.6, Quantitative Analysis, might be used to analyse information in a problem. For example, in a linear programming application, students could be asked to abstract information from a final tableau given in the question but will not be asked to use the technique by requiring them to formulate and solve the relevant model.

Students should be encouraged to see management accounting as part of an overall information system and not in isolation. It is not restricted to monetary measurements alone, but also includes relevant measurements and ratios based on physical measurements, eg scrap expressed in litres or as a percentage of input quantity.

Problems concerning the application of management accounting to the public sector and not-for-profit organisations are considered to be within the syllabus, although no specialised knowledge of the particular sector will be required.

The format of the paper will be similar to previous papers, with no compulsory questions and a choice of give or six questions to be answered from seven or eight respectively. The first part of the paper will include mainly computational questions but these will also test students' ability to extract information from data given, to apply it, to evaluate it and criticise it. The second part will contain essay questions each with two sections. The standard of questions and the volume of information contained in them will be approximately the same as in recent past papers.

Wherever possible, terminology will be standardised in the questions. However, since this is sometimes impossible to achieve, students should be exposed to as many alternative terminologies as possible.

Students should be advised that variation from the published suggested answers, is and will continue to be, acceptable and they will not be penalised for valid deviation or valid and proper, albeit unusual, approaches. Wherever possible the published answers will provide an explanation of complex calculations rather than merely showing the result.

With regard to the reading guide for Paper 2.4 any one of the texts included in List A should provide sufficient coverage to enable a good student to pass the examination as a whole. However, it is unlikely that any single text will provide sufficient coverage to permit a pass on every question in an examination. No one text covers the whole syllabus.

The application of contingency theory may be examined.

Calculation of working capital may be set but will not be major in nature.

Specific sections

Section 1: Accounting for Products and Services

Some of the topics in this section appear to have been covered already in Paper 1.2. Paper 2.4 will focus more on the relevance of a range of approaches in planning control and decision-making; for example, in process costing it is possible to indicate, within the framework of the accounting system, the incremental profits or losses by using a profit centre approach.

Section 1 will also cover service cost situations and how they might be charged out, for example, nil value or opportunity cost. It will focus on the implications of using these methods particularly in terms of providers and users and their attitudes to the acceptability of the methods.

Papers will be checked to ensure that they clarify whether costs are variable or fixed. If a question does leave students in doubt they will not be penalised provided they make their own assumptions clear to the Examiner and their approach is consistent.

Section 2: Budgets and Budgetary Control

Discounting techniques are introduced in Paper 1.2, therefore some knowledge of discounted cash flows (DCF) may be required for Paper 2.4 where questions incorporate a longer time span. However, the main thrust of DCF will be in Paper 3.2, Financial Management.

Section 3: Standard Costing

With regard to mix and yield variances, the question of input mix variances is relevant in the context of standard process costing in that they are linked to the abnormal losses which occur. Students should be able not only to calculate variances but also to appraise the use of this technique and assess the various ways in which it can be used. They will be expected to understand the concept of making use of a planning and operational approach to variance analysis and why it is of benefit. Questions may consider variance trends and their materiality, and the behavioural implications of standard costing as applied in various situations.

Section 4: Information for Decision-making

Students will be required to have a knowledge of micro economic theory from Paper 1.3 in relation to pricing and to make simple calculations of elasticity in the price demand relationship in a linear context.

Questions on conditional probability and the purchase of perfect and imperfect information may be set in the context of a management accounting problem.

With regard to the consideration of non-quantifiable factors relevant in reaching decisions, students should consider any aspect of the environment economic, IT etc, from their previous studies – which might influence the decisions.

Students will not be expected to utilise partial differentiation in this paper.

Questions will not be set on current cost accounting or current purchasing power but students will be expected to utilise indices.

Section 5: Performance Evaluation and Control

Students will not be required to calculate shadow prices from first principles; they will be given the relevant information in the question and will be expected to demonstrate how shadow pricing could be applied to transfer price situations.' END OF ACCA PUBLISHED MATERIAL ON THE SYLLABUS.

COMMENTARY ON THE REVISED SYLLABUS

The Association have produced comprehensive study guides and commentary on the new Cost and Management Accounting II examination. Students are advised to study these carefully as they provide clear guidance to the thinking behind the new syllabus and what the examiners will be looking for.

Your attention is particularly drawn to the following points:

1. The new syllabus and examination format will apply from the December 1988 examinations.

2. It is stated that Management Accounting must be considered as part of the general information system of the organisation and this is the approach adopted in this manual. There is special chapter on information and management and exploration of the problems of providing relevant information.

3. Throughout the syllabus guides and official commentary there is reference to quantitative and statistical techniques and the specific advice is given to study Paper 2.6 Quantitative Analysis either before Paper 2.4 or concurrently with it. The importance of these techniques is recognised in this manual by including at appropriate places, relevant mathematical and statistical techniques. Examples include; probability in decision making, setting statistical control limits and so on. In addition, because of its particular relevance to accounting and the special mention in the official commentary, Linear Programming (LP) is dealt with in detail in a separate chapter.

4.   The official commentary states that a thorough understanding of Stage I knowledge will be assumed. This includes; costing, economics and aspects of business mathematics. When appropriate in this manual relevant material is incorporated in the text and, because of its central importance there is a revision chapter on cost accounting.

5.   Although the syllabus is divided into sections and topics you must not assume that examination questions - and real life problems - will naturally fall into watertight compartments. Many questions span several areas of the syllabus and this makes them even more testing and, it must be said, more realistic.

6.   Students must develop a questioning, critical attitude to cost and management accounting and the ability to interpret results achieved. In this way genuine understanding is developed rather than simply the mechanical use of standard formulae. This is brought out in the ACCA notes and is stressed repeatedly throughout this manual. You must try to develop this attitude in your studies. Continually ask, why is it done this way? Could it be done differently and better? What are the problems with the conventional approach and assumptions? What do the figures *really* mean?

SECTION 2

THE STUDY MANUAL

Containing 21 chapters covering all aspects of the ACCA Paper 2.4, Cost and Management II Syllabus

EXAMINATION AND STUDY TECHNIQUE

Examinations are important, but they should be the culmination of a period of carefully planned preparation not a frantic last minute attempt to digest sufficient information to scrape up just enough marks to pass. Why? Firstly, because poor preparation turns an examination into an ordeal and lack of confidence about your performance in one examination can affect your performance in other papers taken at the same sitting. Secondly, examinations in cost and management accounting test skills which will be found invaluable in later professional life.

For these reasons a thorough, planned study programme covering all relevant aspects of cost and management accounting is vital both for the immediate target, ie your examination in Paper 2.4 and as an essential element in achieving your longer term goal of becoming a qualified accountant.

HINTS ON HOW TO STUDY

1. Syllabus and Question Analysis

Study thoroughly the syllabus in Section 1 of the manual and familiarise yourself with the pattern of questions set from the Question Analysis. Before studying a topic, for example marginal costing, get into the habit of referring to the syllabus in order to refresh your memory regarding the exact requirements.

2. Allocating your Study Time

Begin by being realistic. Decide how many hours on which days of the week you will be able to study. Then consult your diary, or your memory if you don't keep a diary, and be ruthless in crossing out those hours when you watch a favourite TV programme, play sport, or relax in any way. Your studies should not become a burden or you are likely to tire quickly and start making excuses for not working.

An effective approach is to divide your study time into periods of 45 minutes to one hour, followed by a break. Where more than one subject is being studied concurrently, it is advisable to alternate between quantitative subjects such as costing and literary topics like law. This can also be done within a subject, eg 45 minutes reading and note-making from your textbook - coffee break - attempt an exercise in the manual.

Once you have allocated a realistic period of time, you should refer to the syllabus and, leaving four clear weeks before the examination for revision purposes, divide the time into topics (reflecting syllabus weighting). This done you have to keep to your plan. If a particular interruption is likely then plan ahead and try to 'earn' the time off in advance by foregoing a little of your other leisure time. The key to success is:

REGULAR AND SYSTEMATIC STUDY

3. Study and Learning

Study means 'the systematic pursuit of understanding' and done effectively results in learning. But, if it is not done effectively then it is merely time wasted. Having allocated your study time, you must now ensure that it is used effectively by creating the right ambiance - ie by approaching your study periods in the right frame of mind, equipped with the required 'tools' and in an appropriate setting. The 'right frame of mind' means in a positive manner aiming through a structured and systematic programme of work to develop understanding and, of course, to achieve high marks in your examination. Therefore, you must intend to concentrate on the subject not wonder about your friends' activities, what is on TV etc.

The 'tools' for the job means your syllabus, your work programme, a pad, pens, pencils, your text book, your manual, calculator etc. The remaining factor is where you study. Few students will have a private office with adequate lighting, a large desk and soundproofed walls, but most can find a room which is reasonably quiet, warm and well-lit with a table and chair. Once you have developed the art of study through regular practice, you will find that you can concentrate on trains, buses or in a room full of people. But, first develop the habit of making yourself comfortable.

4. Systematic Methods of Study

Read a chapter in the manual quickly to give yourself a feel for the topic. Then read it again more slowly and make notes as you read. Later you can set yourself targets by trying to condense the important points in a chapter on a single sheet of paper. This will help you to identify the key words and phrases and provides a usefully brief set of notes for your eventual revision purposes.

Use the self review questions at the end of each chapter as a basis for your revision of the chapter and always make some attempt at the questions before checking back to the chapter. Similarly, always make some attempt at the end of chapter exercises and past examination questions. Just checking through the answers at the back of the manual without having made a genuine attempt yourself will not provide real understanding.

Remember:

    (a) Always make NOTES when reading

    (b) PRACTICE MAKES PERFECT

    (c) The most useful weapon you can possess is DETERMINATION TO SUCCEED

    (d) REVISION is a daily, weekly and monthly HABIT - always review what you have just done.

5. Final Revision

Use Section 3 of the manual as the basis of your planned revision programme. By the end of your study and revision you should be able to answer *every* question in the manual which will mean that you have become familiar with the whole range of questions set in ACCA examinations.

6. The Examination

Hints on Examination Technique are given in Section 3, the Revision Section of the manual, and you are strongly advised to study the hints as part of your revision programme.

At this stage the most important thing is to ensure that you enter for the examination at the earliest opportunity and obtain official confirmation of your acceptance. Do *not* leave this until the last minute.

The correct address is:

Chartered Association of Certified Accountants
29 Lincoln's Inn Fields
London Wc2A 3EE

1. What is Management Accounting?

INTRODUCTION

1.   This chapter provides an outline of the scope, principles and objectives of Management Accounting and serves as introduction to the manual as a whole. It introduces themes which are developed throughout the manual and seeks to instil in the student a critical, forward looking approach to the collection, analysis and presentation of information to management.

MANAGEMENT ACCOUNTING DEFINED

2.   In the sense that management will be interested in **any** information produced by an accounting system, all accounting could be said to be management accounting whether it was for example, published accounts mainly for external consumption or routine product costs for internal use. However, for practical purposes, such a description is too broad and imprecise. Although there are many definitions of management accounting the following would gain general acceptance:

Management Accounting is concerned with the **provision and interpretation of information** required by management of all levels for the following purposes:

(a)   Formulating the policies of the organisation.
(b)   Planning the activities of the organisation in the long, medium and short term, ie strategic through to operational planning.
(c)   Controlling the activities of the organisation.
(d)   Decision making, ie the process of choosing between alternatives.
(e)   Performance appraisal at strategic, departmental and operational levels.

Management accounting therefore is primarily concerned with data gathering (from internal and external sources) analysing, processing, interpreting and communicating the resulting information for use within the organisation so that management can more effectively plan, make decisions and control operations.

To carry out this task efficiently the management accountant will use data from the financial and cost accounting systems, he will conduct special investigations to gather required data, he will use accounting techniques and appropriate techniques from statistics and operations research, he will take account of the human element in all activities, he will be aware of the underlying economic logic, he will do all these things and many others so that **at all times he will produce information which is relevant for the intended purpose.**

RELATIONSHIP OF MANAGEMENT ACCOUNTING, COST ACCOUNTING AND FINANCIAL ACCOUNTING

3.   Financial accounting evolved from the stewardship function and is concerned in the main with such matters as: financial record keeping, the preparation of final accounts, dealing with debtors and creditors, the raising of finance, and dealing with all aspects of taxation. Financial accounting has a different emphasis to management accounting and, whilst outside the scope of this manual, it is important that the concepts underlying financial accounting are thoroughly understood.

However, there is no realistic dividing line between cost accounting and management accounting particularly with regard to the provision of information for planning and control. Cost accounting is at a more basic level than management accounting and in many organisations is primarily concerned with the ascertainment of product costs. Because the cost accounting system is an important source of data for management accounting purposes, students must be totally familiar with basic cost accounting principles and methods and their conventions and limitations. A chapter covering the outlines of cost ascertainment and basic cost accounting principles is included in this manual for revision purposes but students are recommended to study a comprehensive book on cost accounting* before tackling this manual.

MAJOR THEMES OF MANAGEMENT ACCOUNTING

4.   There are a number of important themes which prevade all aspects of management accounting and which are covered in detail at various points in the manual. These themes are briefly introduced below under the following headings - Future Orientation, Economic Reality, Goal Congruence, Information Systems, Statistical and Operational Research Techniques, Uncertainty. These themes are developed and exemplified throughout the manual.

FUTURE ORIENTATION

5.   Much of the work of the management accountant is concerned with the future, for example, the provision of information for policy formulation, for planning, and for decision making. In detail these activities may involve - forecasting future costs and revenues - estimating future rates of taxation, interest and inflation - considering the

* For example COSTING, T. LUCEY, DP PUBLICATIONS.

reactions of markets and competitors to the introduction of new products or prices – analysing the likely changes in cost structures and productivity consequent upon the introduction of new methods and equipment – assessing the effect of government policies on the operations of the organisation, and many other similar considerations.

Because of this future orientation, information from conventionally prepared historical records (for example, last period's product costs) is only of value if it provides a guide to future outcomes. This factor is a considerable influence (or should be!) on the methods used for coding, recording and aggregating data used in the financial and cost accounting systems of the organisation.

ECONOMIC REALITY

6.   Accounting data and information are used to represent the underlying economic activities of the organisation which include: buying materials, selling products, manufacturing, and financing the organisation. Accordingly, it is essential that the records of past performance and the information derived from the records which is used to guide future planning and decision making, represents the underlying economic realities in a clear and unambiguous manner unfettered by accounting conventions.

As a simple illustration of this principle assume that a firm has some raw material called Zeon in stock which cost £500 per ton to purchase. A new contract is being considered which could use Zeon. What is the appropriate cost to include for Zeon in the following circumstances?

(a)   Where Zeon is in regular use for many existing products and use for the new contract would require an immediate replenishment order at a cost of £600 per ton, and

(b)   Where Zeon has no alternative productive use but could be sold for scrap at £200 per ton?

Assuming (a) applied the appropriate price to use would be the replacement cost of £600 per ton and if (b) were applicable then the scrap value of £200 per ton would be the appropriate figure to use. It will be noted that the recorded historical cost is not relevant in either case.

GOAL CONGRUENCE

7.   This rather ugly piece of jargon simply means that the management accounting system should encourage all employees, including management, to act in a fashion which contributes to the overall objectives of the organisation, ie the employees' objectives and the organisation's objectives would, in ideal circumstances, coincide. More broadly the theme which is stressed repeatedly throughout this manual is that the behavioural aspects of management accounting are of supreme importance. The systems and the approach adopted by the management accountant should motivate staff by means of genuine participation, good communications, rapid feedback and in many other ways, all of which are dealt with in detail later in the manual.

INFORMATION SYSTEMS

8.   An organisation comprises a number of information systems or networks, frequently computer based. Sometimes there are separate information systems dealing with sales, production, personnel, financial and other matters, sometimes there is integration of these sub-systems. Rarely, if ever, is the information system a totally integrated one dealing with all aspects of management's requirements for planning, control and decision making. In many organisations the management accounting information system is the most developed of all the information systems and it is therefore critical that management accounting systems are designed in accordance with the principles of systems theory otherwise they will be less efficient. An example of this could be where a poorly designed budget system causes a manager to act in a manner which, although advantageous to his department, is detrimental to the overall objectives of the organisation. This is an example of sub-optimality.

STATISTICAL AND OPERATIONAL RESEARCH TECHNIQUES

9.   Certain aspects of management accounting, particularly in the areas of planning and decision making, lend themselves to the use of appropriate statistical and operational research techniques. The use of such techniques does not alter the underlying objectives of management accounting but helps to improve or refine a particular solution. Frequently these techniques are implemented by means of computer packages and the accountant's role is to provide relevant input data and to interpret and present the results produced. There are numerous areas where such techniques have been found to assist management accounting. Examples include: statistical forecasting for cost and sales extrapolations, linear programming for resource allocation problems such as production planning, economic order quantity models to help solve inventory control problems and so on.

It is important the management accountant has sufficient familiarity with such techniques to recognise where their use will be beneficial and cost effective. The use of relevant techniques should be seen as a normal part of the work of the modern management accountant and accordingly this manual deals with the various techniques at appropriate points throughout the book and not in a separate chapter where they would appear divorced from main stream management accounting.

Because of their particular importance in planning, control and decision making certain techniques (for example, linear programming and statistical forecasting) are dealt with in this manual but for full coverage of statistical and operational research techniques students are advised to refer to an appropriate text*

UNCERTAINTY

10. Conditions of certainty are said to exist when a single point estimate can be made which will be exactly achieved. Conversely, uncertainty exists where there are various possible outcomes or results or values. It will be apparent that uncertainty, to a greater or lesser degree, is present in more aspects of management accounting, particularly in the areas of planning and decision making. The influence of uncertainty usually increases the longer the planning or decision period but it is frequently present in short run circumstances as well.

There may be uncertainties about the measurement of data, the economic climate, wage rates, performance levels, material costs, the actions of competitors, the rate of inflation or indeed any of the myriads of factors involved in a typical decision.

Accordingly, the management accountant must recognise the all pervasive influence of uncertainty and incorporate its effects into his analysis of a problem. This may involve statistical tests or in depth investigations on uncertain source data, the use of probablistic analysis when processing the data, and/or presenting and interpreting the results for the decision maker in ways that show the effects of uncertainty. In many circumstances it can be positively misleading to show a single figure of profit or contribution when many of the factors involved are likely to be subject to uncertainty.

CENTRAL ROLE OF DECISION MAKING

11. Underlying all the activities of management and therefore all the activities of the management accounting, is decision making.

Planning process, control systems, performance appraisal, resource allocation and all the other facets of the managerial task, directly or indirectly involve decision making. This is a key point to bear in mind when studying the whole of the manual and not just the sections involved with particular decision making techniques.

INFLATION AND MANAGEMENT ACCOUNTING

12. Inflation is but one element, albeit an important one, of the general problem of uncertainty. As pointed out earlier in the chapter the management accountant must consider the effects of uncertainty in every facet of his work and this applies equally to inflation.

Although the Accounting Profession has had difficulties in developing a comprehensive system of accounting for inflation in published accounts, this is no excuse for the management accountant to ignore the effects of inflation when preparing information for planning, control and decision making for use within the firm.

The general effect of inflation, assuming normal accounting procedures and no special adjustments, is that there is an overstatement of profits and an understatement of asset values. These features lead to several undesirable effects which include: higher tax payments (the fiscal drift effect beloved by governments), liquidity problems and an erosion of real income. As a primary task of the management accountant is to show economic realities it is important that the changing value of money is reflected in the information provided to management. Whilst the effects of inflation impinge on every aspects of accounting there are areas where its effects may be particularly significant, eg investment appraisal, pricing decisions, performance appraisal and budgeting, and accordingly there are sections on dealing with inflation in these areas at appropriate points throughout the manual.

CHANGING ROLE OF THE MANAGEMENT ACCOUNTANT

13. There have been dramatic changes in the nature of industry over the past ten years and it is likely that the 1990s will bring even more change. The environment and industrial conditions have become more volatile, there is increasing usage of microelectronics in the factory and office, there is increase and everchanging competitive threats especially from overseas. In addition, the role of the management accountant as the sole or primary supplier of information to management is being challenged by other information specialists, including systems analysts, operational

* For example QUANTITATIVE TECHNIQUES, T. LUCEY. DP PUBLICATIONS.

researchers, managerial economists and business studies graduates. To meet these challenges the management accountant must be adaptable with a sufficient knowledge of a range of relevant disciplines so as to be able to provide the right information at the right time. He must be prepared to keep up-to-date and master new concepts, principles and techniques. At all times he must be critical of existing systems and information to ensure their continuing relevance in the future. The position of management accountants in the future will not be a comfortable one but it will be challenging and worthwhile.

MANAGEMENT ACCOUNTING AND COMPUTERS

14. Nowadays much of the routine aspects of management accounting is dealt with by computers. This includes; cost analysis and forecasting, all forms of ledger keeping, product cost calculations, routine reports production, variance analysis and so on. In addition there is a tendency for computers to be used for more and more of the sophisticated aspects of management accounting such as the provision of information for planning and decision making. Accordingly it is vital that the management accountant becomes fully conversant with computers and understands their advantages and disadvantages in dealing with management accounting. As more and more of the routine work is dealt with by computers, interpretation of results and professional judgement will play an increasing role.

The final chapter of this manual deals with the application of computers in management accounting and information systems generally and, in addition to studying this chapter and other material on computers, students are urged to gain as much practical experience as possible with computers.

SCOPE OF THE MANUAL

15. The manual has been written to provide a comprehensive, integrated coverage of management accounting. The manual structure is shown in Figure 1 from which it will be seen that, after initial study of certain fundamentals, the manual is arranged in four main sections that cover the key areas of work with which the management accountant is involved - **planning, control, decision making,** and **performance appraisal**. Each section covers the necessary theoretical background before discussing the ways that the particular topic is dealt with in practice. In this way the student is better able to understand the limitations of some of the techniques and procedures that are conventionally used whilst at the same time appreciating the practical difficulties involved in implementing a theoretically optimum solution.

SUMMARY

16. (a) Management accounting is concerned with the provision and interpretation of information which assists management in planning, controlling, decision making and appraising performance.

(b) The key feature of information is that it must be relevant for the intended purpose.

(c) The information supplied by the management accountant is future oriented and must reflect economic realities unfettered by accounting conventions.

(d) The management accountant must be aware of the behavioural consequences of his actions and information. Goal congruence must be encouraged.

(e) Management accounting systems should be designed in accordance with system principles and are improved by the judicious use of appropriate statistical and operational research techniques.

(f) Uncertainty exists in all business situations and the information supplied by the management accountant must reflect the uncertainties and variabilities of the situation.

(g) Regardless of whether or not inflation adjustments are made in the organisation's published accounts, the requirement to show economic reality dictates that the management accountant should take account of the changing value of money.

(h) The structure and scope of the manual is shown in Figure 1.

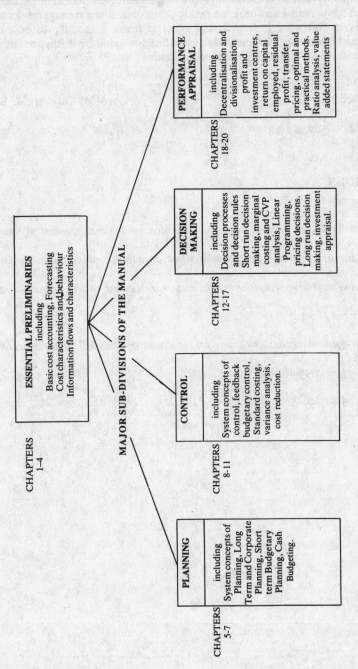

STRUCTURE AND SCOPE OF MANUAL   FIGURE 1.

POINTS TO NOTE

17. (a)   The concept of 'consistency'. so necessary for many aspects of accountancy, is inappropriate for management accounting purposes. The only consistent rule is that the information must be **relevant for the intended purpose.** This may mean, for example, that for different purposes an asset might be valued in several ways. It might be historical cost, net book value, replacement cost, resale value, scrap value, whichever is the most relevant for the intended purpose.

(b)   The management accountant has no exclusive rights to be the sole supplier of information to management. Other specialists, for example, systems analysts, operational researchers, economists and so on are increasingly providing information for planning and decision making purposes. If the management accountant is to maintain his pre-eminent position in this area it is essential that he takes a broadly based multi-disciplinary view of business operations and is able to appreciate the contributions made by disciplines such as operations research, economics, computer science, and the behavioural sciences.

ADDITIONAL READING

Topics in Management Accounting   Arnold, Carsberg & Scapens, PHILIP ALLAN

Perspectives in Management Accounting   Sizer, HEINEMANN/CIMA

An insight into Management Accounting   Sizer, PITMAN

SELF REVIEW QUESTIONS

1.   *Define management accounting. (2)*

2.   *What is the key characteristic of ALL information supplied by the management accountant? (3)*

3.   *Why must the information produced by the management accountant concerned with the future? (5)*

4.   *Why must the information produced by the management accountant reflect economic reality? (6)*

5.   *What is goal congruence? (7)*

6.   *In what areas of management accounting can statistical and operational research techniques be employed? (9)*

7.   *Why is the treatment of uncertainty important? (10)*

8.   *Why must the effects of inflation be considered? (12)*

2. Cost Accounting and Cost Ascertainment − A Revision

INTRODUCTION

1.   This chapter provides a brief outline of basic cost accounting terminology, principles and methods. Because product cost information from the cost accounting system provides a considerable amount of the input data used for management accounting purposes it is necessary for the limitations and conventions involved to be thoroughly understood. The chapter does not purport to cover all aspects of cost accounting and students are advised to refer to a comprehensive book on cost accounting* to resolve any difficulties.

HISTORICAL EMPHASIS

2.   The whole process of cost ascertainment is directed towards the establishment of what it actually cost to produce an article, run a department or complete a job. The costs involved are **past costs**, ie those that have already been incurred. Thus the cost ascertainment process (like financial accounting) is concerned with collecting, classifying, recording, analysing and reporting upon the financial consequences of past actions. For many purposes it is vital to know the results of past activities (for example for control, inventory valuations and profit determination) but this historic emphasis is in sharp contrast to the future orientation of much management accounting work; for example, the provision of information for planning and decision making. It is **future** costs and revenues which are relevant for these purposes so that past costs are only of importance if they provide a guide to the future. It is because of this, and the fact that cost ascertainment involves numerous conventions and assumptions, that any information derived from the cost accounting system is critically examined and, if necessary, adjusted before it is used for management accounting purposes. This is an important point which should be borne in mind whilst studying this chapter.

SOME BASIC DEFINITIONS

3.   Before the procedures of cost ascertainment are discussed, certain preliminary definitions need to be dealt with.

Cost unit. This is a unit of output or service to which costs can be related. The unit chosen is what is most relevant for the activities of the organisation.

Examples

Units or production	Tables, TV sets, tons of cement, litres of paint, a job, a contract, a barrel of beer.
Units of service	Consulting hours, guest-nights, kilowatt hours, passenger-mile.

Within a given organisation there may be several different cost units in order to cost various products or activities.

As costs are incurred they are classified in various way by means of the accounts coding system. An important, primary classification is that into **direct costs** and **indirect costs**.

Direct costs. These costs comprising direct materials, direct labour, and direct expenses, are those which can be directly identified with a job, a product or a service.

Examples

Direct materials	Raw materials used in the product; parts and assemblies incorporated into the finished product; bricks, timber, cement used on a contract.
Direct labour	Wages paid to production workers for work directly related to production, salaries directly attributable to a saleable service (for example, a draughtsman's salary in a contract design office).
Direct expense	Expenses incurred specifically for a particular job, project or saleable service (for example, royalties paid per unit for a copyright design, tool hire for a particular job).

The total of direct costs is known as PRIME COST thus

DIRECT MATERIALS + DIRECT LABOUR + DIRECT EXPENSES = PRIME COST

*For example, COSTING, T. LUCEY, DP PUBLICATIONS

Indirect costs. All material, labour and expense expenditure which cannot be identified with the product are termed indirect costs. The total of indirect costs is known as OVERHEAD which is normally separated into categories such as Production Overheads, Administration Overheads, Selling Overheads and so on.

It will be clear that the sum of direct and indirect costs will equal total cost, thus:

PRIME COST + OVERHEADS = TOTAL COST

ESTABLISHING OVERHEADS

4.   The process of establishing overheads is more involved than for direct costs. The conventional process includes defining a number of **cost centres** and then **allocating** or **apportioning** costs to the cost centres. These terms are defined below:

Cost centre. A location, function, or items of equipment in respect of which costs may be ascertained and related to cost units for control purposes. *Terminology*.

Thus, via the cost centre coding system, costs are gathered together according to their incidence. The gathering together of the indirect costs results in the establishment of the overheads relating to each cost centre which is an essential preliminary to spreading the overheads over cost units.

Cost allocation. This is the term used where the whole of a cost, **without splitting or separation,** can be attributed to a cost unit or cost centre.

All direct costs being identifiable with a cost unit can be allocated without difficulty. Allocation is less frequent with indirect costs but for some items it is possible. For example, fuel oil for a heating boiler which supplies heat to the whole factory could be allocated to the Boiler cost centre.

Apportionment. This process, which is common for indirect costs, involves the **splitting or sharing of a common** cost over the receiving cost centres on some basis which is deemed to reflect the benefits received. The following table gives examples of typical bases of apportionment.

Basis	Costs which may be apportioned on this basis
Floor Area	Rates, Rent, Heating, Cleaning, Lighting, Building Depreciation
Volume or Space Occupied	Heating, Lighting, Building Depreciation
Number of Employees in each Cost Centre	Canteen, Welfare, Personnel, General Administration, Industrial Relations, Safety
Book (or Replacement) Value of Plant, Equipment, Premises, etc.	Insurance, Depreciation
Stores Requisitions	Store-Keeping
Weight of Materials	Store-Keeping, Materials Handling

Note: The process of apportionment, although commonly used for cost ascertainment purposes, is a **convention** only and as such **its accuracy cannot be tested.** Furthermore, the use of data which involves apportionments for planning, control or decision making purposes is likely to give misleading results. Accordingly the management accountant must carefully analyse the methods by which cost data are prepared and make appropriate adjustments before using such data for management accounting purposes.

OVERHEAD ABSORPTION

5.   Overheads form part of total cost but cannot be directly identified with a given cost unit in the way that direct costs can be. Accordingly, overheads are spread over the cost unit by the process known as overhead absorption or overhead recovery.

This is usually done by calculating an overhead absorption rate (OAR) based on the estimated overheads for a cost centre and the expected number of direct labour hours or machines hours for the cost centre. Labour and machine hours are the most common bases chosen for production cost centres. It is conventionally assumed that time based methods such as these more accurately reflect the incidence of overheads in labour or machine intensive departments, respectively.

Basic Cost Ascertainment. Having defined the various terms the build up of total cost can be shown.

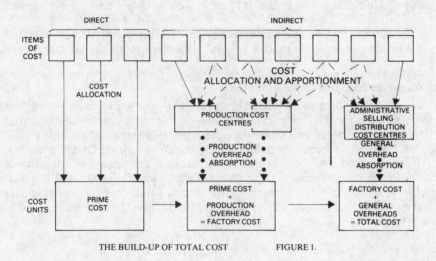

THE BUILD-UP OF TOTAL COST   FIGURE 1.

ABSORPTION COSTING

6.   The procedure outlined so far by which all overheads are absorbed into production is known as **absorption costing** or sometimes **total absorption costing**. Because total overheads contain items which are fixed in nature (those which do not change when the level of activity changes, eg rates) and items known as variable costs (those which vary more or less directly with activity changes, eg raw material usage), absorption costing has implications for stock valuation and performance measurement which are subject to criticism from some accountants. An alternative method of costing, known as marginal costing, excludes fixed costs from the absorption process and charges them in total against the period's results. The implications of these two alternative approaches are explored in the following paragraphs and later in the manual.

MARGINAL COSTING

7.   Marginal costing distinguishes between fixed costs and variable costs. The marginal cost of a product is its variable cost, ie it includes direct labour, direct materials, direct expenses and the variable part of overheads. Marginal costing can be defined as "a principle whereby variable costs are charged to cost units and the fixed cost attributable to the relevant period is written off in full against the contribution for that period". *Terminology.*

The term 'contribution' mentioned in the formal definition is the term given to the difference between Sales and Marginal Cost. Thus

MARGINAL COST = VARIABLE COST   = DIRECT LABOUR

+

DIRECT MATERIAL

+

DIRECT EXPENSE

+

VARIABLE OVERHEADS

CONTRIBUTION = SALES - MARGINAL COST

The term marginal cost sometimes refers to the marginal cost per unit and sometimes to the total marginal costs of a department or batch or operation. The meaning is usually clear from the context.

Note: Alternative names for marginal costing are the 'contribution approach' and 'direct costing'.

There are two main uses for the concept of marginal costing:

(a)   As a basis for providing information to management for planning and decision making. It is particularly appropriate for short run decisions involving changes in volume or activity and the resulting cost changes. This is an important area of study for students and it is dealt with in detail later in the manual.

(b)   It can also be used in the routine cost accounting system for the calculation of costs and the valuation of stocks. Used in this fashion, it is an alternative to total absorption costing. This facet of marginal costing is dealt with below.

MARGINAL COSTING AND ABSORPTION COSTING

8.   Absorption costing, sometimes known as total absorption costing, is the basis of all financial accounting statements and was the basis used for the first part of this chapter. Using absorption costing, all costs are absorbed into production and thus operating statements do not distinguish between fixed and variable costs. Consequently the valuation of stocks and work-in-progress contains both fixed and variable elements. On the other hand, using marginal costing, fixed costs are not absorbed into the cost of production. they are treated as period costs and written off each period in the Costing Profit and Loss account. The effect of this is that finished goods and work-in-progress are valued at marginal cost only, ie the variable elements of cost, usually prime cost plus variable overhead. At the end of a period the marginal cost of sales is deducted from sales revenue to show the contribution, from which fixed costs are deducted to show net profit.

The two approaches are illustrated below using the following data:

Example 1

In a period, 20,000 units of Z were produced and sold. Costs and revenues were:

	£
Sales	100,000
Production Costs:	
:- variable	35,000
:- Fixed	15,000
Administrative + Selling	
overheads:- Fixed	25,000

Operating Statements

Absorption Costing Approach		Marginal Costing Approach		
	£		£	£
Sales	100,000	Sales		100,000
less Production Cost of sales	50,000	*less* Marginal Cost		35,000
= Gross Profit	50,000	= Contribution		65,000
less Admin + Selling				
Overheads	25,000	*less* Fixed Costs		
		Production	15,000	
		Admin S + D	25,000	40,000
= Net Profit	£25,000	= Net Profit		£25,000

The above illustration, although simple, illustrates the general characteristics of both approaches.

The key figure arising in the Marginal statement is the contribution of £65,000. The total amount of contribution arising from Product Z (and other products, if any) forms a pool from which fixed costs are met. Any surplus arising after fixed costs are met becomes the Net Profit.

2. *Cost Accounting and Cost Ascertainment - A Revision*

CHANGES IN THE LEVEL OF ACTIVITY

9.   When changes occur in the level of activity, the absorption costing approach may cause some confusion. In example 1 the activity level was 20,000 units and using the absorption approach, the profit per unit and cost per unit can be calculated as follows:

		£
Selling Price per unit		5
less Total cost per unit =	$\dfrac{£75,000}{20,000}$	3.75
	Profit per unit	£1.25

If these figures were used as guides to results at any activity level other than 20,000, they would be incorrect and may mislead. For example, if the level of activity of Example 1 changed to 25,000 units, it might be assumed that the total profits would be 25,000 x £1.25 = £31,150. However, the results are likely to be as follows:

Operating Statement (Absorption approach)

		£
	Sales (25,000 x £5)	125,000
less	Production Cost (£35,000 x 125% + 15,000)	58,750
	= Gross Profit	66,250
less	Admin + Selling overheads	25,000
	= Net Profit	£41,250

The difference is, of course caused by the incorrect treatment of the fixed cost. In such circumstances the use of the marginal approach presents a clearer picture. Based on the data in Example 1 the marginal cost per unit and the contribution per unit are calculated as follows:

Marginal cost/unit =	$\dfrac{\text{Marginal Cost}}{\text{Quantity}}$	=	$\dfrac{35,000}{20,000}$
		=	£1.75
	∴ contribution/unit	=	Sales Price – Marginal cost/unit
		=	£5 – £1.75
		=	£3.25

If, once again, the activity is increased to 25,000 units, the expected profit would be:

(25,000 units x Contribution/unit) – Fixed Costs
= (25,000 x £3.25) – £40,000
=   £41,250 and the operating statement on marginal costing lines would be

		£
	Sales	125,000
less	Marginal cost (25,000 x 1.75)	43,750
	= Contribution	£81,250
less	Fixed costs	40,000
	Net profit	£41,250

Note: Students will note that the marginal cost and contribution per unit are assumed to be constant and that the fixed costs remain unchanged.

STOCKS AND MARGINAL COSTING

10.   Although the method of presentation was different, both marginal and absorption costing produced the same net profit for the data in Example 1. This was because there was no stock at the beginning or end of the period. Because the two methods differ in their valuation of stock, they produce different profit figures when stocks arise. This is illustrated below.

Example 2

Assume the same data as Example 1 except that only 18,000 of the 20,000 units produced were sold, 2,000 units being carried forward as stock to the next period.

Operating statements based upon marginal costing and absorption costing principles are shown below.

Operating Statements

	Absorption Costing		£		Marginal Costing			£
	Sales (18,000 x £5)		90,000		Sales			90,000
		£					£	
less	Production			*less*	Marginal cost	35,000		
	Cost of Sales	50,000			– Closing Stock			
	– Closing Stock				(2,000 x £.175)	3,500		31,500
	(2,000 x £2.50)	5,000	45,000					
	= Gross Profit		£45,000		= Contribution			£58,500
less	Admin + Selling			*less*	Fixed costs			
	overheads		25,000		Production	15,000		
					Admin S + D	25,000		40,000
	= Net Profit		£20,000					£18,500

(a) The closing stock valuations using the two approaches are:

Absorption Costing   =   Average Production Cost (including fixed costs)

$$= \frac{£50,000}{20,000} = £2.50$$

Marginal Costing   =   Marginal cost, ie variable costs only

$$= \frac{£35,000}{20,000} = £1.75$$

(b) By including fixed costs in stock valuation, absorption costing transfers some of this period's fixed costs into next period when they will be charged against the revenue derived from the stock carried forward (assuming it is sold). Marginal costing always writes off all fixed costs in the period they are incurred.

(c) In a period with increasing stocks (as the one illustrated) absorption costing will show higher profits than marginal costing. Conversely in a period of decreasing stocks marginal costing will show the higher profits. The difference is of course, entirely due to the different treatment of fixed costs in the stock valuation.

MARGINAL COSTING OR ABSORPTION COSTING?

11. The arguments below relate to the use of these techniques in the **routine cost accounting system** of the organisation and not to their use for decision making or control.

Arguments for the use of marginal costing in routine costing:

(a) Simple to operate.

(b) No apportionments, which are frequently on an arbitrary basis, of fixed costs to products or departments. Many fixed costs are indivisible by their nature, eg Managing Director's Salary.

(c) Where sales are constant, but production fluctuates (possibly an unlikely circumstance) marginal costing shows a constant net profit whereas absorption costing shows variable amounts of profit.

(d) Under or over absorption of overheads is almost entirely avoided. The usual reason for under/over absorption is the inclusion of fixed costs into overhead absorption rates and the level of activity being different to that planned.

(e) Fixed costs are incurred on a time basis, eg salaries, rent, rates etc., and do not relate to activity. Therefore it is logical to write them off in the period they are incurred and this is done using marginal costing.

(f)   Accounts prepared using marginal costing more nearly approach the actual cash flow position.

Arguments for the use of total absorption in routine costing.

(a)   Fixed costs are a substantial and increasing proportion of costs in modern industry. Production cannot be achieved without incurring fixed costs which thus form an inescapable part of the cost of production, so should be included in stock valuations. Marginal costing may give the impression that fixed costs are somehow divorced from production.

(b)   Where production is constant but sales fluctuate, net profit fluctuations are less with absorption costing than with marginal costing.

(c)   Where stock building is a necessary part of operations, eg timber seasoning, spirit maturing, firework manufacture, the inclusion of fixed costs in stock valuation is necessary and desirable. Otherwise a series of fictitious losses will be shown in earlier periods to be offset eventually by excessive profits when the goods are sold.

(d)   The calculation of marginal cost and the concentration upon contribution may lead to the firm setting prices which are below total cost although producing some contribution. Absorption cost makes this less likely because of the automatic inclusion of fixed charges.

(e)   SSAP 9 (Stocks and Works in Progress) recommends the use of absorption costing for financial accounts because costs and revenues **must be** matched in the period when the revenue arises, not when the costs are incurred. Also it recommends that stock valuations must include production overheads incurred in the normal course of business even if such overheads are time related, ie fixed. The production overheads **must be based upon normal** activity levels.

CONCLUSIONS REGARDING MARGINAL AND ABSORPTION COSTING

12.   No generalised, all embracing answer can be given as to which technique should be used. Having regard to all the factors, the accountant should make a judgement as to which technique is more appropriate for the requirements of a particular organisation. Although any technique can be used for internal purposes, SSAP 9 is quite clear that absorption costing must be the basis of the financial accounts. It would appear that the use of a full marginal costing system in the routine cost ascertainment procedures of an organisation is relatively rare. This does not mean that marginal costing principles are unimportant. An understanding of the behaviour of costs and the implications of contribution is vital for accountants and managers. The use of marginal costing principles in planning and decision making, dealt with later in the manual is universal and is of considerable important.

MULTI PERIOD EXAMPLE OF MARGINAL AND ABSORPTION COSTING

13.   To bring together the various points covered in the chapter, a fully worked example is shown below.

Example 3

Stock, production and sales data for Industrial Detergents Ltd are given below.

		Period 1	Period 2	Period 3	Period 4
Production	(litres)	60,000	70,000	55,000	65,000
Sales	"	60,000	55,000	65,000	70,000
Opening Stock	"	–	–	15,000	5,000
Closing Stock	"	–	15,000	5,000	–

The company has a single product, for which the financial data, based on an activity level of 60,000 litres/period, are as follows:

	Cost per litre £
Direct Material	2.50
Direct Labour	3.00
Production Overheads	
= 200% of direct labour	6.00
= Total cost/litre	£11.50
Selling price per litre	£18.00

Administrative overheads are fixed at £100,000 per period and half of the production overheads are fixed.

From the above information prepare operating statements on marginal costing and absorption costing principles.

Solution:

The first step is to establish the amount of fixed production overheads per period. The cost data shown above are based on 60,000 litres.

Labour for 60,000 litres   =   60,000 x £3   =   £180,000

Total production overheads   =   200% x £180,000 =   £360,000

∴ Fixed production overheads   = $\dfrac{£360,000}{2}$ =   £180,000

The variable overhead recovery rate is accordingly 100% of direct wages so that marginal cost per litre can be established as follows:

	£
Material	2.50
Labour	3.00
Variable overhead 100% of wages	3.00
	£8.50

Operating Statement using Marginal Costing

	Period 1 £	Period 2 £	Period 3 £	Period 4 £
Sales		1,080,000	990,000	1,170,000	1,260,000
Marginal cost of Production	510,000	595,000	467,500	552,500
+ opening stock			127,500	42,500
- closing stock		127,500	42,500	
= Marginal cost of Sales		510,000	467,500	552,500	595,000
Contribution		570,000	522,500	617,500	665,000
Fixed Costs (Admin + Production)		280,000	280,000	280,000	280,000
NET PROFIT		£290,000	£242,500	£337,500	£385,000

Note: Stocks are valued at marginal cost.

Operating Statement using Absorption costing in Accordance with SSAP 9

	Period 1 £	Period 2 £	Period 3 £	Period 4 £
Sales		1,080,000	990,000	1,170,000	1,260,000
Total Cost of production	690,000	805,000	632,500	747,500
+ opening stock			172,500	57,500
- closing stock		172,500	57,500	
= Total Cost of Sales		690,000	632,500	747,500	805,000
GROSS PROFIT		390,000	357,500	422,500	455,000
Administration Costs		100,000	100,000	100,000	100,000
NET PROFIT		£290,000	£257,500	£322,500	£355,000
Planned Activity Level		60,000	60,000	60,000	60,000
Actual Activity Level		60,000	70,000	55,000	65,000
Difference		–	+ 10,000	– 5,000	+ 5,000
Overhead Over or (under) Absorption		–	+ £30,000	(£15,000)	+ £15,000

Notes:

(a) Stocks are valued at full production cost including fixed production overheads, ie in this example £11.50 per litre. This represents the cost at normal activity levels in accordance with SSAP 9 recommendations.

(b) The amount of over or under absorbed overhead represents the over or under recovery of fixed overheads caused when activity is above or below the planned activity level. In this example the fixed overheads are recovered at £3 per litre. ∴ in period 2 production was 70,000 litres as compared with 60,000 planned so the over absorption was 10,000 litres at £3 per litre = £30,000.

(c) The over/under absorption could be taken direct to P & L a/c or, more usually, taken to a suspense account from which the net balance at the end of the year would be written off to P & L.

(d) The amount over absorbed would be deducted from total cost; the amount under absorbed would be added to total cost.

(e) Because in this example, production and sales were equal over the periods concerned the profits using the two techniques can be reconciled thus:

Profits using Marginal Costing

	£
Period 1	290,000
2	242,500
3	337,500
4	385,000
	£1,255,000

Profits using Absorption Costing

	£
Period 1	290,000
2	257,500
3	322,500
4	355,000
+ Net over absorption	30,000
	£1,255,000

ELEMENTS OF COST - MATERIAL, LABOUR AND OVERHEADS

14. There are a number of costing problems associated with the three elements of cost and these are dealt with below.

Materials. For many organisations the expenditure on materials is a large proportion of total cost and it is essential that all aspects of material control are dealt with efficiently. This involves purchasing, receipt, storage and accounting functions.

There are two main areas with which accountants are concerned. Firstly, the management of the investment in materials and stocks through inventory control procedures which are dealt with in this manual under the general section dealing with Control. Secondly, the costing problems involved in pricing issues of materials to production. The pricing system should be consistent and realistic and should not involve undue administrative complications.

The major pricing systems are FIFO (First in First Out), LIFO (Last in First Out), Average price and Standard price.

FIFO - Issues are priced at the price of the oldest batch in stock until all units have been issued when the next oldest batch is used. It is an actual cost system which has the effect of charging the oldest prices to production and valuing stocks at the more recent. The system is recommended by SSAP 9 and is acceptable to the Inland Revenue.

LIFO - Issues are priced at the price of the most recent batch until a new batch is received. It is an actual cost system which causes product costs to be based fairly closely on current prices and stocks to be valued at the oldest prices. It is not recommended by SSAP 9 and is not acceptable to the Inland Revenue. Like FIFO it is administratively cumbersome because it requires the recording system to keep track of batches.

Average Price - This is a perpetual weighted average system where the issue price is calculated after each receipt taking into account both quantities and money value. This system has an effect on product costs and stock valuation somewhere between LIFO and FIFO. The system makes cost comparisons between jobs somewhat easier and is simpler to administer. It is recommended by SSAP 9 and acceptable to the Inland Revenue.

Standard Price - This is a predetermined price based on consideration of all factors which are expected to affect the price. If a realistic price can be set then purchasing efficiency can be monitored to some extent.

Pricing methods - a summary. Apart from the rare occasions when the specific price paid for materials can be charged into product costs, the price charges will be based on a pricing convention such as described above. It is because of this that product costs from the costing system which are to be used for planning and decision making purposes need to be used with discretion by the management accountant. For planning and decision making purposes the appropriate material cost may be the future replacement cost, the net realisable value or the value of the material in some alternative use (opportunity cost). **Rarely will the historical cost be appropriate.**

LABOUR COST

15. Payment systems for production workers are frequently complex and difficult to administer. Although there are innumerable variations they are essentially of two types; those where straight time rates are paid and wages are not related to production levels, and those where payment is related directly or indirectly to production levels.

Obviously, where the payment system is related in some way to activity, for example, by straight or differential piecework or by individual and/or group bonus systems, labour costs will have some variable characteristics but rarely, if ever, will labour costs behave in a truly variable, linear fashion. The existence of guaranteed minima, in-lieu bonuses, high day rate systems, the tendency for more production workers to become salaried employees, all have implications for the management accountant when considering labour costs in planning and decision making.

SERVICE COST CENTRES

16. As previous described, overheads are aggregated by the process of classification, allocation and apportionment and are then spread over the cost units produced, by the process known as overhead absorption.

A typical complication which occurs in most costing systems relates to service cost centres. These are departments which, although providing essential services to production departments and each other, do not take part in actual production, eg maintenance and stores. Naturally, service cost centres incur costs which may be allocated to them (eg storeman's wages to stores) or apportioned to them (eg an appropriate share of the rates, heating costs to the maintenance shop) by the normal cost accounting process. The service department costs have to be shared over the production departments by the process of secondary apportionment, the base for which is chosen so as to reflect the use made of each service. This process is necessary so that all the service department costs are eventually included in the costs of the production cost units. Typical bases for the secondary apportionment, ie the apportionment of service costs to production cost centres, are shown below:

Service Department	Possible Bases of Apportionment of Service Department Costs to Production Cost Centres
Stores	No. of Requisitions Weight of Materials Issues No. of Items Issued
Maintenance	Maintenance Labour Hours Maintenance Wages Plant Values
Power Generation	Metered Usage Notional Capacity
Personnel	No. of Employees per Department Gross Wages per Department

SERVICE DEPARTMENT COSTS WITH RECIPROCAL SERVICING

17. Prior to the secondary apportionment of costs to production departments it is necessary to establish the costs of each service department. Particular problems arise when service departments provide reciprocal servicing for each other as well as for Production. For example assume that Maintenance (M) do work for Power Generation (PG) who supply power to maintenance. The total cost of M cannot be found until the charge for PG's services is known whilst PG's costs cannot be found until the charge for M's work is known. There are three conventional methods of breaking this circular problem; continuous allotment, the elimination method and the algebraic method using simultaneous equations which is illustrated below in Example 3.

Example 3

A factory has two service departments maintenance (M) and Power Generation (PG) and three production departments (P1, P2 and P3). There is reciprocal servicing as well as servicing the production departments. It has been agreed that the most appropriate bases of apportionment for service departments costs are: Capital equipment values for maintenance and motor horse power for power generation. The appropriate data are summarised below.

Department	M	PG	P1	P2	P3
Overheads	£4,800	£14,600	£14,000	£22,000	£33,000
Capital Values		£100,000	£550,000	£760,000	£640,000
Proportion	-	5%	25%	38%	32%
Horse Power	9000	-	24000	16200	10800
Proportion	15%	-	40%	27%	18%

It is required to establish the total overheads of the production departments.

Solution using simultaneous equations

Let m = Total overheads for maintenance when the power generation charges have been allotted.

Let pg = Total overheads for power generation when the maintenance charges have been allotted.

$$\therefore m = 4800 + 0.15pg$$
$$pg = 14600 + 0.05m$$

which rearranged give

$$m - 0.15\ pg = 4800 \ldots\ldots\ldots \text{Equation I}$$
$$pg - 0.05m = 14600 \ldots\ldots\ldots \text{Equation II}$$

These equations are solved in the normal manner (in this case Equation II is multiplied by 20 and added to Equation I) thus

$$
\begin{aligned}
m - 0.15\ pg &= 4800 \qquad &\text{Equation I}\\
\underline{20pg - m} &= \underline{292,000} \qquad &\text{20 x Equation II}\\
19.85pg &= 296,800
\end{aligned}
$$

$$\therefore pg = \underline{£14952}$$

and by substitution, m is found to be £7,043.

These values of notional overheads are used to make the final secondary apportionments thus (rounded to the nearest £).

Departments

	M	PG	P1	P2	P3
Original Allotment	£4,800	£14,600	£14,000	£22,000	£33,000
Notional overheads for M apportioned over serviced departments	-7,043	352	1,761	2,676	2,254
Notional overheads for PQ apportioned over serviced departments	2,243	-14,952	5,981	4,037	2,691
	-	-	£21,742	£28,713	£37,945

The final apportioned overheads equal the original total allotments, ie £88,400.

Notes:

(a)   The processes of primary and secondary apportionments and establishing the costs of service departments are conventions only and as such their accuracy cannot be tested. The use of such data for decision making should therefore be subject to close scrutiny to ensure its appropriateness for the intended purpose.

(b)   Reciprocal service cost problems can also be solved using matrix algebra, which is described in detail in 'Quantitative Techniques' Ibid.

COSTING METHODS

18.   These are methods of costing which are designed to suit the way products are manufactured or processed or the way that services are provided. Examples of costing methods are: job costing, batch costing, contract costing and process costing which are explained below. It must be clearly understood that, whatever costing method is used, basic costing principles relating to classification, allocation, apportionment and absorption will be used.

JOB COSTING

19.   The main purposes of job costing are to establish the profit or loss on each completed job and to provide a valuation of uncompleted jobs, ie the Work-in-Progress (WIP). This done by creating a Job Cost Card for each job on which would be entered the following details:

Direct Labour costs - including time based and piecework earnings.
Direct Material costs - based on stores issues, special purchases, bills of materials.
Direct expenses - expenses incurred specifically for the particular job, eg tool hire, royalties.

Based on these details and labour and machine time bookings the production departmental overheads would be calculated using the times recorded and the predetermined overhead absorption rates for labour or machine time as appropriate. A job is normally valued at factory cost until it is dispatched when an appropriate amount of selling and administration overheads would be added usually as a percentage of the works cost. The total of the partly complete job cost cards represent the firms work-in-progress and on completion the costs are removed from W-I-P and charged to the Cost of Sales account (DR Cost of Sales CR WIP).

BATCH COSTING

20.   This is a form of costing which is used where a quantity of identical articles are produced together as a batch. The general procedures are very similar to costing jobs. The batch would be treated as a job during manufacture and the various costs (material, labour and expenses) collected in the usual manner. On completion of the batch the total batch cost would be divided by the number of good articles produced so as to provide the average cost per article. Batch costing procedures are common in a variety of industries including clothing, footwear, engineering components.

CONTRACT COSTING

21.   This has many similarities to job costing and is usually adopted for work which is: site based, of a relatively long duration and undertaken to the customer's special requirements. Because of the self contained nature of most site operations more costs than normal can be identified as direct and thus charged to the contract, eg telephones on site, design and planning salaries, site vehicle costs. A particular feature associated with contracts is the provision for progress payments to be made by the client which are necessary because of the length and value of some contracts. The basis for these interim payments is an architect's certificate of work satisfactorily completed. The amount paid is

usually the certified value less a percentage retention which is released by the client when the contract is fully completed. Because contracts often extend over more than one financial year it is necessary to estimate the profit on uncompleted contracts so as to avoid undue fluctuation in company results. The profit to be taken is conservatively estimated and is restricted to a proportion ($\frac{2}{3}$ or $\frac{3}{4}$) of the difference between the **cost** and **value** of work certified and further reduced by the retention percentage. For example:

> Contract price £1,000,000
> Value of Work certified to date £475,000
> Cost of work certified £392,000
> Retention percentage 15%

Solution

		£
	Value of work certified	475,000
less	Cost of work certified	392,000
		83,000

$$\text{2/3 proportion} = £55,333$$
$$\text{Reduced by retentions} = 85\% \times £55,333$$
$$\therefore \quad \text{Profit to be taken on period} = £47,033$$

PROCESS COSTING

22. This form of costing is appropriate where the product follows a series of sequential, frequently automatic processes, eg paper making, refining, paint manufacture, food processing. The essence of process costing involves the averaging of the total costs of each process over the total throughput of that process (including partly completed units) and charging the cost of the output of one process as the raw material input to the next process. Any partly complete units at the end of the period are, for cost calculation purposes, expressed as 'equivalent units'. This merely means the equivalent number of fully complete units which the partly complete units represents. For example, assume that at the end of a period the output of a process was as follows:

1300 fully complete units and 400 partly complete with the following degree of completion

> Material   80% complete
> Labour   60% complete
> Overheads   50% complete

The number of equivalent units is:

	Fully complete Units	+	Equivalent Units in W.I.P.	=	Total Effective Production
Material	1300	+	400 x 80%	=	1620
Labour	1300	+	400 x 60%	=	1540
Overheads	1300	+	400 x 50%	=	1500

The cost of each element of the total effective production is calculated from the material, labour and overhead costs of the period, aggregated, and a total cost per unit calculated.

JOINT PRODUCT AND BY-PRODUCT COSTING

23. Joint and by-products frequently arise from the production process. Although the dividing line between the two is difficult to determine, a joint product is usually the term used when two or more products arise simultaneously in the course of processing, each of which has a significant sales value in relation to one another. Where one of the products arises incidentally in the course of manufacture and has relatively little sales value it is termed a by-product, eg sawdust and bark in timber processing. The most common method of dealing with by-products is to credit the net realisable value of the by-product against the total cost of production. Because of the greater value of joint products more elaborate costing systems are used. The various products become separately identifiable, at a point known as the 'split-off point'. Up to that point all costs are joint costs and, after it, any cost incurred for a particular product is readily identifiable with that product.

APPORTIONING JOINT COSTS

24. For income determination and stock valuation purposes it is conventional to apportion the common costs (ie those prior to split-off point) between the joint products. The two methods most frequently used are: the **physical unit basis** (where costs were apportioned in proportion to the weight or volume of the products), and the **sales value basis** (where costs are apportioned according to the sales value of the products). These two methods are illustrated in Example 4.

Example 4

A process produces three joint products, M, N and O. The appropriate data were as follows:

M - 400 Kgs sold at £12.50 Kg	Sales value =	£5,000
N - 300 Kgs sold at £20 Kg	Sales value =	£6,000
O - 200 Kgs sold at £25 Kg	Sales value =	£5,000
		£16,000

Total joint costs were £11,000

Cost apportionment

Physical unit basis

		Apportionment			Costs Apportioned £
M	400 Kgs	$\frac{400}{900}$	x £11,000	=	4,889
N	300 Kgs	$\frac{300}{900}$	x £11,000	=	3,667
O	200 Kgs	$\frac{200}{900}$	x £11,000	=	2,444
	900 Kgs				£11,000

Sales value basis

					£
M	400 Kgs	$\frac{5000}{16000}$	x £11,000	=	3,437
N	300 Kgs	$\frac{6000}{16000}$	x £11,000	=	4,126
O	200 Kgs	$\frac{5000}{16000}$	x £11,000	=	3,437
	900 Kgs				£11,000

Notes:

(a) It will be seen that the two methods can product substantially different results giving, in this example, gross profit percentages of 2%, 39% and 51% on the physical unit basis and a constant 31% on the sales value basis. The sales value basis always produces a constant margin.

(b) On occasions, products are not saleable at the split-off point and need further processing before a sales value can be established. In such circumstances the post split-off costs are deducted from the final sales value so as to establish a **notional sales value** at the split-off point which is used for the cost apportionment.

(c) It will be apparent that ANY method of apportioning joint costs is only a convention and accordingly is of **no value for decision making.**

SUMMARY

25. (a) Cost accounting systems are largely concerned with the analysis of past costs and operations. management accounting is largely (but not exclusively) concerned with future costs and revenues.

(b) Cost units should be chosen that are the most relevant for the activities of the particular organisation.

(c)   The total of direct cost + direct labour + direct expense is Prime Cost. The total of indirect costs is Overhead.

(d)   Overheads are conventionally established by defining cost centres and then allocating and apportioning costs to the cost centres using bases of apportionment which are deemed to reflect the benefits received. The process of apportionment is a convention only.

(e)   Overheads are spread over cost units by using overhead absorption rates usually based on labour or machine hours.

(f)   Where all costs, both fixed and variable, are included in production costs, the system is known as absorption or total absorption costing. Where fixed costs are excluded from production costs and charged against the period's results, the system is known as marginal costing.

(g)   Contribution is the difference between sales and marginal cost (ie all the variable costs).

(h)   Where there are no opening and closing stocks marginal and absorption costing produce the same net profit. Because the two systems differ in their valuation of stock, differences in net profit arise when stocks exist.

(i)   The major pricing systems for charging materials to production are FIFO, LIFO, Average price and Standard price. Although widely used in cost ascertainment the use of such systems for management accounting purposes has doubtful validity.

(j)   Labour remuneration systems vary widely but are either wholly time based or related, directly or indirectly, to production levels. Labour costs rarely behave in a truly variable, linear fashion.

(k)   A particular problem which arises with the ascertainment of overheads is dealing with service department costs where there is reciprocal servicing.

(l)   The major costing methods are: job costing, batch costing, contract costing and process costing.

(m)   Job, batch and contract costing have broad similarities. Because of the large scale and long term nature of many contracts, conventional arrangements are made to include a proportion of the total contract profit into each years accounts. Typically the amount of profits is a proportion ($\frac{2}{3}$ or $\frac{3}{4}$) of the difference between the cost and value of the work certified which is reduced by the cash retention percentage.

(n)   Process costing involves the averaging of total costs over the total throughput of the process, including any partly completed units.

(o)   Where a process produces joint or by products it is conventional to apportion the common costs on either the physical unit basis or the sales value basis.

POINTS TO NOTE

26.   (a)   In most organisations the cost accounting system has been developed to aid routine purposes. It does not follow that the system will produce appropriate information for management accounting purposes.

(b)   The cost accounting system of the organisation must itself be cost effective. Is the cost accounting system of your organisation just another part of overheads or does it make a positive contribution to organisational efficiency?

ADDITIONAL READING

Cost accounting: a managerial emphasis   Horngren, PRENTICE-HALL

Costing   Lucey, DP PUBLICATIONS

SELF REVIEW QUESTIONS

1.   Why should the management accountant critically examine the bases and assumptions used to produce information from the cost accounting system? (2)

2.   Define cost unit, direct cost, indirect cost and prime cost. (3)

3.   What is the process by which overheads are established? (4)

4. *What is overhead absorption and typically how is this done?* (5)

5. *Distinguish between absorption and marginal costing.* (6)

6. *What is contribution?* (7)

7. *What is the difference between stock valuations using absorption and marginal costing?* (8)

8. *If stocks are increasing will absorption or marginal costing show the higher profits? Why?* (10)

9. *What does SSAP 9 recommend as the basis of Stock Valuation?* (11)

10. *Describe the FIFO, LIFO, Average price, and Standard price systems of pricing stock issues.* (14)

11. *What are some typical bases on which service department costs are apportioned to production cost centres?*

12. *What are three methods of dealing with service department costs where reciprocal servicing takes place?* (17)

13. *Describe job costing.* (19)

14. *How is the profit calculated on incomplete contracts?* (21)

15. *Describe process costing and equivalent units.* (22)

16. *What are the conventional methods of apportioning joint costs?* (23)

EXAMINATION QUESTIONS WITH ANSWERS COMMENCING PAGE 337

A1. *The Waverley Co Ltd has just been set up in order to manufacture and sell three products; A, B and C. Details of planned production and sales quantities for each of these for the next two years are shown below:*

Planned activity – units (000's)

	Year 1			Year 2		
	A	*B*	*C*	*A*	*B*	*C*
Production	30	20	10	30	20	10
Sales	24	16	4	24	10	12

The proposed pattern of production is considered to be the normal long-term pattern but the sales expected in the first two years are not representative of the anticipated long term position.

It is expected that the sales price and the variable cost per unit will be stable for at least two years – the details of these are:

	Sales price (per unit) £	Variable cost (per unit) £
A	8	2
B	12	4
C	12	3

The manufacturing process requires that all production be subjected to both manual operations and mechanical processing. Details of labour and machine production hours required for each unit produced are:

	Labour hours (per unit)	Machine hours (per unit)
A	2	1
B	3	1
C	2	2

Total fixed production overhead costs will be £280,000 in each year.

The managing director wishes to ascertain both the total profit (before administration costs etc.) expected for each of the first two years and the profitability of each product. Accordingly he has asked each of the three applicants for the job of management accountant to produce the information he requires but is surprised that the figures they produce display little similarity. It appears that one candidate has utilised direct costing whereas the other two have utilised absorption costing but with each using a different basis for overhead recovery. Before making a decision as to whom to employ the managing director wishes to ascertain which one of the sets of figures provided is 'correct' and which two sets are, therefore, 'wrong' and so seeks your advice.

Required:

(a) Prepare the three statements the managing director is likely to have received and which show –

    (i)   the total profit (before considering administration costs etc.) for each of the first two years; and
    (ii) the profitability of each product.

(b) Comment on the reasons for any similarities and/or differences in the three sets of figures provided in (a) above. In your comments suggest any improvements which could be made to the application of the absorption costing methods. Advise the managing director which candidate's set of figures provides the 'correct' answer and which are 'wrong'.

(c) It is decided to increase the production of the **first year only** by 20% in order to provide additional buffer stocks. Calculate the cost to Waverley Ltd of holding such additional stocks for a full year if the appropriate cost of financing the additional stocks is 12% per annum. (Ignore any obsolescence and costs of storage).

ACCA, Management Accounting.

A2. Stover Chemicals operates four manufacturing processes. Process 1 yields three joint products (X, Y and Z) in fixed proportions. Although each of these products could be sold at the split-off point (and there exists a ready market for each in this state) they are normally processed further; X in process 2, Y in process 3 and Z in process 4. This additional processing enhances their saleable values as follows:

Selling Prices per Litre

	X	Y	Z
Product sold at split-off point	£0.80	£0.30	£1.30
Product sold after further processing	£1.20	£0.70	£1.75

The process accounts for the last operating period, when the plant was operating at full capacity, can be summarised as follows:

Process 1

	Litres	£		Litres	£
Opening Work in Progress	4,000	1,200	Production Transferred		
Direct Material	99,000	9,900	X to process 2	50,000	25,000
Processing Expense		39,500	Y to process 3	30,000	15,000
			Z to process 4	20,000	10,000
			Closing Work in Progress	3,000	600
	103,000	£50,600		103,000	£50,600

Process 2

	Litres	£		Litre	£
Opening Work in Progress	2,000	1,267	Sales Revenue	50,000	60,000
Input from process 1	50,000	25,000	Closing Work in Progress	2,000	1,267
Processing Expense		13,333			
Profit to Profit and Loss Account		21,667			
	52,000	£61,267		52,000	£61,627

Process 3

	Litres	£		Litres	£
Opening Work in Progress	1,000	650	Sales Revenue	30,000	21,000
Input from process 1	30,000	15,000	Loss to Profit and Loss Account		3,000
Processing Expense		9,000	Closing Work in Progress	1,000	650
	31,000	£24,650		31,000	£24,650

Process 4

	Litres	£		Litres	£
Opening Work in Progress	2,000	1,700	Sales Revenue	20,000	35,000
Input from process 1	20,000	10,000	Closing Work in Progress	2,000	1,700
Processing Expense		14,000			
Profit to Profit and Loss Account		11,000			
	22,000	£36,700		22,000	£36,700

 The costs incurred and the processing efficiency for the period to which the above accounts relate, can be assumed to be representative of current conditions. The joint costs in process 1 have been apportioned on the basis of the output (in litres) of X, Y and Z. All work in progress is complete as far as material content is concerned and (except for the closing work in progress in process 1) it is half processed. The closing work in progress in process 1 is one quarter processed.

 You are required:

 (a) To comment on the relative profitability of the products, in particular consider the loss arising on product Y in process 3.

 (b) To comment on the company's policy of processing all three products beyond the split-off point.

 (c) To restate the process accounts for processes 3 and 4 using sales values (at the split-off point) as the basis for the joint cost allocation.

 (d) To restate the process accounts for processes 1 and 4 using the sales values at the split-off point as transfer prices in transferring production from process 1 to the other processes.

 (e) To discuss the utility of each version of the process accounts (one version in the question and two in your solution) and to comment on the joint cost allocation problem.

ACCA, Management Accounting.

3. Cost Behaviour

INTRODUCTION

1. This chapter discusses the importance of the study of cost behaviour to the management accountant. The accounting classifications of fixed and variable costs, and the problems associated with the classification conventions are discussed. Linear and curvi-linear cost functions are described together with stepped and discontinuous functions. Cost forecasting using accounts classification, industrial engineering and statistical methods is explained. The frequently encountered methods of forecasting; scattergraphs, high-low points, and simple linear regression analysis, are described and ways of assessing the predictive quality of the calculated regression line are explained, including correlation coefficients and the coefficient of determination. Multiple linear regression is briefly described and the chapter concludes with an explanation of learning curves.

WHAT WILL OUR COSTS BE NEXT YEAR?

2. This deceptively simple sounding question - and many others of a like nature - is typical of the problems that the management accountant has to face. Such questions can occur in virtually every aspect of his work and knowledge of the patterns of cost behaviour and ways that future costs (and, of course, other factors such as sales) can be predicted is a fundamental requirement for the management accountant, particularly when he is supplying information for planning and decision making.

COST CLASSIFICATION

3. The classification of costs into fixed and variable, according to their behaviour and characteristics, is an essential preliminary to being able to make any form of cost prediction.

The behaviour of a cost in relation to changes in the level of activity forms the basis of the usual accounting classifications thus:

a **Fixed Cost** is one which, within certain output limits, tends to be unaffected by variations in the level of activity.

a **Variable Cost** is one which tends to vary in direct proportion to variations in the level of activity.

Such a classification should not be a once off exercise to sort costs into rigid absolute categories for all time and for all conditions. The accountant must look at the actual and forecast behaviour of the cost, and the purpose for which the cost is intended so that there is a flexible approach to the classification of costs.

The normal process of cost classification into fixed and variable is only valid within specific, limiting assumptions, ie

(a) When the time period being considered is relatively short, typically a year. Over longer periods, methods, technology and other factors alter, causing changes in the classification of costs and in their behaviour.

(b) When the activity variation being considered is relatively small; for example, normal capacity ± 10%. Outside a limited activity range costs are unlikely to behave in accordance with their original classification.

(c) Over the time period being considered the state of technology, management policies and the methods employed are deemed to remain unchanged.

PROBLEMS ASSOCIATED WITH CONVENTIONAL COST CLASSIFICATIONS

4. There are numerous pitfalls contained in the conventional classifications of fixed and variable cost and the management accountant must constantly keep these in mind to avoid taking too superficial a view of cost classification and prediction.

Typical of the problems involved are the following:

(a) The usual assumption regarding the behaviour of variable costs is that they behave in a linear fashion, ie a variable cost is deemed to alter in direct proportion to changes in volume. This **may** be correct, but a cost may also vary in a non-linear, or curvi-linear, fashion or may change in a series of steps. Whatever the cost function, linear, curvi-linear or stepped, it should be established by analysis of the cost in question and not by some overall, simplistic assumption.

(b) Fixed costs can and do change, for example, local rates virtually always increase each year as do many other fixed costs. The main point is that although costs which are classified as fixed often alter, they do so usually because of factors other than changes in volume. The adherence to quite arbitrary conventions may cause a cost to be classified as fixed, semi-fixed, or variable in different organisations or even in different parts of the same organisation. An example of such a cost is depreciation which, by convention, may be deemed to range from wholly time related through to being directly related to the amount produced.

So that the individual characteristics of costs are not overlooked and in consequence dealt with incorrectly it is useful to subdivide fixed costs into four categories:

(i)   The time period classification. Those types of cost which are not likely to change significantly in the short term, usually a year. In the long term all costs may change or become avoidable.

(ii)   The volume classification. Costs which are fixed for small, but not large changes in output or capacity.

(iii)   The joint classification. Where a cost is incurred jointly with another cost and is only capable of being altered jointly. For example, if an organisation leases a showroom which has a warehouse attached then the fixed cost element applies to both parts of the asset acquired whether or not they are both wanted.

(iv)   The policy classification. These are costs which are fixed by management policy and bear no causal relationship to volume or time. They are usually items which are dealt with by appropriation budgets, eg expenditure on advertising, research and development. These types of costs are sometimes known as programmed fixed costs and typically are reviewed annually.

It will be apparent that a cost may be classed as fixed for some purposes and not others and the management accountant must continually appraise the classification of a cost to ensure its appropriateness for the intended purpose.

(c)   Rarely can a cost be classified as purely variable or purely fixed even though such classifications are, for simplicity, frequently made. More often a cost displays both fixed and variable characteristics and is termed a semi-fixed, or semi-variable, or a mixed cost. With all such costs it is necessary to separate the fixed and variable elements so as to be able to make predictions about the behaviour of the cost in relation to the changes being considered. Various methods are possible which can be sub divided into two categories; by judgement, and by statistical methods.

(i)   by judgement. The characteristics of the cost are established by studying the cost coding system and discussing with the managers and departments involved those costs which cannot be readily identified as fixed or variable. Typically the manager would be asked what the cost in question would be if there was little or no activity and in this way a crude estimate of the fixed element would be obtained.

(ii)   by statistical methods. These methods are of varying sophistication but all rely on some form of analysis of past data of the behaviour of the cost being studied. These methods include: the high-low points method, the scatter chart, regression analysis and are described in detail later in the chapter.

(d)   Irregularity of behaviour. Unfortunately, costs do not behave in regular patterns and care must be taken not to classify say, a variable cost as having a regular, linear function for all activity levels when further analysis might show that it is linear between 90% - 115% of normal activity and thereafter has a curvi-linear function.

(e)   Multiple causes of variation. Different variable costs (or the variable portions of semi-fixed costs) react to different activity measures. For example, direct wages may vary with the number of orders received, distribution costs may vary with the deliveries made and so on. It is an oversimplification, frequently made in examinations, that **all** variable costs vary in relation to the **same** measure of activity and this may give misleading results. Care must be taken only to make this assumption when the context makes it clear that it is the only one possible.

TYPICAL COST PATTERNS

5.   Having considered some of the problems inherent in cost classification some typical cost patterns are shown below in diagrammatic form.

Variable cost patterns – Linear

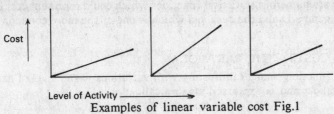

Examples of linear variable cost Fig.1

This pattern is the simplest possible and represents costs which vary in direct proportion to the level of activity. Examples include: direct materials, royalties per unit, power usage (without a standing charge).

A perfectly linear variable cost over all activity levels, as shown in Figure 1 is extremely unlikely. More realistically, a cost may be linear (or a linear approximation assumed) only over the normal range of activity levels and extrapolations outside this range are likely to have less validity. See Figure 2.

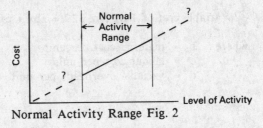

Normal Activity Range Fig. 2

Notes:

(a) The slope of the line, usually represented by b, is the variable cost per unit of activity.

(b) The activity level in units is usually represented by x. Accordingly a variable cost with a linear relationship is expressed thus:

$$y = bx$$

where y is the expected cost.

VARIABLE COST PATTERNS – CURVI-LINEAR

6. Where costs do not vary in direct proportion to activity changes the function is non-linear or **curvi-linear** thus:

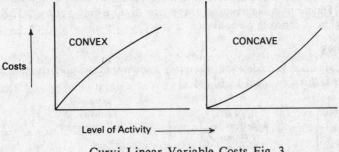

Curvi-Linear Variable Costs Fig. 3

CONVEX – where each extra unit of output causes a **less than proportionate** increase in cost, ie economies of scale operate.

CONCAVE – where each extra unit of output causes a **more than proportionate** increase in cost, ie diminishing returns operate.

Many variable costs may display curvi-linear characteristics. for example, in some processes the amount of waste material remains more or less constant so that when output increases the unit cost for material reduces (economies of scale).

Conversely, when it is necessary to pay increasing differential piece rates so as to increase output, diminishing returns operate and some form of concave curvi-linear function will result.

If a given curve has particular characteristics it may be categorised as a known statistical function by the technique of **curve fitting**. There are numerous statistical functions which could represent cost behaviour, for example, logarithmic, simple exponential, gompertz and the parabola which is one of the more common types and is illustrated below.

CURVI-LINEAR VARIABLE COSTS – THE PARABOLA

7. Where the slope of the cost function changes uniformly with variations in the level of activity (as shown in Fig. 3) the curve is known as a Parabola and is expressed algebraically thus:

$$\text{Variable Cost} = bx + cx^2 + dx^3 + \ldots + px^n$$

where b, c, d, ..., p are constants and x is the level of activity.

Example

Analysis of cost and activity data shows that the variable costs of Part No. 329 can be represented by the function:

$$\text{Variable cost of Part No. 329} = £bx + cx^2 + dx^3$$

where   b = material cost per unit   =   £3
         c = labour cost per unit   =   £0.8
         d = variable overheads per unit   =   £0.06

Calculate

(i) Variable cost when production is 10 units
(ii) Variable cost when production is 15 units

Solution

(i) Production 10 units
    Variable cost   = $£(3 \times 10) + (0.8 \times 10^2) + (0.06 \times 10^3)$
                     =   £170

(ii) Production 15 units
    Variable cost   = $£(3 \times 15) + (0.8 \times 15^2) + (0.06 \times 15^3)$
                     =   £427.5

It will be seen that there is a more than proportionate increase in cost compared with the increase in production thus demonstrating that the function is **concave**, ie there are diminishing returns. The values of the constants determine whether the function is concave or convex.

LINEAR APPROXIMATIONS

8. Frequently a linear approximation is made even when it is known that the underlying cost function is curvi-linear (or indeed any other function). this is shown in Fig. 4.

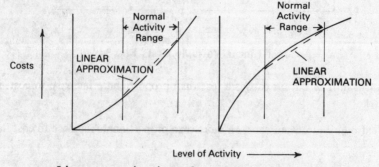

Linear approximations of curvi-linear functions Fig. 4

Such approximations greatly simplify calculations and there is empirical evidence from cost studies that they are reasonably accurate providing that there is only a limited range of activity variation covering a short time period.

Care should be taken, in practice and in examinations, not to make the assumption of linearity where this could produce misleading results.

OTHER COST PATTERNS

9. Some typical cost patterns are shown below:

Fixed cost patterns

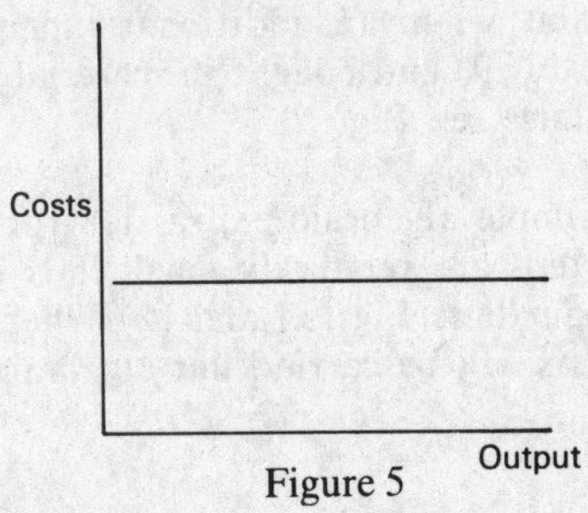

Figure 5

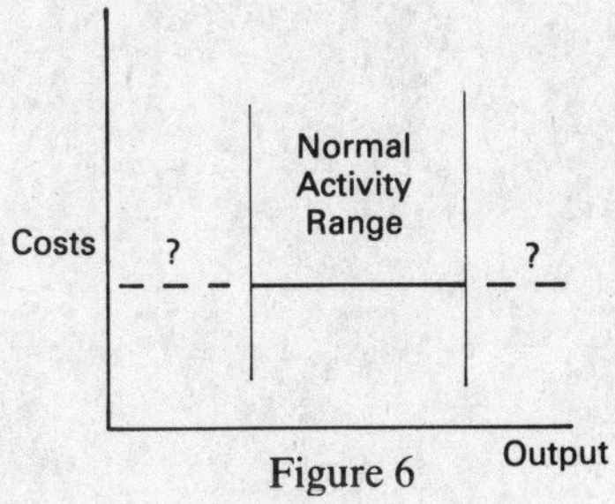

Figure 6

Notes:

(i) Fig. 5 depicts the conventional assumption for a fixed cost constant at all levels of activity. However, a cost is unlikely to be fixed at all levels and Fig. 6 shows a more realistic situation.

(ii) Examples of fixed costs include: rates, time based depreciation, most salaries, rent.

(iii) A fixed cost can be described algebraically as y = a, where y is the cost and a is a constant.

Semi-variable cost patterns

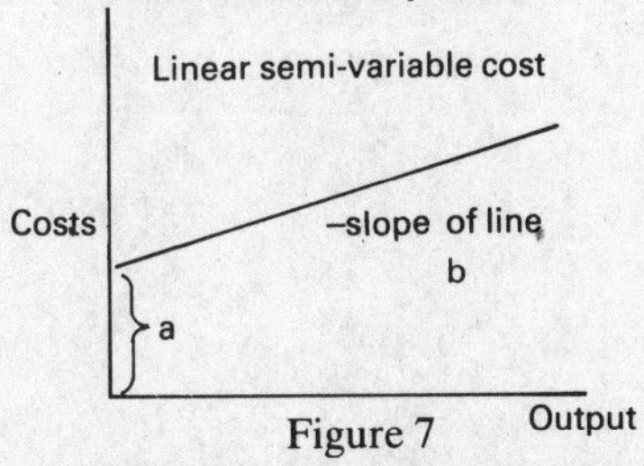

Figure 7

Curvi-linear semi-variable cost

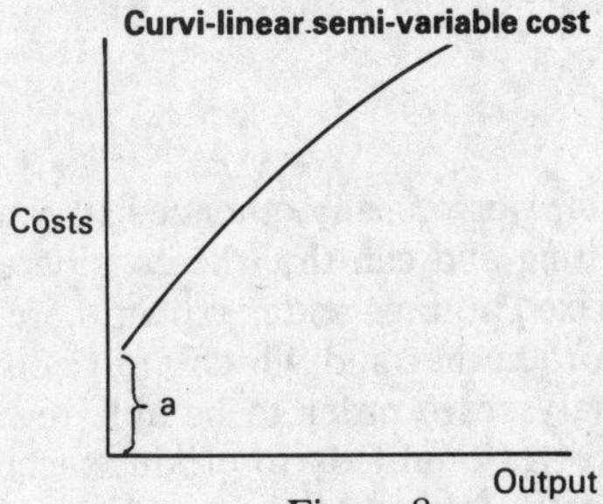

Figure 8

Notes:

(i) The variable element of a semi-variable cost may be **linear**, as shown in Fig. 7, or **curvi-linear** as shown in Fig. 8.

(ii) Examples of semi-variable cost include: power and telephone charges, computer bureau costs with a standing charge and extra costs for the level of service, some direct wage schemes with a piecework and guaranteed minimum payment system.

(iii) These costs can be represented algebraically as follows.

Linear semi-variable cost

$$y = a + bx$$

Curvi-linear semi-variable cost (where the variable portion can be approximated by a parabola)

$$y = a + bx + cx^2 + \dots\dots\ px^n$$

'Stepped' costs

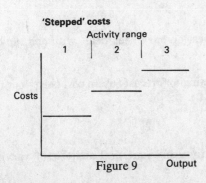

Figure 9

Notes:

(a) These are costs which have continuous characteristics - of a fixed or variable nature - for a given range of activity then, when the activity changes, the cost varies sharply producing a discontinuous function.

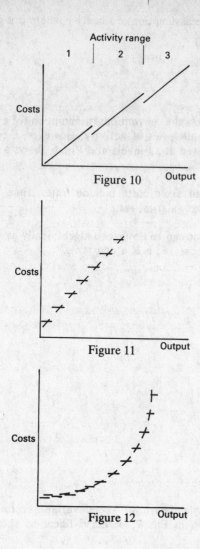

Figure 10

Figure 11

Figure 12

(b)   If the range of activity being considered lies within one step, say activity range 2 on Figs. 9 and 10, then for analysis purposes the cost can be considered as fixed or variable as appropriate within the given activity range.

(c)   Two typical examples of step costs are, **supervisory salaries** (up to a certain activity level, one is sufficient but there comes a point when an additional supervisor becomes necessary see Fig.9) and bought in material costs when there are **discounts** see Fig. 10.

(d)   There is not a simple algebraic expression for step costs but where the steps are relatively small it is usual to make a linear approximation (Figs. 11 and 12). When that is done the cost analysis can be carried out algebraically.

The above diagrams illustrate some commonly encountered cost functions but, of course, many others exist. A given cost may be purely variable up to a certain activity level when it reaches a ceiling and can then be considered as fixed. There may be declining (or increasing) rates paid say, as commission, within fixed minima and maxima; there may be costs which have linear characteristics for one activity range, curvi-linear for another and which are fixed at a third. In all cases the **individual characteristics of the specific cost** must be analysed in order to be able to make realistic predictions. Overall, simplistic assumptions about cost characteristics are very unlikely to produce accurate forecasts and in many cases the quality of planning and decision making is directly related to the accuracy of the forecasts involved.

COST FORECASTING

10.   So far in this chapter the various problems associated with cost classification have been dealt with and typical cost behaviour patterns have been described.

This background is vital to the management accountant when he is attempting to forecast future cost behaviour for use in planning and decision making.

There are three broad approaches to the problem of cost forecasting:

(i)   that based on extrapolation of historical costs and data, frequently using statistical analysis of varying degrees of sophistication,

(ii)   the accounts classification method, and

(iii)   the industrial engineering approach.

These are dealt with below.

INDUSTRIAL ENGINEERING APPROACH

11. Where there are no previous cost records, for example, the launching of a completely new product or where conditions have changed substantially, any form of statistical analysis is likely to be of little or no value. It is in such circumstances that the engineering approach can be used. This method uses a detailed, elemental approach to establish the required level of inputs (materials, labour, facilities, capital equipment) for a particular level of output. These physical inputs are then converted into money costs. The engineering approach is lengthy and can be expensive but when used for the right purposes it can be quite accurate.

It is most appropriate for estimating production costs and where there are clear, physical relationships between inputs and outputs. In addition to separating the fixed and variable elements of cost the method will also establish efficiency targets for different levels of activity which can be used for subsequent monitoring and control purposes.

The engineering approach is not so useful when there is a less direct relationship between costs, activity levels and outputs; for example, maintenance - administration and other overhead items.

The engineering approach uses work study and production engineering techniques and seeks to establish what a cost should be. It will be apparent that this is the same approach which is used to establish the basis of standard costs.

THE ACCOUNTS CLASSIFICATION METHOD

12. This method involves examination of the accounting records and classifying each item on the basis of its assumed behaviour, eg rent and rates as fixed, material cost as variable.

Considerable difficulties arise with the large number of costs which are semi-variable. For each of these costs an estimate must be made of the fixed and variable components. This may be relatively easy for some costs (electricity charges can be analysed into fixed and variable charges by studying published tariffs) but much more difficult for others, for example, maintenance.

The accounts classification method is quick and inexpensive but suffers from several limitations:

(a)   The initial classification has a considerable subjective element.

(b)   The method of dealing with semi-variable costs is often arbitrary.

(c)   By their nature, step costs are likely to be forced into either a fixed or variable category with a subsequent loss of accuracy.

(d)   For this method it is normal to use the latest details from the cost accounts which naturally relate to past events. These may not be representative of future conditions which are of prime importance as far as cost forecasting is concerned.

FORECASTING USING HISTORICAL DATA

13. Frequently data will be available on the past costs incurred, performance levels, output, sales and similar matters which are used as a basis for forecasting future values. Numerous techniques have been developed to help with this process ranging from simple arithmetic and visual methods to advanced, computer based statistical systems. The more important ones from the point of view of the management accountant are dealt with later in this chapter. Regardless of the sophistication of the technique uses there is the presumption that the past will provide some guidance to the future, as indeed it often does. However, before using any method based on historical data for extrapolation into the future the data must be critically examined to ensure their appropriateness for the intended purpose.

Typical of the steps to be taken are the following.

(a)   Check the time period over which the data were collected.

The time scale chosen should be long enough for periodic costs to be included but short enough to avoid the averaging of variations in the level of activity. Averages tend to hide the underlying relationships between cost and level of activity.

(b)   Check that non-volume factors are comparable.

Most cost forecasting exercises are carried out to explore the effect on cost of changes in the level of activity. However many other factors influence cost: for example, changes in technology, production and administrative methods, changes in efficiency, changes in material, labour and other input costs, strikes, weather conditions and numerous other factors. These non volume factors tend to obscure the cost fluctuations due to volume alone and the data must be examined closely to ensure that the non volume factors were broadly similar in the past to the forecasted future conditions. Frequently adjustments have to be made to the data before it can be used for forecasting purposes. Unexamined and unadjusted historical data will only be suitable for forecasting purposes in the most exceptional circumstances.

(c) Examine the accounting methods and policies used for the data.

The ways in which the data are collected and the accounting policies used can introduce bias in the data which may require adjustment.

Examples include: the ways in which apportionments have been made, the treatment of by-products, depreciation policies, cost data being out of phase with the activity to which they relate (eg wages and bonuses paid in arrears).

(d) Choice of the independent variable.

To make cost predictions some form of cost function is required. This will contain a **dependent variable**, usually called y, (ie the cost) and one or more **independent variables** usually called x.

The dependent variable is expressed as a function of the independent variable thus

$$y = f(x)$$

for example, the cost of petrol consumed (the dependent variable) could be expressed as a function of the miles travelled (the independent variable) thus:

$$\text{cost of petrol} = f(\text{miles travelled})$$

Frequently for accounting purposes only one independent variable is used but more than one independent variable may be employed, in which case more sophisticated statistical techniques will be necessary. At the stage of reviewing the basic data it is necessary to establish whether one independent variable will result in acceptable accuracy and, if so, which of the possible independent variables should be chosen? Should it be units or production, labour hours, sales volume, machine hours, weight processed, orders handled? For examination purposes the independent variable is usually clearly stated but in practice it is frequently very difficult to select a single independent variable which provides acceptable accuracy.

LINEAR REGRESSION LINES

14. If it is decided that a linear relationship is a reasonable representation of the cost function there are numerous methods of establishing the fixed and variable characteristics so as to be able to forecast the anticipated future cost. The methods described in detail in this manual are the 'high-low' technique, the visual method using scattergraphs, and the least squares method of simple linear regression analysis. In addition there is some discussion on multiple regression analysis. The methods are described below.

'HIGH-LOW' TECHNIQUE

15. The recorded cost and activity data are plotted on a graph and the two points representing the highest cost and the lowest cost respectively are joined by a straight line. The slope of the line represents the variable cost per unit and the intercept with the vertical axis represents the fixed cost. This is illustrated in Fig. 13.

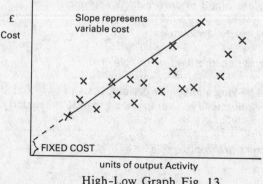

High-Low Graph Fig. 13

The high-low method is simple, crude and because it relies on two extreme points, it may not be very representative of the data. For example the line in Figure 13, probably overstates the variable cost and understates the fixed cost of the data represented. Graphical methods need not be used for the high-low system. Simple arithmetic readily gives the required answers.

For example, assume the following data have been collected on production levels and associated costs

	PRODUCTION LEVEL (UNITS)	COSTS £
LOWEST LEVEL	2,000	8,000
HIGHEST LEVEL	4,000	12,000

$\therefore$ Variable costs per unit $= \dfrac{\text{Difference in costs}}{\text{Difference in activity}} = \dfrac{£4,000}{2,000}$

$= £2 \text{ per unit}$

The fixed element can be calculated by deducting the total variable cost from the cost at either level, as follows:

Fixed Cost $=$ Total Cost – Variable Costs
$=$ £8,000 – (2,000 x £2) = £4,000

The high-low method ignores all other observations save for the two extreme values and is likely to be unrepresentative of all the data. Its use is not recommended because of its inherent limitations.

THE SCATTERGRAPH METHOD

16. Cost and activity data are plotted in a similar manner to that above and a line drawn at an angle which is judged to be the best representation of the slope of the plottings.

This is illustrated in Fig. 14.

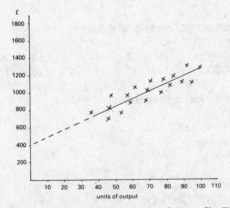

Scattergraph showing visual line of best fit Fig. 14

The dotted line is drawn to show the intersection with the vertical axis and thus gives an estimate of the fixed content of the cost being considered, in this case £400. The slope of the line, ie the variable element, is found as follows:

cost @ zero activity $=$ £400
cost @ 100 units activity $=$ £1250

$\dfrac{1250 - 400}{100 - 0} = £8.5$

$\therefore$ the estimate cost function
$= £400 + 8.5x$ where x = units of output, ie the independent variable.

The graphical method is simple to use and provides a visual indication of approximate cost behaviour. Because each individual is likely to draw a different line with a different slope the method is subjective and approximate. A more objective and accurate approach is to calculate the line of best fit mathematically using the least squares method.

LEAST SQUARES METHOD OF REGRESSION ANALYSIS

17. When it has been established that a causal relationship exists in the data and that a linear function is appropriate the statistical technique known as **least squares** is frequently used to establish values for the coefficients a and b (representing fixed and variable cost respectively) in the linear cost function

$$y = a + bx$$

where y is total cost – the dependent variable
and x is the agreed measure of activity – the independent variable

There are many computer packages available to calculate the coefficients but for simple regression analysis (ie as illustrated above with one independent variable) the coefficients are easily calculated using one of the following approaches, either:

Solve the following two equations

$$\Sigma y = an + b\Sigma x \ldots \ldots I$$
$$\Sigma xy = a\Sigma x + b\Sigma x^2 \ldots \ldots II$$

These are known as the NORMAL EQUATIONS

or: Transpose the normal equations and calculate the coefficients directly.

$$a = \frac{\Sigma y \Sigma x^2 - \Sigma x \Sigma xy}{n(\Sigma x^2) - (\Sigma x)^2}$$

$$b = \frac{n\Sigma xy - \Sigma x \Sigma y}{n(\Sigma x^2) - (\Sigma x)^2}$$

Both approaches are illustrated in the following example.

Example 1

The following data have been collected on costs and output:

Output (000's)	1	2	3	4	5	6	7
Costs (£'000s)	14	17	15	23	18	22	31

Calculate the coefficients in the linear cost function
y = a + bx
using   (i) the Normal Equations and
          (ii) the coefficient formulae.

Solution

Output (x)	Costs (y)	xy	x²
1	14	14	1
2	17	34	4
3	15	45	9
4	23	92	16
5	18	90	25
6	22	132	36
7	31	217	49
Σx = 28	Σy = 140	Σxy = 624	Σx² = 140

where n = 7 (ie number of pairs of readings)

   (i)   Using the normal equations

$$140 = 7a + 28b \ldots \ldots I$$
$$624 = 28a + 140b \ldots \ldots II$$

and eliminating one coefficient thus

$$624 = 28a + 140b \quad \ldots\ldots \text{ II}$$
$$560 = 28a + 112b \quad \ldots\ldots \text{ 1 x 4}$$

$$64 = 28b$$

∴   b = 2.286 and, substituting this value in one of the equations, the value of a is found to be 10.86

∴   Regression line is   y = 10.86 + 2.86x

(ii)   Using the coefficient formulae

$$a = \frac{(140 \times 140) - (28 \times 624)}{7(140) - 28^2} = \underline{10.86}$$

$$b = \frac{7(624) - (28 \times 140)}{7(140) - 28^2} = \underline{2.286}$$

When the coefficients have been calculated the cost function can be used for forecasting simply by inserting the appropriate level of activity, ie a value for x, and calculating the resulting total cost.

For example, where are the predicted costs at output levels of:

              (a)   4,500 units (ie 4.5 in '000s)
and   (b)   8,000 units (ie 8 in '000s)?

(a)   y   =   10.86 + 2.286 (4.5)
            =   £21.147

Note: A prediction *within* the range of the original observations (1 to 7 in Example 1) is known as an INTERPOLATION.

(b)   y   =   10.86 + 2.286 (8)
            =   £29,148

Note: A prediction *outside* the range of original observations is known as an EXTRAPOLATION.

USING LEAST SQUARES IN PRACTICE

18.   A line of best fit can be calculated for any set of data however widely scattered by mechanically using the least squares method. However the values of fixed and variable costs obtained may be of little practical use unless:

(a)   There is a clear causal relationship between the data.
(b)   There is good evidence of correlation.
(c)   The line of best fit calculated is a good predictor of the trend in data.

These three factors are dealt with below.

CAUSAL RELATIONSHIP

19.   There must be a cause and effect relationship between the variables. This can only be established by a knowledge of the practicalities of the situation being studied. Correlation calculations merely tell us if two variables move together not if the movement of one causes the movement of the other. There is, unfortunately, no simple test which enables causal relationships to be determined.

CORRELATION

20.   Having established that a causal relationship exists between the data, it is worthwhile to test for evidence of good correlation prior to carrying out a least squares calculation.

This can be done by carrying out a significance test of the correlation between the two variables using a t-test.

This is illustrated using the data from Example 1 above.

x	y	x^2	y^2	xy
1	14	1	196	14
2	17	4	289	34
3	15	9	225	45
4	23	16	529	92
5	18	25	324	90
6	22	36	484	132
7	31	49	961	624
$\Sigma = 28$	140	140	30,008	624

∴   the calculated t value is

$$t = r \sqrt{\frac{n - 2}{1 - r^2}}$$

$$\text{where } r = \frac{n\Sigma xy - \Sigma x\Sigma y}{[n\Sigma x^2 - (\Sigma x)^2][n\Sigma y^2 - (\Sigma y)^2]}$$

$$= \frac{7 \times 624 - 28 \times 140}{[7 \times 140 - 28^2][7 \times 3008 - 140^2]}$$

$$= \underline{0.839}$$

$$\therefore t = 0.839 \; \frac{\sqrt{7-2}}{\sqrt{1 - (0.839^2)}} = \underline{3.45}$$

The values of t from statistical tables for 5 degrees of freedom are:

at the 95% level = 2.57
at the 99% level = 4.03

∴ we may conclude that as the calculated t value is greater than the value at the 95% level there is evidence of real correlation at the 95% level of significance but not at the 99% level.

PREDICTIVE QUALITY OF THE CALCULATED REGRESSION LINE

21. Having calculated the regression line we now wish to know if the calculated regression coefficients have good predictive qualities. This is done by calculating the COEFFICIENT OF DETERMINATION (r^2).

This coefficient calculates what proportion of the variation in the actual values of y (costs in the example above) may be predicted by changes in the value of x (activity in this example)

∴ $r^2 = \dfrac{\text{Explained Variation}}{\text{Total Variation}}$

and as r has been calculated above

$$r^2 = .839^2$$
$$= \underline{.704} \text{ or } \underline{70.4\%}$$

This can be interpreted in the example above that 70.4% of the variations in costs may be predicted by changes in the output level. Alternatively, factors other than output changes influence costs to the extent of (100 - 70.4)%, ie 29.6%.

Note: Alternative methods exist for assessing the predictive quality of the regression line. One common method is to calculate confidence intervals for the value of the regression coefficient, b. These intervals show for a given probability, say 95%, the range which contains the true variable cost.

How to calculate confidence intervals and other more advanced aspects of regression analysis are described in detail in *Quantitative Techniques, T. Lucey, DP Publications.*

MULTIPLE LINEAR REGRESSION ANALYSIS

22. There are occasions when the accuracy of cost prediction can be improved by basing the forecast on two or more independent variables rather than the single variable used so far. For example, assume that it has been discovered that total cost depend on a linear function of labour hours, weight handled, and machine hours, then the cost function would be:

$$y = a + bx_1 + cx_2 + dx_3 + \mu$$

Where a, b, c and d are coefficients similar to those discussed previously.

μ is a disturbance term that includes the net effect of other factors,

$$
\begin{aligned}
\text{and } x_1 &= \text{labour hours} \\
x_2 &= \text{weight handled} \\
x_3 &= \text{machine hours} \\
\text{and } y &= \text{total cost}
\end{aligned}
$$

The manual calculation of multiple regression coefficients is laborious but most computer systems have statistical packages which can calculate the values of the individual coefficients, their standard errors, the overall value of y, confidence intervals for the regression line and so on.

As an example of the application of multiple regression consider a firm which has found that its total overheads are dependent on labour hours, machine hours and units produced. Analysis has produced the following multiple regression formula:

$$y = £25,000 + 7.3x_1 + 4.8x_2 + 3.1x_3$$

$$
\begin{aligned}
\text{Where } y &= \text{total overheads} \\
x_1 &= \text{labour hours} \\
x_2 &= \text{machine hours} \\
x_3 &= \text{units produced}
\end{aligned}
$$

What are the predicted overheads in a period when there were 16,500 labour hours, 7,300 machine hours and 13,400 units were produced?

Solution

$$
\begin{aligned}
y &= £25,000 + 7.3(16,500) + 4.8(7,300) + 3.1(13,400) \\
&= \underline{£222,030}
\end{aligned}
$$

In a similar manner to the methods shown for simple regression, the coefficient of multiple determination and the standard errors of the individual coefficients can be calculated. Those wishing to study this in greater detail are advised to see *Quantitative Techniques, Ibid.*

THE LEARNING CURVE

23. Cost predictions especially those relating to direct labour costs should allow for the effects of learning process. During the early stages or producing a new part or carrying out a new process, experience and skill is gained, productivity increases and there is a reduction of time taken per unit.

Studies have shown that there is a tendency for the time per unit to reduce at some constant rate as production mounts. For example, an 80% learning curve means that as cumulative production quantities double the average time per unit falls by 20%.

This is shown in Table 1.

Cumulative Production (units)	Cumulative Time Taken (mins)	Average Time Per Unit
20	400	20
40	640	16(20 x 80%)
80	1024	12.8(20 x 80% x 80%)
160	1638.4	10.24(20 x 80% x 80% x 80%)

Illustration of an 80% Learning Curve Table 1

The general form of such a learning curve is a geometric function of the form

$$y = ax^b$$

where
$$y = \text{average labour hours per unit}$$
$$a = \text{number of labour hours for the first unit}$$
$$x = \text{cumulative number of units}$$
$$b = \text{the learning coefficient}$$

The learning coefficient is calculated as follows:

$$b = \frac{\log(1 - \text{Proportionate decrease})}{\log 2}$$

thus for a 20% decrease (ie an 80% learning curve)

$$b = \frac{\log(1 - 0.2)}{\log 2} = \frac{\bar{1}.90309}{0.30103} = \underline{-0.322}$$

Note: It will be remembered from foundation mathematics that the log of 0.8 is conventionally written as $\bar{1}.90309$ but is actually $-1+0.90309$, ie -0.09691 which, divided by 0.30103, gives -0.322.

Having established the values for the function it can be used to find the expected labour time per unit. For example, with an 80% learning curve and a time of 10 minutes for the first unit, what is the expected time per unit when cumulative production is 20 units?

$$y = ax^b = 10 \times 20^{-0.322} = \underline{3.812 \text{ mins}}$$

Notes

(a)   Whilst it is clear that learning does take place and that average times are likely to reduce, in practice it is highly unlikely that there will be a regular consistent rate of decrease as exemplified above. Accordingly, any cost predictions based on conventional learning curves should be viewed with caution (as should any form of prediction!).

(b)   Whilst the regularity of conventional learning curves can be questioned it would be wrong to ignore the learning effect altogether when making labour cost predictions.

APPLICATIONS OF LEARNING CURVE THEORY

24.   The original studies of learning curves were in connection with aircraft construction in World War 2. Aircraft manufacture is labour intensive and complex and these features are characteristic of industries where learning curves might reasonably be applied; for example, shipbuilding, electronics, construction and so on. The more capital intensive an industry, the more automated, the greater the use of robots and so on, the less likely there is to be any form of regular learning curve. Where they are applicable, learning curves typically vary between 70% and 90%. Although 80% learning curves are commonly encountered, as previously illustrated, students are advised that *any* value may be encountered in an examination so it is essential to be able to calculate the learning coefficient from first principles.

Where learning takes place with a regular pattern it is important to take account of the reduction in labour hours and costs per unit. This is important in such areas as; production planning and work scheduling, standard costing, overhead absorption (where this is based on labour hours), pricing policy (where this is based on costs).

COST BEHAVIOUR AND TIME SCALE

25.   The methods and techniques illustrated in this chapter are most appropriate for short run planning and decision making purposes. This means that the relationship between costs and activity and the classifications of the costs themselves are only likely to hold good over a relatively short time span. What is a 'relatively short time span' depends on the particular circumstances, it may be three months, six months, a year; it is unlikely to be as long as five years. Over longer time periods, unpredictable factors are bound to occur, technology will improve, materials may become scarce, so that predictions of cost behaviour, based on examination of historical data, are likely to be increasingly unreliable. For longer term forecasting, qualitative factors and judgement play an increasing role. For example, in the **Delphi Method** of forecasting a panel of experts independently answers a sequence of questionnaires in which the answers to one questionnaire are used to produce the next questionnaire. Thus information is shared and subsequent judgement become more refined. In this way qualitative judgements are used in a systematic fashion to produce long term forecasts.

SUMMARY

26. (a)   The ability to predict costs (and other factors such as sales) is a vital part of supplying information for planning and decision making.

(b)   An essential preliminary to cost prediction is the consideration of what costs (or parts of cost) are fixed and which are variable.

(c)   There are difficulties with the usual cost classifications. Variable costs are not always linear, fixed costs can and do change, and many costs are semi-fixed or semi-variable.

(d)   Costs frequently do not behave in regular fashions and a cost may be linear, curvi-linear or stepped at different activity levels.

(e)   Cost extrapolations outside normal activity ranges are likely to be less accurate.

(f)   A convex function is one in which there are economies of scale. A concave function is one where diminishing returns operate.

(g)   A common curvi-linear function is a parabola which has the form

$$f = bx + cx^2 + dx^3 \ldots \ldots px^n$$

(h)   For simplicity, linear approximations of curvi-linear functions are frequently made.

(i)   There are three approaches to cost forecasting; extrapolation based on historical data using statistical techniques, accounts classification, and the industrial engineering approach.

(j)   Before using any statistical technique the data to be worked on should be checked for their appropriateness.

(k)   Common methods used for linear regression analysis are the 'high-low' technique, scattergraphs, and the lest square method of simple, linear regression analysis.

(l)   The least squares methods produces values for the coefficients a and b in the linear function,

$$y = a + bx$$

(m)   The coefficients are found by solving the Normal Equations or directly by using transpositions of the Normal Equations.

(n)   Although the coefficients can always be calculated, they are of little value for predictive purposes unless there is a causal relationship in the data, there is evidence of correlation, and the line of best fit is a good predictor of the trend.

(o)   The correlation between the two variables can be established by using a t test and the predictive quality of the trend line can be assessed by calculating the coefficient of determination, r^2.

(p)   Multiple regression analysis is where the function has two or more independent variables. The use of multiple regression may be necessary where total cost is a function of two or more activity indicators, eg labour hours, tonnage produced, and machine hours.

(q)   A learning curve is the term given to the function representing the reduction in time taken per unit due to experience and development of skill. It is represented by the function $y = ax^b$. An 80% learning curve (when cumulative production doubles average unit time falls by 20%) is represented by $y = ax^{-0.322}$.

(r)   When longer term forecasting is required extrapolations from historical data become less relevant, and judgement and qualitative factors become increasingly important.

POINTS TO NOTE

27. (a)   Forecasting is a large and complex subject and the intending management accountant is advised to master the introduction contained in this chapter and pursue the subject in one of the specialist books on the subject.

(b)   A factor which should always be considered when making cost and revenue forecasts is the rate of inflation. In general, the management accountant is concerned with values in real terms so care must be taken to allow for the projected rate of inflation particularly when considering such items as labour and material costs, selling prices, and bought in services.

ADDITIONAL READING

Applied Regression Analysis	Draper and Smith, WILEY
Forecasting Methods in Business and Management	Firth, Arnold
Statistical Cost Analysis	Johnston, MCGRAW HILL
Forecasting Costs and Prices	Morrell, CIMA
Forecasting for Business	Wood and Fildes, LONGMAN

SELF REVIEW QUESTIONS

1. *For cost prediction purposes what are the essential cost classifications? (3)*

2. *Why must the management accountant continually review conventional cost classifications and the conventional assumptions regarding cost behaviour? (4)*

3. *Why is it unlikely that all variable costs vary in relation to the same measure of activity? (4)*

4. *What is a concave function? - a convex function? (6)*

5. *What is the formula for a parabolic cost function with four independent variables? (7)*

6. *Why are linear approximations used? (8)*

7. *What is a stepped cost? (9)*

8. *What is the accounts classification method of cost forecasting? (12)*

9. *What questions should be asked regarding the data to be used for forecasting? (13)*

10. *Describe the 'high-low' technique (15)*

11. *How is a scattergraph drawn and used? (16)*

12. *Give the Normal Equations used in the least squares method. (17)*

13. *What is a causal relationship? (19)*

14. *How is a significance test of the correlation between the two variables used for regression analysis?*

15. *What is the coefficient of determination and what is its meaning? (21)*

16. *Why is multiple regression analysis used? (22)*

17. *What is an 80% learning curve? (23)*

18. *Why are statistical and other techniques based on historical data of less validity for long term forecasting? (24)*

EXAMINATION QUESTION WITH ANSWER COMMENCING PAGE 340

A1. *'Some costs are escapable in some sense but not in others' (from* **Overhead** *Costs by W. Arthur Lewis).*

   Required:

   An examination of categories of fixed costs and the implications of the analysis of these groups for decision making purposes.

   ACCA, Management Accounting.

4. Information and Management Accounting

INTRODUCTION

1.   As an information specialist the management accountant must be aware of the nature of information and its attributes. This chapter discusses the distinction between data and information and explains the nature and elements of communications.

Noise and redundancy are described and the desirable properties of management accounting information are discussed. Finally, ways in which the effects of uncertainty can be included in information are explained.

DATA AND INFORMATION

2.   The terms 'data' and 'information' are commonly used interchangeably but from a technical viewpoint they can be distinguished from each other. Data can be defined as groups of non random symbols which represent quantities, events, actions and things. Data are made up of characters which may be alphabetic or numeric or special symbols.

Information is data which have been processed into a form which is meaningful to the recipient and which is of real or perceived value for the intended purpose which, as far as the management accountant is concerned, is likely to be for planning, control or decision making. Thus data are the raw materials from which information is produced. It also follows that which is information for one purpose or level in the organisation may be used as data for further processing into information for a different purpose and level.

Note: This latter point is a key element in management accounting. Information produced must be relevant for the intended purpose otherwise it is useless. This means that, for example, a cost prepared for use in today's selling price quotation may need to be reanalysed and reprocessed to be able to use it for a make or buy decision. This approach is summed up in the well known management accounting phrase, 'different costs for different purposes'. The relevancy requirement may make much of the information produced by the costing system (eg product costs) inappropriate for management accounting purposes without further analysis. This requirement emphasises the need for the management accounting system to be flexible so that the information produced by the system is use specific.

INFORMATION ATTRIBUTES

3.   From a system's viewpoint information possesses a number of attributes

(a)   It reduces uncertainty. Rapid feedback of information helps to reduce uncertainty. This is the main rationale for the introduction of any information system.

(b)   It may be true or false. If the recipient of false information believes it to be true the effect is the same as if it were true.

(c)   It may be incremental. It may update or add new increments to information already available.

(d)   It may be a correction of past false information.

(e)   It may confirm existing information. Note that such information may be of value because it increases the recipient's perception of the correctness of the information.

(f)   It has surprise value. This is the attribute which above all determines the information content of a message or report. The greater the probability of an event occurring the smaller will be the amount of information in a message saying that the event has occurred. The greater the surprise, the more informative the message.

The message, 'It will be dark tonight' has no surprise value and hence contains no information.

COMMUNICATIONS SYSTEMS

4.   Data arise from both internal and external sources and frequently are derived from the day to day operations of the organisation – buying and using materials, selling to customers, making products, receiving and paying cash and so forth. Invoices and other documents are coded, analysed and the data recorded. Subsequently the data are processed perhaps using particular decision or planning techniques, comparisons are made, inferences are drawn and information for a particular purpose is produced. This information is used to prepare a report or statement or a display on a terminal which is then communicated to the manager for his use.

The above very brief outline describes a typical communication system of which the management accounting system is but one example. The various parts of a typical communication system are shown in Figure 1 related to a management accounting example and several important terms are described.

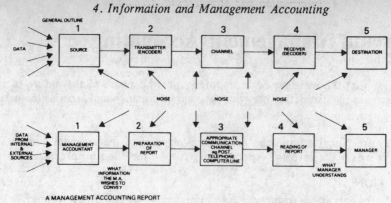

A MANAGEMENT ACCOUNTING REPORT

Fig. 1   Communication Systems

NOISE

5.   This is the term used in communication theory for any influences or factors which cause the message at the receiver being different to the message transmitted. In a general business sense, noise makes the perceived content of a message different from that intended to be conveyed. Noise may arise from numerous factors including: wrong coding, poor presentation, bad form design, illegible writing, misinterpretation, actual physical noise, unexplained jargon. it is clearly important that noise is kept to a minimum and the management accountant should examine each of the gathering, processing, transmitting and receiving stages so that maximum effectiveness is achieved.

REDUNDANCY

6.   This means that more symbols, figures or words are used to represent the message than is strictly necessary.

However, the additional material helps the presence of errors to be detected and, in some instances, can provide for the correction of those errors. The effects of noise can be reduced by the use of some redundancy. Redundancy may consist of repetition of words or figures, multiple copies, confirmatory letters following telephone calls, hard copy printouts following a visual display etc. Normal messages in English exhibit varying degrees of redundancy and it is this fact which makes poor handwriting decipherable and enables the comprehension of messages. Too much redundancy is to be avoided as the amount of repetition and/or extraneous material may obscure the essential information contained in a message.

PERCEPTION

7.   For our purpose this can be defined as the understanding a person obtains from a message or report.

This is an obvious area of importance to the management accountant must of whose output is in the form of reports and statements. A communication can have at least three meanings:

(a) What the sender intended to send
(b) What is actually contained in the message, and
(c) What meaning the receiver understands from the message.

The process of perception in any individual varies from time to time and people attach meanings to messages in accordance with their attitudes, past experiences, and their knowledge of the source of the message. Because only the receivers perception of a message is relevant - he presumably will be taking some action based on the message - it is vital for the sender to reduce possible ambiguities and noise so as to bring the understanding of the receiver as close as possible to that of the sender. The receiver's perception will be enhances if the following points are observed.

(a) Avoidance of unfamiliar technical or accounting jargon. Where its use is unavoidable clear explanations should be provided.

(b) Collaboration with the receiver on the content, format and presentation of reports and statements.

(c) Regular feedback of comments and criticisms from the managers to the management accountant on the effectiveness of the information system.

(d) Gain the confidence of the managers involved by showing that the management accounting system is supportive and not threatening and can be relied upon to produce relevant, accurate and timely information.

(e) The avoidance of excessive detail. Detail should not be confused with accuracy. Every superfluous character means more processing, more delay, extra assimilation and possibly poorer decisions. The basic rule, as with the volume of information, is as little as possible consistent with effective managerial action.

VALUE OF INFORMATION

8.   Information has no value in itself; its value derives from the changes in decision behaviour caused by the information being available. It follows from this that more detailed information, more accurate information, earlier information is not necessarily better information. Only if it improves the resulting decisions is it better information. The production of information only incurs costs which are frequently considerable. Benefits only arise from **actions**. A typical relationship between costs and values is shown in Figure 2.

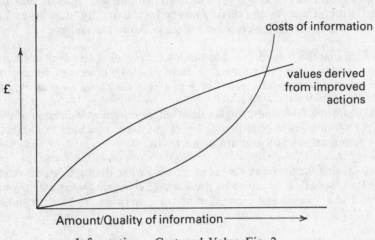

Information - Cost and Value Fig. 2

It follows from economic principles that additional information should be produced only if the additional expected value is greater than the additional expected costs.

Remember - information can only produce costs and only actions can produce benefits.

DESIRABLE PROPERTIES OF MANAGEMENT ACCOUNTING INFORMATION

9.   Investigations into information systems, including accounting ones, have shown that much of the information produced is ignored by the managers concerned. It follows that information which is ignored cannot influence the decision making process and therefore can have no value. To ensure that management accounting information is used effectively the following actors must be considered.

(a)   **Economic reality**. The information should correctly reflect the underlying economic realities. This is the prime requirement and may mean adjusting conventionally prepared accounting information to show more effectively the real economic consequences.

(b)   **Relevance**. The information must be relevant for the person and purpose intended. As an example, information prepared for performance and control purposes should cover only those items for which the manager is responsible.

(c)   **Timing**. The information must be produced in time for it to be used effectively.

(d)   **Accuracy**. The information should be sufficiently accurate for the intended purpose. A reputation for accuracy will enhance the value of the information to the recipient and will make it more likely to be used.

Note: There is no such thing as absolute accuracy. What is required is information, prepared according to correct principles, that can be relied upon for the intended purpose. This may mean that a realistic, speedily prepared estimate may be more useful than a more precise answer produced some time later.

(e)   **Understandability**. The information must be capable of being understood by the recipient. Typical of the ways to increase comprehension are the following:

   (i)   avoidance of unexplained terminology
   (ii)   use of charts, diagrams and tabulated information where appropriate
   (iii)   use of exception reporting and comparative figures
   (iv)   good report and statement layouts
   (v)   a reasonable, but not excessive, amount of redundancy
   (vi)   eliciting the recipient's views and suggestions regarding the understandability of the information.

(f)   **Detail**. Frequently the amount of detail in a statement or report will depend on the recipients level in the organisation. There is a tendency for information to be aggregated (summarised, totalled, precised) more and more according to the recipient's level in the hierarchy. There are usually sound reasons for this but it should be remembered that aggregation reduces the information content of a message or report. The amount of detail should be that which is sufficient for the intended purpose.

UNCERTAINTY AND MANAGEMENT ACCOUNTING INFORMATION

10.   Uncertainty to a greater or lesser degree is present in all planning and decision making situations. It may be the possibility of machine failure, it may be the difficulties of forecasting inflation or exchange rates, it may be the effects of competitors, changing tastes, government actions - the list is endless.

Accordingly, it is vital that the preparer of information for planning and decision making purposes presents the information in a manner which helps the manager to understand the effects of uncertainty on the problem being considered and in particular, now uncertainty is likely to affect the range of possible outcomes.

Information which is presented showing a single valued outcome with no indication of possible uncertainties can be positively misleading for the manager concerned. Some of the ways in which the effects of uncertainties can be presented in reports, statements and analyses are given below.

(a)   Presenting results and outcomes as ranges of values rather than single point estimates. This may be as a simple range (highest - lowest) or it may be by presenting the outcome(s) as a distribution of values represented by the mean or most likely value and a measure of the dispersion of the distribution - usually the standard deviation.

(b)   Using three point estimates (high, low and most likely) for analysis and presentation purposes.

(c)   Associating probabilities with the values and outcomes. The probabilities are likely to be **subjective probabilities**, ie the quantification of judgement rather than objective or statistical probabilities but in spite of this, such probabilities can provide valuable insights to the underlying uncertainties.

(d)   The use of sensitivity analysis. This is a process by which the factors involved in the situation (eg sales volume, cost per unit, inflation rate, selling price per unit and so on) are varied one at a time and the effect on the outcome noted. In this way sensitive factors - those that influence outcomes most - are identified so that they may receive further attention and analysis before a final decision is taken.

(c)   The use of confidence limits. This is particularly appropriate when forecasts are being supplied. Instead of merely a single line representing say, a forecasted cost, confidence limits each side of the line can be calculated so that the uncertainty inherent in the forecast is clearly shown. Narrow confidence limits would demonstrate a higher degree of certainty than confidence limits which are widely spaced.

Note: The treatment of uncertainty, subjective, probability, sensitivity analysis, and confidence limits is dealt with in more detail in Quantitative Techniques, T. Lucey, DP Publications.

SUMMARY

11.   (a)   Information is data processed into a form relevant for the intended purpose.

(b)   Information reduces uncertainty and has surprise value.

(c)   The major elements of a communications system are source - transmitter - channel - receiver - destination.

(d)   Noise is the term used for factors which cause the message received to be different from that transmitted.

(e)   Redundancy means that more figures or words are used than is absolutely necessary. Some redundancy is useful but too much is to be avoided.

(f)   The perception of messages and information by the receiver is all important for the management accountant and good form design, avoidance of jargon, avoidance of excessive detail, all help to improve perception.

(g)   The value of information can only come from better decisions or planning brought about by the information.

(h)   For maximum effectiveness, information produced by the management accounting system should: reflect economic reality, be relevant, timely, accurate, and understandable to the recipient.

(i)   Uncertainty is always present and the effects of uncertainty should be reflected in information produced by the management accountant. This might be by the use of ranges of outcomes, three point estimates, the use of probabilities, sensitivity analysis, the use of confidence limits and so on.

POINTS TO NOTE

12. (a)   It must be remembers that ALL information is incomplete and to some extent inaccurate. It follows from this that many so called 'optimal' solutions are only optimal in relation to the (imperfect) information on which they are based.

(c)   Much management information is now produced by computer. This has many advantages, eg greater depth of analysis, use of statistical and operational techniques, speed and so on. However, great care must still be taken to ensure that the information produced is **relevant for the intended purpose**. Speediness and volume of information are no substitutes for relevance.

ADDITIONAL READING

Report writing in business   Bentley, CIMA

Cybernetics and Management   Beer, ENGLISH UNIVERSITIES PRESS

Accounting Information Systems   Bodnar, ALLYN & BACON

Management Information systems   Lucey, DP PUBLICATIONS

SELF REVIEW QUESTIONS

1.   Distinguish between data and information. (2)

2.   Give six attributes of information. (3)

3.   What are the elements in a communication system? (4)

4.   What is noise? (5)

5.   What is redundancy and why is a certain amount necessary in a message? (6)

6.   How can the receiver's perception be increased? (7)

7.   How is the value of information derived? (8)

8.   Give five desirable properties of management accounting information. (9)

9.   How can the effects of uncertainty be incorporated in reports and statements? (10)

EXAMINATION QUESTION WITH ANSWER COMMENCING PAGE 340

A1. *What are the desirable characteristics of effective management information statements or reports? Why are the characteristics desirable and to what extent to those desirable attributes conflict with each other?*

ACCA, Management Accounting.

Planning

The Management Accountant is one of the major providers of information for planning purposes and to do this effectively it is essential that he understand the nature of planning, how plans are established, the distinction between long term and short term planning, the place of budgeting in the planning process, how to derive individual budgets and the overall Master Budget, and how planning relates to control.

The following three chapters cover these and related matters and commence with an introduction to some important system concepts which are highly relevant to the planning and subsequent control process.

Statistical and Operational research techniques can provide invaluable assistance in planning. Examples include the statistical aids to forecasting cost behaviour already dealt with in Chapter 3 and such operational research techniques as Linear Programming dealt with later in the manual.

5. Planning – Systems Concepts

INTRODUCTION

1. This chapter covers the aspects of General System Theory (GST) which are most relevant in relation to planning. Systems and the systems approach are defined and three of the main types of systems are described. Open and closed systems are explained together with the problem of sub-optimality. Finally, the relationship of planning and control is discussed.

WHAT IS A SYSTEM?

2. Systems exist in every facet of life. There are mechanical systems, biological systems, information systems, social systems, organisational systems and innumerable others. Two simple and typical definitions are:

'A system is a set of interrelated components directed to some purpose'.

'A system is a set of parts co-ordinated to accomplish a set of goals'.

Various other definitions existing but they all contain the essential elements of **parts** and **relationships** and, in the case of organisational systems, they seek to accomplish agreed objectives.

SYSTEMS APPROACH

3. The systems approach avoids taking a piecemeal approach to problems and directs the activities of the components or sub systems of the total system towards meeting overall objectives. The systems approach recognises that changes cannot be made to some parts of the system without considering the effect on the system as a whole and that the overall system characteristics are greater than the sum of the separate parts. This latter is known as the **synergy** or the 2 + 2 = 5 effect.

In relation to a particular organisation the systems approach would require consideration of the following factors:

(a) the system must be defined. This requires establishing the **boundaries** (real or arbitrary) which encompass the system being studied.

(b) The **real objectives** of the system must be specified.

(c) The **environment** in which the system operates, the interactions with the environment, and the constraints which it imposes.

(d) The indicators which will be used to measure the performance of the system as a whole.

(e) The current and anticipated resources available to operate the system.

(f) The parts of the system (ie the sub systems) their relationships, activities and objectives must be studied to ensure conformity with overall system objectives.

(g) The way that the system is managed, ie the planning and controlling of the system through information networks.

Note: It will be seen how the systems approach aligns closely to good management practice. It is objective oriented, an overall view is taken and the effects of the environment are considered.

TYPES OF SYSTEMS

4. For our purposes the three most relevant types of systems are Deterministic, Stochastic and Adaptive.

Deterministic or Mechanistic Systems. These are the simplest systems which are perfectly predictable, ie given the inputs the outputs can be predicted accurately. Machines and computer programs are examples of deterministic systems.

Stochastic or Probabilistic Systems. In these systems some states can be predicted from a previous state but only in terms of probable behaviour. Predictions will always have a certain degree of error because of the existence of random variations in the values of the system components caused by internal and external influences. For example, in an inventory control system the **average** stock or **average** demand can be predicted but the exact value of these factors at a future time cannot be predicted. Various control systems (eg Inventory Control, Production Control, Quality Control) are installed to detect and control the variations in order that they do not become of such magnitude as to endanger the fulfilment of the system objectives.

Adaptive or Self Organising or Cybernetic Systems. These are highly complex systems which adapt to the environment by altering their structure and/or parts and/or behaviour. This adaption is of the system itself and not merely the alteration of some parameter (eg a stock level) within the system. This class of system includes all living systems - animals, plants, social groups and organisations. It is a primary task of management to ensure that organisations continually adapt to changes in the environment to ensure survival and development. It is the essence of long term planning that recognition is given to the fact that organisations are adaptive systems and that environmental influences are all important.

SYSTEM RELATIONSHIPS WITH THE ENVIRONMENT

5.   The environment of a system is all other systems outside its own boundaries. Thus the environment of an organisation are the systems (ie the markets, suppliers, competitors, distribution and so on) in the sector of the economy in which it operates. The environment of a production system in an organisation is the other interacting systems within the organisation.

Systems may be **closed** or **open** systems:

Closed systems: These are systems which are self contained and do not exchange material, information or energy with the environment. In the strict sense no business or organisation system can be a closed system but for many planning and control purposes, systems are designed to be relatively closed with only minimal interactions with their environment. This greatly aids the prediction and monitoring of system performance.

Open systems: These are systems which interact and exchange information, energy and materials with their environment. To ensure survival (the primary organisational objective) adaption to changes in the environment is vital and only open systems have this capability.

These various types of systems are shown in Figure 1.

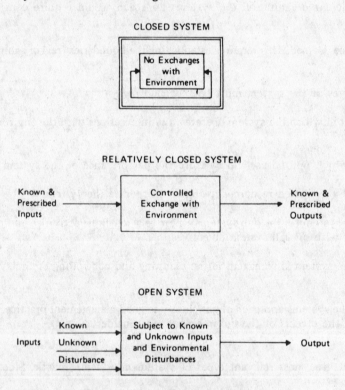

Figure 1 Relationship with Environment

Thus it will be seen that an organisation is an open, adaptive system containing within it a number of sub-systems which may be adaptive, probabilistic or deterministic.

SUB OPTIMISATION

6.   This is where the objectives of sub-systems are pursued to the detriment of the overall system goals. Each sub-system may be working at peak efficiency but this does not necessarily mean that the system as a whole is acting optimally. Sub-optimisation is probably more common than is realised and may be caused by departmental pressures and rivalries, poor communications, lack of co-ordination, poor information systems, or lack of centralised direction and

control. The avoidance of sub-optimisation is an important objective of the planning and control process. The key way of avoiding sub-optimisation is to ensure that the overall objectives of the organisation dominate the objectives of each of the sub systems. This factor must be borne in mind when planning, controlling and monitoring performance.

PLANNING AND CONTROL

7. Planning precedes control and planning without consideration of the type, frequency and method of control will largely be a waste of time. It follows from this, that part of the planning process involves the design of an appropriate control system. Control is an important element of the work of the management accountant and is dealt with in detail in a major section later in the manual after this section on planning. Students should study the following section on planning having regard to the necessity to develop concurrently appropriate control mechanisms in order to monitor the implementation of the agreed plans.

SUMMARY

8. (a) Various definitions exist of a system but all contain the essential elements of parts and relationships.
(b) The systems approach directs attention to overall objectives and thus attempts to avoid sub-optimality.
(c) Three of the most relevant types of system are, deterministic or mechanistic, stochastic or probabilistic, and adaptive or cybernetic.
(d) Open system interact with the environment, closed systems are self contained.
(e) Sub-optimisation means that the objectives of sub-systems (eg departments) are pursued to the detriment of overall objectives.
(f) Part of the planning process includes consideration of an appropriate control system.

POINTS TO NOTE

9. (a) There are few, if any, organisations where sub-optimal activities do not take place. As a primary provider of planning and control information the management accountant must seek to highlight such activities so that corrective action can be taken.

(b) Do not dismiss the basic system principles as obvious, commonsense platitudes. How many recent company failures are due to lack of recognition of the fact that the organisation (ie the system) must adapt to changes in the environment in order to survive?

ADDITIONAL READING

Management accounting: a conceptual approach   Amey & Egginton, LONGMAN

Planning and control systems - a framework for analysis   Anthony, HARVARD UNIVERSITY PRESS

Systems behaviour   Beishon, HARPER & ROW

SELF REVIEW QUESTIONS

1. *Define a system. (2)*

2. *What factors constitute the systems approach? (3)*

3. *Define a deterministic, a stochastic, and a cybernetic system. (4)*

4. *What is the difference between an open and closed system? (5)*

5. *What is sub-optimisation and why should it be avoided? (6)*

6. *When should a control system be considered? (7)*

6. Long Term Planning

INTRODUCTION

1.   This chapter defines planning in general and then specifically considers long term strategic planning which, when applied to organisations, is termed Corporate Planning (CP). The stages in CP are detailed, namely the Assessment, Objective, Evaluation and Agreement stages and the relationship with short term operational planning and control is explained. The contents of the agreed Corporate Plan are described and the advantages and disadvantages of CP are discussed. The chapter concludes with a brief discussion of computer based planning models.

PLANNING DEFINED

2.   Planning is an inescapable part of all rational human activity. Because of its importance to organisations their planning processes have become refined and structured in order to improve their efficiency.

Planning can be defined as:

"The establishment of objectives , and the formulation, evaluation and selection of the policies, strategies, tactics and action required to achieve these objectives. Planning comprises long term/strategic planning, and short term operational planning. The latter usually refers to a period of one year". *Terminology*.

Thus it will be seen that the overall process of planning covers both the long and short term. Short term tactical planning or budgeting works within a framework set by the long term plans and is dealt with in the next chapter.

LONG TERM STRATEGIC PLANNING

3.   This is variously termed 'long range planning', 'strategic planning' or, when applied to organisations, 'corporate planning'. Long term planning covers periods longer than one year and typically embraces 3, 5, 10 years or even longer periods. it can be defined as follows:

"The formulation, evaluation and selection of strategies involving a review of the objectives of an organisation, the environment in which it is to operate, an assessment of its strengths, weaknesses, opportunities and threats for the purpose of preparing a long term strategic plan of action which will attain the objective set." *Terminology*.

Note: Because the readers of this manual are likely to be more concerned with long term planning in organisations, the term **Corporate Planning** (CP) will be used subsequently.

HOW IS THE CORPORATE PLAN DEVELOPED?

4.   The process of CP consists of various stages which focus attention on four key areas: the environment, the objectives, the factors which influence the achievement of the objectives, and the choice of strategies and tactics to achieve the objectives.

The various stages are shown in Figure 1 and explained below.

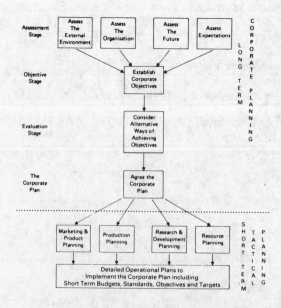

Figure 1   Corporate Planning

THE ASSESSMENT STAGE

5.   This is also known as a **Position Audit** and seeks to provide detailed answers to the following questions.

What is the existing state of the organisation and the environment in which it operates?
and

What is the environment in which the organisation will have to operate in the future?

The four aspects of the assessment stage are:

The external environment.

This includes an assessment of:

Economic, Political, Social and Technological factors affecting the organisation.

Detailed analysis of competitive activity for established products and product developments.

An assessment of current marketing and distribution policies, the degree of market penetration and acceptability and possible market development and product diversification.

Analysis of resources available to the organisation including finance, raw materials, skilled labour.

The organisation.

This is a detailed study of the organisation's strengths and weaknesses, its results, limitations and constraints. Typical of the factors to be studied are:

Analysis of production facilities, age and sophistication of plant, bottlenecks.

Analysis of personnel, their qualities, skills, age profiles, industrial relation policies and record.

Analysis of trading results, profits, turnover, contributions for product groups, sales areas and divisions.

Analysis of research and development activities including projects in progress.

Analysis of financial procedure, investment policies, working capital management.

The future.

Clearly the most difficult to assess yet the most crucial over the medium to long term covered by the CP period. There is a very wide range of factors to be considered, including:

Economic forecasts of GNP, Disposable income, Markets, Inflation, Taxation.

Political problems relating to raw materials, energy, embargos, tariffs.

Social trends in taste, purchasing power, leisure.

Technological forecasting regarding likely developments affecting the organisation.

Competitors likely actions, mergers and acquisitions.

The expectations.

A major influence on corporate objectives are the expectations of the groups involved:

Employees - their expectation of job security and satisfaction, income, pensions, leisure.

Customers - their expectations of quality, delivery, price, product availability.

Shareholders - their expectations of dividends, capital growth.

General Public - their expectations regarding environmental and pollution matters, the contribution of the organisation to the economy.

THE OBJECTIVES STAGE

6.   This is the key stage in the CP process and seeks to answer the question, Where does the organisation want to go?

The essence of CP (as in the system approach outlined earlier) is to define objectives first then consider how they can be achieved. This approach avoids major errors of sub-optimisation by ensuring that the long term corporate objectives are defined **before** the short term tactical objectives covering various facets of operations. The short term objectives and targets contribute towards the achievement of the long term corporate objectives thus encouraging co-ordination and goal congruence on the part of management.

There are very real problems in establishing corporate objectives because of the multi-facetted nature of modern business.

Drucker suggests that there are eight areas in which objectives of performance and results have to be set, ie

> Market standing
> Innovation
> Productivity
> Physical and financial resources
> Profitability
> Manager performance and development
> Worker performance and attitude
> Public responsibility

The setting of objectives is a detailed, iterative task involving much discussion but eventually objectives must be set, within each area, in clear quantifiable terms.

For example within the 'Market Standing' area specific statements would need to be made about such matters as:

> Target sales of each product
> Target sales of product ranges
> Target market share of each product
> Target market share of product ranges
> Target home/export sales of each product/product range
> Target proportions of sales by distribution channel/industrial sector
> Target proportion of sales from new/existing products
> Target new market development,
> and so on

Similar detailed objectives will be set for each of the other areas. The area most familiar to accountants, relating to profitability and finance, would include: target return on capital employed, earnings per share, operating profit, dividends, asset growth and so on.

It will be apparent that objectives covering the whole range of organisational activities are extremely diverse and because of this it is unlikely that a single performance measure, such as Return on Capital Employed, could adequately represent the whole spectrum of corporate objectives. It has been convincingly argued by Simon and others that satisficing rather than classical profit maximising behaviour is more usual. This means that the aim is to obtain a **satisfactory level** of achievement across a set of objectives rather than attempting to optimise a single measure.

The problems associated with this area are developed further in the section on Performance Appraisal.

THE EVALUATION STAGE

7.   This stage is concerned with considering the best way of moving from where the organisation is **now** (determined during the Assessment Stage) to where the organisation **wishes to be in the future** (its Objectives).

Alternative strategies, acquisitions, new products, elimination of low earning products, expansion and rearrangements of facilities, alteration of management practices and other activities are explored so as to be able to achieve the objectives. It is during this process that differences between the performance of credible plans and corporate objectives become apparent. These are called **planning gaps** and the process by which they are investigated is called **gap analysis.** Objectives should not be readily altered. The planning gap would be thoroughly investigated and all possible combinations of new activities, and strategies would be explored to establish whether the identified gaps can be filled.

Eventually at the end of the evaluation process the Corporate Plan is produced which must include the control and performance monitoring process considered necessary. This is so that there will be **information feedback** which is vital in all planning processes to ensure that the implementation of the plan is proceeding satisfactorily and to provide information on which necessary adjustments to the plan can be made. This is developed further in the sections on Control.

THE CORPORATE PLAN

8. The Corporate Plan serves as the overall background and target for the organisation over the medium to long term. It is vital that it is published and made widely available so as to avoid sub-optimisation, to encourage goal congruence, increase motivation and to provide a sense of direction and purpose to the whole organisation.

The content and size of the corporate plan will vary from organisation to organisation by typically the contents will include:

Introduction including remarks on previous plans, appropriate past and current developments, major successes, failures, structural changes. It forms a link between previous plans and the current plan.

Forecast of relevant environmental factors including the expected economic, political, social, technological, competitive and other factors which will impinge on the organisation over the time period of the plan. This makes clear the assumptions about the environment within which the plan has been developed.

Corporate Objectives. The agreed objectives in each of the areas considered necessary should be defined in as specific a manner as possible. This means quantifying even those factors which may be of qualitative nature.

Strategies. The agreed strategies to meet the objectives should be given in broad terms with time scales attached so that the progression towards the fulfilment of objectives by the end of the agreed planning period can be seen.

Divisional/Departmental Plans. These support the strategies and show in greater detail the plans for each of the divisions or departments (these are the long term plans which form the starting point for the tactical planning/budgeting discussed in the next chapter).

Personnel Implications. This section will show the effects of the Corporate Plan on the personnel of the organisation and could include:

Manpower projections over the life of the plan (age, structure, numbers)
Retraining and redeployment policies
Staff development programmes necessary to support the plan
Recruitment or redundancy programmes necessary.

Financial Implications. This will be a substantial section and should include:

Forecasted financial statistics (Turnover, Capital Employed, Net Assets Employed, Contribution %, Profit %, Return on Capital Employed) for each of the years covered by the plan

Forecasted Operating Statements for each year

Forecasted balance sheets for each year

Forecasted source and disposition of funds statements

Forecasted Capital expenditure programme over the period of the plan.

IMPLEMENTATION OF THE CORPORATE PLAN

9. With the full corporate plan serving as an overall, long term target, detailed operational planning covering the short-term (usually one year periods) is then undertaken. Sub-objectives, subordinate to and consistent with corporate objectives, would be developed for departments, functions and sections, and operating targets and budgets would be evolved.

THE NEED for FLEXIBILITY

10.   Corporate plans are developed using forecasts, judgements and assumptions about an increasingly uncertain future. This uncertainty must be recognised and frequently forecasts and assumptions are shown as ranges of values rather than as single point estimates. The inherent uncertainty also requires that the plan itself may need modification and adjustment in the light of unexpected, major occurrences. The process of CP must be dynamic and flexible and not static and inflexible.

The process of reviewing the plan would be done regularly and typically plans might require updating:

(a)   When an unexpected event occurs which has a significant effect on the organisation, eg the sudden loss of a large market or source of supply of raw materials caused by a coup or war, the merger of major competitors, a major technological breakthrough.

(b)   In the light of the organisation's actual progress. This would form part of the annual review of the plan when the year's results were known.

(c)   At longer term intervals (say 3/5 years), the underlying objectives may require redefining with appropriate revisions to corporate strategies.

ADVANTAGES OF CP

11.   (a)   The processes and discussions involved in setting corporate objectives clarify policies and strategies and provide the essential framework for realistic operational planning and budgeting.

(b)   The processes of CP and the associated operational planning help to co-ordinate the differing aspects of the organisation and helps to avoid sub-optimality.

(c)   Having CP as a background avoids undue concentration on short-term factors and facilitates those policies which by their nature are long term in nature, eg capital investment, organisational restructuring, acquisitions and divestments, career planning.

(d)   The CP process exposes weaknesses in the organisation's information systems and forces improvements to be made.

(e)   The all important psychological effect on motivation of having clear targets may be substantial. Furthermore, goal congruence by middle and senior management may be improved.

DISADVANTAGES OF CP

12.   (a)   The processes may become somewhat bureaucratic and absorb a considerable amount of management time.
(b)   Unrealistic objectives may be a disincentive.
(c)   A corporate plan which is rigidly applied may make the organisation inflexible and less capable of responding to major changes.

In spite of the possible disadvantages and the genuine problems of developing and monitoring corporate plans it appears that an increasing number of organisations think that the process is worthwhile.

CP AND THE SYSTEMS APPROACH

13.   The systems approach outlined previously emphasises objective setting, the necessity of taking an overall view, the avoidance of sub-optimisation and the installation of appropriate controls to monitor performance against the plan. It will be apparent that CP aligns itself very closely indeed to the systems approach and is the prime organisational example of systems principles being applied in practice.

CP AND BUDGETING

14.   A budget is a short term plan (usually extending over a year) developed within the framework of the medium to long term CP. The budgetary process, encompassing budgetary planning and budgetary control, is the way that the CP is implemented, period by period. The budgetary process is dealt with in detail in the next chapter.

COMPUTER BASED PLANNING MODELS

15.   The preparation of a full CP complete with comprehensive statements of all the financial consequences is a daunting task to carry out manually. It becomes even more difficult and time consuming to prepare if it is also required to show the effects of changes in the assumptions upon which the plan has been based. For example, an apparently minor change in the assumed inflation rate from 10% to 12% projected over the life of the CP is likely to involve many thousands of calculations, changes in operating, statements, balance sheets, cash flow projections and many other such alterations.

It is because of this that many organisations use computer based models to assist in the overall CP process. The models are sometimes called corporate models or financial models or planning models. Very simply these models are computer programs which depict the operations and relationships of the organisation. Usually the model consists of a large number of interrelated equations representing various facets of the organisations activities. Input of primary assumptions (eg sales level, sales price, wages cost etc., etc.,) into the model enables the resulting operating statements, projections, balance sheets, to be quickly and easily produced by the machine.

The real power and advantage of such computer based models is not merely to produce a single result but is to enable management to ask and obtain answers to questions of the following types:

'What would happen if ....?'

'What would be the result of ....?'

For example, what would be the result of the sales volume growing by 5% p.a., costs increasing by $6\frac{1}{2}$% p.a. and selling prices increasing by 4%?

The computer would speedily calculate the results of such a question and it is this facility to test out various possibilities that makes this development so important for the management accountant.

It should be recognised that whilst computer based models help to illustrate and quantify the uncertainties attached to long term planning they do not eliminate them. Managerial judgement and expertise are still key factors.

MODEL DEVELOPMENT

16. To develop a model which is realistic and has adequate predictive qualities is a collaborative effort between management and information specialists such as systems analysts, accountants and so on.

The key points are:

- The model should have a purpose and be objective orientated.

- Model building is an iterative, creative process with the aim of identifying those variables and relationships which must be included in the model so that it is capable of predicting overall system performance. It is not essential or indeed possible, to include all variables in a model. The variables in a model of greatest importance are those which govern, to a greater or lesser extent, the achievement of the specified objectives. There are the *critical* variables.

- The best model is the simplest one with the fewest variables that has adequate predictive qualities. To obtain this ideal there must be a thorough understanding of the system. The management who operate the system have this understanding and must be involved in the model building, otherwise over elaborate and overly mathematical models may result if the model building exercise is left to systems professionals.

Figure 2 shows an outline of the way models are developed and used.

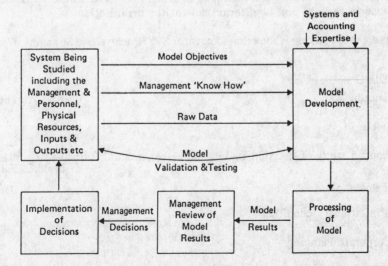

Figure 2 Model Development and Use

SUMMARY

17. (a)   Planning is an essential part of business activity and can be defined as the process of setting objectives and deciding upon the ways that the objectives will be achieved.

(b)   Long-term strategic planning or corporate planning covers periods longer than one year and typically involves the 5 to 10 year term.

(c)   Corporate planning consists of several stages: the assessment stage (position audit), the objective stage, the evaluation stage, all of which lead to the formulation of the corporate plan.

(d)   The assessment stage answers the question 'Where is the organisation now?, by examining the external environment, the organisation itself, the future, and the expectations of the major groups involved.

(e)   The objective stages answers the question 'Where does the organisation wish to go? After much analysis and discussion objectives would be set in each area of corporate activity and responsibility.

(f)   The evaluation stage is concerned with the best way of moving from where the organisation is **now** and where it wishes to be in the **future**. During this stage the planning gaps become apparent.

(g)   Finally the Corporate Plan is produced which serves as the background and target for the organisation over the medium to long term.

(h)   When the Corporate Plan is agreed detailed short term or operational planning takes place usually covering one year periods.

(i)   The uncertainty of the future must be recognised and the Corporate Plan must be flexible and capable of revision if required.

(j)   Corporate planning has a number of advantages including: the clarification of policies and strategies, the avoidance of sub-optimality, taking a long term view, the exposure of weaknesses, and motivational effects.

(k)   The disadvantages include: time consuming, makes for inflexibility, possible bureaucratic procedures.

(l)   Corporate planning is the prime organisation example of the systems approach in action.

(m)   Computer based planning models enables various options and assumptions to be tested easily and speedily.

POINTS TO NOTE

18. (a)   To be effective Corporate Planning must have the total support and involvement of top management. It is not a process which can be left to technical specialists. Their assistance and advice can be extremely useful but management involvement is **essential**.

(b)   Budgetary and short term planning are unlikely to be very effective unless such operational planning takes place within a properly thought out, long term plan for the organisation.

(c)   The corporate appraisal process is sometimes known as SWOT analysis, ie Strengths, Weaknesses, Opportunities, Threats.

ADDITIONAL READING

Practical Corporate Planning   Argenti, ALLEN & UNWIN

Financial planning models   Carr, ACCA

Administrative behaviour: a study of decision-making processes in administrative organisations
                                                                                                      Simon, COLLIER MACMILLAN

The practice of management   Drucker, HEINEMANN

Corporate Planning in inflationary conditions   Hussey, CIMA

Financial aspects of Corporate Planning   Lawton, ICA

SELF REVIEW QUESTIONS

1. *Define planning. (2)*

2. *What are the stages in Corporate Planning? (4)*

3. *What does the position audit seek to do? (5)*

4. *What are the various stages in the position audit? (5)*

5. *What are the areas in which Drucker suggests objectives should be set? (6)*

6. *What is gap analysis? (7)*

7. *What are the typical contents of a full Corporate Plan? (8)*

8. *What is the relationship of operational planning and corporate planning? (9)*

9. *What are the advantages and disadvantages of corporate planning? (11 & 12)*

10. *What are computer based planning models and how can they assist the corporate planning process? (15)*

7. Budgeting

INTRODUCTION

1.   The full budgetary process comprises budgetary planning, dealt with in this chapter, and budgetary control which is dealt with in the subsequent section on control. In this chapter budgetary planning is defined and the benefits that can be obtained from a well designed budgetary system are described. These include co-ordination, clarification of responsibility, communication, control, motivation and goal congruence. The difference between planning and control budgets is discussed and the conditions for successful budgeting are described. The principal budget factor is explained together with the steps in the budgetary process. Various types of budgets are discussed including: sales, production, service, policy and cash budgets and build-up to the Master Budget is illustrated. Fixed and flexible budgets are described and the chapter concludes with a discussion of Zero-base budgeting and PPBS.

BUDGETARY PLANNING

2.   Short term tactical planning or budgetary planning is the process of preparing detailed, short term (usually 1 year) plans for the functions, activities and departments of the organisation thus converting the long term Corporate Plan into action. In general plans are developed using physical values, for example, the number of units to be produced, the number of hours to be worked, the amount of materials to be consumed and so on. When monetary values are attached the plan becomes a **budget**. Budgets are prepared for departments, for functions such as production, inspection, marketing, or for financial and resource items such as capital expenditure, cash, materials, etc.

   The annual process of budgeting should be seen as stages in the progressive fulfilment of the long term plan for the organisation. The budgetary process steers the organisation towards the long term objectives defined in the Corporate Plan.

THE BENEFITS OF BUDGETING

3.   Benefits do not automatically arise from the budgetary process, they have to be worked for. Narrowly conceived budgetary systems or those which are insensitively applied may produce **dysfunctional effects**, ie behaviour and actions from management and staff which oppose or do not contribute to the fulfilment of organisational objectives. Well organised and thought out schemes can however bring positive and significant benefits. These are dealt with below under the following headings: co-ordination, clarification of authority and responsibility, communication, control, motivation and goal congruence, and performance evaluation.

CO-ORDINATION

4.   The budgeting process requires that feasible, detailed budgets are developed covering each activity, department or function in the organisation. This can only be done when the effects of one department's budget are related to the budget of another department. In this way the budgeting process provides for the co-ordination of the activities, departments and functions of the organisation so that each aspects of the operation contributes to the overall plan. This is expressed in the form of a **Master Budget** which summarises all the supporting budgets (fully described in para. 19).

   A well co-ordinated budgeting system helps to ensure that, for example, inventory and purchasing plans are geared to production requirements, that production schedules are related to sales budgets, that arrangements are made for overdraft facilities (if necessary) to coincide with the cash flow budget and similar relationships. Co-ordination is necessary to avoid sub-optimality.

CLARIFICATION OF AUTHORITY AND RESPONSIBILITY

5.   Budgeting (with standard costing) is known as **responsibility accounting**. This means that plans and the resulting information on the performance of the plans is expressed in terms of human responsibilities because it is people that control operations not reports.

   The process of budgeting, particularly for the control aspects, makes it necessary for the organisation to be organised into responsibility or budget centres with clear statements of the responsibilities of each manager who has a budget. The adoption of a budget authorises the plans contained within it. This process enables **management by exception** to be practised. This is where a subordinate is given a clearly defined role with the requisite authority and resources to carry out that part of the overall plan assigned to him and, if activities do not proceed according to plan, the variations are reported to a higher authority. Thus the full budgeting process forces the organisation to clarify roles and responsibilities of its managers and is an excellent example of management by exception in practice.

COMMUNICATION

6.   The full budgetary process involves liaison and discussion between all levels of management. It is an important, formal avenue of communication between top and lower levels of management regarding the organisation's long term objectives and the practical problems of implementing those objectives. When the Master Budget and supporting budgets

are agreed and finalised they provide the formal means of communicating the agreed plans embodied in the budgets to all the staff involved. As well as vertical communication between levels, the budgetary process requires lateral communication between functions and departments to ensure that activities are co-ordinated.

CONTROL

7.   This aspect of budgeting is the one most likely to be encountered by the ordinary staff member. The process of comparing actual results with planned or budgeted results and reporting upon variations, which is the principle of budgetary control, sets a control discipline which helps to accomplish the plans within agreed expenditure limits. In most practical circumstances the same budgets appear to serve as both plans and controls. However, students should be aware that this need not be the case and separate budgets for planning and for control could be developed. As Charnes and Cooper have remarked 'a good plan ..... does not necessarily yield a good control'. The reason for this is that two distinctly different functions are involved. Planning is concerned with internal resource allocation to achieve certain objectives whereas control is concerned with the task of co-ordinating and using the allocated resources (labour, machinery, space, finance) to achieve predetermined levels of efficiency. There are, of course, very real practical problems in developing separate budgets but the fact remains that a single budget used for both planning and control, which appears to be the norm, is attempting to achieve two different objectives which may conflict.

MOTIVATION AND GOAL CONGRUENCE

8.   A well organised budgeting system which encourages the genuine participation and involvement of operating management in the preparation of budgets and the establishment of agreed performance levels, has been found to have a motivating effect. The success of a budgeting system should be judged by the extent to which it encourages goal congruence by the budget holders. This is a recognition of the fact that it is the behavioural aspects of budgeting, rather than the technical ones, which are of primary importance. If the budgetary system is not acceptable to the people who are involved with it, it is likely to be manipulated or opposed to such an extent that it will become unworkable. There are many factors to be considered in relating to the behavioural aspects of budgeting and these are developed in greater detail in the chapter on budgetary control.

PERFORMANCE EVALUATION

9.   A manager's performance is often judged partly by his ability to meet budgets. When considering a manager for promotion or for a salary increase or for some other form of recognition, a manager's budget record and his ability to meet the targets incorporated in budgets is often an important factor. Budgets used as a target can also assist a manager in monitoring his own performance. The knowledge that a budget will be used for performance evaluation causes changes in the manager's attitude to the whole budgeting process. These, and other behavioural factors concerned with budgeting are dealt with in the chapter on Budgetary Control.

CONDITIONS FOR SUCCESSFUL BUDGETING

10.   There are benefits to be gain from budgeting systems but, as previously pointed out, these do not automatically arise. It has been found that a budgeting system is more likely to be successful when the following conditions are found:

(a)   The involvement and support of top management.

(b)   Clear cut definition of long term, corporate objectives within which the budgeting system will operate.

(c)   A realistic organisation structure with clearly defined responsibilities.

(d)   Genuine and full involvement of the line managers in all aspects of the budgeting process. This is likely to include a staff development and education programme in the meaning and use of budgets.

(e)   An appropriate accounting and information system which will include: the records of expenditure and performance related to responsibility, a prompt and accurate reporting system showing actual against budget, the ability to provide more detailed information or advice on request; in short the accounting system should be seen as supportive and not threatening.

(f)   Regular revisions of budgets and targets (where necessary).

(g)   Budgets should be administered in a flexible manner. Changes in conditions may call for changes in plans and the resulting budgets. Rigid adherence to budgets which are clearly inappropriate for current conditions will cause the whole budgeting system to lose credibility and effectiveness. Indeed, if budgets are not subject to revision they are effectively decisions and not plans.

PRINCIPAL BUDGET FACTOR

11. The principal budget factor (or limiting factor or key factor) is a factor which, at any given time, is an overriding planning limitation on the activities of the organisation. The principal budget factor may be production capacity, shortage of labour, materials, finance or, commonly, the level of demand for the goods or services. Because such a constraint will have a pervasive effect on all operational plans and budgets the limiting factor for the planning period must be identified so that the various budgets can be developed having regard to the expected limitation.

The factor can and does change - when one constraint is removed some other limitation will occur otherwise there would be no limit to the organisation's activities.

The assumption of a single principal budget factor is often too simplistic. In a complex organisation, for example, a divisionalised multi-product company, two or more factors may operate simultaneously. In such cases care must be taken to optimise the contribution to the organisation **as a whole** and not merely try to maximise contribution related to any one limiting factor which would cause sub-optimality. Where several constraints arise simultaneously the use of mathematical programming techniques, such as linear programming which is described later, can be invaluable in determining the optimum use of resources.

PREPARING THE BUDGET

12. Figure 1 shows an outline of the overall budgetary process. This is time consuming but vital task. The diagram shows the process as a sequential series of steps but in practice the process is less straightforward. Steps are repeated, revisions are made and there is considerable discussion and argument. Generally a **budget committee** meet at regular intervals and would be serviced by a **budget officer**, usually the accountant. The committee's task to co-ordinate and review the budget programme, establish procedures and timetables, product and update a **budget manual** (described below) explaining the objectives, role and procedures involved in the budgetary system, in short to oversee the administration of the whole process. It is **NOT** the committee's task to prepare individual budgets for particular departments or functions. It is a cardinal feature of budgeting that managers are personally involved with the development of their own budgets and accept responsibility for them. This is a key element in motivating managers and encouraging goal congruence. It is unrealistic to expect a manager to accept responsibility for an externally prepared budget which is imposed on him.

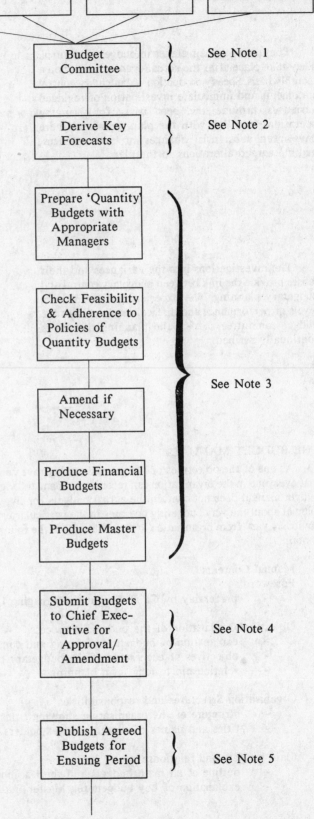

Notes

1.   The budget committee is given responsibility for the task of developing and co-ordinating budgets. The membership varies between organisations but usually comprises people from various functions of the company. The committee would be serviced by the budget officer, usually the accountant. His responsibility is to administer the budget when agreed and to provide technical assistance and data during the budget preparation. The budget planning process takes place prior to the budget period and where budgets are prepared on a rolling basis, budget planning is a regular, continuous activity.

2.   An essential preliminary to making plans and budgets is to prepare forecasts. A forecast is a prediction of future events which are expected to happen, whereas a budget is a planned series of actions to achieve a given result. Invariably the primary forecast, from which most of the subsequent planning derives, is the sales forecast. Forecasting is a large and complex field frequently involving advanced statistical and mathematical techniques.

3.   These steps comprise the bulk of the planning process. Co-ordination and communication between functions is essential to ensure interlocking, feasible budgets which accord to company policies and objectives. Many of these steps need to be repeated during the budget development as inconsistencies become apparent. The testing of one budget against another for feasibility and practicability is a key element in co-ordinating the budget process.

4.   The Budget, comprising the individual departmental and functional budgets and the master budget, is submitted to the Chief Executive or the Board of Directors for examination and approval after any revisions thought necessary. When approved, the budget becomes an executive order and shows for each budget centre an approved level of expenditure. (A budget centre is a section of the organisation so designated for budgetary purposes. It may be a cost centre, a group of cost centres or a department. It will be the responsibility of a designated person, the budget holder).

5.   The agreed budgets are published and distributed to all the budget holders and budget centres. In this way budgets serve as a means of communicating plans and objectives downwards. In addition, that part of the budgetary process concerned with monitoring results, known as budgetary control provides upward feedback on the progress made towards meeting plans.

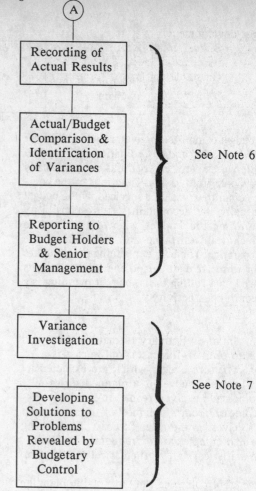

Figure 1 Outline of the Budgetary Process

6.   These are the main stages in budgetary control. They take place after the actual events, usually on a monthly basis. Speedy production of budgetary control statements and immediate investigation of revealed variances provide the best basis for bringing operations into line with the plan, or where there have been substantial changes in circumstances, making agreed alterations to the plan.

7.   The investigations into the variances and their causes provide the link between budgetary control and budgetary planning. The experience of operations, levels of performance and difficulties are fed to the budget committee so that the planning process is continually refined.

THE BUDGET MANUAL

13.   As one of the objectives of budgeting is to improve communications it is important that a manual is produced so that everyone in the organisation can refer to the manual for guidance and information about the budgetary process. The budget manual does not contain the actual budgets for the ensuing period – it is more of an instruction/information manual about the way budgeting operates in the particular organisation and the reasons for having budgeting. Contents obviously vary from organisation to organisation but the following are examples of the information such a manual should contain.

Manual Contents
Foreword
-    preferably by Chief Executive/Managing Director

Objectives/explanation of the budgetary process
-    explanation of budgetary planning and control
-    objectives of each stage of the budgetary process
-    relationship to long term planning

Organisation Structures and responsibilities
-    structure of the organisation showing titles, responsibilities and relationships
-    titles and names of current budget holders

Main budgets and relationship
-    outline of all main budgets and their accounting relationships
-    explanation of key budgets (eg Master Budget, Cash Budget, Sales Budget)

Budget development
-    Budget committee, membership and terms of reference
-    sequence of budget preparation
-    timetable for budget preparation and publication

Accounting procedures
-    name and terms of reference of the budget officer (usually the accountant)
-    coding lists
-    sample forms
-    timetable for accounting procedures, production of reports, closing dates.

BUDGET RELATIONSHIPS

14. The various budgets found in an organisation and their relationships will be specific to that organisation and are unlikely to be found elsewhere in exactly the same form. In spite of this there are broad similarities in the budgets prepared in various types of organisations. As an example, Figure 2 shows the major budgets found in a typical manufacturing concern with their main relationships.

Notes:

(a) Only the main functional budgets are shown. Usually these are subdivided into departmental budgets for day to day control purposes.

(b) The diagram shows only the major formal accounting relationships. It does not purport to show the links and communication flows necessary during budget preparation which are obviously many and varied.

CATEGORIES OF BUDGETS

15. Budgets may be categorised in numerous ways but for a typical manufacturing organisation they could be grouped as follows:

(a) Budgets in the SALES area, ie the Sales Budget and those budgets which are functionally related to the Sales Budget, eg selling and distribution cost budgets and, to some extent, the advertising and promotion budgets.

(b) Budgets in the PRODUCTION area, ie the Production Budget and the related production input budgets (labour, materials, production services).

(c) Budgets for SERVICES. These are the budgets relating to the general services of the organisation, eg administration, personnel, welfare.

(d) Budgets determined by POLICY. These are budgets which are less directly related to day to day activities and are usually determined by top management. Monies and resources would be allocated for these budgets, usually on a longer term basis than normal operating budgets, in order that long term objectives can be met. The main examples of these types of budget are the Capital Expenditure Budget, the Research and Development Budget, and, to some extent, the Advertising Budget. The activities covered by these budgets are, of course, related to current operations but their major emphasis is more far reaching and is to ensure that the organisation is able to meet future challenges by developing new products and techniques, increasing productivity by investment, and preparing for new markets. Although these budgets are reviewed periodically they usually cover periods longer than one year, which is the typical duration for normal operating budgets.

(e) The SUMMARY BUDGETS. These are budgets which derive from the various budgets outlined above and provide valuable summaries of the effects of the organisation's plans. The two budgets in this category are the Master Budget and the Cash Flow Budget.

These various categories are expanded below:

SALES AND RELATED BUDGETS

16. For many organisations the principal budget factor is sales volume so that the sales budget is the primary budget from which the majority of the other budgets are derived.

Before the sales budget can be developed it is necessary to make a **sales forecast**. A forecast is a prediction or estimate of the events which are likely to occur in the future. The forecast becomes a budget only if management accepts it as the objective. Frequently, consideration of the forecasted sales leads management to make adjustment to their plans so that the agreed sales budget differs from the original sales forecast.

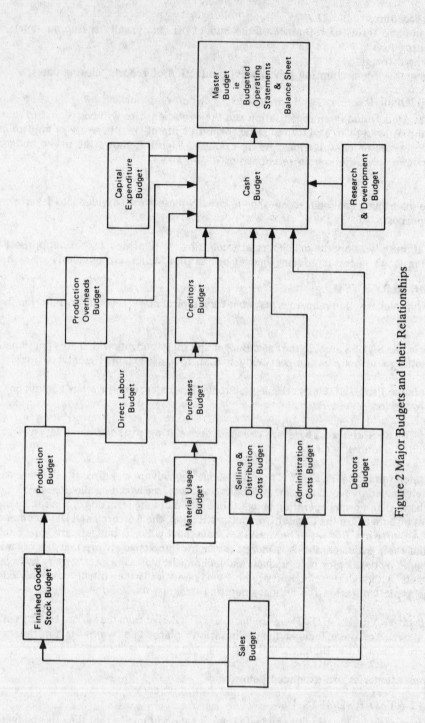

Figure 2 Major Budgets and their Relationships

Figure 2 Major Budgets and their Relationships

Sales forecasting is a complex and difficult task and involves consideration of numerous factors, including:

(a) Past sales patterns - absolutes and trends.
(b) General economic indicators, eg G.D.P., personal income, consumer spending patterns, unemployment, inflation.
(c) Results of market research studies and test marketing.
(d) Advertising and promotion policies and anticipated expenditures.
(e) Pricing and discount policies to be adopted.
(f) Distribution and quality of sales outlets and personnel.
(g) Interaction with competitors on quality, pricing, advertising, product range, availability.
(h) Impact on new technology, where appropriate.
(i) Consumer tastes and legislation.
(j) Environmental, ecological, and safety factors, where appropriate.

Having regard to the sales forecast and the productive capacity of the organisation the sales budget will be prepared which will be subdivided in several ways - by personal responsibility, by sales area, by product or product group. When the sales budget has been drawn up and agreed it becomes the organisation's plan which the sales managers will try to turn into actual sales.

When the sales budget has been finalised the related budgets such as the selling cost budget, the distribution cost budget and similar supporting budgets can be developed relatively easily. A budget which is also related, to a greater or lesser extent, to the level of sales is the advertising and promotion budget. This budget is, however, likely to be set by a policy decision of senior management.

PRODUCTION AND RELATED BUDGETS

17. If the principal budget factor was lack of production capacity then this budget would be the first to be prepared. More normally, when sales volume is the constraint, the production budget would be prepared after the sales budget and would be co-ordinated with that budget and the finished goods stock budget.

The production budget will show the quantities and costs involved for each product and product group and will be scheduled to dovetail with the sales and inventory budgets. This co-ordinating process is likely to show shortfalls or excesses in capacity at various times over the budget period. Where temporary shortfalls are anticipated then consideration would be given to extra overtime or shift working, subcontracting, buying in more parts or machine hire or some other short term way of increasing output. Where there is a more significant shortfall this means that production capacity **is** the limiting factor and consideration will have to be given to providing more substantial increase in capacity (which will have implications for the Capital Expenditure Budget).

When production capacity exceeds the anticipated sales level for significant periods then consideration will have to be given to product diversification, additional promotional effort, reducing selling prices (if demand is considered to be price elastic) or, if all else fails, selling off the excess production capacity.

When the production budget is finalised the production input budgets (labour, materials, production services) are developed based on the budgeted activity levels, existing stock positions and projected labour, material and service costs. Where standardised goods and services are produced then the production input budgets can be developed relatively easily but in jobbing type industries the process is much less precise. In such circumstances some percentage of the sales budget is used for the the various inputs. This percentage is based on previous experience but will, of course, only be valid if the pattern and mix of production in the future is broadly the same as in the past.

BUDGETS FOR SERVICES

18. Within this area there may be a number of individual budgets depending on the size and complexity of the support functions of the organisation although for small organisations a single administration budget may be found acceptable. The major problem in determining the size of these budgets is their indirect relationship with the level of activity, whether expressed as sales volume or units produced. Because of this they are frequently determined by adjusting last year's budget by a percentage. This process, sometimes known as **incremental budgeting**, obviously lacks any rigour and may conceal inefficiencies. Consequently it requires careful study by the Budget Committee before it can be deemed to be acceptable.

BUDGETS DETERMINED BY POLICY

19. These budgets, which include Capital Expenditure, Research and Development, Advertising, have some relationship to current operations but also contain substantial elements which are of a long term nature determined by top management policy. As an example, the Capital Expenditure Budget may contain authorisations for expenditure in connection with replacements and/or enhancements of facilities for current product lines and also provision for equipment and

facilities to cope with new products or new methods to be introduced in the future. It is because of this that these budgets may well move in different directions to the normal operating budgets. For example, a declining Sales Budget may cause management to **increase** the Advertising and/or Research and Development, and/or Capital Expenditure budgets.

The policy budgets are the key ways in which current facilities, products and operations are progressively adjusted in order to meet the long term objectives specified in the Corporate Plan.

THE SUMMARY BUDGETS

20. The two main summary budgets are the master budget and the cash budget.

(a)   The master budget is usually presented in the form of budgeted operating statements, a budgeted trading and profit and loss account and a budgeted balance sheet. The master budget represents a consolidation of all the supporting budgets and represents the financial effects of the total plan for the business as a whole. Each of the parts of the master budget is prepared in the conventional manner except that **budgeted** costs, revenues, investments and so on, are used instead of **historical** figures.

The master budget, supported by the subsidiary budgets, is presented to top management for approval. If approval is given the master budget becomes the financial summary of the agreed plan for the budget period being considered, usually for the year ahead. Often however the master budget is not given immediate approval in which case amendments will have to be made in the underlying budgets (eg the sales budget, the production budget, etc) in order to bring about the desired effects on the master budget. Such amendments should, of course, only be made if they are realistically capable of attainment.

(b)   Cash budget. Liquidity and cash flow management are key factors in the successful operation of any organisation and it is with good reason that the cash budget should receive close attention from both accountants and managers.

The cash budget shows the effect of budgeted activities - selling, buying, paying wages, investing in capital equipment and so on - on the cash flow of the organisation. Cash budgeting is a continuous activity with budgets being rolled forward as time progresses. The budgets are usually subdivided into reasonably short periods - months or weeks.

Cash budgets are prepared in order to ensure that there will be just sufficient cash in hand to cope adequately with budgeted activities. The cash budget may show that there is likely to be a deficiency of cash in some future period - in which case overdraft or loans will have to be arranged or activities curtailed - or alternatively the budget may show that there is likely to be a cash surplus, in which case appropriate investment or use for the surplus can be planned rather than merely leaving the cash idle in a current account.

The typical cash budget has the general form shown in Figure 3.

Cash Budget

	Period 1	Period 2	Period 3	etc.
Opening Cash Balance b/f	XXX	YYY	ZZZ	AAA
+ Receipts from Debtors				
+ Sales of Capital Items				
+ Any Loans Received				
+ Proceeds for Share Issues				
+ Any other Cash Receipts				
= Total Cash Available				
- Payments to Creditors				
- Cash Purchases				
- Wages and Salaries				
- Loan Repayments				
- Capital Expenditure				
- Dividends				
- Taxation				
- Any Other Cash Disbursements				
= Closing Cash Balance c/f	YYY	ZZZ	AAA	

Figure 3

Cash budgets are good examples of the **rolling budgets**, ie where the process of **continuous budgeting** takes place whereby regularly each period (week, month, quarter as appropriate) a new future period is added to the budget whilst the earliest period is deleted. In this way the rolling budget is continually revised so as to reflect the most up to date position. The process of continuous budgeting could, of course, be carried out for any type of budget, not just cash budgets.

CASH BUDGET EXAMPLE

21. The opening cash balance on the 1st January was expected to be £30,000. The sales budgeted were as follows:

	£
November	80,000
December	90,000
January	75,000
February	75,000
March	80,000

Analysis of records shows that debtors settle according to the following pattern:

60% within the month of sale.
25% the month following.
15% the month following.

Extracts from the Purchases budget were as follows:

	£
December	60,000
January	55,000
February	45,000
March	55,000

All purchases are on credit and past experience shows that 90% are settled in the month following purchase and the balance settled the month after.

Wages are £15,000 per month and overheads of £20,000 per month (including £5,000 depreciation) are settled monthly.

Taxation of £8,000 has to be settled in February and the company will receive settlement of an insurance claim of £25,000 in March.

Prepare a cash budget for January, February and March.

Solution
Workings

The receipts from sales are as follows:

	January Cash
November (15% x 80,000)	£12,000
December (25% x 90,000)	22,500
January (60% x 75,000)	45,000
	£79,500

	February Cash
December (15% x 90,000)	£13,500
January (25% x 75,000)	18,750
February (60% x 75,000)	45,000
	£77,250

	March Cash
January (15% x 75,000)	£11,250
February (25% x 75,000)	18,750
March (60% x 80,000)	48,000
	£78,000

Payments for purchases:

	January Cash
December (10% x 60,000)	£6,000
January (90% x 55,000)	49,500
	£55,500

	February Cash
January (10% x 55,000)	£5,500
February (90% x 45,000)	40,500
	£46,000

	March Cash
February (10% x 45,000)	£4,500
March (90% x 55,000)	49,500
	£54,000

Cash Budget

		January £	February £	March £
	Opening balance	30,000	24,000	17,250
	Receipts from sales	79,500	77,250	78,000
	Insurance claim			25,000
=	Total Cash Available	109,500	101,250	120,250
	Payments			
	Purchases	55,500	46,000	54,000
	Wages	15,000	15,000	15,000
	Overheads (less dep'n)	15,000	15,000	15,000
	Taxation		8,000	
=	Total Payments	85,500	84,000	84,000
	Closing balance c/f	24,000	17,250	36,250

RECONCILIATION OF CASH BALANCE AND PROFITS

22. Organisations prepare both cash budgets and operating budgets which show the budgeted profits for each period. These two forms of statements are prepared on totally different bases; the cash budget on the practical, objective basis of measuring positive and negative cash flows whereas budgeted profits are based on the normal conventions of accounting. These include, for example, the accruals concept, the charging of cost which do not create a cash flow – eg depreciation, the distinctions between capital and revenue expenditure and so on.

It is sometimes required to reconcile the budgeted cash and profit figures and the simplest approach to this is to use the Bank Reconciliation Statement approach and commence with one of the figures, say the budgeted cash balance, and then add or subtract the various elements in the budgets so as to agree with the figure of budgeted profit.

In practice there are innumerable items which cause differences between the two figures but the following examples include the major categories:

Sales/Purchases used in profit calculation whereas actual receipts from debtors and payments to creditors used in cash budgets.

Various items in cash budgets which do not appear in profit calculations, eg capital expenditure, taxation and dividends, increases and decreases in loans, sales or fixed assets etc.

Notional cost items such as depreciation and imputed charges appear in profit statements but not in cash budgets.

Changes in credit policies and stock levels affect cash budgets but not profit statements.

Accruals and prepayments are normal features of profit statements but do not appear in cash budgets.

FIXED AND FLEXIBLE BUDGETS

23. 'A fixed budget is one which is designed to remain unchanged irrespective of the volume of output or turnover attained.' *Terminology*

Thus a fixed budget is a single budget with no provision for adjustment should actual activity turn out to be different from that planned. The major purpose of a fixed budget is at the planning stage when it serves to define the broad objectives of the organisation. It is likely to be of little value for control purposes unless by chance the actual activity level turns out to be exactly as planned – an unlikely circumstance.

A flexible budget is one which is designed to adjust the budgeted cost levels to suit the level of activity actually attained. This is achieved by analysing each item of cost contained in the budget into fixed and variable elements. In this way an estimate can be made of the expected costs for the actual activity level experienced. This process is often known as 'flexing' the budget. The procedure for developing a flexible budget is, in principle, quite simple but the results are only accurate if the costs behave in the predicted fashions. Too often simplistic assumptions are made about cost behaviour which are unrealistic.

Examples include – the frequent arbitrary assumption of cost linearity – the assumption of continuity when the cost may actually behave in a stepped or discontinuous manner – the often arbitrary classifications used to determine the fixed and variable elements of costs – the fact that often all variable costs are flexed in relation to the same activity indicator (eg sales or output) when in reality different variable costs vary in sympathy with different activity indicators. These and other problems make it necessary to treat any flexed budget with caution.

A flexible budget is useful for the control aspect of budgeting but as it is an important part of the planning process to consider what control procedures will be necessary, it is usual to carry out the required cost analyses and breakdowns at the planning stage so that the budget may be flexed in due course if this is necessary.

The following simplified example illustrates the general principle.

A machinery department produces a variety of components and its output is measured in standard hours produced (SHP). The anticipated production level is 2000 SHP. This level has been agreed as the basis for the other budgets throughout the organisation and for the Master budget.

The Machinery Department's costs, their classification and behaviour in relation to output levels, have been studied and, after discussion, have been agreed with the departmental manager, who is the budget holder, and his superior, the Works Manager.

BUDGET

Period 09
Department: MACHINING
Activity Level. 2000 Standard Hours

Budget Holder: A.N. OTHER
Budget Relationships
  Upwards: Factory Cost
  Downwards: Nil

Nature of Expense	Budgeted cost for anticipated activity level of 2000 standard hours	Cost Classification	Cost Function (x = activity level)
	£		
Materials	10,000	Variable (linear)	$5x$
Wages	8,200	Semi-variable (linear)	$2600 \times 2.8x$
Salaries	3,200	Fixed	$3200 + 0x$
Maintenance	4,600	Semi-variable (curvi-linear)	$1000 + 0.0009x^2$
Consumable Materials	2,500	Variable (curvi-linear)	$0.000625x^2$
⋮	⋮	⋮	⋮

Notes:

(a) Only a few items of cost are shown. In practice there is likely to be far more detail.

(b) It has been assumed that the variable and semi-variable items vary in relation to the same activity indicator, ie Standard Hours Produced. Although this is a common assumption, particularly in examinations, it is not always an accurate reflection of reality.

Such a budget with its cost breakdowns can be flexed for any required activity level. For example, the budgeted cost allowances for 1800 and 2200 SHP are shown below compared with the original 2000 SHP.

Cost	Cost Function	ACTIVITY LEVEL		
		1800 SHP	2000 SHP	2200 SHP
		£		
Materials	$5x$	9,000	10,000	11,000
Wages	$2600 + 2.8x$	7,640	8,200	8,760
Salaries	$3200 + 0x$	3,200	3,200	3,200
Maintenance	$1000 + 0.0009x^2$	3,916	4,600	5,356
Consumables	$0.000625x^2$	2,025	2,500	3,025

The point must be stressed again that any such cost projection is only as good as the original cost classifications and functions. It has been said with considerable truth that the budgeting process is more a test of forecasting skill than anything else.

LEVEL OF ATTAINMENT

24. It is relatively easy to determine the level of **activity** of an organisation or a department but much more difficult to determine the level of **attainment** to be incorporated into the budget for the planned level of activity. Conventionally the most appropriate level is often described as a tough but realistically attainable standard of achievement. It has to be recognised that the level of attainment incorporated into the budget is likely to influence the motivation of the managers responsible for the achievement of the target. Ideally, the level of attainment should be such that perfect goal congruence is achieved both between individual and organisational goals and between departmental and organisational objectives but this is unlikely to happen.

If impossibly high levels of attainment are incorporated into budgets then it is likely that there will be strong disincentives to management involvement with the budgetary process and a corresponding low level of motivation and goal congruence. If levels are set which are too low than a condition will exist which is called **budgetary slack**. This means that managers can easily keep within the budgeted cost levels for the level of activity even though there may be many inefficiencies. Budgetary slack exists more widely than is realised and is often characterised by the spending sprees which occur towards the end of the budget period so that departments 'spend up to their budget'.

BUDGET VARIABILITY AND UNCERTAINTY

25. Due to the uncertainty attached to the level of attainment (and many of the other factors in budget preparation) attempts have been made to recognise these inherent variabilities by the use of subjective probabilities and elementary probability and statistical theory in budget preparation. Several approaches are possible, for example, instead of the traditional single point estimates, three estimates could be made of the level expected for each factor, pessimistic, most likely and optimistic, each with a subjective probability attached. Alternatively, control bands could be calculated for budget values based on the statistical concept of confidence limits which are calculated from the mean or most likely value of the budget and a measure of the budget's dispersion, the estimated standard deviation.

A simple illustration follows:

Example

A department's budget consists of three items: sales, variable costs and fixed costs. Discussions with management, supported by analysis of records, has produced the following data.

Expected Sales for period: Most Likely   £20,000 Probability 0.7
                                      Optimistic   £25,000 Probability 0.3

Variable costs (for £20,000 sales level)

Optimistic	£12,000	P = 0.2
Most likely	£14,000	P = 0.6
Pessimistic	£15,000	P = 0.2

Variable costs (for £25,000 sales level)

Optimistic	£14,000	P = 0.3
Most likely	£16,800	P = 0.5
Pessimistic	£18,500	P = 0.2

Fixed Costs £4,000

What is the expected value of budgeted profit?

What is the range of possible outcomes?

Solution

	£
Sales	20,000
less Expected value of variable costs	
(12,000 x 0.2 + 14000 x 0.6 + 1500 x 0.2) =	13,800
= Contribution	6,200

	£
Sales	25,000
less Expected value of variable costs	
(14000 x 0.3 + 16800 x 0.5 + 18500 x 0.2)	16,300
	8,700

∴ Expected contribution	
= (6200 x 0.7) + (8700 x 0.3) =	6,950
less Fixed Costs	4,000
∴ Expected value of budgeted profit =	£2,950

The range of outcome is from:

lowest   £20,000 sales combined with the pessimistic variable cost of £15,000

highest   £25,000 sales combined with the optimistic variable cost of £14,000, ie

| from | £20,000 - £15,000 | = | £5,000 contribution | = | £1,000 profit |
| to | £25,000 - £14,000 | = | £11,000 contribution | = | £7,000 profit |

Note: The procedure for establishing a control band of values is illustrated in connection with budgetary control in a later chapter.

ALTERNATIVE APPROACHES TO BUDGETING

26. Whilst there are undoubted advantages in properly planned conventional budgeting systems, too often budgeting tends to reinforce the status quo and budgets are often merely extrapolations of the past (including its inefficiencies). Cost levels are frequently determined by what was spent last year plus a percentage for inflation. This process is known as an *incremental budgeting* and is commonly encountered in both public and private sector organisations.

In stable conditions where there are few changes in the environment in which the organisation operates and objectives remain unchanged then incremental budgeting is a reasonable procedure. However, care will always be needed to ensure that existing expenditure levels - to which will be added an increment - do not conceal gross inefficiencies. Using incremental budgeting, change is inhibited and rarely are the relationships between costs, benefits and objectives subjected to any searching scrutiny. In an attempt to overcome these very real problems, alternative approaches to budgeting have been developed, particularly in North American, two of which Zero-base Budgeting and the Programme Planning and Budgeting System, are described below.

ZERO-BASE BUDGETING (ZBB) DEFINED

27. ZBB is a cost-benefit approach whereby it is assumed that the cost allowance for an item is zero, and will remain so until the manager responsible justifies the existence of the cost item and the benefits the expenditure brings. In this way a questioning attitude is developed whereby each cost item and its level has to be justified in relation to the way it helps to meet objectives and how the expenditure benefits the organisation. This is a forward looking approach as opposed to the all too common method of extrapolating past activities and costs, which is a feature of the incremental budgeting approach.

ZBB is formally defined by the CIMA thus; 'A method of budgeting whereby all activities are re-evaluated each time a budget is formulated. Each functional budget starts with the assumption that the function does not exist and is at zero cost. Increments of cost are compared with increments of benefit, culminating in the planning maximum benefit for a given budgeted cost' *(Terminology).*

The use of ZBB was pioneered by P Phyrr in the United States in the early 1970s and has gained wide acceptance probably because it is a simple idea obviously based on commonsense. ZBB is concerned with the evaluation of the costs and benefits of alternatives and, implicit in the technique, is the concept of opportunity cost.

WHERE CAN ZBB IS APPLIED?

28. ZBB can be applied in both profit seeking and non-profit seeking organisations. The technique gained wide publicity when the then President Carter directed that all US government departments adopt ZBB.

In a manufacturing firm, ZBB is best applied to service and support expenditure including; administration, marketing, personnel, information and computer services, research and development, finance and accounting,production planning and so on. These activities are less easily quantifiable by conventional methods and are more discretionary in nature. Manufacturing costs such as direct materials and labour and production overheads can be more easily controlled by well established methods which compare production outputs with resource inputs rather than using ZBB. Budgeting and controlling manufacturing expenditure uses techniques such as work study and standard costing which are described later in the manual.

ZBB can successfully be applied to service industries and to a wide range of non-profit seeking organisations, for example local and central government departments, educational establishments, hospitals and so on. ZBB could be applied in any organisation where alternative levels of provision for each activity are possible and the costs and benefits can be separately identified. ZBB is concerned with alternatives and means that established activities have to be compared with alternative uses of the same resources. ZBB takes away the implied right of existing activities to continue to receive resources, unless it can be shown that this is the best use of those resources.

IMPLEMENTING ZBB

29.   There are several formal stages involved in implementing a ZBB system but of greater importance is the development of an appropriate questioning attitude by all concerned. There must be a 'value for money' approach which challenges existing practices and expenditures and searching questions must be asked at each stage; typical of which are the following:

(a)   Does the activity need to be carried out at all? What would be the effects, if any, if it ceased?

(b)   How does the activity - existing or proposed - contribute to the organisation's objectives?

(c)   What is the correct level of provision? Has too much or too little been provided in the past?

(d)   What is the best way to provide the function? Have all alternative possibilities been considered?

(e)   How much should the activity cost? Is this expenditure worth the benefits achieved?

(f)   Is the activity essential or one of the frills?

and so on.

STAGES IN IMPLEMENTING ZBB

30. The overall process of implementing a ZBB system can be sub-divided into three stages thus:

(a) *Definition of decision packages*
A decision package is a comprehensive description of a facet of the organisation's activities or functions which can be individually evaluated. The decision package is specified by the managers concerned and must show details of the anticipated costs and results expected expressed in terms of tasks accomplished and benefits achieved.

Two types of decision package are possible:

Mutually-exclusive decision packages.

These are *alternative* forms of activity, tasks and expenditure to carry out the same job. The best option among the mutually exclusive packages is selected by comparing costs and benefits, and the other packages are then discarded. Naturally, mutually-exclusive packages would only be prepared when there are quite clearly different approaches for dealing with the same function. As an example, an organisation with a distribution problem might consider two alternative decision packages: Package 1 might be an in-house fleet of lorries, whereas Package 2 could involve contracts with independent hauliers.

Incremental decision packages

These packages reflect different levels of effort in dealing with a particular activity. There will be what is known as the *base package*, which represents the minimum feasible level of activity, and other packages which describe higher activity levels at given costs and resulting benefits. As an example, a base package for a Personnel Department might provide for staff engagement and termination procedures and payroll administration. Incremental packages might include; education and training, welfare and social activities, pension administration, trade union liaison and negotiations etc. Each package would have its costs and benefits clearly tabulated.

(b) *Packages are evaluated and ranked*
When the decision packages have been prepared, management will then rank all the packages on the basis of their benefits to the organisation. This is a process of allocating scarce resources between different activities, some of which already exist and other that are new.

Minimum requirements which are essential to get the job done and activities necessary to meet legal or safety obligations will naturally receive high priority. It will be found that the ranking process focuses management's attention on discretionary or optional activities.

Because of the large number of packages prepared throughout the organisation the ranking process can become onerous and time consuming for senior management. One way of reducing this problem is for lower level managers to rank the packages for their own budget centre and for these rankings to be consolidated, with others, at the next level up the hierarchy. Alternatively, there could be a cut-off limit for expenditure so that packages for a lower amount, say less than £2,000, could be ranked within the department and need not be referred higher.

(c) *Resources are allocated*
When the overall budgeted expenditure level is decided upon the packages would be accepted in the ranked priority sequence up to the agreed expenditure level.

Where the ranking of lower cost packages has been delegated to departments the proportion of the expenditure budget remaining after the more expensive packages have been ranked would be allocated to individual departments. The departments would then rank their own small packages up to their allocated expenditure level.

ADVANTAGES OF ZBB
31. (a) Properly carried out, it should result in a more efficient allocation of resources to activities and departments.

(b) ZBB focuses attention on value for money and makes explicit the relationship between the input of resources and the output of benefits.

(c) It develops a questioning attitude and makes it easier to identify inefficient, obsolete or less cost-effective operations.

(d) The ZBB process leads to greater staff and management knowledge of the operations and activities of the organisations and can increase motivation.

(e) It is a systematic way of challenging the status quo and obliges the organisation to examine alternative activities and existing cost behaviour patterns and expenditure levels.

DISADVANTAGES OF ZBB

32.   (a)   It is a time consuming process which can generate volumes of paper work especially for the decision packages.

(b)   There is considerable management skill required in both drawing up decision packages and for the ranking process. These skills may not exist in the organisation.

(c)   It may encourage the wrong impression that all decisions have to be made in the budget. Circumstances change and new opportunities and threats can arise at any time and organisations must be flexible enough to deal rapidly with these circumstances when they occur.

(d)   ZBB is not always acceptable to staff or management or trade unions who may prefer the cosy status quo and who see the detailed examination of alternatives, costs and benefits as a threat not a challenge.

(e)   There are considerable problems in ranking packages and there are inevitably many subjective judgements. Political pressures within organisations also contribute to the problem of ranking different types of activity, especially where there are qualitative rather than quantitative benefits.

(f)   It may emphasise short term benefits to the detriment of longer term ones which in the end may be more important.

Undoubtedly the major drawback to ZBB is the amount of time the system takes. One way of obtaining the benefits of ZBB is to apply it selectively on a rolling basis throughout the organisation. This year Marketing, next year, Personnel, the year after Research and Development and so on. In this way, over a period, all activities will receive a thorough scrutiny, the benefits of which should last for years.

PROGRAMME PLANNING AND BUDGETING SYSTEMS (PPBS)

33.   Non-profit seeking organisations such as local and central government, hospitals, charities and so on, often prepare detailed conventional budgets showing the different categories of expenditure, classification by classification. A particular problem of such organisations is that the measurement of outputs is difficult and sometimes impossible. As a consequence the budgeting process frequently just compares current expenditure to budgeted expenditure with little or no attempt to compare expenditure against performance achieved. By contrast, in profit seeking organisations the comparison of expenditure on resource inputs to outputs in terms of revenue and profits is much more straightforward.

In addition to the problems of relating inputs to benefits achieved, non-profit seeking organisations also have difficulties with long term strategic planning and realistic resource allocation. The short-term financial process of annual expenditure budgets is, on occasions, also being used for long term policy planning with obvious disadvantages.

In an attempt to overcome these problems the PPBS system was evolved.

PPBS is a sophisticated concept developed in North America and is usually considered in relation to State and Federal government activities although there is no reason why the system principles could not be more widely applied.

PPBS is based on systems theory and is output and objective oriented with a substantial emphasis on resource allocation based on economic analysis. The system is based, not on traditional organisational structures and divisions, but on 'programmes' - grouping of activities with common objectives. PPBS is similar to the corporate planning process for profit-seeking organisations, described in Chapter 6, but it is not identical. As with corporate planning, conventional short-term budgeting - year by year - takes place within the PPBS long term framework.

PPBS requires that the organisation prepares a long term plan relating to the objectives of the organisation subdivided into programmes. These programmes are expressed in terms of objectives to be achieved over the medium to long term, say 3 to 5 years. The key point is that the programmes are objective related and spread across several conventional departments. The total estimated costs are for the programme as a whole and are not initially expressed in relation to departments. When the various programmes for the organisation have been agreed they form the long term plan for the organisation. PPBS covers activities spanning several years and conventional annual expenditure budgeting would take place within this framework. Each year the departments contributing to a given programme would prepare, and be monitored by, normal expenditure budgets for their share of the programme's activities for the year in question.

PPBS requires a sophisticated information system able to monitor progress towards meeting systems objectives. The PPBS reporting system should be able to report upon results in terms of the programmes of activities unlike conventional reporting which is geared to existing organisational sub-divisions and usually deals only with expenditures.

A PPBS EXAMPLE

34. Assume that a Local Authority operates PPBS and has a programme concerned with the welfare of children. The programme might extend over 5 years and objectives would be agreed covering all aspects of children's welfare, including:

    (a) Births, health, diseases, dental care and so on
    (b) Nursery school attendance, primary and secondary school attendance, achievements and so on
    (c) Home conditions parental care, one parent family problems, etc
    (d) Discipline and behavioural aspects
    (e) Sports and leisure activities and provision
    (f) Safety and counselling services

and so on.

It will be immediately apparent that numerous departments would contribute to the 'Children's Programme' and this can be represented diagrammatically as shown in Figure 4.

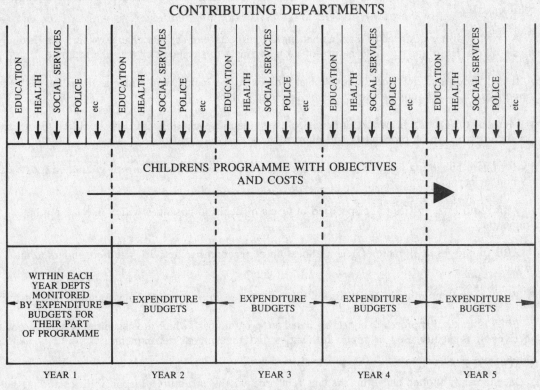

CONTRIBUTING DEPARTMENTS

PPBS — Children's Programme

Figure 4

SUMMARY

35. (a) Budgetary or short-term planning is the process by which the long term corporate plan is converted into action.

    (b) Properly organised budgetary systems can bring substantial benefits including: co-ordination, clarification of responsibilities, communication, control, motivation, and goal congruence.

    (c) Properly developed budgets co-ordinate departments and activities and thus help to avoid sub-optimality.

    (d) The budgetary process is an important formal means of horizontal and vertical communication.

    (e) The budgetary process includes the all important control aspect. Although the same budgets frequently appear to serve for both planning and control, separate planning and control budgets could be prepared.

    (f) The success of a budgetary system should be judged by the extent it encourages goal congruence.

(g)   The budgeting system is likely to be successful if it has top management support, clear definitions, full involvements, appropriate accounting systems, and is administered in a flexible manner.

(h)   The principal budget factor is the factor which imposes the overall limitation on the activities of the organisation. In complex organisations the assumption of a single limiting factor may be too simplistic.

(i)   The whole budgetary process is detailed with many steps and is shown in Figure 1.

(j)   The Budget Manual is an important aid to communications and is an instructional/information manual not a list of agreed financial budgets.

(k)   All budgets are related and interconnect so as to form part of the Master Budget.

(l)   Key summary budgets are the Cash Budget and the Master Budget which are effectively summaries of all other budgets.

(m)   The control of cash and liquidity is a continuous process and cash budgets are updated frequently, usually on a rolling basis.

(n)   A fixed budget is designed to remain unchanged irrespective of activity changes whereas a flexible budget (by analysis of the fixed and variable nature of costs) adjusts to the level of activity attained.

(o)   It is difficult to determine the level of attainment to be included in budgets. If set too high there will be low motivation, if set too low there will be budgetary slack.

(p)   Many of the factors in budget preparation are subject to variation and this should be recognised. Possible ways include the use of probability and elementary statistical concepts.

(q)   Zero base budgeting is a method of budgeting whereby all activities are re-evaluated (costs c.f. benefits) each budget period.

(r)   ZBB requires activities to be specified in terms of decision packages which may be mutually exclusive or incremental.

(s)   ZBB should result in more efficient allocation of resources to activities and engenders a value for money attitude.

(t)   ZBB creates voluminous quantities of paperwork and takes considerable managerial time to implement.

(u)   PPBS is a radical approach to budgeting based on 'programmes', which are groupings of activities with common objectives. It is mainly used in public authorities and government departments.

POINTS TO NOTE

36. (a)   Mechanically applied budgeting systems reinforce existing structures, responsibilities and methods and may inhibit change.

(b)   Budgeting systems are no substitute for good management. Too often budgeting systems concentrate almost entirely on internal factors whilst neglecting the all important interactions and necessary adaptions to the environment.

ADDITIONAL READING

Budgeting and Cash Management   Accounts Digest No. 108, ICA

Budget planning and control systems   Amey, PITMAN

Programme budgeting; concept and application and practical problems of implementation   CIPFA

SELF REVIEW QUESTIONS

1. *What is the difference between a plan and a budget? (2)*

2. *In what ways does budgeting help co-ordination? (4)*

3. *How does the budgetary process assist communication? (6)*

4. *What are the conditions for successful budgeting? (9)*

5. *What is the principal budget factor and why must it be identified? (11)*

6. *What are the steps in the budgetary process? (12)*

7. *Give the contents of a typical budget manual. (13)*

8. *Show the relationships of the main budgets with the Master Budget. (14)*

9. *What is the Master Budget? (20)*

10. *Why is the CAsh Budget important and what is a typical format? (20)*

11. *Distinguish between fixed and flexible budgets. (23)*

12. *How is a flexible budget adjusted? (23)*

13. *What is budgetary slack? (24)*

14. *How can the variability of budget factors be dealt with? (25)*

15. *What is zero base budgeting and what is its objective? (26)*

16. *What is a decision package? (30)*

17. *Why is ranking necessary and how is it done? (30)*

18. *What are the advantages of ZBB? (31)*

19. *What are the disadvantages of ZBB? (32)*

20. *Define PPBS. (33)*

EXAMINATION QUESTIONS WITH ANSWERS COMMENCING PAGE 340

A1. *Dyer Ltd manufactures a variety of products using a standardised process which takes one month to complete. Each production batch is started at the beginning of a month and is transferred to finished goods at the beginning of the next month. The cost structure, based on current selling prices, is*

	%	%
Sales price		100
Variable costs		
Raw materials	30	
Other variable costs	40	
Total variable cost-used for stock valuations		70
Contribution		30

Activity levels are constant throughout the year and annual sales, all of which are made on credit, are £2.4 million. Dyer is now planning to increase sales volume by 50% and unit sales price by 10%. Such expansion would not alter the fixed costs of £50,000 per month, which includes monthly depreciation of plant of £10,000. Similarly raw material and other variable costs per unit will not alter as a result of the price rise.

In order to facilitate the envisaged increases several changes would be required in the long term. The relevant points are:

(i)   The average credit period allowed to customers will increase to 70 days.
(ii) Suppliers will continue to be paid on strictly monthly terms.
(iii) Raw material stocks held will continue to be sufficient for one month's production.
(iv) Stocks of finished goods held will increase to one month's output or sales volume.
(v)   There will be no change in the production period and 'other variable costs' will continue to be paid for in the month of production.
(vi) The current end of month working capital position is:

	(£000's)	(£000's)
Raw materials	60	
WIP	140	
Finished goods	70	270
Debtors		200
		470
Creditors		60
Net working capital - excluding cash		410

Compliance with the long term changes required by the expansion will be spread over several months. The relevant points concerning the transitional arrangements are:

(i)   The cash balance anticipated for the end of May is £80,000.
(ii) Up to and including June all sales will be made on one month's credit.
From July all sales will be on the transitional credit terms which will mean

60% of sales will take 2 month's credit
40% of sales will take 3 month's credit.

(iii) Sales **price** increase will occur with effect from August's sales.
(iv) Production will increase by 50% with effect from July's production. Raw material purchases made in June will reflect this.
(v)   Sales **volume** will increase by 50% from October's sales.

Required:

(a)   Show the long term increase in annual profit and long term working capital requirements as a result of the plans for expansion and a price increase. (Costs of financing the extra working capital requirements may be ignored).

(b)   Product a monthly cash forecast for June to December, the first seven months of the transitional period.

(c)   Using your findings from (a) and (b) above make brief comments to the management of Dyer Ltd on the major factors concerning the financial aspects of the expansion which should be brought to their attention.

                                                                    ACCA, Management Accounting.

A2. (a) Describe, provide an example and discuss the importance for budgetary planning of, the principal budget (or limiting) factor. Indicate circumstances in which the concept of a single principal budget factor is not realistic and specify how the problems posed by such circumstances can be overcome.

(b) Explain how the use of quantitative methods can assist the practice of management accounting. Illustrate your answer with reference to a management accounting application of any quantitative method (other than any mentioned in (a) above), show how the technique has assisted in the practice of management accounting and outline any difficulties of its application.

                                                                    ACCA, Management Accounting.

A3. *Synchrodot Ltd manufactures two standard products, product 1 selling at £15 and product 2 selling at £18. A standard absorption costing system is in operation and summarised details of the unit cost standards are as follows:*

Standard Cost Data – Summary

	Product 1	Product 2
	£	£
Direct Material Cost	2	3
Direct Labour Cost	1	2
Overhead (Fixed and Variable)	7	9
	£10	£14

The budgeted fixed factory overhead for Synchrodot Ltd is £180,000 (per quarter) for product 1 and £480,000 (per quarter) for product 2. This apportionment to product lines is achieved by using a variety of 'appropriate' bases for individual expense categories, eg floor space for rates, number of work-staff for supervisory salaries etc. The fixed overhead is absorbed into production using practical capacity as the basis and any volume variance is written off (or credited) to the Profit and Loss Account in the quarter in which it occurs. Any planned volume variance in the quarterly budgets is dealt with similarly. The practical capacity per quarter is 30,000 units for product 1 and 60,000 units for product 2.

At the March board meeting the draft budgeted income statement for the April/May/June quarter is presented for consideration. This shows the following:

Budgeted Income Statement
for April, May and June 1981

	Product 1		Product 2	
Budgeted Sales Quantity		30,000 units		57,000 units
Budgeted Production Quantity		24,000 units		60,000 units
Budgeted Sales Revenue		£450,000		£1,026,000
Budgeted Production Costs				
Direct Material		£48,000		£180,000
Direct Labour		24,000		120,000
Factory Overhead		204,000		504,000
		£276,000		£840,000
Add:				
Budgeted Finished Goods				
Stock at 1 April 1981	(8,000 units)	80,000	(3,000 units)	42,000
		£356,000		£882,000
Less:				
Budgeted Finished Goods				
Stock at 30 June 1981	(2,000 units)	20,000	(6,000 units)	84,000
Budgeted Manufacturing Cost of Budgeted Sales		£336,000		£798,000
Budgeted Manufacturing Profit		£114,000		£228,000
Budgeted Administrative and Selling Costs (fixed)		30,000		48,000
Budgeted Profit		£84,000		£180,000

The statement causes consternation at the board meeting because it seems to show that product 2 contributes much more profit than product 1 and yet this has not previously been apparent.

The Sales Director is perplexed and he points out that the budgeted sales programme for the forthcoming quarter is identical with that accepted for the current quarter (January/February/March) and yet the budget for the current quarter shows a budgeted profit of £120,000 for each product line and the actual results seem to be in line with the budget.

The Production Director emphasises that identical assumptions, as to unit variable costs, selling prices and manufacturing efficiency, underly both budgets but there has been a change in budgeted production pattern. He produces the following table:

Budgeted Production	Product 1	Product 2
January/February/March	30,000 units	52,500 units
April/May/June	24,000 units	60,000 units

He urges that the company's budgeting procedures be overhauled as he can see no reason why the quarter's profit should be £24,000 up on the previous quarter and why the net profit for product 1 should fall from £4.00 to £2.80 per unit sold, whereas, for product 2 it should rise from £2.11 to £3.16.

You are required:

(a) To reconstruct the company's budget for the January/February/March quarter.
(b) To restate the budgets (for both quarters) using standard marginal cost as the stock valuation basis.
(c) To comment on the queries raised by the Sales Director and the Production Director and on the varying profit figures disclosed by the alternative budgets.

ACCA, Management Accounting.

A4. Tomm Ltd has three manufacturing departments. One of these is regarded, for responsibility accounting purposes, as a cost centre whereas the other two are classified as profit centres. Cost centre 1 (CC1) produces two joint products, P12 and P13. P12 is processed further in profit centre 2 (PC2) to yield P2. P13 is processed further in profit centre 3 (PC3) to yield P3.

The draft budgets for the three departments are as follows:

Departments	CC1	PC2	PC3
Budgeted output	20,000 kilos of P12 40,000 kilos of P13	40,000 units of P2	20,000 units of P3
	£'000	£'000	£'000
Budgeted sales revenue	–	1,600	800
Cost of goods sold			
Bought in raw material	100	20	30
Internal transfers	(600)	200	400
Direct labour	120	150	110
Processing cost	150	115	145
Administrative salaries	55	135	150
General overhead allocation	175	30	15
	–	650	850
Budgeted profit (loss)	–	950	(50)

The processing costs can be analysed as follows:

Departments	CC1	PC2	PC3
	£'000	£'000	£'000
Variable			
Identifiable with individual departments and varying with output	120	20	5
Fixed			
Identifiable with individual departments and controllable by departmental management	25	90	130
Central computer services not controllable by departmental management – allocated on basis of floor area	5	5	10

If the centrally provided computer facilities were obtained from outside the organisation on an individual basis by the individual departments, it is estimated that this would cost:

	CC1	PC2	PC3
	£'000	£'000	£'000
	25	20	5

The costs of CC1 have been allocated to PC2 and PC3 on the basis of the weight of material transferred during the period. This basis has been used in the past but it is now being questioned as it seems to bias the figures in favour of PC2. An investigation of this, and other aspects of the budgeting system, has been undertaken and the following recommendations have been made:

1.   Fixed and variable costs should be separated in the budgets.

2.   Controllable and uncontrollable costs should be clearly distinguished.

3.   Joint costs (both fixed and variable) should be allocated so that both profit centres show the same profit rate (as a percentage of sales value).

4.   Central computer costs should be allocated in a manner which recognises the cost savings achieved by using a central facility.

You are required to redraft the budget in a way that conforms to these recommendations. Make (and state) any assumptions that you consider necessary or appropriate.

ACCA, Management Accounting.

A5. *(a)* 'A budget is a forecast'.
   'A budget is a target'.
   'A budget is an allocation of resources'.
   'A budget is a measuring rod'.

   Discuss any conflicts that are inherent in the above views of budgets. Discuss the general validity of each of the statements and give your own views on the nature of budgets.

(b) *Discuss the problems that are likely to be involved in setting and agreeing the budget for an organisation's Research and Development Department and in instituting a system of financial control for such a department.*

ACCA, Management Accounting.

Control

The next four chapters cover the important topic of control and control systems. The implementation of plans without well designed control systems is largely a waste of time so that the management accountant must be considering the problems of implementation and control at the planning stage.

The essence of control is the comparison of performance against plan or target. The monitoring of progress and the comparisons with target reveal variations from the original plan which can either be used to guide activities back towards the original plan or, if the monitoring of actual results and conditions shows that unforeseen conditions have arisen, can be used to revise the original plans. This latter process if of great strategic importance and is part of general plan reviews which are vital in volatile, uncertain conditions.

8. Control – Concepts and System Principles

INTRODUCTION

1. This chapter defines control and discusses the steps in the control cycle. Control system theory and single and double feedback are described together with the concepts of negative and positive feedback. The importance of the timing of control actions is emphasised together with the relationship of reward structures to control systems.

Finally the law of requisite variety relating to the control of complex systems is briefly introduced.

CONTROL DEFINED

2. Control is concerned with the efficient use of resources to achieve a previously determined objective, or set of objectives, contained within a plan. It will be recalled that a plan is the method by which it has been decided that the objectives will be most effectively achieved. In an organisational sense, control is exercised by the feedback of information on **performance compared with plan**. Thus it will be seen that planning and control are inextricably linked and indeed in practice the distinction between the two functions is often blurred.

TYPES OF CONTROL SYSTEMS

3. The main accounting control systems are **budgetary control** and **standard costing**, dealt with in the following chapters. These are important quantitative control systems but they are by no means the only ones found in a typical organisation. Other quantitative control systems include: Quality Control, Production Control and Inventory Control.

In addition to the quantitative systems outlined above there are also control systems concerned with **qualitative** factors. Two important examples are systems for monitoring product quality and schemes of staff appraisal.

An organisation is a network of interacting control systems which, in the ideal world, should complement one another and should help to steer the activities of the organisation towards meeting the corporate objectives. Perhaps inevitably this is not always the case and sometimes the systems may be in direct conflict. An example of this is where a narrowly conceived and rigidly applied budgetary control system which concentrated on short term cost reductions might cause a lack of staff recruitment and development with an inevitable long term reduction in overall staff efficiency.

BASIC ELEMENTS OF CONTROL

4. Control is the activity which measures deviations from planned performance and provides information upon which corrective action can be taken (if required) either to alter future performance so as to conform to the original plan, or to modify the original plans.

The elements of the control cycle are:

(a) A standard specifying the expected performance. This can be in the form of a budget, a procedure, a stock level, an output rate or some other target.

(b) A measurement of actual performance. This should be made in an accurate, speedy, unbiased manner and using relevant units or measures. For example, time taken, £'s spent, units produced, efficiency ratings and so on.

(c) Comparison of (a) and (b). Frequently the comparison is accompanied by an analysis which attempts to isolate the reasons for any variations. A well known example of this is the accounting process of **variance analysis**, described in Chapter 11.

(d) Feedback of deviations or variations to a control unit. In an organisational context the 'control unit' would be a manager. This type of feedback is 'single-loop' feedback which is described more fully in the next paragraph.

(e) Actions by the control unit to alter performance in accordance with the plan.

(f) Feedback to a higher level control unit regarding large variations between performance and plan and upon the results of the lower level control unit's actions.

This is 'double-loop' feedback which is also described more fully in the next paragraph.

FEEDBACK LOOPS

5. Control is exercised in organisational systems by feedback loops which gather information on **past** performance from the **output** side of a system, department or process, which is used to govern **future** performance by adjusting the **input** side of the system.

Systems theory gives special names to certain parts of the control and feedback cycle - illustrated in Figure 1 and explained below.

Sensor
These are the measuring and recording devices of the system. In mechanical systems this is some form of automatic metering but in organisational systems the usual sensor is some form of paperwork. Care must be taken to ensure that the sensor is appropriate for the system, is sufficiently accurate and timely and does not introduce bias.

Comparator
This is the means by which the comparison of actual results and the plan is achieved. Typically in information systems this is done by a clerk or by a computer program.

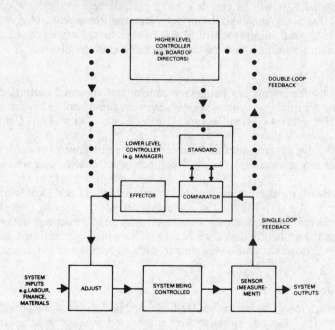

Figure 1   Control and Feedback Cycle

Effector
In an information system the usual effector is a manager or supervisor acting on the report containing the results of the comparisons and issuing the instructions for adjustments to be made.

Single Loop Feedback
Single-loop feedback, usually expressed simply as 'feedback', is the conventional feedback of relatively small variations between actual and plan in order that corrective action can be taken to bring performance in line with the plan. The implications of this is that existing performance standards and plans remain unchanged. This type of feedback is that associated with the normal budgetary control or standard costing statement.

Double-Loop Feedback
This is a higher order of feedback designed to ensure that plans, budgets, organisational structures and the control systems themselves are revised to meet changes in conditions. Ross Ashby maintains that double-loop feedback is essential if a system is to adapt to a changing environment and, as already pointed out, adaptability is the primary characteristic of organisations that survive. The business environment abounds with uncertainties - competitor's actions, inflation, industrial disputes, changes in tastes and technology, new legislation - and the monitoring of trends and performance so that appropriate adjustments can be made to plans is likely to be more productive than the rigid adherence to historical plans and budgets which were prepared in earlier and different circumstances.

NEGATIVE FEEDBACK
6.   This is feedback which seeks to dampen and reduce fluctuations around a norm or standard. Control systems incorporating negative feedback are inherently more stable and are more likely to conform to previously agreed levels or standards. A typical example is that of a Stock Control system with a planned level of stock holding. In such systems the monitoring of stock levels and usage rates and the ordering of replenishments at appropriate times seeks to maintain stocks at the planned level. This is depicted in Figure 2.

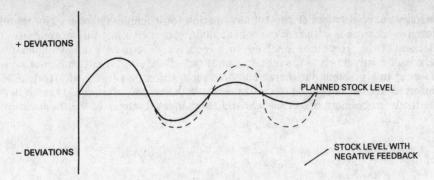

+ DEVIATIONS

PLANNED STOCK LEVEL

− DEVIATIONS

STOCK LEVEL WITH
NEGATIVE FEEDBACK

Figure 2   Effect of Negative Feedback

Negative feedback produces corrective action in the opposite direction to the deviation.

A **homeostat** is a control device for holding a process or system within desired limits so that it becomes self regulating. A control system using negative feedback is homeostatic in nature but it may be far from a perfect homeostat.

POSITIVE FEEDBACK

7.   Positive feedback causes the system to amplify an adjustment or action. Positive feedback acts in the same direction as the measured deviation. Negative feedback is more commonly found in control systems but positive feedback does sometimes occur in information systems. An example is where advertising expenditure is linked to sales - as sales increase beyond the original expectation, positive feedback causes the advertising appropriation to be increased.

Unplanned positive feedback, perhaps caused by excessive delays in producing information, can cause system instability and loss of control.

CLOSED LOOP AND OPEN LOOP SYSTEMS

8.   A closed loop system is one where output measurement is fed back so that appropriate adjustments are made to the input side of the system. Some mechanical systems, eg thermostats in heating installations, are totally closed loop systems.

Organisational and business systems containing feedback control loops which have been designed as an integral part of the system are essentially closed loop systems although influences other than output monitoring can effect decisions.

Open loop systems are where no feedback loop exists and control is external to the system and not an internal part of it. This means that control is not an automatic process within the system but has to be dealt with by external intervention. Because of the obvious dangers of such imperfectly controlled systems, open loop systems are not consciously designed into business organisations but some of the effects of an open loop system may accidentally occur. Where the feedback control loop breaks down (eg reports not prepared, not read, or prepared too late for action etc.) the effects of an open loop system would be achieved.

TIMING OF CONTROL ACTION

9.   Control action is likely to be most effective when the time lag between the output and corrective action - via the information loop - is as short as possible. Not only will the control action be able to commence earlier but it will be more appropriate. Too great a time lag may cause the resulting control action to be the opposite of what it should be.

Figure 3 shows the effect of time lag in control actions which transforms what should be negative feedback (ie damping oscillations) to positive feedback (ie amplifying oscillations).

Two factors which influence the speed of control are the organisational structure and the reporting period.

If an item of information has to pass through several levels of organisation's hierarchy before effective action can be taken then there will inevitably be delays.

Peter Drucker has said that decisions should always be made at the lowest possible level, consistent with the nature of the decision and as close to the scene of action as possible. Effective control and organisational protocol may thus be in conflict.

There is a tendency for some types of control information for example budgetary control and standard costing reports, to be produced in accordance with conventional accounting periods - monthly or four weekly - for all levels in the organisation. Because of the procedures involved, such reports are frequently not available until halfway through the next period and consequently much of the information is out-of-date and is misleading as a guide to action. There is no complete answer to this problem but there should be recognition that the most effective **control period** is not necessarily the same as an **accounting period**. At lower levels in the organisation, rapid feedback of a relatively small range of matters is likely to be more effective whilst at higher levels there is less immediacy.

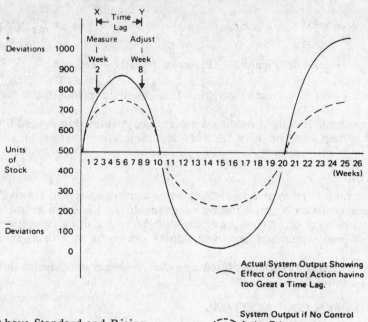

Point X. Measurement - Above Standard and Rising

Point Y. Adjustment - As Consequence of Measurement at Point X, Adjust in Downward Direction.

(Note that system at Point Y is already moving downward. Adjustment, because of Time Lag, Exaggerates Oscillation).

Figure 3   Effect of Time Lag in Control Actions

CONTROL SYSTEMS AND REWARD STRUCTURES

10.   The targets and levels of performance which are developed at the planning stage are used subsequently during the control process to monitor performance and to provide guidance as to the corrections required, if any. Performance targets should be set so that goal congruence is encouraged, ie the employee is given the maximum incentive to work towards the firm's goals. Control is effective when it induces behaviour which is in accord with achievement of the firm's objectives as specified in the planning budget. Where the organisation's reward-penalty system is consistent with the control systems there is evidence from Stedry, Arrow and others, that goal striving behaviour is encouraged.

The reward-penalty system of an organisation is the whole range of benefits and advantages which can be offered to, or withheld from, an employee. Typically these could include: promotions, wage and salary increments, bonuses, share options, profit sharing, company cars and other 'perks, holidays and so on.

If the control system is seen to be unconnected to the reward-penalty system of the organisation it will be perceived to be of little importance by the managers concerned and consequently it will tend to be ignored and so, by inference, will the organisation's objectives.

The incentive element discussed above is but one of the behavioural aspects of control systems, albeit an important one. Other behavioural considerations related directly to budgetary control are dealt with in the next chapter.

LAW OF REQUISITE VARIETY

11.   Complex systems such as commercial and industrial firms, public authorities and other types of organisations contain a large number of elements and pursue a range of objectives. The law of requisite variety, discussed by Beer, Ashby and others, states that for full control the control system should contain variety at least equal to the system

it is wished to control. The effect of this is that relatively simple control systems such as, for example, budgetary control, cannot be expected to control the multi-facetted activities of a complex organisation. At best such control systems may only control a relatively narrow aspect of the organisation's activities.

A major source of the disturbances and variations in organisations is the influence of external variables upon the achievement of the firm's objectives. Many of these external factors are non-controllable so would not be included in a conventional control system which concentrates on controllable internal factors. However where external factors interact with internal variables it is necessary to include them in the overall control system in order that the interactions can be monitored. Examples of external factors which, although uncontrollable by the organisation, are likely to make changes necessary within the organisation, are a sudden increase in advertising expenditure by a competitor or the introduction of a discount campaign by a competitor.

CONCENTRATION OF CONTROL EFFORT

12. The full control cycle - continual monitoring of results, comparisons with plans, analysis of variations and reporting - is an expensive and time consuming process. Accordingly it is important that the effort is concentrated where it can be most effective such as areas of high expenditure, vital operations and process, departments whose objectives are vital elements in the fulfilment of overall objectives and other similar areas.

A good example of this is the use of **Pareto analysis** (sometimes called ABC analysis or the 80/20 rule) in stock control. It is commonly found that 20% of the items account for 80% of the total inventory value and accordingly the major control effort would be concentrated on these items and correspondingly less time spent on detailed analysis and control of items which have insignificant values. The application of this simple concept is, of course, much wider than just inventory control and its use makes it more likely that control activities will be cost effective.

FEEDFORWARD

13. Close examination of any socio-technical system such as a private or public sector organisation will show that there are two types of control loop; *feedback loops* which *monitor* past results to detect and correct disturbances to the plan and *feedforward loops* which *react* to immediate or forthcoming dangers by making adjustments to the system in advance in order to cope with the problem in good time. In any organisation it is unlikely that pure feedforward or pure feedback control would operate in isolation. Feedback control on its own may be too slow nd feedforward control too risky, so that some balance between the two is desirable. *Feedback monitors, feedforward warns.*

Figure 4 shows an outline of the two types of control.

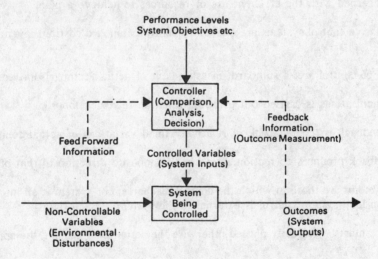

Figure 4 FEED FORWARD AND FEEDBACK LOOPS

Feedforward uses flair and insight and relies heavily on information about the environment to anticipate critical changes in the non-controllable variables *before* they have an effect on the system. Feedforward is open-loop and does not feed back through the process as does closed-loop feedback control. The ability to sense impending problems and to take prior corrective action, which is the essence of feedforward control, are also the hallmarks of successful managers and businessmen.

EXAMPLES OF FEEDFORWARD

14. Practical examples of feedforward include the following: news of political instability in a country which was a major supplier of an important raw metal would cause astute buyers to buy before prices went up and their own stocks were depleted (in contrast a pure feedback system would not react until stocks had actually fallen), a company hearing of a possible industrial dispute would make alternative production arrangements, such as sub-contracting or engaging non-union labour, in advance of the withdrawal of labour and so on.

Figure 5 provides an example of feedforward and feedback in a marketing system.

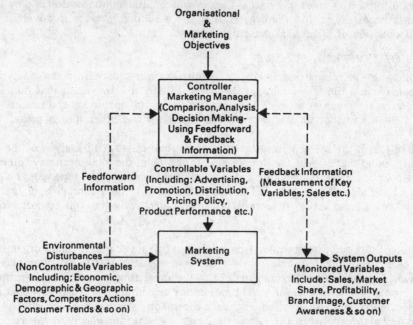

Figure 5 FEEDFORWARD FEEDBACK IN A MARKETING SYSTEM

SUMMARY

15. (a) Control is concerned with the efficient use of resources to achieve a plan.

(b) Major quantitative control systems are budgetary control, standard costing, inventory control, production control.

(c) The elements of control are: a standard, measurement of actual, comparison, feedback, adjustment.

(d) Control in organisations is carried out using information feedback loops.

(e) Single loop feedback is the feedback of relatively small variations of actual compared to plan.

(g) Negative feedback produces correction action in the opposite direction to that of the deviation.

(h) Closed loop systems are those in which the control mechanism or system is an integral part of the system whereas in an open loop system control is external to the system.

(i) Control actions must be correctly phased otherwise the action may become the opposite of that intended.

(j) Where the reward-penalty system is consistent with the organisation's control system, goal striving behaviour is encouraged.

(k) The law of requisite variety states that the control system should contain variety at least equal to the system it is wished to control.

(l) Feedforward loops react to immediate or future disturbances in order to take corrective action.

POINTS TO NOTE

16. (a) In practice it is very difficult to distinguish between control variations which arise from uncertainties in the environment and poor forecasting, and those due to sub-standard performance on the part of the manager concerned.

(b)   In Chapter 1 it was stressed that the overriding requirement for the management accountant was to produce information which is relevant for the intended purpose. This principle applies also to control information and it is vitally necessary that the information produced by the control system is based on **genuine** economic realities and not upon arbitrary conventions and assumptions.

(c)   When a variation between performance and plan occurs (eg a standard costing variance) always ask 'Is this due to managerial inefficiency or some other form of sub-standard performance or does the variation arise because the plan is inappropriate for current conditions?

ADDITIONAL READING

Management accounting: a conceptual approach	Amey & Egginton, LONGMAN
An introduction to cybernetics	Ashby, METHUEN
Management control and information	Gee and Dew, MACMILLAN
Management information systems	Lucey, DP PUBLICATIONS

SELF REVIEW QUESTIONS

1.   *What is the relationship of planning and control? (2)*

2.   *What are the elements of the control cycle? (4)*

3.   *Draw a feedback loop. (5)*

4.   *What is the distinction between single and double level feedback? (5)*

5.   *Describe negative feedback. (6)*

6.   *Distinguish between closed loop and open loop systems. (8)*

7.   *What is the reward-penalty system of the organisation? (10)*

8.   *Define the law of requisite variety. (11)*

9.   *What is the 80/20 rule? Why is it important? (11)*

10. *What is feedforward? (13)*

9. Budgetary Control

INTRODUCTION

1. This chapter discusses the control aspect of budgeting which follows budgetary planning.

Controllable and non-controllable items are discussed together with the typical hierarchy of control. The effectiveness of control reports is analysed together with the ways in which significant variances can be identified. The all important behavioural aspects of budgeting are explained including: goal congruence, motivation and the problems of dysfunctional behaviour and the chapter concludes with a summary of the benefits and problems of budgeting.

RESPONSIBILITY ACCOUNTING AND BUDGETARY CONTROL

2. Budgetary control, with budgetary planning described in chapter 7, is part of the overall system of **responsibility accounting** within an organisation.

Responsibility accounting is a system of accounting in which costs and revenues are analysed in accordance with areas of personal responsibilities so that the performance of the budget holders can be monitored in financial terms.

Once the plans for the department have been agreed and embodied in a budget (ie budgetary planning), the budgetary control process begins. The process follows the classical control cycle whereby each period, usually monthly, the **actual costs** incurred are compared with the **planned costs** and the differences or **variances** are highlighted. Budgetary control is an example of management by exception where attention is directed to the few items which are not proceeding according to plan. The usual method of feedback is via budgetary control reports to the manager concerned (ie the effector) with copies to his superior.

The aim of budgetary control is to provide a formal basis for monitoring the progress of the organisation as a whole and of its component parts, towards the achievement of the objectives specified in the planning budgets. The budgetary control system provides some of the feedback necessary to be able to make corrections to current operations and activities in order to meet the original objectives and plans (ie single-loop feedback) and also some of the feedback upon which alterations to the plans are made, if necessary (ie double-loop feedback).

Budgetary control should not be viewed merely as a penny pinching, cost saving exercise but as a positive and integral part of the organisation's planning and control activities which should give due regard to organisational objectives, the needs and aspirations of the personnel involved, and to longer term as well as short term considerations.

FLEXIBLE BUDGETS FOR CONTROL

3. To be able to make valid comparisons between actual costs incurred and a **realistic** budget allowance it is necessary for there to be flexible budgets. It will be recalled from Chapter 7 that these are budgets with each item of cost analysed into fixed and variable elements so that when the actual activity level is known the budget can be 'flexed' to produce a target cost allowance against which actual costs can be legitimately compared. From a control viewpoint a fixed budget is likely to be inappropriate unless by pure chance the actual level of activity turns out to be the same as the planned level. Thus the only feasible type of budget for control purposes is a flexible budget and all subsequent references in this chapter to 'budgets' mean 'flexible budgets'.

CONTROLLABLE AND NON-CONTROLLABLE ITEMS

4. The basis of responsibility accounting is the partitioning of the whole organisation into responsibility or control centres. In the feedback comparisons the manager of a responsibility centre, the budget holder, should not be held responsible for an item over which he has no control.

Thus the items over which a manager has significant, though not necessarily complete, influence within a given time span are deemed **controllable** items and other items as **non controllable**. The terms, controllable and non controllable, only have meaning related to a particular responsibility centre. What is non-controllable for a lower level budget centre will be controllable at some higher level. It is important that budgetary control reports are consistent with the assigned responsibility at each level of the organisation and that a budget holder is only held responsible for items which he can genuinely influence.

Non controllable items may sometimes be included in the feedback reports purely for information and communication. This is particularly appropriate for higher level responsibility centres.

Every elements which appeared in the planning budgets will be controllable by someone in the organisation and should thus appear in their budget. This applies equally to such matters as working capital, cash flow, research and development, capital expenditure as well we to the more normal items such as wages, salaries and expenditure on materials.

THE HIERARCHY OF CONTROL

5. The system of responsibility accounting and budgetary control feedback is designed round the organisation structure of the firm. The feedback reports of the system should be designed to reflect the different levels of the organisation and the duties and scope of responsibility of the managers concerned. Each level of reporting should be interrelated with levels which are above and below the one concerned. In this way each manager is kept informed of his own performance and of the progress of budget holders junior to him for whom he is responsible. He also knows that managers senior to him will receive reports, suitably summarised and edited, on his own performance. This linked, hierarchial reporting system would, of course, be supported by regular meetings between budget holders and their superiors to review progress and performance and to discuss actions to be taken and the results of actions already taken.

The procedures outlined above are the very core of the control process from which it is to be hoped that appropriate corrective actions will result.

As an example, Figure 1 shows several typical levels of reporting from Production Supervisors through to the Managing Director. As each item of cost is reported at the ascending levels its treatment becomes less and less detailed with the scope of the budgetary control report becoming broader and broader in line with the increase in responsibilities.

Figure 2 shows for one item of cost, direct labour, the typical aggregation process that takes place as the level ascends together with the increase in scope of the budget reports for the particular budget holder. The reports range from those containing **all** the cost performance data of the **whole** organisation prepared for the Managing Director to the directly controllable production costs and expenses of a small section in one factory for a factory foreman.

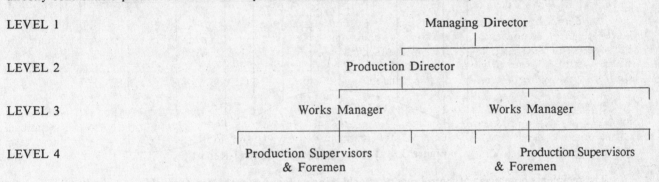

LEVEL 1		Managing Director
LEVEL 2		Production Director
LEVEL 3	Works Manager	Works Manager
LEVEL 4	Production Supervisors & Foremen	Production Supervisors & Foremen

Figure 1   The Hierarchy of Reporting

Budget v Actual

LEVEL 1	Managing Director	Total labour costs (plus costs and performance for **whole organisation**)
LEVEL 2	Production Director	Total labour cost analysed works by works (plus costs and performance for the **production function**)
LEVEL 3	Works Manager	Labour costs for works analysed by section, product group and labour type supported by summary of standard cost variances (plus costs and performance for the **works**)
LEVEL 4	Production Supervisor	Labour costs analysed by section, by product group, by labour type and by operation. Supported by detailed standard costing variance analysis (plus costs and performance for **section**).

Figure 2 Report Interrelationships for Labour Costs and Scope of Reports

EFFECTIVE CONTROL REPORTS

6.   The budgetary control report is a major vehicle in the feedback process and to ensure maximum effectiveness it is important that its design, content, timing and general impact is given careful consideration. The general characteristics of information have been dealt with in Chapter 4 from which it will be remembered that it is **actions** which produce **benefits** whilst **information** only produces **costs**. It follows that a budgetary control report which is ignored or misunderstood will not lead to effective actions and so will be useless.

The key items which should be shown are:

(a)   The budgeted level of costs and revenues for the period and year to date.
(b)   The actual level of costs and revenues for the period and year to date.
(c)   The variances between (a) and (b) together with the trends in variances.
(d)   An indication of what variances are significant together with, where possible, analysis and comment which can be used to bring the variances under control.

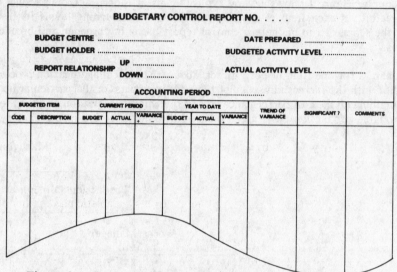

Figure 3   Typical Budgetary Control Report

The recipients of budgetary control reports should be encouraged to make constructive criticisms of all aspects of the reporting procedure so that it is improved and made more effective.

A typical budgetary control report is shown in Figure 3. It should be noted that the budgeted amounts would be the flexed budget allowances appropriate to the actual level of activity achieved.

THE SIGNIFICANCE OF VARIANCES

7.   As pointed out in the previous chapter it is good practice to concentrate control efforts where they will be most useful. Rather than dissipating scarce and expensive managerial and accounting time into detailed investigations of all variances it is more cost-effective to focus attention on those variances which are considered significant. This means that there should be some way of deciding what is a 'significant variance'.

From a practical viewpoint a variance can be considered significant when it is of such a magnitude, relative to the budget or standard, that it will influence management's actions and decisions. Variances may arise for a number of reasons of which the following three are the most important.

(a)   Failure to meet a correctly set and agreed budget or standard.
(b)   An incorrectly set or out of date budget or standard.
(c)   Random deviations.

Variances arising from reasons (a) and (b), if of sufficient relative magnitude, are variances which require further investigation and possible management action. This action may be to bring operations into line with the agreed plans or it may be to make adjustments to the plan itself. Random deviations, ie variations which have arisen by chance are, by definition, uncontrollable.

The problem remains of how to determine whether a variation from a budget or standard is attributable to chance and therefore not significant or whether it is due to a controllable cause and is of sufficient magnitude to be classed as significant.

BUDGETS AND STANDARDS AS RANGES

8.   Typically a budget allowance or a standard cost is shown as a single figure but more realistically it should be considered as a band or range of values with the budgeted allowance or standard as the centre value.

This is illustrated in Figure 4.

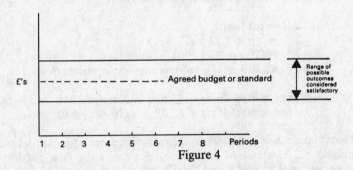

Figure 4

If the actual result falls within the band it is considered satisfactory and the variance would be deemed to be not significant. If the actual result was outside the range it would be considered to be **significant** and a fuller investigation would probably be mounted. When used in this way the range of values shown in Figure 4 is known as a Control Band and the upper and lower limits known as **Control Limits**.

SETTING CONTROL LIMITS

9.   The control limits may be set by **estimation** or **statistical analysis**.

(a)   Estimation. This approach is the most commonly used and bases the control limits on judgement and experience. Typically a figure of ± 5% is used and variances within this range would be deemed not significant. Although obviously lacking any statistical rigour this approach is a pragmatic one and implicitly uses the same concepts as more sophisticated methods.

(b)   Statistical analysis. Up until now the term 'significant' has been used in a general sense. More precisely a variance which is statistically significant is one which is of such a magnitude that it is unlikely to have arisen by chance.

Statistical probability tests based on the properties of normal distributions can be used to determine whether differences from budget or standard arise from chance (ie not significant) or from controllable causes (ie significant).

To be able to set control limits which can be used to determine statistical significance is dependent on a number of statistical assumptions and upon being able to calculate or estimate the standard deviation.

The major assumptions are:

(i)   The actual values which are compared with the budgeted allowance or standard are drawn from a single, homogeneous population.

(ii)   The budgeted allowance or standard is the arithmetic mean of the population. This means that the budget or standard is set at an attainable level.

(iii)   Any variations from budget are deemed to arise from chance.

These various assumptions are necessary in order to utilise the known properties of the normal distribution.

Therefore assuming that the population (used in the statistical sense) of actual values is normally distributed about the mean (or budget), control limits can be set at any required level, for example:

   5%   control limits are set at mean ± 1.96 standard deviations
   2%   control limits are set at mean ± 2.33 standard deviations
   1%   control limits are set at mean ± 2.57 standard deviations
   0.2%   control limits are set at mean ± 3.09 standard deviations

For example, the budgeted allowance for a given cost is £2,500 and from analysis of past records of cost behaviour the standard deviation is estimated to be £90.

- what are the 2% control limits?
- what is the meaning of such limits?
- show the limits graphically.

2% control limits
mean ± 2.33 s.d.
= £2,500 ± 2.33 (90)
= £2,500 ± 210 (to nearest whole number)

Upper control limit = £2,500 + 210 = £2,710
Lower control limit = £2,500 - 210 = £2,290

Meaning of control limits. If chance alone causes variations from standard, then 98% of deviations should fall within the range of the mean (or budget) ± 2.33 standard deviations. If a deviation falls outside these limits, ie above £2,710 or below £2,290 then the variance is said to be **significant at the 2% level**.

Graph of control limits.

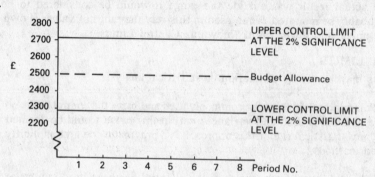

Although setting control limits by statistical methods appears to be more rigorous it must be realised that some of the necessary statistical assumptions regarding the distribution of actual values may not be valid in practice and also that the calculation or estimation of the standard deviation may be difficult.

TO INVESTIGATE OR NOT TO INVESTIGATE

10. Judgement will always be required whether to investigate the causes of a variance. Investigations cost money and may cause disruptions to production whilst the benefits gained may be slight. Mechanical rules could be set up to decide upon an investigation, for example, 'investigate all variances which fall outside the control limits described previously'. Such rules formalise the decision process but are not necessarily cost-effective in deciding whether a system is out of control. If it was required to derive a quantitative decision rule whether to investigate or not this could be done using elementary decision theory, provided the necessary information was available. To illustrate this, assume the following factors:

p   =   probability of budget being found to be *under control* when a variance is investigated.

1 - p   =   probability of budget being found to be *out of control* when a variance is investigated.

I   =   Investigation costs

B   =   Benefits gained from an investigation.

These factors can be set out as follows:

Decision	Budget under control (p)	Budget out of control (1 - p)	Expected value of decision
Investigate	- I	B - I	- pI + (1 - p)(B - I)
Do not investigate	0	0	0

Example

Detailed records have been kept of a department's budget variances, the average costs of previous investigations and the benefits gained when an out of control state is corrected; thus:

$$p = \text{probability of budget been found to be under control} = 0.8$$
$$I = £240 \qquad B = £2,000$$

Assuming that past conditions will apply in the future is it worth investigating a significant variance?

Solution

EV of decision to investigate $= -(0.8 \times 240) + (1 - 0.8)(2,000 - 240) = + £160$

∴ worthwhile to investigate.

It will be realised that the above procedure is only superficially objective. It presupposes knowledge of probabilities, costs and revenues that is unlikely to be encountered in practice. As previously stated, judgement will always be required.

Note: The whole of the above section on the significance of variances, the setting of control limits and the decision to investigate variances is applicable to both budgets and standard costs, which are dealt with in the following chapter.

QUANTITIES NOT PRICES

11. The statistical concepts covered in the preceding paragraphs deal with the random variations which arise from the human element. This could be variations in the time taken to produce a part or the different amounts of material used by an operative. Because of human factors there will always be some variances even if there is no specific cause. This makes variances which arise from human induced quantity fluctuations more suitable for statistical analysis. These variances include: labour and overhead efficiency, material usage and overhead volume.

Price and expenditure variances are different in character to quantity variances and are less suitable for the type of statistical analysis described.

BEHAVIOURAL ASPECTS OF BUDGETING

12. An understanding only of the technical aspects of the budgetary process is not sufficient for the management accountant. The human, social and organisational factors which are involved at all stages in budgeting are of critical importance and cannot be ignored. There has been considerable research into the behavioural aspects of budgeting but as with many other facets of human behaviour the findings are complex, imperfectly understood and sometimes contradictory so broad generalisations are difficult to make. On one point there does seem to be agreed and that is that budgeting is not considered by participants as a neutral, objective, purely technical process which is a view adopted by many accountants.

The human, subjective elements cannot be overemphasised - budgeting is not a mechanistic, technical procedure. Its success is totally dependent upon the goodwill and co-operation of the participants. Without this budgeting will become merely a paper exercise with no real impact on the operations of the organisation except perhaps negatively.

Many of the behavioural problems with budgeting arise from managements' attempts to make the budget perform different functions; some of which are to an extent incompatible. These functions include:

(a) acting as a target.
(b) acting as a plan.
(c) being a control measure.
(d) a means of motivating managers.
(e) acting as a device for measuring performance.
(f) promoting a goal congruence.
(g) acting as a medium of communication and co-ordination.
(h) acting as a framework for the delegation of authority

and so on.

It will be apparent from the above list that it is almost inevitable that difficulties will arise in setting and using budgets which attempt to cope with so many disparate tasks.

The following paragraphs explore some of the more relevant behavioural research findings about budgets and the budgeting process.

BUDGETS AS TARGETS

13. Numerous researchers (for example Argyris, Hofstede, French, Kay and Meyer) have found that clearly defined quantitative targets can improve motivation and thus produce better performance than if no target existed. This raises the problem of the level of performance to be incorporated as the target. Should the budget targets reflect senior management's expectations or employee aspirations (ie the level of performance the employee hopes to attain)?

Hofstede's research indicated that:

(a) very easy targets will be achieved but do not motivate managers to achieve their full potential.

(b) very difficult targets will not be accepted and cause managers to give up trying, so that their performance will be lower than if realistic targets had been set.

(c) the best performance levels are likely to be achieved by setting the toughest target that will be accepted by the manager as his own personal goal, ie equivalent to the manager's aspiration level.

Research has shown that budgets do not necessarily lead to improved performance and that the budget level which leads to the best performance is likely to be set on the majority of occasions. If budgets are set at the level which will achieve maximum performance then adverse variances are likely. These must be treated sympathetically; if they are used as a pressure device budget holders will try to obtain looser budgets in the future either by under performing or by political bargaining. These easier budgets will produce fewer adverse variances but overall performance will be lower.

Aspiration levels are not constant and are affected by the budget holders previous performance compared with the budget level. Becker and Green found that:

(a) where performance is well below the budget then the budget should be revised downward sufficiently for it to be perceived as attainable. If this is not done the budget holder will become discouraged and his aspiration level, and future performance, will fall.

(b) where performance is just below the budget level (resulting in an adverse variance) sympathetic and non-punitive feedback of results will normally lead to an increase in aspiration level and performance.

(c) where performance meets or slightly exceeds the level in the budget it is likely that the aspiration level will increase and the budget holder's potential performance will be greater. In these circumstances a budget revision could be made.

MOTIVATION

14. Motivation is the need to achieve a selected target or objective and the resulting drive and determination that influences actions directed towards the selected target. It is clearly desirable that managers and supervisors are motivated by the budgeting system and there is some evidence that clearly defined targets and objectives can influence motivation in a positive manner.

Research shows that although budgeting systems sometimes gave positive motivational effects all too often they produce undesirable negative reactions.

The adverse effects can occur at both the planning and the implementation stages thus:

at the *planning stage* managers may

(a) build in slack unnecessarily.

(b) complain of lack of time for budgeting.

(c) argue that a formal budget is too restrictive and that they should be allowed more flexibility in making operational decisions.

(d) not co-ordinate their budgets with those of other budget centres.

(e) base future plans purely on past results with no examination of alternative options and new ideas.

(f) set out to show the budget is unworkable especially if they have not been connected with the budget's preparation and it has been decided for them by senior management.

at the *implementation stage* managers may

(a) not co-operate and co-ordinate with other budget holders.

(b) put in just enough effort to achieve budget targets without trying to beat those targets.

(c) tolerate poor and inaccurate recording and classification of costs.

(d) ensure that they spend up to their budget, even if not necessary, to ensure it is not tightened in the future.

(e) concentrate on short-term factors to the detriment of more important longer term consequences.

(f) seek to blame the budgeting system for any problems which occur.

It is obviously of importance that accountants and senior management try to develop and implement budgeting systems in a manner that is acceptable to the budget holders and produces positive effects.

However, Argyris in his researches often found that budgets were considered as pressure devices and were viewed as part of a management policing system. Naturally enough in such circumstances the budgeting system had a demotivating effect - the opposite to that intended. To foster motivation, acceptance by the managers concerned of their budgets and of the levels of performance contained in the budgets is absolutely vital.

The effect on motivation of incentives should not be underestimated. As pointed out in the previous chapter, research studies carried out by Stedry and others show that there are positive gains in motivation when the reward - penalty systems of the organisation is consistent with its control system.

There is an intuitive feeling that participation by budget holders in the budget and target setting process is likely to affect motivation and this aspect of budgeting has been extensively researched.

PARTICIPATION IN BUDGETING

15. Participation in budget and target setting means that, before budgets are finalised, there are frank discussions with budget holders who are thus in a position to influence the levels of their budgets and targets. Thus defined, it would seem to be self evidently a good thing but the research does not produce a clear cut picture.

Some studies show that participation leads to more positive attitudes and higher performance whilst others find the opposite. For example studies by Kenis and Collins showed a positive correlation of attitude and performance with participation whilst other studies by such researchers as, Bryan and Locke, Stedry and others showed a negative relationship between participation and performance.

An additional problem is that different organisations use the word participation to describe quite different activities. These can range from true participation, which is where the budget holder can exert real influence, to what is described by Argyris as 'pseudo-participation'. This is where budgets are discussed with lower level management but with the primary aim of obtaining formal acceptance of budgets and performance levels previously determined by top management.

MAKING PARTICIPATION WORK BETTER

16. The research has identified various factors which help the organisation to decide whether or not participation is worthwhile and, if so, how it can be made most effective. The factors include; the cultural setting of the organisation, the work situation, the management style of the organisation, the relationship between supervisors and the supervised, the extent of decentralisation, the type of structure and business, and so on.

As examples; Stedry found that a more authoritarian and less participative management style led to higher performance, Hopwood found that in constrained and programmed environments, participation was much less effective than those where flexibility and motivation were important.

Where individuals feel that they have more control over their own destinies and the organisation has genuine decentralised decision making participation appears to have positive effects. Conversely some people do not welcome independence and respond more positively to a more authoritative and less participative approach. It does seem that participation in the right circumstances can improve the budget holder's attitude to the budget system and make it more likely that he will accept the targets contained in the budget. However, it is apparent from the research that participation must be used with care and applied selectively having regard to social and behavioural factors. On occasions, imposed budgets and an authoritarian style will lead to higher performance.

GOAL CONGRUENCE

17. This is there the goals of individuals and groups coincide with the goals and objectives of the organisation so that individuals and groups acting in their own self interest are also acting in accordance with the higher organisational goals. This ideal is difficult to achieve in its entirety but recognition must be given to the fact that organisational objectives cannot be set and implemented through the budgeting system without consideration of the interaction of local group and departmental objectives.

Hopwood's researches suggest that there are numerous problems in achieving goal congruence. Objectives are rarely clearly defined and there may be numerous objectives in the one organisation, some of which may conflict. Further, different managers may perceive their objectives differently and imperfect information, departmental rivalries, different and conflicting reward structures and other practical realities make perfect goal congruence extremely unlikely.

BUDGETS AND PERFORMANCE EVALUATION

18. Budgets are one of the accounting measures which are used to assess a manager's performance. The reward system of the organisation (ie pay, promotion, etc) is often linked to the achievement of certain levels of performance, frequently measured in accounting terms. It is conventionally assumed that by establishing formal performance measurement and rewarding individuals for their performance they will be encouraged to maximise their contribution towards the organisation's objectives. In this way it is assumed that goal congruence will be achieved. On the other hand, if performance measures and the way they are used, motivate managers in ways that do *not* contribute to organisational objectives this is a dysfunctional consequence and leads to a lack of goal congruence.

Unfortunately, the research evidence suggests that all too often accounting performance measures lead to a lack of goal congruence. Managers seek to improve their performance on the basis of the indicator used even though this is not in the best interests of the organisation as a whole. For example Likert found that concentration on short term cost reductions produced damaging longer term effects on labour turnover and absenteeism which were dysfunctional. This problem occurs not only with budgets but with other types of accounting measurement. For example, assessing management performance by the Return on Capital Employed (discussed in detail later in the manual) has been found by Dearden to cause managers to delay making new investments which are in the interests of the organisation as a whole but which would cause their own R.O.C.E. to fall. This is a clear example of sub-optimality discussed earlier.

We should not be surprised that concentration on a single measure or target causes problems. The Law of Requisite Variety, explained in the previous chapter, states that for full control the control system must have as much variety as the system being controlled so that concentration on a single measure (a budget level, return on capital employed or whatever) cannot hope to control adequately a complex system. Numerous organisations have attempted to deal with the problem of assessing managerial performance using multiple criteria and one of the pioneers was the General Electric Company of America.

General Electric identified eight key result areas which are summarised below:

Productivity
Personnel development
Profitability
Market position
Product leadership
Employee attitudes
Public responsibility
Balance between short - and long-term goals.

Within each key area various performance targets were established and a manager would be expected to achieve a satisfactory performance level across all eight facets. A high score on profitability would not compensate for poor performance elsewhere.

HOW BUDGETS ARE USED

19. Behavioural problems also arise from the way that senior management use the budgeting system. Budgets and indeed all accounting information should be interpreted and used with care and tact.

Hopwood found three distinct styles of using budget and cost data:

(a) Budget-constraint style:

This is where the accounting information was primarily to ensure adherence to short-term cost levels. Adverse cost variances would be used to censure a budget holder regardless of performance elsewhere.

(b) Profit-conscious style:

Here the emphasis was on the long run effectiveness of the budget holder's contribution to the organisation's goals. In this case the minimisation of long run costs was seen as most desirable.

(c) Non-accounting style:

Accounting data played only a minor role in assessing performance.

Hopwood found that the first two styles were more effective in concentrating attention on costs than the non-accounting style. There was evidence that the profit-conscious style promoted a more positive attitude whereas the short-term emphasis on cost levels caused tensions, budget manipulation and a less active involvement with the financial well being of organisation.

From this and other research it is clear that accountants must use budget and accounting data in a supportive not threatening manner without an over emphasis on short-term budget compliance. Accounting information should *assist* managers to manage their departments more efficiently. It should not be seen as negative and something which is used to find faults. If the budgeting and accounting systems are seen as providing genuine assistance to a manager there will be fewer behavioural problems, motivation will increase, and dysfunctional effects minimised.

BENEFITS AND PROBLEMS OF BUDGETING

20. Budgetary planning and control systems, in varying degrees of complexity and coverage, can be found in most organisations of any size in both the public and private sectors. There are genuine benefits to be gained from the use of such systems but these benefits do not automatically accrue. They have to be worked for and there must be continual appraisal of all aspects of the budgetary system and of its administration. An awareness of the problems which may be encountered and of the factors which prevent the most effective use of budgetary systems is also valuable in order that, where possible, these may be overcome.

BENEFITS OF BUDGETING

21. (a) It is the major formal way in which the organisational objectives are translated into specific plans, tasks and objectives related to individual managers and supervisors. It should provide clear guidelines for current operations.

(b) It is an important medium of communication for organisational plans and objectives and of the progress towards meeting those objectives.

(c) The development of budgets (done properly) helps to achieve co-ordination between the various departments and functions of the organisation.

(d) The involvement of all levels of management with setting budgets, the acceptance of defined targets, the two way flow of information and other facets of a properly organised budgeting system all help to promote a coalition of interest and to increase motivation.

(e) Management's time can be saved and attention directed to areas of most concern by the 'exception principle' which is at the heart of budgetary control.

(f) Performance of all levels is systematically reported and monitored thus aiding the control of current activities.

(g) The investigation of operations and procedures, which is part of budgetary planning and the subsequent monitoring of expenditure, may lead to reduced costs and greater efficiency.

(h) The regular systematic monitoring of results compared to plan (ie the budget) provides information upon which either, to adjust current operations to bring them into line with the previous plan or, to make adjustments to the plan itself where this becomes necessary.

(i) The integration of budgets makes possible better cash and working capital management and makes stock and buying policies more realistic.

PROBLEMS ASSOCIATED WITH BUDGETING

22. Various problems and difficulties which may occur in connection with budgeting are given below but it does not necessarily follow that they **will** occur in any given organisation.

(a) There may be too much reliance on the technique as a substitute for good management.

(b) The budgetary system, perhaps because of undue pressure or poor human relations, may cause antagonism and decrease motivation.

(c) Variances are just as frequently due to changing circumstances, poor forecasting or general uncertainties as due to managerial performance.

(d) Budgets are developed round existing organisational structures and departments which may be inappropriate for current conditions and may not reflect the underlying economic realities.

(e) The very existence of well documented plans and budgets may cause inertia and lack of flexibility in adapting to change.

(f) There is a major problem in setting the levels of attainment to be included in budgets and standards. Although much research has been done in this area by Stedry, Becker and Green and others, knowledge is still incomplete. There are many factors to be considered including: the aspiration level of individuals, group pressures, the extent of participation, past performances and so on. This is an unresolved problem which is present in **every** budgetary and standard costing system.

(g) The inherent lags and delays in the system. For example the actual results for June are typically available mid to late July and would be compared with June's budget which itself would be based on estimates and forecasts which were **made up to 12 months previously**. The resulting variances may then be used to guide management's actions for August. Because of these delays and lags there is the real possibility that the budgets and resulting variances are of little value as a guide to current operations.

SUMMARY

23. (a) Budgetary control is part of the organisation's system of responsibility accounting.

(b) Flexible budgets are essential to produce realistic budget allowances against which to compare actual results.

(c) A budget holder can only be held responsible for controllable items, ie those items over which he has significant influence.

(d) Budgets and the subsequent reporting procedures are developed in accordance with the organisation structure of the firm.

(e) The design, content and timing of budgetary control reports must be given careful consideration to ensure maximum effectiveness.

(f) To concentrate attention it is necessary to determine what are significant variances.

(g) Budgets or standards should more properly be considered as a range of values round the agreed budget or standard.

(h) Control limited can be set by estimation or statistical analysis based on certain assumptions and the properties of the normal distribution.

(i) Variances which are within the control limits are not significant and those outside would be deemed significant.

(j) Typical control limits are:

5% control limits   mean $\pm$ 1.96 s.d.
1% control limits   mean $\pm$ 2.57 s.d.

(k) The behavioural aspects of budgeting are of critical importance even though imperfectly understood.

(l) Goal congruence should be encouraged and is where individual and organisational goals coincide.

(m) Where budgets are seen merely as pressure devices and as part of a management policing system, motivation likely to decrease. Real participation promotes a coalition of interests which increases goal congruence and motivation.

(n) Dysfunctional behaviour is any behaviour which reduces organisational efficiency and should be minimised where possible.

(o) The major benefits of budgeting systems, assuming they are properly planned and administered are: communication, co-ordination, motivation, the promotion of goal congruence, better control and possible cost reductions.

(p) The main problems which may be encountered with budgetary systems include: antagonism and demotivation, difficulties in determining real variances, may cause inflexibility, setting the appropriate level of attainment, lags and delays in the system.

POINTS TO NOTE

24. (a) The type of responsibility centres discussed in this chapter are **budget centres**, which may be a single cost centre or a group of cost centres. With increasing amounts of responsibility accorded to managers, responsibility centers may be termed **profit centres** or **investment centres**. These latter types of responsibility centres are dealt with in the section on Performance Appraisal.

(b) Care must be taken that, with so much attention directed to the exceptions or variances, the levels of the standards and budgets themselves are not neglected.

(c) Even if a variance is deemed to be significant it does not follow that there will be a full investigation. The decision to investigate or not is a cost/benefit exercise whereby the investigation costs are compared with the likely benefits.

(d) The variance control chart shown in the chapter is similar to those used in Quality Control Procedures. In such applications measurements of, say, the diameter of a component are plotted on the chart so that the trend of deviations can be seen easily and this enables corrections to be made, if necessary, even before a deviation goes beyond the control limits.

(e) Most readers of this manual will be accountants or intending accountants so that it is worth pointing out that one of the common attitudes of accountants is a potential source of friction particularly when related to control systems. Accountants regard it as a success when they are able to show evidence of waste or inefficiency and a considerable part of their training is directed to this end. To the line managers and staff involved in the control system these events are effectively failures or mistakes and it is a natural reaction, to a greater or lesser extent, to resent failures being pointed out.

ADDITIONAL READING

Behavioural Aspects of Budgeting — Accountants' Digest No. 49 ICA

Management Accounting and Behavioural Science — Caplan, ADDISON-WESLEY

Management Control and Information — Dew and Gee, MACMILLAN

The Game of Budget Control — Hofstede, TAVISTOCK

Accounting and Human Behaviour — Hopwood, PRENTICE HALL

Budget Control and Cost Behaviour — Stedry, PRENTICE HALL

Some Personality Determinants of the Effects of Participation — Vroom, PRENTICE HALL

SELF REVIEW QUESTIONS

1. What is responsibility accounting? (2)

2. What is the major aim of budgetary control? (2)

3. What type of budgets should be used in budgetary control? (3)

4. Distinguish between controllable and non-controllable items. (4)

5. What relationship is there between the organisation structure and budgetary control? (5)

6. What are the key items which should appear on a budgetary control report? (6)

7. How do variances arise? (7)

8. What is a significant variance? (7)

9. How can control limits be set? (8)

10. What are the major assumptions necessary in order to set control limits by statistical methods? (9)

11. What are the different functions a budget attempts to achieve? (12)

12. What level of target should be incorporated into a budget? (13)

13. What is a person's aspiration level? (13)

14. What is motivation and how is it affected by the budget process? (14)

15. What is participation and is it always effective? (15)

16. What is pseudo-participation? (15)

17. In what circumstances is participation most effective? (16)

18. What is goal congruence and why is it difficult to achieve? (17)

19. What are the behavioural problems associated with accounting measures for performance evaluation? (18)

20. How can Requisite Variety be included in performance measurement? (18)

21. What are the behavioural consequences of the way that budgets are used? (19)

22. Give six benefits of a properly organised budgeting system. (21)

23. What problems may be encountered in implementing and operating a budgeting system? (22)

EXAMINATION QUESTIONS WITH ANSWERS COMMENCING PAGE 344

A1. In discussing the standard setting process for use within budgetary control and/or standard costing systems, the following has been written: 'The level of standards appears to play a role in achievement motivation ....'

Required:

(a) Briefly distinguish between the motivational and managerial reporting objectives of both budgetary control and standard costing. Describe the extent to which these two objectives place conflicting demands on the standard of performance utilised in such systems.

(b) Describe three levels of efficiency which may be incorporated in the standards used in budgetary control and/or standard costing systems. Outline the main advantages and disadvantages of each of the three levels described.

(c) Discuss the advantages and disadvantages of involving employees in the standard setting process.

ACCA, Management Accounting.

A2. *Gray Ltd will commence operations at the beginning of the year and the budgets for activity and costs for the first 3 quarters of operation are shown below.*

Budgets – Quarters I – III			
Period covered – months	QI 1-3	QII 4-6	QIII 7-9
Activity	(000's)	(000's)	(000's)
Sales – units	9	17	15
Production	10	20	15
Costs	(£000's)	(£000's)	(£000's)
Direct materials – A	50	100	75
– B	40	80	60
Production labour	180	285	230
Factory overheads – excluding depreciation	80	110	95
Depreciation of production machinery	14	14	14
Administration expenses	30	30	30
Selling and distribution expenses	29	37	35
TOTAL COSTS	423	656	539

The figures in the budget for quarters I and III reflect Gray's cost structures which have the following major features:

(i)   the fixed element of any cost is completely independent of activity levels;

(ii)   any variable element of each cost displays a simple linear relationship to volume except that the variable labour costs become 50% higher for activity in excess of 19,000 units per quarter due to the necessity for overtime working;

(iii)   the variable element of selling and distribution expenses is a function of sales, ALL other costs with a variable element are a function of production volume.

In quarter IV the sales volume could range from an extreme low volume of 15,000 units to an extreme high volume of 21,000 units but with a most likely volume of 18,000 units. In month 9 it will be possible to accurately estimate sales for quarter IV and the production level of that quarter will be set equal to the sales volume. Activity for each quarter is spread evenly throughout that quarter.

Cost structures will remain the same in quarter I to III but are expected to differ in quarter IV **only** in the following respects:

(i)   Material A will rise in price by 20%.

(ii)   All production labour wage rate will rise by 12½%.

(iii)   Variable labour input per unit of output will decrease, due to the learning curve effect, such that only 80% of the previous labour input per unit of output is required in quarter IV. The threshold for overtime working remains at 19,000 units per quarter.

(iv)   Fixed factory overheads and the fixed element of selling and distribution costs will each rise by 20%. (The variable element of selling and distribution costs will be unaltered).

The effect of these changes is considered too small to require a change in the standard cost per unit of £30 which is used for stock valuation.

Sales price in quarter IV, £40, will be identical to the price charged in the previous three quarters. All sales are made on terms which are strictly net and allow two months credit. However, the actual payment pattern expected will lead to:

70% of all sales being paid in accordance with the credit terms.
100% of all sales being paid for within 3 months.

All cash expenses relating to production are paid for in the month production takes place and similarly expenses relating to selling and distribution are paid for in the month of sale.

Required:

(a)   Produce a statement which analyses, under each cost classification given in the budgets, the variable cost per unit and the fixed costs which will be effective in quarter IV.

(b)   Prepare a flexible budget of estimated production costs for quarter IV. The budget should be drawn up with step points which will facilitate simple interpolation of costs for production levels between those presented in the budget and will also show expected costs for the most likely production level.

(c)   (i) Prepare statements showing the profit and the cash flow to be derived during quarter IV at the expected, extreme high and extreme low levels of activity.

(ii) Briefly comment on the reasons for any differences between the behaviour of cash flow and profit at the three levels of activity.

ACCA, Management Accounting.

A3. *(a)   In the context of budgeting, provide definitions for **four** of the following terms:*

> *aspiration level;*
> *budgetary slack;*
> *feedback;*
> *zero-base budgeting;*
> *responsibility accounting.*

(b)   Discuss the motivational implications of the level of efficiency assumed in establishing a budget.

ACCA, Management Accounting.

10. Standard Costing − I

INTRODUCTION

1.   This chapter, the first of two dealing with Standard Costing defines standard costing and the main types of standards.

   The relationship with budgeting and the ways that standards can be developed are described. Variances and variance analysis are introduced and descriptions, formulae and examples are given for a number of commonly encountered variances relating to material, labour and overheads. The chapter concludes with a description of control ratios related to variances.

STANDARD COSTING EXPLAINED

2.   Standard costing is an important control technique which follows the feedback control cycle discussed previously. Standard costing establishes predetermined estimates of the cost of products or services, collects actual costs and output data and compares the actual results with the predetermined estimates. The predetermined costs are known as STANDARD COSTS and the difference between standard and actual is known as a VARIANCE. The process by which the total variance or difference between standard and actual cost is subdivided is known as VARIANCE ANALYSIS. In practice, standard costing is a detailed process requiring considerable accounting and technical development work before it can be used effectively. It can be used in a variety of costing situations, batch and mass production, process manufacture, transport, certain aspects of repetitive clerical work and even in jobbing manufacture where there is some standardisation of components or parts. In principle there is no reason why standard costing should not be applied in service industries providing that a realistic cost unit can be established. Undoubtedly, however, the greatest benefit is gained when the manufacturing or production process involves a substantial degree of repetition. The major applications in practice are in mass production and repetitive assembly work.

OBJECTIVES OF STANDARD COSTING

3.   (a)   To provide a formal basis for assessing performance and efficiency.

   (b)   To control costs by establishing standards and analysing variances.

   (c)   To enable the principle of 'management by exception' to be practised at the detailed, operational level.

   (d)   To assist in setting budgets.

   (e)   The standard costs are readily available substitutes for actual average unit costs and can be used for stock and work-in-progress valuations, profit planning and decision making, and as a basis of pricing where 'cost-plus' systems are used.

   (f)   To assist in assigning responsibility for non-standard performance in order to correct deficiencies or to capitalise on benefits.

   (g)   To motivate staff and management.

   (h)   To provide a basis for estimating.

   (i)   To provide guidance on possible ways of improving performance.

STANDARD COST DEFINED

4.   This can be formally defined as:

   'A predetermined calculation of how much costs should be under specified working conditions.

   It is built up from an assessment of the value of cost elements and correlates technical specifications and the quantification of materials, labour and other costs to the prices and/or wage rates expected to apply during the period in which the standard cost is intended to be used. Its main purposes are to provide bases for control through variance accounting, for the valuation of stock and work in progress and, in some cases, for fixing selling prices'. *Terminology*.

   This is a long, technical description but it will be seen that a standard cost should be based on sound technical and engineering studies, specified production methods, work study and work measurement, clearly defined material specifications, and price and wage rate projections. The above represents the position under ideal circumstances and standards produced following such a thorough process are likely to be accepted as truly representative and realistic. However, standards produced less rigorously can also be of some value particularly in service areas and in industries where a detailed engineering basis is inappropriate.

It will be noted that a standard cost is NOT an average of past costs. These are likely to contain the results of past mistakes and inefficiencies. Furthermore, changes in methods, technology and prices make comparisons with the past of doubtful value for control purposes and assessing current efficiency.

TYPES OF STANDARD

5.   There are various types of standards which could be established and the type or types to be used in a particular organisation is dependent upon the requirements and objectives of the standard costing system. The type of standard used naturally affects the nature and scale of the variances and the meaning which can be attributed to them.

Four main types of standard are described: basic, ideal, attainable, and current.

Basic Standards: These are long term standards which could remain unchanged over the years. They could be used to show trends over time for such items as material prices, labour rates and efficiency and the long term effects of changing methods. Also they could be used as a basis for setting current standards. Basic standards would not normally form part of the reporting system as any variances produced would have little or no meaning being an unknown mixture of controllable and uncontrollable factors.

Ideal Standards: These are based on optimal operating conditions, no breakdowns, no wastage, no stoppages or idle time. Ideal standards would be adjusted periodically to reflect improvements in materials, methods and technology. Clearly such standards would be unattainable in practice and accordingly ideal standards are unlikely to be used for routine reporting purposes. If they were used there would continually be adverse variances which are likely to affect morale and motivation. Ideal standards may however be considered as long term targets and used for long term development purposes but are of little value for day-to-day control activities.

Attainable Standard: This is by far the most commonly encountered standard. Such a standard is based on efficient (but not perfect) operating conditions. Allowances would be made for normal material losses, fatigue and machine and tool breakdowns. Attainable standards should be based on high performance levels which can, with effort, be achieved. Such standards aim to provide tough but realistic targets and as such should motivate staff; they can be used for product costing, for cost control, for stock valuation, for estimating and as a basis for budgeting. Attainable Standards would be revised periodically (usually annually) to reflect the conditions, prices, methods etc. which are expected to prevail during the ensuing control period. These standards are the ones normally used for routine control purposes and from which variances are calculated. If the standard remains a realistic target over the whole of the control period then the cumulative sum of the variances should be small and any variances calculated will represent controllable matters which, if significant, would merit attention. Unless otherwise stated subsequent references in this manual to standards mean **attainable standards**.

Current Standard: This is a standard which is set for use over a short period to reflect current conditions. Where conditions are stable then a current standard will be the same as an attainable standard but where, for example, a temporary problem exists with material quality or there is an unexpected price rise, then a current standard could be set covering, say, two or three months to deal with the particular circumstances. It follows that any variances arising when a current standard is used will be controllable variances.

A particular example of the use of current standards is in inflationary circumstances where current standards could be set, perhaps on a month by month basis, using the performance levels agreed for the attainable standard for the year with the price levels adjusted by suitable indices for month by month control.

Note: As mentioned in the previous chapter there are very real problems in determining the level of attainment in budgets or standards. It follows therefore, to a greater or lesser extent, **all** standards contain a subjective element.

STANDARDS AND BUDGETS

6.   Both standards and budgets are concerned with setting performance and cost levels for control purposes. They therefore are similar in principle although they differ in scope. Standards are a **unit** concept, ie they apply to particular products, to individual operations or processes. Budgets are concerned with **totals**; they lay down cost limits for functions and departments and for the firm as a whole. As an illustration the standard material cost of the various products in a firm could be as follows:

		Standard Material cost/unit	Planned Production	Total Material Cost
		£		£
Product	X321	3.50	5000 units	17,500
Product	Y592	7.25	1500 units	10,875
Product	Y728	1.50	2500 units	3,750
etc		etc	etc	etc
etc		etc	etc	etc

OVERALL TOTAL = MATERIALS BUDGET =   £275,000

In this way the detailed unit standards are used as the basis for developing meaningful budgets. This is particularly so for direct material and direct labour costs which are more amenable to close control through standard costing whereas overheads would normally be controlled by functional and departmental budgets. Further differences are that budgets would be revised on a periodic basis, frequently as an annual exercise, whereas standards are revised only when they are inappropriate for current operating conditions. Such revisions may take place more or less frequently than budget revisions. The accounting treatment of standards and budgets also differs. Budgets are memorandum figures and do not form part of the double entry accounting system whereas standards and the resulting variances are included.

SETTING STANDARDS

7.   Meaningful standards which can be used for control purposes rest on a foundation of properly organised, standardised methods and procedures and a comprehensive information system. It is little point trying to develop a standard cost for a product if the production method is not decided upon. A standard cost implies that a target or standard exists for every single element which contributes to the product; the types, usage and prices of materials and parts, the grades, rates of pay and times for the labour involved, the production methods and layouts, the tools and jigs and so on. Considerable effort is involved in establishing standard costs and keeping them up to date. Traditionally, the standard cost for each part or product is recorded on a standard cost card and an example is given later in this chapter. With the increased usage of computers for costing purposes frequently nowadays there is no physical standard cost card. When a computer is used, the standard costs are recorded on a magnetic disk or tape file and can be accessed and processed as required. Whether a computer or manual system is used, there are no differences in the principles of standard costing, although there are many differences in the method of day to day operation. The following paragraphs explain some of the detailed procedures involved in setting standards.

SETTING STANDARDS - MATERIALS

8.   The materials content of a product: raw materials, sub-assemblies, piece parts, finishing materials etc is derived from technical and engineering specifications, frequently in the form of a Bill of Materials. The standard quantities required include an allowance for normal and inevitable losses in production, that is, machining loss, evaporation, and expected levels of breakages and rejections. The process of analysis is valuable in itself because savings and alternative materials and ways of using materials are frequently discovered. The responsibility for providing material prices is that of the buying department. The prices used are not the past costs, but the forecast expected costs for the relevant budget period. The expected costs should take into account trends in material prices, anticipated changes in purchasing policies, quantity and cash discounts, carriage and packing charges and any other factor which will influence material costs.

SETTING STANDARDS - LABOUR

9.   Without detailed operation and process specifications it would be impossible to establish standard labour time. The agreed methods of manufacture are the basis of setting the standard labour times. The techniques of work measurement are involved, frequently combined with work study projections based on elemental analysis when a part is not yet in production. The labour standards must specify the exact grades of labour to be used as well as the times involved. Planned labour times are expressed in standard hours (or standard minutes). The concept of a standard hour is important and can be defined as: "The quantity of work achievable at standard performance, expressed in terms of a standard unit of work in a standard period of time". *Terminology*.

Frequently output is expressed as to many 'standard hours' or 'standard minutes' rather than a quantity of parts. When the times and grades of labour have been established a forecast of the relevant wage rates for the control period can be made, usually by the Personnel Department.

Note: In setting the time element of a labour standard full account must be taken of any learning effects so that the standard set will be a realistic one under operational conditions. The 'learning curve' and its effect on labour times was described in Chapter 3.

SETTING STANDARDS - OVERHEADS

10. It will be recalled from Chapter 2 how overhead absorption rates are established. These predetermined overhead absorption rates become the standards for overheads for each cost centre using the budgeted standard labour hours as the activity base. For realistic control, overheads must be analysed into their fixed and variable overheads thus:

Standard Variable O.A.R   = $\dfrac{\text{Budgeted variable overheads for cost cost centre}}{\text{Budgeted standard labour hours for cost centre}}$

and

Standard Fixed O.A.R.   = $\dfrac{\text{Budgeted fixed overheads for cost centre}}{\text{Budgeted standard labour hours for cost centre}}$

The level of activity adopted, expressed in standard labour hours, is the budgeted expected annual activity level which is the basis of the Master budget. For reporting and control purposes this would be classed as 100% capacity.

SETTING STANDARDS - SALES PRICE AND MARGIN

11. Fundamental to any form of standard costing, budgeting and profit planning is the anticipated selling price for the product. The setting of the selling price is frequently a top level decision and is based on a variety of factors including: the anticipated market demand, competing products, manufacturing costs, inflation estimates and so on. Finally, after discussion and investigation, a selling price is established at which it is planned to sell the product during the period concerned. This becomes the standard selling price. The standard sales margin is the difference between the standard cost and the standard selling price. Where a standard marginal costing system is used, the standard contribution is calculated following normal marginal costing principles.

Notes:

(a) Normally when 'standard cost' is mentioned it means total standard cost, ie total absorption cost principles are used incorporating fixed and variable costs. Standard marginal costing is also employed, but students should assume that total absorption cost principles are involved whenever the term standard cost is used without qualification. This nomenclature is adopted in this manual. When marginal costing principles are used the term **standard marginal cost** is used.

(b) The problems of setting selling prices and the ways that the Management Accountant can assist in the pricing decision are dealt with in detail later in the manual.

(c) It follows that a standard costing system works within a framework of a budgeting system. A budgetary control system without a standard costing system is quite usual but a standard costing system without the discipline and structure provided by a budgetary system could not be recommended.

RESPONSIBILITY FOR SETTING STANDARDS

12. The line managers who have to work with and accept the standards must be involved in establishing them. There are strong behavioural and motivational factors involved in this process as mentioned in the previous chapter. Work study staff, engineers, accountants and other specialists provide technical assistance and information but the line managers must be involved in the critical part of standard setting, that of agreeing the level of attainment to be included in the standard.

THE STANDARD COST CARD

13. The process of setting standards results in the establishment of the standard cost for the product. The makeup of the standard cost is recorded on a standard cost card. In practice there may be numerous detail cards together with a summary card for a given product, or the standard cost details may be on a computer file. The principles, however, remain the same. A simple standard cost card is shown below:

		Standard Cost Card			

Standard Cost Card

PART NO *X291* DESCRIPTION *Stub Joint* BATCH QUANTITY *100*

TOOL REF. *T5983* WORK STUDY REF. *WS255* DRAWING NO. *D59215*

REVISION DATE *3/12/82* REVISED BY *G.R.P.*

COST TYPE AND QUANTITY	STANDARD PRICE or RATE	DEPT 7	DEPT 19	DEPT 15	TOTAL
		£	£	£	£
Direct Materials					
2.5Kg P101	£14.8kg	37.00			37.00
1000 units A539	£3.75 100		37.50		37.50
					74.50
Direct Labour Machine Operation					
Grade 15					
4.8 hrs	£2.5 hr	12.00			12.00
9.2 hrs	£2.5 hr		23.00		23.00
Assembly					
Grade 8					
16.4 hrs	£1.75 hr			28.70	28.70
					63.70
Production Overhead					
Machine Hour Rate	£11 hr	52.80	101.12		153.92
Labour Hour Rate	£6 hr			98.40	98.40
		101.80	161.62	127.10	252.32

STANDARD COST SUMMARY	
	£
DIRECT MATERIALS	74.50
DIRECT LABOUR	63.70
PRODUCTION OVERHEADS	252.32
STANDARD COST PER 100	£390.52

Figure 1   STANDARD COST CARD

REVISION OF STANDARDS

14. To show trends and to be able to compare performance and costs between different periods, standards would be rarely changed. On the other hand, for day to day control and motivation purposes, standards which reflect the most up to date position are required and consequently revisions would need to be made continually. The above positions reflect the extremes of the situation. There is no doubt that standards which are right up to date provide a better target and are more meaningful to the foremen and managers involved, but the extent and frequency of standard revision is a matter of judgement. Minor changes in rates, prices and usage are frequently ignored for a time, but their cumulative effect soon becomes significant and changes need to be made. Prior to computer maintained standard cost files, standard cost revisions were a time consuming chore as it was necessary to ensure that all the effects of a change were recorded. For example, a price change of a common raw material would necessitate alterations to

(a) the standard cost cards of all products, parts and assemblies using the material;
(b) any price lists, stock sheets and catalogues involving the material and products derived from the material;

Because of such factors, commonly all standard costs are revised together at regular, periodic intervals such as every six or twelve months, rather than on an individual, random basis.

BEHAVIOURAL ASPECTS OF STANDARDS

15. The points made in the previous chapter regarding the importance of the human aspects of budgeting apply equally to standard costing. Both techniques employ similar principles and both rely absolutely upon the people who have to work to the budgets and standards. Because of the detailed nature of standard costing and its involvement with foremen and production workers, communication becomes of even greater importance. Production workers frequently regard any form of performance evaluation with deep suspicion and if a cost-conscious, positive attitude is to be developed, close attention must be paid to the behavioural aspects of the system. Full participation, realistic standards, prompt and accurate reporting, no undue pressure or censure - all contribute to an acceptable system. Remember if the system is not accepted by the people involved it will be unworkable.

CONTROL THROUGH VARIANCE ANALYSIS

16. An important objective of standard costing is to be able to monitor current operational performance against standards by the use of variance analysis. This procedure follows the control cycle explained earlier and is identical in principle to that used in budgetary control except that the analysis of variances is much more detailed.

It will be recalled that a variance is a difference between standard cost and actual cost. The term variance is rarely used on its own.

Invariably it is qualified in some way, for example: labour efficiency variance, direct material yield variance and so on. The process by which the total difference between standard and actual costs is analysed is known as variance analysis. Variances arise from differences between standard and actual quantities, efficiencies and proportions and/or differences between standard and actual rates or prices. These are the **causes** of variances; the **reasons** for the differences have to be established by investigation.

Notes:

(a)   Variances may be ADVERSE ie where actual cost is greater than standard or they may be FAVOURABLE where actual cost is less than standard. Alternative terms are MINUS or PLUS variances, respectively.

(b)   The accounting use of the term variance should not be confused with the statistical variance which is a measure of the dispersion of a statistical population. In statistical terminology, an accounting variance would be known as a **deviation**.

THE PURPOSE OF VARIANCE ANALYSIS

17. The only purpose of variance analysis is to provide practical pointers to the causes of off-standard performance so that management can improve operations, increase efficiency, utilise resources more effectively and reduce costs. It follows that overly elaborate variance analysis which is not understood, variances that are not acted upon and variances which are calculated too long after the event do not fulfil the central purpose of standard costing. The types of variances which are identified must be those which fulfil the needs of the organisation. The only criterion for the calculation of a variance is its usefulness - if it is not useful for management purposes, it should not be produced. Most text books (and this one is no exception!) give lists of commonly encountered variances but it cannot be emphasised too strongly that these should not be automatically produced **unless** they provide specific, relevant and useful information. It is highly likely, in a given organisation, that specialised variances will be found to be most relevant and that some or all of the conventionally encountered variances will be of little value.

RESPONSIBILITY IDENTIFICATION THROUGH VARIANCE ANALYSIS

18. In ideal circumstances, variances are analysed in sufficient detail so that responsibility can be assigned to a particular individual for a specific variance. This is a worthwhile objective which, if achieved, considerably assists cost control. Because of the importance of this principle, standard costing and budgetary control are known as responsibility accounting. A particular example of this principle is the conventional assumptions behind the subdivision of the direct materials cost variance, that is, the total difference in material costs between actual and standard. The total variance comprises a price component, which is deemed to be the responsibility of the buyer, and a usage component, which is deemed to be the responsibility of the foreman or line manager.

However, it must be realised that in practice divisions of responsibility are rarely perfectly clear cut. There are many interdependencies and shared responsibilities in a typical organisation which make simplistic assumptions about the location of responsibilities highly suspect. For example, where Department A receives parts and materials from another section within the organisation, the labour efficiency of Department A is to some extent dependent on the regular and timely flows of correct specification parts and materials from elsewhere. This means that labour efficiency, and the resulting variances, which are conventionally deemed to be the sole responsibility of Department A are to some extent uncontrollable by the management of Department A. This is only a simple example of an interdependency and other more subtle examples can be found in most organisations.

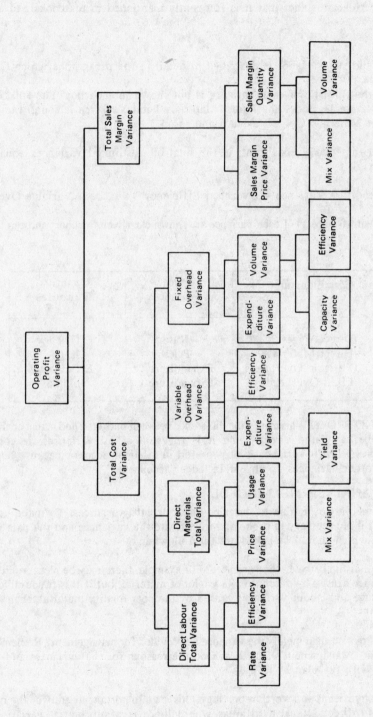

Figure 2   Chart of commonly encountered variances

THE RELATIONSHIP OF VARIANCES

19. The overall objective of variance analysis is to subdivide the total difference between budgeted profit and actual profit for the period into the detailed differences (relating to material, labour, overheads and sales) which go to make up the total difference. The particular variances which are computed in any given organisation are those which are relevant to its operations and which will aid control. Figure 2 shows a hierarchy of commonly encountered variances but, as pointed out above, relevance and specific appropriateness to management are the only criteria which justify the calculation of any variance, not the fact that it is frequently mentioned in textbooks and examinations.

Notes on Figure 2

(a)   Each variance and sub-variance is described in detail in the paragraphs which follow.

(b)   For simplicity the full title of each variance is not shown in each box. The full titles are easily derived from the chart. For example, under the Direct Materials Total Variance is found the **Direct Materials** Price Variance, the **Direct Materials** Usage Variance and so on.

(c)   The chart is arithmetically consistent, ie the total of the linked variances equals the senior variance shown. For example.

Variance Overhead Expenditure Variance + Overhead Efficiency Variance = Variable Overhead Variance

(d)   The price and quantity aspects of each variance are shown clearly on the chart and can be summarised as shown in the table below.

Cost Element	Price Variances	Quantity Variances
Direct Wages	Rate	Efficiency
Direct Materials	Price	Usage
Variable Overheads	Expenditure	Efficiency
Fixed Overheads	Expenditure	Volume

(e)   The 'OPERATING PROFIT' variance is the difference between budgeted and actual operating profit for a period. This variance can be calculated directly and it is the sum of all variances, ie cost variances and sales variances. The operating profit variance is not entered in a ledger account because budgeted profit does not appear therein. All other variances do appear in ledger accounts.

MAKING VARIANCE ANALYSIS MEANINGFUL

20. It is not sufficient merely to be able to describe and calculate variances. To make variance analysis into a useful aid to management it is necessary to probe and investigate the variances and the data used to calculate them. Typical of the questions which should be asked are the following:

(a)   Is there any relationship between the variances? For example, there may be pleasure in observing a favourable materials price variance caused by purchase of a job lot of material, but if this favourable variance is more than offset by adverse usage and labour variances caused by the poor quality material, then there is little cause for rejoicing.

(b)   Can further information than merely the variance be provided for management? Remember, variance analysis is but a means to an end. Management's task is to find the reasons for the variances and to take action to bring operations into line with the plan.

(c)   Is the variance significant and worth reporting? This is an important matter for the management accountant because it is vital to direct attention to areas where there is a substantial variation between actual and standard. The meaning of significant variances and the methods by which they can be identified have been dealt with previously in connection with budgetary control. The methods and principles described are equally applicable to standard costing variances as well as those which arise in budgetary control.

(d)   Are the variances being reported quickly enough to the right people, with sufficient or too much detail, with explanatory notes and background data?

(e)   Do the variances and trends indicate that the standards need amendment? This is the double loop or higher order feedback previously described.

THE VARIANCES DESCRIBED IN DETAIL

21. Each of the variances shown in Figure 2 is described in the following paragraphs. Each variance is defined and explained, a formula and typical causes of the variance are given together with a worked example.

The worked examples for the basic material and labour variances are based on the following extract from the Standard Cost Card for Part No. 50Y and actual results for period 2.

Extract from a Standard Cost Card for a Part No. 50Y

	Standard Cost/Unit £
Raw materials 60 kgs @ £3.5 Kg	210
Direct labour 15 hrs @ £2.75/hour	41.25
	251.25

Actual Results for Period 2

Production	140 parts
Direct Material Purchases	8000 Kgs at a cost of £30,000
Opening stock direct material	1800 Kgs
Closing stock direct material	1450 Kgs
Direct wages	£5805 for 2150 hours

THE BASIC MATERIALS VARIANCES

22. This paragraph deals with the Direct Materials Total Variance and the primary sub divisions, the Direct Materials Price Variance and the Direct Materials Usage VAriance.

A particular problem arises with material variances because materials could be charged to production either at actual prices or standard prices. This affects when the prices variance is calculated, ie either at the time of purchase or at the time of usage. Although both these approaches are possible, the procedure where materials are charged to production at standard price has many advantages and will be adopted in this manual. This method means that variances are calculated as soon as they arise, (ie a price variance when the material is purchased) and that they are more easily related to an individual's responsibility (ie a price variance would be the buyer's responsibility). Accordingly for materials variances (and ALL other variances), price variances are calculated first and thereafter the material is at standard price. The individual material variances can now be considered.

Direct material total variance – definition
'The difference between the standard direct material cost of the actual production volume and the actual cost of direct material.' *Terminology.*

Direct material price variance – definition
'The difference between the standard price and actual purchase price for the actual quantity of material.' *Terminology.*

Direct material usage variance – definition
'The difference between the standard quantity specified for the actual production and the actual quantity used, at standard purchase price'. *Terminology.*

FORMULAE

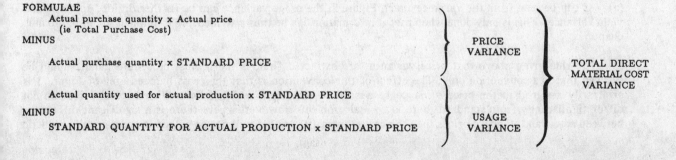

Actual purchase quantity x Actual price
   (ie Total Purchase Cost)
MINUS

Actual purchase quantity x STANDARD PRICE

                                              PRICE
                                              VARIANCE

Actual quantity used for actual production x STANDARD PRICE
MINUS
STANDARD QUANTITY FOR ACTUAL PRODUCTION x STANDARD PRICE   USAGE
                                                VARIANCE

TOTAL DIRECT MATERIAL COST VARIANCE

Example 1 (based on data from para 21.)

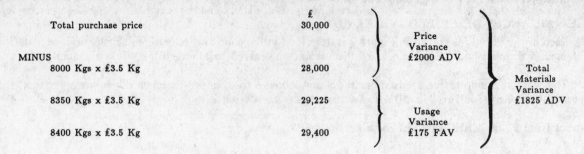

	£	
Total purchase price	30,000	Price Variance £2000 ADV
MINUS		
8000 Kgs x £3.5 Kg	28,000	
8350 Kgs x £3.5 Kg	29,225	Usage Variance £175 FAV
8400 Kgs x £3.5 Kg	29,400	

Total Materials Variance £1825 ADV

Notes:

(a)   Although rules can be given regarding the sequence of the formulae so that a minus variance is always adverse and a plus is favourable, it is easier and less error prone to determine the direction of the variance by common sense, ie if the price/usage is less than standard the variance is favourable, if more, then the variance is adverse.

(b)   The price variance is based on the actual quantity purchased and is extracted first. Thereafter the actual price is never used for variance calculations.

(c)   In the above example, the actual usage (8350 Kgs) was calculated as follows:

Opening Stock + Purchases – Closing Stock = Usage
ie 1800 + 8000 – 1450 = 8350 Kgs

(d)   It follows from the above calculations that a price variance could arise even if there was no usage, provided that there were purchases during the period.

(e)   Students should note how the formulae develop from actual values (in lower case) progressively to STANDARD VALUES (in capitals). This layout is used throughout the manual.

Typical causes of material variances
Price variances

(a)   Paying higher or lower prices than planned.
(b)   Losing or gaining quantity discounts by buying in smaller or larger quantities than planned.
(c)   Buying lower or higher quality than planned.
(d)   Buying substitute material due to unavailability of planned material. (Both (c) and (d) may affect usage variances).

Usage Variances

(a)   Greater or lower yield from material than planned.
(b)   Gains or losses due to use of substitute or higher/lower quality than planned.
(c)   Greater or lower rate of scrap than anticipated.

Notes:

(a)   As can be seen from the variance chart, Figure 2, the usage variance can be further divided into mix and yield variances. This is only done when useful information can be thus provided. An example is given in the next chapter.

(b)   The rule given above that price variances are extracted first, is the normal procedure but it should be realised that is a convention only. The effect of this convention is that the cross hatched area of Figure 3 is arbitrarily assigned to the price variance because that variance is isolated first. Where actual prices do not differ significantly from standard there is no real problem. However, where there is a significant difference between actual and standard prices then the usage/quantity variance will not be valued in economically realistic terms. This problem exists throughout variance analysis and means that the sequence of variance analysis (conventionally price or rate first) determines to which variance the 'increment x increment' amount is assigned. This means that many variances have an inbuilt imprecision which should be remembered when interpreting variances.

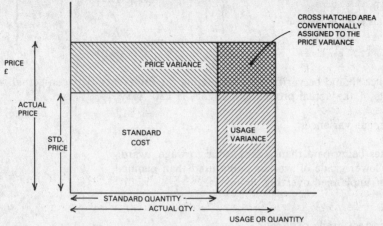

Figure 3 Diagrammatic representation of Price and Usage Variances

LABOUR VARIANCES

23. This paragraph deals with the Direct Labour Total Variance, The Direct Labour Rate Variance (the 'price' variance), and the Direct Labour Efficiency Variance (the 'usage' variance). These are defined below:

Direct Labour Total Variance – definition
'The difference between the standard direct labour cost and the actual direct labour cost, incurred for the production achieved'. *Terminology.*

Direct Labour Rate Variance – definition
'The difference between the standard and actual direct labour rate per hour for the total hours worked'. *Terminology.*

Direct Labour Efficiency Variance – definition
'The difference between the standard hours for the actual production achieved and the hours actually worked, valued at the standard labour rate'. *Terminology.*

The formulae are given below and follow a similar pattern to the material variances.

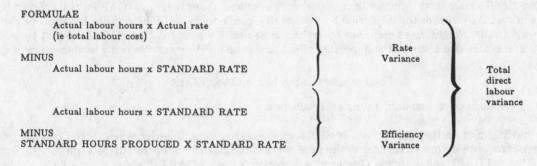

Notes:

(a) It will be seen that the second line of the rate variance and the first line of the efficiency variance are identical.

(b) Where appropriate records exist and it is considered that useful information will result, an idle time variance can be calculated by multiplying the hours of idle time by the standard rate. The variance so calculated, together with the efficiency variance, forms the labour usage variance. Where no idle time variance is calculated, as in the formulae shown above, the efficiency variance is equivalent to the labour usage variance. As with labour efficiency, the effect of idle time on variable and fixed overheads can also be calculated.

Example 2 (based on data from para 21.)

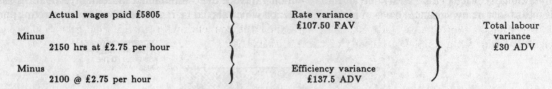

Actual wages paid £5805		Rate variance £107.50 FAV	
Minus 2150 hrs at £2.75 per hour			Total labour variance £30 ADV
Minus 2100 @ £2.75 per hour		Efficiency variance £137.5 ADV	

The total variance should be verified by calculating the difference between actual wages paid, £5805 and the standard labour costs of the actual production, £5775, ie £30 ADV.

Typical causes of labour variances:
Rate
    (a) Higher rates being paid than planned due to wage award.
    (b) Higher or lower grade of worker being used than planned.
    (c) Payment of unplanned overtime or bonus.

Efficiency
    (a) Use of incorrect grade of labour.
    (b) Poor workshop organisation or supervision.
    (c) Incorrect materials and/or machine problems.

Note: It will be apparent that the assumption behind the labour efficiency variance is that labour is a variable cost and that output is directly related to labour hours. In modern circumstances where output may be machine dominated and the amount of labour may be more or less constant, the calculation of such a ratio is unlikely to produce any meaningful information for control purposes.

BASIC VARIANCE ANALYSIS

24.   So far only the basic material and labour variances have been dealt with. The illustrations have been deliberately kept simple in order to emphasise the major principles of variance analysis. There is considerable similarity between the methods of calculating all types of variance and students are advised to master the first part of this chapter before proceeding to the overhead and other variances which follow. An important general principle which should be apparent at this stage is that actual prices or rates are never used in variance analysis, except to calculate the price or rate variance which is **always done first.**

INTRODUCTION TO OVERHEAD VARIANCE ANALYSIS

25.   Before dealing with the individual variances it is necessary to recall some of the earlier material in the manual. Overheads are absorbed into costs by means of predetermined overhead absorption rates (OAR) which are calculated by dividing the budgeted overheads for the period by the activity level anticipated. The activity level can be expressed in various ways (units, weight, sales etc.), but by far the most useful concept is that of the Standard Hour. It will be recalled that the 'Standard Hour' is a unit measure of production and is the most commonly used measure of activity level. thus:

$$\text{Total overhead absorbed} = \text{OAR} \times \text{SHP}$$

where SHP is the number of Standard Hours of Production.

Where the Standard costing system uses total absorption costing principles (ie where both fixed and variable overheads are absorbed into production costs) the total overheads absorbed can be subdivided into Fixed Overhead Absorption Rates (FOAR) and Variable Overhead Absorption Rates (VOAR) thus:

FIXED OVERHEADS ABSORBED =   FOAR X SHP
VARIABLE OVERHEADS ABSORBED =   VOAR X SHP
TOTAL OVERHEADS ABSORBED =   (FOAR + VOAR) X SHP

When standard **marginal** costing is used, only variable overheads are absorbed into production costs and thus only variances relating to variable overheads arise; fixed overheads being dealt with by the budgetary control system. Thus it will be seen that overhead variance analysis is considerably simplified when standard marginal costing is employed.

There are several possible approaches to overhead variance analysis and one commonly encountered approach, that shown in Figure 2, is described with worked examples and diagrammatic representations. Students should be aware that much of conventional overhead variance analysis is subject to criticism as being of little value for control purposes. The various criticisms that can be made are dealt with after the conventional principles have been explained and exemplified. The various examples are based on the following data.

Budget for Department No. 13
for period No. 5

Fixed overheads	£15,360
Variable overheads	£20,480
Labour hours	5,120
Standard hours of Production	5,120

Actual for period

Fixed overheads	£15,850
Variable overheads	£21,220
Labour hours	5,100
Standard hours produced	5,050

From the budget the overhead absorption rates have been calculated using standard hours as the absorption base.

$$\text{F.O.A.R.} = \frac{\text{Budgeted fixed overheads}}{\text{Budgeted activity (Std. Hrs)}} = \frac{£15,360}{5,120} = £3 \text{ per hour}$$

$$\text{V.O.A.R} = \frac{\text{Budgeted variable overheads}}{\text{Budgeted activity (Std. Hrs)}} = \frac{£20,480}{5,120} = £4 \text{ per hour}$$

and the total absorption rate is £3 + 4 = £7 per hour

Notes:

(a) It will be seen that **budgeted** labour hours and the **budgeted** standard hours production are the same. This is the normal planning basis. If actual labour hours and the standard hours actually produced also were the same, then efficiency would be exactly as planned and no efficiency variances would arise. It will be seen from the data that this is not the case on this occasion.

(b) It will be apparent that because absorption rates for fixed overheads have been calculated the examples will be based on total absorption costing principles.

VARIABLE OVERHEAD VARIANCES

26. This paragraph describes the variable overhead variance, the variable overhead expenditure variance and the variable overhead efficiency variance.

Variable overhead variance - definition
The difference between the actual variable overheads incurred and the variable overheads absorbed.
(This variance is simply the over or under absorption of overheads.)

Variable overhead expenditure variance - definition
The difference between the actual variable overheads incurred and the allowed variable overheads based on the actual hours worked.

Variable overhead efficiency variance - definition.
The difference between the allowed variable overheads and the absorbed variable overhead.

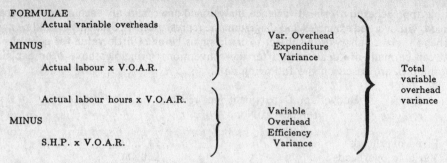

FORMULAE
    Actual variable overheads

MINUS

    Actual labour x V.O.A.R.   } Var. Overhead
                                                    Expenditure
                                                    Variance
                                                                        } Total
                                                                          variable
                                                                          overhead
    Actual labour hours x V.O.A.R.   }   variance

MINUS   Variable
                                                  Overhead
    S.H.P. x V.O.A.R.   Efficiency
                                                  Variance

Note: It will be realised that, based on the VOAR, the budget is flexed to suit the actual hours worked.

Example 3 (based on data from para 25.)

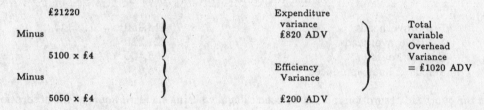

    £21220   Expenditure
                                                 variance
Minus   £820 ADV
                                                                        } Total
                                                                          variable
    5100 x £4   }   Overhead
                                                                          Variance
Minus   Efficiency   = £1020 ADV
                                                 Variance
    5050 x £4   } £200 ADV

As usual, the total variance can be verified by taking the difference between what the variable overheads actually cost and the amount absorbed by the actual production.

$$£21,220 - 20200 = £1020$$

Variable overhead variances can be depicted as shown in Figure 4.

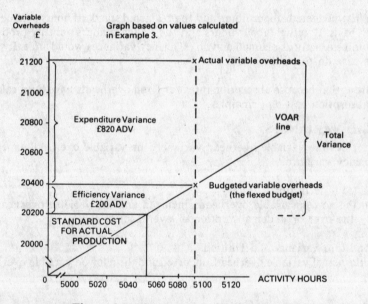

Figure 4 Variable Overhead Variances

FIXED OVERHEAD VARIANCES

27.   This paragraph describes one approach to fixed overhead variance analysis and covers the Fixed overhead Variance, the Fixed Overhead Expenditure Variance, the Fixed Overhead Volume Variance and its sub variances, the Capacity Variance and the Efficiency or Productivity Variance.

Fixed overhead total variance – definition
The total difference between the fixed overhead absorbed by the actual production and the actual fixed overhead for the period.

Note: As with the variable overhead variance the fixed overhead total variance simply represents under or over absorption of overheads.

Fixed overhead expenditure variance – definition
The difference between actual fixed overheads and allowed or budgeted fixed overheads for the period.

Fixed overhead volume variance – definition
The difference between the fixed overhead absorbed by the actual production and budgeted fixed overheads for the period.

The volume variance arises from the actual volume of production differing from the planned volume. If required, the volume variance can be subdivided into an efficiency variance and a capacity variance.

Fixed overhead efficiency variance – definition
This is the difference between the standard hours of production achieved and the actual labour hours, valued at the F.O.A.R.

Fixed overhead capacity variance
This is the difference between the budgeted hours and actual hours, valued at the F.O.A.R.

The formulae for these variances are as follows:

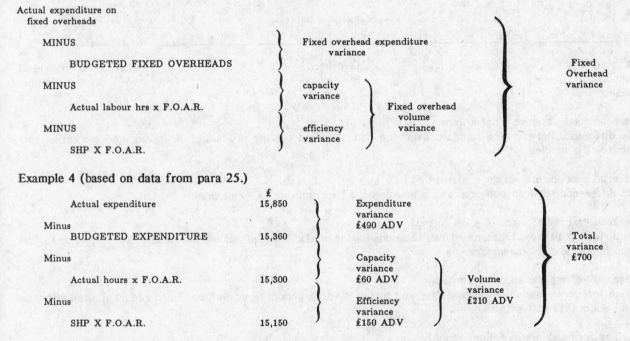

Actual expenditure on
fixed overheads

    MINUS   } Fixed overhead expenditure
                                                  variance
        BUDGETED FIXED OVERHEADS   Fixed
                                                                               Overhead
    MINUS   } capacity   variance
                                               variance
        Actual labour hrs x F.O.A.R.   } Fixed overhead
                                                            volume
    MINUS   } efficiency   variance
                                               variance
        SHP X F.O.A.R.

Example 4 (based on data from para 25.)

	£			
Actual expenditure	15,850	Expenditure variance £490 ADV		
Minus				Total variance £700
BUDGETED EXPENDITURE	15,360			
Minus		Capacity variance £60 ADV		
Actual hours x F.O.A.R.	15,300		Volume variance £210 ADV	
Minus		Efficiency variance £150 ADV		
SHP X F.O.A.R.	15,150			

Once again the total variance can be verified by comparing actual expenditure and the amount of fixed overheads absorbed by the actual production, ie £15,850 – 15150 = £700 ADV

The fixed overhead variances can be depicted as shown in Figure 5.

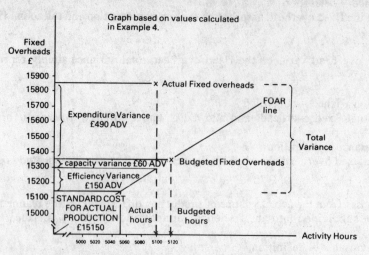

Figure 5 Fixed Overhead Variances

ALTERNATIVE OVERHEAD VARIANCES

28. The overhead variances illustrated so far have been based on the separation of the total overheads into fixed and variable components. An alternative, and simpler, approach is to calculate variances based on the total overheads, that is fixed and variable combined.

In such circumstances the following variances could be calculated

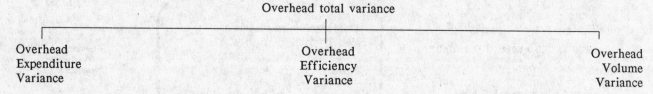

Overhead total variance - definition
'The difference between the standard overhead cost specified for the production achieved, and the actual cost incurred'. *Terminology*.

Overhead expenditure variance -definition
'The difference between budgeted and actual overhead expenditure'. *Terminology*.

Overhead efficiency variance - definition
'The difference between the standard over head rate for the production achieved and the standard overhead rate for the actual hours taken'. *Terminology*.

Overhead volume variance - definition
'The difference between the standard overhead cost of the actual hours taken and the flexed budget allowance for the actual hours taken'. *Terminology*.

The formulae are as follows

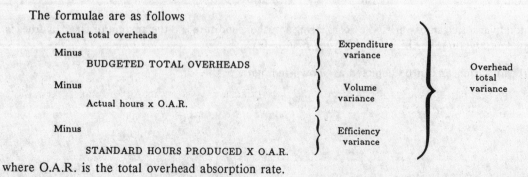

where O.A.R. is the total overhead absorption rate.

Example 5 (based on the data in Para 25.)

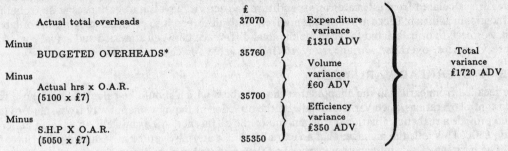

	£	
Actual total overheads	37070	Expenditure variance £1310 ADV
Minus BUDGETED OVERHEADS*	35760	
Minus Actual hrs x O.A.R. (5100 x £7)	35700	Volume variance £60 ADV
Minus S.H.P X O.A.R. (5050 x £7)	35350	Efficiency variance £350 ADV

Total variance £1720 ADV

This can be verified by calculating the difference between the actual total overheads and the total overheads absorbed by the actual production. £37070 - 35350 = £1720 ADV

*The budgeted overheads are calculated by the normal process of flexing a budget, ie

Budgeted total overheads	=	Budgeted Fixed overheads + Actual hours x V.O.A.R
	=	£15360 + 5100 x £4
	=	£35760

It will be seen that the volume variance is equivalent to the under-recovery of the fixed overheads caused by working 5100 instead of the budgeted 5120 hours, ie

(Actual hours - budgeted hours) x F.O.A.R.
(5100 - 5120) x £3 = £60 ADV

The above variances can be depicted as shown in Figure 6.

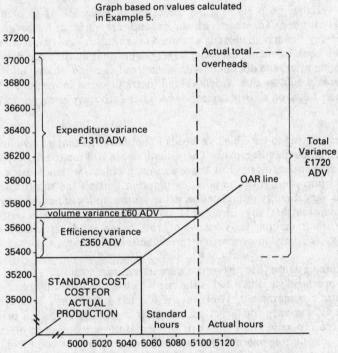

Figure 6 Total Overhead Variances

Note: It will be realised that this second approach to overhead variance analysis is merely an aggregation of the approach outlined previously in para 27.

REASONS FOR OVERHEAD VARIANCES

29. Overhead variances largely arise because of the conventions of the overhead absorption process. Overhead absorption rates are calculated from estimates of expenditure and activity levels and variances arise from differences in both these factors. In addition, because overheads are frequently absorbed into production by means of labour hours, overhead variances need to be calculated to reconcile the total difference between standard and actual cost. Apart from the expenditure variances, overhead variances are of limited value for control purposes.

A CRITIQUE OF OVERHEAD VARIANCES

30. It will be recalled from earlier in the chapter that the variances which should be calculated are those which help management to control operations. Such variances indicate the direction of the movement away from standard (adverse or favourable) and provide a realistic valuation of the amount of the difference. An example is an adverse materials usage variance of say, £500. This tells the manager that an extra £500 of materials, valued at standard price, have been used in production. The meaning of this information is clear and the manager has a realistic valuation of the improvement he might make by bringing operations in line with standard, assuming that the standard price is a reasonable figure.

How do overhead variances measure up to these criteria? In general, the answer is, not very well. The following are some of the specific criticisms that can be made of overhead variance analysis especially the fixed overhead content.

(a)   A major factor in calculating overhead variances is the overhead recovery rates. These rates arise from the conventions of **cost ascertainment** whereby costs are absorbed into cost units by means of labour hour or machine hour rates. The use of such rates for the quite different purpose of **cost control** has obvious limitations.

(b)   Both the numerator and denominator of a department overhead absorption rate contain subjective and possibly quite arbitrary values. The fixed costs in the numerator may include apportionments of general company fixed costs to the various departments and the choice of the output level for the denominator is arbitrary. These and other factors determine the amount of the overhead absorption rate which in turn determines the values assigned to the overhead variances.

(c)   The volume variance purports to show the effect of not working to planned capacity but its use in this respect is extremely limited. Together with the expenditure variance however it does show to what extent the overhead absorption system has adequately absorbed overheads for cost ascertainment purposes. It will be realised that this is simply a book balancing exercise, largely dependent on the accuracy of the original estimates used in calculating absorption rates, and does not assist managerial decision making or operational control. A more useful variance in this area would be one which valued losses or gains in output in terms of realisable contribution rather than variances based on absorption rates which have arbitrary elements and which were designed for a quite different purpose.

(d)   The variances relating to variable overheads to not have the major flaws inherent in those relating to fixed overheads but some problems still remain. The valuations are still related to overhead absorption rates which have the same caveats as mentioned above. A more serious problem, which considerably limits their usefulness for operational control purposes, is the implicit assumption that **all** the multifarious items which go to make up variable overheads vary directly in proportion to the **same** activity indicator, conventionally labour hours. It may be a realistic assumption that, say, direct materials vary in proportion to output but it is far too simplistic a view that all the items making up variable overheads (eg indirect materials, power, lighting, supervision, maintenance and so on) vary in proportion to **one** activity indicator.

(e)   The expenditure variance (the difference between actual expenditure and the flexed budget) is probably the most useful of the overhead variances and is the one which would generally be considered to be controllable by the responsibility centre's management. However, it too has limitations. The overhead expenditure variance is analogous to the total variance for direct costs in that it consists of both a **price** and a **usage** component. The expenditure variance can arise from either price increases, eg increase in electricity charges, salary increases or by changes in quantity, eg more telephone calls, more staff, or some combination of price and quantity differences. Accordingly, without further analysis, perhaps by detailed item-by-item budgetary comparisons, the overall expenditure variance is of limited value for control purposes.

DISPOSITION OF VARIANCES

31. It is general practice at the end of a control period to write off all variances to the Costing Profit and Loss account and to carry all items in the Cost Accounts at standard cost. Provided that the variances are relatively small this is a reasonable practice and is one which should be adopted. However, certain difficulties may arise from this practice particularly when the variances are significant; for example:

(a)   Typically, material price variances are isolated at the time of purchase and materials are thereafter maintained at standard price. This process breaks the normal matching rule used in calculating the profits of an accounting period, ie the accruals concept of SSAP 2.

(b)   Where the variances are significant the valuations (at standard cost) of materials, work-in-progress, and finished goods stocks may not be considered acceptable for balance sheet purposes. In such circumstances it may be necessary to apportion variances over the various categories to achieve more acceptable valuations.

(c)   Where significant **favourable** price, usage and efficiency variances arise and stock exist, this could mean that an unrealised profit may be taken. Because of this, favourable variances are sometimes retained in the accounts until the relevant production is actually sold.

CONTROL RATIOS

32.   As an alternative to overhead efficiency and volume variances ratios can be calculated using the same basic data of budgeted and actual labour hours and standard hours produced.

The three ratios are:

$$\text{ACTIVITY RATIO} = \frac{\text{Standard hours produced}}{\text{Budgeted labour hours}} \times 100$$

$$\text{CAPACITY RATIO} = \frac{\text{Actual labour hours worked}}{\text{Budgeted labour hours}} \times 100$$

$$\text{EFFICIENCY RATIO} = \frac{\text{Standard hours produced}}{\text{Actual labour hours worked}} \times 100$$

Based on the data from para 25. the three ratios can be calculated.

Data		
Budgeted labour hours	5120
Actual labour hours	5100
Standard hours produced	5050

$$\text{Activity Ratio} = \frac{5050}{5120} \times 100 = 98.6\%$$

$$\text{Capacity Ratio} = \frac{5100}{5120} \times 100 = 99.6\%$$

$$\text{Efficiency Ratio} = \frac{5050}{5100} \times 100 = 99\%$$

These ratios are statements in relative terms of the absolute measures provided by variances.

The Activity ratio is equivalent to the Fixed Overhead Volume variance.

The Capacity ratio is equivalent to the Fixed Overhead Capacity variance.

The Efficiency ratio is equivalent to the Fixed and Variable Overhead and Labour Efficiency variances.

SUMMARY

33.   (a)   Standard costing involves comparing actual costs with predetermined costs and analysing the differences, known as variances.

(b)   There are four main types of standard: Basic standards, ideal standards, attainable standards and current standards.

(c)   Basic standards are long term standards which remain unchanged for long periods; ideal standards represent perfect working conditions and performances; attainable standards are currently attainable standards based on high but not impossible performance levels. Attainable standards are the most common.

(d)   Standards relate to individual items, processes and products; budgets relate to totals.

(e)   Setting standards is a detailed, lengthy process usually based on engineering and technical studies of times, materials and methods. Standards are set for each of the elements which make up the standard cost: labour, materials and overheads.

(f)   Accountants, work study engineers and other specialists provide technical advice and information, but do not set the standards. This is the responsibility of the line managers and their superiors.

(g)   The culmination of the standard setting process is the preparation of a standard cost card for the product showing the target cost for the following periods.

(h)   Difficulties arise with the too frequent revision of standards. Consequently it is common practice to revise them on a periodic basis, half yearly or yearly.

(i)   The behavioural aspects of standard costing, like budgeting, are all important. The system must be acceptable to the people who will have to operate it.

(j)   Variance analysis is the process of analysing the total difference between planned and actual performance into its constituent parts.

(k)   Variance analysis must be useful to management otherwise it is pointless.

(l)   Variances should be calculated in accordance with responsibilities but this is often difficult.

(m)   Although there are different names, each type of variance; materials, wages and overheads has a PRICE element and a QUANTITY element.

(n)   The relationship between variances must be considered. Variances should not be considered in isolation. Invariably there are interdependencies which conventional variance analysis does not reveal.

(o)   The basic materials variances measure the differences between actual and standard price and actual and standard usage.

(p)   Price variances are ALWAYS extracted first. Thereafter all variance calculations use standard price.

(q)   The basic labour variances measure the difference between actual and standard wage rates and actual and standard labour efficiency.

(r)   An important factor in overhead absorption and overhead variance analysis is the activity level. Frequently this is measured in standard hours. A standard hour is a unit measure of production, not of time.

(s)   Using total absorption principles both fixed and variable overheads are absorbed into production, so variances relating to both fixed and variable overheads will arise. Using standard marginal costing only variable overheads are absorbed into production overheads so that fixed overhead variances cannot arise.

(t)   Variable overhead variances reflect differences in variable overhead expenditure and labour efficiency. Fixed overhead variances also reflect differences in expenditure and labour efficiency and in addition differences between the planned capacity (activity level) and actual capacity. Apart from the expenditure variances the usefulness of overhead variances is questionable except for balancing purposes.

(u)   The Total Cost Variance, shown in Figure 1, is merely the total of all the variances, ie the Direct Materials cost variance, the Direct Wages cost variance and the Variable and Fixed Overhead variances.

POINTS TO NOTE

34.   (a)   Variances are related to responsibilities. It follows, therefore, that a manager should only be held responsible for a variance when he has control over the resource or cost element being considered.

(b)   It must be stressed that variance analysis merely directs attention to the cause of off-standard performances. It does not solve the problem, nor does it establish the reasons behind the variance. These are management tasks.

(c)   The variances described are ones commonly found, but many others exist. It would be impossible to describe or remember all the possible variances, but of far greater importance is to understand the principles underlying variance analysis; once this is done any given variance can be calculated easily.

(d)   The relationships between variances must always be considered. Rarely is a single variance of great significance. Is a favourable variance offset by a larger adverse one?

(e)   Although budgetary control and standard costing are techniques which use the same underlying principle, an important difference is that standard costs and variances form part of the double entry system whereas budgetary control is in memorandum form.

(f)   The overhead volume variances can be criticised because information which is intended for product costing purposes (ie absorption of fixed overheads into cost units) is used as a basis for control information. Fixed overheads are based more on time than activity so that it becomes very difficult to trace responsibility for an adverse volume variance. Because of this, the fixed overhead expenditure variance is probably the most relevant fixed overhead variance for control purposes.

(g)   Standard costing can only exist realistically within the framework of a budgeting system. On the other hand budgetary control systems are frequently found without a standard costing system. Standard costing should only be employed when it suits the product, type of manufacture and the organisation and when its use is cost-effective.

(h)   The significance of variances and variance control bands have been dealt with in the chapter on Budgetary Control. The principles and techniques described apply equally to standard costing variances.

(i)   Although it is conventional to value usage and efficiency variances at standard prices or rates students should be aware that they could alternatively be valued at actual price. It is argued that such a procedure gives a valuation that is economically realistic, more up to date and is thus a better guide for management action.

ADDITIONAL READING

Management Accounting Guidelines No. 5 'Standard Costing: some aspects of implementation'   CIMA

Management Accounting   Amey and Egginton, LONGMAN

Cost accounting: a managerial emphasis   Horngren, PRENTICE HALL

SELF REVIEW QUESTIONS

1.   *What is standard costing? (2)*

2.   *What are the objectives of standard costing? (3)*

3.   *Define standard cost. (4)*

4.   *What are the four main types of standard? (5)*

5.   *What is the relationship between budgets and standards? (6)*

6.   *What factors need to be considered when setting standards? (7-9)*

7.   *What is a 'standard hour'? (9)*

8.   *Whose responsibility is it ultimately for setting the level of attainment in a standard? (12)*

9.   *Describe a standard cost card. (13)*

10.   *Why are the behavioural aspects of standard costing so important? (15)*

11.   *What is the purpose of variance analysis and what variances should be calculated? (17)*

12.   *Why is the location of responsibility for variances desirable but difficult to achieve? (18)*

13.   *What is the operating profit variance and how could this be analysed? (19)*

14.   *How can the significance of a variance be established? (20)*

15.   *Define the common materials variances and give their formulae. (22)*

16.   *Define the common labour variances and give their formulae. (23)*

17. *What is the basis of overhead variance analysis? (25)*

18. *What are typical variable overhead variances and what are their formulae? (26)*

19. *Describe a four way variance analysis of fixed overheads. (27)*

20. *What is a possible alternative approach to overhead variance analysis? (28)*

21. *Why do overhead variances arise? (29)*

22. *What specific criticisms can be made of overhead variances as a means of management control? (30)*

23. *What happens to variances at the period end? (31)*

24. *Describe the control ratios. (32)*

EXAMINATION QUESTIONS WITH ANSWERS COMMENCING PAGE 347

A1. *The Britten Co Ltd manufactures a variety of products of basically similar composition. Production is carried out by subjecting the various raw materials to a number of standardised operations, each major series of operations being carried out in a different department. All products are subjected to the same initial processing which is carried out in departments A, B and C; the order and extent of further processing then depending upon the type of end product to be produced.*

It has been decided that a standard costing system could be usefully employed within Britten and a pilot scheme is to be operated for six months based initially only on department B, the second department in the initial common series of operations. If the pilot scheme produces useful results then a management accountant will be employed and the system would be incorporated as appropriate throughout the whole firm.

The standard cost per unit of output of department B is:

	£	£
Direct labour (14 hours at £2 per hour)		28
Direct materials		
(i) output of department A (3 Kg at £9 per Kg)	27	
(ii) acquired by and directly input to department B		
material X (4 Kg at £5 per Kg)	20	47
Variable overhead (at £1 per direct labour hours worked)		14
Fixed production overheads		
(i) directly incurred by department B - (note 1)		
manufacturing overhead (per unit)	3	
(ii) allocated to department B		
general factory overhead (per unit)	8	11

Note 1. Based on normal monthly production of 400 units.

In the first month of operation of the pilot study (month 7 of the financial year), department B had no work in progress at the beginning and the end of the month. The actual costs allocated to department B in the first month of operation were:

	£	£
Direct labour (6,500 hours)		14,000
Direct materials		
(i) output of department A (1,400 Kg) - (note 2)	21,000	
(ii) material X (1,900 Kg)	11,500	32,500
Variable overhead		8,000
Fixed overhead		
(i) directly incurred manufacturing overhead	1,600	
(ii) allocated to department B - (note 3)	2,900	4,500
		£59,000

Note 2. Actual cost of output of department A.

Note 3. Based on the actual expenditure on joint manufacturing overheads and allocated to departments in accordance with labour hours worked.

The production manager feels that the actual costs of £59,000 for production of 500 units indicates considerable inefficiency on the part of department B. He says, 'I was right to request that the pilot standard costing system be carried out in department B as I have suspected that they are inefficient and careless – this overspending of £9,000 proves I am right'.

Required:

(a) Prepare a brief statement which clearly indicates the reasons for the performance of department B and the extent to which that performance is attributable to department B. The statement should utilise variance analysis to the extent it is applicable and relevant.

(b) Comment on the way the pilot standard costing system is currently being operated and suggest how its operation might be improved during the study period.

ACCA, Management Accounting.

A2. *(a) Specify and explain the factors to be considered in determining whether to investigate a variance which has been routinely reported as part of a standard costing system.*

(b) Describe how accumulated production variances should be treated at the end of an accounting period.

ACCA, Management Accounting.

A3. *(a) A budget might be construed around the activities requires to meet a given goal or, alternatively, a budget might be a forecast derived from past experience. Similarly standards might be regarded as targets or they might be set at an average level of performance achieved in the past.*

Discuss the considerations that should be borne in mind when establishing appropriate bases for setting standards and budgets.

(b) The quality control chart is suggested as having applicability in deciding whether or not to investigate a cost variance.

Describe and discuss the suggested approach.

ACCA, Management Accounting.

11. Standard Costing – II

INTRODUCTION

1.   This chapter continues the study of variance analysis by considering mix and yield variances and the sales margin variances. Standard marginal costing is explained and contrasted with standard costing based on total absorption costing principles. The concept of planning and operational variances is discussed and exemplified and the chapter concludes with a survey of cost reduction techniques such as variety reduction, value analysis and work study which are used in an attempt to reduce costs and increase efficiency.

MORE DETAILED MATERIAL VARIANCES

2.   The basic material variances were described in the previous chapter. In certain circumstances it is conventional for sub-variances to be calculated, known as the Direct Materials Mix Variance and the Direct Materials Yield Variance. Typical circumstances in which such calculations are considered appropriate are those where the production process involves mixing different material inputs to make the required output. Examples include: the manufacture of fertilisers, steel, plastics, food products and so on. A feature of such processes is the existence of process losses through impurities, evaporation, breakages, machinery failures and other such factors which affect the yield from the process.

There are several methods of calculating mix and yield variances; some treat the mix variance as part of the price variance, others that there should be a combined mix/price variance, whilst another approach is that the mix and yield variances are sub-variances of the usage variance. This latter approach is illustrated in Figure 2 in the previous chapter and is the system included in the CIMA Terminology of Management Accounting.

There are two alternative ways of sub-dividing the usage variance. One uses the individual standard prices of the ingredients whilst the other uses a weighted average price for all ingredients. For the variance calculations these prices are applied to slightly different ingredient quantities. Both methods produce the *same mix and yield variances in total*; all that differs is the amount attributed to each constituent ingredient.

For identification the methods will be termed the 'individual price' and the 'weighted average price' methods and both are defined and illustrated below using the same data for comparative purposes. The individual price method (which is that in the CIMA terminology) is illustrated first.

Definitions (Individual price method)

Direct Materials Mix Variance

'The difference between total quantity in standard proportion, priced at the standard price and the actual quantity of material used priced at the standard price'. *Terminology*.

Direct Material Yield Variance

'The difference between the standard yield of the actual material input and the actual yield, both valued at the standard material cost of the product'. *Terminology*.

MIX AND YIELD FORMULAE (INDIVIDUAL PRICE METHOD)

3.   FORMULAE

Direct Materials Mixture Variance	=	STANDARD COST of the actual quantity of the actual mixture	minus	STANDARD COST of the actual quantity of the STANDARD MIXTURE
Direct Materials Yield Variance	=	STANDARD COST of the actual quantity of the STANDARD MIXTURE	minus	STANDARD COST of the STANDARD QUANTITY of the STANDARD MIXTURE

Notes:

(a)   Because the price variance is always dealt with first, the mix and yield variances use only standard prices.

(b)   Note how the expressions move from **actual** to STANDARD values and that the second part of the mix variance is the same as the first in the yield variance.

(c)   The yield variance measures abnormal process losses or gains.

Example 1

A fertiliser is made by mixing and processing three ingredients, P, N and Q. The standard cost data are as follows

		Standard Proportions	Standard Cost
Ingredient	P	50%	£20 per tonne
	N	40%	£25 per tonne
	Q	10%	£42 per tonne

A standard process loss of 5% is anticipated.

In a period the output was 93.1 tonnes and the inputs were as follows:

		Actual usage	Actual price	Actual cost £
Ingredient	P	49 tonnes	£16 per tonne	784
	N	43 tonnes	£27 per tonne	1,161
	Q	8 tonnes	£48 per tonne	384
				£2,329

Calculate all relevant material variances using the individual price method.

Solution

The total variance is calculated thus:

Standard cost for 1 tonne

Ingredient	P	0.5 tonne @ £20	=	£10
	N	0.4 tonne @ £25	=	£10
	Q	0.1 tonne @ £42	=	£4.2
				£24.2

1 tonne of input at standard produces 0.95 tonnes of output so the standard cost per tonne of output is

$$£24.2 \quad \times \quad \frac{100}{95} = £25.473684$$

∴ Standard cost of actual output = 93.1 x £25.473684 = £2371.6

Actual cost of output = £2329

∴ Total Variance = £42.6(FAV)

The three relevant variances are: Price, Mix and Yield which are to be calculated in that order. The usage variance is merely the total of the mix and yield variances.

The summary of the variance calculations is given below followed by explanatory notes.

Notes:

(a) Actual usage
     Actual mix   £2,329
     Actual price

(b) Actual usage
     Actual mix
     STANDARD PRICE   £2,391

(c) Actual usage
     STANDARD MIX
     STANDARD PRICE   £2,420

(d) STANDARD USAGE
     STANDARD MIX
     STANDARD PRICE   £2,371.6

DIRECT MATERIALS PRICE VARIANCE £62 (FAV)

MIXTURE VARIANCE £29 (FAV)

YIELD VARIANCE £48.4 (ADV)

USAGE VARIANCE £19.4 ADV

DIRECT MATERIALS COST VARIANCE £42.6 FAV

It will be seen how the factors involved, usage-mix-price, start all at **actual** and move stage by stage to become all at STANDARD. This is the key to remembering the method of calculation.

Notes:

(a) Actual usage, actual mix, actual price is the cost given in the question, ie £2,329.

(b) The actual usage in the actual proportions is evaluated at the standard price, ie
£(49 x 20) + (43 x 251) + (8 x 42) = £2,391

(c) The standard mix is found by putting the actual total quantity (100 tonnes) into the standard proportions (50%, 40% and 10%), ie 50P, 40N and 10Q.

These are evaluated at the standard prices and compared with the values from (b).

INGREDIENT	ACTUAL USAGE	TOTAL USAGE IN STANDARD PROPORTIONS	DIFFERENCE	STANDARD PRICE	VARIANCE
	Tonnes	Tonnes	Tonnes	£	£
P	49	50	+ 1	20	20 FAV
N	43	40	- 3	25	75 ADV
Q	8	10	+ 2	42	84 FAV
	100	100	TOTAL MIX VARIANCE		29 FAV

(d) The standard usage is found by working back from the actual output (93.1 tonnes) to determine what the standard total quantity of inputs should be, assuming a normal process loss of 5%.

ie standard output quantity = 95% of standard input quantity

∴ Standard input quantity = $\frac{100}{95}$ x actual output quantity

= $\frac{100}{95}$ x 93.1

= 98 tonnes

This value is pro rated in the standard proportions, calculated at the standard price and compared with the values from (c) thus:

INGREDIENT	TOTAL USAGE IN STANDARD PROPORTIONS		STANDARD USAGE FOR OUTPUT IN STD PROPORTIONS	DIFFERENCE	STANDARD PRICE	VARIANCE	
	Tonnes		Tonnes	Tonnes	£	£	
P	50	(98 x 50%)	49	– 1	20	20	ADV
N	40	(98 x 40%)	39.2	– 0.8	25	20	ADV
Q	10	(98 x 10%)	9.8	– 0.2	42	8.4	ADV
	100		98	TOTAL YIELD VARIANCE		48.4	ADV

The alternative 'weighted average price' method is now defined and illustrated.

ALTERNATIVE METHOD FOR MIX AND YIELD VARIANCES

4.   Definitions (weighted average price method)

Direct Materials Mix Variance
The difference between the standard quantity of inputs for the output achieved and the actual quantity used priced at the difference between individual standard prices and weighted average standard price.

Direct Materials Yield Variance
The difference between the standard quantity of inputs for the output achieved and the actual quantity used priced at the weighted average standard price.

Example 1 is reworked below based on these alternative definitions.

The Total Variance is £42.6 ADV and the Price Variance is calculated in exactly the same manner and is, as previously, £62 Favourable.

To calculate the weighted average mix and yield variances the input quantity differences and the weighted average standard ingredient price have to be calculated.

INGREDIENT	STANDARD USAGE FOR OUTPUT IN STD PROPORTIONS	ACTUAL USAGE	INPUT DIFFERENCES
	Tonnes	Tonnes	Tonnes
P	49	49	–
N	39.2	43	– 3.8
Q	9.8	8	+ 1.8
	98	100	– 2.0

Weighted Average Standard ingredient price.

From the original data the standard cost of 1 tonne is:

				£
Ingredient	P	0.5 x £20	=	10
	N	0.4 x £25	=	10
	Q	0.1 x £42	=	4.2
				24.2

∴ Weighted average ingredient cost is £24.2 per tonne

These values are used in the variance calculations

MIX VARIANCE:

INGREDIENT	INPUT DIFFERENCES	X	STANDARD PRICE	= VARIANCE
	Tonnes		*less* WEIGHTED AVERAGE PRICE £	£
P	–			–
N	– 3.8		(£25 – 24.2) = 0.80	3.04 ADV
Q	+ 1.8		(£42 – 24.2) = 17.80	32.04 FAV
			TOTAL MIX VARIANCE	29.00 FAV

YIELD VARIANCE:

INGREDIENT	INPUT DIFFERENCES	X	WEIGHTED AVERAGE STANDARD PRICE	= VARIANCE
	Tonnes		£	£
P	–			
N	– 3.8		24.2	91.96 ADV
Q	+ 1.8		24.2	43.56 FAV
			TOTAL YIELD VARIANCE	48.40 ADV

Thus it will be seen that the alternative approaches produce the same total mix and yield variances but differ in the amount attributed to each ingredient. Which is the correct method?

No one method of calculating variances or any given variance is more correct than any other. The 'correct' variances are those which assist management to make the right decisions. Accordingly, management would use whichever of the above methods is deemed to provide the most relevant information if, in fact, mix and yield variances are thought to provide any useful information. However, students should be aware that there are serious doubts about the usefulness and meaning of conventionally prepared mix and yield variances. These doubts are explored below.

PROBLEMS WITH CONVENTIONAL MIX AND YIELD VARIANCES

5.   The standard mix is, by definition, the cheapest possible combination of materials, which fulfils the technical requirements of the output, having regard to the relative prices and characteristics of the materials and the process yield expected when the standard was set. Typical conventional variances, as the example calculated above, show the effect of changes from the original standard (based on implicit assumptions discussed below) but give no indication of whether the results were optimal given the relative prices, qualities and availability of materials at the time of production. Where substitutability of materials is possible and/or where the characteristics of materials are variable and/or where there are relative price changes then the optimal mix may be continually changing and a static, historical standard, as implied in conventional variance calculations, is unlikely to be appropriate.

The choice of the optimum mix of materials in any given circumstances is a subtle one involving the balancing of current material prices, availability and characteristics, the extent of technical substitutability and the requirements of the finished production. Because of this many process industries use computer based linear programming techniques (described in a later chapter) on a continual basis to select the optimal mix for the current production.

The likelihood that the original standard will be out of date is but one problem with conventional mix and yield variance analysis. Other problems are as follows:

(a)   The conventional analysis presupposes a constant correlation between physical inputs and output regardless of the mix of inputs, ie if the mix of inputs changes the same relationship is assumed between the new mix and output as between the original standard mix and output. Such an assumption is illogical and contravenes the concept of an optimum mix.

(b)   The conventional analysis ignores the technical acceptability of the output by assuming that the output is acceptable regardless of the input mix of materials.

(c)   Conventionally a linear substitutability between material inputs assumed. If this reasoning were pursued to the extreme it would result in a mix consisting of one material only, the cheapest! This mix would produce a large, favourable mix variance which seems a strange measure of what would be a production impossibility.

(d)   Based on the premise that the standard represents the optimum position, conventional analysis should never produce a favourable mix variance because the lower standard cost of the actual mix means that it should have been the original standard in the first place, assuming the technical acceptability of the output. Examination questions based on conventional analysis which produce favourable mix variances are therefore internally inconsistent. The figures in Example 1 earlier in the chapter were chosen to give a favourable mix variance to illustrate this point.

(e) Even when the current circumstances are exactly as envisaged (ie same prices, technical qualities etc) if one of the sub-variances (mix or yield) is adverse then the other will be favourable and vice versa. Accordingly even in such stable conditions there would seem to be little value in calculating the sub-variances. The usage variance will be adverse at all conditions other than standard.

(f) The conventional analysis abstracts any differences between actual and standard prices first, and then uses standard price for the mix and yield variances. However, when prices vary from standard it is these very changes in relative prices which may make changes in mix and yield worthwhile. The exclusion of them from mix and yield calculations makes it more difficult to judge the correctness, or otherwise, of managerial decisions.

It will be seen from the above that conventional mix and yield variance analysis has serious deficiencies and is unlikely to produce information that assists management. Meaningful variance analysis is possible in this area but it cannot be achieved by the mechanical application of a few simple formulae. It will always be based on a thorough understanding of the principles and objectives of variance analysis and of the technical and commercial factors affecting the process being considered. Typical of the factors to be considered are:

(i) The relative prices, availabilities and technical characteristics of the input materials at the time of the mix.

(ii) The extent of the technical substitutability of materials.

(iii) The planned yield from **any** given actual mix of materials, not merely the yield from the standard mix.

(iv) The interdependencies between the material variances and the other process inputs. For example, a given material mix, based on relative prices and other factors may show an overall favourable materials variance but which may be more than outweighed by extra labour costs.

SALES MARGIN VARIANCES

6. A number of the more commonly encountered cost variances have now been dealt with and it will be recalled that the objective of cost variance analysis was to help management to control costs. However, costs are only one factor contributing to the achievement of planned profits. Another important factor is the margin on sales; either the profit margin when absorption costing is used or the contribution margin when marginal costing is used.

Accordingly sales margin variances can be calculated and because cost variance analysis extracts all the differences between planned and actual costs, the products are always treated at **standard manufacturing cost for the purpose of sales margin variance analysis.**

Part of Figure 2 from the preceding chapter is reproduced below showing the sales margin variances.

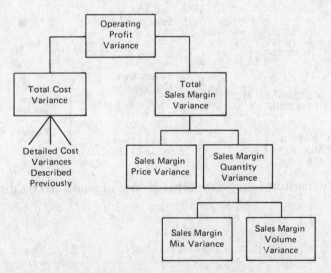

Extract from Figure 2. Preceding Chapter

Notes:

(a)   The standard sales margin is the difference between the standard selling price of a produce and its standard cost and is the same as the standard profit for the product.

(b)   The 'standard cost' referred to above is the 'total standard cost', ie it includes both fixed and variable costs. When fixed costs are excluded it becomes the standard marginal cost and the difference between standard selling price and standard marginal cost is known as the **standard sales contribution.**

SALES MARGIN VARIANCES - DEFINITIONS

7.   Definitions

Total sales margin variance

The difference between the budgeted margin from sales and the actual margin when the cost of sales is valued at the standard cost of production.

Sales margin price variance

That portion of the total sales margin variance which is the difference between the standard margin per unit and the actual margin per unit for the number of units sold in the period.

Note: This is a normal price variance and could equally well be described as the 'sales turnover price variance'.

Sales margin quantity variance

The portion of the total sales margin variance which is the difference between the budgeted number of units sold and the actual number sold valued at the standard margin per unit.

Note: This is a normal usage variance, analogous to the direct materials usage variance previously described.

When more than one product is sold, the Sales Margin Quantity Variance can be subdivided into a Mix Variance and a Volume Variance. The mix variance shows the effect on profits of variations from the planned sales mixture, and the volume variance shows the effect of the unit volume varying from standard. These sub-variances are defined below.

Sales margin mixture variance

That portion of the sales margin quantity variance which is the difference between the actual total number of units at the actual mix and the actual total number of units at standard mix valued at the standard margin per unit.

Sales margin volume variance

That portion of the sales margin quantity variance which is the difference between the actual total quantity of units sold and the budgeted total number of units at the standard mix valued at the standard margin per unit.

The formulae for these variances are given below.

Formulae

Note: There is considerable similarity in approach between these variances and the direct materials variances shown previously.

Example 2

A company makes and sells three products Q, R, and S. During a period, budget and actual results were as follows:

Product	Total Sales £	Budget Unit Volume units	Budget Unit Price £	Budget Unit Margin £	Total Margin £	Total Sales £	Actual Unit Volume units	Actual Unit Price £	Actual Unit Margin £	Total Margin £
Q	18,000	600	30	10	6,000	14,560	520	28	8	4,160
R	13,500	300	45	15	4,500	14,210	290	49	19	5,510
S	6,500	100	65	25	2,500	5,670	90	63	23	2,070
	38,000	1,000			13,000	34,440	900			11,740

Calculate all relevant sales margin variances.

Solution

Notes:

The similarity of these calculations and those for material variances can be seen by comparing the above solution with that for Example 1 in para 3.

Notes:

(a) This is the actual total margin as shown in the original data, ie £11,740.

(b) This is the actual units in the actual proportions but at budgeted margins, ie
£(520 x 10) + (290 x 15) + (90 x 25) = £11,800

(c) This is the actual number of units sold (900) but at the standard proportions (60%, 30%, 10%), valued at standard
£(540 x 10) + (270 x 15) + (90 x 25) = £11,700

(d) This is the total budgeted margin as given in the question, ie £13,000.

As usual, the total variance can be verified by comparing the budgeted position with the actual position, ie
£11,740 - £13,000 = £1,260 ADV

Note:

In similar fashion to the material mix and yield variances, the sales margin mix variance and the volume variance can alternatively be calculated using the weighted average standard margin rather than the individual standard margins as used above.

LIMITATIONS OF SALES MARGIN VARIANCE ANALYSIS

8.   The purpose of all variance analysis is to aid management control. To do this variances must be relevant and within a manager's control. Because there are so many external factors involved, the control of sales volume, sales margins and sales mix is extremely difficult and it is somewhat doubtful whether full variance analysis in this area is useful. In certain circumstances however, some of the variances may provide useful information; for example, where the sales price is under the control of the selling organisation and prices are stable, then the sales margin price variance could be useful, alternatively, when a manager is responsible for two or more products which are substitutes for one another (different qualities of paint) then the mix variance would show the effect of changes in demand and therefore might be useful.

Note: In the above example the standard proportions were based on the number of units. On occasions where there are substantial differences in the selling prices of the various products within a firm (eg bicycle tyres and tractor tyres) standardising on the number of units could produce distortions. In such cases the proportions for the standard mix would be based on sales turnover, not units. This procedure would only alter the balance between the mix and volume variances. The overall quantity variance would remain unchanged.

SALES VARIANCES c.f. SALES MARGIN VARIANCES

9.   Historically variance analysis in the sales are commenced with variances based on sales turnover, ie if actual sales were above budget there was a favourable sales variance even if profits fell, perhaps because the sales of low profit items had increased. Although information on variations in sales turnover is important, nowadays it is likely to be supplied by detailed sales analyses, not through variance analysis. Management need to have information about profit performance related to budget and for this reason sales margin variances are generally of much greater importance and so have been described in the preceding paragraphs.

STANDARD MARGINAL COSTING

10.   Most standard costing systems are based on total absorption cost principles and the standards and variances described in the last two chapters are typical of such systems. Standard costing can also incorporate marginal cost principles and is then termed standard marginal costing. It will be recalled that marginal costing involves the separation of costs, and those which remain unaffected by activity changes, known as fixed costs. Fixed costs are not absorbed into individual units of production and are deducted in total from the contribution (sales − marginal cost) earned from units sold. Standard marginal costing incorporates these principles and has the following characteristics.

(a)   Standards are developed in the normal manner and entered as usual on the standard cost card, except that fixed costs do not appear. The standard cost card includes

> Direct materials
> Direct labour
> Direct expenses
> Variable overheads
> ie no fixed costs

(b)   A standard contribution is set for each product and added to the standard margin cost. This sets the standard selling price. The standard contribution becomes the standard sales margin.

(c)   A budgeted profit statement is prepared for the next period with budgeted levels of sales and fixed overheads. Typically this would appear as follows:

Budgeted Profit Statement for Period

		£
	Budgeted sales	XXX
	(Budgeted no. of units x standard selling price)	
less	Budgeted cost of sales	XXX
	(Budgeted no. of units x standard marginal cost per unit)	—
=	Budgeted Contribution	XXX
less	Budgeted fixed costs	XXX
=	Budgeted profit	XXX

(d) Variance analysis is simplified because of the disappearance of the fixed overhead volume variance and its sub-variances, the capacity and efficiency variances. All other variances are identical or very similar. The different categories are listed below.

TYPES OF VARIANCE	CHARACTERISTICS OF STANDARD MARGINAL COST VARIANCES
DIRECT MATERIALS DIRECT LABOUR VARIABLE OVERHEADS	IDENTICAL TO ABSORPTION STANDARD COST VARIANCES " "
FIXED OVERHEADS	ONLY VARIANCE IS THE FIXED OVERHEAD EXPENDITURE VARIANCE ALL OTHER FIXED OVERHEAD VARIANCES DISAPPEAR

SALES VARIANCES	WITH THE EXCEPTION THAT THE STANDARD SALES MARGIN IS NOW THE STANDARD CONTRIBUTION. THE VARIANCES ARE CALCULATED IN AN IDENTICAL MANNER.
	THE NEW TITLES ARE:
	
	- Sales contribution variance
	   (was sales margin variance)
	- Sales contribution price variance
	   (was sales margin price variance)
	- Sales contribution quantity variance
	   (was sales margin quantity variance)
	- Sales contribution mixture variance
	   (was sales margin mixture variance)
	- Sales contribution volume variance
	   (was sales margin volume variance)

STANDARD MARGINAL COSTING EXAMPLE

11. Example 3

The following data relate to the budget and actual results of a firm which produces and sells a single product and which employs standard marginal costing.

Budget			Actual		
Production	12000 units		Production	11,200	
Sales	1200 units		Sales	11,200	
		£			£
Sales		192,000	Sales		190,400
less Standard Marginal Cost			less Actual Marginal Cost		
	£			£	
- materials	48,000		- materials	50,400	
- labour	60,000		- labour	50,400	
- variable overheads	36,000	144,000	- variable overheads	39,200	140,000
= Contribution		48,000	= Contribution		50,400
less Fixed Costs		25,000	less Fixed Costs		28,400
= Profit		23,000	= Profit		22,000

Extracts from the Standard Cost Card for the products are:

		£
	Material 4 Kgs @ £1 Kg	4
	Labour 2 hours @ £2.50	5
	Variable overheads 2 hours @ £1.50	_3_
=	Standard marginal cost	12
	Standard contribution	_4_
	Standard selling price	_16_

During the period 44,800 Kgs of material were used and 21,000 labour hours were worked.

Calculate all relevant variances and show a reconciliation between budgeted and actual profit.

Solution

The total variance is the Operating Profit variance which is the difference between budgeted and actual profit, ie £23,000 - 22,000 = £1000 ADV

The total of all other variances will equal this amount.

The cost variances are extracted first.

Materials Variances

	£		
Actual price Actual quantity	50,400	Price variance £5,600 ADV	
Actual quantity STANDARD PRICE (44800 @ £1)	44,800		Materials variance £5,600 ADV
STANDARD QUANTITY STANDARD PRICE (44800 @ £1)	44,800	Usage variance NIL	

Labour Variances

	£		
Actual hours Actual rate	50400	Rate variance 2100 FAV	
Actual hours STANDARD RATE (21000 @ £2.50)	52500		Labour variance £5600 FAV
STANDARD HOURS STANDARD RATE (22400 @ £2.5)	56000	Efficiency variance £3500 FAV	

Variable Overhead Variance

	£		
Actual variable overheads	39200	Expenditure variance £7700 ADV	
Actual hours x VOAR (21000 x £1.50)	31500		Variable Overhead variance £5600 ADV
SHP x VOAR (22400 x £1.5)	33600	Efficiency variance £2100 FAV	

Fixed overhead expenditure variance
= £28,400 - 25000 = £3400 ADV

Summary of Cost Variances

	£
Materials	5600 ADV
Labour	5600 FAV
Variable overheads	5600 ADV
Fixed overheads	3400 ADV
Total	£9000 ADV

Sales variances (when standard contribution is £4 per unit and standard selling price is £16).

	£			
Actual contribution when Sales valued at std. cost (£190,400 - (11200 x 12)	56000	} Price variance £11200 FAV		} Total Contribution variance £8000 FAV
Actual units @ STANDARD CONTRIBUTION	44800	} Quantity variance £32000 ADV		
BUDGETED UNITS STANDARD CONTRIBUTION (12000 x £4)	48000			

Variance Summary

	£
Total cost variance	9000 ADV
Total sales variance	8000 FAV
= Operating Profit variance	£1000 ADV

PLANNING AND OPERATIONAL VARIANCES

12. The approach to variance analysis so far explained is the traditional one whereby actual performance is compared with a predetermined standard and a variance calculated. If the standard, which will have been prepared some time previously, is still a realistic attainable target in current conditions then the calculated variances will be of some value. However, if there have been uncontrollable changes in internal or external operating conditions then the standard may not now be a realistic one and the calculated variances will be of little or no value and may even be misleading.

This is a real problem particularly in volatile conditions and an attempt to overcome this is to separate out the total variances into **planning variances** and **operating variances**.

Planning variances seek to explain the extent to which the original standard needs to be adjusted in order to reflect changes in operating conditions between the current situation and that envisaged when the standard was originally calculated, in effect it means that the original standard is brought up to date so that it is a realistic attainable target in **current conditions**.

Operating variances indicate the extent to which attainable targets (ie the adjusted standards) have been achieved. Operating variances would be calculated after the planning variances have been established and are thus a realistic way of assessing performance.

The separation of that part of the total variation which is due to planning deficiencies makes possible a clearer definition of what is an attainable, current target. In traditional variance analysis there is the implicit assumption that the **whole** of the variance is due to operating deficiencies and that the planning associated with setting the original standard was perfectly accurate, which is hardly realistic.

One of the leading exponents of the theory of planning variances, Professor Demski, has argued that because of the traditional emphasis on the comparison between actual and planned results, without regard to changes in planned results, the traditional accounting method does not act as an opportunity cost system. He argues that variances ought to be calculated by taking as the comparison level, not the original budget or standard, but a budget or standard which can be seen with hindsight, to be the optimum that should have been achievable. The original budget and standards are known as *ex-ante* standards, the ones that are set which are deemed to be currently attainable are known as *ex-post* standards.

OPPORTUNITY COST APPROACH USING EX-ANTE AND EX-POST STANDARDS

13. The opportunity cost approach seeks to calculate variances that provide a realistic measurement of the gains or losses arising from *controllable* operating results, ie the operating variances. The *ex-post* standards, ie the planning variances, are largely uncontrollable by operating management so are best separated in order to show more clearly the efficiency or inefficiency of operations.

The relationships are shown in Figure 1.

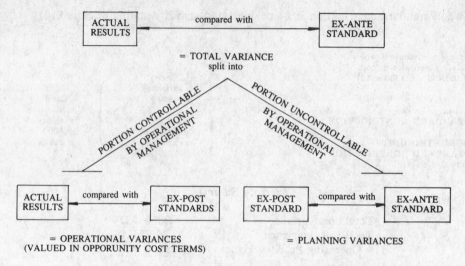

Figure 1   Planning and Operational Variances

The following examples illustrates the calculation of planning and operational variances.

EXAMPLES OF PLANNING AND OPERATING VARIANCES

14. Example 2

A raw material, Zeta, is used in the production of Alpha and an extract from the standard cost card for Alpha showing the rates of usage and expected price is as follows:

> **Alpha Standard Cost Card** (extract)
> material per unit.
> 10 Kgs of Zeta @ £6 Kg = £60 = standard material cost.

During the current period 270 units of Alpha were produced and the usage was 2850 Kgs with an actual material cost of £16,530. Due to world wide price movements Zeta was freely available at £5.5 Kg during the period.

Calculate

(i)   the traditional variances

(ii) the planning and operating variances.

Solution

(i)   **Traditional variances**

		£
Material Price Variance		
£16530 – (2850 x £6)	=	570 FAV
Material Usage Variance		
(2850 – 2700) x £6 =		900 ADV
∴ Total Material Cost Variance	=	£330 ADV

(ii) **Planning Variance (uncontrollable)**

		£
(£2700 x £6) – (£2700 x £5.5)	=	1350 FAV

Operating Variances (controllable)

Operating Price variance
£16530 − (2850 x £5.5)   =   855 ADV

Operating Usage variance
(2850 − 2700) x £5.5   =   825 ADV
Total Operating Material Variance   =   £1680 ADV

Planning variance + Operating variances = Traditional variance = £1350 FAV + 1680 ADV = £330 ADV.

Notes:

(a) The planning variance shows the total difference due to uncontrollable factors, ie the world wide price change, and is the difference between the old standard price and the new standard price for the standard quantity of material that should be used. If the planning variance is correct all that is left are controllable factors which are analysed by the operating variances.

(b) The operating variances follow the normal procedures for material variances except that the new standard price of £5.5 is used. It will be noted that the operating price variance shows that there **have** been purchasing inefficiencies which contrasts with the traditional price variance which showed apparent purchasing efficiency.

Example 3

In a four week period Acme Ltd budgeted to make and sell 800 units of its single product with a budget as follows:

BUDGET FOR 4 WEEK PERIOD

	£
Production and Sales (8000 units at £15 each)	120,000
less Variable costs (8000 at £5 each)	40,000
= Contribution	80,000
less Fixed Costs	45,000
= Profit	35,000

Due to storm damage there was an external power line failure and 3 days production out of the possible 20 days were lost. The actual results were:

	£
Production and Sales (7150 units at £15 each)	107,250
less Variable costs (7150 at £5 each)	35,750
	71,500
less Fixed costs	45,000
= Profit	26,500

Calculate

(i)   the traditional variances
(ii) the planning and operational variances

Solution

(i)   Traditional Variances

Inspection shows that there has been no change in selling prices, variable costs and margin so the only variance is the sales volume variance, ie

(Original Budget − Actual Sales) x Standard Margin = (8000 − 7150) x £10 = £8500 ADV

(ii) Planning and Operational Variances

With hindsight a more realistic ex-post budget for the period would have been 8000 units less 3 days standard production, ie 8000 − 1200 = 6800 units.

Thus the planning variance would be the ex-ante budget less the ex-post budget at the standard margin, ie
(8000 − 6800) x £10 = £12,000 ADV

The operational variance, which is deemed to be the controllable portion, is the difference between the more realistic ex-post budget and actual output at the standard margin thus:

$$(6800 - 7150) \times £10 = \underline{£3500 \text{ FAV}}$$

Planning Variance + Operational Variance = Total Variance
£12,000 ADV + £3,500 FAV = £8,500 ADV

It will be seen that the above variances have used the contribution foregone as a reasonable equivalent to opportunity cost. Also it can be claimed that they show a more realistic picture of the effects of planning errors and of operating efficiency or inefficiency than traditional variances which assume that *all* differences arise from operational factors.

BENEFITS AND PROBLEMS OF PLANNING AND OPERATING VARIANCES

15.   The segregation of traditional variances into those which are due to planning deficiencies and those which are due to controllable factors is probably not widely used in the U.K. but it does have certain benefits.

(a)   It makes standard costing and variance analysis more realistic and meaningful in volatile and changing conditions.

(b)   Operational variances provide an up to date guide to current levels of operating efficiency as the standards have been recalculated using up to date information.

(c)   Having up to date standards and therefore more meaningful variances is likely to make the standard costing system more acceptable and to have a positive effect on motivation.

(d)   It emphasises the importance of the planning function in the preparation of standards and helps to identify planning deficiencies.

(e)   The calculation of such variances provides a systematic method of reviewing standards and the assumptions contained within them.

As is to be expected there are problems in using such variances.

(a)   There is an element of subjectivity in determining after the event (ie ex-post) what is a realistic price. This makes the allocation between planning and operational causes a subjective matter susceptible to political pressures.

(b)   There is undeniably more clerical and managerial time involved in continually establishing up to date standards and calculating additional variances.

(c)   Where the planning and operating functions are carried out in the same responsibility centre there is likely to be pressure to put as much as possible of the total variance down to outside, uncontrollable factors rather than internal, controllable actions. However, these pressures exist in the interpretation of any type of variance.

ADVANTAGES OF STANDARD COSTING

16.   (a)   Standard costing is an example of 'management by exception'. By studying the variances, management's attention is directed towards those items which are not proceeding according to plan. Management are able to delegate cost control through the standard costing system knowing that variances will be reported.

(b)   The process of setting, revising and monitoring standards encourages reappraisal of methods, materials and techniques so leading to cost reductions.

(c)   Standard costs represent what the parts and products should cost. They are not merely averages of past performances and consequently they are a better guide to pricing than historical costs. In addition, they provide a simpler basis of inventory valuation.

(d)   A properly developed standard costing system with full participation and involvement creates a positive, cost effective attitude through all levels of management right down to the shop floor and thereby increases motivation and goal congruence.

DISADVANTAGES OF STANDARD COSTING

17. (a) It may be expensive and time consuming to install and to keep up to date.

(b) In volatile conditions with rapidly changing methods, rates and prices, standards quickly become out of date and thus lose their control and motivational effects. This can cause resentment and loss of goodwill. A possible method of overcoming this problem is by the use of planning and operational variances but this involves more subjectivity and more work.

(c) There is research evidence to show that overly elaborate variances are imperfectly understood by line managers and thus they are likely to be ineffective for control purposes.

(d) Virtually all aspects of setting standards involves forecasting and subjective judgements with inherent possibilities of error and argument.

(e) The usefulness of a number of variances relating to overheads, sales margins, mix and yield is questionable.

(f) All forms of variance analysis are post mortems on past events. Obviously the past cannot be altered so that the only value variances can have is to guide management if identical or similar circumstances occur in the future. This implies stable, repeating situations which is not always a reflection of reality. Indeed if the conditions were as stable as postulated then simpler 'point of action' controls and checks are likely to have more effect than variance reporting. For example, if a purchase order was being contemplated at above standard price then it could be arranged that the order would need to be countersigned (and investigated) by the Purchasing Director. This type of control is likely to be more effective than reporting an adverse price variance weeks or months after the event.

COST REDUCTION

18. Budgetary Control and Standard Costing are examples of **cost control** techniques which have the broad objective of containing costs within a pre-determined target. On the other hand **cost reduction** is a concept which has the aim of reducing costs from some previously accepted norm or standard whilst at the same time maintaining the effectiveness or performance of the product or service. Cost reduction is an active, dynamic concept which attempts to extract more from the factors of production without loss of effectiveness.

The most effective cost reduction programmes are those which embrace all aspects of the firm's operations, systems and products and are those which have full top management support and co-operation. Significant cost reductions can often be made simply by the application of common sense but there are several formal techniques which have been found to be of value in improving products, reducing waste, streamlining systems and thereby reducing costs. Some of the more important ones are explained briefly below - variety reduction, value analysis, work study and organisation and methods.

VARIETY REDUCTION

19. Examination of the product range may show that it is too extensive and that some of the products are uneconomic because they are produced in small quantities. Variety reduction when applied to components is often called **standardisation** and is widely used because it is often cost effective to be able to produce a range of finished products from a common, relatively small, pool of components. In general fewer varieties makes for longer production runs, increases the scope for automation, and is likely to reduce costs. It goes without saying that the sales and marketing aspects of variety reduction must be closely considered otherwise any production gains may be nullified.

VALUE ANALYSIS

20. Value analysis or value engineering is an assessment process carried out by a team during the design stages of a product. The team would consist of engineering, technical and production personnel together with an accountant and has as its objective the task of designing a product which meets the essential design objectives at minimum cost. Value analysis is a systematic, conscious attempt to eliminate inessentials and unnecessary costs and is carried out by detailed questioning of every aspect of the products functions, materials, methods of manufacture, components, finish etc.

Typical of the questions to be asked are the following:
-   Can the function of the product be achieved in some other way?
-   Are all of the functions of the product essential?
-   Can the product be made lighter, smaller or from cheaper material?
-   What standardisation of components, materials, methods of manufacture etc. can be made?
-   Can the design be modified so that the product can be made more easily and cheaply?
-   and so on.

The full application of value analysis would mean that periodically each product in the firm would come under searching scrutiny and thereby there would be a continual, planned search for cost reduction.

WORK STUDY

21.   This is a technique used in factories to determine the most efficient methods of using labour, materials and machinery. The main subdivisions of work study are **method study** and **work measurement**. Method study is the recording and analysis of existing methods of doing work and comparing these with proposed methods in order to implement new and more effective procedures. Work measurement is the process of establishing times for a qualified worker to carry out a task at a defined level of performance. It will be apparent from this that Work Study is the basis of much of standard costing.

Work Study is a valuable technique for improving efficiency and reducing waste in factories and can be applied in many areas including: Factory layouts and work flow, materials handling, tool design, scheduling, line balancing, workplace methods and layout.

ORGANISATION AND METHODS (O & M)

22.   O & M has been described as 'work study in the office' and the broad objectives of the two techniques are similar. Administrative and overhead costs are a significant proportion of the costs of an organisation and are a fruitful area for cost reduction programmes. O & M is the systematic analysis of administrative and office procedures in order to produce more efficient methods. O & M is carried out by a process of investigation, analysis, design and implementation of improved methods, equipment and procedures and there are many areas where it can be applied in the office. These include: form design, office layout, departmental procedures, office mechanisation, work flows, paperwork elimination, telephone and communication services and many other examples.

A development of O & M called **systems analysis** has evolved to deal with those procedures which require the use of computers. Whilst having the same broad objectives as O & M and using the same questioning approach, naturally there are many differences in the technical expertise required.

COST REDUCTION – CONCLUSION

23.   Any or all of the above techniques may be used in cost reduction programmes often with great success. However, of probably greater importance is the motivation of all levels of staff to achieve more effective results from every facet of their work. This is an aspect of goal congruence and it is essential that the accounting system supports, not hinders, this process.

It is important that long term as well as short term factors are kept in mind when seeking cost reductions as some cost reduction activities may be counter-productive in the long term. There are numerous examples where short term savings are easily made but which are likely to produce significant adverse results in the longer term. Examples include maintenance, advertising, staff development, research and development.

SUMMARY

24.   (a)   Where it can provide useful information the material usage variance can be subdivided into a mix variance and a yield variance.

(b)   These are variances which arise due to the actual mixture/yield varying from the standard mixture/yield where mixture means proportions.

(c)   Sales margin variances have the objective of helping to control the profit, ie margin, on sales.

(d)   The standard sales margin is the difference between the standard selling price and the standard cost of an item.

(e)   The total sales margin variance can be subdivided into Price and Quantity variances. Where more than one product is sold, the Quantity variance can be subdivided into mixture and volume variances.

(f)   The method of calculating the sales margin variances is very similar to the methods used for calculating materials variances.

(g)   Standard costing can employ marginal costing principles and becomes known as Standard Marginal Costing. Fixed costs are not absorbed into individual units of production.

(h)   A standard marginal cost is the total of all standard variable costs. A standard contribution is added to give a standard selling price.

(i)   Using standard marginal costing, variance analysis is simplified because all fixed overhead variances disappear, except for the fixed overhead expenditure variance.

(j)   Material, labour and variable overhead variances are identical and, with the exception that the standard contribution becomes the sales margin, so are the sales variances.

(k)   Traditional variances can be separated into planning variances and operational variances.

(l)   Planning variances seek to measure that part of the total variance which is due to planning deficiencies whilst the operating variances seek to measure operating results as compared to a realistic, current standard.

(m) Cost reduction seeks to extract more from the factors of production without loss of effectiveness.

(n)   Techniques of cost reduction include: variety reduction, value analysis, work study, organisation and methods, systems analysis.

POINTS TO NOTE

25   (a)   The decision to make a detailed investigation into a particular variance is a cost/benefit appraisal depending on the cost of investigation compared with a subjective assessment of the benefits expected to result, having due regard to the probabilities involved.

(b)   It is important that higher management help to generate a positive attitude towards variances rather than the adverse reaction from operating management which will inevitably occur if variances are always associated with apportioning blame and criticism. The approach to be fostered is that variances and variance analysis are a way of learning how to do better in the future.

(c)   There is evidence that there is a tendency in practice to adopt an asymmetric approach to variances giving unfavourable variances more attention than favourable ones of similar magnitude. This may mean that opportunities are lost to improve operations by investigating the reasons for favourable variances.

(d)   A positive cost reduction programme having due regard to the long term effects, is essential for every organisation. It is not sufficient merely to have cost control procedures.

(e)   The greatest possible care is necessary when interpreting variances even ones that are apparently straightforward. For example, an adverse price variance may be due to the Purchasing Department buying in advance of a much larger price increase which is astute purchasing rather than the below par performance conventionally associated with an adverse variance.

(f)   Conventional variance analysis does not illustrate the interdependencies which abound in every organisation. These interdependencies makes interpretation of **ANY** variance a difficult task.

ADDITIONAL READING

Topics in Management Accounting	Arnold, Carsberg and Scapens, PHILIP ALLAN
Contemporary Cost Accounting and Control	Benston, DICKENSON PUBLISHING COMPANY
Accounting and its Behavioural Implications	Bruns and DeCoster, MCGRAW HILL
Variance Accounting	Laidler, MACMILLAN/CIMA
Cost Accounting: A managerial Emphasis	Horngren, PRENTICE HALL
Accountants' Digest No. 18, Clerical Work Measurement	ICA
Studies in Cost Analysis	Solomons, SWEET AND MAXWELL
Budget Control and Cost Behaviour	Stedry, MARKHAM

SELF REVIEW QUESTIONS

1.   When would mix and yield variances be calculated? What are their formulae? (2 & 4)

2.   Why do mix and yield variances occur? (2 – 4)

3.   What are the deficiencies of conventional mix and yield variances? (5)

4.   What product cost is used in sales margin variance analysis? (5)

5.   What is the standard sales margin? (6)

6.   What is the standard sales contribution? (6)

7.   What are the sub divisions of the total sales margin variance? (7)

8.   What drawbacks are there in sales margin variance analysis? (8)

9.   Distinguish between sales variances and sales margin variances. (9)

10. What are the major differences between standard marginal costing and standard costing based on total absorption costing principles? (10)

11. What is the purpose of planning and operating variance analysis? (12)

12. How is the planning variance calculated?, the operating variances? (13 – 14)

13. What are the benefits of planning variances? What are their limitations? (15)

14. What is cost reduction? (18)

15. What is the objective of variety reduction and standardisation? (19)

16. What is value analysis? (20)

17. Distinguish between work study and O & M. (21 & 22)

EXAMINATION QUESTIONS WITH ANSWERS COMMENCING PAGE 349

A1. *A year ago Kenp Ltd entered the market for the manufacture and sale of a revolutionary insulating material. The budgeted production and sales volumes were 1,000 units. The originally estimated sales price and standard costs for this new product were:*

	£	£
Standard sales price – per unit		100
Standard costs – per unit		
Raw materials – Aye 10 lbs at £5	50	
Labour – 6 hours at £4	24	74
Standard contribution – per unit		£26

Actual results were:

First Year's Results

	£(000's)	(£000's)
Sales – 1,000 units		158
Production costs – 1,000 units		
Raw materials – Aye 10,800 lbs	97.2	
Labour – 5,800 hours	34.8	132
Actual contribution		26

'Throughout the year we attempted to operate as efficiently as possible, given the prevailing conditions' stated the Managing Director. 'Although in total the performance agreed with budget, in every detailed respect, except volume, there were large differences. These were due, mainly, to the tremendous success of the new insulating material which created increased demand both for the product itself and all the manufacturing resources used in its production. This then resulted in price rises all round.'

'Sales were made at what was felt to be the highest feasible price but, it was later discovered, our competitors sold for £165 per unit and we could have equalled this price. Labour costs rose dramatically with increased demand for the specialist skills required to produce the product and the general market rate was £6.25 per hour – although Kenp always paid below the general market rate whenever possible.'

'Raw material Aye was chosen as it appeared cheaper than the alternative material Bee which could have been used. The costs which were expected at the time the budget was prepared were, per lb, Aye, £5 and Bee, £6. However the market prices relating to efficient purchases of the material during the year were:

> Aye £8.50 per lb, and
> Bee £7.00 per lb.

Therefore it would have been more appropriate to use Bee, but as production plans were based on Aye it was Aye that was used'.

It is not proposed to request a variance analysis for the first year's results as most of the deviations from budget were caused by the new product's great success and this could not have been fully anticipated and planned for. In any event the final contribution was equal to that originally budgeted so operations must have been fully efficient.'

Required:

(a) Compute the traditional variances for the first year's operations.

(b) Prepare an analysis of variances for the first year's operations which will be useful in the circumstances of Kenp Ltd. The analysis should indicate the extent to which the variances were due to operational efficiency or planning causes.

(c) Using, for illustration, a comparison of the raw material variances computed in *(a)* and *(b)* above, briefly outline two major disadvantages of the approach applied in part *(b)* over the traditional approach.

ACCA, Management Accounting.

A2. *Explain, and clearly distinguish between, the meaning of the terms*

(a) 'cost reduction programme', and
(b) 'zero based budgeting'

Describe two applications within any of the functions of management accounting which could be assisted by the utilisation of either of these two techniques. Outline a major difficulty in their application.

ACCA, Management Accounting.

Decision Making

The next six chapters cover various facets of the all important activity of decision making. A significant part of the task of the management accountant is to supply information for decision making purposes and it is essential that there is full awareness of the decision process and of the techniques that may be of help in choosing between alternatives.

Throughout this section the importance of **relevancy** is stressed again and again. The characteristics of relevant information are described and the stages in the decision process are explained.

Formal decision rules such as expected value are described and short run decision criteria based on marginal costing and cost-volume-profit analysis are analysed in typical decision making situations. The particular requirements of pricing decisions are dealt with in detail including the theoretical economic background and the important resource allocation technique of Linear Programming and the way it can provide assistance to the management accountant, is described and exemplified.

Long run decision making or investment appraisal is covered in some depth including the use of discounted cash flow and methods for dealing with risk, inflation, and capital rationing.

12. Decision Making — An Introduction

INTRODUCTION

1.   This chapter discussed the overall decision process and analyses the stages in the process ranging from the definition of objectives through to the final selection of the correct course of action. The importance of information being specified in economically relevant terms is emphasised and avoidable, differential and opportunity costs are described and exemplified. The use of formal decision rules such as expected value, maximin, maximax and minimax regret is discussed and the use of probabilities and probability trees in analysing complex decision sequences is described and exemplified.

BACKGROUND TO DECISION MAKING

2.   Decision making is an all pervasive activity taking place at every level in the organisation covering both the short and long term. Plans are activated by decisions and a significant number of decisions require some form of financial or quantitative analysis in order that a rational choice can be made. It is because of this that the practising management accountant is heavily engaged in producing relevant information for decision making purposes. A knowledge of the decision process, the importance and meaning of relevancy and of the techniques which can provide assistance with the analysis of information for decision making are vital knowledge for the student of management accounting and are the subject of the next six chapters.

The emphasis in this manual is on decisions which have a quantitative basis. However, it must be realised that regardless of the amount of quantitative information available, the actual decision process invariably includes consideration of qualitative, psychological, behavioural and social factors as well as the quantitative ones. Some decisions, often of great importance, are based entirely on qualitative factors, for example, staff appointments, new designs for a fashion house and other of a similar nature. In spite of this there is a vast range of business situations for which quantitative and financial analysis plays a crucial part in making rational decisions. These range from long term strategic decisions such as acquisitions, launching new products or buying capital equipment to shorter term tactical problems such as product planning, make or buy, product pricing and so on. A common element of all these problems is that they rely on information on costs and revenues which is correctly specified in **economically relevant** terms for the particular decision being considered. This is the overriding requirement of the information that should be supplied. Consistency of treatment in the traditional accounting sense is not possible in these circumstances, **relevancy** is all important. What are relevant costs and how they can be identified are dealt with in detail later in this chapter.

Decision making can be defined as making choices between future, uncertain alternatives. It must be emphasises that **all decision making** relates to the **future** and that a decision is a **choice** between **alternatives** in pursuit of an objective(s). Where no alternatives exist no decision can be made and nothing can be done now that will alter the past. These fundamentals of decision making are of critical importance in determining what information the management accountant should supply to the decision maker.

THE DECISION PROCESS

3.   The overall decision process can be subdivided into stages although in practice the divisions between the stages may be blurred. The stages are:

(a)   definition of objective(s)
(b)   consideration of alternatives
(c)   evaluation of alternatives in the light of the objective(s)
(d)   selection of the course of action.

The whole process may extend over a long period - for example, there were several years of analysis and exploration before the final decision to drill for oil in the North Sea - or it may take place within seconds for some routine, operational decision.

The stages in the decision process are expanded below.

DEFINITION OF OBJECTIVES

4.   The decision maker must be aware of the objective(s) of the organisation which should be stated in explicit terms. An organisation may have multiple objectives and where this situation exists it is essential that they are consistent with one another. For example, it may be inconsistent to pursue the objective of maximising profits whilst at the same time attempting to maximise market share.

Although the single objective of profit maximisation appears to be the norm, particularly for examination purposes, students should be aware that research by H.A. Simon and others indicates that satisficing behaviour (ie acceptance of a satisfactory level of achievement) appears to be more usually encountered in practice than the 'optimising' behaviour implied by profit maximisation. This is probably a realistic acceptance of the practical difficulties of information feedback, computation, and forecasting in a typical organisation.

The link between plans, objectives and decisions is that plans are the embodiment of the organisation's objectives and decisions are the implementation of plans. Wherever possible the objectives should be quantified and indeed this is essential if one or other of the powerful mathematical decision models is to be used as a basis for choosing the best alternative. Where the objective can be quantified it is known as an **objective function**. As previously stated, this manual concentrates on those decision problems which lend themselves to quantitative analysis so it follows that we are only concerned with problems where the objective(s) can be quantified and an objective function established.

The definition of objectives will inevitably cause initial consideration to be given to the constraints or limitations of the problem. Constraints may be shortages of labour, materials, space, machine capacity, finance or they may be requirements on sales or stock levels or they may be the need to achieve particular results. For example, the organisation's objective may be to maximise sales turnover subject to the constraint that the return on capital employed is 15% or more. If a given constraint limits the values of the objective function it is called a **binding constraint** or a **limiting factor**. Constraints are dealt with further when the ways that alternatives can be evaluated are discussed.

CONSIDERATION OF ALTERNATIVES

5.   Decision making always involves predictions and this is also true when selecting the set of alternatives from which the final decision will be made. There is the possibility that, although the best choice will hopefully be made from the selected set of alternatives, there exists some other alternative which would better fulfil the organisation's objectives. Attractive alternatives do not automatically submit themselves to the decision process, they have to be continuously and actively sought out. An aid to this process is the development of effective information systems which gather information from external internal sources in order to ensure that opportunities are not overlooked.

On occasions there may appear to be only one action open to the organisation and it might thus appear that the necessary conditions for decision making (ie choice between alternatives) do not exist. This is not true because one of the alternatives should be to take no action now in order to be in a position to undertake a more attractive alternative in the future which uses the same resources.

Ideally, the set of alternatives to be considered should be an exhaustive list but because of information deficiencies and uncertainty this is rarely, if ever, possible. The effect of this is that so called 'optimal' solutions produced by various techniques are only optimal in a restricted sense.

EVALUATION OF ALTERNATIVES

6.   Although the management accountant must be familiar with the whole of the decision process, undoubtedly his major contribution is in that part of the process concerned with making quantitative comparisons between the alternatives so that the decision maker is provided with a relevant and correctly specified financial basis for the ultimate decision.

To carry out this task effectively the management accountant must be totally familiar with a range of concepts and techniques including: the determination of economically relevant costs and revenues, the use of various formal decision rules or models, the use of probabilities in decision analysis, the construction of decision trees, the use of Cost-Volume-Profit analysis, resource allocation using linear programming, and the use of investment appraisal techniques such as Discounted Cash Flow (DCF). DCF, linear programming and Cost-Volume-Profit analysis are dealt with in subsequent chapters whilst the other material is dealt with later in this chapter.

An important part of the evaluation of alternatives is concerned with the assessment of risk and uncertainty. Because all decision making is concerned with the future, uncertainty is ever present and in general it would be misleading to present information for decision making purposes which ignored the possible consequences of such matters as: competitor's actions, inflation, imperfect forecasting, interest and finance changes, new government legislation, possible material/labour shortages, possible industrial disputes and all the factors which contribute to uncertainty. This chapter and subsequent ones cover a range of methods of incorporating uncertainty into the appraisal process.

SELECTION OF THE COURSE OF ACTION

7.   This is the stage where the actual choice between the alternatives is made. Decisions have been classified by Simon into **programmed** and **non-programmed** categories.

Programmed. These are relatively structured decisions within a clearly defined operational area. The decision rules are known and generally there is a clear cut, single objective. Because of the nature of these decisions they are the first to be incorporated into computer based information systems because they can be made automatically, given normal circumstances.

A typical example of a programmed decision is a replenishment decision based on usage and re-order levels in an inventory control system.

Non-programmed. These are decisions for which decision rules and procedures cannot or have not yet been devised. Generally they involve non-repetitive circumstances and may include a number of external and internal factors many of which have a substantial degree of uncertainty. As a consequence there is the necessity to supply a variety of information tailored to the particular situation rather than the narrower, restricted range of information suitable for programmed decisions.

Ad-hoc decision problems are severe tests for information systems and as a consequence there is the tendency to try to make the decision problem under consideration fit existing decision rules or models so that a decision can be made more easily. This approach is only correct when the current problem is **truly suitable** for the decision model envisaged. An example of this is the assumption, frequently made, that all the costs and factors in a problem behave in a linear fashion. If this assumption is made then various solution techniques exist, ranging from simple contribution and cost-volume-profit analysis to linear programming models. If the linearity assumption is valid then the techniques will be of value but if the assumption is invalid then an incorrect decision could easily be made.

The **real** situation must be studied and only information and techniques **relevant** to the **actual problem** should be used.

An important factor in decision making is the individual's attitude to risk. Individual attitudes range from **risk seeking** to **risk aversion** so in consequence, given the same information, different individuals are quite likely to make different decisions. Research has shown that people making business decisions tend towards risk aversion and as a result do not necessarily choose alternatives which have the highest calculated returns if those returns are associated with significant chances of failure. The importance of this for the management accountant is that it is essential to provide information for decision making which shows the effects of risk and uncertainty and the range of likely outcomes. In this way the decision maker is better able to appreciate the background to the alternatives and hopefully will be able to make more informed decisions.

RELEVANT COSTS AND REVENUES

8. The importance of relevancy for decision making has already been stressed and it is now time to consider in detail what are relevant costs and revenues for decision making purposes. In summary, relevant information concerns:

(a) Future costs and revenues.
Decision making is concerned with the future so that it is **expected future costs and revenues** which are of importance to the decision maker. This means that past costs and revenues are only useful insofar as they provide a guide to future values. Sunk costs are irrelevant.

(b) Differential costs and revenues.
Only those costs and revenues which alter as a result of a decision are relevant. Where factors are common to all of the alternatives they can be ignored; only the differences are relevant. In many short run situations the fixed costs remain constant for each of the alternatives being considered so that the marginal costing approach showing sales, marginal cost and contribution is useful. However great care is necessary when dealing with traditional accounting classifications of cost in order not to mislead or be misled. So called 'fixed' costs can and do change and thus become relevant factors for the decision being considered. This is the key factor and not the recorded cost classification - with its implied behaviour patterns - contained within the cost accounting system.

Differential costs and revenues are costs that can be **avoided** or **revenues foregone** if the particular alternative is not adopted. The differential approach is an essential one for decision making and can be used for both short and long run decision making. The major operational difference between the two is that for long run decisions, usually called investment decisions, the time value of money has to be considered and discounting techniques need to be used. Investment decisions are dealt with later in the manual.

OPPORTUNITY COST

9.   So far the economically relevant costs for decision making have been defined as future, avoidable costs but in economic theory the correct cost for evaluating a decision is termed the **opportunity cost**. Opportunity cost can be defined as the value of the next best alternative, ie it is the net receipts foregone by not accepting the best available alternative. It will be noted that the definition of opportunity cost emphasises **alternatives** which, of course, are the basis of decision making.

Thus there would seem to be two types of relevant costs for decision making – opportunity costs and avoidable costs. However, this is not so as the two are identical and are merely different ways of looking at the same thing.

Economically relevant cost ≡ opportunity cost ≡ avoidable cost.

In a given problem where there are exchange transactions (buying or selling) then opportunity costs are measured by the money outlays. In other circumstances where the resources used are not represented by outlay costs it may be necessary to impute a value for opportunity cost.

Whether it is best to use solely avoidable (differential) costs or avoidable costs plus imputed opportunity costs depends entirely on what is more convenient in a given problem. Properly used, either method will give the correct decision.

A number of examples follow which illustrate typical problems encountered in determining relevant costs.

RELEVANT COST EXAMPLES

10. Example 1

A 1 year contract has been offered which will utilise an existing machine that is only suitable for such contract work. The machine cost £25,000 five years ago and has been depreciated £4,000 per year on a straight line basis and thus has a book value of £5000. The machine could be sold now for £8000 or in 1 year's time for £1000. Four types of material would be needed for the contract as follows:

| | Units | | Price per Unit | | |
Material	In Stock	Required for Contract	Purchase Price of Stock	Current Buying-in Price	Current Resale Price
			£	£	£
W	1200	300	1.80	1.50	1.20
X	200	1100	0.75	2.80	2.10
Y	3000	600	0.50	0.80	0.60
Z	1800	1200	1.80	2.00	1.90

W and Z are in regular use within the firm. X could be sold if not used for the contract and there are no other uses for Y, which has been deemed to be obsolete.

What are the relevant costs in connection with the contract (ignoring the time value of money)?

Solution

Machine costs. The historic cost is a sunk cost and is not relevant. The depreciation details given relate to accounting conventions and are not relevant.

The relevant cost is the opportunity cost caused by the reduction in resale value over the one year duration of the contract, ie £8000 - 1000 = **£7000.**

Material costs
W
Although there is sufficient in stock the use of 300 units for the contract would necessitate the need for replenishment at the current market price.

∴ Relevant cost   =   300 x £1.50   =   **£450**

X
If the contract were not accepted 200 units of X could be sold at £2.10 per unit. The balance of 900 units required would be bought at the current buying-in price of £2.80.

$$
\begin{array}{lll}
 & & \pounds \\
\therefore \text{ Relevant cost} = & 200 \times \pounds2.10 = & 420 \\
 & 900 \times \pounds2.80 = & \underline{2520} \\
 & & \underline{\underline{\pounds2940}}
\end{array}
$$

Y
If the 600 units were used on the contract they could not be sold so the opportunity cost is the current resale price of £0.60 per unit.

$$\therefore \text{ Relevant cost} = 600 \times \pounds0.60 = \underline{\underline{\pounds360}}$$

Z
Similar reasoning to W, ie replenishment at current buying-in price

$$\therefore \text{ Relevant cost} = 1200 \times \pounds2 = \underline{\underline{\pounds2400}}$$

Note: It will be seen from the above examples that the recorded historical cost, which is the 'cost' using normal accounting conventions, is not the relevant value in any of the circumstances considered.

Example 2

A decision has to be taken by a firm whether or not to initiate manufacture of a new product called Wizzo. The following data have been established.

(a) A market research study carried out three months ago into the sales potential of Wizzo cost £25,000.

(b) A new machine would require to be purchased at a cost of £100,000 solely to make Wizzo. A nil scrap value is anticipated and it is the firm's policy to write of depreciation on a straight line basis over 5 years.

(c) Wizzo would be manufactured in a factory owned by the firm, the annual depreciation charge of which is £8,000. At present the factory is sub-let at £17,500 p.a.

(d) The labour requirements for Wizzo are

	Hours/Unit of Wizzo	Normal Wage Rates/Hour	
		First Year	Subsequent Years
		£	£
Skilled	4	3.00	3.50
Semi-Skilled	3	2.20	2.60
Unskilled	2	1.80	1.85

It is expected that there will be shortage of skilled labour in the first year only so the manufacture of Wizzo will make it necessary for the skilled labour to be diverted from other work on which a contribution of £4.50 per hour is earned, net of wage costs. The firm currently has a surplus of semi-skilled labour paid at full rate but doing unskilled work. The labour concerned could be transferred to provide sufficient labour for the manufacture of Wizzo and would be replaced by unskilled labour.

(e) Overhead costs are allocated to manufacture at the rate of £18 per skilled labour hour as follows:

$$
\begin{array}{lr}
 & \pounds \\
\text{Fixed overheads} & 13.00 \\
\text{Variable overheads} & \underline{5.00} \\
 & \underline{\underline{18.00}}
\end{array}
$$

(f) The manufacture and sale of Wizzo is expected to cause sales of an existing product, Bango, to fall by 3000 units per annum. The contribution on Bango is £9 per unit.

(g) The manufacture of Wizzo would require the services of an existing manager who would be paid £12,000 p.a. If not required for Wizzo the manager would be made redundant and would receive £3,000 p.a. under a service agreement.

What are the relevant costs from the above data in deciding whether or not to manufacture Wizzo (ignoring the time value of money).?

Solution

(a) The market research cost of £25,000 is a sunk cost and is irrelevant to the current decision.

(b) The purchase of the machine is a relevant cash flow. The depreciation charges are non-cash flows and are irrelevant to the current decision.

Machinery:- Relevant Cost **£100,000**

(c) Manufacture of Wizzo would mean that the present rental received would be foregone so it is a relevant cost. The depreciation charge is not relevant.

Factory:- Relevant Cost **£17,500 p.a.**

(d) The out of pocket wages costs per unit of Wizzo are as follows:

		£	1st Year £	Subsequent Years £
Note (i)	Skilled	4 x 3.50		14
Note (ii)	Semi-skilled	3 x 1.80	5.40	
		3 x 1.85		5.55
Note (iii)	Unskilled	2 x 1.80	3.60	
		2 x 1.85		3.70

Notes:

(i)   There is a shortage of skilled labour in year 1 so there will be no additional cash flow for wages but there will be an opportunity cost of alternative work foregone (see Note iv)

(ii)   The relevant cost of the semi-skilled labour is the replacement cost of the new unskilled labour.

(iii) The relevant costs are the normal wage rates.

(iv)   The diversion of skilled labour to Wizzo causes a loss of net contribution of £4.50 per hour plus a loss of the recoupment of skilled wages of £3.00 per hour, ie a total opportunity cost of £7.50 per hour making a total cost per unit of Wizzo of 4 x £7.50 = **£30.**

∴ Relevant wages and opportunity costs of labour
Year 1 = £5.40 + 3.60 + 30.00 = **£39 per unit**
Year 1 = £14 + 5.55 + 3.70 = **£23.25 per unit**

(e) It is assumed that the fixed overhead proportion of the overhead rate relates to existing fixed overheads which do not change. Accordingly the relevant costs are the variable overheads, thus

Overheads:- Relevant cost = 4 x £5 = **£20 per unit**

(f) If the manufacture of Wizzo causes a sales loss elsewhere then this is a relevant cost applicable to the Wizzo decision

Sales loss:- Relevant cost = 3000 x £9 = **£27,000 p.a.**

(g) If Wizzo is manufactured then the manager will have to be paid £12,000 p.a. However, employing him full time will avoid the £3,000 p.a. redundancy payment which is an opportunity benefit arising from the manufacture of Wizzo. Thus the net avoidable cost of the manager is £12,000 - 3000 = £9,000 p.a.

Manager:- Relevant cost = **£9,000 p.a.**

FORMAL DECISION RULES

11. It is often considered useful to process the alternatives being considered according to particular decision rules or decision models. In this way the ultimate decision maker is presented with a ranking of the alternatives according to some previously agreed criteria so making the actual decision a more routine matter, provided of course that the decision maker considers the particular rule appropriate for the decision being considered.

The decision rules covered in this manual are Expected Value, the Maximin rule, the Maximax rule and the Minimax regret criterion.

EXPECTED VALUE (EV)

12. Expected value is an averaging process which can be used where the alternatives being considered have two or more possible outcomes and where, objectively or subjectively, a probability can be assigned to each outcome. Thus, expected value is a simple way of bringing some of the effects of uncertainty into the appraisal process.

Rarely are objective probabilities (ie those verifiable by repeated tests, eg tossing coins) available in business so that the probabilities with which we are invariably concerned are **subjective probabilities**, which are the quantification of judgements and assessments by the people involved. Once assigned, subjective probabilities obey the normal rules of probability.

The expected value of an event is the total of the **probability** of each possible outcome **times** the **value** of each possible outcome.

Example 3

Three alternatives are being considered each of which has several outcomes with associated probabilities and it is required to calculate the Expected Values.

Alternative A Outcomes		Alternative B Outcomes		Alternative C Outcomes	
Probability	Contribution £	Probability	Contribution £	Probability	Contribution £
		0.1	2,500		
0.2	6,000	0.2	5,000	0.4	8,000
0.6	10,000	0.4	9,000	0.6	11,500
0.2	12,500	0.2	11,500		
		0.1	16,000		

Solution

Expected Values

A
(0.2 x 6,000) + (0.6 x 10,000) + (0.2 x 12,500)   =   **£9,700**

B
(0.1 x 2,500) + (0.2 x 5,000) + (0.4 x 9,000) + (0.2 x 11,500) + (0.1 x 16,000)   =   **£8,750**

C
(0.4 x 8,000) + (0.6 x 11,500)   =   **£10,100**

∴ on basis of expected value C would be preferred and the ranking would be CAB.

Notes:

(a) In each case it will be seen that the probabilities total 1 which indicates that all outcomes have been included.

(b) The number of outcomes can vary as shown in this example but a commonly encountered situation is that depicted for Alternative A where there are three outcomes: often termed Optimistic – Most Likely – Pessimistic.

(c) Expected value calculations use the two basic rules of probability. It will be recalled from foundation statistics that these are the multiplication rule (AND) and the addition rule (OR).

(d)   The reporting of the expected value alone may mislead the decision maker because it has the effect of masking the characteristics of the underlying distribution of outcomes and probabilities. Where more information is required on the uncertainties additional information must be supplied utilising various statistical techniques. Examples of such techniques are dealt with later in the manual.

EXPECTED VALUE – ADVANTAGES AND DISADVANTAGES

13.   Expected Value is a useful summarising technique, but suffers from similar advantages and disadvantages to all averaging methods.

Advantages:

(a)   Simple to understand and calculate.
(b)   Represents whole distribution by a single figure.
(c)   Arithmetically takes account of the expected variabilities of all outcomes.

Disadvantages:

(a)   By representing the whole distribution by a single figure it ignores the other characteristics of the distribution, eg the range and skewness.

(b)   Makes the assumption that the decision maker is risk neutral, ie he would rank equally the following two distributions:

	£	p	
Pessimistic Outcome	18000	.25	
Most likely Outcome	20000	.5	EV = £20,000
Optimistic Outcome	22000	.25	
and			
Pessimistic Outcome	6000	.2	
Most likely Outcome	18000	.6	EV = £20,000
Optimistic Outcome	40000	.2	

It is of course unlikely that any decision maker would rank them equally due to his personal attitude to risk and, assuming a typical 'risk aversion' attitude, the first of the above distributions would normally be preferred.

Although it appears to be widely used for the purpose, the concept of expected value is not particularly well suited to one off-decisions. Expected value can strictly only be interpreted as the value that would be obtained if a large number of similar decisions were taken with the same ranges of outcomes and associated probabilities. Hardly a typical business situation!

OPTIMISATION OF LEVELS OF ACTIVITY UNDER CONDITIONS OF UNCERTAINTY

14.   Expected Value concepts can be used to calculate the maximum stock or profit level when demand is subject to random variations over a period.

Example 4

A distributor buys perishable articles for £2 per item and sells them at £5. Demand per day is uncertain and items unsold at the end of the day represent a write off because of perishability. If he understocks he loses profit he could have made.

A 300 day record of past activity is as follows:

Daily Demand (units)	No. of Days	p
10	30	.1
11	60	.2
12	120	.4
13	90	.3
	300	1.0

What level of stock should he hold from day to day to maximise profit?

Solution

It is necessary to calculate the **Conditional Profit** (CP) and **Expected Profit** (EP). CP = profit that could be made at any particular conjunction of stock and demand, eg if 13 articles were bought and demand was 10 then

$$CP = (10 \times 5) - (13 \times 2) = £24$$
$$EP = CP \times \text{probability of the demand}$$
eg the CP above is £24 and p (demand = 10) = .1
$$EP = £24 \times .1 = £2.4$$

CONDITIONAL AND EXPECTED PROFIT TABLE

Stock Options

Demand	p	10 CP £	10 EP £	11 CP £	11 EP £	12 CP £	12 EP £	13 CP £	13 EP £
10	.1	30	3	28	2.8	26	2.6	24	2.4
11	.2	30	6	33	6.6	31	6.2	29	5.8
12	.4	30	12	33	13.2	36	14.4	34	13.6
13	.3	30	9	33	9.9	36	10.8	39	11.7
	1.0		30		32.5		*34.0		33.5

Optimum

Table 1

The optimum stock position, given the pattern of demand, is to stock 12 units per day.

VALUE OF PERFECT INFORMATION

15. Assume that the distributor in Example 4 could buy market research information which was perfect, ie it would enable him to forecast the exact demand on any day so that he could stock up accordingly. How much would the distributor be prepared to pay for such information? To solve this type of problem, the profit with perfect information is compared with the optimum EP from Table 1.

Profit with perfect Information

					£
When demand is 10, stock 10	Profit	=	(10 x £3) x .1	=	3.0
When demand is 11, stock 11	Profit	=	(11 x £3) x .2	=	6.6
When demand is 12, stock 12	Profit	=	(12 x £3) x .4	=	14.4
When demand is 13, stock 13	Profit	=	(13 x £3) x .3	=	11.7
					£35.7

As the EP from Table 1 was £34, the distributor could pay up to £1.70 (£35.7 - 34) for the information. The principles behind this type of problem seem to be the subject of frequent examination questions so clear understanding is vital. The shortfall between the **expected value** of outcome and the **maximum possible** outcome with perfect information is the upper limit of the amount that would be paid for such information.

Obviously there is no such thing as perfect information and the calculation of the amount to pay for such information would seem to be a totally theoretical exercise with no practical value. This is not so, because the calculation provides the upper limit which any information could be worth. Having this ceiling value relates the costs of information production to the maximum value which could possibly be obtained. It makes explicit the fact that producing more information, with the resulting increase in costs, is not automatically worthwhile. The extra costs must be compared with the extra benefits expected.

ALTERNATIVE DECISION RULES

16. The rule so far covered in this chapter is to choose the alternative which maximises the expected value. This is the most commonly encountered decision rule and is the one which should be used unless there are clear instructions to the contrary. However alternative rules do exist and these include

the MAXIMIN rule
the MAXIMAX rule
the MINIMAX REGRET rule

These rules are illustrated using the following payoff table showing potential profits and losses which are expected to arise from launching various products in three market conditions thus.

Pay off table in £'000s

	Boom Conditions	Steady State	Recession
Product A	+ 8	1	- 10
Product B	- 2	+ 6	+ 12
Product C	+ 16	0	- 26

Pay Off Table. Table 2

The probabilities are, Boom 0.6, Steady State 0.3 and Recession 0.1 so that the expected values are

$$\text{Product A} = (0.6 \times 8) + (0.3 \times 1) + (0.1 \times -10) = 4.1$$
$$\text{Product B} = (0.6 \times -2) + (0.3 \times 6) + (0.1 \times 12) = 1.8$$
$$\text{Product C} = (0.6 \times 16) + (0.3 \times 0) + (0.1 \times -26) = 7$$

So using the expected value rule the ranking would be C, A, B.

What are the rankings using the alternatives?

MAXIMIN the 'best of the worst'
This is a cautious decision rule based on maximising the minimum loss that can occur. The worst losses are:

$$\begin{array}{ll} A & -10 \\ B & -2 \\ C & -26 \end{array}$$

∴ Ranking using the MAXIMIN rule is B, A, C.

MAXIMAX the 'best of the best'
This is an optimistic rule and maximises the maximum that can be gained.

The maximum gains are:-

$$\begin{array}{ll} A & +8 \\ B & +12 \\ C & +16 \end{array}$$

∴ Ranking using the MAXIMAX rule is C, B, A.

MINIMAX REGRET

17.   This decision seeks to 'minimise the maximum regret' that there would be from choosing a particular strategy. To see this clearly it is necessary to construct a **regret table** based on the payoff table, Table 2. The regret is the **opportunity loss** from taking one decision given that a certain contingency occurs; in our example whether there is boom, steady state, or recession.

Regret Table in £'000s

	Boom	Steady State	Recession
Product A	8	5	22
Product B	18	0	0
Product C	0	6	38

Table 3

Note: The above opportunity losses are calculated by setting the best position under any state to zero and then calculating the amount of shortfall there is by not being at that position. For example, if there is a recession product B gains +12 but if Product A had been chosen there is a loss of -10 making a total shortfall, as compared with B, of 22, which is the opportunity loss.

The maximum 'regrets' are:-

$$
\begin{array}{ll}
A & 22 \\
B & 18 \\
C & 38 \\
\end{array}
$$

∴ the ranking using the MINIMAX REGRET rule is B, A, C.

OPPORTUNITY LOSS AND EXPECTED VALUE

18. As a loss is the negative aspect of gain it is to be expected that opportunity loss and expected value are related. This is indeed so and the opportunity losses multiplied by the probabilities, ie the expected opportunity loss (EOL) can be used to arrive at the same ranking as the expected value (EV) rule except that where the **maximum** EV is chosen, the **minimum** EOL is required.

∴ MINIMISING EOL gives the same decision as MAXIMISING EV.

For example, the EOL'S of Table 3 are:-

$$
\begin{array}{lll}
A & (0.6 \times 8) + (0.3 \times 5) + (0.1 \times 22) & = 8.5 \\
B & (0.6 \times 18) + (0.3 \times 0) + (0.1 \times 0) & = 10.8 \\
C & (0.6 \times 0) + (0.3 \times 6) + (0.1 \times 38) & = 5.6 \\
\end{array}
$$

∴ ranking in order of minimum EOL gives C, A, B, which is identical to the ranking given by the expected value method.

USE OF DECISION RULES

19. The calculation of expected value or a ranking based on the alternative decision rules is but one input of information to the ultimate decision maker. The calculations may give some broad guidance but in practice it is unlikely that the recommended decisions would be automatically adopted in all cases. There are too many political, behavioural and other factors involved in a typical business situation to allow the act of decision making to become an automatic process dictated by a simple decision criterion. However, if no guidance is given in an examination, then the use of some form of expected value would be recommended, although it would be prudent to mention some of the inherent limitations of the technique.

DECISION TREES

20. These are a pictorial method of showing a sequence of inter-related decisions and outcomes and can provide assistance in the clarification of complex decisions. They invariably involve multiple outcomes and associated probabilities and are usually based on expected values although, in principle, there is no reason why any other decision rule could not be used.

STRUCTURE OF DECISION TREES

21. The structure and typical components of a decision tree are shown in the following illustration:

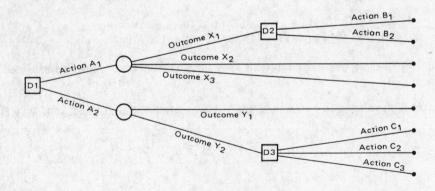

Figure 1

Notes:

(a) It will be seen that there are two types of nodes. Decision nodes depicted by squares and Outcome nodes depicted by circles.

(b) The Decision nodes are points where a choice exists between alternatives and a managerial decision is made based on estimates and calculations of the returns expected.

(c) The Outcome nodes are points where the events depend on probabilities, eg assume that Action A_1 in Figure 1 was - Build branch factory - then outcomes, X_1, X_2, and X_3 could represent various possible sales: high, medium, and low, each with an estimated probability.

DRAWING DECISION TREES

22. The procedure for drawing decision trees and evaluating the returns expected will be illustrated by using the following example.

Example 5

A firm making widgets have been considering the likely demand for widgets over the next 6 years and think that the demand pattern will be as follows:

	High demand for 6 years	p	=	.5
	Low demand for 6 years	p	=	.3
	High demand for 3 years			
followed by	Low demand for 3 years	p	=	.2

(No possibility is envisaged of Low demand followed by High demand).

Enlargement of capacity is required and the following options are available:

Option   A   Install fully automatic facilities immediately at a cost of £5.4m.

           B   Install semi-automatic facilities immediately at a cost of £4m.

           C   Install the semi-automatic facilities immediately as in B and upgrade to fully automatic at an additional cost of £2m in 3 years time providing demand has been high for 3 years.

The returns expected for the various demand and capacity options are estimated to be

		IF HIGH DEMAND	IF LOW DEMAND
OPTION	A	£1.6m p.a.	£0.6m p.a.
	B	£0.9m p.a. for 3 years then £0.5m p.a. for 3 years	£0.8m p.a.
	C	£0.9m p.a. for 3 years then £1.1m for 3 years	£0.8m p.a. for 3 years then £0.3m p.a. for 3 years.

What decision(s) should the firm take assuming that the objective is to maximise expected value?

Solution

The decision tree is developed in two stages, the FORWARD PASS and the BACKWARD PASS.

FORWARD PASS

23. Draw the decision tree starting from the left showing the two Decision points and the various demand options thus:

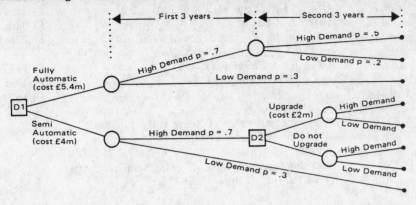

Figure 2

THE BACKWARD PASS

24. It will be seen that ther are two decision points D_1 at the start and D_2 at the end of the first three years. To evaluate D_1 it is necessary to evaluate D_2 first, because the values of the D_1 actions depend upon the D_2 values. This is why this stage is known as the backward pass, ie evaluate the decision points from right to left.

D_2 can be depicted as follows:

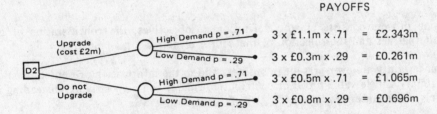

Figure 3

∴ The expected value of upgrading is
£2.343 + £0.261 = **£0.604m**

The expected value of **NOT** upgrading is
£1.065 + £0.696 = **£1.761m**

Note: The probability of high demand being .71 as shown in Figure 3 is obtained by the following reasoning. D_2 will only be reached if there is high demand for the first three years. The probability that high demand will be following by high demand is 0.5 and by low demand 0.2.

∴ P(High demand in second 3 years) $= \dfrac{0.5}{0.5 + 0.2} = 0.71$

Figure 2 can now be redrawn with D_2 having an expected value of £1.761m.

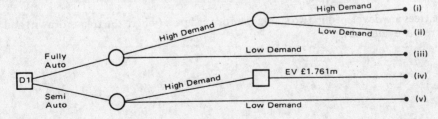

Figure 4

	PAYOFFS		EV
(i)	6 x £1.6m x 0.5	=	£4.8m
(ii)	(3 x £1.6m + (3 x £0.6m) x 0.2	=	£1.32m
(iii)	6 x £0.6m x 3	=	£1.08m
			£7.20m
(iv)	(3 x £0.9m + £1.76m) x 0.7	=	£3.1227m
(v)	6 x £0.8m x 0.3	=	£1.44m
			£4.5627m

The expected value of being fully automatic
= £7.2m - £5.4m = **£1.8m**

and the expected value of being semi-automatic
= £4.5627m - £4m = **£0.5627m**

The D_2 decision would be go for option A, ie put in the fully automatic machinery at the outset.

SUMMARY

25. (a) Plans are activated by decisions and the decision process includes consideration of political, psychological and social factors as well as quantitative and financial ones.

(b) Relevancy is the all important characteristic of information supplied for decision making.

(c) Decision making is making choices between future, uncertain alternatives. Where no alternatives exist no decision making is possible.

(d) The decision process consists of: the definition of objectives, the consideration of alternatives, the evaluation of alternatives and the selection of the course of action.

(e) Risk and uncertainty are ever present in business and so the information presented must clearly show the effects of uncertainty. Single value profit or contribution figures can be positively misleading if some or all of the factors involved are uncertain.

(f) The relevant costs and revenues for decision making are differential future costs and revenues. Sunk costs are irrelevant.

(g) Opportunity cost is the value of the next best alternative and, properly specified, is equivalent to future avoidable costs.

(h) In appropriate circumstances formal decision rules can be useful. The rules include: expected value, maximin, maximax, and the minimax regret criterion.

(i) Expected value is value x probability and is a useful averaging technique but suffers from several disadvantages.

(j) Maximin is a cautious decision rule, maximax is an optimistic rule and minimax regret seeks to minimise the maximum regret that could occur.

(k) Decision trees are a pictorial method of showing an interrelated series of decisions and outcomes. Generally they are evaluated using expected value.

(l) Decision trees are developed in two stages the forward pass (where the tree is drawn) and the backward pass (where the tree is evaluated).

POINTS TO NOTE

26. (a) Programmed decisions, as defined by Simon, are the ones in which the use of formal decision rules (expected value, minimax regret and so on) is likely to be the most appropriate.

(b) It is a common misconception to assume that all decision making in conditions of certainty (ie where all outcomes and values are known) is trivially easy. This is not so because there are some problems where there are thousands or indeed millions of possible combinations and where the optimum choice is by no means obvious. Some of these types of problems can be solved by mathematical programming techniques, one of which, Linear Programming, is dealt with later in the manual.

(c) The importance of relevancy for costs and revenues in decision making has been emphasised in this chapter. Where there is difficulty in establishing relevant costs or revenues ask the basic question: 'Will it change?' If the cost or revenue item does alter as a result of the decision, then it is relevant.

ADDITIONAL READING

Management Accounting: a conceptual approach	Amey and Egginton, LONGMAN
Topics in Management Accounting	Arnold, Scapens and Carsberg, PHILIP ALLAN
Economics of Business Decisions	Carsberg, PENGUIN
Managing for Results : Economic tasks and risk taking decisions	Drucker, HEINEMANN
Information for decision making	Rappaport, PRENTICE HALL
Studies in Cost Analysis	Solomons, SWEET & MAXWELL

SELF REVIEW QUESTIONS

1. What is the relationship between objectives, plans and decisions? (2)

2. What are the stages in the decision process? (3)

3. What is 'satisficing' behaviour? (4)

4. What are constraints or limitations? (4)

5. Why should the analysis of decisions include the effects of uncertainty? (6)

6. Distinguish between programmed and non-programmed decisions. (7)

7. Define relevant cost and revenues. (8)

8. What are opportunity costs? (9)

9. Explain expected value and its use in decision making. (12)

10. What is conditional profit? (14)

11. How is the value of perfect information calculated? (15)

12. Define the maximin, maximax, and the minimax regret rules. (16 & 17)

13. What is opportunity loss? (18)

14. What is a decision tree and what are the types of nodes it contains? (21)

15. How is a decision tree drawn? (22)

EXAMINATION QUESTIONS WITH ANSWERS COMMENCING PAGE 350

A1. *At the Purcell Co. Ltd a proposed expansion, which would entail the setting up of a separate department to produce a new product, had previously been rejected on various, non-financial, grounds. However, the project was being re-examined. Details of the proposed expansion are as follows:*

(i)   A new department would be set up.

(ii) Planned sales and production quantities are shown in the table below:

<table>
<tr><td colspan="6" align="center">Planned sales and production quantities
(000's units)</td></tr>
<tr><td>Month</td><td>Sales
quantity</td><td>Production
quantity</td><td>Month</td><td>Sales
quantity</td><td>Production
quantity</td></tr>
<tr><td>January</td><td>Nil</td><td>6</td><td>April</td><td>10</td><td>21</td></tr>
<tr><td>February</td><td>4</td><td>8</td><td>May</td><td>14</td><td>22</td></tr>
<tr><td>March</td><td>6</td><td>14</td><td>June</td><td>18</td><td>21</td></tr>
<tr><td></td><td></td><td></td><td>July and
onwards</td><td>20</td><td>20</td></tr>
</table>

(iii)   Standard labour costs are £5 per unit produced but there is a guaranteed minimum wages payment per month of £75,000. Any production in excess of 20,000 units in any one month will cause additional labour costs of 50% per unit on the excess production only. All wage payments will be made in the month during which production takes place.

(iv)   Raw materials will usually be purchased, on one month's credit, in the month preceding manufacture, but the raw materials for the production of both January and February will be obtained early in January. Raw materials costs will be £7 per unit.

(v)   Delivery costs will be £10,000 per month plus £2 per unit sold, paid for in the month of sale. The £2 charge per unit relates to the amount to be paid to an external carrier for delivery to customers of the goods from Purcell's various central warehouses. The £10,000 is a standing charge made by Purcell's transport department for delivering the goods to warehouses – the transport department will however only have to incur additional costs of £2,000 per month as a result of the proposed expansion. All delivery costs commence in February.

*(vi)   Overhead costs **directly** incurred by the new department will be:*

(a) Variable production overhead – £2 per unit produced, paid for in the month of production.
(b) Fixed production overhead – £12,000 per month including £2,000 depreciation. Cash expenditure being paid monthly from January onwards.

*(vii)   Overhead costs **allocated** to the new department will be:*

(a) Fixed production overhead – £28,000 per month.
(b) Administration costs – £25,000 per month.

These allocated overheads are apportionments of general overheads none of which will alter as a result of the expansion.

(viii) Sales price per unit will be £20. The standard cost of production, based on the long term monthly production, is £16 comprising:

	£	£
Direct labour		5
Direct material		7
Variable overhead		2
Fixed production overhead		
directly incurred	0.6	
allocated	1.4	
		2
		£16

This standard cost is to be used for stock valuation purposes.

(ix) Sales are to be made on two months credit. However it is felt that the following payment pattern will be operative:

60% of sales paid for in accordance with the credit terms
30% of sales paid one month late
10% of sales paid for two months late

There are no settlement discounts.

Purcell's managing director stated 'The main reason for reconsidering this expansion is liquidity. Purcell is expected to have a low cash balance at the end of July when we are committed to pay for substantial capital commitments already entered into. This expansion should help to provide the needed funds. However profit is also important and so I need to know by how much Purcell Ltd will be better off as a result of this expansion. Just how much profit will appear in the accounts of the new department?'

Required:

(a) For the period January to July, ascertain

(i)   the profit which will appear in the management accounts as relating to the new department, and
(ii)   the incremental benefit to Purcell Ltd as a result of the expansion.

(b) Using an appropriate cash forecast, calculate the effect the expansion will have on Purcell's cash balance as at the end of July.

ACCA, Management Accounting.

A2. *(a) Joint cost apportionments pervade accounting but there are strong arguments for claiming that they should be avoided whenever possible.*

Explain the case against joint cost apportionments in relation to:
costs prepared for planning purposes;
costs prepared for control purposes;
costs used for pricing;
costs used for decision making.

(b) Comment briefly on the applicability of game theory to joint cost apportionment.

ACCA, Management Accounting.

A3. *Itervro Ltd, a small engineering company, operates a job order costing system. It has been invited to tender for a comparatively large job which is outside the range of its normal activities and, since there is surplus capacity, the management are keen to quote as low a price as possible. It is decided that the opportunity should be treated in isolation without any regard to the possibility of its leading to further work of a similar nature (although such a possibility does exist). A low price will not have any repercussions on Intervero's regular work.*

The Estimating Department has spent 100 hours on work in connection with the quotation and they have incurred travelling expense of £550 in connection with a visit to the prospective customer's factory overseas. The following Cost Estimate has been prepared on the basis of their study:

Inquiry 205H/81
Cost Estimate

		£
Direct Material and Components		
2,000 units of A at £25 per unit		50,000
200 units of B at £10 per unit		2,000
Other material and components to be bought in (specified)		<u>12,500</u>
		64,500
Direct Labour		
700 hours of skilled labour at £3.50 per hour		2,450
1,500 hours of unskilled labour at £2 per hour		3,000
Overhead		
Department P - 200 hours at £25 per hour		5,000
Department Q - 400 hours at £20 per hour		8,000
Estimating Department		
100 hours at £5 per hour		500
Travelling Expenses		550
Planning Department		
300 hours at £5 per hour		<u>1,500</u>
		£85,500

The following information has been brought together:

Material A This a regular stock item. The stock holding is more than sufficient for this job. The material currently held has an average cost of £25 per unit but the current replacement cost is £20 per unit.

Material B A stock of 4,000 units of B is currently held in stores. This material is slow moving and the stock is the residue of a batch bought seven years ago at a cost of £10 per unit. B currently costs £24 per unit but the resale value is only £18 per unit. A foreman has pointed out that B could be used as a substitute for another type of regularly used raw material which costs £20 per unit.

Direct Labour The workforce is paid on a time basis. The company has adopted a 'no redundancy' policy and this means that skilled workers are frequently moved to jobs which do not make proper use of their skills. The wages included in the cost estimate are for the mix of labour which the job ideally requires. It seems likely, if the job is obtained, that most of the 2,200 hours of direct labour will be performed by skilled staff receiving £3.50 per hour.

Overhead - Department P Department P is the one department of Intervero Ltd that is working at full capacity. The department is treated as a profit centre and it uses a transfer price of £25 per hour for charging out its processing time to other departments. This charge is calculated as follows:

	£
Estimated Variable Cost per machine hour	10
Fixed Departmental Overhead	8
Departmental Profit	<u>7</u>
	<u>£25</u>

Department P's facilities are frequently hired out to other firms and a charge of £30 per hour is made. There is a steady demand from outside customers for the use of these facilities.

Overhead - Department Q Department Q uses a transfer price of £20 per charging out machine processing time to other departments. This charge is calculated as follows:

	£
Estimated Variable Cost per machine hour	8
Fixed Departmental Overhead	9
Departmental Profit	<u>3</u>
	<u>£20</u>

Estimating Department The Estimating Department charges out its time to specific jobs using a rate of £5 per hour. The average wage rate within the department is £2.50 per hour but the higher rate is justified as being necessary to cover departmental overheads and the work done on unsuccessful quotations.

Planning Department This department also uses a charging out rate which is intended to cover all department costs.

(a) You are required to restate the Cost Estimate by using an opportunity cost approach. Make any assumptions that you deem to be necessary and briefly justify each of the figures that you give.

(b) Discuss the relevance of the opportunity cost approach to the situation described in the question and consider the problems which are likely to be encountered if it is used in practice.

(c) Briefly discuss the general applicability of opportunity cost in business decision making where a choice exists among alternative courses of action.

ACCA, Management Accounting.

A4. (a) A small contractor has been asked to quote for a contract which is larger than he would normally consider. The contractor would like to obtain the job as he does have surplus capacity.

The estimating and design department has spent 200 hours in preparing drawings and the following cost estimate:

		£
Cost Estimate		
Direct materials:		
3,000 units of X at £10 (original cost)	– see note 1	30,000
100 units of Y (charged out using FIFO)	– see note 2	
50 units at £100 £5,000		
50 units at £125 £6,250		
		11,250
Direct material to be bought in:	– see note 3	12,000
Direct labour:		
– Skilled staff	– see note 4	
2,720 hours at £5 per hour		13,600
– Trainees	– see note 5	
1,250 hours at £2 per hour		2,500
Depreciation on curing press	– see note 6	
Annual depreciation (straight line) £12,000		
One month's depreciation		1,000
Subcontract work	– see note 7	20,000
Supervisory staff	– see note 8	6,150
Estimating and design department	– see note 9	
200 hours at £10 per hour £2,000		
Overtime premium for 50 hours £500		
		2,500
		99,000
Administration overhead at 5% of above costs	– see note 10	4,950
		103,950

The following notes may be relevant:

(1) A sufficient stock of raw material X is held in the stores. It is the residue of a quantity bought some 10 years ago. If this stock is not used on the prospective contract it is unlikely that it will be used in the foreseeable future. The net resale value is thought to be £20,000.

(2) Material Y is regularly used by the contractor on a variety of jobs. The current replacement cost of the material is £130 per unit.

(3) This is the estimated cost of the required material.

(4) Staff are paid on a time basis for a 40 hour week. The labour hour rate includes a charge of 100% of the wage rate to cover labour related overhead costs. It is estimated that, at the current level of operations, 80% of the overheads are variable. It is considered that one extra worker will be required temporarily for 3 months if the contract is obtained. His salary of £100 per week (and the associated amount of labour related overhead expense) is included in the estimate of £13,600.

(5) No additional trainees would be taken on. The trainees' wage rate is £1 per hour but their time is charged out at £2 to allow for labour related overhead on the same basis as in note 4 above.

(6) The curing press is normally fully occupied. If it is not being used by the contractor's own workforce it is being hired out at £500 per week.

(7) This is the estimated cost for the work.

(8) It is not considered that it would be necessary to employ any additional supervisory staff. The estimated cost of £6,150 includes an allowance of £1,000 for overtime which it may be necessary to pay to the supervisors.

(9) The expense of this department is predominantly fixed but the overtime payments were specifically incurred to get the drawings and plans out in time.

(10) The administrative expense is a fixed cost. This is the established method of allocating the cost to specific contracts.

It is considered that any quotation higher than £100,000 will be unsuccessful. You are required to prepare a revised cost estimate using an opportunity cost approach. State whether you consider that the revised calculations can provide support for a quotation below £100,000.

(b) Comment on the use of opportunity cost:
  (i)   for decision making and
  (ii) for cost control purposes.

ACCA, Management Accounting.

A5. *(a) It has been claimed that managers do not find opportunity costs useful in making decisions. If a manager is considering a range of alternative proposals, the opportunity costs can only be obtained by ranking the proposals in order of their attractiveness. When the alternatives are so ranked, the best alternative is immediately known and opportunity cost is not needed.*

Discuss the above criticism of opportunity cost and state your views as to the usefulness of the concept.

(b) 'Fixed costs can be relevant for decision making' – Discuss.

ACCA, Management Accounting.

13. Marginal Costing and CVP Analysis

INTRODUCTION

1.   This chapter deals with the use of marginal costing and cost-volume-profit analysis in short run decision making. Examples are given of the use of marginal costing principles including make or buy, special order, product elimination and decisions involving limiting factors. The main formulae involved in cost-volume-profit analysis are provided and various break-even charts and profit graphs are depicted. The economist's approach to cost-volume-profit analysis is contrasted with that of the accountant and the chapter concludes with an explanation of the use of differential calculus in optimising activity levels.

USES OF THE MARGINAL COSTING APPROACH

2.   The concept of marginal costing - the separation of costs into fixed and variable, the calculation of contribution, and the treatment of fixed costs as period costs - was introduced in Chapter 2 where the effects of using the concept in the routine cost accounting system was explored. The key aspect of the approach, that of the separation of fixed and variable elements of cost, is widely used in cost and management accounting. Examples include: forecasting cost behaviour (dealt with in Chapter 3), flexible budgeting (dealt with in Chapter 7), transfer pricing (dealt with later) and short run decision making which is dealt with in this chapter.

SHORT RUN TACTICAL DECISIONS

3.   These are decisions which seek to make the best use of existing facilities. Typically, in the short run, fixed costs remain unchanged so that the marginal cost, revenue and contribution of each alternative is relevant. In these circumstances the selection of the alternative which maximises contribution is the correct decision rule. In the long term (and sometimes in the short term) fixed costs do change and accordingly the differential costs must include any changes in the amount of fixed costs. Where there is a decision involving no changes in fixed costs normal marginal costing principles apply. Where the situation involves changes in fixed costs a more fundamental aid to decision making called **differential costing** is used. Marginal costing is covered first in this chapter and then differential costing.

ALTERNATIVE CONCEPTS OF MARGINAL COST

4.   To the economist, marginal cost is the additional cost incurred by the production of one extra unit. To the accountant, marginal cost is average variable cost which is presumed to act in a linear fashion, ie marginal cost per unit is assumed to be constant in the short run, over the activity range being considered.

These views can be contrasted in the following graphs:

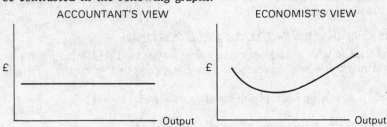

Figure 1   Marginal Cost per Unit

This difference of viewpoint regarding marginal cost per unit results in the following alternative views of a firm's total cost structure.

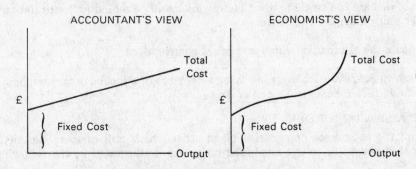

Figure 2   Total Cost Structures

The economic model is an explanation of the cost behaviour of firms in general, whereas the accounting model is an attempt to provide a pragmatic basis for decision making in a particular firm. However, it is likely that differences between the two viewpoints are more apparent than real. A number of investigations have shown that marginal costs are virtually constant per unit over the range of activity changes studied. Accordingly for short run decision making purposes the marginal cost per unit is normally assumed to be constant. Thus if the marginal cost per unit was £5 per unit, the total marginal cost for

100 units would be	£500
150 units would be	£750
200 units would be	£1000

and so on.

Great care must be taken not to make this assumption unles it is realistic. Where economies or diseconomies of scale are expected or if there is any other factor which will make the costs behave in a non-linear fashion then the traditional assumption of linearity should not be made and a deeper analysis should be undertaken to determine the true underlying cost function.

KEY FACTOR

5.   Sometimes known as a limiting factor or principal budget factor. This is a factor which is a binding constraint upon the organisation, ie the factor which prevents indefinite expansion or unlimited profits. It may be sales, availability of finance, skilled labour, supplies of material or lack of space. Where a single binding constraint can be identified, then the general objective of maximising contribution can be achieved by selecting the alternative which **maximises the contribution per unit of the key factor.** It will be apparent that from time to time the key factor in an organisation will change. For example, a firm may have a shortage of orders. It overcomes this by appointing salesmen and then finds that there is a shortage of machinery capacity. The expansion of the productive capacity may introduce a problem of lack of space and so on.

Note: The 'maximising contribution per unit of the limiting factor' rule can be of value, but can only be used where there is a single binding constraint and where the constraint is continuously divisible, ie it can be altered one unit at a time. Where several constraints apply simultaneously, the simple maximising rule given above cannot be applied because of the interactions between constraints. In such situations mathematical techniques can be used to establish the optimal position. One of the more important mathematical techniques that can be used for such problems, known as Linear Programming (LP), is described later in the manual. LP represents a readily available means of extending C-V-P analysis to cope with practical problems.

EXAMPLE OF DECISIONS INVOLVING MARGINAL COSTING

6.   Several typical problems in which marginal costing can provide useful information for decision making are given below. Once the general principles are understood, they can be applied in any other similar circumstances.

The steps involved in analysing such problems are as follows:

(a)   Check that fixed costs are expected to remain unchanged.

(b)   If necessary separate out fixed and variable costs.

(c)   Calculate the revenue, marginal costs and contribution of each of the alternatives.

(d)   Check to see if there is a single limiting factor which will be a binding constraint and if so, calculate the contribution per unit of the limiting factor.

(e)   Finally, choose the alternative which maximises contribution.

The situations shown below are decisions involving acceptance of a special order, dropping a product, choice of product where a limiting factor exists and make or buy.

ACCEPTANCE OF A SPECIAL ORDER

7.   By this is meant the acceptance or rejection of an order which utilises spare capacity, but which is only available if a lower than normal price is quoted. The procedure is illustrated by the following example.

Example 1

Zerocal Ltd manufacture and market a slimming drink which they sell for 20p per can. Current output is 400,000 cans per month which represents 80% of capacity. They have the opportunity to utilise their surplus capacity by selling their product at 13p per can to a supermarket chain who will sell it as an 'own label' product.

Total costs for the last month were £56,000 of which £16,000 were fixed costs. This represented a total cost of 14p per can.

Based on the above data should Zerocal accept the supermarket offer?

What other factors should be considered?

Solution

The present position is as follows:

			£	
	Sales (400,000 x 20p)	=	80,000	
less	Marginal cost		40,000	(= 10p/can)
=	Contribution		40,000	
less	Fixed Costs		16,000	
=	NET PROFIT		£24,000	

On the assumption that fixed costs are unchanged, the special order will produce the following contribution

			£
	Sales (100,000 x 13p)	=	13,000
less	Marginal cost		
	(100,000 x 10p)	=	10,000
=	CONTRIBUTION		£3,000

∴ the new order brings in more contribution which, because fixed costs are already covered, results in increased net profit. Thus, purely on the cost figures, the order would be acceptable.

However, there are several other factors which would need to be considered before a final decision is taken.

(a) Will the acceptance of one order at a lower price lead other customers to demand lower prices as well?

(b) Is this special order the most profitable way of using the spare capacity?

(c) Will the special order lock up capacity which could be used for future full price business?

(d) Is it absolutely certain that fixed costs will not alter.

Notes:

(a) Although the price of 13p is less than the total cost of 14p per can, it does provide some contribution, so may be worthwhile.

(b) The process of marginal cost pricing to utilise spare capacity is widely used, eg hotels provide cheap weekend rates, railways and airlines have cheap fares for off peak periods, many manufacturers of proprietary goods produce own label products and so on.

(c) The contribution from the special order can also be calculated by multiplying the quantity by the contribution per can, ie 100,000 x 3p = £3,000.

DROPPING A PRODUCT

8.   If a company has a range of products one of which is deemed to be unprofitable, it may consider dropping the item from its range.

Example 2

A company produces three products for which the following operating statement has been produced:

	Product X	Product Y	Product Z	Total
	£	£	£	£
Sales	32,000	50,000	45,000	127,000
Total Costs	36,000	38,000	34,000	108,000
Profit/(Loss)	(£4,000)	£12,000	£11,000	£19,000

The total cost comprise $\frac{2}{3}$ variable $\frac{1}{3}$ fixed.

The directors consider that as Product X shows a loss it should be discontinued.

Based on the above cost data should Product X be dropped?

What other factors should be considered?

Solution

First calculate the fixed costs, ie
$\frac{1}{3}(36,000) + \frac{1}{3}(38,000) + \frac{1}{3}(34,000) = £36,000$

Rearranging the operating statement in marginal costing form products:

	Product X £	Product Y £	Product Z £	Total £
Sales	32,000	50,000	45,000	127,000
less				
Marginal Cost	24,000	25,333	22,667	72,000
= CONTRIBUTION	£8,000	£24,667	£22,333	£55,000

less Fixed Costs	36,000
= NET PROFIT	£19,000

From this it will be seen that Product X produces a contribution of £8,000. Should it be dropped the position would be:

	£
Contribution Product Y	24,667
Contribution Product Z	22,333
Total Contribution	47,000
less Fixed Costs	36,000
= NET PROFIT	£11,000

Thus dropping Product X with an apparent loss of £4,000 **reduces** total profits by £8,000 which is, of course, the amount of contribution lost from Product X.

Other factors which need to be considered:

(a) Although Product X does provide some contribution, it is at a low rate and alternative, more profitable products or markets should be considered.

(b) The assumption above was that the fixed costs were general fixed costs which would remain even if X was dropped. If dropping X results in the elimination of the fixed costs originally apportioned to X, then the elimination would be worthwhile. However, this is unlikely.

CHOICE OF PRODUCT WHERE A LIMITING FACTOR EXISTS

9.   This is the situation where a firm has a choice between various types of products which it could manufacture and where there is a single, binding constraint.

Example 3

A company is able to produce four products and is planning its production mix for the next period. Estimated cost, sales, and production data are given below.

Product	W		X		Y		Z	
	£		£		£		£	
Selling Price/unit	20		30		40		36	
	£		£		£		£	
Labour (@ £2/hr)	6		4		14		10	
Materials (@ £1 kg)	6	12	18	22	10	24	12	22
Contribution		£8		£8		£16		£14
Resources/Unit								
Labour (hours)	3		2		7		5	
Materials (Kgs)	6		18		10		12	
Maximum Demand (Units)	5000		5000		5000		5000	

Based on the above data, what is the most appropriate mix under the two following assumptions?

(a) If labour hours are limited to 50,000 in a period **or**
(b) If material is limited to 110,000 Kgs in a period.

Whatever products have a positive contribution and there are no constraints, there is a prima facie case for their production.

However, when, as in this example, constraints exist, the products must be ranked in order of contribution per unit of the constraint and the most profitable product mix established.

Accordingly, the contribution per unit of the inputs is calculated.

Product	W	X	Y	Z
	£	£	£	£
Contribution/Unit	8	8	16	14
Contribution/Labour Hour	2.67	4	2.29	2.8
Contribution/Kg of Material	1.33	0.44	1.6	1.17

Answer:

(a) To make all the products up to the demand limit would require:
(5000 x 3) + (5000 x 2) + (5000 x 5) = 85,000 labour hours but as there is a limit of 50,000 hrs in a period, the products should be manufactured in order of attractiveness related to labour hours which is X, Z, W and finally Y.

	Produce	5000 units X using	10,000	labour hours
		5000 units Z using	25,000	labour hours
		5000 units W using	15,000	labour hours
	and no units of Y			
	which uses the total of		50,000	hours available.

(b) If the constraint is 110,000 kgs of material, then a similar process produces a ranking of Y, W, Z and finally X which will be noted is the opposite of the ranking produced if labour is the constraint.

When material is the constraint, the optimum production mix is:

	5000 units of Y using	50,000	Kgs material
	5000 units of W using	30,000	Kgs material
	2500 units of Z using	30,000	Kgs material
and no units of X		-	
which uses the total of		110,000	Kgs of material

Notes:

(a) The above process of maximising contribution per unit of the limiting factor can only be used where there is a single binding constraint.

(b) Most practical problems involve various constraints and many more factors than the example illustrated. In such circumstances, if linearity can be assumed, linear programming will indicate the optimum solution.

(c) In general where no constraint is identified, a reasonable decision rule is to choose the alternative which maximises contribution per £ of sales value.

MAKE OR BUY

10. Frequently management are faced with the decision whether to make a particular product or component or whether to buy it in. Apart from overriding technical reasons, the decision is usually based on an analysis of the cost implications.

In general, the relevant cost comparison is between the marginal cost of manufacture and the buying in price. However, when manufacturing the component displaces existing production, the lost contribution must be added to the marginal cost of production of the component before comparison with the buying in price. The two situations are illustrated below.

Example 4

A firm manufactures component BK 200 and the costs for the current production level of 50,000 units are:

COSTS/UNIT

	£
Materials	2.50
Labour	1.25
Variable overheads	1.75
Fixed overheads	3.50
TOTAL COST	£9.00

Component BK 200 could be bought in for £7.75 and, if so, the production capacity utilised at present would be unused.

Assuming that there are no overriding technical considerations, should BK 200 be bought in or manufactured?

Solution

Comparison of the buying in price of £7.75 and the full cost of £9.00 might suggest that the component should be bought in.

However, the correct comparison is between the MARGINAL COST of manufacture (ie £5.50) and the buying in price of £7.75. This indicates that the component should be manufactured, not bought in.

The reason for this is that the fixed costs of £175,000 (ie 50,000 units at £3.50) would presumably continue and, because the capacity would be unused, the fixed overheads would not be absorbed into production.

If BK 200 was bought in, overall profits would fall by £112,500, which is the difference between the buying in price and the marginal cost of manufacture, ie (£7.75 - 5.50) x 50,000.

Example 5

A firm is considering whether to manufacture or purchase a particular component 2543. This would be in batches of 10,000 and the buying in price would be £6.50. The marginal cost of manufacturing Component 2543 is £4.75 per unit and the component would have to be made on a machine which was currently working at full capacity. If the component was manufactured, it is estimated that the sales of finished product FP97 would be reduced by 1000 units. FP97 has a marginal cost of £60/unit and sells for £80/unit.

Should the firm manufacture or purchase component 2543?

Solution

A superficial view, based on the preceding example, is that because the marginal cost of manufacture is substantially below the buying in price, the component should not be bought in and thus further analysis is unnecessary. However, such an approach is insufficient in this more realistic situation and consideration must be given to the loss of contribution from the displaced product.

Cost analysis - Component 2543 in batches of 10,000

	£
Marginal Cost of manufacture	
= £4.75/unit x 10,000	47,500
+ Lost contribution for FP97	
= £20/unit x 1000	20,000
	67,500
Buying in price	
= £6.50/unit x 10,000	65,000

There is a saving of £2,500 per 10,000 batch by buying in rather than manufacture.

Note: The lost contribution of £20,000 is an example of an opportunity cost discussed in the previous chapter. This is the value of a benefit sacrificed in favour of some alternative course of action. Where there is no alternative use for the resource, as in Example 4, then the opportunity cost is zero and can thus be ignored.

DIFFERENTIAL COSTING

11. This is a term used in the preparation of ad-hoc information when the cost and income differences between the various options being considered are high-lighted so that clear comparisons can be made of all the financial consequences. In one sense differential costing is a wider concept than marginal costing because all cost changes are considered, both fixed and variable, whereas the presumption when marginal costing is used is that only variable costs change.

A simple example of the application of differential costing is as follows:

A company is considering whether to expand activities by 20% (Option B) or remain at their present level (Option A). The expansion will increased fixed costs and, because of overtime, also marginal costs. To sell the extra output some selling price reductions will be necessary. Summaries of the positions and of the differential between them are shown below.

	Option A Current Activity	Option B Current Activity + 20%	Differential B - A
	£	£	£
Sales	300,000	350,000	50,000
less Marginal Cost	180,000	220,000	40,000
= Contribution	120,000	130,000	10,000
less Fixed Costs	90,000	96,000	6,000
= Net Profit	£30,000	£34,000	£4,000

Thus, on the basis of the figures and with the usual caveats regarding the quality of estimates the expansions would seem to be worthwhile.

This simple procedure should be recognised as merely a restatement of the relevant cost principles discussed in Chapter 14, that is the relevant costs and revenues are those **which will change as a result of the decision.**

COST-VOLUME PROFIT (C-V-P) ANALYSIS

12. C-V-P analysis, sometimes termed Break-Even analysis, is an application of marginal costing and seeks to study the relationship between costs, volume and profit at differing activity levels and can be a useful guide for short-term planning and decision making. It is more relevant where the proposed changes in activity are relatively small so that established cost patterns and relationships are likely to hold good. With greater changes in activity and over the longer term, existing cost structures, eg the amount of fixed costs and the marginal cost per unit, are likely to change so C-V-P analysis is unlikely to produce useful guidance.

Typical short run decisions where C-V-P analysis may be useful include: choice of sales mix, pricing policies, multi-shift working and special order acceptance.

C-V-P ANALYSIS ASSUMPTIONS

13. Before any formulae are given or graphs drawn, the major assumptions behind C-V-P analysis must be stated. These are:

    (a) All costs can be resolved into fixed and variable elements.
    (b) Fixed costs will remain constant and variable costs vary proportionately with activity.
    (c) Over the activity range being considered costs and revenues behave in a linear fashion.
    (d) That the only factor affecting costs and revenues is volume.
    (e) That technology, production methods and efficiency remain unchanged.
    (f) Particularly for graphical methods, that the analysis relates to one product only.
    (g) There are no stock level changes or that stocks are valued at marginal cost only.
    (h) There is assumed to be no uncertainty.

It will be apparent that these are over simplifying assumptions for most practical situations so that C-V-P analysis should be used with caution and only as an approximate guide for decision making.

C-V-P ANALYSIS BY FORMULA

14. C-V-P analysis can be undertaken by graphical means which are dealt with later in this chapter, or by simple formulae which are listed below and illustrated by examples

(a)   Break-even point (in units) $= \dfrac{\text{Fixed Costs}}{\text{Contribution/unit}}$

(b)   Break-even point (£ sales) $= \dfrac{\text{Fixed costs}}{\text{Contribution/unit}} \times \text{Sales Price/unit}$

     or Fixed Costs $\times \dfrac{1}{\text{C/S ratio}}$

(c)   C/S ratio $= \dfrac{\text{Contribution unit}}{\text{Sales Price per unit}} \times 100$

(d)   Level of sales to result in target profit (in units) $= \dfrac{\text{Fixed Cost} + \text{Target Profit}}{\text{Contribution/unit}}$

(e)   Level of sales to result in target profit after tax (units) $= \dfrac{\text{Fixed Cost} + \left(\dfrac{\text{Target Profit}}{1 - \text{Tax Rate}} \right)}{\text{Contribution/unit}}$

(f)   Level of sales to result in Target profit (£ sales) $= \dfrac{(\text{Fixed Cost} + \text{Target Profit}) \times \text{Sales price/unit}}{\text{Contribution/unit}}$

Note: The above formulae relate to a single product firm or one with an unvarying mix of sales. With a multi product firm it is possible to calculate the break even point as follows:

Break-even point (£ sales) $= \dfrac{\text{Fixed Costs} \times \text{Sales Value}}{\text{Contribution}}$

Example 6

A company makes a single product with a sales price of £10 and a marginal cost of £6. Fixed costs are £60,000 p.a.

Calculate

    (a) Number of units to break even
    (b) Sales at break-even point
    (c) C/S ratio
    (d) What number of units will need to be sold to achieve a profit of £20,000 p.a.?
    (e) As (d) with a 40% tax rate.
    (f) What level of sales will achieve a profit of £20,000 p.a.?

(g) Because of increasing costs the marginal cost is expected to rise to £6.50 per unit and fixed costs to £70,000 p.a. If the selling price cannot be increased what will be the number of units required to maintain a profit of £20,000 p.a.?

Solution:

Contribution	=	Selling price - marginal cost	
	=	£10 - 6	
	=	£4	

(a) Break-even point (units)
$$= \frac{£60,000}{4}$$
$$= 15,000$$

(b) Break-even point (£ sales)
$$= 15,000 \times £10$$
$$= £150,000$$

(c) C/S Ratio
$$= \frac{£4}{10} \times 100$$
$$= 40\%$$

(d) Number of units for target profit
$$= \frac{£60,000 + 20,000}{£4}$$
$$= 20,000$$

(e) Number of units for target profit with 40% tax
$$= \frac{£60,000 + \left(\frac{20,000}{1 - 0.4} \right)}{£4}$$
$$= 23,333$$

(f) Sales for target profit
$$= 20,000 \times £10$$
$$= £200,000$$

(Alternatively, this figure can be deduced by the following reasoning. After break-even point the **contribution** per unit becomes **net profit** per unit, so that as 15,000 units were required at break-even point, 5000 extra units would be required to make £20,000 profit.

∴ total units = 15,000 + 5,000 = 20,000 x £10 = £200,000)

(g) Note that the fixed costs, marginal cost and contribution have changed

No. of units for target profit
$$= \frac{£70,000 + 20,000}{£3.50}$$
$$= 25,714 \text{ units}$$

Note: The C/S ratio is sometimes known as the P/V ratio.

GRAPHICAL APPROACH

15. This may be preferred

(a) Where a simple overview is sufficient.

(b) Where there is a need to avoid a detailed, numerical approach when, for example, the recipients of the information have no accounting background.

The basic chart is known as a Break Even chart which can be drawn in two ways. The first is known as the traditional approach and the second as the contribution approach. Whatever approach is adopted, all costs must be capable of separation into fixed and variable elements, ie semi-fixed or semi-variable costs must be analysed into their components.

THE TRADITIONAL BREAK-EVEN CHART

16. Assuming that fixed and variable costs have been resolved, the chart is drawn in the following way:

(a) Draw the axes
-   Horizontal: showing levels of activity expresses as units of output or as percentages of total capacity.
-   Vertical: showing values in £'s or £000s as appropriate for cost and revenues.

(b) Draw the cost lines
-   Fixed cost. This will be a straight line parallel to the horizontal axis at the level of the fixed costs.
-   Total cost. This will start where the fixed cost line intersects the vertical axis and will be a straight line sloping upward at an angle depending on the proportion of variable cost in total costs.

(c) Draw the revenue line
This will be a straight line from the point of origin sloping upwards at an angle determined by the selling price.

Example 7

A company makes a single product with a total capacity of 400,000 litres p.a. Cost and sales data are as follows:

Selling price	£1 per litre
Marginal cost	£0.50 per litre
Fixed costs	£100,000

Draw a traditional break-even chart showing the likely profit at the expected production level of 300,000 litres.

From Figure 3 it will be seen that break-even point is at an output level of 200,000 litres and that the width of the profit wedge indicates the profit at a production level of 300,000. The profit is £50,000.

Notes: The 'margin of safety' indicated on the chart is the term given to the difference between the activity level selected and break-even point. In this case the margin of safety is 100,000 litres.

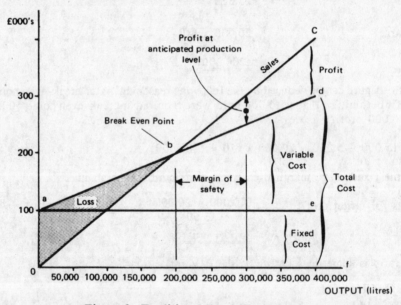

Figure 3   Traditional Break Even Chart

THE CONTRIBUTION BREAK-EVEN CHART

17. This uses the same axes and data as the traditional chart. The only difference being that variable costs are drawn on the chart before fixed costs resulting in the contribution being shown as a wedge.

Example 8

Repeat Example 7 except that a contribution break-even chart should be drawn

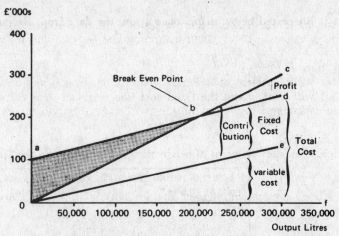

Figure 4   Contribution Break Even Chart

Notes:

(a)   The area c.o.e. represents the contribution earned. There is no direct equivalent on the traditional chart.

(b)   The area of d.a.o.f. represents total cost and is the same as the traditional chart.

(c)   It will be seen from the chart that the reversal of fixed costs and variable costs enables the contribution wedge to be drawn thus providing additional information.

An alternative form of the contribution break-even chart is where the net difference between sales and variable cost, ie total contribution, is plotted against fixed costs. This is shown below once again using the same data from Example 7

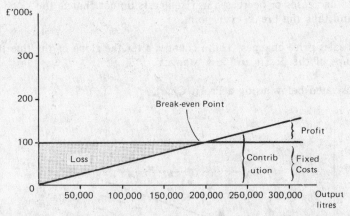

Figure 5   Alternative Form of Contribution Break Even Chart

Notes:

(a)   Sales and variable costs are not shown directly.

(b)   Both forms of contribution chart. Figures 4 and 5, show clearly that contribution is first used to meet fixed costs and when these costs are met, the contribution becomes profit.

PROFIT CHART

18. This is another form of presentation with the emphasis on the effect on profit of varying levels of activity. It is a simpler form of chart to those illustrated so far because only a contribution line is drawn.

The horizontal axis is identical to the previous charts, but the vertical axis is continued below the point of origin to show losses. A contribution line is drawn from the loss at zero activity, which is equivalent to the fixed costs, through the break-even point.

The contribution line is drawn by plotting the amount of contribution at various sales levels which is readily calculated using the CS ratio; 50% in Example 7. By commencing the line at the amount of the fixed costs, 'loss' and 'profit' wedges are shown which are identical to those in the earlier charts.

This type of chart is illustrated below using, once again, the data from Example 7.

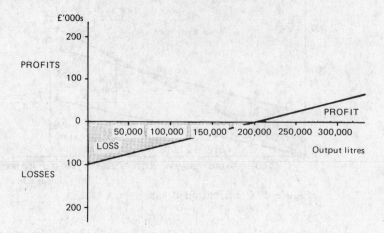

Figure 6   Profit Chart

Note: Lines for variable and fixed costs and sales do not appear, merely the one summary profit line.

CHANGES IN COSTS AND REVENUES

19.   Several of the main types of chart have been described and it should be apparent that they are all able to show cost/revenue/volume/profit relationships in a simple, effective form. It is also possible to show the effect of changes in costs and revenues by drawing additional lines on the charts. The changes are of two types:

(a)   Fixed cost changes. Increases or decreases in fixed costs do not change the slope of the line, but alter the point of intersection and thus the break-even point.

(b)   Variable cost and sales price changes. These changes alter the slope of the line thus affecting the break-even point and the shape of the profit and loss 'wedges'.

These changes are illustrated below using a Profit Chart.

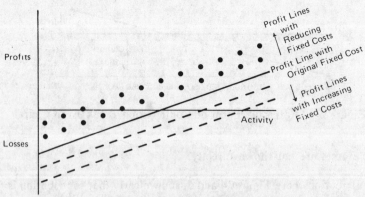

Figure 7   Profit Chart Showing Changes in Fixed Costs

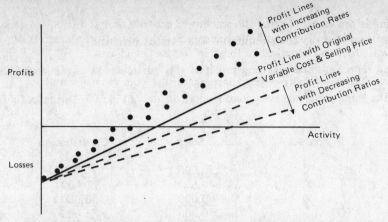

Figure 8   Profit Chart Showing Changes in Contribution Ratio

Note: The above chart shows the effect of variable cost and/or sales price changes which have a net effect on contribution. If, say, an increase in variable costs was exactly counterbalanced by an increase in sales price, the contribution would be the same and the original profit line would still be correct.

A MULTI-PRODUCT CHART

20.   All of the charts illustrated so far have assumed a single product. Equally they could have illustrated a given sales mix resulting in an average contribution rate equivalent to a single product. An alternative method is to plot the individual products each with their individual C/S characteristics and then show the resulting overall profit line. This is shown below:

Example 9

A firm has fixed costs of £50,000 p.a. and has three products, the sales and contribution of which are shown below.

Product	Sales £	Contribution £	C/S ratio
X	150,000	30,000	20%
Y	40,000	20,000	50%
Z	60,000	25,000	42%

Plot the products on a profit chart and show the break-even sales.

Solution

The axes on the profit chart are drawn in the usual way and the contribution from the products, in the sequence of their C/S ratio, ie Y, Z, X, drawn on the chart.

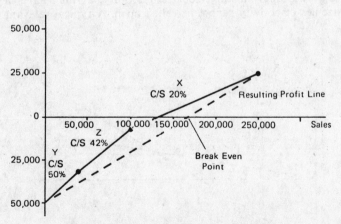

Figure 9   Multi-Product Profit Chart

Notes:

(a) The solid lines represent the contributions of the various products.

(b) The dotted line represents the resulting profit of this particular sales mix and C/S ratios.

(c) Reading from the graph the break-even point is approximately £170,000. The exact figure can be calculated as follows:

Product	Sales £	Contribution £
X	150,000	30,000
Y	40,000	20,000
Z	60,000	25,000
TOTALS	250,000	75,000

$$\text{Overall C/S ratio} \quad = \quad \frac{£75,000}{£250,000} = 30\%$$

$$\therefore \text{Break-even point} \quad = \quad \frac{\text{Fixed Costs}}{\text{C/S Ratio}}$$

$$= \quad \frac{£50,000}{.3}$$

$$= \quad £166,667$$

The above result could also be found using the formula for a multi product firm given earlier in the Chapter thus:

$$\text{Breakeven point for Multi product firm} \quad = \quad \frac{\text{Fixed Costs x Sales Value}}{\text{Contribution}}$$

$$= \quad \frac{£50,000 \text{ x } 250,000}{75,000}$$

$$= \quad £166,667$$

LIMITATIONS OF BREAK-EVEN AND PROFIT CHARTS

21. The various charts depicted show cost, volume and profit relationships in a simplified and approximate manner. They can be useful aids, but whenever they are used the following limitations should not be forgotten.

(a) The charts are reasonable pointers to performance within normal activity ranges, say 70% – 120% of average production. Outside this relevant range the relationship depicted almost certainly will not be correct. Although it is conventional to draw the lines starting from zero activity, as they have been drawn in this chapter, relationships at the extremes of activity cannot be relied upon. A typical relevant range of activity could be shown as follows.

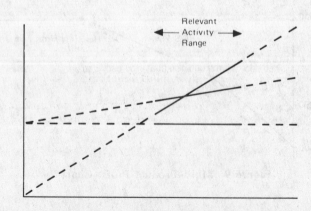

Figure 10   Break-Even Chart Showing Relevant Activity Range

(b)   Fixed costs are likely to change at different activity levels. A stepped fixed cost line is probably the most accurate representation.

(c)   Variable costs and sales are unlikely to be linear. Extra discounts, overtime payments, the effect of the learning curve, special price contracts and other similar matters make it likely that the variable cost and revenue lines are some form of curve rather than a straight line.

(d)   The charts depict relationships which are essentially short term. This makes them inappropriate where the time scale spans several years.

(e)   C-V-P analysis, like marginal costing, makes the assumption that changes in the level of output are the sole determinant of cost and revenue changes. This is likely to be a gross over-simplification in practice although volume changes, of course, do have a significant effect on costs and revenues.

(f)   It is assumed that either, there is a single product or a constant mix of products or a constant rate of mark-up on marginal cost.

(g)   Risk and uncertainty are ignored and perfect knowledge of cost and revenue functions is assumed.

(h)   It is assumed that the firm is a price taker, ie a perfect market is deemed to exist.

(i)   It is assumed that revenues and all forms of variable cost (materials, labour and all the components of variable overheads) vary in accordance with the same activity indicator. This is an over-simplification in most realistic situations.

ALTERNATIVE FORMS OF BREAK-EVEN CHARTS

22.   So far the charts depicted have had conventional linear cost and revenue functions but as pointed out in the previous paragraph, these are not always realistic. There is no reason why the charts should not be drawn using other, perhaps more appropriate representations of costs and revenues, eg stepped costs and revenues, curvi-linear functions, linear functions with variable slopes and so on. The permutations and possibilities are endless and a few of the possibilities are shown below.

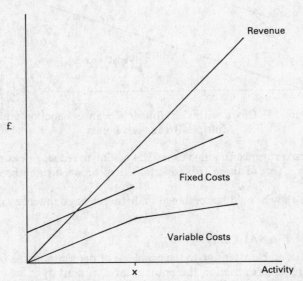

Figure 11   Chart with Stepped Linear Cost Function

Figure 11 shows a stepped increase in fixed costs at activity x and a reduction in the variable cost slope from that point. A possible cause might be the introduction of equipment which increases fixed charges but reduces labour costs.

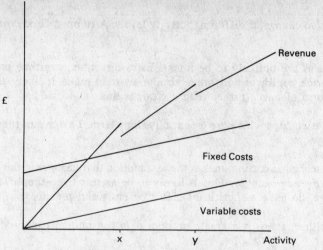

Figure 12   Chart with Stepped Linear Revenue Function

Figure 12 shows a stepped revenue function with break points at x and y and reductions in the slope at these two points. A possible explanation is that the points x and y represent discount break points and that to increase sales it is necessary to reduce unit selling prices as well as have discounts.

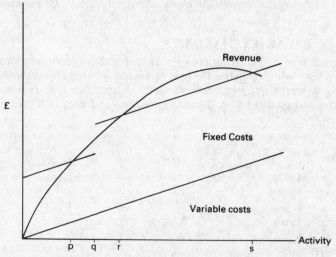

Figure 13   Chart with Curvilinear Revenue Function and
Multiple Breakeven Points

Figure 13 shows a curvi-linear revenue function caused by having to reduce prices to increase sales and a stepped cost function at activity q. The effect of these two functions is to produce three break-even points at p, r and s.

The various characteristics shown could be combined in different ways and many other representations could be drawn.

ECONOMIST'S VIEW OF C-V-P ANALYSIS

23.   Economists have given considerable attention to the problems of determining the optimal level of activity of the firm. Given the objective of profit maximisation the optimal level of activity is when marginal cost (MC) equals marginal revenue (MR).

A typical representation of short run economic relationships under conditions of imperfect competition is shown in Figures 14 and 15.

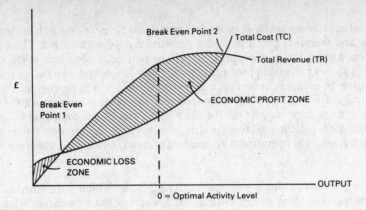

Figure 14

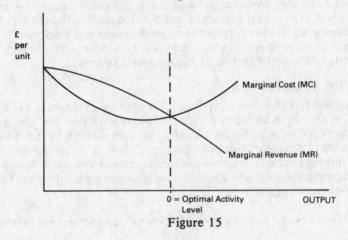

Figure 15

The following characteristics should be noted regarding the economist's approach compared with that of the accountant.

(a) The economic model, like the accountant's model assumes that volume is the sole determinant of cost and revenue changes.

(b) Economic theory treats the total cost function as curvi-linear as opposed to the simpler accounting assumption of linearity. The economic model reflects decreasing marginal cost at lower output levels and increasing marginal cost at higher levels. Although there are conflicts between the assumptions contained in both models regarding input prices and production efficiencies, probably the major reason for the differences between the cost functions is the range of activity levels encompassed by the models. The economic model covers a range of outputs sufficient to cause significant changes in efficiency whereas the simpler cost-volume relationships assumed in the accounting model would only be valid over a smaller activity range.

(c) The economic model is based on opportunity costs which include a normal rate of profit. A normal rate of profit is considered by economists to be a cost that has to be met if the firm is to stay in business. Profit is a reward to one of the factors of production (eg the entrepreneurial input supplied by shareholders) for risk-taking and for enterprise. This means that Break-Even point No 1 in Figure 14 is NOT equivalent to the break-even point shown in a typical accounting break-even chart such as Figure 3. The accounting break-even point would be to the left of the economist's break-even point No 1 because it does not include any profit element being merely the balancing of accounting costs and revenues. The accounting break-even chart should be based, like all information for decision making purposes, on expected future costs and revenues not on historical costs.

(d) The point o in Figures 14 and 15 indicates the optimal level of activity where profit is at a maximum. The 'envelope' between the two break-even points, in Figure 14 represents the 'super-profit' potential which, according to conventional economic theory, could only be achieved over a short period in a competitive market. In the long run it would be expected that firms would earn the normal level of profits included at the first break-even point assuming free entry to the market. The typical accounting break-even chart has a single break-even point and, because of the linearity assumptions, predicts - unrealistically - that profits can continually be increased by expanding output. Without further analysis, the traditional accounting break-even approach cannot be used to establish the optimum output level.

(e)   The conventional accounting break-even model has a linear revenue function with a constant price per unit at all production levels and therefore profit increases proportionately with output. The assumption is that the firm operates under perfect competition and is a price taker. The particular economic model depicted assumes a curvi-linear function which shows increasing profits at low activity levels and decreasing profits at higher levels. The model shown in Figure 14 assumes imperfect market conditions where pricing and output decisions are interdependent. The validity of either model depends upon the type of market in which the firm operates although in practice the position is more complicated than the simplistic assumptions contained in both of the models. Product differentiation, promotion policies, tactical pricing, changes in the marketing mix, foreign competition at subsidised prices and other such operating disturbances all tend to cloud the clear cut relationships embodied in both models.

(f)   The economist's approach produces a general analytical model which is designed to produce predictions about the behaviour of market variables (price, output, etc.) whereas the accountant's model has the more limited objective of attempting to provide practical assistance for decision making within a given firm. Both models suffer from the disadvantage that they are based on single cost and revenue values for every output level and thus ignore the uncertainties which exist in every planning and decision making situation. Provided that the relevant activity range is being considered and the cost and revenue functions are valid then both models are likely to give similar solutions to a given problem although care will be needed in the interpretation because of the inclusion of normal profits in the cost function of the economic model.

OPTIMISING THE LEVEL OF ACTIVITY

24.   Where the cost and/or revenue functions are curvi-linear, for example as shown in Figure 14, then it is possible to determine the optimal level of activity in accordance with the objectives of the firm. This can be done in two ways, either by drawing graphs of the functions as in Figure 14 and 15 or more directly by the use of differential calculus. It will be recalled that the process of differentiation provides a ready means of finding the rates of change of curvi-linear functions and of their turning points. If the curvi-linear functions represent cost and revenue then the rates of change are marginal cost and marginal revenue respectively and the turning points of the functions are the point of minimum cost and maximum revenue respectively.

The following example illustrates the use of differentiation to find the optimal level of activity.

Example 10

A firm has the following cost and revenue functions:

Variable cost function c	=	£($\frac{1}{2}q^2 + 10q$)
Demand function p	=	£($150 - \frac{3}{4}q$)
where p	=	price in £'s
c	=	variable cost in £'s
q	=	number of units sold per period

The fixed costs are £1,000 per period

It is required to determine:

(a)   The price, quantity and resulting profit if the firm's objective is to maximise sales revenue.

(b)   The price, quantity and resulting profit if the firm's objective is to maximise profit.

Solution

(a)

$$\text{Let } R = \text{revenue}$$

$$\text{then } R = pq = (150 - \tfrac{3}{4}q)q$$
$$= 150q - \tfrac{3}{4}q^2$$

for maximum revenue

$$\frac{dR}{dq} = 0 \text{(with a negative second derivative)}$$

$$\therefore 150 - 1\tfrac{1}{2}q = 0 \left(\text{with } \frac{d^2R}{dq^2} = -1\tfrac{1}{2} \right)$$

$$\therefore q = 100 \text{ at maximum revenue point}$$

$$\therefore p = £(150 - \tfrac{3}{4}q) = £(150 - \tfrac{3}{4}(100)) = £75$$

$$\therefore R = pq = £(75 \times 100) = \underline{£7500}$$

Profit at maximum revenue point is,

$$
\begin{array}{lr}
 & \pounds \\
\text{Revenue} & 7{,}500 \\
less \quad \text{Costs} = \pounds(\tfrac{1}{2}(100)^2 + 10(100) + 1000) & \underline{7{,}000} \\
\therefore \text{ Profit per period} = & \underline{\underline{\pounds 500}}
\end{array}
$$

(b) For maximum profit, marginal revenue should equal marginal cost, ie

$$\frac{dR}{dq} = \frac{dC}{dq}$$

$$dR = 150 - 1\tfrac{1}{2} \text{ and } \frac{dC}{dq} = q + 10$$

$$\therefore 150 - 1\tfrac{1}{2} = q + 10$$

$$\therefore q = \underline{56} \text{ at maximum profit point}$$

The resulting price per unit is

$$
\begin{array}{rl}
p & = \pounds(150 - \tfrac{3}{4}q) \\
 & = \underline{\pounds 108}
\end{array}
$$

Profit at maximum profit point is

$$
\begin{array}{lr}
 & \pounds \\
\text{Revenue} = \pounds(56 \times 108) & 6{,}048 \\
less \text{ costs} = \pounds(\tfrac{1}{2}(56)^2 + 10(56) + 1{,}000) & \underline{3{,}128} \\
\therefore \text{ Profit per period} & \underline{\underline{\pounds 2{,}920}}
\end{array}
$$

Note: If the processes of differentiation are unfamiliar to you or you wish to revise the principles you are advised to refer to a suitable text book covering this topic, eg Quantitative Techniques, T. LUCEY, DP Publications.

SUMMARY

25. (a) The principles of marginal costing (the separation of fixed and variable costs and the calculation of contribution) have many uses in management accounting including short run decision making.

(b) To the accountant marginal cost is average variable cost which is generally assumed to behave linearly whilst to the economist it is the cost incurred by the production of one extra unit.

(c) The key factor is a binding constraint upon the organisation. Where a single binding constraint can be identified then maximising contribution per unit of the limiting factor will produce the maximum contribution. LP is necessary to deal with more than one constraint.

(d) Marginal costing principles can be used for numerous types of short run decisions, eg special order acceptance, make or buy, expansions or contraction of activity and other similar problems.

(e) Care must be taken in identifying the relevant costs and revenues that an applicable opportunity cost is not overlooked.

(f) Cost-volume-profit (CVP) analysis is an application of marginal costing principles and seeks to estimate the profit or loss at differing activity levels. Basic CVP analysis has many simplifying assumptions and any results must be viewed with caution.

(g) CVP analysis can be dealt with by the use of formulae or by using charts which are generally termed break-even charts.

(h) Break-even charts can be drawn in a variety of ways and probably the most informative way is known as the contribution break-even chart where variable costs are drawn first and the contribution 'wedge' is produced.

(i) Profit charts are simpler representations whereby a single line representing profit is drawn commencing at the loss value equivalent to fixed costs. Multi-product charts can also be drawn based on their C/S ratios.

(j)   Traditionally drawn break-even charts have many limitations including: linearity assumptions, based on single products or constant product mixes, risk and uncertainty are ignored.

(k)   The economist's view of C-V-P analysis is based on curvi-linear functions. One of the other major differences in approach is the inclusion of a normal rate of profit in economic costs.

(l)   The inclusion of curvi-linear functions enables the optimal level of activity to be determined either graphically or by means of differential calculus.

(m) Given the assumptions contained in the economic model the price, quantity and profit can be established whether the firm's objective is sales or profit maximisation.

POINTS TO NOTE

26. (a)   Marginal costing and C-V-P analysis can be useful guides in short term decision making but they are based on a number of restrictive assumptions. These must be thoroughly understood so that the techniques are not used in circumstances where they could give misleading information.

(b)   Finding the optimal price, quantity and profit values as illustrated for the economist's approach to C-V-P analysis has a satisfying air of completeness but it must be remembered that the information upon which the analysis is based is rarely, if ever, fully available. This applies particularly to the revenue functions.

(c)   Providing that linearity of all factors can be assumed then Linear Programming (LP) provides a powerful extension to basic CVP analysis. LP is able to deal with many more factors, numerous binding constraints and, because most computers have LP packages, the effects of uncertainty can readily be incorporated into the analysis.

ADDITIONAL READING

Management Accounting: A decision emphasis	De Coster and Schafer, WILEY
Statistical Cost Accounting	Johnston, MCGRAW HILL
Quantitative Techniques	Lucey, DP PUBLICATIONS
Analysing Business Strategy: The use of CVP analysis	Quereshi, CIMA
Marginal Costing	Rickwood and Piper, CIMA
Information for Decision Making	Solomons, PRENTICE HALL

SELF REVIEW QUESTIONS

1.   Why is the marginal costing approach suitable for analysing short run decisions? (3)

2.   What are the differences between the accountant's and economist's views of marginal cost? (4)

3.   What is the limiting factor and what is the basic decision rule where a limiting factor exists? (5)

4.   What are the general steps involved in analysing a decision when marginal costing is to be used? (6)

5.   When should costs **and** opportunity costs be considered? (10)

6.   What is differential costing? (11)

7.   What are the assumptions behind C-V-P analysis? (13)

8.   What are the formulae for: break-even point (units); break-even point (sales); level of sales to achieve a target profit? (14)

9.   Draw a traditional break-even chart. (16)

10. How does the contribution break-even chart differ from the traditional one? (17)

11. What is a profit chart? (18)

12. What would be the effect on a chart of altering fixed costs? Variable costs? (19)

13. *How is a multi-product profit chart drawn? (20)*

14. *What are the limitations of break-even and profit charts? (21)*

15. *What alternative representations could be included in such charts? (22)*

16. *What are the major differences between the accountant's and economist's views of C-V-P analysis? (23)*

17. *Using differential calculus what are the main steps in establishing the price, quantity and profit if the firm's objective is to maximise profit? (24)*

EXAMINATION QUESTIONS WITH ANSWERS COMMENCING PAGE 353

A1. *The accountant's approach to Cost-Volume-Profit Analysis has been criticised in that, among other matters, it does not deal with the following:*

  (a) *situations where sales volume differs radically from production volume;*
  (b) *situations where the sales revenue and the total cost functions are markedly non linear;*
  (c) *changes in product mix;*
  (d) *risk and uncertainty.*

  Explain these objections to the accountant's conventional cost-volume-profit model and suggest how they can be overcome or ameriorated.

ACCA, Management Accounting.

A2. *The Central Co Ltd has developed a new product and is currently considering the marketing and pricing policy it should employ for this. Specifically it is considering whether the sales price should be set at £15 per unit or at the higher level of £24 per unit. Sales volume at these two prices are shown in the following table:*

Sales price £15 per unit		Sales price £24 per unit	
Forecast sales volume (000's)	Probability	Forecast sales volume (000's)	Probability
20	0.1	8	0.1
30	0.6	16	0.3
40	0.3	20	0.3
		24	0.3

The fixed production costs of the venture will be £38,000.

The level of the advertising and publicity costs will depend on the sales price and the market aimed for. Within a sales price of £15 per unit the advertising and publicity costs will amount to £12,000. With a sales price of £24 per unit these costs will total £122,000.

*Labour and variable overhead costs will amount to £5 per unit produced. Each unit produced requires 2 Kg of raw material and the basic cost is expected to be £4 per Kg. However the suppliers of the raw material are prepared to lower the price in return for a firm agreement to purchase a guaranteed minimum quantity. If Central Ltd contracts to purchase at least 40,000 Kg then the price will be reduced to £3.75 per Kg for **all** purchases. If Central contracts to purchase a minimum of 60,000 Kg then the price will be reduced to £3.50 per Kg for **all** purchases. It is only if Central Ltd guarantees either of the above minimum levels of purchases in advance that the appropriate reduced prices will be operative.*

If Central Ltd were to enter into one of the agreements for the supply of raw material and was to find that it did not require to utilise the entire quantity of materials purchased then the excess could be sold. The sales price will depend upon the quantity which is offered for sale. If 16,000 Kg or more are sold then the sales price will be £2.90 per Kg for all sales. If less than 16,000 Kg are offered the sales price will be only £2.40 per Kg.

Irrespective of amount sold the costs incurred in selling the excess raw materials will be, per Kg, as follows:

Packaging	£0.30
Delivery	£0.45
Insurance	£0.15

Central's management team feels that losses are undesirable while high expected money values are desirable. Therefore it is considering the utilisation of a formula which incorporates both aspects of the outcome to measure the desirability of each strategy. The formula to be used to measure the desirability is:

$$\text{'Desirability'} = L + 3E$$

where   L   =   *Lowest outcome of the strategy*
         E   =   *Expected monetary value of the strategy.*

The higher this measure the more desirable the strategy.

The marketing manager seeks the advice of you, the management accountant, to assist in deciding the appropriate strategy. He says 'We need to make two decisions now –

(i)   which price per unit should be charged; is it £15 or £24 per unit?; and

(ii)   should all purchases of raw materials be at the price of £4 per Kg or should we enter into an agreement for a basic minimum quantity? If we enter into an agreement, then was minimum level of purchases should we guarantee?

As you are the management accountant I expect you to provide me with some useful relevant figures.'

Required:

(a) Provide statements which show the various expected outcomes of each of the choices open to Central Co Ltd.

(b) Advise on its best choice of strategies if Central Ltd's objective is:

(i)   to maximise the expected monetary value of the outcomes;
(ii)   to minimise the harm done to the firm if the worst outcome of each choice were to eventuate;
(iii)   to maximise the score on the above mentioned measure of 'Desirability'.

(c) Briefly comment on either

(i)   two other factors which may be relevant in reaching a decision;
OR
(ii)   the decision criteria utilised in (b) above.

ACCA, Management Accounting.

A3. 'A breakeven chart must be interpreted in the light of the limitations of its underlying assumptions .....' (from Cost Accounting: a managerial emphasis by C.T. Horngren.)

Required:

(a) Discuss the extent to which the above statement is valid and both describe and briefly appraise the reasons for FIVE of the most important underlying assumptions of break even analysis.

(b) For any THREE of the underlying assumptions provided in answer (a) above, give an example of circumstances in which that assumption is violated. Indicate the nature of the violation and the extent to which the breakeven chart can be adapted to allow for this violation.

ACCA, Management Accounting.

A4. *(a) The accountant of Laburnum Ltd is preparing documents for a forthcoming meeting of the budget committee. Currently, variable cost is 40% of selling price and total fixed costs are £40,000 per year.*

The company uses an historical cost accounting system. There is concern that the level of costs may rise during the ensuing year and the chairman of the budget committee has expressed interest in a probabilistic approach to an investigation of the effect that this will have on historic cost profits. The accountant is attempting to prepare the documents in a way which will be most helpful to the committee members. He has obtained the following estimates from his colleagues:

	Average Inflation Rate over ensuing year	Probability
Pessimistic	10%	0.4
Most likely	5%	0.5
Optimistic	1%	0.1
		1.0

	Demand at Current Selling Prices	
Pessimistic	£50,000	0.3
Most Likely	£75,000	0.6
Optimistic	£100,000	0.1
		1.0

The demand figures are given in terms of sales value at the current level of selling prices but it is considered that the company could adjust its selling prices in line with the inflation rate without affecting customer demand in real terms.

Some of the company's fixed costs are contractually fixed and some are apportionments of past costs; of the total fixed costs, an estimated 85% will remain constant irrespective of the inflation rate.

You are required to analyse the foregoing information in a way which you consider will assist management with its budgeting problem. Although you should assume that the directors of Laburnum ltd are solely interested in the effect of inflation on historic cost profits, you should comment on the validity of the accountant's intended approach. As part of your analysis you are required to calculate:

(i) The probability of at least breaking even, and
(ii) the probability of achieving a profit of at least £20,000.

(b) It can be argued that the use of point estimate probabilities (as above) is too unrealistic because it constrains the demand and cost variables to relatively few values. Briefly describe an alternative simulation approach which might meet this objection.

ACCA, Management Accounting.

A5. (a) 'Cost-volume-profit analysis should not be restricted by the limitations of break-even analysis and the break-even chart.' Comment on this quotation.

Outline the limitations of the conventional break-even chart and **give your views** on whether cost-volume-profit analysis can provide an improved approach.

(b) **Give your views** on the statement that 'The fixed overhead volume (denominator) variance is a measure of the utilisation of capacity'.

ACCA, Management Accounting.

14. Pricing Decisions

INTRODUCTION

1.   This chapter deals with one particular type of decision, that of pricing the firm's products. Not all firms are able, or wish, to pursue an independent pricing policy but for those that have to make these types of decision the chapter provides an introduction to the factors which need to be considered.

The theoretical economic background to pricing, known as marginal analysis, is reviewed together with the concept of demand elasticity. Formula pricing methods based on cost plus systems are described and their limitations discussed. The contribution approach or marginal cost pricing method of setting short run prices is explained and the chapter concludes with a brief discussion of non-price methods of influencing demand such as advertising and sales promotion.

INTERNAL AND EXTERNAL PRICING

2.   A firm may be concerned with two types of pricing decisions. Those for sales external to the firm, ie to its customers and those relating to prices used for internal transfers between parts of the same organisation. This latter process is known as **transfer pricing** and is dealt with in this manual in the section on Performance Appraisal.

Pricing decision for external sales are dealt with in the rest of this chapter.

THE PRICING PROBLEM

3.   The pricing problem is a complex one with numerous, interacting factors and no simplistic solution. Typical of the factors which may need to be considered - explicitly or implicitly - in a pricing decision are the following:

The firm's objective(s).
Is the firm a profit or revenue maximiser or is it pursuing satisficing objectives?

The market in which the firm operates.
Perfect or imperfect competition or oligopolistic or monopolistic conditions?

The demand for the firm's product.
Are the quantities known which are expected to be sold at various prices?

The elasticity of demand for the product.
Is the demand elastic or inelastic?

The cost structure of the firm and the product.
What are the expected future marginal costs, fixed costs?

The competition.
What is the extent and nature of the competition?

The product.
What is the stage in the product life cycle?

The relative position of the firm.
Is the firm dominant enough to be a price maker or is it a price taker?

Level of activity.
Will the firm be working at full or below capacity? What is the position of competitors?

Government restrictions or legislation.
Are there regulations or laws governing prices?

Inflation
Is inflation rising, falling, high, low?

The availability of substitutes.
Is the product clearly differentiated or are there close substitutes?

Naturally not all these points are explicitly considered in every pricing decision and it is quite possible for some factor not included above to be significant for a particular situation.

THEORETICAL BACKGROUND TO PRICING

4.   Micro-economics has provided much of the theoretical background to pricing and, whilst there are difficulties in applying the basic theory in practice, it serves as a useful starting point.

The theory states that firms should seek the price which maximises profit and will thereby obtain the most efficient use of the economic resources held by the firm. This price is at that level of sales where the addition to total revenue from the sale of the last unit (the marginal revenue, MR) is equal to the addition to total costs resulting from the production of that last unit (the marginal cost, MC).

This is illustrated below in relation to one particular type of market; that where there is monopolistic or imperfect competition and differentiated products thus enabling the firm to pursue an independent pricing policy.

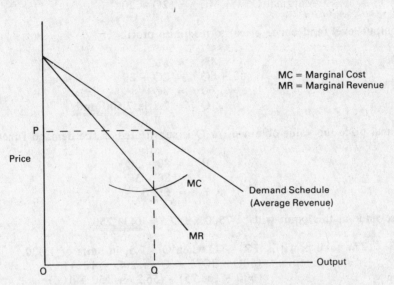

Figure 1   Optimum Pricing in Imperfect Competition

At price P, output is the level of Q and profit is at a maximum. The optimal price P represents the price ceiling in any situation. The **price floor** could theoretically be zero if the goods are already produced, or if it is still to be produced and there is spare capacity, the price floor could be marginal cost. If there are scarce resources then the price floor will include the opportunity cost of the scarce resources.

It follows from Figure 1 that the firm operating in imperfect competition can determine either price or output but not both. This also applies to the monopolist. A firm operating under conditions of perfect competition, where the price is determined by the market, can only determine its output. In an oligopolistic market (where there are few sellers) firms recognise their interdependence and are influenced by each other's decisions, particularly regarding prices. All the oligopolists will tend to charge similar prices even if there is no overt collusion and in such market structures there is likely to be a price leader who will provide the bench mark for the prices of the whole industry. In such market conditions there is likely to be considerable non-price competition, eg advertising, hidden discounts, extended credit and similar activities.

ESTABLISHING THE THEORETICAL OPTIMAL PRICE

5.   Assuming that the required information on demand and cost functions is available the optimal price can be determined easily by the use of differential calculus.

For example, assume that a firm has the following demand and cost functions:

Demand function
P = 80 – 3Q, where P is the unit selling price and Q is quantity in thousands.

Cost function
$TC = Q^2 + 20Q + 100$, where TC is total cost in £'000s.

What is the optimal price to maximise profits? What is the maximum profit and what is the sales revenue at that point?

Solution

$$\begin{aligned}
\text{If demand function} &= P = 80 - 3Q \\
\text{then Total Revenue} = TR &= Q(80 - 3Q) \\
&= 80Q - 3Q^2
\end{aligned}$$

and Marginal Revenue is obtained by using differential calculus thus

$$\text{Marginal Revenue} = MR = \frac{dR}{dQ} = 80 - 6Q$$

$$\begin{aligned}
\text{The total cost function} = TC &= Q^2 + 20Q + 100 \\
\therefore \text{Marginal Cost} = MC &= 2Q + 20
\end{aligned}$$

$\therefore$ To find the output level (and hence price) to maximise profits

$$\begin{aligned}
MR &= MC \\
80 - 6Q &= 2Q + 20 \\
60 &= 8Q \\
\therefore Q &= 7.5 \text{ ie } \underline{\textbf{7,500 units}}
\end{aligned}$$

To find the optimal price the value obtained for Q is substituted in the demand functions,

$$\begin{aligned}
P &= 80 - 3Q \\
&= 80 - 3(7.5) \\
\therefore P &= \underline{\textbf{£57.5}}
\end{aligned}$$

The total sales revenue at this point will be 7500 x £57.5 = $\underline{\textbf{£431,250}}$

The total profit is TR - TC when Q = 7.5, in units of 1,000.

$$\begin{aligned}
\therefore \quad &(80Q - 3Q^2) - (Q^2 + 20Q + 100) \\
&(600 - 168.75) - (56.25 + 150 + 100)
\end{aligned}$$

Maximum Profit = 125, which converted into '000s = $\underline{\textbf{£125,000.}}$

PRICE ELASTICITY OF DEMAND

6.   An important consideration for a supplier is the reaction of consumers to alterations in price. The concept of price elasticity of demand has been developed to provide a measure of the degree to which demand responds to a change in price.

The basic formula is

$$\text{Price Elasticity of Demand} = \frac{\text{\% Change in quantity demanded}}{\text{\% Change in price}}$$

Note: It is important to remember that it is the **percentage changes** in quantity and price that are used and **not absolute changes**. Price elasticity is normally negative but by convention the minus sign is omitted.

The measurement of elasticity can range from zero to infinity; from perfect inelasticity to perfect elasticity but naturally the extremes of values have only theoretical interest. Three important ranges of values are discussed below.

Elasticity of demand greater than 0 but less than 1
A commodity with this value is said to have an INELASTIC demand. This means that a fall in price results in a less than proportionate extension of demand and thus total revenue falls.

Elasticity of demand = 1
Such a value is known as UNIT elasticity which means that a percentage fall in price is exactly matched by a percentage extension of demand so total revenue remains constant.

Elasticity of demand greater than 1 but less than infinity
In these circumstances the demand is said to be ELASTIC. The demand changes by a greater proportion than the change in price and accordingly the total revenue rises when price falls. The greater the elasticity the greater the effect on revenue from a reduction in price.

Although the concept of elasticity of demand is of considerable importance there are obvious practical problems in obtaining meaningful values. Two particular difficulties which arise are the differing reactions to large and to small price movements and to the fact that it is very unlikely for a demand curve to have constant elasticity along its entire length.

Whilst the price elasticity of demand is the most important measure of the sensitivity of demand, two other types of elasticity are associated with changes in the condition of demand, the formulae of which are given below:

$$\text{Cross elasticity of demand} = \frac{\text{\% change in quantity of X demanded}}{\text{\% change in price of Y}}$$

This shows the effect of a change in the price of one good on the demand for another good.

$$\text{Income elasticity of demand} = \frac{\text{\% change in quantity demand}}{\text{\% change in income}}$$

This shows the effect on demand of a change in income.

LIMITATIONS TO THE CLASSICAL THEORY

7.   The classical theoretical approach, often called marginal analysis, has numerous limitations which makes practical application of the pure theory very difficult. The following are some of the main limitations.

(a) Marginal analysis assumes perfect knowledge of all the factors involved. The practical difficulties of finding such information are great particularly relating to knowledge of the demand schedule, ie how much will be sold at any price. Finding the true marginal cost also poses considerable difficulties.

(b) Marginal analysis assumes a single maximising objective with the firm acting with complete economic rationality. Studies of practical situations show that firms do not pursue single objectives and satisficing rather than maximising behaviour appears to be commonly encountered.

(c) Marginal analysis assumes that changes in the volume of sales are solely a function of price changes where as many non-price factors, eg advertising and sales promotion and changes in the conditions of demand such as income changes, produce significant changes in sales volume.

(d) Marginal analysis assumes rational decision guided by purely economic factors. Decision makers in practice are influenced by moral, social, political as well as economic considerations. The behavioural factors which impinge upon decision makers are reflected in such common phrases as 'a fair price' or 'a reasonable rate of return'.

Despite the limitations outlined above, economic analysis makes an important contribution to pricing theory by emphasising the interaction of demand and cost information and directs attention to the importance of marginal changes in costs and revenues. This emphasis has encouraged more flexible pricing policies and has caused traditional accounting 'cost-based' pricing methods to be reassessed and to be used in a more circumspect manner.

PRICING IN PRACTICE

8.   Like many other types of problem the pricing decision suffers from the lack of accurate and relevant information. This is particularly so in relation to demand information and many firms incur considerable costs in an attempt to discover likely demand and how demand will vary with changes in price - its elasticity. Ways in which this is done include: surveys, market research, econometric analysis, test marketing, simulation models, representative's feedback and other such methods.

However difficult the task may be, it is important to try to establish some form of information on demand because it is a crucial element. Pricing is not simply a cost based decision which has been a traditional view and accounts for the frequent use of some form of cost plus system.

Pricing is always an important decision although the frequency of such decisions and the level at which they are taken varies from firm to firm. For example, the price for a car would be a decision taken at Board level in a car manufacturers and, even in inflationary conditions, would only be infrequently altered. On the other hand, in a jobbing engineering company making a variety of items to order, pricing decisions are frequent and likely to be delegated to a relatively low level in the organisation. It is in such organisations that pricing formulae and prescribed mark ups are found. In this way senior management attempt to control pricing policy whilst at the same time avoiding the detailed, day to day work of setting individual prices.

COST PLUS PRICING SYSTEM

9. Empirical studies have shown that firms frequently employ some form of formula based on costs to arrive at a selling price. In general these systems are concerned with two elements - what is the relevant cost to include in the price?, and - what is the 'profit' margin which must be added to the costs to arrive at the selling price?

Two cost plus systems are described below: full-cost pricing and rate of return pricing.

FULL COST PRICING

10. This system, sometimes known as absorption cost pricing, uses conventional cost accounting principles to establish the total cost for a product to which is added a mark up, say 20%, to arrive at a selling price. The total cost includes all the variable costs, the measurement of which should present few problems, plus apportioned fixed costs based on normal volumes and normal production mixes. It is this latter point which causes the major problems. The costs so established will only be appropriate when the actual volume/mix is the same as the estimated volume/mix even assuming there was some non-arbitrary way of assigning fixed costs to products which there is not. Alterations in selling prices affect the volume of sales which in turn affect the unit fixed costs which raises the possibility of further price changes thus causing a circular problem to be ever present when full-cost pricing is employed.

A further problem with this method of pricing, which is common to all cost-plus systems, is the amount of the mark-up.

There are numerous factors which govern the mark-up percentage. For example, the mark-up may be related to risk and rates of stock turnover (eg higher for jewellers than greengrocers), it may be influenced by general market conditions and the expected elasticity of demand for the product and it may be governed by what is normal for a given trade. The most inflexible system would be where a fixed percentage is applied to the total cost of each product regardless of changes in conditions. This approach could cause a firm that is operating below capacity to turn away business which is available at less than normal price even though such business may be priced above marginal cost and would thus make a contribution to fixed cost.

However, it must be realised that in the long run prices must be sufficiently high to recover all costs, both fixed and variable, together with a reasonable rate of profit otherwise the survival of the firm will be in jeopardy.

RATE OF RETURN PRICING

11. Where an organisation uses the concept of return on capital employed, ie

$$\frac{\text{Profit}}{\text{Capital Employed}} \quad \%$$

as a measure of performance, management may wish to know what selling price would be necessary to achieve a given rate of return on capital employed. This procedure involves deciding upon a target rate of return on capital employed, estimating the total costs for a 'normal production year, and the amount of capital employed. These figures can be used in the following formula:

$$\frac{\text{Percentage mark}}{\text{up on cost}} = \frac{\text{Capital Employed}}{\text{Total Annual Costs}} \text{ x } \frac{\text{Planned Rate of Return}}{\text{on Capital Employed}}$$

For example, assume that the target rate of return on capital employed is 18%, the amount of capital employed is £1.5m and the estimated annual total costs are £2.25m, what is the required mark up on cost?

$$\text{Mark up \%} = \frac{1.5}{2.25} \text{ x } 18\%$$

$$= \underline{12\%}$$

Notes:
    (a) The ratio Capital employed: Total Annual Costs is known as the capital turnover ratio.
    (b) Return on capital employed (ROCE) is fully described later in the manual.

This method of calculating a mark-up does have the advantage of relating pricing to longer term financial objectives but it will be apparent that it is only a variant of full-cost pricing with the same potential inflexibility. The claim is sometimes made that the method removes the arbitrary element from establishing what is a 'fair' mark up, but the arbitrariness is simply transferred to the target rate of return. A further element of arbitrariness is that in order to make the calculation in a multi-product firm it would be necessary to apportion capital employed by product group which could only be done in an arbitrary manner.

Both full-cost and rate of return pricing are essentially long term pricing strategies which, rigidly applied, lack the flexibility to deal with short-term pricing decisions.

USING COST PLUS SYSTEMS

12. A number of criticisms can be levelled at cost plus systems particularly when they are used in a mechanical fashion.

The main ones are as follows:

(a) The systems do not take demand explicitly into account and assume that prices are solely cost related.

(b) Where the systems are incorporated in routine decision making there is the tendency to base the costs on past cost levels rather than consider what the costs will be in the future.

(c) Cost plus systems tend to ignore the inherent arbitrariness of fixed cost allocation and absorption procedures and the apportionment of capital employed in a multi-product organisation.

(d) Cost plus is a long run pricing concept which lacks flexibility in dealing with short run pricing where the interaction of volume, price and profit are all important.

Frequently, of course, cost plus systems are used in a more flexible fashion and the notional cost plus price is but the starting point in a pricing decision. Management may vary the mark up percentage by some intuitive consideration of demand, competition, capacity and other relevant matters, thus adjusting the price to suit current circumstances.

MARGINAL PRICING

13. This method of pricing, sometimes referred to as the variable cost or contribution method of pricing, is simply the application of cost-volume-profit analysis to pricing decisions. Using marginal pricing, the firm sets prices so as to maximise contribution towards fixed cost and profit.

As in any decision the costs and revenues to be used for pricing are FUTURE costs and revenues. All past outlays are inescapable, they are sunk costs. For short term decisions marginal pricing can increase pricing flexibility and profits but needs to be used judiciously.

A typical example of its application in practice is where hotel chains cater for full price business during the week and offer the spare capacity at weekends at some price above marginal cost, but less than normal price, thus increasing profits. This process is known as price discrimination and enables the firm to sell at different prices in different markets. A further example of marginal pricing is the familiar one where a firm is experiencing reduced demand and obtains the best possible price above marginal cost in order to provide some contribution to fixed costs.

Marginal pricing policies may also be relevant when dealing with the variables involved in managing marketing strategies. For example, a typical product moves through what is known as the **product life-cycle**, ie introduction, growth, maturity, saturation and decline. At each stage management will require marginal cost and separable period cost data relevant to that stage in the cycle in order to make appropriate pricing decisions. Because volumes will vary at each stage the marginal approach will assist in choosing the most appropriate combination of price, advertising and, where necessary, price discrimination without the issue being clouded by the inclusion of unit fixed costs.

Marginal pricing makes explicit the consideration of demand and volume and thus more nearly approaches the theoretical framework of classical economics dealt with in the early part of the chapter. However, few if any firms are able to optimise prices by the MC = MR equation.

Used with care, marginal pricing can assist in short run price setting but care must be taken that marginal pricing does not become the long run norm. It is worth restating that in the long run prices must cover all costs plus a reasonable margin of profit.

Marginal pricing differs from the cost plus systems in that there is no automatic percentage mark up on cost to arrive at a selling price. When the marginal cost is known, the selling price is established in order to maximise contribution having regard to the expected demand, volume and other factors.

ALTERNATIVE WAYS OF INFLUENCING DEMAND

14. So far, this chapter has concentrated on pricing as the sole means by which a firm can influence demand for its products but pricing is only one way of influencing demand; others include advertising, improving quality, better service, more representatives and numerous other devices. Where markets are oligopolistic or near oligopolistic, common in industrial societies, price is not generally considered a competitive device and advertising and other forms of sales promotion become all important.

Advertising is invariably associated with product branding and seeks to shift the demand curve of the firm to the right and/or to make it more inelastic thus giving the firm more flexibility in its pricing. The possible effect of a successful advertising campaign is shown below.

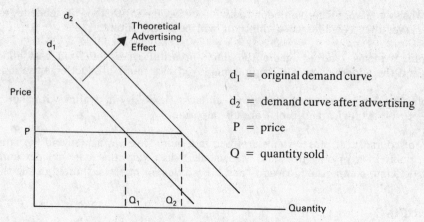

Figure 2   Demand Curves and Advertising

Figure 2 shows the position where the demand curve is moved to the right thus moving the quantity sold from Q_1 to Q_2. It will be noted that the price is unchanged and also that in this illustration the elasticity of demand (the slope) is unchanged.

If advertising has any success then there are two possible results. One is a **market widening effect** where the total market is expanded and increased sales by a single firm are not at the expense of others. The other is a **substitution** or **market sharing** effect where the result is a revision of market share. As is to be expected, the two effects may well interact in practice.

SUMMARY

15. (a)   Pricing is a complex problem with numerous interacting factors including: objectives, markets, demand and demand elasticity, costs, competition, level of activity and so on.

(b)   Economic theory states that firms should seek the price which maximises profit. Given the demand schedule the intersection of the marginal cost and marginal revenue is the optimum point and either price or output (but not both) can be determined.

(c)   If the appropriate functions are known, the optimal price can be determined using differential calculus.

(d)   Price elasticity of demand is a measure of the degree to which demand responds to price changes. Price elasticity can vary from zero (perfectly inelastic demand) to infinity (perfectly elastic demand).

(e)   Marginal analysis is difficult to apply in practice. Difficulties include: lack of information, multiple objectives, non-price factors influencing demand.

(f)   A typical pricing system used in practice is full cost pricing where a mark-up, say 30%, is added to total cost. There are difficulties associated with the fixed element of the cost and with the amount of mark up.

(g)   Rate of return pricing is but a variant of cost plus pricing. Both these pricing policies are essentially long term strategies which may lack flexibility in the short term.

(h)   Marginal or variable cost or contribution pricing is the application of cost-volume-profit analysis to pricing decisions where management aims to maximise contribution. It increases pricing flexibility but should be considered only as a short run policy if applied to all products and services.

(i)   Advertising is another means of influencing demand and has the general objective of pushing the demand schedule to the right. Advertising may have a market widening or a market sharing effect.

POINTS TO NOTE

16. (a)   One particular use of cost plus pricing is concerned with some Government contracts where the price is determined by a formula whereby the firm recovers all its agreed costs plus a percentage mark-up.

(b)   Like all decision making, pricing decisions must be concerned with **future** costs and revenues.

(c)   'Standby' air tickets are a well publicised example of marginal pricing in practice.

(d)   Two possible pricing policies are price skinning and pricing penetration. Price skimming is where a firm exploits the market by charging a high initial price perhaps to capitalise on the novelty appeal of a product. Price skimming is not feasible when there are already numbers of close substitutes and the high profits, if successful, may induce competitors to enter the market. Pricing penetration is in effect the opposite policy where low prices are charged initially in order to gain a large part of the market.

ADDITIONAL READING

Pricing and Output Decisions	Arnold, HAYMARKET
Pricing	Boston, CIMA
Pricing in Business	Hague, ALLEN & UNWIN
Advanced Management Accounting	Kaplan, PRENTICE HALL
Insight into Management Accounting	Sizer, PITMAN

SELF REVIEW QUESTIONS

1.   *Give twelve factors which may need to be considered in a pricing decision. (3)*

2.   *Given a profit maximising objective what is the theoretically optimum level of sales? (4)*

3.   *Define price ceiling and price floor. (4)*

4.   *How can calculus be used to determine the optimal price? (5)*

5.   *What is the price elasticity of demand and why is it important? (6)*

6.   *What is the characteristic of sales revenue when the price elasticity of demand is unity? (6)*

7.   *What are the major limitations associated with theoretical marginal analysis? (7)*

8.   *What are the characteristics of cost plus systems? (9)*

9.   *What is full cost pricing and what are the problems associated with the system? (10)*

10.   *What is 'rate of return' pricing and what are its advantages and disadvantages? (11)*

11.   *What criticisms can be made of cost plus pricing systems? (12)*

12.   *What is marginal pricing and when is it best applied? (13)*

13.   *What is the main objective of advertising? (14)*

EXAMINATION QUESTIONS WITH ANSWERS COMMENCING PAGE 356

A1.   *French Ltd is about to commence operations utilising a simple production process to produce two products, X and Y. It is the policy of French to operate the new factory at its maximum output in the first year of operations. Cost and production details estimated for the first year's operations are as follows:*

Product	Production resources per unit		Variable cost per unit		Fixed Production overheads directly attributable to product	Maximum production
	Labour hours	Machine hours	Direct labour	Direct materials	(£000's)	(000's)
			£	£		
X	1	4	5	6	120	40
Y	8	2	28	16	280	10

There are also general fixed production overheads concerned in the manufacture of both products but which cannot be directly attributed to either. This general fixed production overhead is estimated at £720,000 for the first year of operations. It is thought that the cost structures of the first year will also be operative in the second year.

Both products are new and French is one of the first firms to produce them. Hence in the first year of operations the sales price can be set by French. In the second and subsequent years it is felt that the market for X and Y will have become more settled and French will largely conform to the competitive market prices that will becomes established. The sales manager has researched the first year's market potential and has estimated sales volumes for various ranges of selling price. The details are:

Product X		Product Y	
Range per unit sales price	Sales volume	Range of per unit sales price	Sales volume
£ £	(000's)	£ £	(000's)
Up to 24.00	36	Up to 96.00	11
24.01 to 30.00	32	96.01 to 108.00	10
30.01 to 36.00	18	108.01 to 120.00	9
36.01 to *42.00	8	120.01 to 132.00	8
		132.01 to 144.00	7
		144.01 to *156.00	5

*Maximum price.

The managing director of French wishes to ascertain the total production cost of X and Y as, he says, 'Until we know the per unit cost of production we can not properly determine the first year's sales price. Price must always ensure that total cost is covered and there is an element of profit – therefore I feel that the price should be total cost plus 20%. The determination of cost is fairly simple as most costs are clearly attributable to either X or Y. The general factory overhead will probably be allocated to the products in accordance with some measure of usage of factory resources such as labour or machine hours. The choice between labour and machine hours is the only problem in determining the cost of each product – but the problem is minor and so, therefore, is the problem of pricing.'

Required:

(a) Produce statements showing the effect the cost allocation and pricing methods mentioned by the managing director will have on

(i)   unit costs,
(ii)   closing stock values, and
(iii) disclosed profit for the year of operation.

(b) Briefly comment on the results in (a) above and advise the managing director on the validity of using the per unit cost figures produced for pricing decisions.

(c) Provide appropriate statements to the management of French Ltd which will be of direct relevance in assisting the determination of the optimum prices of X and Y for the first year of operations. The statements should be designed to provide assistance in each of the following, separate, cases:

(i)   year II demand will be below productive capacity;
(ii)   year II demand will be substantially in excess of productive capacity.

In both cases the competitive market sales price per unit for year II are expected to be

> *X - £30 per unit*
> *Y - £130 per unit*

Clearly specify, and explain your advice to French for each of the cases described.

(Ignore taxation and the time value of money.)

ACCA, Management Accounting.

A2. *(a) Briefly describe the differences between absorption and direct (marginal or variable) costing.*

(b) Discuss the extent to which cost data is useful in the determination of pricing policy. Explain the advantages and disadvantages of presenting cost data for possible utilisation in pricing policy determination using an absorption, rather than a direct, costing basis.

ACCA, Management Accounting.

15. Linear Programming

INTRODUCTION

1. This chapter describes the important resource allocation technique known as Linear Programming (LP). The characteristics which enable problems to be solved by LP and the ways of expressing problems in a standarised manner are described. The graphical solution method is discussed and an outline of the simplex technique is provided. The interpretation of simplex tableaux is explained both for maximising and minimising problems and the meaning and identification of shadow prices is described in detail both for graphical and simplex solutions. The chapter concludes with a summary of the limitations of LP.

LP DEFINITION

2. LP is a mathematical technique to optimise the allocation of scarce resources. Many management decisions are essentially resource allocation decisions and LP enables optimal solutions to be found to a range of problems where the number of factors involved and their relationships would make simpler solution methods difficult, if not impossible. LP can be used for a range of problems and typical applications include: product mix problems, production planning capital rationing and aspects of financial modelling. LP is an important technique for the management accountant because it provides an extension of cost-volume-analysis capable of dealing with practical problems which, because of the large number of interactions and the presence of more than one bind constraint, cannot be solved by the more basic approaches.

REQUIREMENTS FOR LP

3. LP is a technique to optimise the value of some objective (eg to maximise contribution) when the factors involved (eg labour hours) are subject to some constraint or limitation.

Thus LP can be used to solve problems which have the following characteristics:

(a) Can be stated in numeric terms.

(b) All factors have linear relationships, ie if one unit requires 5 man hours, 2 units require 10 hours and so on. It must be stressed that every relationship in the problem must be linear or able to be linearly approximated.

(c) The problem must permit a choice or choices between alternative courses of action.

(d) There must be one or more restrictions on the factors involved. These may be restrictions on the availability of resources, for example, only 3,000 machine hours are available per week or they may relate to particular characteristics, for example, a fertiliser mix must contain a minimum of 15% phosphates and 25% nitrogen.

(e) Fractional solutions must be feasible.

EXPRESSING LP PROBLEMS IN A STANDARD MANNER

4. Before considering methods of solving LP problems it is necessary to be able to express any given problem in a standardised manner. This is a common examination requirement which facilitates the solution and ensures that no important element of the problem is overlooked. The two main aspects of this process are determining the **objective** (and hence the objective function) and the **limitations** or **constraints**.

THE OBJECTIVE FUNCTION

5. This is the objective of the problem expressed in a simple mathematical form. The objective may be to maximise contribution or net present value or profit or it may be to minimise cost or time or some other appropriate measure. Examples follow of both maximising and minimising problems.

Example 1

A company produces three products A, B and C with contributions of £10, £15 and £20 per unit respectively and it is required to maximise total contribution.

The objective function is:

$$\text{MAXIMISE} \qquad 10x_1 + 15x_2 + 20x_3$$

$$\begin{aligned} \text{where } x_1 &= \text{number of units of A produced} \\ x_2 &= \text{number of units of B produced} \\ x_3 &= \text{number of units of C produced} \end{aligned}$$

Note: This problem has three **unknowns** or **decision variables**: x_1, x_2, x_3.

Example 2

A company mixes four raw materials to produce a plastic. Material W costs 40p per kilogram, material X costs £1.20 per kilogram, material Y cost 90p per kilogram and material Z cost £2.60 per kilogram. Each of the materials contribute some essential quality to the plastic and it is required to use the least cost mix.

The objective function is:

$$\text{MINIMISE} \quad 40x_1 + 120X_2 + 90x_3 + 260x_4 \text{ (in pence)}$$
or
$$\text{MINIMISE} \quad 0.40x_1 + 1.20x_2 + 0.90x_3 + 2.60x_4 \text{ (in £'s)}$$

$$
\begin{aligned}
\text{where } x_1 &= \text{kgs of W}\\
x_2 &= \text{kgs of X}\\
x_3 &= \text{kgs of Y}\\
x_4 &= \text{kgs of Z}
\end{aligned}
$$

Note: This problem has four decision variables.

It is necessary to be clear about the number of decision variables because this influences the choice of solution method. It must be emphasised that an LP problem can only pursue **one objective at a time**. If the objective is changed it becomes a new problem.

LIMITATIONS OR CONSTRAINTS

6.   The limitations in any given problem must be clearly identified, quantified, and expressed mathematically. To be able to use LP they must, of course, be linear.

The following example follows the typical pattern for maximising problems.

Example 3

A company produces three products and wishes to plan production to maximise contribution.

The objective function is

$$\text{MAXIMISE} \quad 16x_1 + 8x_2 + 5.5x_3$$

$$
\begin{aligned}
\text{where } x_1 &= \text{number of units of A}\\
x_2 &= \text{number of units of B}\\
x_3 &= \text{number of units of C}
\end{aligned}
$$

and the coefficients of the objective function (16, 8 and 5.5) represent the contributions per unit of the products.

The company employs 150 skilled and 80 unskilled workers and works a 40 hour week.

The times to produce 1 unit of each product by the types of labour are shown below

	Products		
	A	B	C
Skilled Labour Hours	3	2.5	1
Unskilled Labour Hours	3.5	6	4

The three products are made from two raw materials, Argon and Zenon. There are limitations on the availability of the materials and only 25,000 kgs of Argon and 18,000 kgs of Zenon are available in a period. The usage of the materials in the products is as follows:

	Product			
	A	B	C	
Argon	7.5	3.0	4.5	kgs/unit
Zenon	6	5	3	kgs/unit

Labour and material limitations expressed in the standard manner

$$
\begin{array}{llllll}
3x_1 & + 2.5x_2 & + & x_3 & \leqslant & 6000 & \text{(skilled labour)} \\
3.5x_1 & + 6x_2 & + & 4x_3 & \leqslant & 3200 & \text{(unskilled labour)} \\
7.5x_1 & + 3x_2 & + & 4.5x_3 & \leqslant & 25000 & \text{(Argon)} \\
6x_1 & + 5x_2 & + & 3x_3 & \leqslant & 18000 & \text{(Zenon)}
\end{array}
$$

In addition there is a general limitation applicable to all maximising problems which is a formal means of ensuring that negative quantities of a product do not result, ie

$$x_1, x_2, x_3 \geqslant 0$$

Notes:

(a)   The above constraints are all of the 'less than or equal to' type ($\leqslant$) which are the most commonly encountered in the maximising problems.

(b)   'Greater than or equal to' ($\geqslant$) constraints can also occur. For example if in Example 3 it was necessary to produce at least 500 units of product C to fulfil a contract a new restriction would have to be included thus:

$$x_3 \geqslant 500 \text{ (contract restriction)}$$

FIXED COSTS

7.   LP is concerned with **changes** in cost and revenues so it follows that a factor such as fixed costs which would be unchanged over the range of output being considered should not be included in the LP formulation. To eliminate the effect of fixed costs and to maintain linear relationships it is normal to use contribution (ie sales less marginal cost) rather than profit in the objective functions.

SOLVING LP PROBLEMS

8.   When the problem has been expressed in the standardised manner it can be solved by either of two methods. If there are only TWO unknowns or decision variables then the problem can be solved by graphical methods. If there are THREE or more unknowns then the usual solution method is the Simplex technique. Graphical methods are dealt with first followed by a description of the Simplex method.

GRAPHICAL LP SOLUTIONS

9.   Graphical methods are the simplest to use and should be employed wherever possible. The following are the major features of the approach.

(a)   Can only be used where there are 2 unknowns.

(b)   Graphical methods can deal with any number of limitations but as each limitation is a line on the graph a large number of lines may make the graph difficult to read. This is rarely a problem in examination questions.

(c)   Both maximising and minimising problems can be dealt with graphically and the method can deal with constraints of the 'greater than or equal to' ($\geqslant$) type and the 'less than or equal to ($\leqslant$) type.

(d)   The axes of the graph represents the unknowns and each constraint is drawn as a straight line on the graph. The area on the graph which does not contravene any of the constraints is known as the **feasible region**.

(e)   The solution point is always at a vertex of the constraints on the edge of the feasible region. If a line is drawn representing the objective function the solution point for **maximising** problems is the corner of the feasible region furthest to the **right** which can be touched by the objective function line; for **minimising** problems it is the corresponding point furthest to the **left** of the feasible region. When the solution point is found the values of the decision variables can be read directly from the axes of the graph.

GRAPHICAL LP EXAMPLE

10.   **Example 4**

A manufacturer produces two products, Klunk and Klick. Klunk has a contribution of £3 per unit and Klick £4 per unit. The manufacturer wishes to establish the weekly production plan which maximises contribution.

Production data are as follows:

PER UNIT

	Machining (Hours)	Labour (Hours)	Material (lbs)
Klunk	4	4	1
Klick	2	6	1
Total Available per week	100	180	40

Because of a trade agreement sales of Klunk are limited to a weekly maximum of 20 units and to honour an agreement with an old established customer at least 10 units of Klick must be sold per week.

Solution

It will be seen that this is a problem with two unknowns (the quantities of the two products) and five constraints (machining hours, labour hours, materials and the two sales constraints). Four of the constraints are of the $\leqslant$ type whilst the sales constraint for Klick is of the $\geqslant$ type.

The problem in the standardised format is as follows:

$$\text{MAXIMISE } 3x_1 + 4x_2 \text{ (objective function)}$$

SUBJECT TO
CONSTRAINTS
A	$4x_1$	$+$	$2x_2$	$\leqslant$	100	(Machining hours constraint)
B	$4x_1$	$+$	$6x_2$	$\leqslant$	180	(Labour hours constraint)
C	x_1	$+$	x_2	$\leqslant$	40	(Materials constraint)
D	x_1			$\leqslant$	20	(Klunk sales constraint)
E			x_2	$\geqslant$	10	(Klick sales constraint)

$$x_1 \geqslant 0$$

where x_1 = number of units of Klunk
x_2 = number of units of Klick

Note: As it is impossible to make negative quantities of the products it is necessary formally to state the non-negative constraint (ie $x_1 \geqslant 0$). Constraint E, being of the $\geqslant$ type already ensures that negative quantities of x_2 will not appear in the solution.

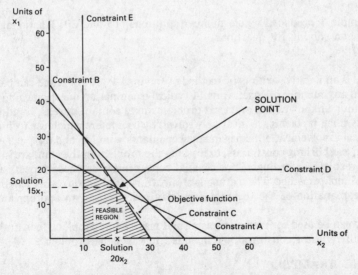

Figure 1 Graphical Solution to Example 4

The optimal solution is 15 units of x_1 and 20 units of x_2 giving a contribution of $£(15(3) + 20(4)) = £125$.

Notes:

(a)   Each constraint is plotted on the graph as an equality. Using Constraint A as an example, the plotting points are found as follows.

$$\text{Constraint } 4x_1 + 2x_2 = 100$$

$$\text{Plotting point on } x_1 \text{ axis} = \frac{100}{4} = 25$$

$$\text{Plotting point on } x_2 \text{ axis} = \frac{100}{2} = 50$$

The area to the left of each $\leqslant$ constraint, ie A to D, and the area to the right of the $\geqslant$ constraint E, is the area which does not violate that particular constraint. As each constraint is drawn the area that does not violate any constraint - the feasible region - generally becomes smaller.

(b)   The values of x_1 and x_2 at the optimal activity can be inserted into the constraints to find out the utilisation of each constraint thus,

Resource Constraint A	4(15)	+	2(20)	=	100 (Machining hours fully utilised)
Resource Constraint B	4(15)	+	6(20	=	180 (Labour hours fully utilised)
Resource Constraint C	1(25)	+	1(20)	=	35 (5 lbs material spare)
Sales Constraint D	1(15)			=	15 (Sales agreement honoured)
Sales Constraint E			1(20)	=	20 (Sales agreement honoured)

It will be seen that the two resource constraints which are fully utilised, A and B, formed the vertex at the optimum point. Constraint C which is not fully utilised did not touch the feasible region and is an example of a **redundant** or non-binding constraint.

(c)   The line representing the objective function is sloped to reflect the relative contributions of the two unknowns. Such a line is known as an **Iso-profit** or **Iso-cost** line and the line shown is only one of an infinite number of such lines that can be drawn. The lines could be drawn, parallel to each other, increasingly further to the right from the point of origin of the graph. For maximising problems the optimum point is that vertex of the feasible region furthest to the right that can be touched by an iso-profit line. In many examples, including Figure 1, the optimal point is obvious without drawing the iso-profit line but students are advised ALWAYS to draw the iso-profit line which can help to determine the optimum point where there are a number of vertices close together. Also, in examinations, more marks will be gained for a complete graph. Similar principles apply to minimising problems except that the converse applies, ie the optimum point is the point furthest to the LEFT that can be touched by an iso-profit line.

(d)   Although Example 1 produced whole number solutions (15 and 20) fractional solutions are possible and frequently occur when solving LP questions.

SIMPLEX METHOD

11.   The Simplex method is an iterative arithmetic method of solving LP problems and can be used for problems with any number of unknowns and any number of constraints. A typical examination question using the Simplex method would typically have three or four unknowns but practical problems may contain dozens, hundreds and even thousands of unknowns and constraints. Such problems are invariably solved by computers which use techniques based on the Simplex method. The main practical involvement of management accountants with LP, and a typical examination requirement, is calculating contributions, establishing constraints, expressing the problem in the standardised manner and interpreting the computer produced results. Accordingly, this manual concentrates on these aspects and does not deal with the detailed processes of the Simplex method. The method is straightforward but somewhat lengthy and tedious and students wishing to have a full explanation of the technique are advised to study an appropriate text book.*

The Simplex method can be used for both minimising and maximising problems, constraints of the $\leqslant$ and $\geqslant$ type and situations where the both types of constraint are included in the same problem.

SIMPLEX MAXIMISING EXAMPLE

12.   The following example will be used as a basis for explaining the use of the Simplex method. The explanations include: expressing the problem in the standardised manner, setting up the first Simplex tableau and finally how the final solution tableau can be interpreted.

*For example, Quantitative Techniques, T. LUCEY, DP Publications.

Example 5

A company can produce three products, A, B and C. The products yield a contribution of £8, £5 and £10 respectively.

The products use a machine which has 400 hours capacity in the next period. Each unit of the products uses 2, 3 and 1 hour respectively of the machine's capacity.

There are only 150 units available in the period of a special component which is used singly in products A and C.

200 kgs only of a special alloy is available in the period. Product A uses 2 kgs per unit and Product C uses 4 kgs per unit.

There is an agreement with a trade association to produce no more than 50 units of Product B in the period.

The company wishes to find out the production plan which maximises contribution.

Solution

As always, the first step is to express the problem in the standardised manner as described in the first part of the chapter.

The standardised format

Objective function:

$$\text{Maximise } 8x_1 + 5x_2 + 10x_3$$

Subject to:-

$$
\begin{array}{rcrcrclll}
2x_1 & + & 3x_2 & + & x_3 & \leqslant & 400 & \text{(Machine hours constraint)} \\
x_1 & & & + & x_3 & \leqslant & 150 & \text{(Component constraint)} \\
2x_1 & & & + & 4x_3 & \leqslant & 200 & \text{(Alloy constraint)} \\
& & x_2 & & & \leqslant & 50 & \text{(Sales constraint)} \\
\end{array}
$$

$$x_1 \geqslant 0, \quad x_2 \geqslant 0, \quad x_3 \geqslant 0$$

where
x_1 = no. of units of Product A
x_2 = no. of units of Product B
x_3 = no. of units of Product C

It will be seen that this is a problem with 3 unknowns and four constraints which are all of the $\leqslant$ type.

The next stage is to change the inequalities in the constraints into equalities by adding a **slack variable** in each constraint. This is done so that arithmetic can take place on the constraints during the Simplex iterations. The slack variables represent the spare capacity in the constraints and the Simplex method automatically assigns a value to the slack variables. The values can range from the full amount of the constraint when there is no production to a value of zero when the constraint is fully utilised. For example when a slack variable, s_1, is added to the machining constraint the constraint appears as follows

$$2x_1 + 3x_2 + x_3 + s_1 = 400$$

The slack variable, s_1, can take any value from:
400 hours - ie the position of zero production and therefore maximum unused capacity
0 hours - ie the position of the is fully utilised and there is zero unused capacity.

The full formulation with slack variables is as follows:

$$\text{Maximise } 8x_1 + 5x_2 + 10x_3$$

Subject to:-

$$
\begin{array}{rcrcrcrcl}
2x_1 & + & 3x_2 & + & x_3 & + & s_1 & = & 400 \\
x_1 & + & & & x_3 & + & s_2 & = & 150 \\
x_1 & & & + & x_3 & + & s_3 & = & 200 \\
& & x_2 & & & + & s_4 & = & 50 \\
\end{array}
$$

Note: s_1, s_2, s_3, s_4 are the slack variables and represent the spare capacity in the limitations.

The initial Simplex tableau can now be set up ready for the step-by-step solution method to take place.

INITIAL SIMPLEX TABLEAU

SOLUTION VARIABLE	PRODUCTS			SLACK VARIABLES				SOLUTION QUANTITY
	x_1	x_2	x_3	s_1	s_2	s_3	s_4	
s_1	2	3	1	1	0	0	0	400
s_2	1	0	1	0	1	0	0	150
s_3	2	0	4	0	0	1	0	200
s_4	0	1	0	0	0	0	1	50
Z	8	5	10	0	0	0	0	0

Table 1

Notes:

(a) It will be seen that the values in the body of the table are the values from the objective function and constraints in the formulation where the slack variables were added.

(b) The variable 'Z' has been used for the objective function and represents total contribution.

(c) The tableau shows that $s_1 = 400$, $s_2 = 150$, $s_3 = 200$, $s_4 = 50$ and $Z = 0$.

(d) The tableau shows a feasible solution, that of nil production, nil contribution, and maximum unused capacity as represented by the values of the slack variables.

(e) It will be seen that the columns under the slack variables contain a single figure 1 with the rest of the column being zeros. In a Simplex tableau the solution value for a variable is ALWAYS found opposite the figure 1 where the rest of the column is zeros.

(f) Although this initial Simplex tableau does show a feasible solution - as does every succeeding tableau - it can obviously be improved upon and this is the task of the Simplex solution technique. After a number of iterations the optimum solution is reached giving a final tableau as follows.

SOLUTION VARIABLE	PRODUCTS			SLACK VARIABLES				SOLUTION QUANTITY
	x_1	x_2	x_3	s_1	s_2	s_3	s_4	
s_1	0	0	-3	1	0	-1	-3	50
s_2	0	0	-1	0	1	$-\frac{1}{2}$	0	50
x_1	1	0	2	0	0	$\frac{1}{2}$	1	100
x_2	0	1	0	0	0	0	1	50
Z	0	0	-6	0	0	-4	-5	-1050

Table 2

Note: This is recognised as the optimum position because there are no positive values in the bottom row, ie no further gains in contribution can be made by altering production levels.

INTERPRETING THE FINAL TABLEAU

The solution can be read directly from Table 2 in each row where there is a figure 1 in a column of zero's, ie

$$s_1 = 50$$
$$s_2 = 50$$
$$x_1 = 100$$
$$x_2 = 50$$

This means that the optimum production plan is:

100 units of Product A (ie x_1)
50 units of Product B (ie x_2)

This production plan results in a contribution of **£1050** found in the Table at the end of the Z row. Because s_1 and s_2, the slack variables, have values at optimum this means that there is some unused capacity, ie

s_1 = 50 - means that there are 50 hours of unused machine capacity
s_2 = 50 - means that there are 50 unused components.

It will be realised that x_3, s_3 and s_4 do not have values in the final volume of Table 2. This means that, at optimum,

- there is no production of x_3
- that the 200 kgs of special alloy are fully utilised
- that the sales constraint is binding

Note: This minus sign against the £1050 contribution in the Z row is merely a result of the Simplex arithmetic and can be ignored.

The values shown for the production plan, contribution and unused capacities can be verified as follows

At optimum when x_1 = 100 and x_2 = 50

Contribution	=	£(100(8) + 50(5))	=	£1050
Matching hours	=	100(2) + 50(3)	=	350 leaving 50 spare
Components usage	=	100(1)	=	100 leaving 50 spare
Alloy usage	=	100(2)	=	200 fully utilised

Further information can be obtained from Table which is of considerable importance from an accounting viewpoint. It will be seen the bottom row of Table 2 contains three minus figures

x_3 column − 6
s_3 column − 4
s_4 column − 5

The values, which are an automatic and useful by-product of the Simplex method, are known as **shadow prices** or **shadow costs** or **dual prices** and are discussed below.

SHADOW PRICES

13.   The shadow price of a scarce resource is the increase in the value of the objective function which would be achieved if one more unit of the resource was available. In the terms of Example 2 above, if one more kilogramme of the special alloy was made available, contribution would increase by £4 (ie the s_3 value).

The shadow price of a resource is the opportunity cost of that resource and the valuation produced by the Simplex method results from the effects of one more unit of the resource on the output of the products: A and B in our example.

At the margin, shadow prices can provide guidance to decision makers on, for example, the value to the business of relieving existing constraints, but they will normally only apply to relatively small changes in the resource levels. If the change in the amount of the resource is of a significant magnitude then the problem should be re-solved using the revised resource levels when new shadow prices will result.

A constraint only has a shadow price when it is binding. Where resources are not fully utilised the shadow price is zero. This accords with common sense for there can be no benefit in increasing the amount of a resource of which there is already a surplus.

Reverting to the interpretation of Table 2 the shadow prices and interpretations are as follows.

x_3 shadow price £6

This means that if any units of Product C were manufactured (it will be recalled that it was not in the optimal production plan) overall contribution would FALL by £6.

s₃ shadow price £4

This means every extra kilogramme of the alloy would INCREASE contribution by £4.

s₄ shadow price £5

This means that if the sales constraint could be lifted every extra unit of product B that could be sold would increase overall contribution by £5.

Machine hours and components, slack variables s_1 and s_2, have zero shadow prices as shown in Table 2. This is to be expected as there are surplus machine hours and components available.

The shadow prices of the binding constraints can be used to prove the contribution, thus:

Alloy constraint	200 x £4	=	£800
Sales constraint	50 x £5	=	£250
	= Total contribution		£1050

PRIMAL AND DUAL PROBLEMS

14. Every LP problem has an equal but opposite formulation. For every maximising problem there is an equal but opposite minimising problem and for every minimising problem, an equal but opposite maximising problem. Correctly interpreted the same answers can be obtained from either formulation. The original problem is known as the **primal** problem and the equal but opposite formulation as the **dual** or **inverse**. For example, in a given set of circumstances, the same optimal plan for the organisation might be obtained from either a primal problem to maximise contribution or the dual problem to minimise cost.

A particular use of the dual formulation is concerned with minimisation problems which it is required to solve by the Simplex method. The method can be used to solve both minimising and maximising problems but because solving maximising problems by the Simplex method is a more straight forward process, it is normal to convert a minimising problem into a maximising one and solve the resulting dual formulation by the usual Simplex technique. This is illustrated below.

MINIMISATION EXAMPLE

15. Example

A plastics manufacturer can utilise three raw materials, Poly, Gimp and Mox in varying proportions to produce three products A, B and C. The firm wishes to produce at least 200 units of A, 300 units of B and 80 units of C.

Each kilo of Poly yields 4 of A, 3 of B and 2 of C
Each kilo of Gimp yields 5 of A, 6 of B and 1 of C
Each kilo of Mox yields 1 of A, 3 of B and 1 of C.

If Poly costs 20p a kilo, Gimp costs 30p per kilo and Mox costs 50p what is the minimum purchase plan to produce the required output?

Solution

Step 1. Express the problem in the standardised manner, ie

Minimise $20x_1 + 30x_2 + 50x_3$

Subject to:-

$$4x_1 + 5x_2 + x_3 \geqslant 200 \quad \text{Product A}$$
$$3x_1 + 6x_2 + 3x_3 \geqslant 300 \quad \text{Product B}$$
$$2x_1 + x_2 + x_3 \quad G \quad 80 \quad \text{Product C}$$

$$x_1, x_2, x_3 \geqslant 0$$

where x_1 = kgs of Poly
x_2 = kgs of Gimp
x_3 = kgs of Mox

Step 2. Form the DUAL and INVERSE of the formulation above. make the problem into a MAXIMISING one by making a COLUMN for each LIMITATION and a CONSTRAINT row for each ELEMENT in the objective function, thus:

$$
\begin{array}{llllll}
\text{Maximise} & 200A & + & 300B & + & 80C \\
\text{Subject to} & 4A & + & 3B & + & 2C & \leqslant 20 \\
& 5A & + & 6B & + & 1C & \leqslant 30 \\
& 1A & + & 3B & + & 1C & \leqslant 50
\end{array}
$$

It will be seen that the original quantity **column** has become the objective function **row** and that the original costs (20, 30 and 50) have become the amounts of the constraints. It will also be noted that the constraints are of the $\leqslant$ type, ie as a normal maximising problem.

Step 3. Set up the first Simplex tableau complete with slack variables.

INITIAL SIMPLEX TABLEAU

SOLUTION VARIABLE	A	B	C	s_1	s_2	s_3	COST
s_1	4	3	2	1	0	0	20
s_2	5	6	1	0	1	0	30
s_3	1	3	1	0	0	1	50
QUANTITY	200	300	80	0	0	0	0

Step 4. The normal Simplex procedure for maximising is worked through resulting in the following optimum position.

FINAL SIMPLEX TABLEAU

SOLUTION VARIABLE	A	B	C	s_1	s_2	s_3	COST
C	1	0	1	2/3	-1/3	0	3 1/3
B	2/3	1	0	-1/9	1/9	0	4 4/9
s_3	-2	0	0	-1/3	-2/3	1	33 1/6
QUANTITY	-80	0	0	-20	-40	0	-1600

The above is the normal result of a maximising problem. However, to obtain the solutions to the original minimising problem some differences in the usual interpretation are required.

Quantities to be purchased

These are the figures under the slack variable columns, ie

$$
\begin{array}{lll}
s_1 & = -20 & \text{Purchase 20 kgs of Poly} \\
s_2 & = -40 & \text{Purchase 40 kgs of Gimp} \\
s_3 & = 0 & \text{Nil purchases of Mox}
\end{array}
$$

Total Cost

This is the value at the bottom right hand corner, ie **£1600**, which can be verified as follows:
$$£(20 \times 20 + 30 \times 40) = \underline{£1600}$$

Shadow Prices

These are read from the cost column, ie

$$
\begin{array}{lll}
C & = & 3\ 1/3 \\
B & = & 4\ 4/9 \\
s_3 & = & 33\ 1/6
\end{array}
$$

Explanations. If either of the two quantity constraints C or B is changed by one unit then the total cost will change by £3 1/3 or £4 4/9 respectively.

The s_3 valuation means that if any of the material, Mox, is purchased, total cost will increase by £33-1/6 per kg purchased.

Overproduction

The -80 under column A indicates an overproduction of Product A by 80 units.

Proof: 20 kgs Poly + 40 kgs Gimp yields

Product A: 80 units + 200 units = **280 units**, ie 80 surplus
Product B: 60 units + 240 units = **300 units**, ie minimum required
Product C: 40 units + 40 units = **80 units**, ie minimum required

CALCULATING THE SHADOW PRICES

16. As explained above, the Simplex method produces the shadow prices as an automatic by-product. However, on occasions it is required to calculate the shadow prices for problems that have been solved graphically, ie those with two unknowns. The shadow prices cannot be read from the graph and some simple calculations are required. It will be recalled from para 14 that every primal problem has a dual. The dual formulation of a problem gives the shadow prices so all that is necessary for a two decision variable problem is to form the dual and to solve by simultaneous equations.

The problem given in Example 4, Figure 1 will be used to exemplify the method.

The objective function and the two binding constraints (the only ones that can have shadow prices) were as follows:

$$\text{Maximise } 3x_1 + 4x_2$$

$$\text{Subject to } \quad 4x_1 + 2x_2 \leqslant 100 \text{(materials)}$$
$$4x_1 + 6x_2 \leqslant 180 \text{(labour)}$$

and the optimal solution was 15 units of x_1 and 20 units of x_2 giving a contribution of £125.

The shadow prices are found thus:

If M = shadow price per machining hour
L = shadow price per labour hour

the dual formulation is

$$4M + 4L = 3 \ldots\ldots\ldots \text{ Equation I}$$
$$2M + 6L = 4 \ldots\ldots\ldots\text{Equation II}$$

Halving Equation I and deducting from Equation II

$$
\begin{array}{rrcl}
      & 2M + & 6L = & 4 \\
\text{less} & 2M + & 2L = & 1\frac{1}{2} \\
\hline
\text{gives} & & 4L = & 2\frac{1}{2} \qquad \therefore L = 0.625
\end{array}
$$

and substituting gives M = 0.125

Thus the shadow prices are £0.125 per machining hour and £0.625 per labour hour. These values can be verified by evaluating the total availability of the two resources by their respective shadow prices thus:

Contribution = £(100 x 0.125 + 180 x 0.625) = **£125**

SENSITIVITY ANALYSIS

17. In practice, management are interested in more than just the solution to the LP problem as indicated either graphically or by the Simplex method. They need to know about the **sensitivity** of the solution. An optimal solution may hold for only a narrow range of constraint or contribution values and would thus be termed as **sensitive** solution. Alternatively, the indicated solution may hold good over a wide range of values and would be termed **robust**. The examination over which range of values the original solution still applies is termed **sensitivity analysis**. The output of LP packages on computers usually provides sensitivity analysis information which gives guidance on the amount of variation that can be tolerated before there is a change in the solution.

For smaller problems sensitivity analysis can be carried out by making some simple calculations. As an illustration assume that having found the solution to Example 4, shown on Figure 1, you are asked the following question.

What is the maximum contribution to which Klick can be raised without the original solution of 15 units of Klunk and 20 units of Klick being changed? (The contribution of Klunk is to remain at £3 per unit).

Examination of Figure 1 will show that the angle of the objective function (determined by the relative contributions) can be increased to that of constraint B before a change in solution occurs.

∴ Ratio of constraint B = 45 : 30 = $1\frac{1}{2}$: 1
∴ As Klunk is to remain at the same contribution, Klick can increase in the ratio of $1\frac{1}{2}$: 1 in relation to the £3 contribution of Klunk

∴ x : £3 = $1\frac{1}{2}$: 1
∴ x = £4.50

Klick can increase up to £4.50 without the solution changing. When the contributions are £4.50 and £3 exactly the objective function is at the same angle as constraint B and there is an infinite number of solutions ranging from the original solution ($15x_1, 20x_2$) to $30x_2$. When the price of Klick goes above £4.50 there will be a single solution of $30x_2$, ie 30 units of Klick and no production of x_1.

LIMITATIONS OF LP

18. LP is a useful, practical technique but naturally there are some drawbacks to its use. The main ones are summarised below.

(a) Assumption of certainty. The LP model is a deterministic one where certain knowledge is assumed of the input values and the uncertainties surrounding most business situations are not included. (Sensitivity analysis is a means of attempting to include some of the problem's uncertainties).

(b) Assumption of linearity. The objective function and the constraints must all be linear or capable of being approximated by a linear function. This may not be appropriate for many practical situations which may be better represented by curvi-linear functions.

(c) Assumption of continuity. In ordinary LP it is assumed that the functions are continuous variable. In some situations only whole number solutions are realistic and rounding of Simplex or Graphical solution values may cause serious errors.

(d) Single objectives. An LP formulation can only pursue one objective at a time whereas a practical problem may have multiple objectives.

It will be apparent that a number of the limitations of LP apply with equal or greater force to management accounting techniques such as marginal costing or C-V-P analysis. Consequently it is important to be aware of the limitations of ANY technique used for decision making.

SUMMARY

19. (a) LP is a resource allocation technique which provides a valuable extension to cost-volume-profit analysis.

(b) The major requirements of problems which can be solved by LP are: numeric, linearity, alternatives must exist, restrictions or constraints must exist.

(c) Before solving, LP problems must be expressed in a standardised manner whereby the objective function and the constraints are clearly set out in mathematical form.

(d) LP is concerned with changes in costs and revenues so fixed costs are not included. It is because of this that maximising contribution rather than profit is generally the objective.

(e) If there are only 2 unknowns or decision variables LP problems can be solved by graphical means regardless of the number of constraints.

(f) The axes represent the unknowns and each constraint is drawn as a straight line. The area which does not contravene any constraint is known as the feasible region.

(g)   The optimum point is always a vertex of the constraints at the edge of the feasible region, the furthest to the **right** for maximising problems and the furthest to the **left** for minimising problems.

(h)   The Simplex method is an iterative, arithmetic method of solving LP problems which can be used for problems of any size and for maximising and minimising problems.

(i)   A typical examination requirement is to interpret the final Simplex tableau which shows: the solution quantities, the value of the objective function, the unused capacities or resources, and the shadow prices.

(j)   The shadow price of a scarce resource (ie fully utilised at optimum) is the opportunity cost of the constraint and is a valuable by-product of the Simplex method.

(k)   For every LP problem there is an equal but opposite formulation known as the primal and dual formulations, respectively. Although there are different layouts in the final tableau, the required results can be obtained from either formulation.

(l)   Shadow prices cannot be read directly from a graphical solution but can be obtained by simple calculation.

(m)   Sensitivity analysis is the process of varying factors in the problem to see the effect on the solution and to see the range of variation permitted before the solution changes.

(n)   The major limitations of LP are: the assumptions of linearity, certainty and continuity.

POINTS TO NOTE

20.   (a)   The importance of opportunity costs (ie shadow prices) are automatically produced by the Simplex method of solving LP problems and can be easily determined from graphical solutions. This makes LP an extremely useful technique for the management accountant when advising on resource allocation problems.

(b)   LP is a valuable extension of C-V-P analysis using similar principles and assumptions.

ADDITIONAL READING

Linear Programming	Accountant's Digest No. 65, ICA
An introduction to mathematical programming for accountants	Carsberg, ALLEN & UNWIN
Quantitative Techniques	Lucey, DP PUBLICATIONS
Linear programming in financial planning	Salkin & Kornbluth, ACCOUNTANCY AGE

SELF REVIEW QUESTIONS

1.   *What is LP and why is it of value to the management accountant? (2)*

2.   *What are the characteristics of problems that can be solved by LP? (3)*

3.   *How are problems expressed in the standardised manner? (4-6)*

4.   *When can graphical solution methods be used and how is the graph drawn? (9)*

5.   *How is the graph interpreted? (10)*

6.   *When is the Simplex method used? (11)*

7.   *What are slack variables and why are they necessary? (12)*

8.   *How is the final tableau recognised and how is it interpreted? (12)*

9.   *What are shadow prices and what constraints have shadow prices? (13)*

10.   *Distinguish between the primal and dual. (14)*

11.   *What differences in interpretation are necessary when considering the final tableau of a maximising dual formulation of a primal minimising problem? (15)*

12. How can shadow prices be obtained when the Simplex method has not been used to find a solution? (16)

13. What is a sensitive solution and what is sensitivity analysis? (17)

16. Investment Appraisal I

INTRODUCTION

1. This chapter considers the reasons for investment and explains in detail the various appraisal criteria. The 'traditional' techniques of accounting rate of return and payback are described together with their limitations. Discounted Cash Flow (DCF) is explained and the two principal techniques of Net Present Value (NPV) and Internal Rate of Return (IRR) are discussed in detail. Their use in typical situations is shown and a detailed comparison is made of their relative advantages and disadvantages. The latter part of the chapter discusses the problems associated with establishing an appropriate discount rate, known as the cost of capital. The Weighted Average Cost of Capital (WACC) approach using the dividend valuation model is described and the chapter concludes with a brief description of an alternative method of estimating the cost of equity capital known as the Capital Asset Pricing Model (CAPM).

LONG RUN DECISION MAKING

2. Investment decisions are long run decisions where consumption and investment alternatives are balanced over time in the hope that investment now will generate extra returns in the future. There are many similarities between short-run and long-run decision making, for example, the choice between alternatives, the need to consider future costs and revenues and the importance of incremental changes in costs and revenues but there is the additional requirement for investment decisions that, because of the time scale involved, the time value of the money invested must be considered. The time scale also makes the consideration of uncertainty and inflation of even greater importance than when considering short term decisions.

Assuming that finance is available the decision to invest will be based on three major factors:

(a) The investor's belief in the future. In business the beliefs would be based on forecasts of internal and external factors including: costs, revenues, inflation and interest rates, taxation and numerous other factors.

(b) The alternatives available in which to invest. This is the stage at which the various techniques used to appraise the competing investments would be used. The various techniques are covered in detail in this chapter.

(c) The investor's attitude to risk. Because investment decisions are often on a large scale, analysis of the investor's attitude to risk and the project uncertainty are critical factors in an investment decision and are dealt with in the following chapter.

Investment decision making is variably a top management exercise. This is because of the scale and long term nature of the consequences of such decisions. The accountant's task is to gather the essential data from various sources, consider the financing and taxation implications, analyse the data using one or more of the appraisal techniques and present the decision maker with the results of the exercise so that the decision maker may make more informed and hopefully better decisions.

There is strong research evidence* that overly elaborate appraisal methods, notwithstanding their theoretical correctness, are seen by practical decision makers as largely irrelevant. What is crucial is that the accountant should provide information which improved real investment decision making.

TRADITIONAL INVESTMENT APPRAISAL TECHNIQUES

3. Two particular methods of comparing the attractiveness of competing projects have become known as the 'traditional techniques'. These are the Accounting Rate of Return and Payback which are described below.

ACCOUNTING RATE OF RETURN

4. This is the ratio of average annual profits, after depreciation, to the capital invested. This is a basic definition only and variations exist, for example

- profits may be before or after tax
- capital may or may not include working capital
- capital invested may mean the initial capital investment or the average of the capital invested over the life of the project.

Note: An alternative term is return on Capital Employed (ROCE). The use of ROCE in divisional performance appraisal is dealt with later in the manual.

---

*For example 'Capital budgeting in the 1980's: A major survey of investment practices in large companies'. DR.R. PIKE, CIMA, 1982

Example 1. Accounting Rate of Return

A firm is considering three projects each with an initial investment of £1000 and a life of 5 years. The profits generated by the projects are estimated to be as follows:

AFTER TAX AND DEPRECIATION PROFITS

Year	Project I £	Project II £	Project III £
1	200	350	150
2	200	200	150
3	200	150	150
4	200	150	200
5	200	150	350
TOTAL	1000	1000	1000

Calculate the accounting rate of return (ARR) on
- (a) Initial Capital
- (b) Average Capital

Accounting rate of return on Initial Capital:

		Project I	Project II	Project III
Average Profits	=	$\dfrac{1000}{5}$	$\dfrac{1000}{5}$	$\dfrac{1000}{5}$
	=	£200 p.a. =	£200 p.a. =	£200 p.a.
ARR is		$\dfrac{200}{1000}$ = 20%	$\dfrac{200}{1000}$ = 20%	$\dfrac{200}{1000}$ = 20%

Accounting rate of return on Average Capital:

		Project I	Project II	Project III
Average Capital	=	$\dfrac{1000}{2}$	$\dfrac{1000}{2}$	$\dfrac{1000}{2}$
	=	£500 =	£500 =	£500
ARR is		$\dfrac{200}{500}$ = 40%	$\dfrac{200}{500}$ = 40%	$\dfrac{200}{500}$ = 40%

Note: Average capital is calculated according to the usual accounting convention that the initial investment is eroded steadily to zero over the life of the project so that the average capital invested is

$$\frac{\text{Initial Investment}}{2}$$

ADVANTAGES AND DISADVANTAGES OF ARR

5.   The only advantage that can be claimed for the ARR is simplicity of calculation, but the disadvantages are more numerous.

Disadvantages:

(a) Does not allow for the timing of outflows and inflows. The three projects in Example 1 are ranked equally even though there are clear differences in timings.

(b) Uses as a measure of return the concept of accounting profit. Profit has subjective elements, is subject to accounting conventions and is not as appropriate for investment appraisal purposes as the cash flows generated by the project.

(c) There is no universally accepted method of calculating ARR.

PAYBACK

6. Numerous surveys have shown that payback is a popular technique for appraising projects either on its own or in conjunction with other methods. Payback can be defined as the period, usually expressed in years which it takes for the project's net cash inflows to recoup the original investment. The usual decision rule is to accept the project with the shortest payback period. The following example demonstrates the technique.

Example 2

Calculate the payment periods for the following three projects:

NET CASH FLOWS

Year	PROJECT I		PROJECT II		PROJECT III	
	Cash Flow	Cumulative Cash Flow	Cash Flow	Cumulative Cash Flow	Cash Flow	Cumulative Cash Flow
0	-1500	-1500	-1500	-1500	-1500	-1500
1	+ 600	- 900	+ 400	-1100	+ 300	-1200
2	+ 500	- 400	+ 500	- 600	+ 500	- 700
3	+ 400	NIL	+ 600	NIL	+ 400	- 300
4	–		–		+ 300	NIL
5	–		–		+ 300	+ 300
6	–		–		+ 300	+ 600

(Note: The usual investment appraisal assumptions are adopted for the above table and all subsequent examples, that Year O means now, Year 1 means at the end of 2 year, year 2 the end of 2 years and so on, and that a negative cash flow represents a cash outflow and a positive sign represents a cash inflow).

Payback Periods	Project I	= 3 years
	Project II	= 3 years
	Project III	= 4 years

ADVANTAGES AND DISADVANTAGES OF PAYBACK

7. Advantages:

(a) Simple to calculate and understand.

(b) Uses project cash flows rather than accounting profits and hence is more objectively based.

(c) Favours quick return projects which may produce faster growth for the company and enhance liquidity.

(d) Choosing projects which payback quickest will tend to minimise those risks facing the company which are related to time. However, not all risks are related merely to time.

Disadvantages:

(a) Payback does not measure overall project worth because it does not consider cash flows after the payback period. In Example 2, Project III is ranked after Projects I and II, even though it produces cash flows over a 6 year period.

(b) Payback provides only a crude measure of the timing of project cash flows. In example 2, Projects I and II are ranked equally, even though there are clear differences in the timings of the cash flows.

In spite of any theoretical disadvantages, payback is undoubtedly the most popular appraisal criterion in practice.

DISCOUNTED CASH FLOW (DCF)

8. There is growing use of DCF techniques for appraising projects and for assisting investment decision making. The use of DCF overcomes some of the disadvantages of the traditional techniques but it must be stressed that DCF itself has problems and contains many assumptions so that it should be used with care and with an awareness of its limitations. The main DCF techniques of Net Present Value (NPV) and Internal Rate of Return (IRR) are described in this chapter but it is necessary first to consider two features common to all DCF methods: the use of cash flows and the time value of money.

USE OF CASH FLOWS

9.   All DCF methods use cash flows and not accounting profits. Accounting profits are invariably calculated for stewardship purposes and are period orientated (usually monthly, quarterly or annually) thus necessitating accrual accounting with its attendant conventions and assumptions. For investment appraisal purposes a project orientated approach using cash flows is to be preferred for the following reasons.

(a)   Cash flows are more objective and in the end are what actually count. Profits cannot be spent.

(b)   Accounting conventions regarding revenue/capital expenditure classifications, depreciation calculations, stock valuations become largely redundant.

(c)   The whole life of the project is to be considered, therefore it becomes unnecessary and misleading to consider accounting profits which are related to periods.

(d)   The timing or expected timing of cash flows is more easily ascertained.

WHAT CASH FLOWS SHOULD BE INCLUDED?

10.   The all embracing answer to this question is the **net after tax incremental cash flow** effect on the firm by accepting the project, ie the comparison of cash flows with and without the project. Many of the cash flow items are readily identifiable, eg the initial outlay on a new machine, but others are less easily identified yet are nevertheless just as relevant, eg the increase or reduction in sales income of an existing product when a new product is introduced. Typical cash flow items include:

(a)   Cash Inflows
  (i)   The project revenues
  (ii)   Government grants
  (iii)   Resale or scrap value of assets
  (iv)   Tax receipts
  (v)   Any other cash inflows caused by accepting the project.

(b)   Cash Outflows
  (i)   Initial investment in acquiring the assets
  (ii)   Project costs (labour, materials etc)
  (iii)   Working capital investment
  (iv)   Tax payments
  (v)   Any other cash outflow caused by accepting the project.

Notes:
(a)   The relevant costs in investment decisions, as with all other decisions, are opportunity costs and not historical accounting costs. For example, if a project occupies storage space rented by the firm at £5/square metre which could be sublet by the firm at £7/square metre, then the relevant cash flow is the benefit foregone of £7/square metre.

(b)   It will be noted that depreciation is not included. Depreciation is **NOT** a cash flow but an accounting convention. The capital outlay is already represented by the cash outflow of the initial investment, so to include depreciation would involve double counting. The only role of depreciation in investment appraisal is in determining the tax payments of the project, which are, of course, real cash flows.

(c)   Similarly, interest payments are not included because the discounting process itself takes account of the time value of money and to include interest payments and to discount would be to double count.

TIME VALUE OF MONEY

11.   Investment appraisal is concerned with long run decisions where costs and income arise at intervals over a period. Monies spent or received at different times cannot be compared directly, they must be reduced to equivalent values at some common date. This could be at any time during the the project life but appraisal methods which take account of the time factor use either now, the present time, or the end of the project as the common date.

Both discounting and compounding methods allow for the time value of money and could thus be used for investment appraisal but on the whole discounting methods are more frequently used. In general it is preferable to receive a given sum earlier rather than later because the sum received earlier can be put to use by earning interest or some productive investment within the business, ie money has a time productivity.

It should be noted that the time value of money concept applies even if there is zero inflation. Inflation obviously increases the discrepancy in value between monies received at different times but it is not the basis of the concept.

ASSUMPTIONS IN BASIC DCF APPRAISAL

12. In describing the two main DCF methods certain assumptions are made initially so that the underlying principles can be more easily understood. These are as follows:

(a) Uncertainty does not exist
(b) Inflation does not exist
(c) The appropriate discount rate to use is known
(d) A perfect capital market exists, ie unlimited funds can be raised at the market rate of interest.

Subsequently these assumptions will be removed and the problems of dealing with uncertainty, inflation, choosing a discount rate and capital rationing dealt with.

NET PRESENT VALUE (NPV)

13. The NPV method utilises discounting principles which should be familiar to management accounting students from earlier studies but for those whose knowledge is incomplete in this area the principles of discounting and the use of discount tables are reviewed in Appendix I of this chapter.

The NPV method involves calculating the present values of expected cash inflows and outflows (ie the process of discounting) and establishing whether in total the present value of cash inflows is greater than the present value of cash outflows.

The formula is

$$NPV = \sum_{i=0}^{i=n} \frac{C_i}{(1 + r)^i}$$

where C is the net cash flow in the period, i is the period number, and r is the discount rate.

Where the discount rate is the cost of capital of the firm (described in para 22) the usual decision rule, given the assumptions in para 12, is that a project is **acceptable if it has a positive NPV.**

Example 3

An investment is being considered for which the net cash flows have been estimated as follows:

Year 0	Year 1	Year 2	Year 3	Year 4
-9,500	+3,000	+4,700	+4,800	+3,200

What is the NPV if the discount rate is 20%? Is the project acceptable?

Note: Conventional year end cash flows have been assumed, ie Year 0 means now, Year 1 means after 1 year and so on.

Solution

From Table A the discount factors are 0.833, 0.694, 0.579 and 0.482.
∴   NPV = 9,500 + (0.833 x 3,000) + (0.694 x 4,700) + (0.579 x 4,800) + (0.482 x 3,200)

NPV = + £582 and, given the assumptions contains in the basic DCF model the investment would be acceptable.

MEANING OF NPV

14. If the NPV of a project is positive this can be interpreted as the potential increase in consumption made possible by the project valued in present day terms. This is illustrated by Table 1 based on Example 3 which shows the position if £9,500 is borrowed at 20% p.a. to finance the project on overdraft terms where interest is paid on the balance outstanding at the end of each year.

	Amount Owing b/fwd	+	Year's Interest	-	Year's Cash Flow	=	Balance o/s c/fwd
End year 1	9500	+	1900	-	3000	=	8400
End Year 2	8400	+	1680	-	4700	=	5380
End Year 3	5380	+	1076	-	4800	=	1656
End Year 4	1656	+	331	-	3200		

giving a final surplus of £1213

Table 1

This shows that if £9500 is borrowed at 20% the principal and interest could be repaid from the project cash flows leaving a cash balance at the end of Year 4 of £1213. This balance is known as the **Net Terminal Value** and has a present value of £584 (£1213 x 0.482) which, allowing for the approximations contained in three figure tables, is the NPV of Example 3.

INTERNAL RATE OF RETURN (IRR)

15. Alternative names for the IRR include: DCF yield, marginal efficiency of capital, trial and error method, discounted yield and the actuarial rate of return.

The IRR can be defined as the discount rate which gives zero NPV. Except by chance the IRR cannot be found directly; it can be found either by drawing a graph known as a **present value profile** or, more normally, by calculations involving linear interpolation. Both methods are illustrated below using the data from Example 3.

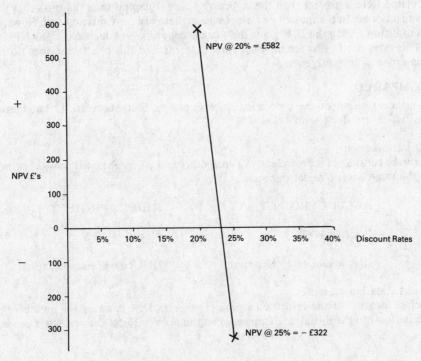

Figure 1   Present Value Profile

Notes on Figure 1

(a)   At least one discount rate must be chosen which gives a negative NPV so that the present value line crosses the horizontal axis.

(b)   The present value line crosses the axis at approximately 23% which is a close enough estimate for most practical purposes.

FINDING THE IRR BY LINEAR INTERPOLATION

16. Based on the data from Example 3 the IRR can be calculated as follows:

$$\text{IRR} = \underset{\text{(a)}}{20\%} + \underset{\text{(b)}}{5\%} \; \underset{\text{(d)}}{\overset{\text{(c)}}{\frac{582}{904}}}$$

$$= \; 23.2\%$$

Where

    (a)   is a discount rate which gives a positive NPV. In this example 20% gives £582.
    (b)   is the difference between (a) and the rate which gives a negative NPV. In this example 25% -20% = 5%.
    (c)   is the positive NPV at the discount rate chosen in (a). In this example it is £582.
    (d)   is the total range of NPV at the rates chosen. In this example +582 to -322 is a range of £904.

Notes:

    (a)   A simple way of obtaining a rough estimate of the IRR is to take the reciprocal of the payback periods. With short payback periods as in Example 3 the method is a poor estimator.

    (b)   As there is a non-linear relationship between discount rates and NPV, linear interpolation does not give a strictly accurate results. However, where the two discount rates that give positive and negative results are fairly close then the result is accurate enough for all practical and examination purposes.

DECISION RULE USING IRR

17. Where the calculated IRR is greater than the company's cost of capital then the project is acceptable, given the assumptions already mentioned. In the majority of cases where there are conventional cash flows, ie an initial outflow followed by a series of inflows, then the IRR gives the same accept or reject decision as the NPV which is the case in Example 3 above. This does not follow for all cash flow patterns and the two techniques do not necessarily rank projects in the same order of attractiveness.

NPV AND IRR COMPARED

18. In many circumstances either of these decision criteria can be used successfully but there are differences in particular situations which are dealt with below.

    (a) Accept/Reject decisions.
Where projects can be considered independently of each other and where the cash flows are conventional then NPV and IRR give the same accept/reject decision.

	ACCEPT PROJECT	REJECT PROJECT
NPV	Positive NPV	Negative NPV
IRR	IRR above cost of capital	IRR below cost of capital

    (b) Absolute and Relative measures
NPV is an absolute measure of the return on a project whereas IRR is a relative measure relating the size and timing of the cash flows to the initial investment. Thus the NPV reflects the scale of a project whereas the IRR does not.

Example 4

    Assume a project has the following cash flows:

	Year 0	Year 5
Project X	-£20,000	+£40,241

NPV @ 10%	=	£4,990
IRR	=	15%

∴ Project acceptable by both methods - assuming 10% is the cost of capital.

Now assume that the project is scaled up by a factor of 10

	Year 0	Year 5
Project 10X	-£200,000	+£402,410

NPV @ 10%	=	£49,900
IRR	=	15%

The NPV method clearly discriminates between Project X and Project 10X whereas the IRR remains unchanged at 15%.

(c) Mutually Exclusive Projects

An important class of projects is that concerned with mutually exclusive decisions, eg where only one of several alternative projects can be chosen. For example, where several alternative uses of the same piece of land are being considered, when one is chosen the other are automatically excluded.

Mutually exclusive decisions are commonly encountered and make it necessary to rank projects in order of attractiveness and to choose the most profitable. In such circumstances NPV and IRR may give conflicting rankings.

Example 5 (Mutually exclusive projects of differing scale)

A property company wishes to develop a site it owns. Three sizes of properly are being considered and the costs and revenues are as follows:

	Year 0 Expenditure £m	Year 1 to perpetuity Rentals p.a. £m
Small development	2	0.6
Medium development	4	1
Large development	6	1.35

The cost of capital is 10% and it is required to rank the projects by NPV and IRR and to select the most profitable.

The projects are mutually exclusive because the building of one size of development excludes the others.

Solution

	Expenditure £m	P.V. of rentals £m	NPV £m	IRR %
Small	2	6	4	30
Medium	4	10	6	25
Large	6	13.5	7.5	22.5

The ranking obtained by NPV and IRR differ and in such circumstances the NPV ranking is preferred (ie large development in this example) because it leads to the greatest increase in wealth for the company.

Although safer the simpler to rank by NPV, IRR can be used by adopting an incremental approach and comparing the incremental IRR at each increment with the cost of capital. Example 5 is reworked using this approach.

	Incremental Expenditure £m	Incremental Rental £m	Incremental IRR %
Stage 1 (small)	2	0.6	30
Stage 2 (medium-small)	2	0.4	20
Stage 3 (large-medium)	2	0.35	17.5

It will be seen that the IRR of each successive stage, although declining, is greater than the 10% cost of capital so that each successive increment is worthwhile. Although this method leads to the correct conclusion it is cumbersome and the simpler, more direct NPV method is preferable.

Example 6 (Mutually exclusive projects, same scale)

Two mutually exclusive investments have cash flows as follows:

	Year 0	Year 1	Year 2	Year 3
Project A	−24000	+ 8000	+12000	+16000
Project B	−24000	+16000	+10000	+ 8000

The cost of capital is 10%.

The NPV and IRR of these projects is as follows:

	NPV @ 10%	IRR
		%
Project A	+5200	20.65
Project B	+4812	22.8

Thus it will be seen that the rankings differ and, assuming that 10% is the appropriate discount rate, the ranking given by the NPV, ie Project A being preferred, gives the maximum wealth to the company.

Note: The conflict in ranking shown above is but a reflection of the differing time profile of the project cash flows. Such time profiles produce different NPV rankings using different discount rates; for example, the NPV's of the above projects at 20% discount rate are £256 and £900 respectively, giving a B - A ranking instead of the A - B ranking at 10%.

NON-CONVENTIONAL CASH FLOWS. (THE MULTIPLE RATE PROBLEM)

19. The projects considered so far have had conventional cash flows, ie an initial outflow followed by a series of inflows. Where the cash flows vary from this they are termed non-conventional. The following are examples.

Example 7. Non-Conventional Cash-flow Patterns

	Year 0	Year 1	Year 2
Project X	−2000	+4700	−2750
Project Y	+2000	−4000	+4000

Project X has 2 outflows and is thus non-conventional

Project Y has an outflow in a year's time instead of initially and is thus non-conventional.

When a project has non-conventional cash flows it may have

(i)   one IRR
(ii) multiple IRR's
(iii) no IRR

Multiple Rates:- If the present value profile for Project X in Example 7 is drawn it can be seen that it is a multiple IRR project having two IRR's, at 10% and 25%.

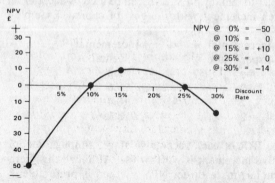

Figure 2 Present Value Profile of Project X

No IRR: Project Y in Example 7 above is an example of a project where it is not possible to calculate a real rate of return.

To be able to calculate a real IRR it is necessary to solve for i in the following expression:

$$+2000 \quad - \quad \frac{4000}{(1+i)^1} \quad + \quad \frac{4000}{(1+i)^2} \quad = \quad 0$$

Solving for i produces $i = \sqrt{-1}$ which is not a real number.

In circumstances with non-conventional cash flow patterns which produce multiple IRR's or no real IRR the use of IRR is not recommended.

The NPV method gives clear, unambiguous results whatever the cash flow pattern.

Project X above has positive NPV's at discount rates between 10% and 25% and negative NPV's at lower and higher rates. Project Y has a positive NPV at any discount rate.

SUMMARY OF NPV AND IRR COMPARISON

20. (a) NPV is technically superior to IRR and is simpler to calculate.

(b) Where cash-flow patterns are non-conventional there may be nil or several internal rates of return making the IRR impossible to apply.

(c) NPV is superior for ranking investments in order of attractiveness.

(d) With conventional cash flow patterns both methods give the same accept or reject decision.

(e) Where discount rates are expected to differ over the life of the project such variations can be readily incorporated into NPV calculations, but not in those for the IRR.

(f) Notwithstanding the technical advantages of NPV over IRR, IRR is widely used in practice so that it is essential that students are aware of its inherent limitations.

EXCESS PRESENT VALUE INDEX (EVPI) OR PROFITABILITY INDEX

21. The EVPI is merely a variant of the basic NPV method and is the ratio of the NPV of a project to the initial investment

$$\text{ie EVPI} \quad = \quad \frac{\text{NPV}}{\text{INITIAL INVESTMENT}}$$

Thus the index is a measure of relative and not absolute profitability. Because of this it suffers from the same general criticisms when used for ranking purposes as the IRR. The EVPI is not suitable for ranking mutually exclusive projects, but because it is a measure of relative profitability it can be used where there are a number of divisible projects (ie fractional parts of projects may be undertaken) which cannot all be implemented because of a shortage of capital in the current period. In such circumstances the projects can be ranked in order of their EVPI's and implemented in order of attractiveness until the capital available is exhausted. If, however, the projects being considered covered two or more periods where funds were limited then the EVPI could not be used. In general the EVPI is of limited usefulness and the use of NPV is considered safer.

COST OF CAPITAL

22. So far in this chapter the discount rate or the target rate of return has been assumed. Obviously in practice the rate is not automatically provided and it is necessary to estimate or calculate some appropriate discount rate. This rate is known as the **cost of capital**. The calculation of the cost of capital is a complex subject involving many aspects of financing and company financial structures. Inevitably there are many subjective judgements to be made even in the most sophisticated calculations and there is empirical evidence that any businessmen estimate the cost of capital in an intuitive manner without too much regard for theoretical niceties. In spite of this it is necessary for accountancy students to be aware of some of the more generally accepted theoretical background to cost of capital calculations. Two possible approaches to this problem are discussed in this manual, one based on the estimated costs of the elements which make up the overall supply of capital known as the **Weighted Average Cost of Capital** and a more theoretical view based on the relationship in the capital market between risk and return known as the **Capital Asset Pricing Model**.

THE WEIGHTED AVERAGE COST OF CAPITAL APPROACH

23. Companies, particularly large ones, are complex entities and are funded from a large number of sources. These range from long term sources such as equity capital to short term sources such as bank overdrafts. They also range from those with a fixed contractual rate of interest such as debentures and preference shares to those with no specified cost such as ordinary shares. It is this diversity which complicates the situation, but fortunately there are two generally accepted principles which help to clarify the situation somewhat. These are that **long term funds only** should be included in the cost of capital calculation and that the cost of capital should be **representative** of the overall **pool of long term capital.**

(a) Long term funds only. The reasoning behind this is that investment appraisals are essentially concerned with long-term investments and short-term finance, for example, bank overdrafts, is not generally available for these investments. Short-term finance such as bank overdrafts and hire purchase provide valuable ancillary forms of finance and can be taken into account in the cash flows of the project, ie as changes in the working capital requirements or as the cash payments under the hire purchase agreements.

(b) Representative Cost of Pool of long-term Capital. It is generally considered incorrect to identify the particular source of capital with particular projects. It is incorrect to discount one project, financed by an issue of debentures, at the cost of those debentures and some other project at an imputed cost of equity capital. The reasons for this are that the coupon cost of the debentures almost certainly does not reflect the overall impact on the company's cost of capital, and also because the matching of projects with particular sources of funds is very much a random matter. What is more important is that projects earn at least the average cost of capital of the pool of long-term capital resources available to the firm. This cost of capital is known as the **weighted average cost of capital (WACC).**

Note: The above principles are not absolute rules and differences exist in practice and in examination questions. A typical variation is for a regularly occurring bank overdraft (normally considered a short term method of finance) to be included in the pool of capital resources available for investment purposes and thus the cost of the bank overdraft would need to be included in the weighted average cost of capital calculation.

The WACC is found by calculating the average of the cost of each component of the firm's finance (equity, preference, debentures) weighted according to its proportionate share of the total pool of capital available. The weighting normally used is the current market valuation of the shares and loan stock, not the nominal book values.

Example 8

Acropolis Ltd has the following long term sources of capital

10 million £1 Ordinary shares with a current market price of £1.40
2 million £1 Preference shares with a current market price of 92.5p
£7.5 million Debenture Stock with a current market price of £90 per £100 nominal value.

The individual component costs have been estimated at 16%, 12% and 8% respectively.

Calculate the WACC using market value weighting.

Solution

Component	Market Value		Proportion	Individual Cost	Weighted Cost %	
Ord. Shares	10m x £1.4 =	£14m	62%	16%	.62 x 16% =	9.92
Pref. Shares	2m x 0.925 =	£1.85m	8%	12%	.08 x 12% =	0.96
Debentures	7.5m x 0.9 =	£6.75m	30%	8%	.3 x 8% =	2.4
		£22.6m total			TOTAL =	13.28%

∴ Weighted average cost of capital = 13.28%.

In the example above, the individual component costs were provided but normally these have to be estimated or calculated. The major factors to be considered in this process are discussed below.

COST OF THE COMPONENTS OF WACC

24. Preference shares and debentures have known costs associated with them, either the dividend rate of the shares or the fixed rate of interest attached to the debentures. Accordingly, having due regard to the different taxation treatment of debentures and preferences shares, an estimate of their costs can be made relatively easily. The position is more complicated with ordinary shares or equity and many more assumptions are required.

Debentures and preference shares are dealt with first followed by discussion of the problems associated with estimating the cost of equity.

FIXED INTEREST CAPITAL (DEBENTURES AND PREFERENCE SHARES)

25. Fixed interest sources of funds, debentures and preference shares, may be irredeemable or redeemable at a given date. Interest paid on debentures, unlike preference dividends, is an allowable charge against corporation tax. These factors give rise to four possible situations shown below.

	IRREDEEMABLE	REDEEMABLE
Preference Shares	Case 1	Case 2
Debentures	Case 3	Case 4

Except for the taxation deduction Case 1 and Case 3 are identical and so are Case 2 and Case 4.

IRREDEEMABLE SOURCES (Cases 1 and 3)

26. The cost of a perpetuity is

$$r = \frac{a}{v} \, 100\% \quad \text{where } r = \text{rate of interest or dividend}$$

$$a = \text{annual income}$$

$$v = \text{current market value.}$$

This simple formula is used in the examples below.

Example 9 (Case 1)

A company finds that its £1 9% Preference shares are currently quoted at 82p. What is the effective cost?

Solution

$$r = \frac{a}{v} \, 100\% = \frac{.09}{.82} \times 100 = 10.97\%$$

$$\underline{\text{say } 11\%}$$

Example 10 (Case 3)

Assume the same data as in Example 9 except that debentures are involved and the corporation tax rate is 55%.

Solution

The after tax cost of interest $= r(1 - c)$
where c = corporation tax rate

∴ Based on Example 9 data and 55% corporation tax:-

After tax cost of interest	$= 11(1 - 0.55)$
	$= 4.95$
	$= \underline{\text{say } 5\%}$

REDEEMABLE SOURCES OF CAPITAL

27. The cost of redeemable debentures and preference shares consists of two elements.

(a) The costs of servicing, by interest or dividends, the loan stock for a finite number of years and,
(b) The redemption costs at the end of the stated number of years.

The annual servicing costs can be considered as an annuity and, if debenture interest is involved, are an allowable charge against corporation tax. The redemption costs at the end of the period ar not tax deductible so must be included gross in the cost of capital calculation.

Example 11 (Case 2)

Assume the same data as in Example 9 except that the stock is redeemed at par (£1) after 20 years. No taxation is involved because the stock is in the form of preference shares.

The cost to the company is the discount rate (x) which equates the future income and amount of the redemption to the current purchase price, ie

$$0.09A_{\overline{20}|} x + 1.00 \qquad \frac{1}{(1 + x)20} \qquad - 0.82 \quad = \quad 0$$

$$\text{(i)} \qquad\qquad\qquad \text{(ii)} \qquad\qquad \text{(iii)}$$

Notes:

(i)   Is the present value of a 20 year annuity of the 9p income at x% (Table B)
(ii) Is the present value of the amount redeemed (£1) after 20 years at x% (Table A)
(iii) Is the current price.

To find the value of x we try a given percentage in the equation above. Try 12%

$$.09 \times 7.47 + .104 - .82 = -0.0437$$
$$\therefore 12\% \text{ is too high.}$$

Try 10%

$$.09 \times 8.514 + 0.149 - .82 = +0.0953$$
$$\therefore 10\% \text{ is too low.}$$

As usual the value is found by linear interpolation

$$x \quad = \quad 10 + 2 \left(\frac{0.0935}{0.1390} \right)$$

$$= \quad \underline{11.37\%}$$

Example 12 (Case 4)

Once again the position is as Example 11 except that debentures are involved and thus the taxation aspects must be considered. Because of the differing tax treatments of the two elements which make up the total cost to the firm (ie interest - allowable against tax, redeemable element - not allowable) it is necessary to consider the elements separately.

Effective interest rate for 10 years of interest payments at 9% nominal when purchased at 82p is found as follows:-

$$0.82 = .09 \times 20 \text{ year annuity factor at } x\%$$

$$\therefore \quad \frac{0.82}{0.09} \quad = \quad 9.11$$

and looking along the 20 year annuity line the rate will be seen to be between 8% and 10% (ie between 9.818 and 8.514). This rate can be approximated as follows

$$8\% + 2\% \left(\frac{0.60}{1.304} \right) \quad = \quad 8.92\%, \text{ say } \underline{9\%}$$

$$\therefore \text{ After tax interest rate} \quad = 9(1 - 0.55)$$
$$\simeq \underline{4\%}$$

The redemption yield for a 20 year debenture paying a 9% coupon rate redeemable at par is made up of the interest payments over the 20 years plus the amount received at redemption, ie 11.37% as calculated in Example 11.

As the interest payments account for 9% of this, the extra non tax allowable element is 2.37% (11.37 - 9).

$$\therefore \quad \text{the overall, net, after tax cost to the firm is}$$
$$4\% + 2.37\% = 6.37\% \text{ say } \underline{6\tfrac{1}{2}\%}$$

EQUITY CAPITAL

28. Although of great importance in the financial structures of most organisations equity capital does not have a known, fixed rate of dividend associated with it but obviously it does have a cost. There is general acceptance that the returns to equity should be higher than the returns to fixed interest investments such as debentures, and also that there is a relationship between the returns to equity shareholders and the risk class of the company – the higher the risk, the higher the expected return.

One approach to the estimation of the cost of equity is the use of the Gordon growth model, sometimes termed the dividend valuation model.

GORDON GROWTH MODEL

29. This is a theory of share price movements based on the assumption that the sole determinant of the price of shares (and thus the return received by the investor) is the present value of the anticipated future stream of dividends. The model is based on numerous assumptions the major ones of which are:

(a) Investors act rationally with regard to future returns.

(b) Investors all have the same time preference which can be evaluated by discounting at the investor's personal discount rate.

(c) There is no inflation or taxation and that the future is known with certainty by all investors.

Clearly these assumptions may make the model totally invalid in practice, but the application of the theory may be a useful starting point in the estimation of the cost of equity. Two further assumptions frequently made for examination purposes which considerably simplify the calculations, involved are that either constant dividends are paid each year to perpetuity, or that there is a constant compound growth rate of dividends to perpetuity, ie the dividend each year increases by the same percentage. The formulae for the dividend valuation model are as follows:

(i) CONSTANT DIVIDENDS TO PERPETUITY

$$i \;=\; \frac{d}{v}$$

(ii) CONSTANT COMPOUND GROWTH RATE OF DIVIDENDS TO PERPETUITY

$$i \;=\; \frac{d(1+g)}{v} + g$$

where v = current market value for share
  d = dividend per share
  i = personal discount rate
  g = growth rate of dividends.

Example 13

Pitprop Ltd has just paid a dividend of 35p on its ordinary shares which are currently priced at £3.20. What is the investor's personal discount rate if:

(a) dividends are expected to remain constant?
(b) dividends are expected to grow at 15% compound p.a.?

Solution

(a) $i \;=\; \dfrac{d}{v} \;=\; \dfrac{0.35}{£3.20} \;=\; 10.93\%$ say <u>11%</u>

(b) $i \;=\; \dfrac{d(1+g)}{v} + g \;=\; \dfrac{0.35(1+0.15)}{3.20} + 0.15 \;=\; 27.58\%$, <u>say 27½</u>

Notes:

(a) The investor's personal discount rate is known as the COST OF EQUITY CAPITAL.

(b) With constant dividends it will be recognised that the cost of equity capital is the dividend yield.

(c) If a company was entirely equity financed, as postulated in the basic Gordon model, then the cost of capital to be used for discounting should be the cost of equity as outlined above and thus the NPV of projects is directly related to their impact on share prices as shown in Example 14.

(d) Estimates of g, the growth factor, may be based on past growth rates of dividends or on the expected results of current and future investment opportunities and changes in the financing strategies of the firm.

Example 14

Wye Ltd is financed entirely by equity and has 5000 £1 shares in issue which have a market price of £4 each. From existing projects a constant dividend of 50p per share has been and can continue to be paid. A new project is being considered which has an outlay now of £2000 and which is expected to generate £650 p.a. cash flows to perpetuity. Assuming that the finance for the new project is raised by a right issue and that all project proceeds will continue to be paid out as dividends, calculate:

    (a) the new dividends per share
    (b) the new market value per share assuming a 2.5 rights issue
    (c) the overall gain to the shareholders.

Solution

Shareholders personal discount rate (cost of equity)

$$= \frac{50p}{£4} = .125 = 12\tfrac{1}{2}\%$$

(a) New dividend per share

$$= \frac{\text{old dividend payment + project proceeds}}{\text{new number of shares}}$$

$$= \frac{£(500 \times .50) + 650}{7000} = 45p/share$$

(b) New market value per share

$$= \frac{\text{new dividend}}{\text{cost of equity}} = \frac{45}{.125} = £3.60$$

(c) Overall gain to shareholders

$$\text{Project NPV} = (\frac{650}{.125} - 2000) = £3,200$$

which is reflected in the changed market valuation of the company thus

		£
Net Market Valuation 7000 x £3.60 =		25,200
less Old Market Valuation	20,000	
Cost of Rights Issue	2,000	22,000
Gain to Shareholders		3,200

Note: The actual terms of the rights issue whether 2:5. 1:2 or whatever, are irrelevant because the overall valuation and the amount to be contributed by shareholders is unaffected. The project NPV is obtained by calculating the present value of a £650 p.a. perpetuity and deducting the original investment of £2,000.

NEW ISSUES RIGHTS ISSUES AND RETAINED EARNINGS

30. There are various forms in which equity finance may appear. These may be public issues to the market, rights issues to existing shareholders and the use of retained earnings which are an alternative to the payment of dividends. In general, some estimate of the cost of each source could be based on the 'growth model' but there are detail differences. For example, both rights issues and public issues incur issue costs which may be considerable. On the other hand, retained earnings have no issue expenses and reduce the tax liability on income for shareholders. However, if the retained earnings can only be obtained by reduction in anticipated dividends then there may be a fall in the share price and a loss of confidence in the firm.

In general all types of equity are relatively expensive forms of finance compared with, for example, the tax allowable interest on debentures.

GEARING AND THE WACC

31. The relationship between fixed interest capital sources (debentures and preferences shares) and equity sources is known as the gearing of the firm (leverage in American terminology) and is usually expressed as percentage. Various gearing ratio formulae exist. Typical examples are:

$$\text{Capital Gearing} = \frac{\text{Fixed interest capital}}{\text{Fixed interest capital} + \text{Equity Capital}}$$

The fixed interest capital and the equity capital may be expressed either in terms of **Book Values** or **Market Values.**

$$\text{Income Gearing} = \frac{\text{Fixed interest charges}}{\text{Operating profit before fixed interest charges and taxation}}$$

Because many variants of the gearing ratio exist students must take particular care when comparing gearing ratios of different companies that they are calculated on the same basis.

EFFECTS OF CHANGES IN GEARING

32. The general effect of increases in the gearing ratio is to increase the risks of both equity and fixed interest investors but particularly those of the equity shareholder, because of the fixed interest entitlement whether or not profits are made or whether profits are high or low. Thus, as the gearing ratio increases, holders of both equity and fixed interest capital are likely to require higher returns to compensate for the increased vulnerability of their dividends or interest. What gearing ratio to aim for, that is, the optimum financial structure of the company, is a matter of some debate with two contrasting positions, what has become known as the 'traditional view' and the Modigliani-Miller hypothesis.

THE TRADITIONAL VIEW OF GEARING AND WACC

33. Because fixed interest investors historically have not required such a high return as equity investors, making a company more highly geared by introducing fixed interest capital, such as debentures and preferences shares, lowers the WACC at least in the early stages. As the gearing increases equity holders start to demand a higher return to compensate for the increased risks involved and at even higher gearing ratios the fixed interest investors start to demand higher returns so that eventually the WACC starts to rise. This movement results in a U shaped WACC curve indicating that for a given company there is some optimum mix of debt and equity. This is summarised in Figure 3.

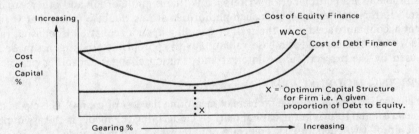

Figure 3 Traditional View of Gearing and WACC

THE MODIGLIANI-MILLER HYPOTHESIS (MM)

34. The essential core of the MM view is that firms of the same size with the same operating risks will have the same total value and hence WACC regardless of their individual gearing ratios. Their view that the proportion of debt to equity does not affect the WACC results in a straight line WACC rather than a U shaped curve as in the traditional view. The MM view is shown in Figure 4.

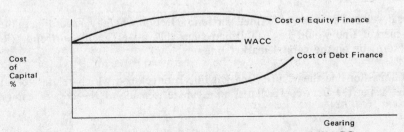

Figure 4 Modigliani Miller View of Gearing and WACC

To obtain a straight line WACC, MM advance two basic arguments.

(a)   The issue of more debt causes the return required by equity shareholders to rise so that the advantages of using the cheaper debt finance is exactly offset. This process they suggest works by investors altering their own personal gearing through personal borrowing, and switching investments. This process is known as arbitrage.

(b)   At high levels of gearing, risk seeking investors will buy shares for the first time.

The MM view is based on a number of assumptions the major ones of which are that there is no taxation and capital markets are perfect. In practice the market is not perfect and taxation does exist which has the effect of reducing the cost of debt finance substantially. Since the early 1960's whe MM first published their thesis much academic discussion and empirical research has taken place to verify or disprove their arguments. So far this has been inconclusive.

From a student's point of view the importance of the MM view is that it prevents too ready acceptance of the apparently common-sense 'traditional view'. It should be clear that a broad view of the cost of fixed interest capital should include not only the effective rate of interest calculations as shown above but also the effect on the returns required by equity investors.

WACC - A SUMMARY

35.   The WACC appears to be a commonly used method of obtaining the discounting rate for use in investment appraisal but it must be recognised simply as an operational tool with a number of subjective elements and theoretical limitations.

If the WACC is based simply on historical capital structures then its use can be severely criticised because it is the anticipated future structures that are relevant particularly if the capital for the proposed project makes a significant change in the financial structure of the company, for example by changing the gearing ratio. In general, WACC would seem to be more appropriate when the proposed investment is of a similar nature to existing operations so that the general business risk is unchanged. WACC makes the implicit assumption that the two types of risk with which the company is concerned, (ie **business risks** caused by trading and operations and **financial risks** which are a function of gearing) remain unchanged.

Although there is an accounting logic to WACC, whereby the average value of the various elements is used, it will be apparent that the estimated cost of an important element, the equity based sources, is dependent on the validity of the dividend valuation model with its inherent assumptions and estimates, eg the estimate for g and the assumption that dividends are the sole determinant of share price.

These and other problems lead a number of writers, eg Williams and Gordon and others, to doubt if the cost of capital can be measured in the real world. Whilst such authorities are no doubt correct, that is little comfort to the practising management accountant faced with the task of deciding upon a realistic discounting rate. It is because of such realities that the WACC is often used as a base valuation with appropriate adjustments made for such matters as the risk elements caused by the project, future interest and taxation changes and other practical considerations.

CAPITAL ASSET PRICING MODEL (CAPM)

36.   The CAPM is an alternative approach to the problem of measuring the cost of capital. The model attempts to measure the relationship between risk and return in the capital market. Underlying the model is the assumption that the return to an investor is made up of two parts: a risk free rate of interest to which is added a premium to cater for the particular level of risk in a given security. Where the risk is greater so is the additional premium. The premium is calculated by using what is known as the β (Beta) coefficient.

The beta-coefficient is a measure of the volatility of the individual security's returns relative to market returns and thus, when a risk-return profile for the market is calculated, the cost of capital for a given company can be established. Assuming that such a value is available, it can be used as the discount rate being a fair approximation of opportunity cost representing as it does the market's expected rate of return for shares in its risk class.

The CAPM was developed as an aid to optimal portfolio selection whereby, according to the attitude to risk of the investor, a **capital market line** would be established such that all efficient portfolios (ie preferred trade-offs between risk and return) lie on the capital market line.

From the capital market line the **security market line** is developed which relates to individual securities and firms. From this line, using the Beta coefficients, an estimate is made of the cost of capital.

Although this process is involved and somewhat theoretical it is an attempt to obtain an objective estimate of the required return of shareholders and seeks to measure the very real trade-off that exists between risk and return in the capital market.

Like all theoretical models the CAPM incorporates numerous assumptions which may limit its application in practical situations. Some of the major assumptions are:-

(a)   Investors are wealth maximisers who base their choice of portfolios on the mean and variance (ie the measure of risk) of the returns expected from the security.

(b)   All investors can borrow or lend unlimited amounts at a given risk free rate of interest.

(c)   All investors have identical subjective estimates of the return and variance of return (riskiness) of a particular security.

(d)   There are no transaction costs and no taxes.

(e)   All investors are price takers. This means that no investor operates on a scale large enough to have any significant influence on the price of a security.

Note: These are restrictive assumptions and the CAPM can be criticised on these grounds but it would be remembered that some criticisms can be made against ALL investment appraisal techniques.

USING CAPM TO ESTIMATE THE COST OF EQUITY

37.   The steps involved in using CAPM to estimate the cost of equity capital are as follows:

1.   Estimate the market parameters.
That is the risk-free rate of return, the expected return on the market and the variance of the market return.

2.   Estimate the firm's beta coefficient.
This is based on an historical analysis of the shares performance, ie the prices, price changes, dividend yields, variances of return and covariances with market returns over as long a period as possible. Risk-less securities have beta coefficients equal to nil; an average security has a beta value of 1.0; lower risk securities have values less than 1 and relatively higher risk securities have beta values greater than 1.

3.   Estimate the cost of equity using the market parameters and the firm's beta coefficient.
Figure 5 provides a representation of the process.

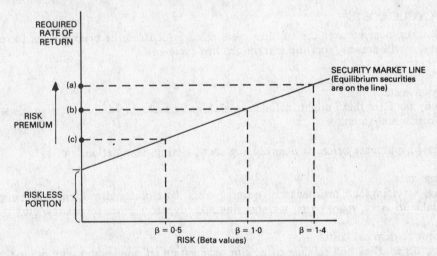

Figure 5 Security Market Line Showing Trade Off Between Risk and Return

Notes on Figure 5: Three possible beta values have been shown which result in three estimates of the required rate of return.

(a)   Beta value 1.4 - higher than average return and risk
(b)   Beta value 1.0 - security with an average return and risk
(c)   Beta value 0.5 - lower than average return and risk.

The intercept with y axis is the riskless rate of return and is generally taken as the return on government stocks.

The appropriate equation for establishing the expected return is as follows:

$$R_a = R_f + (R_m - R_f)\beta$$

where R_a = the expected return on the security
   R_f = the risk free interest rate
   R_m = the expected return on a market portfolio
   β = the beta coefficient which measures the volatility of the security's return relative to market return.

For example, if the risk free interest rate is 9%, the market return 13% and the beta coefficient is 1.4 then:

$$R_a = 9 + (13 - 9)1.4$$
$$= \underline{18.2\%}$$

which would be the cost of capital estimate according to the Capital Asset Pricing Model.

Note: The β coefficient is found by dividing the covariance of the return on the new investment and the return on the market portfolio by the variance of the market return, ie

$$\beta = \frac{COV.(R_a, R_m)}{Variance (R_m)}$$

LIFE CYCLE COSTING - A DEFINITION

38. Life cycle costing or terotechnology can be defined as: 'A combination of management, financial, engineering and other practices applied to physical assets in pursuit of economic life cycle costs, ie its aim is to obtain the best use of physical assets at the lowest cost to the entity'. *Terminology.*

The concept of terotechnology was publicised by the Department of Industry in the 1970s with the aim of getting industry to take account of the total cost of acquiring, operating and eventually disposing of an asset over its whole life rather than merely concentrate on one aspect of cost, that of acquisition. Of course enlightened management have always taken the long view and have avoided the trap of making undue economies at the purchasing stage to the detriment of operating and maintenance costs later on. This is false economy but is all too prevalent. The original concept addressed only physical assets (see definition above) but the more modern view is that the principles of life cycle costing should apply equally to products and services as well as conventional fixed assets.

TYPICAL LIFE CYCLE COSTS

39. In general all costs incurred over the full life cycle of an asset from the original idea for purchase or design through to disposal or withdrawal from the market are life cycle costs.

Examples include:

(a) Acquisition costs
-   if made by the firm these might include research and development costs, design costs, consultancy fees, testing, production and so on.

-   if purchased; purchase price, any purchasing costs, testing, installation, etc.

(b) Operating costs
   including; servicing and maintenance, training costs, cost of standby facilities, energy costs, overhead costs attributable to asset, spare parts, warehousing and inventory costs for spares, etc.

(c) Retirement or disposal costs
   including; dismantling and salvage costs, site reclamation (if applicable), any other form of termination costs.

At any of the stages there may be fees for technical services or costs to bring the equipment up to current legal standards. Examples include the costs of eliminating excess noise, fumes or noxious discharges and waste products and of meeting more stringent safety regulations.

OPTIMISING LIFE CYCLE COSTS

40. It will be apparent that the aim is to minimise the overall costs over the asset's life cycle. This will be achieved best by considering the impact of, and interactions between, **all** costs prior to acquisition rather than considering the elements in a piecemeal fashion. All too often the initial capital costs are considered in isolation in a conventional project appraisal and the budgeting of maintenance and operating costs are considered separately after the asset has been acquired. If the interactions between the two are studied it may well be cost effective to incur higher initial capital costs to reduce later servicing and maintenance charges and to ensure more trouble free production.

To keep life cycle costs to a minimum, apart from initial acquisition costs, three areas need close examination.

Utilisation: What is the proportion of time that the asset is capable of functioning or producing to the required standard?

Maintainability: How easy is the asset to service and maintain and what is the availability and cost of parts?

Disposal: What will be the costs and problems of disposal or destruction?

Each of these areas requires technical, engineering, scientific and production expertise; they cannot be assessed by accountants alone. If any of these vital areas are overlooked it is unlikely that life cycle costs will be minimised. As an example of the problems encountered, consider the difficulties and costs faced by the Nuclear Industry in decommissioning obsolete reactors and disposing of nuclear waste.

An important point for accountants to remember is that reports and cost analyses should be related to the variable length of an asset's life cycle and not to the conventional reporting periods of months and years commonly encountered. Terotechnology does not involve any new accounting techniques or principles; rather it is a way of integrating types of information in order to examine a problem in its entirety.

EXAMPLE – LIFE CYCLE COSTS

41. A firm with a 10% cost of capital is considering the purchase of two machine tools, X and Y. Both can produce the same component at identical rates per working hour and the relevant data on the machines is as follows:

	Machine X	Machine Y
Capital Cost		
Operating costs per working hour		
Energy	£3	£5
Consumables	£6	£8
Variable overheads	£6	£7
Maintenance Costs		
Service intervals	12 p.a.	10 p.a.
Cost of Services	£1000	£800
Random breakdowns	3 p.a.	1 p.a.
Cost of breakdowns	£2000	£3000
Expected Availability		
(working hours per annum)	1500	2000
Contribution from production		
per hour (excluding mc. costs)	£50	£50
Expected life	5 years	5 years
Net salvage value at the end of		
year 5	£10,000	£25,000

Solution

	Machine X	Machine Y
Gross contribution/hour	£50	£50
less Operating costs	£15	£20
Contribution/hour	£35	£30
Hours available	1500	2000
Total contribution p.a.	52,500	60,000

		Machine X		Machine Y	
less	Maintenance				
	Service	12000		8000	
	Breakdowns	6000	18,000	3000	11,000
Net contribution p.a.			£34,500		£49,000

$$\therefore \quad \text{PV of X} = -100{,}000 + 3.791 \times 34{,}500 + 0.621 \times 10{,}000 = £37{,}000$$
$$\text{PV of Y} = -160{,}000 + 3.791 \times 49{,}000 + 0.621 \times 25{,}000 = £41{,}284$$

Thus machine Y would be preferred because, although having a greater capital cost, it is available for more hours per year for production, it has lower servicing costs and a greater resale value. Over the whole life cycle it is more cost effective.

SUMMARY

42. (a)   Investment decisions are long run decisions where consumption and investment opportunities are balanced over time.

(b)   The decision to invest is based on many factors including: the investor's beliefs in the future, the alternatives available and his attitude to risk.

(c)   The 'traditional' investment appraisal techniques are the accounting rate of return and payback. Payback is shown by recent surveys to be the most widely used technique.

(d)   Payback is the number of period's cash flows to recoup the original investment. The project chosen is the one with the shortest payback period.

(e)   Discounted Cash Flow (DCF) techniques use cash flows rather than profits and take account of the time value of money.

(f)   The formula for Net Present Value is

$$\text{NPV} = \quad \Sigma \quad \frac{C_i}{(1 + r)^i}$$

and given the assumption of the basic model, a project is acceptable if it has a positive NPV.

(g)   NPV can be interpreted as the potential increase in consumption made possible by the project valued in present day terms.

(h)   Internal Rate of Return (IRR) is the discount rate which gives zero NPV and can be found graphically or by linear interpolation.

(i)   With conventional projects IRR and NPV give the same accept or reject decision. NPV is an absolute measure whereas IRR is a relative one.

(j)   NPV is a more appropriate measure for choosing between mutually exclusive projects and in general is technically superior to IRR.

(k)   The discount rate used in DCF calculations is known as the cost of capital.

(l)   The Weighted Average Cost of Capital (WACC) approach is based on the theory that long term funds only should be included in the cost of capital which should be representative of the overall pool of capital available.

(m) The WACC is found by weighting (according to market values) each of the component costs of the sources of capital.

(n) Fixed interest funds such as debentures and preferences shares have known costs associated with them but equity does not.

(o) One approach to estimating the cost of capital is by the use of the Gordon growth or dividend valuation model.

(p) The dividend valuation model postulates that the sole determinant of the price of shares is the present value of the anticipated future stream of dividends.

(q) Changes in gearing (the relationship between fixed interest and equity capital) is deemed to affect the WACC according to the 'traditional' view whereas the Modigliani–Miller (MM) hypothesis states that the proportion of debt to equity does not affect the WACC.

(r) The Capital Asset Pricing Model (CAPM) attempts to measure the relationship between risk and return in the capital market and is an alternative approach to the measurement of the cost of equity capital. The CAPM, like all investment appraisal techniques, has numerous assumptions.

(s) Using the CAPM involves: estimating the market parameters and the firm's beta coefficient and using these values to calculate the expected return on the security using the formula

$$R_a = R_f + (R_m + R_f)\beta$$

(t) Life cycle costing or terotechnology aims to obtain the best use of an asset over the **whole** life taking into account acquisition, maintenance, operating and disposal costs.

POINTS TO NOTE

43. (a) It is arguable that the existence of a stream of potentially worthwhile investment opportunities is of far greater importance to the firm than the particular appraisal method used.

(b) A recent survey of the capital budgeting practices of large companies by Dr. R. Pike showed that over 75% of companies used payback as an appraisal method, often in conjunction with other techniques. The same survey showed that only 17% on companies used NPV as their primary evaluation technique in spite of the generally acknowledged technical superiority of NPV over payback. This would seem to suggest that much the academic preoccupation with refining measurement techniques may be misplaced.

(c) Successful investment appraisal is entirely dependent on the accuracy of cost and revenue estimates. No appraisal technique can overcome significant inaccuracies in this area.

(d) The CAPM was developed to assist in portfolio management which has the general objective of maintaining an efficiently diversified portfolio of investments. This means studying the relationship between risk and return in the market place. The research has indicated that risk consists of two elements; systematic or undiversifiable risk, ie the volatility or movements of the market as a whole, and unsystematic or diversifiable risk, ie the volatility of operations and investments specific to the firm. This is the type of risk measured by the beta coefficient.

ADDITIONAL READING

The economics of capital budgeting	Bromwich, PENGUIN
Capital Budgeting	CIPFA
Capital budgeting: theory, quantitative methods and applications	Herbst, HARPER & ROWE
Managerial finance	Weston & Brigham, HOLT, RINEHART & WINSTON

SELF REVIEW QUESTIONS

1. *Why are investment decisions important? (2)*

2. *Define the accounting rate of return and give its advantages and disadvantages. (4)*

3. *What is payback and what is the normal decision rule using payback? (6)*

4.   Why are cash flows used in DCF calculations and not accounting profits? (9)

5.   What cash flows should be included in the appraisal? (10)

6.   Why has money a time value? (11)

7.   Define NPV and state the basic formula. (13)

8.   What is Net Terminal Value? (14)

9.   What is the Internal Rate of Return and how is it calculated? (15 and 16)

10. What are the major differences between NPV and IRR? (18)

11. What is the multiple rate problem? (19)

12. What is the EVPI or Profitability Index and when can it be used effectively? (21)

13. What are the two general principles underlying the WACC approach? (23)

14. Given the individual element costs how is the WACC calculated? (23)

15. What is the difference in the calculation of the cost of debentures and preference shares? (25)

16. How is the cost calculated of redeemable sources of capital? (27)

17. What is the Gordon growth model and what are its major assumptions? (29)

18. What is gearing and what is the 'traditional' view of gearing and the WACC? (31-33)

19. What is the MM hypothesis? (34)

20. What is the CAPM? (36)

21. Describe the steps in using the CAPM in estimating the cost of equity capital. (37)

22. What is terotechnology? (38)

EXAMINATION QUESTION WITH ANSWER COMMENCING PAGE 359

A1. *Pavgrange plc is considering expanding its operations. The company accountant has produced* **pro forma** *profit and loss accounts for the next three years assuming that:*

(a) The company undertakes no new investment.
(b) The company invests in Project 1.
(c) The company invests in Project 2.

Both projects have expected lives of three years, and the projects are mutually exclusive.

*The **pro forma** accounts are shown below:*

(a) **No new investment**

Years	1	2	3
	£000	£000	£000
Sales	6,500	6,950	7,460
Operating costs	4,300	4,650	5,070
Depreciation	960	720	540
Interest	780	800	800
Profit before tax	460	780	1,050
Taxation	161	273	367
Profit after tax	299	507	683
Dividends	200	200	230
Retained earnings	99	307	453

(b) **Investment in Project 1**

Years	1	2	3
	£000	£000	£000
Sales	7,340	8,790	9,636
Operating costs	4,869	5,620	6,385
Depreciation	1,460	1,095	821
Interest	1,000	1,030	1,030
Profit before tax	11	1,045	1,400
Taxation	4	366	490
Profit after tax	7	679	910
Dividends	200	200	230
Retained earnings	(193)	470	680

(c) **Investment in Project 2**

Years	1	2	3
	£000	£000	£000
Sales	8,430	9,826	11,314
Operating costs	5,680	6,470	7,230
Depreciation	1,835	1,376	1,032
Interest	1,165	1,205	1,205
Profit before tax	(250)	775	1,847
Taxation	0	184	646
Profit after tax	(250)	591	1,201
Dividends	200	200	230
Retained earnings	(450)	391	971

The initial outlay for Project s is £2 million and for Project 2 £3½ million.

Tax allowable depreciation is at the rate of 25% on a reducing balance basis. The company does not expect to acquire or dispose of any fixed assets during the next three years other than in connection with Projects 1 or 2. Any investment in Project 1 or 2 would commence at the start of the company's next financial year.

The expected salvage value associated with the investments at the end of three years is £750,000 for Project 1 and £1,500,000 for Project 2.

Corporate taxes are levied at the rate of 35% and are payable one year in arrears.

Pavgrange would finance either investment with a three year term loan at a gross interest payment of 11% per year. The company's weighted average cost of capital is estimated to be 8% per annum.

Required:

(a)   Advise the company which project (if either) it should undertake. Give the reasons for your choice and support it with calculations.

(b)   What further information might be helpful to the company accountant in the evaluation of these investments?

(c)   If Project 1 had been for four years duration rather than three years, and the new net cash flows of the project (after tax and allowing for the scrap value) for years four and five were £77,000 and (£188,000) respectively, evaluate whether your advice to Pavgrange would change.

(d)   Explain why the payback period and the internal rate of return might not lead to the correct decision when appraising mutually exclusive capital investments.

ACCA, Financial Management.

Appendix to Chapter 16

Review of discounting formulae and the use of discount tables

COMPOUND INTEREST

1. The principles of compound interest form the basis of discounting and annuity calculation so must be understood.

The basic compounding formula is

$$S \quad = \quad P(1 + r)^n$$

where S   =   a sum arising in the future

r   =   rate of interest usually expressed as an interest rate per annum, eg 10%. It appears in the formula as a decimal, ie 10% = .10

n   =   number of interest bearing periods, usually expressed in years

Example 1

How much will £5000 amount to at 10% compound over 6 years?

$$
\begin{aligned}
S \quad &= \quad £5000 \ (1 + 0.10)^6 \\
&= \quad £5000 \ \text{x} \ 1.772 \\
&= \quad £8860
\end{aligned}
$$

Note: The compound interest factor $(1 + 0.10)^6$, can be found using a calculator or logarithms but tables are more normally used. Look up in Table D under 10% for 6 years and the factor is 1.772.

Example 2

How long will it take for a given sum to treble itself at 17% p.a. compound:

$$\text{i.e. } 3 = 1(1 + 0.17)^n$$

Table D can be used as a shortcut solution method. Look under 17% to find the factor closest to 3. This will be found to be 3.001 opposite 7 years.

∴ a given sum will treble itself in almost exactly 7 years at 17% p.a. compound.

DISCOUNTING

2. Compounding looks forward from a known present sum which, with the addition of re-invested interest, equals some future value. On occasions the future sum is known (or estimated) and it is required to calculate the present value. This process is known as **discounting** and is effectively the obverse of compounding.

The compounding formula given in para 1 can be restated in terms of discounting to a present value thus:

$$P \quad = \quad \frac{S}{(1 + r)^n}$$

Example 3

What is the present value of £15000 received in 10 years time with a discount rate of 14%.

$$
\begin{aligned}
P \quad &= \quad \frac{S}{(1 + r)^n} \\[2mm]
&= \quad \frac{15000}{(1 + 0.14)^{10}} \\[2mm]
&= \quad £4050
\end{aligned}
$$

Note: Once again the expression could be evaluated by calculator or logarithms but tables are normally used. Table A shows the discount factors, ie $\dfrac{1}{(1 + r)^n}$ and at 14% for 10 years the factor is 0.270. Thus the answer to this problem is £15000 x 0.270 = £4050.

DISCOUNTING A SERIES

3.   The most important application of discounting is in connection with investment appraisal and the normal requirement is to discount a series of cash flows and not just a single figure. In such circumstances the formula given in para 2 becomes

$$NPV = \sum_{i=0}^{i=n} \frac{C_i}{(1+r)^i}$$

where NPV is the Net Present Value, C is the net cash flow in the period, i is the period number, and r is the discount rate.

Example 4

What is the present value of the following cash flows, which are deemed to arise at the end of each year, when the discount rate is 15%.

Period:	Now	after 1 year	after 2 years	after 3 years
Cash Flow	- 2000	+ 800	+ 1000	+ 1300

$$\therefore NPV = \frac{-2000}{(1+.15)^0} + \frac{800}{(1+.15)^1} + \frac{1000}{(1+.15)^2} + \frac{1300}{(1+.15)^3}$$

The expression has been given in full for illustrative purposes only and is not normally necessary as the discount factors from Table A can be used thus:

$$NPV = -2000 + 800 \times 0.870 + 1000 \times 0.756 + 1300 \times 0.658$$
$$= +£307.4$$

Where the cash flows vary from year to year, as in Example 4, a separate calculation has to be made for each year but where the cash flows are constant for all years, ie an annuity, the discounting process is simplified considerably.

ANNUITIES

4.   Where a constant cash flow is received each year the series is known as an annuity. The present value could be found by separately discounting each year but the series can be brought together into one expression, as follows:

$$P = \frac{A[1 - (1 + r)^{-n}]}{r}$$

where A is the regular cash receipt, ie, the annuity.

Example 5

What is the present value of an annuity of £1000 p.a. received for 10 years when the discount rate is 12%.

$$P = \frac{1000[1 - (\frac{1}{1 + .12})^{10}]}{0.12}$$
$$= £5,650$$

Because annuities are commonly encountered tables are available for the annuity factor, ie

$$ie \quad \frac{1 - (1 + r)^{-n}}{r} \quad \text{See Table B.}$$

From Table B the factor under 12% for 10 years is 5.650 (It will be noted that the Annuity factors are simply the summation of the discount factors from Table A).

$$\therefore \text{ present value is } £1000 \times 5.650 = £5,650.$$

A shorthand way of expressing the annuity factor is $A_{\overline{n}|r}$ which means the annuity factor for n years at r rate of interest. Thus Example 5 could be shown as

$$£1000A_{\overline{10}|\,0.12} = £5,650.$$

Example 6

Evaluate

(a) $£500A_{\overline{5}|\,0.10}$

(b) $£2000A_{\overline{8}|\,0.20}$

(c) $£4500A_{\overline{6}|\,0.12}$

Solution

(a) $£5000A_{\overline{5}|\,0.10}$ = £500 x 3.791 = £1895.5

(b) $£2000A_{\overline{8}|\,0.20}$ = £2000 x 3.837 = £7674

(c) $£4500A_{\overline{6}|\,0.12}$ = £4500 x 4.111 = £18499.5

Example 7

A firm agrees to pay an employee the following amounts at the end of each year

Year	1	2	3	4
Amount	£6,000	£7,500	£9,000	£10,000

However, the employee prefers to receive the same amount in each of the years. What is the amount given that the discount is 10%?

Solution

It is necessary first to find the NPV of the payments.

$$NPV = 6000 \times 0.909 + 7500 \times 0.826 + 9000 \times 0.751 + 10000 \times 0.683$$
$$= \underline{£25,238}$$

From Table B the annuity factor for 4 years at 10% is 3.170.

$$\therefore \text{Equal payment in each of the 4 years} = \frac{25238}{3.170} = \underline{£7961.5}$$

Note: This process is known as annualising and is a useful procedure for dealing with replacement problems where there are various possible life cycles. If the annualised equivalent to each of the cycles is found a direct comparison is possible.

CASH FLOWS GROWING (OR DECLINING) AT A COMPOUND RATE

5.   It is sometimes necessary to find the present value of a stream of cash flows which are expected to increase (or reduce) at a compound rate. This is as follows:

$$\text{Leg } g = \% \text{ growth p.a.}$$

$$\text{then } A^1 = \frac{A}{(1 + g)} \text{ and } P = A^1{}_{\overline{n}|r_0}$$

$$\text{where } r_0 = \frac{r - g}{1 + g}$$

Example 8

What is the present value of rentals which are expected to commence in a year's time with a rental of £1155 p.a. and thereafter increase at 5% p.a. compound? The rentals will last 10 years and the discount rate is 26%.

Solution

$$r_0 \quad = \quad \frac{r - g}{1 + g} \quad = \quad \frac{.26 - .05}{1.05} \quad = \quad 0.20$$

$$\text{and } \frac{A}{1 + g} \quad = \quad \frac{1155}{1.05} \quad = \quad £1100$$

$$\therefore P \quad = \quad £1100A^1{}_{\overline{10}|\,20\%}$$
$$= \quad £1100 \times 4.192$$
$$= \quad \underline{£4611.2}$$

Example 9

Assume the same problem as Example 8 except that the rental will reduce by 5% p.a.

$$g \quad = \quad -0.05$$

$$r_0 \quad = \quad \frac{.26 + 0.05}{1 - 0.05} \quad = \quad \underline{32.63\% \text{ say } 33\%}$$

$$\text{and } \frac{A}{1 + g} \quad = \quad \frac{1155}{.95} \quad = \quad 1215.7$$

$$\therefore P \quad = \quad £1215.7A^1{}_{\overline{10}|\,33\%}$$
$$= \quad £1215.7 \times 2.937$$
$$= \quad \underline{£3570.5}$$

PERPETUITIES

6.   Where a stream of cash flows goes on for ever the expression in square brackets in the annuity formula given in para 4 reduces to 1 and the formula simplifies considerably to

$$P \quad = \quad \frac{A}{r}$$

Example 10

What is the present value of a perpetual annuity of £1000 at 20% which could alternatively be shown as £1000$A_{\overline{\infty}|}$20%?

$$P \quad = \quad \frac{A}{r} \quad = \quad \frac{1000}{.2} \quad = \quad \underline{£5000}$$

COMPOUNDING/DISCOUNTING AT INTERVALS OTHER THAN ANNUAL

7.   Conventionally, particularly in examinations, it is assumed that all compounding and discounting is at yearly intervals. This need not be so and discounting or compounding can take place at any interval, eg monthly, quarterly, half yearly or continuously.

Continuous discounting or compounding requires special tables but the normal tables (Tables A, B and D) can be used for discrete periods other than yearly as shown in the following example.

Example 11

What is the present value of £30,000 received in 3 years time discounted at half yearly intervals at 20% p.a.?

Solution

Calculate the discount rate per period

$$= \quad \frac{\text{Discount rate p.a.}}{\text{No. of periods p.a.}} \quad = \quad \frac{20\%}{2} \quad = \quad 10\%$$

Look up in Table A for 6 periods at 10% (ie treat the year's column as periods). The discount factor will be found to be 0.564.

$$\therefore \quad \text{Present value} \quad = \quad £30,000 \times 0.564$$
$$= \quad \underline{£16920}$$

Similar principles apply to compounding problems. The more frequently a value is discounted/compounded the more smaller/larger will be the result.

Note: The rule given above only provides an approximate answer. If an exact answer is required the following formula can be used.

true annual rate of interest $\qquad = \qquad [(1 + \frac{r}{n})^n - 1]\ 100\%$

$\qquad$ where n $\qquad = \qquad$ number of times compounded in a year

$\qquad\qquad$ r $\qquad = \qquad$ nominal yearly rate

Example 12

What is the true annual rate of interest if the nominal rate is 10% p.a. but interest is paid half yearly at 5%.

$\qquad$ true rate $\qquad = \qquad [(1 + \frac{.1}{2})^2 - 1]\ 100\%$

$\qquad\qquad\qquad\qquad = \qquad 10.25\%$

17. Investment Appraisal II

INTRODUCTION

1.   This chapter continues the study of investment appraisal and considers the problems caused by inflation, taxation, uncertainty, and capital rationing.

In the section on inflation the problems caused by general and differential inflation are discussed and the difference between money and real cash flows is explained. The impact of taxation, both beneficial and adverse, on investment is analysed and an example is provided showing how taxation effects can be incorporated into the appraisal process. The all important aspect of risk and uncertainty is considered in some depth, including the ways uncertainty can be assessed in relation to the individual project, for combinations of projects (the portfolio effect) and the influence of the decision maker's attitude to risk. The chapter concludes with a review of the capital rationing problem and ways in which single and multi-period capital rationing can be incorporated into the appraisal process.

INFLATION

2.   Inflation can be simply defined as an increase in the average price of goods and services. The accepted measure of general inflation in the UK is the Retail Price Index (RPI) which is based on the assumed expenditure patterns of an average family. General inflation is a factor in investment appraisal but of more direct concern is what may be termed **specific inflation**, ie the changes in prices of the various factors which may up the project being investigated, eg wage rates, sales prices, material costs, energy costs, transportation charges and so on. Every attempt should be made to estimate specific inflation charges and so on. Every attempt should be made to estimate specific inflation for each element of the project in as detailed a manner as feasible. General, overall estimates based on the RPI are likely to be inaccurate and misleading.

SYNCHRONISED AND DIFFERENTIAL INFLATION

3.   Differential inflation is where costs and revenues change at differing rates of inflation or where the various items of cost and revenue move at different rates. This is the normal situation but the concept of synchronised inflation - where costs and revenues rise at the same rate - although unlikely to be encountered in practice, is useful for illustrating various facets of project appraisal involving inflation.

MONEY CASH FLOWS AND REAL CASH FLOWS

4.   Money cash flows are the actual amounts of money changing hands whereas 'real' cash flows are the purchasing power equivalents of the actual cash flows. In a world of zero inflation there would be no need to distinguish between money and real cash flows as they would be identical. Where inflation does exist then a difference arises between money cash flows and their real value and this difference is the basis of the treatment of inflation in project appraisal.

INFLATION IN INVESTMENT APPRAISAL

5.   The following example will be used to illustrate the way that inflation is dealt with in investment appraisal.

Example 1

A labour saving machine costs £60,000 and will save £24,000 p.a. at current wage rates. The machine is expected to have a 3 year life and nil scrap value. The firm's cost of capital is 10%.

Calculate the project's NPV

(a)   With no inflation
(b)   With general inflation of 15% which wage rates are expected to follow (ie synchronised inflation)
(c)   With general inflation of 15% and wages rising at 20% p.a. (ie differential inflation)

Solution

(a)   NPV - no inflation

$$- 60,000 + 24000 \; A_{\overline{3}|10\%}$$
$$= \quad - 60,000 + 24000 \times 2.487 = -£312$$

∴ Project unacceptable as it has a negative NPV at company's cost of capital.

(b) General inflation 15%, wages increasing at 15%

Wage savings p.a. with no inflation	Wage savings p.a. with 15% inflation
24000	27600
24000	31740
24000	36501

With no inflation the appropriate discounting rate was 10%. With inflation at 15%, the 10% discounting rate is insufficient to bring cash sums arising at different periods into equivalent purchasing power terms. Without inflation £1 now was deemed equivalent to £1.10 a year hence. With a 15% inflation rate the sum required would be £1.10(1.15) = £1.265, thus the discount rate to be used is 26½%.

Project NPV with 15% synchronised inflation

Year	Cash Flow	26½% Discount Factors	Present Value
0	-60,000	1.000	-60,000
1	+27,600	0.792	21,859
2	+31,740	0.624	19,806
3	+36,501	0.494	18,031
		NPV =	-£304

∴ Project unacceptable

It will be seen that the answers with no inflation and with 15% synchronised inflation are virtually the same, (the difference being due to roundings in three figure tables). This equivalence is to be expected, as with synchronised inflation the firm, in real terms, is no better or no worse off.

(c) Project with 15% general inflation and wages rising at 20% p.a. (differential inflation).

Wages per annum

$$\text{Year} \quad 1 \quad 24000 \ (1.20) \quad = \quad £28,800$$
$$2 \quad 24000 \ (1.20)^2 \quad = \quad £34,560$$
$$3 \quad 24000 \ (1.20)^3 \quad = \quad £41,472$$

Project NPV with differential inflation

Year	Cash Flows	26½% Discount Factors	Present Value
0	-60,000	1.000	-60,000
1	+28,800	0.792	22,810
2	+34,560	0.624	21,565
3	+41,472	0.494	20,487
		NPV =	£4,862

∴ Project acceptable.

Thus it will be seen that with differential inflation the project is acceptable. In this case this is to be expected because it was a labour saving project so that, in real terms, the firm is better off if the rate of wage inflation is greater than the general rate of inflation.

Frequently differential inflation works to the disadvantage of the firm, for example, when costs are rising faster than prices. Each case is different and detailed, individual analysis is required - not generalised assumptions.

MONEY AND REAL DISCOUNT RATES

6. The 26½% discount rate used in Example 1 was a **money** discount factor and was used to discount the **money** cash flows of the project. The relationship between real and money discount factors is as follows:

$$\text{Real discount factor} \quad = \quad \frac{1 + \text{Money discount factor}}{1 + \text{Inflation Rate}} \quad - 1$$

Using the data from Example 1 the real discount factor can be calculated.

$$\text{Real discount factor} = \frac{1 + .265}{1 + .15} - 1 = 0.1 \text{ ie } \underline{10\%}$$

In this case, of course, the real discount factor was already known and the above calculation is for illustrative purposes only.

The real discount factor can be used providing that the money cash flows are first converted into real cash flows by discounting at the general inflation rate as follows.

Example 2

Rework part (c) of Example 1 using real cash flows and the real discount factor.

Real Cash Flow Evaluation

Year	Money Cash flow	General Inflation 15% Discount Factors	Real Cash Flows	Real Discount Factors 10%	Present Values
0	–60,000	1.000	–60,000	1.000	–60,000
1	+28,800	0.870	25,056	.909	22,776
2	+34,560	0.756	26,127	.826	21,581
3	+41,472	0.658	27,289	.751	20,494
				NPV =	£4,851

From which it will be seen that (table rounding differences apart) the two methods give identical results.

Thus it will be seen that there are two approaches to investment appraisal where inflation is present.

SINGLE DISCOUNTING – MONEY CASH FLOWS DISCOUNTED BY MONEY DISCOUNT FACTOR

TWO STAGE DISCOUNTING – MONEY CASH FLOWS DISCOUNTED BY GENERAL INFLATION RATE AND THE REAL CASH FLOWS PRODUCED DISCOUNTED BY REAL DISCOUNT FACTOR

The two approaches produce the same answer because the money discount factor includes the inflation allowance. Because of this and because money cash flows are the most natural medium in which estimates will be made, it is recommended that money cash flows should be discounted at an appropriate money discount factor. Take GREAT CARE never to discount money cash flows by a real discount factor or real cash flows by a money discount factor. If real cash flows are directly provided in a question take care to discount once only using a real discount factor.

TAXATION AND INVESTMENT APPRAISAL

7.   Because taxation causes a change in cash flows it is a factor to be considered in project appraisal. Indeed in some practical situations the taxation implication are dominant influences on the final investment decision. The following paragraphs cover the general impact of taxation on the appraisal process but make no claim to cover the intricacies of company taxation.

TREATMENT OF TAXATION IN PRINCIPLE

8.   It will be recalled that project appraisal should be based on the net, after tax, incremental cash flows arising from the project. It follows therefore that the general treatment of taxation in project appraisal involves estimating the cash outflows or inflows arising in respect of taxation, incorporating them in the project cash flow estimates, and discounting in the usual manner. Because of the complexities of the taxation system the tax cash flows resulting from a project may have adverse (ie cause a cash outflow) or beneficial (ie product a cash inflow or reduce and outflow) effects on a project. In addition, as project appraisal is concerned with both the amount and timing of cash flows, the inclusion of the effects of taxation may significantly alter project returns because of the timing of taxation payments.

THE MAJOR TAXATION EFFECTS UPON PROJECT APPRAISAL

9.   Taxation effects a project in numerous ways, but probably the most significant three effects are:

(a) Corporate taxes on project profits and losses
(b) Investment incentives (cash grants and/or capital allowances), where applicable.

(c) The reduction of the WACC because interest payments are allowable against tax.

It is somewhat ironic that, notwithstanding what has been said earlier about the inappropriateness of conventionally prepared accounting profits for investment appraisal purposes, it is usually necessary in practical problems to calculate accounting profits to assess the taxation effects on cash flows. This is, of course, because taxation is assessed upon conventionally prepared accounts, not on cash flows. In most examination questions this distinction is usually ignored and project cash flows are deemed to be the appropriate figures on which to base taxation.

CORPORATION TAXES ON PROFITS AND LOSSES

10. Where a project produces profits these are taxed at the appropriate ruling rate of Corporation Tax and payable at the periods of between 9 and 21 months after the end of the period in which the profits were earned. Because project appraisal deals with both the timing and amount of cash flows it is necessary to allow for this time lag and to bring the taxation cash outflow into the appropriate period. Typically in examination questions a one year lag is assumed, ie tax payments are deemed to be paid in the year following that in which profits are earned. Where a specific time lag is not given assume a one year period.

Where a project produces losses, the overall taxation of the firm will be affected as follows:

(a) Where the firm has sufficient profits from other operations the loss on the project will reduce the overall taxation liability of the firm. This reduction of tax is equivalent to a cash inflow to the project (ie loss x corporation tax rate) suitably time lagged.

(b) Where the project loss causes an overall loss, the resulting cash inflow from the loss can be either

(i) Carried back to a previous profit making year. In this case the equivalent cash inflow should be shown against the project in the year in which the reduction of tax liability was possible.

(ii) Carried forward to a future profit making year. Similarly the equivalent cash inflow will be shown against the project in the future year when sufficient profits become available.

INVESTMENT INCENTIVES

11. Although details of investment incentives are altered frequently, the overall objective says the same, ie to encourage investment in fixed assets though the tax system. There are two basic types of investment incentives; cash grants (currently only payable in development areas), and accelerated depreciation allowances (known as capital allowances).

(i) Cash grants. When these are receivable they should be brought into the project appraisal in the period in which they are receivable.

(ii) Capital allowances. These allowances have an equivalent cash inflow value of capital allowance x corporation tax rate assuming sufficient profits are being earned to cover all the allowances. The cash inflow effect will be lagged an appropriate period. One year should be assumed unless stated to the contrary.

TAX AND THE WACC

12. This has already been dealt with in the previous chapter where it was explained that because debenture interest is tax deductible, the WACC is thereby reduced. This concession does not apply to dividends or to the capital redemption portion of the yield on redeemable debentures.

IMPUTATION SYSTEM AND ADVANCE CORPORATION TAX (ACT)

13. The current U.K. system means that the timing of tax payments is affected by the company's dividend policy. The payment of dividends to shareholders is regarded as the net equivalent of a grossed up amount at the standard rate of income tax. The difference must be paid by the company as ACT under the quarterly account system and the amount of ACT paid has the effect of reducing the corporation tax to be paid subsequently (subject to the limitations imposed by the Taxes Acts). Thus, the imputation tax system favours the use of retained earnings since the payment of ACT can be delayed. From the examination point of view it is considered that the combination of investment appraisal, dividend policy, and ACT is unlikely to be encountered.

PROJECT APPRAISAL INVOLVING TAXATION

14. **Example 3**

Electronic Ltd is considering the purchase of a die casting machine at a cost of £20,000. The project cash flows are estimated as follows

Year 0	Year 1	Year 2	Year 3	Year 4
-20,000	+7,000	+5,000	+11,000	+5,000

The following may be assumed

(a) the existence of other taxable profits.
(b) 25% writing down allowances.
(c) 35% rate of Corporation Tax.
(d) The machine was sold for £4,500 at the end of 4 years.
(e) 1 year lag on all tax effects.

The company requires a 10% return after tax.

Calculate the NPV of the project.

Solution

Year	Project Cash Flows £	Tax effect of WDA £	Tax on profits £	Net after Tax Cash Flows £	Discount Factors	Present Values £
0	-20,000			-20,000	1.000	-20,000
1	+ 7,000	+1,750		+ 8,750	0.909	+ 7,954
2	+ 5,000	+1,312	-2,450	+ 3,862	0.826	+ 3,190
3	+11,000	+ 984	-1,750	+10,234	0.751	+ 7,686
4	(+ 5,000	+ 738	-3,850	+ 6,388	0.683	+ 4,363
	(+ 4,500					
5		+ 640	-2,450	- 1,810	0.621	- 1,124
						+ 2,069

Note: The tax effect of the WDA is calculated thus:

		£				£
Capital Cost		20,000				
25% WDA		5,000	@	35%	=	1,750
WDV		15,000				
25% WDA		3,750	@	35%	=	1,312
WDV		11,250				
25% WDA		2,812	@	35%	=	984
WDV		8,438				
25% WDA		2,109	@	35%	=	738
WDV		6,329				
Sold for		4,500				
∴ Balancing allowance		1,829	@	35%	=	640

It will be seen that the project has a positive NPV of £2,069 and, subject to the usual qualifications, the project is acceptable.

UNCERTAINTY IN INVESTMENT APPRAISAL

15. Uncertainty is a major factor to be considered in all types of decision making. It is of particular importance in investment appraisal because of the long time scale and amount of resources involved in a typical investment decision.

In general, risky or uncertain projects are those whose future cash flows, and hence the returns on the project, are likely to be variable - the greater the variability, the greater the risk. Unfortunately, elements of uncertainty can exist even if future cash flows are known with certainty. For example, if a lease is being appraised the future cash flows are known and fixed but their value may vary because of changes in the rate of inflation.

There are three stages of the overall appraisal and decision process in which risk and uncertainty merit special attention:

(a) The risk and uncertainty associated with the individual project.

(b) The effect on the overall risk and uncertainty of the firm when the project being considered is combined with the rest of the firm's operations - the portfolio effect.

(c) The decision maker's attitude to risk and its effect on the final decision. These three elements are dealt with below.

UNCERTAINTY AND THE INDIVIDUAL PROJECT

16. Various methods of considering the uncertainty associated with projects are described below. They have the general objective of attempting to assess or quantify the uncertainty surrounding a project by some form of analysis which goes beyond merely calculating the overall return expected from the project. In this way further information is provided for the ultimate decision maker so that, hopefully, a better decision will be made. It must be emphasised however, that the methods do not of themselves reduce the uncertainties surrounding a proposed investment. If this is feasible, it can only be done by management action.

The methods to be described can be separated into three groups.

(a) Time based
(b) Probability based
(c) Sensitivity analysis and simulation.

TIME BASED

17. The three methods of incorporating uncertainty which are based on time are Payback, Risk Premium and Finite Horizon. These methods rest on the assumption that project risks and uncertainty are related to time, ie the longer the project the more uncertain it is. Whilst it is reasonable to assume that uncertainty does often increase with time it is by no means universally true and there are many projects which are shortlived and risky whilst others are long term and relatively safe. The three methods are described below.

PAYBACK

18. This is the number of periods cash flows required to recoup the original investment. Apart from its use as an accept/reject criterion, payback can be used as a measure of risk, often in conjunction with a DCF measure such as NPV or IRR. If two projects A and B had approximately the same NPV and A had the shorter payback period then A would be preferred.

Advantages

(a) Simplicity of calculation.
(b) General acceptability and ease of understanding.

Disadvantages

(a) Assumes that uncertainty relates only to the time elapsed.

(b) Assumes that cash flows within the calculated payback period are certain.

(c) Makes a single blanket assumption – that uncertainty is a function of time – and does not attempt to consider the variabilities of the cash flows estimated for the particular project being appraised.

RISK PREMIUM

19. On occasions the discount rate is raised above the cost of capital in an attempt to allow for the riskiness of projects. The extra percentage being known as the risk premium. Such an inflated discounted rate raises the acceptance hurdle for projects and can be shown to treat risk as a function of time by more heavily discounting later cash flows as demonstrated in the following example.

Example 4

The cash flows for a project are shown below. The cost of capital is 10% and as the project is considered to be risky, a risk premium of 5% is to be added to the basic rate. The effects of the two discount rates are shown.

Year	0	1	2	3	4	5	NPV
Estimated Cash Flows	–10,000	+2,000	+3,000	+2,500	+3,000	+3,500	
10% Discount Factors	1.000	0.909	0.826	0.751	0.683	0.621	
P.V. @ 10%	–10,000	1818	2478	1877	2049	2173	+395
15% Discount Factors	1.000	0.870	0.756	0.658	0.572	0.495	
P.V. @ 15%	–10,000	1740	2268	1645	1716	1732	–899
Percentage reduction of P.V.s caused by risk premium		4%	8%	12%	16%	20%	

Table 1

The bottom line shows the progressively increased discounting which takes place on later cash flows demonstrating that the risk premium concept treats uncertainty as being related to time elapsed.

Advantages of a risk premium.

(a) Simple to use.

Disadvantages of a risk premium.

(a) Makes the implicit assumption that uncertainty is a function of time.

(b) By making the same overall, blanket assumption for all projects it does not consider the individual project characteristics nor does it explicitly consider the variability of the project cash flows.

(c) It creates the problem of deciding upon a suitable risk premium. Should it be the same for all projects or should it be adjusted for different projects?

Note: One of the theories relating to business profit is that it is the reward for taking uninsurable risks. If this is correct, and it has some intuitive appeal, then a more subtle and long term effect of using a risk premium is that the firm will tend to move towards a portfolio of projects which, although potentially high yielding, have high risks – which is the opposite effect to that intended.

FINITE HORIZON

20. In this method which is the simplest of all to apply, project results beyond a certain period (eg 10 years) are ignored. All projects are thus appraised over the same time period.

Advantage:

(a) Simplicity.

Disadvantages:

(a) The establishment of any fixed time horizon is arbitrary. Projects do vary in length and this should be reflected in the appraisal.

(b) Project cash flows within the time horizon are considered certain.

(c) Does not explicitly consider the variabilities of cash flows.

SUMMARY OF TIME-BASED METHODS OF CONSIDERING UNCERTAINTY

21. These methods are simple to apply and require little, if any, extra calculation. They are for the most part arbitrary and unreliable. Although obviously uncertainty tends to increase with time there is not a straightforward relationship and the time based methods fail to examine the characteristics of individual projects and merely make one blanket assumption covering all projects. The whole purpose of investment appraisal is to distinguish between projects and accepting one overall assumption is likely to mask rather than highlight the differences between the investment opportunities being considered.

PROBABILITY BASED METHODS OF ASSESSING UNCERTAINTY

22. The methods to be described rest on the assumption that meaningful estimates of the subjective probabilities associated with the various cash flows can be established. For example, the project analyst might ask a manager to make three estimates of the cash flow of a period (optimistic, most likely, pessimistic) instead of just a single estimate, and in addition ask the manager to assess the likelihood of each of three estimates. Following such a request the manager might make the following estimate:

Cash Flow in Period x

Optimistic	£8,000	with a probability of 10% (.1)
Most likely	£4,500	with a probability of 65% (.65)
Pessimistic	£3,000	with a probability of 25% (.25)

The estimates thus obtained form a probability distribution of the cash flows. It follows that if the individual cash flows are expected to vary then the overall return for the project will also vary. The main objectives of probability based methods is to demonstrate the likely variation in the result, whether NPV or IRR, due to the estimated variations in the cash flows. In this way the effects of uncertainty are more clearly shown and hopefully a more informed decision may be taken. The three methods to be described which use subjective probabilities are Expected Value, Discrete Probabilistic Analysis and Continuous Probabilistic Analysis.

EXPECTED VALUE (EV)

23. This has been covered in detail in Chapter 14. It will be recalled that EV is Probability x Value and EV can be used for individual cash flows or project NPV's. The following simple example illustrates the technique.

Example 5

The cash flow and probability estimates for a project are shown below.

Calculate

(a) Expected value of the cash flows in each period and
(b) Expected value of the NPV when the initial project outlay is £11,000 and the cost of capital is 15%.

CASH FLOW AND PROBABILITY ESTIMATES

		CASH FLOWS			
	Probability	Period 1	2	3	4
		£	£	£	£
Optimistic	0.3	5000	6000	4500	5000
Most likely	0.5	3500	4000	3800	4500
Pessimistic	0.2	3200	3600	3100	4000
Expected value of cash flows		3890	4520	3870	4550

The NPV is found by discounting the expected value of cash flows in the normal manner.
NPV = -11,000 + (3890 x 0.870) + (4520 x 0.756) + (3870 x 0.658) + (4550 x 0.572) = £950

The advantages and disadvantages of expected value as a decision criterion have already been covered in Chapter 14 and these apply equally to the use of Expected Value in investment appraisal.

It is worth repeating that expected value, in spite of its limitations, is the decision rule which should normally be employed unless the problem clearly indicates something to the contrary.

DISCRETE PROBABILISTIC ANALYSIS (DPA)

24. DPA can be considered as an extension of the expected value procedure described above. As its basis it requires similar estimates of cash flows and associated probabilities, but instead of merely averaging these estimates it uses the component parts of the estimates to show the various outcomes and probabilities possible. The following example illustrates the technique.

Example 6

The NPV of Example 5 was £950 and management consider this somewhat marginal and wish to explore the range of outcomes possible. Further investigation reveals that two capital costs are possible; the £11,000 as stated with a probability of 0.8 and £15,000 with a probability of 0.2. This results in a new expected NPV of +£150 using the new expected capital cost of £11,800. The full range of outcomes and probabilities is shown in Table 2.

	Most Likely Capital Cost P = 0.8 £11,000		Pessimistic Capital Cost P = 0.2 £15,000	
Optimistic Cash Flows P = 0.3	3707	(0.24)	- 293	(0.06)
Most Likely Cash Flows P = 0.5	143 *	(0.4)	-3857	(0.1)
Pessimistic Cash Flows P = 0.2	-1167	(0.16)	-5167	(0.04)

Table 2

The table shows the NPV resulting from each possible combination of the original estimates of cash flows and the capital costs and gives the probability of the combination occurring. For example, the cell marked* is calculated thus

$$
\begin{array}{lll}
\text{Present value of most likely cash flows} & = & £11,142 \\
\textit{less} \text{ most likely capital cost} & & \underline{11,000} \\
\text{NPV} & = & \underline{143} \\
\end{array}
$$

The combination has a probability of 0.5 x 0.8 = <u>0.4</u>

From Table 2 it will be seen that the outcomes range from +£3707 to -£5167 and that the probability of making a loss is 0.16 + 0.06 + 0.1 + 0.04 = <u>0.36</u> or alternatively, the probability of at least breaking even is 0.64.

Management now has more information on which to base a decision.

Advantages of DPA.

(a) Simple to apply and understand.

(b) Gives some indication of the range of possible outcomes and their probabilities.

(c) Considers the detailed variations in the cash flows and investment required for a project rather than merely making one overall assumption such as that uncertainty is directly related to time elapsed.

Disadvantages.

(a) Uses discrete estimates whereas a continuous distribution may be a better representation of a particular project.

(b) Increases the amount of subjective estimation necessary.

CONTINUOUS PROBABILISTIC ANALYSIS (CPA)

25. CPA has the same overall objective as DPA which has been described above. That is, to show the variability of the project outcome which results from the variability of the individual cash flows thus enabling the analyst to make probability assessments of the likelihood of various outcomes. It differs from DPA in that continuous distributions and aspects of statistical theory are used instead of the discrete estimates which are a feature of DPA.

CPA can be shown diagrammatically as follows

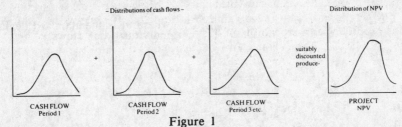

Figure 1

To be able to combine the distributions as shown and to be able to make probability statements about the project outcome, it is first necessary to establish the mean (or most likely value) and a measure of the dispersion of each of the individual period's cash flows.

ESTABLISHING THE MEANS AND DISPERSION OF CASH FLOWS

26. In general, there is little problem in estimating the mean of the period's cash flows, this being equivalent to the most likely value. A more significant problem is to establish a suitable measure of the variability or dispersion of the period's cash flows. The most useful measure for statistical purposes is the standard deviation in the conventional statistical manner so that some form of subjective estimation becomes necessary.

This could be done as follows:

Assume that the most likely value of the cash flow in a given period was estimated to be £30,000 and it was considered that there was likely to be some variability.

The manager responsible for the estimate could be asked a question similar to the following.

'Given that the most likely value of the cash flow is £30,000, within what limits would you expect the cash flow to be 50% of the time?'

Assume that the answer to the above question was £25,000 to £35,000.

It is known from Normal Area Tables that 50% of a distribution lies between the mean $\pm \frac{2}{3}\sigma$ (approximately)

$$\therefore £10,000 \text{ (ie } 35,000 - 25,000) = 4/3\sigma$$

$$\therefore \sigma \simeq \underline{£7500}$$

An alternative to the question asked above would be ask the manager, 'what is the total range of cash flow that might be expected?'

If the manager was consistent he would answer, '£7,500 to £52,500'.

It is known that the whole of a normal distribution is within the range of the mean $\pm 3\sigma$ (approximately). Accordingly, the estimate of the standard deviation would be,

$$\sigma = \frac{£52,500 - 7,500}{6} = \underline{£7,500}$$

It is clear that the estimation process outlined above is crude and lacks statistical rigour. However, subjective estimation is an unavoidable aspect of all investment appraisals and the procedure does enable some sort of assessment to be made of the probability of achieving various outcomes.

Having obtained the estimates of the means and standard deviations these must be combined to give the mean and standard deviation of the overall project NPV.

COMBINING THE MEANS AND STANDARD DEVIATIONS OF THE CASH FLOWS

27. There is little problem in obtaining the mean of the project NPV. This is simply the means, or most likely values, of the cash flows discounted in the usual manner. The project standard deviation is obtained by combining the discounted standard deviations of the individual cash flows using what is known as the **statistical sum**.

Standard deviations cannot be combined directly but it is possible to add variances, when this is done the square root of the result can be taken thus establishing the standard deviation of the project's NPV, ie σ_{NPV}

$$\therefore \quad \sigma^2_{NPV} = \Sigma \left[\frac{\sigma_i}{(1 + r)^i} \right]^2 \quad \text{where } \sigma_i \text{ is the standard deviation of the individual cash flows.}$$

$$\sigma^2_{NPV} = \Sigma \left[\frac{\sigma_i{}^2}{(1 + r)^{i2}} \right]$$

$$\sigma_{NPV} = \Sigma \sqrt{\frac{\sigma_i{}^2}{(1 + r)^{i2}}}$$

This formula is used in the following example

Example 6

The means and standard deviations of the cash flows of a project are shown below and it is required to calculate.

    (a)   The project NPV (ie the mean)
    (b)   The variable of the project NPV (ie σ_{NPV})
    (c)   The probability of obtaining
         –a negative NPV
         –a NPV of at least £20,000

It can be assumed that the cash flows in each period are independent, ie variations in one period are independent of variations in other periods and that the cost of capital is 10%

Period	0	1	2	3	4	5
Net cash flow (most likely value)	-200,000	+55,000	+48,000	+65,000	+70,000	+40,000
Variability expected (ie Standard deviation of cash flow)	0	4,000	4,500	3,500	4,500	3,000
Discount Factors @ Cost of Capital of 10%	1.00	.909	.826	.751	.683	.621

Solution

(a) The project NPV is found in the usual way, ie
-200,000 + (55,000 x 0.909) + (48,000 x 0.826) + (65,000 x 0.751) + (70,000 x 0.683) + (40,000 x 0.621)
    $\therefore$ Project NPV (ie the mean) = **£11,108**

(b) The standard deviation of the NPV is found by inserting the various estimated cash flow standard deviations into the formula.

$$\sigma_{NPV} = \sqrt{\Sigma \left[\frac{4000^2}{(1 + .1)^2} + \frac{4500^2}{(1 + .1)^4} + \frac{3500^2}{(1 + .1)^6} + \frac{4500^2}{(1 + .1)^8} + \frac{3000^2}{(1 + .1)^{10}} \right]}$$

$\therefore \sigma_{NPV} = $ £6,847

It will be seen that the squaring of the denominator has the effect of requiring discount factors at 2, 4, 6, 8 and 10 years instead of the usual 1, 2, 3, 4 and 5 years.

(c) The probability of obtaining a negative NPV (or the probability of any value of NPV) is found by using standard statistical tests of normal area, ie find the 'z' score or standardised variate and obtain the resulting probability from Normal Area Tables as follows.

$$z \quad = \quad \left| \frac{£11,108 - 0}{6847} \right|$$

$$= \quad \underline{1.622}$$

and from the Tables we find that the probability of the NPV being above zero is 0.9474 (ie 0.5 + 0.4474) thus there is approximately a 5.3% chance (1 - 0.9474) of there being a negative NPV.

The probability of there being at least £20,000 NPV is found by a similar process.

$$z \quad = \quad \left| \frac{20,000 - 11,108}{6847} \right|$$

$$= \quad \underline{1.299}$$

and using the Tables we find that the probability of obtaining at least £20,000 NPV is approximately 9.7%.

The distribution of the project NPV can also be shown diagrammatically as in Figure 2.

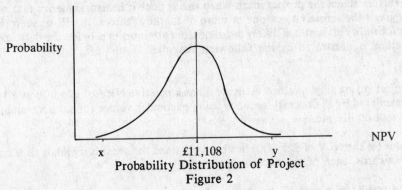

Probability

£11,108

x   y   NPV

Probability Distribution of Project
Figure 2

Point x on the diagram is approximately £11,108 - (3 x 6847) = £ -9433 and point y is approximately £11,108 + (3 x 6847) = £31,649

COMPARISON OF PROJECTS USING CPA

28. Having calculated the means and standard deviations of various projects the project distributions can be compared quite simply. The distributions could be drawn on the same graph and visually examined or the relative variability of the distributions could be calculated using their **coefficients of variation**.

The coefficient of variation is found as follows:

$$\text{Coefficient of variation} \quad = \quad \frac{\sigma}{x} \; 100\%$$

For example, two projects have estimated results as under

Project		
- A	mean = £80,000	s.d. = £12,500
- B	mean = £130,000	s.d. = £17,500

What are the coefficients of variation and which is the relatively less risky project?

$$\text{Coefficient of variation A} \quad = \quad \frac{12,500}{80,000} \; x \; 100\% \; = \; \underline{15.6\%}$$

$$\text{Coefficient of Variation B} \quad = \quad \frac{17,500}{13,000} \; x \; 100\% \; = \; \underline{13.5\%}$$

∴ Project B is relatively less risky assuming that the standard deviation is a reasonable measure of the riskiness of the projects.

SUMMARY OF CPA

29. The analysis outlined above can be extended to cover situations where projects are not independent and/or where the individual distributions are not normal or near normal. All the methods have the same overall objects, which is to find the mean and variability (riskiness) of the project NPV.

Advantages of CPA

(a) Produces a distribution of the NPV rather than a single figure.

(b) Enables probability statements to be made about the project's outcome which reflect the variabilities expected in each period's cash flows.

(c) Enables the NPV distributions of competing projects to be compared.

(d) Uses the more realistic assumption of continuous rather than discrete values.

Disadvantages

(a) Introduces a further element of subjective estimation.

(b) More complex than DPA, so therefore may not be properly understood or used by decision makers.

SENSITIVITY ANALYSIS

30. This is a practical way of showing the effects of uncertainty by varying the values of the key factors (eg sales volume, price, rates of inflation, cost per unit) and showing the resulting effect on the project. The objective is to establish which of the factors affect the project most. When this is done it is management's task to decide whether the project is worthwhile, given the sensitivity of one or more of the key factors. It will be seen that this method does not ask for subjective probability estimates of likely outcomes, but attempts to provide the data upon which judgements may be made. The method is illustrated by the following example.

Example 7

Assume that a project (using single valued estimates) has a positive NPV of £25,000 at a 10% discounting rate. This value would be calculated by the normal methods using particular values for sales volume, sales price, cost per unit, inflation rate, length of life etc, etc.

Once the basic value (ie the NPV of £25,000) has been obtained the sensitivity analysis is carried out by flexing, both upwards and downwards, each of the factors in turn.

An abstract of the results of a sensitivity analysis for the project above might be as follows:

SENSITIVITY ANALYSIS ABSTRACT

Original NPV = £25,000

A Element to be varied	B Alteration from Basic	C Revised NPV £	D Increase + Decrease - £	E Percentage Change	F Sensitivity Factor ie $\frac{E}{B}$
Sales	+15%	46,000	+21,000	84	5.6
Volume	+10%	33,000	+ 8,000	32	3.2
(Basic Value	-10%	17,000	- 8,000	32	3.2
8000 units in					
Period 1,	-15%	14,000	-11,000	44	2.9
8500 in					
Period 2 etc)	-20%	9,000	-16,000	64	3.2
Sales	+20%	42,000	+ 17,000	68	3.4
Price	+10%	31,000	+ 6,000	24	2.4
(Basic Value	-10%	17,000	- 8,000	32	3.2
£6 unit in					
Period 1,	-15%	11,000	-14,000	56	3.73
£6.25 in					
Period 2 etc)	-20%	2,000	-23,000	92	4.6
Cost/Unit	+25%	-12,000	-37,000	148	5.9
(Basic Value	+10%	6,000	-19,000	76	7.6
£2.50 in					
Period 1	-5%	34,000	+ 9,000	36	7.2
£2.60 in					
Period 2 etc)	-10%	47,000	+22,000	88	8.8

Table 3

From such an analysis the more sensitive elements can be identified. Once identified further analysis and study can take place on these factors to try to establish the likelihood of variability and the range of values that might be expected so as to be able to make a more reasoned decision whether or not to proceed with the project.

Advantages of Sensitivity Analysis

(a) Shows the effect on project outcome of varying the value of the elements which make up the project (eg Sales, Costs, etc).

(b) Simple in principle.

(c) Enables the identification of the most sensitive variables.

Disadvantages of Sensitivity Analysis

(a) Gives no indication of the likelihood of a variation occurring.

(b) Considerable amount of computation involved.

(c) Only considers the effect of a single change at a time which may be unrealistic.

RISK AND THE PORTFOLIO EFFECT

31. So far in this Chapter we have studied the risks associated with each project considered in isolation. This is an important matter but it will be apparent that of greater significance to the firm is the **aggregate risk from all projects** accepted which could be termed its **portfolio of projects**.

The effect on the firm of the risks of individual projects may be neutralised or enhanced when all the individual projects are considered together. A simple example would be where a firm is operating in a cyclical industry with variable (ie risky) returns on its existing projects. A new project is being considered which, although variable or risky, is expected to follow a different cyclical pattern to existing operations. When existing operations are experiencing low activity the new project is expected to have substantial activity so that the overall risk to the firm from its portfolio, including the new project, will be minimised. This is, of course, a major reason why firms diversify their operations.

The analysis of this aspect of risk and uncertainty was developed for stock market investment portfolio analysis by Markowitz and others and has already been briefly alluded to when the Capital Asset Pricing Model was discussed earlier. There are many restrictive assumptions behind the analysis and there are some difficulties in applying it to project investment within the firm but the general reasoning is valid and is of considerable importance.

ASSESSING THE PORTFOLIO RISK

32. The general procedure for assessing the extent to which the proposed project(s) add to or subtract from the risk of existing operations is to calculate the covariance between the returns of the project(s) and returns of existing operations and to use the covariance(s) to obtain the coefficient of correlation between the project(s) returns and the returns of existing operations.

The interpretation of the correlation coefficients is as follows:-

Coefficient of correlation	=	-1	risk fully neutralised
	=	0	risk unaltered
	=	+1	risk fully enhanced

The following example illustrates the general procedure.

Example 8

A firm with £100,000 to invest is considering two projects, X and Y each requiring an investment of £100,000. The returns from the proposed projects and from existing operations under three possible views of expected market conditions are shown in Table 4 together with the calculated standard deviations of returns, ie the measure of riskiness used by the company.

MARKET STATE	I	II	III
PROBABILITY OF MARKET STATE	0.3	0.4	0.3
Rate of return PROJECT X	20%	20%	$-1\frac{2}{3}\%$
Standard deviation of returns, Project X = 22%			
Rate of Return PROJECT Y	-2%	15%	27%
Standard deviation of returns, Project Y = 15%			
Rate of Return of existing operations	-9%	$18\frac{1}{4}\%$	28%
Standard deviation of returns on existing operations = 18%			

Table 4

The firm considers that the risk and return of their existing operations are similar to the market as a whole and that a reasonable estimate of a risk free interest rate is 8%.

Which, if either, of the two proposed investments should be initiated and why?

Solution

The first stage is to calculate the expected returns for X and Y and existing operations.

Expected Returns (R)

Project X
$$\overline{R}_X = (0.20 \times 0.3) + (0.20 \times 0.4) + (-0.01667 \times 0.3) = 0.135 = \underline{13.5\%}$$

Project Y
$$\overline{R}_y = (-0.02 \times 0.3) + (0.15 \times 0.4) + (0.27 \times 0.3) = 0.135 = \underline{13.5\%}$$

Existing Operations
$$\overline{R}_O = (-0.09 \times 0.3) + (0.1825 \times 0.4) + 0.28 \times 0.3) = 0.13 = \underline{13\%}$$

It will be seen that the expected returns of Projects X and Y are the same and as the standard deviation of Project Y is lower than Project X then Project Y is the preferred project **if the projects are considered in isolation from existing operations.**

However, this is too superficial a view and further analysis is required on the effect of adding either project to the existing portfolio.

It will be recalled that a project's risk can be separated into two elements – systematic and unsystematic risk. The unsystematic risk is the diversifiable risk which can be reduced or eliminated when the project is part of an appropriate portfolio. The systematic risk is the proportion which cannot be eliminated (it applies to the economy or market as a whole) and thus the project's returns must be considered against this residual element.

Portfolio analysis can be used to find the minimum required return for Projects X and Y given their risk levels by calculating the covariances between project returns and existing operations and using these values to calculate the correlation coefficients thus:

Covariance between Project X return (R_X) and Company Return (R_O)

	$(R_X - \overline{R}_X)^*$	x	$(R_O - \overline{R}_O)^*$	x	Market state probability	=	Covariance
State I	0.065	x	-0.22	x	0.3	=	-0.00429
II	0.065	x	0.0525	x	0.4	=	0.001365
III	-0.15157	x	0.15	x	0.3	=	-0.00682
					Covariance	=	-0.009745

*These values are found by deducting the calculated expected return ($\overline{R}$) from the actual return given in Table 4. For example the value -0.15167 is found as follows: (-0.01667 - 0.135) = -0.15167.

The value of the co-variance is then used to find the correlation coefficient between Project X returns and returns from existing operations (O).

$$\text{Correlation coefficient between X and O} = \frac{covariance\ (x,o)}{\sigma_X . \sigma_O} = \frac{-0.009745}{0.22 \times 0.18}$$

$$\therefore \text{Correlation } (x,o) = \underline{-0.246}$$

Covariance between Project Y return (R_y) and Company Return (R_O)

	$(R_y - \overline{R}_y)$	x	$(R_O - \overline{R}_O)$	x	Market State probability	=	Covariance
State I	-0.155	x	-0.22	x	0.3	=	0.01023
II	0.015	x	0.0525	x	0.4	=	0.000315
III	0.135	x	0.15	x	0.3	=	0.006075
							+0.01662

$$\text{Correlation coefficient between Y and O} = \frac{Covariance\ (y,o)}{\sigma_y . \sigma_O} = \frac{+0.01662}{0.15 \times 0.18}$$

$$\text{Correlation } (y,o) = \underline{\textbf{+0.615}}$$

These values can be used to calculate the required return from projects X and Y given that the risk free interest rate is 8%. (R_F)

Required return of Project X

$$= R_F + \frac{R_o - R_F}{\sigma_o} \cdot \sigma_x \cdot \text{Correlation} (x,o)$$

$$= 0.08 + \frac{0.13 - 0.08}{0.18} \quad .0.22. -0.246$$

$$= 0.08 - 0.015 \qquad = 0.065 = \underline{6.5\%}$$

Required return of Project Y.

$$R_F + \frac{R_o - R_F}{\sigma_o} \cdot \sigma_y \cdot \text{Correlation} (y,o)$$

$$= 0.08 + \frac{0.13 - 0.08}{0.18} \quad .0.15.0.615$$

$$= 0.08 + 0.0256 \qquad = \underline{10.56\%}$$

Based on the Portfolio analysis, Project X is the preferred project for the following reasons.

(a)   Project X provides the greatest excess of actual return over minimum return, ie 13.5% c.f. 6.5% whereas Project Y is 13.5% c.f. 10.56. Thus Project X maximises the company's wealth.

(b)   The negative correlation coefficient of Project X, -0.246 means that its pattern of returns to some extent neutralise the overall portfolio risk when Project X is combined with current operations. Although Project Y has a lower individual risk its correlation coefficient of +0.615 means that it enhances risk when combined with current operations.

Note: It will be seen that the decision following analysis of the Portfolio effects is the opposite to that when the project's riskiness is considered in isolation.

It is feasible to work manually through a problem with as few projects as Example 8 but the number of relationships rises dramatically as the number of projects increases so it is likely that the application of the above principles to any practical sized problem would require computer assistance.

DECISION MAKER'S ATTITUDE TO RISK

33. Having dealt with the riskiness of individual projects and of combinations of projects, the third aspect of risk in investment appraisal can now be considered; that of the decision maker's attitude to risk and its influence on the final investment decision.

Surveys and studies have shown that individual differ in their attitudes to risk and that for serious decision making such as investment appraisals in business, decision makers are **risk averters**. This means that in general, decision makers would prefer a less risky (less variable) investment even though it may have a lower expected value than a higher return yet riskier investment.

This may be demonstrated by the following example.

Two investments are being considered.

Investment A -   Return of £100,000 with a probability of 1, ie certainty

Investment B   Return of £300,000 with a probability of 0.5
                  Return of zero with a probability of 0.5

The expected returns are:

Investment A £100,000

Investment B (£300,000 x 0.5) + (0 x 0.5) = £150,000

It will be apparent that virtually every investor would prefer the certainty of Investment A to the uncertainty or risk involved in Investment B even though it has the higher expected value. Such behaviour is risk aversion.

Implicit in such behaviour is an assumption about the **utility** or satisfaction derived from money. The utility function of a risk averter declines as the level of income or wealth rises, ie a declining marginal utility. A 'risk neutral' investor regards each increment of income or wealth as having the same value whereas a 'risk seeker' is a person whose utility function increases as his level of income or wealth increases. These three possibilities are shown in Figure 3.

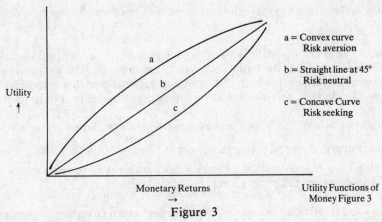

a = Convex curve
Risk aversion

b = Straight line at 45°
Risk neutral

c = Concave Curve
Risk seeking

Utility

Monetary Returns
→

Utility Functions of
Money Figure 3

Figure 3

UTILITY AND CERTAINTY EQUIVALENT

34. Utility theory applied to decision making in risky conditions postulates that individuals attempt to optimise something termed utility and assumes that for any individual a formal, quantifiable relationship can be established between utility and money.

The theoretical way that an individual's utility function is established is by the use of certainty equivalents. These are derived in the following fashion.

Assume that an individual owns a sweepstake ticket which offers a 50% chance of winning £200,000 and a 50% chance of winning nothing. He would be asked what amount of cash he would accept for the lottery ticket. If he would sell the ticket for £75,000 this is the **certainty equivalent**, ie the value at which he is indifferent between the certain £75,000 and the chance of winning £200,000. This certainty equivalent would be assigned a utile value of 0.5 (a utile is the unit of utility). From such questions the person's utility function can be derived and then asked to make choices in investment decisions.

However, whilst these processes have theoretical appeal they are virtually impossible to apply in practice because of the extreme difficulty of establishing any form of meaningful utility function. However, risk aversion and varying individual attitudes to risks are very real phenomena although difficult to quantify. Accordingly, it is essential that the project analyst produces some form of risk analysis, both for projects in isolation and in combination, so that the decision maker has more information upon which to make a decision. There are variable or risky elements of every project and to ignore this aspect in the project appraisal can be positively misleading to the decision maker.

CAPITAL RATIONING – DEFINITION

35. This is where the firm is unable to initiate all projects which are apparently profitable because insufficient funds are available. Under the assumption given for the basic DCF model, a perfect capital market was presumed, ie as much finance as required could be raised at the market rate of interest. In imperfect capital market conditions capital may be raised, but at increasing rates of interest; but there will be some point where there is an absolute limit to the amount that could be raised. Such a situation is known as external capital rationing. Alternatively, the effects of capital rationing may develop for internal purposes, for example, it may be decided that investment should be limited to the amount that can be financed solely from retained earnings or kept within a given capital expenditure budget. The external and internal factors which impose quantitative limits have led to two opposing viewpoints developing, known as the 'hard' and 'soft' views of capital rationing. The 'hard' view is that there is an absolute limit on the amount of money a firm may borrow or raise externally whereas the 'soft' view is that rationing by a quantitative limit such as

an arbitrary capital expenditure budget should only be seen as a temporary, administrative expedient because such a limit is not determined by the market (the assumption being that any amount of funds is available at a price) and such a limit would not be imposed by a profit maximising firm.

Whatever the causes of the limited capital supply available for investment purposes it means that, not only must each project cover the cost of capital, but that the project or batch of projects selected must maximise the return from the limited funds available, ie some form of ranking becomes necessary.

Before considering solution methods some definitions need to be considered.

(a) Single period capital rationing - where there is a limit on the funds available now but where it is anticipated that funds will be freely available in subsequent periods.

(b) Multi-Period Capital rationing - where the limitation of funds extends over a number of periods or possibly indefinitely.

(c) Divisible projects - projects where the whole project or any fraction may be undertaken. If a fractional part is undertaken, then it is assumed that the initial outlay and subsequent cash inflows and outflows are reduced pro rata. Although for most industrial projects this situation seems somewhat hypothetical, the assumption of divisibility is frequently made in solving capital rationing problems, particularly in examination questions.

(d) Indivisible projects - where the whole project must be undertaken or not at all.

PROJECT SELECTION UNDER CAPITAL RATIONING

36. Where capital rationing exists the normal DCF decision rule, ie accept all projects which have a positive NPV at the cost of capital, is insufficient to make the appropriate project selection.

The objective where capital rationing exists is to maximise the return from the batch of projects selected having regard to the capital limitation. This means that the investment decision changes from simply being 'accept or reject' to what is in effect a ranking problem. Ways of achieving this objective are shown below for the following rationing possibilities.

-   single period capital rationing with divisible projects

-   single period capital rationing with divisible projects where some are mutually exclusive

-   single period capital rationing with indivisible projects

-   multi period capital rationing with divisible projects.

SINGLE PERIOD CAPITAL RATIONING - DIVISIBLE PROJECTS

37. This is the simplest case and the solution method is to rank the projects in order of their EVPI (ie NPV per £ of outlay as described earlier) and to choose projects, or fraction of a project, until the supply of capital for investment is exhausted.

Example 9

CR Ltd has a cost of capital of 15% and has a limit of £100,000 available for investment in the current period. It is expected that capital will be freely available in the future. The investment required, the NPV at 15% and the EVPI for each of the 6 projects currently being considered are shown below.

What projects should be initiated?

PROJECT	OUTLAY	NPV @ 15%	EVPI	NPV / OUTLAY
	£	£		
A	20,000	8,000	0.4	
B	40,000	28,000	0.7	
C	35,000	37,500	1.07	
D	50,000	31,500	0.63	
E	15,000	3,500	0.23	
F	45,000	-5,000	-0.11	

Solution

Ranking by EVPI is C, B, D, A and E. Project F cannot be considered because it fails the initial hurdle of achieving a positive NPV.

∴ Optimal Investment Plan

PROJECT	FRACTION UNDERTAKEN	INVESTMENT	NPV
		£	£
C	1.00	35,000	37,500
B	1.00	40,000	28,000
D	0.50	25,000	15,750
		£100,000	£81,250

It will be seen that this solution method uses the well known management accounting principle of maximising return per unit of the limiting factor - in this case NPV per £ of capital available for investment. It will be recalled that this principle is appropriate where there is a **single constraint only** - in this example, investment finance for one period.

SINGLE PERIOD CAPITAL RATIONING WITH MUTUALLY EXCLUSIVE DIVISIBLE PROJECTS

38. Where two or more of the projects are mutually exclusive the solution method of ranking by EVPI can still be used but the projects have to be divided into groups each containing one of the mutually exclusive projects. This is shown below.

Example 10

Assume the same data as Example 9 except that projects B and D are mutually exclusive.

What projects should be initiated?

Solution

It is necessary to divide the projects into two groups, rank by EVPI, select projects up to the capital limit and to compare the total NPV obtainable from each group.

	Group I				Group II	
Project	Investment	EVPI		Project	Investment	EVPI
	£				£	
A	20,000	0.4		A	20,000	0.4
B	40,000	0.7		C	35,000	1.07
C	35,000	1.07		D	50,000	0.63
E	15,000	0.23		E	15,000	0.23

Ranking the groups and choosing the projects up to the investment limit produces the following:

	Group I				Group II		
Project	Fraction	Investment	NPV	Project	Fraction	Investment	NPV
		£	£			£	£
C	1.00	35,000	37,000	C	1.00	35,000	37,500
B	1.00	40,000	28,000	D	1.00	50,000	31,500
A	1.00	20,000	8,000	A	¾	15,000	6,000
E	⅓	5,000	1,167				
		£100,000	£74,667			£100,000	£75,000

It will be seen that, by a narrow margin, Group II with the proportion indicated, has the greater NPV and would be chosen.

SINGLE PERIOD CAPITAL RATIONING - INDIVISIBLE PROJECTS

39. Where projects have to be accepted in their entirety or not at all, then the EVPI ranking procedure does not necessarily produce the optimal solution. Providing that relatively few projects are involved a trial and error approach can be used to find a solution. Where projects are indivisible then it is likely that some of the capital available for investment may be unused and in such circumstances a full analysis should include the returns from external investment of under-utilised funds.

Example 11

Lloyds Ltd has a cost of capital of 10% and has a limit of £100,000 available for investment in the current period. Capital is expected to be freely available in future periods. The following indivisible projects are being considered.

Project	Initial Investment	NPV @ 10%
	£	£
A	35,000	17,500
B	40,000	22,500
C	65,000	38,000
D	48,000	31,500
E	23,000	9,000

It is required to calculate the optimal investment plan when:

(a)   where there are no alternative investments available for any surplus funds
(b)   where surplus funds can be invested to produce 12% in perpetuity.

Solution

(a)   Various combinations are tried to see which combination produces the maximum NPV. Table 5 shows a few examples.

Project Combinations	Total Outlay for Combinations	Surplus Funds	Total NPV of Combination
	£	£	£
AC	100,000	–	55,500
ABE	98,000	2,000	49,000
AD	83,000	17,000	49,000
BD	88,000	12,000	54,000
BE	63,000	37,000	31,500
CE	88,000	12,000	47,000
DE	71,000	29,000	40,500

Table 5

It will be seen from Table 5 that the best investment plan is A and C which utilises all the funds available and produces a combined NPV of £55,500.

(b)   When surplus funds can be invested externally each of the combinations in Table 5 which have surplus funds must be examined to see if the project NPV plus the return on external investment is greater than £55,500.

Each £1,000 invested at 12% in perpetuity yields £200 NPV

$$\text{ie} \quad \left(\frac{1,000 \times .12}{.1}\right) - 1,000 = £200$$

The project combinations and total NPV (Projects + External Investment) are shown in Table 6.

Combination	Total Project Outlay	Funds Externally Investment	External Investment NPV	+	Project NPV	=	Total NPV
	£	£	£		£		£
ABE	98,000	2,000	400	+	49,000		49,400
AD	83,000	17,000	3,400	+	49,000		52,400
BD	88,000	12,000	2,400	+	54,000		*56,400
BE	63,000	37,000	7,400	+	31,500		38,900
CE	88,000	12,000	2,400	+	47,000		49,400
DE	71,000	29,000	5,800	+	40,500		46,300

Table 6

*When external investment is considered then projects B D should he initiated and £12,000 invested externally to produce a total NPV of £54,500. It will be seen that this is slightly better than the A C combination shown in Table 5.

Note: Although ranking by EVPI in conditions of single-period capital rationing with indivisible projects does not necessarily produce the correct ranking it usually provides an excellent guide to the best group of projects.

MULTI-PERIOD CAPITAL RATIONING

40. This has been previously defined as the position where investment funds are expected to be limited over several periods. In such circumstances it becomes difficult to choose the batch of projects (some starting immediately, some one period hence, two periods hence, etc.) which yield the maximum return and yet which remain within the capital limits. The problem becomes one of optimising a factor (eg NPV) where resources are limited, ie the funds available over the periods being considered. This will be recognised as a problem where Linear Programming (LP) can be used and LP has been used successfully in solving Multi-Period Capital Rationing problems.

MULTI-PERIOD RATIONING - LP SOLUTION

41. To use LP as a solution method means making the assumption that projects are divisible, ie fractional parts can be undertaken. This is not necessarily a realistic assumption, but it is one frequently made for examination purposes. The following example will be used to illustrate the LP formulation, solution and interpretation of multi-period capital rationing problems.

Example 12

Trent Ltd has a cost of capital of 10% and is considering which project or projects it should initiate. The following projects are being considered:

		Estimated Cash Flows			
Project	Year 0	Year 1	Year 2	Year 3	Year 4
A	-15,000	-25,000	30,000	30,000	20,000
B	-25,000	-15,000	30,000	29,000	30,000
C	-35,000	-15,000	40,000	44,000	30,000

Capital is limited to £40,000 now and £35,000 in Year 1. The projects are divisible.

Solution

Step 1. Calculate the project NPV's in the usual manner.

These are as follows:

$$A = £23,245$$
$$B = £28,414$$
$$C = £37,939$$

Step 2. Formulate the problem in LP terms which means defining the objective function and the constraints. The objective for Trent Ltd is to maximise NPV and this may be expressed as:

maximise $23,245X_A + 28,414X_B + 37,939X_C$

where X_A is the proportion of Project A to be initiated
X_B is the proportion of Project B to be initiated
X_C is the proportion of Project C to be initiated

The constraints in this problem are the budgetary limitations in Periods 0 and 1.

Capital at time 0
$$15,000X_A + 25,000X_B + 25,000X_C \leqslant 40,000$$

Capital at time 1
$$25,000X_A + 15,000X_B + 15,000X_C \leqslant 35,000$$

In addition it is necessary to specify the formal constraints regarding the proportions of projects accepted to ensure that a project cannot be accepted more than once or that 'negative' projects are accepted.

$$\text{ie} \quad X_A, X_B, X_C < 1$$
$$X_A, X_B, X_C > 0$$

The whole formula appears thus:

Maximise $23,245X_A$	$+28,414X_B$	$+37,939X_C$		
Subject to $15,000X_A$	$+25,000X_B$	$+35,000X_C$	<	40,000
$25,000X_A$	$+15,000X_B$	$+15,000X_C$	<	35,500
X_A			<	1
	X_B		<	1
		X_C	<	1
X_A			>	0
	X_B		>	0
		X_C	>	0

Step 3. Solve the LP Problem.

The above formulation can then be solved by the Simplex method as described previously. It will be apparent that even with a highly simplified problem such as this manual solution methods are exceedingly tedious and accordingly it is unlikely that a student would have to work through the method in examinations.

However, formulation of the problem and interpretation of results are possible topics.

The solution of the above problem is as follows:

Project	Fraction Accepted
A	0.988
B	0
C	0.719

Value of objective function £50,244.

Shadow prices	1st constraint (ie £40,000 Year 0 budget) =	0.922
	2nd constraint (ie £35,000 Year 1 budget) =	0.3755

Step 4. Interpretation of Solution

The solution indicates that 0.988 of Project A and 0.719 of Project C should be initiated. This investment plan uses all the funds available in Years 0 and 1.

The shadow prices indicate the amount by which the NPV of the optimal plan (ie £50,244) could be increased if the budgetary constraints could be increased. For every £1 relaxation of the constraint in Period 0, £0.922 extra NPV would be obtained. The shadow prices indicate that extra funds in Period 0 are worth approximately three times those in Period 1. This fact may give management some guidance in their consideration of various alternative sources of capital.

Note: It will be remembered the assumption made in this example is that these projects are divisible. This is not necessarily a very practical assumption, but it appears to be one frequently made in examinations. Being divisible the NPV is scaled down by the proportion of the project accepted. This is a way of checking the result obtained. In this example the value of NPV obtained is £50,244, ie (0.988 x £23,245) + (0.719 x 37,939).

Where projects are not divisible the only feasible solution method is Integer Programming which is outside the scope of the syllabus at which this book is aimed.

RESERVATIONS OVER THE LP METHOD OF SOLVING CAPITAL RATIONING PROBLEMS

42. There is no doubt that in the right circumstances LP can be a useful method of dealing with multi-period capital rationing problems. There are, however, numerous assumptions and limitations which must be kept in mind if the use of the technique is being considered. The major ones are as follows:

(a) Is the assumption of linearity for all functions realistic?

(b) Are projects truly divisible and capable of being scaled in a linear fashion?

(c) Are all investment opportunities included for each of the periods contained in the model?

(d) Are all projects and constraints independent of one another as assumed in the LP model?

(e) Are all cash flows, resources, constraints known with the certainty assumed in the model? (The way that uncertainty is ignored is possibly the most significant reservation).

(f) Is the choice of discount rate a realistic one? Under 'hard' capital rationing (ie externally imposed) the opportunity cost of funds cannot be known until the investments plan is formulated which, of course, requires the cost of funds to be known - a classic circular argument!

SUMMARY

43. (a) Specific inflation is of more direct concern in investment appraisal and differential inflation is commonly encountered.

(b) The general treatment of inflation in investment appraisal is concerned with distinguishing between the real and nominal value of money and can be dealt with by either single or double discounting.

(c) Because taxation affects the cash flows of a project it is a factor to be considered. It affects a project in three ways: taxes on profits, investment incentives, and its effect on the cost of capital.

(d) Some taxation implications have beneficial effects on projects, eg investment incentives and the fact that interest payments are an allowable charge.

(e) Uncertainty and risk are important factors to be considered in investment appraisal. Three aspects are of special concern: individual project uncertainty, the 'portfolio' effect, and the decision makers' attitude to risk.

(f) Individual project uncertainty can be analysed by three groups of techniques: time based, probability based, and sensitivity analysis and simulation.

(g) The main problem with the time based methods is that they do not explicitly consider the variability of cashflows.

(h) The probability based methods use subjective probabilities and range from expected value through to methods employing statistical analysis based on the properties of distributions.

(i) Arguably of more importance than individual project risk is the aggregate risk of the firm's portfolio of projects. New projects may, to some extent, neutralise or enhance existing risks.

(j) Using the covariance of project returns and returns on existing operations the correlation coefficients of new and existing projects can be calculated.

(k) The decision maker's attitude to risk is of critical importance but is extremely difficult to quantify. In general, decision makers are risk averters.

(l) Capital rationing is where all apparently profitable projects cannot be initiated because of shortage of capital.

(m) The decision rule where capital rationing exists is to maximise the return from the project(s) selected rather than simply accept/reject decisions of projects in isolation.

(n) Single period rationing with divisible projects is dealt with by ranking in order of EVPI, having due regard to mutually exclusive projects. Where the projects are indivisible then a trial and error combination approach can be used.

(o) Multi-period capital rationing with divisible projects is usually solved by LP which produces the optimal solution quantities (ie the projects to be initiated) the value of the objective function (ie the total NPV) and the shadow costs (ie opportunity costs of the binding constraints).

(p) Although useful there are a number of reservations of using LP for solving capital rationing problems.

POINTS TO NOTE

44. (a) The treatment of such matters as inflation and uncertainty have been dealt with in this chapter in the context of investment appraisal. However the concepts and techniques described have a much wider application than just investment decisions. For example, the uses of expected values, sensitivity analysis and the concept of the real as opposed to the nominal value of money are applicable in virtually every area of planning and decision making.

(b) Because of the amount of data involved and the complexity of the techniques used, computers are widely employed for investment appraisals, particularly in the area of risk evaluation and sensitivity analysis. to obtain the maximum benefit from the computer packages it is essential that the management accountant is totally familiar with the appraisal principles and concepts upon which the programs are based.

(c) Valuable information can sometimes be gleaned from carrying out a post audit of a capital project. This should include a review of the forecasts and out-turns for all the factors involved, eg cash flows, length of life, inflation rates and so on as well as the appraisal methods used.

(d) A common application of investment appraisal is the analysis of purchase c.f. leasing. Frequently the decision to purchase or lease depends on the taxation rules in operation at the time. In general, when an organisation leases an item the leasing payments are fully tax deductible but the firm (the lessee) loses the capital allowances which accrue to the leasing company (the lessor). Each case is different and individual analysis is required which should follow the following pattern.

(i)   Calculate the present value of the lease arrangement with the necessary adjustments for taxation including the time lags.

(ii)   Calculate the present value of outright purchase including the taxation effects of capital allowances and any loan repayments made if it is necessary to raise a loan to purchase the asset.

(iii)   Choose the cheapest acquisition method between (i) and (ii), both of which will show negative present values.

(iv)   Calculate the present value of the **trading operations** of the asset and project with the usual taxation adjustment for profits and/or losses. This present value will be positive and care must be taken NOT to include any form of acquisition costs (purchase or lease) in this part of the analysis. This has been dealt with in steps (i) and (ii).

(v)   Compare the best present value of lease or purchase, ie (i) or (ii) with the trading present value form (iv) to decide whether the project is worth while initiating.

ADDITIONAL READING

The Economics of Capital Budgeting	Bromwich, PITMAN
Analysis for Investment Decisions	Carsberg, ACCOUNTANCY AGE
Business Investment Decisions Under Inflation	Carsberg and Hope, ICA
The Evaluation of risk in Business Investment	Hull, PERGAMMON
Investment Appraisal	Lumby, VAN NOSTRAND REINHOLD
Management of Company Finance	Samples and Wilkes, NELSON
Investment Appraisal and Inflation	Westwick and Shoket, ICA

SELF REVIEW QUESTIONS

1.   What is specific inflation and why is it important in investment appraisal? (2)

2.   Distinguish between money and 'real' cash flows. (4)

3.   What is the relationship between real and money discount factors? (6)

4.   Why is it necessary to consider taxation in investment appraisal and in what ways does taxation affect a project?
                                                                                      (7-9)

5.   What are the steps in considering taxation in project appraisals? (14)

6.   In which stages of the appraisal and decision process should uncertainty and risk be considered? (15)

7.   What are the time based methods of considering uncertainty? What is their underlying assumption and their major limitation? (17–21)

8.   Describe the method of using Expected Value in project appraisals. (23)

9.   How does discrete probabilistic analysis extend the expected value technique? (24)

10.   What is continuous probabilistic analysis and, if used, how are the means and dispersions of the cash flows established? (25 & 26)

11.   How is the standard deviation of the NPV established and how is this used? (27)

12.   What is the objective of sensitivity analysis and how is it carried out? (30)

13.   Why is it important to consider not only the risks of individual projects but the aggregate risk of combinations of projects? (31)

14.   What is the general procedure for assessing the portfolio risk? (33)

15.   What are risk averters? (33)

16.   What is a certainty equivalent? (34)

17.   What is the difference between 'hard' and 'soft' capital rationing? (35)

18.   How would the investment decision be made if single period rationing existed with divisible projects? (37)

19.   How would the answer to 18 change if some of the projects were mutually exclusive? (38)

20.   What is multi-period capital rationing and what is a possible solution method? (40)

21.   What reservations existing regarding the use of LP to solve capital rationing problems? (42)

EXAMINATION QUESTIONS WITH ANSWERS COMMENCING PAGE 360

A1. *As the financial consultant of the Bourbon Can Company, a medium sized manufacturing business, you have been asked to advise on the current year's investment proposals. The proposed projects, shown below, are not mutually exclusive.*

PROJECT A   To replace the existing data processing equipment. Initial cost £250,000. Expected life of new equipment 6 years. Expected annual after tax cash inflow £72,500.

PROJECT B   To develop a new type of container. Cost £70,000. All to be incurred in the current year. Expected life of product 5 years. Expected annual after tax cash inflow £30,000, the inflows to commence in one year's time.

PROJECT C   To install safety equipment. Initial cost £90,000. Expected life 3 years. Expected annual after tax cash inflow £45,000.

PROJECT D   To construct a new factory building. Initial cost £210,000. Expected life 8 years. Expected annual after tax cash inflow £57,000.

PROJECT E   To extend the existing loading equipment. Initial cost £170,000. Expected life 4 years. Expected annual after tax cash inflow £70,000.

PROJECT F   To purchase patent rights to a new process. Initial cost £135,000. Expected life 7 years. Expected annual after tax cash inflow £36,000.

You may assume that with the exception of project B, all cash inflows would commence in the current year. For calculation purposes you may assume that the annual cash inflows are always received on the last day of the year. Tax can be assumed to have been paid in the year in which the profits are earned.

The company's marginal cost of capital for the coming year is estimated at 16%. The company is, however, in a capital rationing situation and it estimates it will only have £600,000 to invest on capital projects in the current year.

Required:

(a) Which projects would you recommend the company to undertake? Give the reasons for your choice.

(b) What factors, if any, other than those given in the question, would you advise the company to consider before making a decision?

ACCA, Financial Management.

A2. A division of Bewcast plc has been allocated a fixed capital sum by the main board of directors for its capital investment during the next year. The division's management has identified three capital investment projects, each potentially successful, each of similar size, but has only been allocated enough funds to undertake two projects. Projects are not divisible and cannot be postponed until a later date.

The division's management proposed to use portfolio theory to determine which two projects should be undertaken, based upon an analysis of the projects' risk and return. The success of the projects will depend upon the growth rate of the economy. Estimates of project returns at different levels of economic growth are shown below.

Economic growth (annual average)	Probability of occurrence	Estimated return (%) Project 1	Project 2	Project 3
Zero	0.2	2	5	6
2 per cent	0.3	8	9	10
4 per cent	0.3	16	12	11
6 per cent	0.2	25	15	11

Required:

(a) Using the above information evaluate and discuss which two projects the division is likely to undertake. All relevant calculations must be shown.

(b) What are the weaknesses of the evaluation technique used in (a) above, and what further information might be useful in the evaluation of these projects?

(c) Suggest why portfolio theory is not widely used in practice as a capital investment evaluation technique.

(d) Recommend, and briefly describe, an alternative investment evaluation technique that might be applied by the division.

ACCA, Financial Management.

Performance Appraisal

The work of the management accountant can range from the analysis of detailed aspects of operations such as calculating variances or job costs, to consideration of performance at a broader, macro level.

This may involve assessing the performance of autonomous or semi-autonomous divisions of the same firm or considering the performance and stability of whole companies perhaps for the purpose of investment or acquisition. This aspect of the work of the management accountant, particularly at senior levels, is becoming of increasing importance with the growth of decentralised operations, multi division companies and because of merger and take-over activity.

This section of the manual deals with the objectives, techniques, and limitations of performance appraisal systems in multi-division companies together with a detailed analysis of transfer pricing which becomes necessary when divisions of the same company trade with each other and it is desired to assess the profitability of each division. Ratio analysis relating to internal efficiency, solvency and investment is explained and the section concludes with an outline of value added statements as an aid to performance appraisal.

18. Divisional Performance Appraisal

INTRODUCTION

1. This chapter discusses the principles of decentralisation and divisionalisation and the possible problems which may arise. The need for performance appraisal systems is discussed and the objectives of such systems are specified. The characteristics of profit centres and investment centres are explained and relative and absolute performance measures are introduced. The various measures associated with profit are described in detail. These include: controllable profit, divisional profit, net profit, controllable residual profit and net residual profit. The main relative measure of performance, return on capital employed, is discussed together with the variants commonly encountered. The chapter concludes with a brief review of appraisal measures outside the financial area.

DIVISIONALISATION AND PERFORMANCE APPRAISAL

2. Particularly in large companies, there has been substantial decentralisation of managerial decision making from central management to the operating divisions of the company. This has occurred in existing single companies and also as a consequence of merger activity. Typically, mergers result in a large, diversified group consisting of a number of operating divisions, with various degrees of autonomy, answerable to the holding company or the main board of directors. As a result of such structural changes the financial control of divisions by central management has become a complex and vital task. It is one in which the practising management accountant, particularly at senior levels, has a key role in the design and operation of performance appraisal systems which assist central management to ensure that the company as a whole - including the divisions - fulfills overall company objectives.

Before examining the techniques and methods of performance appraisal it is necessary to consider the reasons why decentralisation occurs and to discuss the potential problems which may arise if the process works imperfectly and there is inadequate monitoring.

WHAT IS DECENTRALISATION?

3. As organisations grow in size and complexity top management find themselves unable to make all the decisions. In such circumstances authority for certain types of decision-making is delegated to subordinate managers and thus some decision making moves away from the centre and decentralisation takes place.

The amount of decentralisation can vary widely. In theory, total decentralisation could occur whereby a division operated completely autonomously with authority to make all types of decisions and would thus in effect be a separate entity. Of course, such a situation is unlikely to be encountered and whilst the amount of delegated authority varies considerably, certain types of decisions invariably seem to be retained by central management. Typically these include: major investment decisions, senior staff appointments and salaries and pricing decisions although in certain types of industries, for example, retailing and jobbing engineering, pricing may be considered an operational responsibility. If central management delegated these and other such major decisions it would lack strategic control of the enterprise.

The main areas of divisional responsibility are connected with the day to day actions of manufacturing, selling and promotion, labour appointments and utilisation, maintenance, and customer and supplier relationships.

There are no absolute standards to judge the extent to which an organisation is decentralised. An organisation may have numerous operating divisions but with all decisions of any significance taken at the centre whilst another may have few or no identifiable divisions yet has genuine, decentralised decision making. The natural consequence of a policy of decentralisation is the creation of semi-autonomous operating divisions where the local management has considerable, but not absolute, discretion and has responsibility for divisional profitability. It is in such circumstances that formal performance appraisal and monitoring systems become necessary.

OBJECTIVES OF DECENTRALISATION

4. The general purpose of decentralisation and the creation of divisional structures is to enhance the efficiency of the enterprise as a whole and to make it more capable of meeting overall objectives.

Properly organised and controlled, decentralisation should:

(a) Improve local decision making.
Divisional management are in close touch with day to day operations and are in a position to make more informed and speedier decisions.

(b) Improve strategic decision making.
Central management are relieved of much lower level and routine decision making and thus able to concentrate on strategic considerations.

(c)   Increase flexibility and reduce communication problems.

The ability to take decisions near the point of action reduces response time and means that adjustments can be made more swiftly to cope with changes in market or supply conditions. The shorter communication lines mean quicker decisions and fewer chances of errors caused by communication channels.

(d)   Increase motivation of divisional management.

This is a key feature of decentralisation and arguably is the most important factor contributing to increased efficiency. Research shows that people value greater independence and respond in a positive manner to increased responsibility particularly when this is linked to the reward system of the organisation. An important factor in the design of performance appraisal systems is to ensure that motivation is not stifled and that goal congruence is encouraged.

(e)   The spread of genuine decision making and the increased responsibility this entails provides better training for junior management. In many organisations there are movements within divisional management and between divisional and central management thus enhancing career opportunities for able and ambitious managers. The existence of these opportunities helps to attract people of the right calibre and increases morale and motivation.

POSSIBLE PROBLEMS WITH DECENTRALISATION

5.   The major potential problem with decentralisation, particularly where the divisions are highly interdependent, is that of sub-optimal decision making. This is caused by decisions where benefits to one division are more than offset by costs or loss of benefits to other divisions. Where there is a lack of congruence between the overall objectives of the organisation and the goals and aims of the local decision maker then sub-optimal decision making is likely unless there is a relevant and well design appraisal system.

Other problems and extra costs which may occur with decentralisation are the duplication of certain services in the divisions and at headquarters, eg market research, computing services, personnel functions. In addition, it is likely that decentralisation will require more sophisticated information. Friction may also occur between divisional managements, particularly where the performance of one division is dependent on that of another division. This problem is aggravated when financial considerations which affect divisional performance are concerned. A particular example of this is the problem of setting **transfer prices** for goods and services supplied by one division to another. The price at which goods or services are transferred affects the financial performance of both divisions involved and is a possible area in which sub-optimal decisions may be taken. The setting of transfer prices and the problems associated with them are discussed in detail in the following chapter.

OBJECTIVES OF PERFORMANCE APPRAISAL

6.   When central management have decided that decentralisation should take place and operating divisions are established, some system of control or performance appraisal becomes necessary. As with any form of information system the performance appraisal system should assist management to plan and control activities, and to make decisions which enable the objectives of the organisation as a whole to be met. In particular, performance appraisal systems for monitoring divisions with substantial delegated powers, ideally should:

(a)   Promote goal congruence.

The performance appraisal system and criteria employed should help local management to direct operations and to make decisions in ways that fulfil overall company objectives. Ideally the goals of local managements should coincide with overall company goals - perfect goal congruence - but of course this is a difficult state to achieve in its entirety.

(b)   Provide relevant and regular feedback to central management.

Central management need regular feedback of appropriate information in order to judge the capability of local management and also to assess the economic worth of the division as an operating unit. These two aspects may be related but involved distinctively different considerations and information requirements.

(c)   Encourage initiative and motivation.

The performance appraisal system should not be narrowly conceived or so rigidly applied that it stifles initiative. For example, if local management see an opportunity which would increase overall company profits but which would reduce the profits of their own division, then the system should be flexible enough for this to take place without local management feeling that they will be penalised. Local management must be encouraged to feel that, within the prescribed limits, they have genuine autonomy.

(d) Encourage long run views rather than short-term expedients.

The long term success of the organisation is the primary objective and the performance appraisal systems and measures should encourage decision making which contributes to this objective. An over emphasis on short run considerations may cause adverse long term effects. Short term improvements in results are relatively easily made by, for example, forgoing proper maintenance, hiring poorer quality but cheaper staff. reducing product quality and other similar expedients. Maintaining improved results over a period is quite a different matter.

RESPONSIBILITY CENTRES

7.   In Chapter 2 one type of responsibility centre was discussed. This was the cost centre which, it will be recalled, is a department or section or function over which a designated individual has responsibility for expenditure. Cost centres generally form the basis of budgetary control systems which are one form of performance appraisal usually with the emphasis on cost items.

When setting up systems to monitor the performance of semi-autonomous operating divisions the basic principles of responsibility accounting are developed beyond cost centres to what are called **profit centres** and **investment centres**.

Profit centre - this is a unit of the organisation, often called a division, which is responsible for expenditures, revenues and profits.

Investment centre - this is a profit centre for which the designated manager is responsible for profit in relation to the capital invested in the division. It should be noted that the term does not necessarily mean that the manager is responsible for the investment decisions within the division. As previously pointed out, above a fairly low limit, investment decisions are frequently the prerogative of central management.

The following table summarises the types of responsibility centres.

Cost Centre	Profit Centre	Investment Centre
Responsible for:	Responsible for:	Responsible for:
COSTS	COSTS	COSTS
-	REVENUES	REVENUES
-	PROFITS	PROFITS
-	-	PROFITS IN RELATION TO INVESTMENT

In practice it appears the the term **profit centre** is frequently used whether the division is responsible for just profit or profit in relation to the capital invested in the division.

CHOICE OF FINANCIAL APPRAISAL MEASURES

8.   Having decided that a division's performance must be monitored the measures to be used need to be chosen. Should the division's performance be judged by its profit and if so on what basis should this be calculated? Or should the basis be some quite different measure such as sales growth? The considerations affecting these and other measures are dealt with below but it must be realised that no one measure can fulfil all the requirements of an ideal appraisal criterion nor can any one measure satisfactorily monitor all aspects of the multi-facetted nature of divisional operations.

Two categories of financial performance measures appear to be commonly used - those based on **absolute values** which are usually profitability criteria of one kind or another, and those based on **relative values** which are generally some form of return on investment or capital employed. These measures are dealt with below.

PROFITABILITY MEASURES OF PERFORMANCE

9.   Profit is a widely used absolute measure of performance and is one familiar to management and acceptable to them; which is an important behavioural consideration. When profit is used as a performance measure it provides a means by which division can be compared with division and one division's performance can be compared period by period. However used, there are substantial control advantages when actual profit is compared with planned or budgeted profit.

When profit is used as measure of performance appraisal it may be defined in a variety of ways and a number of the more important variants are described below, including: controllable profit, divisional profit, net profit, controllable residual profit, and net residual profit.

After the descriptions of each type of profit a table is given showing their relationships. In addition, a worked example is provided showing the calculations necessary for each measure.

CONTROLLABLE PROFIT

10. This can be defined as revenues less costs controllable at the divisional level. The rationale for this concept is sound in that the measure includes only those costs and revenues for which local management has primary responsibility. What costs and revenues to include depends on the degree of tactical responsibility that has been delegated. Particular items that are included or excluded are dealt with below:

Variable items (costs and revenues)

In general those items of cost and revenues which are dependent on local decisions are **included**, for example, sales income, costs of labour, materials, operating expenses including short run interest charges relating to controllable working capital items such as debtors and inventories.

Divisional overheads

Where the items are controllable locally they would be **included**. This would include items which are fixed in relation to activity but can be varied by management action. Examples include administrative and supervisory costs and, where delegated to the division, advertising costs.

Depreciation and fixed asset costs

Normally these items should be **excluded** because the investment and disinvestment of fixed assets and hence depreciation charges are a strategic responsibility and outside the control of local management. Also, depreciation charges are based on past investment decisions and often on historical costs so do not reflect current conditions. Note that if fixed asset investment is controllable by local management then depreciation on controllable items would be **included**.

Apportioned items

Frequently a portion of central administration costs or part of the costs of facilities used jointly by divisions (eg computer costs) are charged to the division. By definition these are non-controllable and all such apportioned costs are excluded.

DIVISIONAL PROFIT

11. Sometimes known as traceable profit or direct profit. This is the profit that arises from divisional operations which can be calculated without arbitrarily apportioned central costs. It is equivalent to controllable profit less depreciation on divisional assets and other non-controllable divisional overheads. It follows that a number of the costs which are identifiable with the division are not controllable by the division.

NET PROFIT

12. This can be defined as revenues less controllable divisional costs and apportioned central administration costs.

The use of this method does allow local management to be aware of all the costs of the division and of its net effect on the group results. However, all methods of apportioning costs are arbitrary and local management have no control over the amount of costs apportioned which may be at a significant level. In such circumstances appraisal by divisional net profit may have adverse behavioural effects, reduce motivation and may lead to sub-optimal decision making.

Conceptually this method does not seem as sound as controllable profit although it appears to be commonly used.

CONTROLLABLE RESIDUAL PROFIT OR INCOME

13. This is sales revenue less controllable divisional costs and interest imputed on the divisional investment. Using residual profit as a performance measure assumes that the level of divisional investment is a responsibility of divisional management. This should be contrasted with the view taken when controllable profit is used as a performance measure that the investment level is a central, strategic responsibility. It follows that depreciation should be charged on fixed assets controlled by the division when residual income is calculated. The imputed interest charge on the amount invested represented the opportunity cost of funds and is normally based n the firm's cost of capital.

It will be apparent that residual profit is a broader concept than any of the simpler profit variants and rests upon a firmer theoretical base.

The advantages and disadvantages and some of the problems associated with the application of controllable residual profit are given below.

Advantages of controllable residual profit

(a)   Goal congruence is encouraged because the process of charging the divisions with the firm's cost of capital ensures that managers are aware of the opportunity cost of funds and that divisional decisions, particularly relating to investment, are compatible with the aims of the organisation as a whole.

(b)   The use of a clear cut objective such as 'maximise residual profit' could have a strong motivating influence and would ensure that growth opportunities will not be missed providing they earn a rate of return above the cost of capital.

(c)   Residual profit concepts take a long run view of divisional performance. Also, an objective expressed in terms of maximising an absolute figure avoids the situation which may occur when investment opportunities would be rejected if they lowered the average divisional rate of return, expressed in relative terms, even though such opportunities earn a rate of return above the company's cost of capital. This is directly analogous to the arguments for NPV as compared with IRR discussed earlier particularly in relation to mutually exclusive investment.

Note: Return on capital employed, which is a **relative** measure of performance has strong affinities with Residual Profit and is discussed in para 18 in this chapter.

(d)   Controllable residual profit is a reasonable measure, albeit with many imperfections, of the performance of local management. The inclusion of controllable items plus the imputed interest charge on controllable divisional investment is a genuine attempt to separate managerial performance from the overall performance of the division as an economic unit.

Disadvantages of controllable residual profit.

(a)   Although central management may like the idea of imputing a cost to the division for use the use of local assets, they may not favour the assumption on investment powers contained within the residual profit approach. It will be recalled that it is assumed that local management are able to take their own investment decisions which is a power that central management may not wish to relinquish.

(b)   Residual profit includes, without distinction, the effects of both past investment decisions and of current operation performance. This is because the depreciation charges included in the residual profit calculations should represent the true loss in economic value of the asset(s), whereas the calculation is usually based on historic values or less frequently on inflation adjusted values, neither of which necessarily reflect any economic changes specific to the assets(s).

Ideally, the effects of past decisions, which are by definition unalterable, should be separated from the effects of current operations, but there are obvious practical difficulties in this process.

(c)   The difficulties of estimating the firm's cost of capital have been discussed earlier but, notwithstanding the problems, the use of the weighted average cost of capital for calculating residual profit is frequently advocated. The WACC, an estimate of the current opportunity cost of funds, is applied to the book value (gross or net) of divisional assets which are the results of past investment decisions. Thus there is an incompatibility in that the interest charge, as conventionally calculated, is a form of review of the past usage of assets rather than a correctly specified opportunity cost relevant for taking decisions about the asset's future. This may lead to sub-optimal decision making on the part of local management. For example, local management may dispose of an asset which in the short run does not meet the required return even though it may be in the long run interest of the firm as a whole to retain the asset within the division.

NET RESIDUAL PROFIT

14. This is controllable residual profit less interest on non-controllable divisional assets and apportioned head office charges. This performance measure attempts to appraise the economic worth of the division as a whole from the viewpoint of the group. It combines both the performance of local management (appraised by controllable residual profit) and an evaluation of the investment in the division and its total costs, including an appropriate share of central charges.

RELATIONSHIP OF THE APPRAISAL MEASURES BASED ON PROFIT

15. The various definitions of profit have been discussed in the preceding paragraphs. What measure to use is a matter of judgement which depends on a variety of factors including: company objectives, degree of decentralisation and divisionalisation, quality of local management, the efficiency of available information systems including the accounting systems, the type of industry and other such considerations.

Table 1 summaries the various measures and shows their relationships. It will be seen that after **controllable** profit there is a divergence of philosophy whereby divisions are considered either as profit centres or, when imputed interest is involved, as investment centres.

Relationship of Divisional Profit Measures

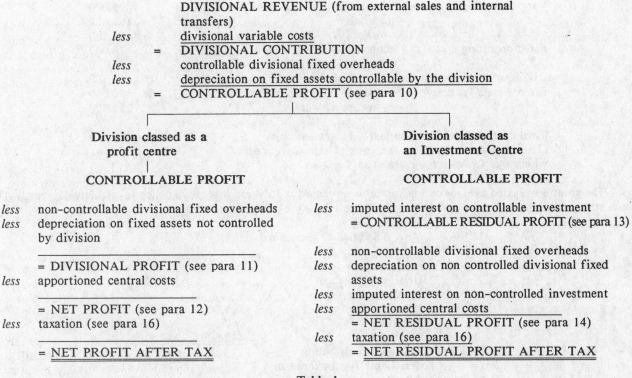

	DIVISIONAL REVENUE (from external sales and internal transfers)
less	divisional variable costs
=	DIVISIONAL CONTRIBUTION
less	controllable divisional fixed overheads
less	depreciation on fixed assets controllable by the division
=	CONTROLLABLE PROFIT (see para 10)

Division classed as a profit centre

CONTROLLABLE PROFIT

less non-controllable divisional fixed overheads
less depreciation on fixed assets not controlled
       by division
_____
       = DIVISIONAL PROFIT (see para 11)
less apportioned central costs
_____
       = NET PROFIT (see para 12)
less taxation (see para 16)
_____
       = NET PROFIT AFTER TAX

Division classed as an Investment Centre

CONTROLLABLE PROFIT

less imputed interest on controllable investment
       = CONTROLLABLE RESIDUAL PROFIT (see para 13)

less non-controllable divisional fixed overheads
less depreciation on non controlled divisional fixed
       assets
less imputed interest on non-controlled investment
less apportioned central costs
_____
       = NET RESIDUAL PROFIT (see para 14)
less taxation (see para 16)
_____
       = NET RESIDUAL PROFIT AFTER TAX

Table 1

SHOULD PROFIT BE BEFORE OR AFTER TAX?

16. Whatever the particular variant of profitability used there is the problem of deciding whether performance should be appraised on a before or after tax basis.

It can be argued that a before tax basis should be used for the divisions because the final tax assessment is based on the results of the company or group as a whole and therefore tax could only be charged to the divisions on some arbitrary basis. An alternative view is that it may be the investment decisions of a particular division which earn the capital allowances or generate the taxable income so that the division concerned should have the appropriate credit or charge. This is particularly relevant for investment centres which have substantial control over investment policies.

Although the decision to appraise on a before or after tax basis is complex and will in practice be based on the circumstances of the particular situation, on balance it would seem that a **before tax basis is preferred**. The main reasons for this are:

(a) The whole purpose of appraisal systems is to appraise the performance of local management and the performance of the division as an economic unit. The effects of the tax system through timing differences, capital allowances and changing rates may obscure the actual underlying managerial and economic performance.

(b) Tax planning is frequently a central function which, quite properly, may impose constraints or cause local decisions to be adjusted for the good of the firm as a whole. Accordingly local performance levels may be misrepresented if based on after-tax considerations.

(c)   In many circumstances the apportionment to divisions of a share of the taxation charge or credit may be on an arbitrary basis.

PROFITABILITY CALCULATIONS

17. Example 1

The following data have been collected relating to the WYMEX division of the MULTICELL group.

Data for WYMEX division

		£
Sales Revenue - external customers		600,000
- internal transfers		350,000
Variable operating costs	- labour	95,000
	- materials	160,000
	- overheads	42,500
Fixed operating costs	- controllable by division	78,000
	- controllable centrally	41,000
Divisional management cost		26,500
Fixed Assets (at cost)	- divisional purchases	450,000
	- central purchases	250,000
Total central administration and management costs		684,210

(These are apportioned on the basis of sales revenue which was £5.2m for the group as a whole)

The group's weighted average cost of capital is estimated at 15% and it is group policy to calculate depreciation on a straight line basis at 25% and to impute interest on a gross investment basis.

Solution to Example 1

			£
	Divisional Revenue		950,000
less	Variable costs		
	labour	95,000	
	materials	160,000	
	overheads	42,500	297,500
=	Divisional contribution		652,500
less	controllable fixed overheads		78,000
less	controllable depreciation		112,500
=	CONTROLLABLE PROFIT		462,000

Profit Centre Approach

		£
	CONTROLLABLE PROFIT b/f	462,000
less	non-controllable fixed overhead	41,000
less	non-controllable depreciation	62,500
=	DIVISIONAL PROFIT	358,500
less	Apportioned central charges	
	(684,210 / 5,200,000 x 950,000)	125,000
=	NET PROFIT before tax	£233,500

Investment Centre Approach

		£
	CONTROLLABLE PROFIT b/f	462,000
less	imputed interest on controllable investment (15% of £450,000)	67,500
=	CONTROLLABLE RESIDUAL PROFIT	394,500
less	non-controllable overheads	41,000
less	non-controllable depreciation	62,500
less	non-controllable imputed interest	37,500
less	apportioned central charges	125,000
=	NET RESIDUAL PROFIT before tax	£128,500

RETURN ON CAPITAL EMPLOYED (ROCE)

18.   Return on capital employed, alternatively termed return on investment (ROI), is a commonly used **relative** measure of divisional performance appraisal. It has the appeal of simplicity in that a single percentage figure, prepared from readily available and understood financial information, is used both as a measure of divisional performance and as a basis of comparison with other divisions and other opportunities available to the firm. However, ROCE has numerous limitations and needs to be used with caution.

ROCE can be defined in various ways but the basis of all the variants is the simple formula.

$$\text{ROCE} = \frac{\text{PROFIT}}{\text{INVESTMENT}} \times 100\%$$

This formula can be disaggregated as follows:

$$\text{ROCE} = \frac{\text{SALES}}{\text{INVESTMENT}} \times \frac{\text{PROFIT}}{\text{SALES}} \times 100\%$$

or ROCE = Capital turnover x Profit percentage on sales.

Profit and investment can be defined in a variety of ways, which are discussed below, but such variations are relatively unimportant compared with the potential problems which may arise from the fact that **any** form of ROCE is a ratio measure. It will be recalled in the discussion of NPV and IRR, that any ratio measure, improperly used, is unsuitable for ranking investments so that improper use of ROCE may cause local management to make sub-optimal decisions. ROCE measures the average return on divisional investment and local management can only improve their ROCE by investing in projects which earn **above** the existing ROCE or by ceasing existing projects which earn **below** their average ROCE. This is a safety first policy which means that local management may act in a manner detrimental to the interests of the firm as a whole. For example, they may reject an investment which, although lowering their divisional ROCE, has a return in excess of the firm's WACC and therefore should be accepted.

The use of ROCE as a divisional appraisal measure makes the same assumption over investment powers as that discussed in para 13 on residual profit, that is divisional management have control over their own investments. When divisional management do not have such control, the denominator (investment) of the ratio is a constant as far as divisional management is concerned so that maximising ROCE is equivalent to maximising profit and the use of the ratio becomes unnecessary.

Any value that ROCE may have as an appraisal measure of divisional performance can only arise when local management have control over both the denominator (investment) and the numerator (profit) of the ratio.

As conventionally calculated (using normal profits and book values of assets) ROCE overstates the rate of return, which may have serious repercussions if decisions are based on the calculated figure. This arises because, in inflationary conditions, profits are overstated owing to depreciation charges being based on historical costs, whilst at the same time the bottom half of the ratio, the capital employed, is understated being the same original costs. The overall effect of this two way bias can be seriously to overstate the ROCE. It follows from this that some form of inflation adjustment should be made, both to profits and to asset values, if a more meaningful ROCE figure is required.

PROFIT IN ROCE CALCULATIONS

19. Depending on circumstances and the objectives of the appraisal process any of the profit measures described in relation to profit centres, as shown on Table 1, could be used in ROCE calculations. This includes Controllable Profit, Divisional Profit and Net Profit. It will be apparent that residual profit already takes account of the investment in the division, via the imputed interest charge, and to use such a profit figure in the ROCE calculation would double count the impact of the investment.

ROCE is an investment centre approach and uses one of the profit measures mentioned applied to the divisional investment. The factors governing the choice of profit measures and whether they should be before or after tax have already been discussed. These factors apply equally to their use in ROCE calculations.

DEFINING THE INVESTMENT BASE IN ROCE CALCULATIONS

20. Several different bases are used to value the capital employed in a division, for example, gross book value, net book value or current replacement cost. Whatever method is used, great care is needed that bias from accounting procedures does not mask the underlying level of operational efficiency. For example, if original cost is used as the base, a division with old assets may be shown to have a higher rate of return than a division with more modern assets, simply as a result of lower original costs. The valuation of assets on an historical basis invariably means that the asset base is an amalgam of assets acquired at different times with correspondingly different monetary values which inevitably creates anomalies.

Consideration of the three valuation bases mentioned above follow:

Gross book value:

If this basis is used comparisons between divisions may be difficult and local management may be induced to make sub-optimal decisions. For example, when a new asset is replaced the gross book value of divisional assets will increase by the difference between the cost of the new asset and the original cost of the old asset. The relevant capital cost for investment appraisal purposes is the new asset cost less the scrap value of the old asset. As the scrap value is likely to be far less than the original cost of the old asset, the capital cost of the new asset is understated when gross book values are used in the ROCE calculation. This means that replacement decisions which did not meet normal investment targets (eg a DCF return above the weighted average cost of capital of the firm) may improve a division's ROCE. The use of gross book values may also cause a manager to dispose of assets which earn less than the divisional average ROCE even though their retention can be justified when the overall return of the company is considered.

Net book values:

The use of net book values has the effect of showing an increasing rate of return over time simply by the diminution of the capital employed base as each period's depreciation is deducted. There is little logic in this and such a result may cause local management to discourage new investment which would reduce an overstated return on capital employed. Such a policy might show increasing rates of return on capital employed whilst at the same time profits could actually be falling.

Current replacement cost:

The theoretically correct valuation for the assets employed is their opportunity cost or economic value to the business. This involves a range of subjective judgements which may be unacceptable to the managements concerned.

Accordingly, a number of firms use the current replacement cost of the assets as an approximation of their economic value. Replacement costs are usually estimated by the use of specially prepared indices which measure the changing costs of various groups of assets. The indices are applied to the historical costs to produce a current valuation. There is no doubt that this method is more defensible than gross or net book values although there are still a number of subjective elements and appropriate indices or estimates of current values will not always be readily available. it follows that if current values are used for the assets employed, profits will have to be adjusted to current values.

Note: Whatever basis is used, it appears to be common practice to use the average value for the year, and not year end values. It will be realised that this is a minor refinement which does not solve the fundamental problems mentioned above.

ROCE c.f. RESIDUAL PROFIT

21. These are the two most frequent advocated financial performance measures, both of which include the impact of the amount invested in the division, one in a relative way - ROCE - and one using absolute values - RESIDUAL PROFIT. Both have numerous limitations but both are defensible as practical performance measures when used with an awareness of their deficiencies and particularly when they are supported by other appraisal information.

Which is to be preferred? The balance of the theoretical argument would favour residual profit. It is a better ranking device and it encourages management to invest in assets which will produce a return greater than the imputed interest charge and thus increase residual income. Also it avoids the problems which may occur when a division is earning a high rate of return on existing assets and is reluctant to invest in lower return yet still worthwhile projects. In spite of these arguments ROCE is the more widely used measure in practice so it is important that the measure is used in its most appropriate form and close attention is given to signs of any sub-optimal decision making based on ROCE computations.

TARGET LEVEL OF PERFORMANCE

22. Notwithstanding their limitations, ROCE and residual profit are used as performance measures so that it is necessary to set some level or standard of performance to be used as the divisional target.

Setting any form of performance target is a controversial exercise with many subjective elements but typical factors which would be considered include:

(a) The company's cost of capital. This, of course, is the absolute minimum acceptable rate of return and the target level would normally be set higher than this.

(b) The returns being achieved by efficient competitors in the same industry. Interfirm comparisons and other published data can provide guidance in this area.

(c) The risk level of the industry, company and division. In general the higher the risk levels the higher the target.

(d) The nature of the industry, the degree of competition and the position of the firm within the industry.

(e) The general economic climate and the extent of under/over capacity within the industry and the firm.

It does not follow that a standard rate or target should be set for all the divisions of a firm. Although this appears to be a 'fair' and consistent approach it must be remembered that the objective of performance appraisal measures and the targets set is to motivate local management into making decisions in accordance with the overall interests of the firm. If divisions operate in different markets with differing risk levels it is extremely likely that different target levels, appropriate to individual divisional conditions, will be more efficient than an overall blanket rate.

APPRAISING MULTIPLE OBJECTIVES

23. ROCE and residual profit are useful summary appraisal measures and, in spite of deficiencies, make a significant contribution to the assessment of financial performance and financial objectives. However, no single measure can hope to assess all of the various objectives that might be set for a company or division. This is in accordance with the Law of Requisite Variety, discussed previously, and means that for full control of a division, ROCE or residual profit should be supported by other appraisal measures appropriate to the particular objective being considered.

Examples of areas in which objectives might be set and possible appraisal measures are as follows:

Objectives set in connection:	Possible appraisal measures
Sales	Sales turnover and trends by product, product range, area, type of distribution etc.
Market share	Proportion of market for individual product and product ranges. Trends and comparison with overall market.
Growth	Appropriately adjusted for inflation, comparisons and trends for sales, assets employed, profits, number of employees, etc.
Labour relations	Labour turnover, absenteeism statistics, number of promotions, transfers, grievances. Number of apprentices and trainees, courses and support.
Productivity	Labour and machine hours per unit, output per shift and hour. Material utilisation. Overheads per £ of sales, value added statistics.
Quality and Reliability	Quantifiable measures include number of goods returns, guarantee claims, item and product acceptability. Percentage of re-worked parts.
Social responsibilities	Difficult to quantify but possible measures include: number of local employees, support given to local institutions, number of school visits, sponsorships, amount spent on anti-pollution measures.

It is likely that objectives will be set in some or all of the above areas, particularly where the firm practises 'management by objectives' (MBO). This phrase was first publicised by Drucker who emphasises the multiple aspects of managerial performance and the need to harmonise individual aspects of managerial performance and the need to harmonise individual managerial goals with organisational goals. Where MBO is practised, informally or formally, appraisal of performance will be required in many areas outside the strictly financial measures discussed in this chapter.

MULTI-NATIONAL PERFORMANCE APPRAISAL

24. An extreme form of divisionalisation occurs in multi-national organisations and companies who typically operate on a world wide scale with operating divisions dispersed in numerous countries and even continents. Whilst in general the principles covered in this chapter apply to such organisations it is obvious that the scale of operations, the diversity of conditions and personnel, and the distances involved make control of such organisations a complex and exacting task.

Typical of the additional problems that these organisations face are the following (not in order of importance).

(a) Distance and remoteness from headquarters which increase delays and information problems.
(b) Variability in the quality of management and workers in the various countries.
(c) Differing local taxation and company rules.
(d) Local trade and government policies and restrictions.
(e) Local pricing and tariff regulations.
(f) Currency exchange difficulties and rate fluctuations.
(g) Transportation delivery problems and transfer pricing difficulties concerned with trade between divisions.
(h) Differences in accounting standards and policies.
(i) Motivation problems with local management remote from headquarters.

SUMMARY

25. (a) The growth of divisionalisation has produced a need for performance appraisal and financial control systems.

(b) Decentralisation takes place when authority is delegated.

(c) Decentralisation should: improve local and strategic decision making, increase flexibility, increase motivation, improve training.

(d) Decentralisation may bring problems. These include: sub-optimal decision making, duplication, more expensive information systems.

(e) Ideally, performance appraisal systems should promote goal congruence, provide meaningful feedback, encourage initiative and the longer term view.

(f) Profit centres are responsible for expenditures, revenues and profits. Investment centres are profit centres where profit is assessed in relation to capital invested.

(g) Financial performance appraisal measures are either absolute measures (some form of profit) or relative measures (return on capital employed).

(h) Controllable profit is revenues less costs controllable at divisional level.

(i) Divisional profit is the divisional profit without apportioned central costs.

(j) Controllable residual profit is revenue less controllable costs and interest imputed on the divisional investment. This measure assumes that divisional investment is the responsibility of divisional management. This measure is a reasonable measure of managerial performance albeit with some limitations.

(k) In general, a before tax basis for profits is preferred because the general objective of performance appraisal is to assess managerial operating efficiency which may be masked by after-tax profit figures.

(l) Return on Capital Employed (ROCE) is a commonly used relative measure of performance appraisal but has numerous limitations which must be understood before its use is advocated.

(m) Any of the profit measures could be used as the numerator of the ROCE ratio with their previously stated meanings.

(n) The investment base may be based on historical asset values on a gross or net basis or may be based on replacement values.

(o) On balance residual profit is technically to be preferred but ROCE is widely used and can be a useful, practical tool provided there is an awareness of its inherent limitations.

(p) Whatever appraisal measure is used a target level of performance must be set. Factors to be considered include: cost of capital, risks, interfirm comparisons, economic conditions and so on.

(q) To control all the facets of divisional operations other appraisal measures should be set in such areas as: sales, growth, productivity, labour relations, quality.

POINTS TO NOTE

26. (a) To design effective performance appraisal systems the objectives and problems associated with decentralisation and divisionalisation should be thoroughly understood.

(b) Divisional performance appraisal can assess the performance of the division as an operating unit jointly with the performance of divisional management. However this need not be so and the performance of the division could be assessed using the measures outlined in this chapter, separately from the performance of the management who could be judged against agreed targets in all the areas for which they have responsibility.

(c) A problem which may occur in performance appraisal is the conflict between the (recommended) use of DCF for investment decision making and the use of conventional accrual accounting conventions for overall performance appraisal. In certain circumstances the choice of the correct project using DCF criteria can lead to a short run fall in profits and ROCE, as conventionally calculated. This may lead a manager into not making an investment which is in the overall group interest because it will have no apparently adverse effect on divisional performance. The potential for this problem always exists but can be mitigated to some extent by the use of residual profit as an appraisal measure and by head office management taking a long run view.

ADDITIONAL READING

Management Accounting : A conceptional approach	Amey and Egginton, LONGMAN
Cost Accounting : A managerial emphasis	Horngren, PRENTICE HALL
Financial Control of Divisional Capital Investment	Scapens, Sale and Tikkas, CIMA
Divisional Performance : Measurement and Control	Solomons, IRWIN
Financial Planning in Divisionalised Companies	Tomkins, ACCOUNTANCY AGE

SELF REVIEW QUESTIONS

1. *What is decentralisation? (3)*

2. *What type of decision making is usually retained by central management? (3)*

3. *What are the objectives of decentralisation? (4)*

4. *What are the possible problems which may arise with decentralisation? (5)*

5. *Where operating divisions exist what are the objectives of performance appraisal? (6)*

6. *Distinguish between profit and investment centres. (7)*

7. *What are the two major categories of financial performance appraisal measures? (8)*

8. *Define: controllable profit, divisional profit, net profit, controllable residual profit and net residual profit.*
   (9-14)

9. *What are the arguments as to\whether appraisal should be based on profits before or after tax? (16)*

10. *How can ROCE be defined? (18)*

11. *Why do conventionally calculated ROCE ratios overstate the return? (18)*

12. *What are the various investment bases which can be used in ROCE calculations and what are their characteristics?*
    (20)

13. *Contrast ROCE and residual profits as financial performance measures. (21)*

14. *What factors are involved in setting target performance levels? (22)*

15. *What non-financial appraisal measures could be used for divisional performance appraisal? (23)*

EXAMINATION QUESTIONS WITH ANSWERS COMMENCING PAGE 363

A1. *Divisionalisation is a common form of organisational arrangement but there is some diversity of opinion as to the best measure of divisional performance.*

Discuss this topic and describe and compare the main performance measures that have been suggested.
ACCA, Management Accounting.

A2. *Alton division (A) and Birmingham division (B) are two manufacturing divisions of Conglom plc. Both of these divisions make a single standardised product, A makes product I and B makes project J. Every unit of J requires one unit of I. The required input of I is normally purchased from division A but sometimes it is purchased from an outside source.*

The following table gives details of selling price and cost for each product:

	Product I	Product J
	£	£
Established selling price	30	50
Variable costs		
Direct material	8	5
Transfers from A	–	30
Direct labour	5	3
Variable overhead	2	2
	15	40
Divisional fixed cost (per annum)	£500,000	£225,000
Annual outside demand with current selling prices (units)	100,000	25,000
Capacity of plant (units)	130,000	30,000
Investment in division	£6,625,000	£1,250,000

Division B is currently achieving a rate of return well below the target set by the central office. Its manager blames this situation on the high transfer price of product I. Division A charges division B for the transfers of I at the outside supply price of £30. The manager of division A claims that this is appropriate since this is the price 'determined by market forces'. The manager of B has consistently argued that intra group transfers should be charged at a lower price based on the costs of the producing division plus a 'reasonable' mark-up.

The board of Conglom plc is concerned about B's low rate of return and the divisional manager has been asked to submit proposal for improving the situation. The board has now received a report from B's manager in which he asks the board to intervene to reduce the transfer price charged for product I. The manager of B also informs the board that he is considering the possibility of opening a branch office in rented premises in a nearby town, which should enlarge the market for product J by 5,000 units per year at the existing price. He estimates that the branch office establishment costs would be £50,000 per annum.

You have been asked to write a report advising the board on the response that it should make to the plans and proposals put forward by the manager of division B. Incorporate in your report a calculation of the rates of return currently being earned on the capital employed by each division and the changes to these that should follow from an implementation of any proposals that you would recommend.

ACCA, Management Accounting.

A3. *(a) The headquarters of the Antioch Group receives regular financial statements from each of its divisions. Since the divisions are regarded as investment centres, there is an emphasis on return on divisional investment.*

XY Division is a new division operating in a completely new plant. The planned investment in the division was £2,200,000 (£1,650,000 for plant and buildings and £550,000 for working capital). At the investment planning stage, Antioch's cost of capital rate was estimated at 10% and it was calculated that the new division would provide an accounting rate of return of 15% p.a. on the investment. A budget achieving this rate of return was prepared for the first year of operations (1985).

The budget for 1985 did not include provision for any intra group transfers but during 1985, although the budgeted level of sales was achieved, 25% of these sales was made to the other divisions in the group. The transfer price for these 'sales' is 85% of the outside price. The transferee divisions were able to resell these goods to outside customers at the full price.

For 1985 the summarised return of XY Division is as follows:

XY Division
Divisional Income Statement for 1985

	£	£
Sales		
- External		750,000
- Internal (to other divisions)		212,500
		962,500
Cost of goods manufactured		
- Direct Material	420,000	
- Direct labour	128,000	
- Overheads	177,000	
	725,000	
Less		
Finished goods stock	62,200	662,800
Selling and distribution expenses	22,500	
Central overhead as per budget	20,000	
		42,500
Divisional net profit		257,200

XY Division
Summarised Balance Sheet at 31 December 1985

	£	£
Fixed assets at written down value		1,600,000
Current assets (excluding current		
accounts with other divisions £212,500)	650,000	
Current liabilities	50,000	
		600,000
		2,200,000
Return on divisional capital		11.7%

The income statement is constructed from the actual income and expense except that the finished goods stock is valued at standard full cost. Selling and distribution expenses are variable costs, varying proportionately with the volume of external sales.

During 1985 the following variances were recorded in the division's costing system:

Variances		Favourable £	Unfavourable £
Direct material	- Price	10,000	
	- Efficiency		39,500
Direct labour	- Rate	2,500	
	- Efficiency		15,000
Overhead	- Spending	5,100	
	- Efficiency		12,000
	- Volume	8,100	
Selling and distribution			1,500
		25,700	68,000

It is considered that the unfavourable efficiency variances were largely attributable to the need for workstaff to familiarise themselves with the new equipment. The volume variance is attributable to the fact that the actual production level was 10% higher than the budgeted production level. The budget assumed a minimal holding of finished goods stock at the end of the year. The budgeted fixed manufacturing overhead is £81,000.

You are required to reconstruct the budgeted 1985 income statement from the foregoing details and to prepare a schedule that explains the difference between the budgeted and actual rate of return figures.

(b) Briefly discuss the relative merits of return on investment and residual income as measures of divisional performance.

ACCA, Management Accounting.

A4. *Discuss the proposition that interest (paid and/or imputed) should be regarded as a cost.*

    (a) in a conventional cost accounting system, and
    (b) in a divisional performance evaluation system.

                                            ACCA, Management Accounting.

A5. *(a) 'Because of the possibility of goal incongruence, an optimal plan can only be achieved if divisional budgets are constructed by a central planning department, but this means that divisional independence is a pseudo-independence.'*

    Discuss the problems of establishing divisional budgets in the light of this quotation.

    (b) 'Head Office' will require a division to submit regular reports of its performance.

    Describe, discuss and compare three measures of divisional operating performance that might feature in such reports.

                                            ACCA, Management Accounting.

19. Transfer Pricing

INTRODUCTION

1.   Transfer pricing becomes necessary when there are internal transfers of goods or services and it is required to appraise the separate performances of the divisions or departments involved. This chapter reviews the objectives which any system of transfer pricing should try to meet and analyses the theoretical background to transfer pricing using relevant aspects of economic theory. This includes the setting of optimum transfer prices, the determination of output levels and the apportionment of company profits between the supplying and buying divisions. The problems involved in setting transfer prices in practice are then discussed and market based, cost based and negotiated pricing are described.

WHY IS TRANSFER PRICING NECESSARY?

2.   Transfer pricing is the process of determining the price at which goods are transferred from one profit centre to another profit centre within the same company. Such internal trading is more prevalent within horizontally and vertically integrated companies than conglomerate operations with their heterogenous groupings.

   If profit centres are to be used, transfer prices become necessary in order to determine the separate performances of both the 'buying' and 'selling' profit centres. If transfer prices are set too high, the selling centre will be favoured whereas if set too low the buying centre will receive an unwarranted proportion of the profits.

   In general germs, transfer pricing is purely an internal, bookkeeping exercise which does not affect the overall profitability of the firm. However, in certain circumstances, transfer pricing may have an indirect effect on overall company profitability by influencing the decisions made at divisional level. For example, based on the proposed transfer price, a divisional manager may decide to purchase an item externally rather than accept the internal transfer even though such a decision may reduce overall company profitability.

OBJECTIVES WHICH TRANSFER PRICES SHOULD MEET

3.   Ideally, transfer prices should be set in a manner and at a level which fulfil three objectives:

   (a)   Goal congruence. The prices should be set so that the divisional management's desire to maximise divisional earnings is consistent with the objectives of the company as a whole. The transfer prices should not encourage sub-optimal decision making.

   (b)   Performance appraisal. The prices should enable reliable assessments to be made of divisional performance. The prices form part of information which should

   -   guide decision making
   -   appraise managerial performance
   -   evaluate the contribution made by the division to overall company profits
   -   assess the worth of the division as an economic unit.

   (c)   Divisional autonomy. The prices should seek to maintain the maximum divisional autonomy so that the benefits of dencentralisation (motivation, better decision making, initiative, etc) are maintained. The profits of one division should not be dependent on the actions of other divisions.

   In practice there are extreme difficulties in establishing prices which meet all these objectives. If prices are set centrally at levels where overall company objectives are met, then the autonomy of divisions is jeopardised, motivation may diminish and some of the benefits of decentralisation will be lost. Alternatively, where divisions act autonomously and freely set transfer prices, sub optimal decision making is hard to avoid. There is no completely satisfactory solution to this problem but research studies suggest that companies are prepared to accept a certain level of sub-optimal decision making on the part of divisions in order to gain the more than compensating advantages which they perceive arise from decentralisation.

THEORETICAL BACKGROUND TO TRANSFER PRICING

4.   Before considering the various methods used in practice for setting transfer prices it is useful to consider the relevant aspects of economic analysis which indicate the theoretically optimum price.

   Given a profit maximising objective, economic theory postulates that the marginal net revenue product of each resource throughout the company should be the same. This means that the equilibrium transfer price would be the marginal cost of the selling division for that output level at which this marginal cost equals the buying division's marginal revenue product from the use of the resource or item transferred.

   This can be shown graphically as follows.

Example 1

A company has two divisions, S and B. S makes an intermediate product which can be sold to division B or on the open market which is perfectly competitive. Division B has complete freedom to buy from S or on the open market. It can be assumed

(a) that there is perfect knowledge of all cost and revenue functions;
(b) that the buying and selling costs on the open market are the same as for internal buying and selling;
(c) that the firm has a profit maximising objective.

Let S   = supplying division
    B   = buying division
   p_i = open market price of intermediate product
 mc_S = marginal cost function of S
nmr_B = net marginal revenue function of B

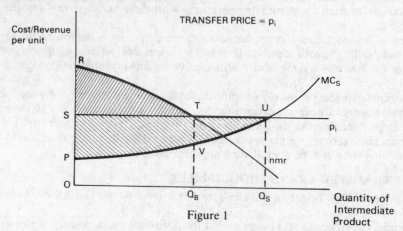

Figure 1

Notes on Figure 1

(a) The **net marginal revenue** function (nmr_B) is the difference between the selling price of the final product and division B's own marginal cost, ie excluding the cost of the intermediate product transferred from Division S.

(b) OQ_S represents the **total output** of intermediate products from Division S. OQ_B represents the amount of output **transferred** to Division B whilst the difference between Q_S and Q_B represents the **amount sold** on the open market.

(c) The shaded area, PSRTU, represents total profits for the company as a whole which could be distributed as follows:

Area RST to division B
Area SUP to division S

The reasoning for this is that RTU is the net marginal revenue function for the firm as a whole resulting from sales of the final product, so that the area above p_i (transfer price of intermediate product) represents the marginal revenue resulting from the inclusion of the intermediate product into the final product. The area SUP shows the difference between the marginal cost of the intermediate product and the price obtained for the intermediate product either as part of the final product (area STVP) or as direct sales of the intermediate product (area TUV).

(d) The optimal quantities, Q_B and Q_S, are found by the usual method of equating marginal revenue to marginal cost. Q_B corresponds to the intersection of the net marginal revenue division B with p_i. Q_S corresponds to the intersection of p_i and the marginal cost of division S.

It will be recalled that in conditions of perfect competition, as assumed in this case, the selling price per unit = average revenue = marginal revenue.

In this particular case, division S will be indifferent as to whether to transfer internally or sell on the open market. Similarly division B can buy internally or externally as desired and in each case the price would be p_i. It should be noted that in other circumstances it may be necessary for the firm to specify that internal transfers should take place up to certain levels in order to avoid sub-optimal decision making. This is dealt with in paras 5 to 8.

(e) Transfer pricing policies are based on the marginal costs of the supplying division plus any opportunity costs to the whole organisation. In this case no opportunity costs were identified so that the optimal transfer price is the stated intermediate product market price, p_i, which also enables the two quantities, Q_B and Q_S, to be determined.

UNEQUAL INTERMEDIATE PRODUCT BUYING AND SELLING PRICES

5.   The theoretical background to transfer pricing can be developed to deal with the problems which occur when there are transaction costs involved in the buying and/or selling of the intermediate product on the external market.

For example, whilst there may be, in all other respects, a perfect intermediate product market with a given selling price per unit, buyers may have to pay packing and delivery charges which effectively creates separate buying and selling prices as far as a firm such as described in Example 1 is concerned.

The analysis to deal with this situation follows the same broad principles covered in paragraph 4 and is shown in connection with Example 2.

Example 2

A company has two divisions, S and B. S makes an intermediate product which can be transferred to division B or sold on the open market. The open market for the intermediate product is perfectly competitive except that if division B buys on the open market it will have to pay packaging and delivery costs. The effect of this as far as the whole firm is concerned is that there are two prices for the intermediate product; P_{OS} which is the price for outside sales from division S and P_{OP} which is the price for outside purchases by division B. It follows that $P_{OP} > P_{OS}$. For each of the three cases specified below it is required to:

(a) derive the optimal transfer price;
(b) show the total profits accruing to each of the divisions and to the firm as a whole;
(c) show the optimum output level of the intermediate product;
(d) state any restrictions central management may place upon divisional management's autonomy in order to avoid sub-optimal decision making.

Case 1. Where the intersection of the marginal cost function of division S(mc_S) and the net marginal revenue function of division B (nmr_B) is below P_{OS}.

Case 2. Where the intersection of mc_S and nmr_B is between P_{OS} and P_{OP}.

Case 3. Where the intersection of mc_S and nmr_B is above P_{OP}.

In each case a diagram is used which follows the same pattern as Figure 1.

SOLUTION CASE 1

6.   Case 1.

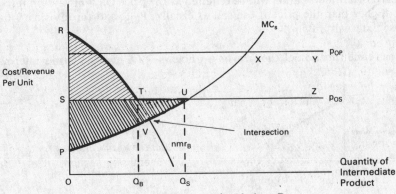

Figure 2 Intersection below P_{OS}

(a) Optimal transfer price is P_{OS}.

(b) The profits accruing to the firm as a whole and the distribution is identical to that shown in Figure 1, ie

area PSRTU	=	total profits
area RST	=	profit to division B
area SUP	=	profit to division S

(c) The total output of the intermediate product is Q_S and Q_B will be transferred to division B. The difference between Q_B and Q_S will be sold on the open market at price P_{OS}.

(d) Some central management intervention is required because although division B will always prefer to buy internally at price P_{OS} rather than buy on the open market at price P_{OP}, the intermediate products may not always be available. Accordingly, management must monitor the situation so that division S always has sufficient (quantity Q_B) to supply all division B's requirements. Division S will be indifferent between selling externally and internal transfers at price, P_{OS}, but to maximise overall company profits it is important that sufficient quantities of the intermediate product are available for internal transfer thus avoiding division B having to buy externally at price P_{OP}.

Note: The net marginal revenue function of the firm as a whole is RTUZ and the firm's intermediate marginal cost function is PXY.

SOLUTION CASE 2

7. Case 2

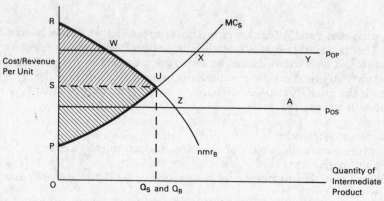

Figure 3 Intersection between P_{OS} and P_{OP}

(a) The transfer price will be set at OS, ie at the intersection of the marginal cost of the supplying division and the net marginal revenue of the buying division.

(b) The profits accruing to the company as a whole are represented by area PRU. The proportion accruing to division B is area RSU and the proportion to division S is area PSU.

(c) The optimum output level and the number to be transferred internally are the same, at point Q_S/Q_B. No intermediate product will be sold externally.

(d) No central management intervention will be required as the price OS is always preferred by both divisions. For division S it is higher than the price it can sell externally, P_{OS}, and for division B the price OS is lower than it can purchase externally, P_{OP}.

Note: The net marginal revenue function of the firm as a whole is RZA and the firm's intermediate marginal cost function is PXY.

SOLUTION CASE 3

8. Case 3

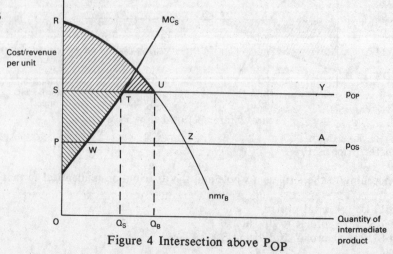

Figure 4 Intersection above P_{OP}

(a) As mc_S and nmr_B intersect **above** the buying in price, P_{OP}, the transfer price must set at P_{OP}.

(b) The profits are as follows:

$$
\begin{aligned}
\text{area PSRUT} &= \text{total company profits} \\
\text{area RUS} &= \text{profit to division B} \\
\text{area PST} &= \text{profit to division S.}
\end{aligned}
$$

(c) The total output of division S, quantity Q_S, must all be transferred to division B. Division B's total requirements is Q_B so the division will have to purchase the difference between Q_S and Q_B on the open market at price P_{OP}. This situation should be contrasted with Case 1, Figure 2, particularly in respect of the positions of Q_S and Q_B.

(d) Some central management intervention is required to ensure that quantity Q_S is made and transferred internally because the marginal cost of the intermediate product is below the buying in price up to point T. It will be apparent that division B will be indifferent between internal transfers and external purchases because these are at the same price, P_{OP}. Accordingly, some central management intervention will be required to avoid sub-optimal decision making. Division S would produce only up to Point W if selling on the open market at P_{OS}.

Note: The net marginal revenue function of the firm as a whole is RZA and firm's intermediate marginal cost function is PTY.

TRANSFER PRICING IN PRACTICE

9. Generally there is insufficient information to set prices using the economic analysis previously described. Firms need to use methods for setting transfer prices which are feasible, which use information that is available without undue costs, and which meet as many of the objectives described in para 3 as possible.

The methods utilised can be divided into three categories:

(a) market based pricing
(b) cost based pricing
(c) negotiated pricing.

MARKET BASED TRANSFER PRICING

10. Where a market exists outside the firm for the intermediate product and where the market is competitive (ie the firm is a price taker) then the use of market price as the transfer price between divisions would generally lead to optimal decision making. Such a price would meet all the objectives described in para 3, ie

- Goal congruence would be achieved as the divisions could act in their own best interest without reducing overall company profits.

- Performance evaluation would be possible in a realistic manner.

- The autonomy of the divisions would be maintained as the selling division could sell on the open market or internally and the buying division would have the option of purchasing in the market place or internally.

Where significant external buying and selling costs exist then a transfer price may be set somewhat lower than market price to reflect the cost savings from internal transfers. These circumstances may lead to negotiated market prices where the total cost savings are apportioned between the buying and selling divisions. In such circumstances an arbitration procedure may be required but too much central intervention of this nature could undermine the autonomy of divisions.

Where appropriate market prices exist then their use represents a feasible ideal. However there are difficulties in applying the concept universally. These include the following:

(a) Frequently there is no market for the intermediate product or service being considered. This is typically the case for specialised components, materials, parts or services.

(b) Even where some form of intermediate market does exist it may be difficult to obtain an appropriate price. A price is only strictly comparable when **all** features are identical - quality, delivery, finish, and so on.

(c)   Where a market does exist it may not be perfectly competitive, which means that the market is affected by the pricing decisions of divisional managers. Where there is an interdependence between output and pricing decisions there is no such thing as a single market price.

(d)   The market prices that are available may be considered unrepresentative. For example, there may be considerable excess capacity in the intermediate market so that current quotations ar well below long run average prices. In such circumstances the use of either the current, abnormally low, price or the long run 'normal' price may lead to sub-optimal decision making on the part of the supplying divisional management or to loss of motivation and autonomy of the purchasing division.

COST BASED PRICING

11.   Cost based transfer pricing systems are commonly used because the conditions for setting ideal market prices frequently do not exist; for example, there may be no intermediate market or the market which does exist may be imperfect.

Without the necessary conditions for establishing market prices there is no simple decision rule which leads to optimal decision making and which meets all the objectives for the ideal transfer price described in para 3. Providing that the required information is available, a rule which would lead to optimal decisions for the firm as a whole, would be to transfer at marginal cost up to the point of transfer, plus any opportunity cost to the firm as a whole. Even assuming that variable outlay costs as conventionally recorded in accounting systems, are a reasonable approximation of economic marginal costs the imposition of such a rule would undermine the concept of profit centres in that the profitability of divisions required to transfer at marginal cost could not be appraised, and the autonomy of divisions would be affected.

Given all the difficulties in establishing ideal prices, firms have to find some answer to the transfer pricing problem so that methods based on costs which are readily available from the normal accounting systems are frequently used. A general problem which arises in such circumstances is that the costs may include inefficiencies of the selling division which would thus be passed on to the buying division. Accordingly standard costs, rather than actual costs should be used as the basis of the transfer price in order not to burden the buying department with the inefficiencies of the supplying department.

The two main cost derived methods are those based on **full cost** and **variable cost**.

FULL COST TRANSFER PRICING

12.   This method, and the variant which is full costs plus a profit markup, has the disadvantage that sub-optimal decision making may occur particularly when these is idle capacity within the firm.

The full cost (or cost plus) is likely to be treated by the buying division as an input variable cost so that external selling price decisions, if based on costs, may not be set at levels which are optimal as far as the firm as a whole is concerned.

A simple example of this follows.

Division S sells to division B at full cost + 33⅓% and division B sells externally at a similar mark up. The following data are available.

Division S	£	Division B	£
Variable costs per unit	26	Transfer Price	48
Fixed costs per unit	10	Own variable costs per unit	15
Total Cost per unit	36	Fixed costs per unit	9
Mark up	12		72
		Mark up	24
Transfer Price	£48	Selling Price	£96

Thus, based on the stated pricing rules, division B would be attempting to sell at £96. If spare capacity exists then B may try to obtain any price above marginal cost but is likely to treat marginal cost as the variable costs of the division, ie £63 (£48 + 15). As far as the firm as a whole is concerned the marginal cost is the variable cost in each division, £41 (£26 + £15) so that the firm may lost a contribution margin if £63 is deemed to be the minimum acceptable figure for marginal pricing.

Full cost transfer pricing suffers from a number of other limitations.

(a) The calculated cost is only accurate at one level of output.

(b) The validity of any pricing decision based on past costs is questionable.

(c) When transfers are made at full cost plus a profit markup the selling division is automatically given a certain level of profit rendering genuine performance appraisal difficult.

(d) When the selling division is inefficient or working at low volume the costs may be unacceptably high as far as the buying division is concerned.

VARIABLE COST TRANSFER PRICING

13. Using this system transfers would be made at the (standard) variable costs up to the point of transfer. Assuming that the variable cost is a good approximation of economic marginal cost then this system would enable decisions to be made which would be in the interests of the firm as a whole as pointed out in para 4. However, variable cost based prices will result in a loss for the selling division so performance appraisal becomes meaningless and motivation will be reduced.

A possible way of resolving this dilemma is to use a variable cost based transfer price so that sub-optimal decision making is minimised and, as a separate exercise, credit the supplying division with a share of the overall profit which eventually results from the transferred item. This dual transfer price approach has an apparent fairness in that credit for profits earned are shared between divisions but performance appraisal based on arbitrarily apportioned profit shares has obvious shortcomings and administrative difficulties.

NEGOTIATED TRANSFER PRICING

14. As an alternative to setting prices based on rules or formulae, transfer prices could be set by negotiation between the buying and selling divisions. This would be appropriate if it could be assumed that such negotiations would result in decisions which were in the interests of the firm as a whole and which were acceptable to the parties concerned.

However, there are difficulties in this approach because it is unlikely that the parties concerned have equal bargaining power and protracted negotiations may be time consuming and divert management energies away from their primary tasks. Disagreements, which are all too likely, will require some form of arbitration by central management which itself undermines the autonomy of divisions and may cause resentment. It must be remembered that the objective of divisionalisation is to enhance the overall efficiency of the organisation so that care must be taken not to nullify any benefits through inter-divisional wrangling over transfer prices.

SUMMARY

15. (a) Transfer pricing is the pricing of internal transfers between profit centres.

(b) Ideally the transfer prices should: promote goal congruence, enable effective performance appraisal, and maintain divisional autonomy.

(c) Economic theory suggests that the optimum transfer price would be the marginal cost of the selling division for that output level at which the marginal cost equals the buying divisions marginal revenue product. Transfer prices should always be based on the marginal costs of the supplying division plus the opportunity costs to the organisation as a whole.

(d) Because of information deficiencies, transfer pricing in practice does not always follow theoretical guidelines. Typically prices are market based, cost based or negotiated.

(e) Where an appropriate market price exists then this is an ideal transfer price. However there may be no market for the intermediate product, the market may be imperfect, or the prices considered unrepresentative.

(f) Where cost based systems are used then it is preferable to use standard costs to avoid transferring inefficiencies.

(g) Full cost transfer pricing (or full cost plus a mark up) suffers from a number of limitations; it may cause sub-optimal decision making, the price is only valid at one output level, it makes genuine performance appraisal difficult.

(h) Providing that variable cost equates with economic marginal cost then transfers at variable cost will avoid gross sub-optimality but performance appraisal becomes meaningless.

(i)   Negotiated transfer prices will only be appropriate if there is equal bargaining power and if negotiations are not protracted.

POINTS TO NOTE

16. (a)   There is a tendency to think of transfer pricing solely in terms of goods or parts being transferred between manufacturing divisions. This is not so, because the principles apply equally to the transfer of services between divisions and to the provision of services from the centre to divisions. A particular example of the latter is the provision of computer services from headquarters to divisions and the problem that arises of determining the level of charges that should be made to the profit centres. This is a form of transfer pricing to which the general principles outlined in this chapter apply.

(b)   The use of transfer prices is fundamental to the profit centre concept where there is significant interdependence between divisions. The rationale for decentralisation and profit centres depends on the local management's freedom and interdependence. Imposed transfer prices and/or lack of buying and selling options severely limits the significance of any form of divisional performance appraisal.

ADDITIONAL READING

Management Control Systems	Anthony and Dearden, IRWIN
Cost Accounting : A Managerial Emphasis	Horngren, PRENTICE HALL
Management Accounting Guidelines No. 1 : Inter Unit Transfer Pricing	CIMA
Divisional Performance : Measurement and Control	Solomons, IRWIN
Financial Planning in Divisionalised Companies	Tomkins, HAYMARKET

SELF REVIEW QUESTIONS

1.   *Why do transfer prices become necessary? (2)*

2.   *What objectives should transfer prices attempt to meet? (3)*

3.   *What is the theoretically optimum transfer price? (4)*

4.   *In what circumstances should central management intervene in setting transfer prices or transfer quantities? (6–8)*

5.   *What is market based transfer pricing and why might there be difficulties in using this approach? (10)*

6.   *Describe full cost transfer pricing and its characteristics. (12)*

7.   *What is variable cost transfer pricing and how might any possible disadvantages be overcome? (13)*

8.   *What is negotiated transfer pricing? (14)*

EXAMINATION QUESTIONS WITH ANSWERS COMMENCING PAGE 365

A1. *Amalgamated Processors plc is a divisionalised organisation which operates a standard costing and budgetary planning and control system in which the preparation of detailed operating budgets is undertaken by the divisions themselves after centrally determined profit targets have been communicated to them.*

The Penbrock Division of the company produces and sells a standardised component which is sold externally at £10 per unit and internally, to other divisions, at a transfer price of £9 per unit. The standard specification for this product is as follows:

	£
Standard Specification	
2m² of material A at £0.20 per m²	0.40
5 units of component B at £0.37 per unit	1.85
15 minutes of labour at £2.00 per hour	0.50
Variable manufacturing overhead – 150% of direct labour cost	0.75
Fixed manufacturing overhead	1.50
Standard unit manufacturing cost	5.00
Central office charge	1.00
Selling and distributive overhead	1.00
Standard unit cost	£7.00

The fixed manufacturing overhead is absorbed on the basis of the 'normal monthly output of 15,000 units. The selling and distributive overhead relates solely to external sales and the monthly divisional budget for this comprises a fixed element of £9,600 and a variable element of £0.20 for each unit of budgeted external sales. The fixed selling and distributive overhead has been unitised assuming a 'normal' monthly external sales level of 12,000 units. The 'central office charge' element of the standard specification relates to a charge made by the 'head office' for central services provided – this has also been unitised assuming the normal monthly activity level of 15,000 units. Unsold stock is carried at standard manufacturing cost.

The following details apply to the Penbrock Division for April 1982:

Profit and Loss Account
April 1982

		Actual		Budget	
		Units	£	Units	£
Sales	- External	10,000	100,000	12,000	120,000
	- Internal	4,000	36,000	3,000	27,000
		14,000	£136,000	15,000	£147,000
Cost of Goods Manufactured		16,000	85,000	15,000	75,000
Less: Stock Adjustment		2,000	10,000	-	-
		14,000	75,000	15,000	75,000
Selling and Distributive Overhead			13,000		12,000
Central Office Charges			15,000		15,000
Profit			33,000		45,000
			£136,000		£147,000

The 'actual cost of goods manufactured can be analysed as follows:

	£
Material A	6,500
Component B	31,745
4,250 Labour hours at £2.10	8,925
Variable manufacturing overhead	12,325
Fixed manufacturing overhead	25,505
	£85,000

The stores records of the Penbrock Division are kept at standard cost so that the material cost figures include both the cost of the actual direct materials used (priced at their standard cost) and the price variance on materials purchased during April. The details of usage and purchases are as follows:

Material A:	Usage	34,000m²
	Purchases	30,000 m² at £0.19 per m²
Component B:	Usage	78,500 units
	Purchases	90,000 units at £0.40 per unit.

The workstaff have complained that the quality of the most recently purchased batch of Material A is inferior to the regular grade, that it gives rise to more waste and that it requires more time to process.

You are required:

(a) To prepare a statement, for the general manager of the Penbrock Division, analysing the reasons for the profit shortfall of £12,000 and to provide a commentary on this statement.

(b) To comment on the practice of isolating material price variances at the time of the material's purchase.

(c) To comment on the transfer pricing method used by the Penbrock Division.

ACCA, Management Accounting.

A2. *(a) Discuss the difficulties of determining (i) an appropriate cost unit and (ii) an appropriate performance indicator in organisational units which provide a free service to the consumer.*

(b) Contingency theory states that there are no universally valid rules of organisation and management but that both are dependent on circumstances. Discuss the implications of this theory for management accounting systems.

ACCA, Management Accounting.

A3. *Division A of a large divisionalised organisation manufactures a single standardised product. Some of the output is sold externally whilst the remainder is transferred to division B where it is a subassembly in the manufacture of that division's product. The unit costs of Division A's product are as follows:*

	£
Direct material	4
Direct labour	2
Direct expense	2
Variable manufacturing overheads	2
Fixed manufacturing overheads	4
Selling and packing expense – variable	1
	15

Annually 10,000 units of the product are sold externally at the standard price of £30.

In addition to the external sales, 5,000 units are transferred annually to Division B at an internal transfer charge of £29 per unit. This transfer price is obtained by deducting variable selling and packing expense from the external price since this expense is not incurred for internal transfers.

Division B incorporates the transferred-in goods into a more advanced product. The unit costs of this product are as follows:

	£
Transferred-in item (from Division A)	29
Direct material and components	23
Direct labour	3
Variable overheads	12
Fixed overheads	12
Selling and packing expense – variable	1
	80

Division B's manager disagrees with the basis used to set the transfer price. He argues that the transfers should be made at variable cost plus an agreed (minimal) mark-up since he claims that his division is taking output that Division A would be unable to sell at the price of £30.

Partly because of this disagreement, a study of the relationship between selling price and demand has recently been made for each division by the company's sales director. The resulting report contains the following table:

Customer demand at various selling prices

Division A			
Selling price	£20	£30	£40
Demand	15,000	10,000	5,000

Division B			
Selling price	£80	£90	£100
Demand	7,200	5,000	2,800

The manager of Division B claims that this study supports his case. He suggests that a transfer price of £12 would give Division A a reasonable contribution to its fixed overheads while allowing Division B to earn a reasonable profit. He also believes that it would lead to an increase of output and an improvement in the overall level of company profits.

You are required:

(a) to calculate the effect that the transfer pricing system has had on the company's profits, and

(b) to establish the likely effect on profits of adopting the suggestion by the manager of Division B of a transfer price of £12.

ACCA, Management Accounting.

20. Ratio Analysis

INTRODUCTION

1.   This chapter describes the objectives of ratio analysis and how to use the technique most effectively. Three major groups of ratios are described and exemplified - those relating to profitability, solvency and investment potential. Return on capital employed and the supporting 'pyramid' of ratios is described in detail together with a fully worked example. The need to make comparisons and identify trends is emphasised and the limitations of ad-hoc ratio analysis are described. The Z score approach to ratio analysis, developed by Professor Altman, is described and the chapter concludes with a summary of value added statements and ratios.

WHAT IS RATIO ANALYSIS AND WHY IS IT USED?

2.   Ratio analysis is the systematic production of ratios from both internal and external financial reports so as to summarise key relationships and results in order to appraise financial performance. Ratio analysis as a practical means of monitoring and improving performance is greatly enhanced when

(a)   Ratios are prepared regularly and on a consistent basis so that trends can be highlighted and the changes investigated.

(b)   Ratios prepared for an individual firm can be compared with other firms in the same industry. This process is greatly facilitated when the firm has ready access to comparative ratios prepared in a standardised manner. Some Trade Associations prepare ratios for their member companies and the Centre for Inter firm Comparison, established by the British Institute of Management and the British Productivity Council, provides such a service on a national basis.

(c)   Ratios are prepared showing the inter-locking and inter-dependent nature of the factors which contribute to financial success. Typically this is done using the so-called 'pyramid of ratios' which is described in detail in para 4.

The information value of any given ratio, considered in isolation, is small. For example, if it is known that the return on capital employed for a company is 12% in a given year, this is not very informative. However if we find that the figure was 18% five years ago and has been declining, or that the average percentage for similar firms in the same industry is 15% then this information becomes of much greater significance and further analysis would be urgently required.

Ratio analysis may direct attention to areas where there are inefficiencies and this it provides a valuable service but it cannot say how the deficiencies will be made good. That can only be done by managerial action.

WHAT RATIOS SHOULD BE PREPARED?

3.   The simple answer to this question is, any ratio which will assist management to plan, control or make decisions. This means that some ratios will be prepared that are unique to the individual firm whilst others will have universal applicability. It will be recalled that this is a similar position to that discussed in the chapters on standard costing variances.

Ratio analysis can be directed towards various aspects of company performance including:

- the financial performance of the company in terms of income generation, ie profitability. Ratios in this area include return on capital employed and the analysis of this ratio into component ratios relating to sales and assets (covered in para 4 to 10).

- the analysis of company solvency. Ratios in this area include those relating to current assets and current liabilities and the breakdown of these measures to show the effects of cash flows, inventory changes and movements in debtors and creditors (covered in paras 11 to 14).

- the assessment of the company's performance in terms of its value to investors. Ratios dealing with this area include PE (price/earnings) ratio, dividend yields and other such investment criteria (covered in paras. 15 and 16).

THE PROFITABILITY RATIOS

4.   For comparative purposes the key ratio in this area is the return on capital employed (ROCE) already discussed. The ROCE is the primary ratio and the factors involved (Profit and Capital Employed or Total Assets) can be progressively subdivided into more and more detailed ratios which highlight the influence of sales, the types of assets, and the various types to costs, on overall company performance as expressed by the ROCE.

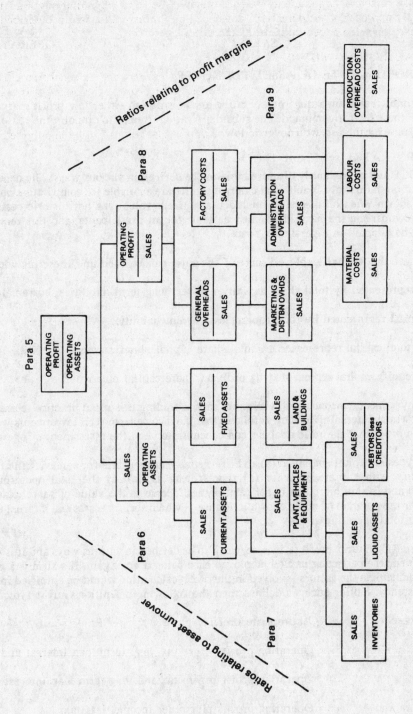

Figure 1 Ratio Pyramid

Typically the ROCE and supporting ratios ar shown as a pyramid of ratios as depicted in Figure 1 which should be studied in conjunction with the paragraphs indicated on the diagram.

Note on Figure 1: The chart shows some typical ratios which can be calculated to show the relationships which exist between the factors which affect the overall return the company obtains on operating assets, ie the operating capital employed. The major division of the ROCE is into the rate of asset turnover and the percentage operating profit on sales, ie

$$\frac{\text{OPERATING PROFIT}}{\text{OPERATING ASSETS}} \quad = \quad \frac{\text{OPERATING PROFIT}}{\text{SALES}} \quad \text{x} \quad \frac{\text{SALES}}{\text{OPERATING ASSETS}}$$

=   PERCENTAGE PROFIT x RATE OF ASSET TURNOVER

This division illustrates that a low return on operating assets is due to either low profit margins or a low rate of asset turnover or both these factors combined. The subsidiary ratios attempt to pinpoint the reasons why there are low profit margins and/or why the asset turnover is low.

ROCE – THE PRIMARY RATIO (see Figure 1)

5.   This ratio is the ROCE and as previously discussed this can be defined in various ways. The definition to be used depends on the purpose of the ratio analysis and what external figures are available for comparative purposes. The most realistic return will be shown when all assets are included at current valuations not historic costs. Naturally, for any form of inter-firm comparison the bases used must be same for all participants, and this requirement usually determines the basis to be adopted in a particular firm.

Various definitions of the 'capital employed' part of the ratio can be used and these include:

(a)   **Total capital** represented by total share capital, reserves, long term liabilities, current liabilities.

(b)   **Long term capital** represented by total capital **less** current liabilities.

(c)   **Shareholders' total capital** represented by total share capital plus reserves.

(d)   **Shareholders' equity capital** represented by ordinary share capital plus reserves.

Where a firm has investments unconnected with their normal trading it is usual practice to exclude these from capital employed when assessing internal efficiency. It follows that the income from such investments would be excluded from operating profits in order that the ratio analysis can concentrate upon the assessment of operating efficiency.

Of the above four types of capital employed (a) and (b) are more appropriate for assessing the firm's efficiency in generating profitability with a preference for (a) representing as it does the total operating assets of the company. Definitions (c) and (d) are more useful for relating net income to the value of shareholder's capital. The basis most appropriate for the pyramid of ratios shown in Figure 1, which seek to assess the internal efficiency of the company, is basis (a), ie total operating assets.

The numerator of the ROCE ratio, profit or income, can also be defined in various ways and it is vital to have the correctly specified profit for the particular capital employed base being used. Again, if a firm is a participant in an interfirm comparison scheme then the factors involved in the profit calculation would be specified in detail to ensure comparability and consistency. Failing such guidelines then the following definitions might typically be used.

Capital Employed base	Appropriate profit
(a) Total capital	Operating profit before tax, long term loan interest and bank interest.
(b) Long term capital	Operating profit before tax and long term loan interest.
(c) Shareholders' total capital	Operating profits plus other income, less tax.
(d) Shareholders' equity capital	Operating profits plus other income less tax and preference dividends.

The factors governing the choice of before or after tax profits have already been discussed previously.

RATE OF ASSET TURNOVER (see Figure 1)

6. This ratio measures the use being made of assets and draws attention to the intensity with which assets are employed. The ratio gives an assessment of past managerial efficiency in the deployment of company assets and is considered to be a good guide to the likely level of future profits.

SUBSIDIARY ASSET RATIOS (see Figure 1)

7. The various subsidiary ratios shown (and other which could be calculated) attempt to answer the question, 'What are the detailed reasons why the rate of asset turnover has declined/increased?' For example, a firm may have too much working capital in relation to sales or it may not have made effective use of the various types of fixed assets. As with all ratios, trends in this area are of great importance and adverse movements should receive close attention so that remedial action can be taken.

PROFITABILITY MARGIN (see Figure 1)

8. This ratio assesses the overall margin on sales which, together with the rate of asset turnover, is a major factor in the return that the company receives on capital employed. Because the margin on sales varies greatly from industry to industry (compare, for example, a clothing manufacturer and a heavy machine tool manufacturer) it is important that comparisons are made only with firms within the same industry or with the previous performance of the same firm.

SUBSIDIARY MARGIN RATIOS (see Figure 1)

9. These ratios relate the various costs, which determine the overall margin, to sales. The ratios are useful measures of internal operating efficiency and may provide guidance as to where further analysis would be worthwhile. The ratios shown are but typical examples and many other more specialised ratios might be calculated to suit particular firms or industries. For example, in a particular industry one raw material may be considered to be of great importance so that a special ratio may be calculated relating that material to the sales value of production.

PROFITABILITY RATIOS – EXAMPLE

10. **Example 1.** Using the Final Accounts given below calculate the profitability ratios shown in Figure 1 for Relationships plc.

Relationships plc
Profit and loss account for year ended 31st December 19..

			£('000s)
	Sales		6,500
less	Factory Cost of Sales		
	Materials	2,610	
	Labour	1,140	
	Production Overheads	725	4,475
=	GROSS PROFIT		2,025
less	Administration Overheads	666	
	Marketing & Distribution Overheads	426	
	Bank Interest	65	
	Loan Interest	240	1,397
=	NET PROFIT BEFORE TAX		628
less	Tax		116
	PROFIT AFTER TAX		512
less	Dividends		
	10% Preference	50	
	Ordinary – Interim (paid)	180	
	Ordinary – Final (proposed)	180	410
	TRANSFERRED TO RESERVES		102

Relationships plc
Balance Sheet as at 31st December 19..

		£	£('000s)
FIXED ASSETS			
Goodwill		50	
Patents		175	
Land and Buildings		2,500	
Machinery and Equipment		3,750	
Vehicles		595	7,070
CURRENT ASSETS			
Stocks – Finished Goods		265	
– W–I–P		195	
– Raw Materials		320	
Debtors		1,025	
Cash and Bank		95	1,900
less **CURRENT LIABILITIES**			
Bank overdraft		850	
Creditors		824	
Taxation payable		116	
Proposed dividend		180	1,970	(70)
			£7,000

Represented by	£
SHARE CAPITAL	
Ordinary Shares £1 each	2,750
10% Preference Shares £1 each	500
RETAINED PROFIT	1,750
DEBENTURES	
12% loan stock	2,000
	£7,000

Solution

As explained in para 5 various definitions of 'Capital Employed' are possible with **Total Capital** being the most appropriate for the calculation of the efficiency ratios as depicted in Figure 1.

$$\therefore \text{ Relationships plc:- total capital}$$
$$= £7,070,000 + 1,900,000 = £8,970,000$$

The appropriate profit to use is also given in para 5 and is operating profit before tax, long term loan interest and bank interest, ie

$$£628,000 + 305,000 = \underline{£933,000}$$

$$\therefore \text{ROCE} = \frac{933,000}{8,970,000} = \underline{10.4\%}$$

The various supporting ratios can now be calculated.

Asset turnover ratios

$$\frac{\text{Sales}}{\text{Operating Assets}} = \frac{6,500,000}{8,970,000} = 0.72:1$$

$$\frac{\text{Sales}}{\text{Current Assets}} = \frac{6,500,000}{1,900,000} = 3.42:1$$

$$\frac{\text{Sales}}{\text{Fixed Assets}} = \frac{6,500,000}{7,070,000} = 0.92:1$$

$$\frac{\text{Sales}}{\text{Inventories}} = \frac{6,500,000}{780,000} = 8.33{:}1$$

$$\frac{\text{Sales}}{\text{Liquid Assets}} = \frac{6,500,000}{1,120,000} = 5.80{:}1$$

$$\frac{\text{Sales}}{\text{Debtors less Creditors}} = \frac{6,500,000}{201,000} = 32.34{:}1$$

Profit Margin Ratios

$$\frac{\text{Operating Profit}}{\text{Sales}} = \frac{933,000}{6,500,000} = 14.35\%$$

$$\frac{\text{General overheads}}{\text{Sales}} = \frac{1,092,000}{6,500,000} = 16.8\%$$

$$\frac{\text{Factory Costs}}{\text{Sales}} = \frac{4,475,000}{6,500,000} = 68.8\%$$

$$\frac{\text{Marketing overheads}}{\text{Sales}} = \frac{426,000}{6,500,000} = 6.5\%$$

$$\frac{\text{Administration Overheads}}{\text{Sales}} = \frac{666,000}{6,500,000} = 10.25\%$$

$$\frac{\text{Material Cost}}{\text{Sales}} = \frac{2,610,000}{6,500,000} = 40.15\%$$

$$\frac{\text{Labour cost}}{\text{Sales}} = \frac{1,140,000}{6,500,000} = 17.54\%$$

$$\frac{\text{Production Overheads}}{\text{Sales}} = \frac{725,000}{6,500,000} = 11.15\%$$

Note: The calculation of the above ratios is only the first step in the full process of Ratio Analysis. Comparisons would be made with the ratios of previous years of Relationships plc, trends would be identified, reasons established for adverse movements and so on. In addition, comparisons would be made with ratios from other similar companies with the overall objective of identifying and rectifying weaknesses.

SOLVENCY RATIOS

11. The analysis of solvency (or potential insolvency) can be assisted by the judicious use of ratio analysis but such analysis has certain limitations. Ratio analysis is of necessity based on normal financial reports (balance sheets, operating statements, profit and loss accounts) so that any ratios prepared relate to **past conditions** whereas solvency relates to the **present**. Conditions may have changed dramatically since the last balance sheet date and a firm which was solvent then may be currently having difficulties, perhaps because of credit facilities being withdrawn. Accordingly, any solvency ratios need to be interpreted with care and adjustments made in the light of more up-to-date information.

Solvency ratios can be grouped into two categories, those relating to short term factors and those concerned with the long term ability of the firm to meet all financial liabilities including those not currently payable.

SHORT TERM SOLVENCY RATIOS

12. Certain of the short-term solvency ratios, particularly the 'current' and 'quick' ratios, are considered to be of great importance in judging the financial stability of companies particularly by financial analysts, investors, bankers and creditors.

Two groups of ratios have been found to be of value: those which relate current assets to current liabilities and those which indicate the rate at which short term assets such as stock and debtors are turned into cash.

Group 1 . Ratios concerned with current assets and liabilities.

$$\text{The current ratio} = \frac{\text{Current Assets}}{\text{Current Liabilities}}$$

$$\text{The quick ratio or acid test} \quad = \quad \frac{\text{Current Assets - Stocks}}{\text{Current liabilities}} \text{(sometimes known as quick assets)}$$

The current ratio effectively assesses the working capital of the firm and is generally expected to be within a band of values appropriate for a given industry. It is wrong to be dogmatic about the 'ideal' value for the current ratio but it appears that analysts consider values in the range of 1.8:1 to 2:1 to be acceptable.

The current ratio considers those assets and liabilities which have life cycles measured in months rather than weeks and whilst this aspect of solvency is of great importance the immediate liquidity position, say the next 6/10 weeks, also needs to be considered. This is assessed by the quick ratio which excludes stocks and thus concentrates attention on more liquid assets such as cash and debtors. Again, whilst there can be no precise norm, it appears that an acceptable range of values for the acid test ratio is between 1:1 and say 0.8:1 (Quick assets: Current liabilities).

If the current liabilities include a bank overdraft which it is known will not be recalled within the short time scale being considered then a more meaningful ratio would be to calculate the following adjusted acid test ratio.

$$\frac{\text{Quick assets}}{\text{Current liabilities - bank overdraft}}$$

This would compare assets and liabilities with approximately the same life cycles.

Note: This principle could also apply to a tax liability with a known payment date.

Group 2. Cash conversion ratios

The firm's day to day liquidity position is largely dependent upon the rate at which cash flows into the business from normal operations. These operations include the conversion of stocks into sales and therefore debtors and the subsequent rate of conversion of debtors into cash.

The two following ratios provide some guidance to the firm's ability to generate cash from normal trading.

$$\text{Average stock turnover ratio} \quad = \quad \frac{\text{Cost of goods sold in period}}{\text{Average stock held during the period}}$$

$$\text{Average collection period} \quad = \quad \frac{\text{Debtors as at balance sheet date}}{\text{Average daily credit sales during period}}$$

Whilst the average stock turnover ratio varies greatly between different industries, comparison with broadly similar companies and with previous periods of the same firm can provide useful guidance. Increasing competition, dated marketing policies and products, unnecessarily high prices and other such factors are likely to be reflected in a deterioration in the average stock turnover ratio.

An important element in cash flow management is to monitor continually the average time that debtors take to settle. The calculation of the average collection period should be only part of a firm's total credit and cash management system. The system would normally include such matters as: regular reminder letters, use of debt collection agencies if necessary, cash discounts, trade discounts related to creditworthiness, prompt invoicing and banking procedures, age analysis of debtors and the application of Pareto analysis (ie the 80:20 rule) to the individual debtors so that the important items can be monitored closely.

LONG TERM SOLVENCY RATIOS

13. These ratios concentrate on the longer term financial stability and structure of the firm and are generally of most interest to financial analysts and investors.

A number of ratios can be calculated in this area and these include:

(a) Gearing ratio $\quad = \quad \dfrac{\text{Fixed Interest Capital}}{\text{Fixed interest capital + Equity Capital}}$

(b) Shareholders equity to assets ratio $\quad = \quad \dfrac{\text{Shareholders equity (capital plus reserves)}}{\text{Total assets}}$

(c) Non-equity claims to assets ratio $\quad = \quad \dfrac{\text{Long term debt plus current liabilities}}{\text{Total assets}}$

(d)   Interest coverage ratio $\qquad$ = $\qquad$ $\dfrac{\text{Profit before tax and interest}}{\text{Interest charges for period}}$

Ratios (a), (b) and (c) are closely related and are merely facets of the same relationship. Analysts consider that too high a gearing ratio is potentially unstable indicating as it does undue dependence on external sources for long term financing. It is important to calculate these longer term solvency factors because favourable short term ratios may disguise a worsening financial position. For example, if a firm incurs a long term liability in the form of debentures this has the effect of improving the current ratio (current assets : current liabilities) but it worsens the firm's gearing and interest coverage ratios. With fluctuating profits this could cause substantial variations in the dividends paid to shareholders which is considered by the market to be one of the signs of financial instability.

The interest coverage ratio assesses the ability of the company to meet the recurring interest charges which arise when long term and short term loans are contracted.

SOLVENCY RATIOS – EXAMPLE
14. Example 2.

Using the data from Example 1 calculate the short term and long term solvency ratios for Relationships plc. It can be assumed that the stock values given in the balance sheet approximate to average stocks held during the year.

Solution

Current ratio $\qquad$ = $\qquad$ $\dfrac{\text{Current assets}}{\text{Current liabilities}}$ $\qquad$ = $\qquad$ $\dfrac{1,900,000}{1,970,000}$ = 0.96:1

Note: With a 'normal' range of 1.8:1 to 2:1 this would be considered an alarming value.

Acid test $\qquad$ = $\qquad$ $\dfrac{\text{Quick assets}}{\text{Current liabilities}}$ $\qquad$ = $\qquad$ $\dfrac{1,120,000}{1,970,000}$ = 0.57:1

If it could be assumed (or ascertained by enquiry) that the bank overdraft will not be recalled then the adjusted acid test ratio could be calculated.

Adjusted acid test ratio $\qquad$ = $\qquad$ $\dfrac{\text{Quick assets}}{\text{Current liabilities - overdraft}}$ $\qquad$ = $\qquad$ $\dfrac{1,120,000}{1,120,000}$ = 1:1

Cash conversion ratios

Average stock turnover $\qquad$ = $\qquad$ $\dfrac{\text{Cost of goods sold}}{\text{Average stock}}$ $\qquad$ = $\qquad$ $\dfrac{4,475,000}{780,000}$ = 5.74 times

Average collection period $\qquad$ = $\qquad$ $\dfrac{\text{Debtors}}{\text{Average daily sales}}$ $\qquad$ = $\qquad$ $\dfrac{1,025,000}{17,808}$ = 57.56 days

Note: In the stock turnover ratio **average stock** is invariably used. Where beginning and end stock values are unrepresentative it may be necessary to calculate an average based on monthly stock values.

Long term solvency ratios

Gearing ratio $\qquad$ = $\qquad$ $\dfrac{\text{Fixed interest capital}}{\text{Fixed interest + Equity Capital}}$ $\qquad$ = $\qquad$ $\dfrac{2,000,000}{7,000,000}$ = 28.6%

Note: The above ratio is based on book values. Alternatively the ratio could be based on market values as shown in para 16.

Equity to assets ratio $\qquad$ = $\qquad$ $\dfrac{\text{Shareholders' equity}}{\text{Total assets}}$ $\qquad$ = $\qquad$ $\dfrac{5,000,000}{8,970,000}$ = 55.74%

Non-equity claims to assets ratio $\qquad$ = $\qquad$ $\dfrac{\text{Long term debt + current liabilities}}{\text{Total assets}}$ = $\dfrac{3,970,000}{8,970,000}$ = 44.26%

Interest coverage ratio $\qquad$ = $\qquad$ $\dfrac{\text{Profit before tax and interest}}{\text{Interest charges}}$ $\qquad$ = $\qquad$ $\dfrac{933,000}{305,000}$ = 3.06 times

Note: Once again trends and comparisons are all important. Based on the conventionally accepted norms Relationships plc would appear to be having severe solvency problems, particularly in the short term.

INVESTMENT RATIOS

15. The overall objective of calculating the various investment ratios is to assess the company in terms of its potential and stability as an equity investment.

The ratios typically calculated cover earnings, dividends and share prices as follows:

$$\text{(a)} \quad \text{Earnings per share} \quad = \quad \frac{\text{Profits after tax less Preference Dividend (Gross)}}{\text{Number of ordinary shares issued}}$$

SSAP 3 recommends that this ratio should be shown in the accounts of all listed companies and students are advised to refer to the Standard for guidance on how to deal with the complications which occur in practice.

$$\text{(b)} \quad \text{Dividend yield} \quad = \quad \frac{\text{Nominal share value x Dividend \%}}{\text{Market price per share}}$$

This ratio measures the rate of return on the amount invested.

$$\text{(c)} \quad \text{Dividend cover} \atop \text{(or Payout ratio)} \quad = \quad \frac{\text{Profit after tax - Preference dividend (gross)}}{\text{Gross equity dividend}}$$

This ratio gives a measure of the margin of available earnings that is available to meet the current dividend declared on ordinary shares. The higher the dividend cover the more certain it is that the dividends on ordinary shares will be maintained.

$$\text{(d)} \quad \text{Price earnings (PE) ratio} \quad = \quad \frac{\text{Market price per share}}{\text{Earnings per share}}$$

The PE ratio relates earnings to market price and is generally taken as measure of the growth potential of an investment. Company earnings after tax and preference dividends, are available to pay ordinary dividends and to plough back into the company. The PE ratio is equivalent to the number of years' purchase of latest earnings, represented by the share price at any given time. The reciprocal of the PE ratio shows the earnings yield, ie

$$\text{(e)} \quad \text{Earnings yield} \quad = \quad \frac{\text{Earnings per share}}{\text{Market price per share}} \quad \text{x } 100\%$$

which can alternatively be expressed as
Dividend cover x Dividend

In addition to the above ratios an investor or analyst will also be interested in the **gearing** of the company (already mentioned in connection with the long term solvency para 13) and to the investor, gearing ratios based on market values are likely to be the most relevant, ie

$$\text{(f)} \quad \text{Capital gearing ratio} \atop \text{(market values)} \quad = \quad \frac{\text{Total market value preference shares + Market value of debentures}}{\text{Total equity market value}}$$

Unduly low gearing ratios indicate that the company is failing to take full advantage of the tax relief available on debenture interest whilst excessively high gearing will force up the cost of debentures (the market will require higher interest rates to compensate for the extra risk) and cause equity earnings to become volatile.

INVESTMENT RATIOS - EXAMPLE

16. Example 3.

Using the data from Example 1 calculate the investment ratios for Relationships plc. The market price for Ordinary Shares is £1.80; for Preference Shares 80p; and debentures are quoted at 92.

Solution

$$\text{Earnings per share} \quad = \quad \frac{\text{Profit after tax less Preference Dividend}}{\text{No. of Ordinary Shares}} \quad = \quad \frac{£462,000}{2,750,000} \quad = \underline{16.8\text{p}}$$

$$\text{Dividend Yield} \quad = \quad \frac{\text{Nominal value x Dividend \%}}{\text{Market price}} = \quad \frac{\text{£1 x 13.5\%}}{\text{£1.80}} \quad = \underline{7.28\%}$$

$$\text{Payout ratio} \quad = \quad \frac{\begin{array}{c}\text{Profit after tax less}\\\text{Preference Dividend}\end{array}}{\text{Equity dividend}} = \quad \frac{\text{£462,000}}{360,000} \quad = 1.28 \text{ times}$$

$$\text{Price earnings ratio} \quad = \quad \frac{\text{Market Price per share}}{\text{Earnings per share}} = \quad \frac{\text{£1.80}}{16.8\text{p}} \quad = 10.7$$

$$\text{Earnings yield} = \quad \frac{1}{\text{P/E ratio}} \% \quad = \quad \frac{1}{10.7} \% \quad = \underline{9.3\%}$$

(alternatively Payout ratio x Dividend yield % = 1.28 x 7.28% = 9.3%)

$$\text{Capital gearing} \quad = \quad \frac{\text{Market value preference + debentures}}{\text{Market value equity}}$$

$$= \quad \frac{\text{£400,000 + £1,840,000}}{\text{£4,950,000}}$$

$$= \quad \underline{45.25\%}$$

Note: Comparisons with alternative yields, cover, earnings and gearing are available from financial analysts, journals and stockbrokers.

DEVELOPMENTS IN RATIO ANALYSIS

17. Historical ratio analysis as described so far in this chapter appears to be a useful management technique, particularly when used on a comparative, interfirm basis but it is not without limitations. Consequently a number of attempts have been made to refine ratio analysis in order to make it more effective and forward looking. A particular example of this is the work of Professor Altman.

Altman and other workers have developed a technique based on identifying a small, selected group of 5 ratios which are combined using calculated weightings to produce a single value, known as Z or Zeta score. The procedure, which is a form of multiple discriminant analysis, is designed to replace the conventional norms which are used in traditional ratio analysis, by empirically tested weights and groups that provide a clear datum level above which the firm is likely to be healthy and profitable and below which there are likely to be financial crises.

The original equation developed by Altman was,

$$Z = 0.012X_1 + 0.014X_2 + 0.033X_3 + 0.006X_4 + 0.010X_5$$

where X_1 to X_5 are the particular ratios chosen by Altman as the most significant predictors of performance and financial health and the coefficients (0.012 et al) are the constant weightings derived from empirical studies.

THE FIVE KEY RATIO

18. The ratios selected by Altman were those which his researches indicated as the best collective predictor of financial stability and hence survival. The detailed make up of each ratio and the definitions used are based on American practice but require little or no adjustment for UK conventions. The selected ratios are as follows:

$$X_1 \quad : \quad \frac{\text{GROSS CURRENT ASSETS}}{\text{GROSS TOTAL ASSETS}}$$

This means that current liabilities are **not** deducted to establish the working capital which is a normal UK convention.

$$X_2 \quad : \quad \frac{\text{RETAINED EARNINGS}}{\text{GROSS TOTAL ASSETS}}$$

$$X_3 \quad : \quad \frac{\text{PROFITS (before interest and tax)}}{\text{GROSS TOTAL ASSETS}}$$

This is the ROCE ratio which, as is to be expected, has the highest weighting (0.033) in arriving at the Z score.

$$X_4 \quad : \quad \frac{\text{MARKET VALUE OF EQUITY}}{\text{BOOK VALUE OF TOTAL DEBT}}$$

$$X_5 \quad : \quad \frac{\text{SALES}}{\text{GROSS TOTAL ASSETS}}$$

Using the above ratios and weights Altman established two indicator values for the X score; above 3% (0.03) there is a high probability that the company would not fail, below 1.8% (0.018) failure was very likely and would probably happen within two years. Obviously there is a grey area between these two values but any value below 3% should be cause for serious concern for the firm in question.

Developments in the procedure have enabled claims to be made that it is possible to make successful predictions as much as five years ahead and the process has been further refined by calculating differing values for the Z score indicators for different industries.

Whilst the calculation of Z scores cannot of itself be a substitute for managerial and financial judgement and expertise there seems little doubt that such a process replaces a particular area of subjectivity by a more objective, quantitative assessment. The procedure is being used for this purpose by some firms of auditors in their assessment of the 'going concern' status necessary to comply with SSAP 2.

VALUE ADDED (or ADDED VALUE)

19. Value added is the difference between sales income and bought in goods and services. Value added statements can help to assess the relative efficiency of the firm without the analysis being obscured by external input costs which may be largely uncontrollable. Value added is the wealth that a firm creates by its own efforts. The value added performance of a company is a good measure of the overall productivity of the firm and it is out of the total amount of the value added that the firm rewards all interested parties, including shareholders, staff, Inland Revenue and others.

The Corporate Report advocated that a statement of Added Value should be prepared as this was considered to be the simplest and most effective way of putting profit into proper perspective in relation to the amount of value added paid out to employees, shareholders, the Government, and suppliers of loan capital.

A typical format of a Value Added Statement is shown in Figure 2.

Statement of Added Value
for year to . . . . .

			£
	SALES		6,500,000
less	Bought in goods and services		4,250,000
=	ADDED VALUE		2,250,000
	APPLIED AS FOLLOWS		£
	To employees		1,750,000
	(Wages, pensions, and other benefits)		
	To suppliers of capital	£	
	Dividends to shareholders	140,000	
	Interest on loans	75,000	215,000
	To pay Government Taxation		50,000
	To provide for maintenance and expansion of assets		
	Depreciation		100,000
	Retained profits		135,000
=	ADDED VALUE		£2,250,000

Figure 2

VALUE ADDED RATIOS

20. In addition to the production of a summary value added statement such as that shown in Figure 2 the concept of value added can be included in ratio analysis.

Value added is a prime measure of productivity and ratios using value added could easily be included in the pyramid of ratios shown in Figure 1. Typical ratios involving value added include:

> Value added/Fixed Assets
> Value added/Current Assets
> Value added/Per Employee
> Value added/per £ of direct wages

and others of a similar nature.

VALUE ADDED AND MOTIVATION

21. It can be argued that value added is a better measure of performance than profit and if this viewpoint is accepted then there is likely to be more favourable motivational effects if performance is judged on value added rather than profit. To change the whole range of management accounting reports and statements from conventional profits and contributions to statements of value added would be a formidable task but on a selective basis the concept might be worthwhile.

RATIO ANALYSIS – A SUMMARY

22. Ratio analysis, particularly when used in a comparative manner, is a useful broad indicator to weaknesses in company operations and policies. All companies can derive some benefits from properly conducted ratio analysis and comparison but clearly the less efficient firms are likely to gain the most pertinent information. Participation in properly organised inter-firm comparison schemes, where consistent bases are employed and information is used that is unavailable from normal published accounts, eliminates many of the difficulties that may occur when comparisons are made based on ratios prepared on an ad hoc basis using information only from published accounts. In such circumstances ratio analysis may be of limited value for a number of reasons, including:

(a) The accounting rules and conventions used for matters such as stock valuations, depreciations, revenue/capital distinctions etc are likely to differ from company to company.

(b) Where accounts are prepared on an historical cost basis without current value and inflation adjustments, comparisons become more difficult and the ratios themselves have less meaning.

(c) Where a company is part of a group, transfer pricing policies and financing arrangements make it difficult to establish genuine operating results for the individual company.

Regular ratio analysis to determine trends **within** a given company is always likely to be of some value and it would be normal to include inter-related ratio analysis as part of the overall performance appraisal systems of the firm.

SUMMARY

23. (a) Ratio analysis uses financial reports and data and summarises key relationships, eg profit to sales, in order to appraise financial performance.

(b) The effectiveness of ratio analysis is greatly improved when trends are identified, comparative ratios are available, and inter-related ratios are prepared.

(c) Ratios can be subdivided into many groups and three typical ones are: profitability ratios, solvency ratios, and investment ratios.

(d) The key ratio dealing with profitability is the ROCE. Typically this is supported by other ratios which progressively analyse asset turnover and profitability.

(e) Key supporting ratios are sales: Operating Assets and Operating profit:sales.

(f) Solvency ratios can be concerned with the short term and the long term.

(g) The main ratios concerned with short term solvency are the current ratio and the 'quick' ratio or acid test. Also, cash conversion ratios such as the average stock turnover and average collection period are useful aids.

(h)   The long term solvency ratios concern the financial stability and structure of the firm. Several of the ratios relate to the firm's gearing and others concern interest coverage.

(i)   The investment ratios include: earnings per share, dividend yield and cover and the price-earnings ratio.

(j)   Conventional ratio analysis has been refined by Altman by developing a value known as the Z score, based on five key ratios. Indicator values have been developed which it is claimed provide good predictors of financial stability or instability.

(k)   Value Added is the wealth that a company creates by its own efforts and value added statements and ratios can provide guidance on the productivity and performance of an organisation with the issue being clouded by input costs.

POINTS TO NOTE

24.   (a)   Ratio analysis, using inter-related ratios, avoids giving undue emphasis to one isolated aspect of company operations and emphasises that financial success is the result of the interaction of numerous contributory factors.

(b)   Comparison between ratios for widely differing types of organisation are usually pointless and misleading. For example the ROCE for a capital intensive food processing company might be 12% whilst the ROCE for a knowledge based organisation (eg designers, architects, solicitors) with virtually no capital assets, might be 2000%.

(c)   There are firms who specialise in publishing ratios for particular trades supported by forecasts and analyses of trends which are likely to affect that sector of the economy.

ADDITIONAL READING

Application of classification techniques in business, banking and finance   Altman, JAI PRESS

Value added   Cox, HEINEMANN/CIMA

Value added reporting: uses and measurement   Gray & Maunders, A.C.C.A.

Industrial performance Analysis: Business Ratios   INTERCOMPANY COMPANY COMPARISONS

SELF REVIEW QUESTIONS

1.   *How can ratio analysis be most effective? (2)*

2.   *What broad groups of ratios can be prepared? (3)*

3.   *What is the 'pyramid' of ratios and what ratios are typically included? (4)*

4.   *In what ways can the 'capital employed' and 'profit' parts of the ROCE ratio be defined? (5)*

5.   *What are the asset ratios? (6 & 7)*

6.   *What are the profitability ratios? (8 & 9)*

7.   *What are the main short term solvency ratios and what are considered 'good' ranges of values? (12)*

8.   *What are the key long term solvency ratios? (13)*

9.   *Define the main investment ratios and show their relationships. (15)*

10.   *What is the objective of calculating the Z score developed by Altman? What are the five key ratios? (17)*

11.   *What is the value added and what is the typical layout for a value added statement? (19)*

12.   *What are the reasons why ad hoc ratio analysis may be of limited value? (22)*

EXAMINATION QUESTION WITH ANSWER COMMENCING PAGE 368

A1. *The XY Engineering Company operates a job order absorption costing system. Although a wide variety of work is undertaken it has been found useful to distinguish two categories of work, these are referred to as X jobs and Y jobs.*

The company's manufacturing activities are carried out in two production departments, X department and Y department. These departments are dealt with as cost centres in the company's costing system. Most of the manufacturing for X jobs is carried out in department X and most of the work on Y jobs is carried out in department Y. There is, however, a certain amount of inter-departmental work and this is charged for at cost, as estimated by the costing system. Department X is more capital intensive than department Y.

Service department expenses, direct labour overtime premiums and administrative overheads are charged to jobs by means of a plant wide overhead absorption rate. For the past year the absorption rate has been £15 per direct labour hour.

At present department X is working at 90% of full capacity whereas department Y is regularly working overtime.

During the past year some concern has been expressed over the profitability of the average Y job. It seems that, whereas X jobs average 22% profit on sales value, the corresponding percentage for Y jobs is 12. The manager of Department Y disputes the use of the profit percentage of sales value to assess the relative profitability of the two departments. He points out that his department's annual profit is 10% higher than that of department X.

You are required:

(a) to comment on the suitability of the costing system for providing information on the relative profitability of the two types of product and the use of the profit on sales value percentage as a measure of relative profitability;

(b) to advise the management on improvements to their costing system. Do not suggest a standard costing system, but specifically include in your report your views on the merits of a profit centre system.

ACCA, Management Accounting.

21. Management Accounting and Computers

INTRODUCTION

1.   This chapter explains why computers provide valuable assistance for management accountants and how management accounting is part of the overall information system of the firm. Data processing and decision support systems are described and relevant aspects of computer applications are explained and exemplified; including, spreadsheets, expert systems and sensitivity analysis.

BACKGROUND COMPUTER KNOWLEDGE

2.   All students taking management accounting examinations will either be concurrently studying computers and data processing or will be exempt from the subject because of their previous studies.

Accordingly no attempt will be made in this manual to explain what computers are or how they operate. The emphasis will be on highlighting some of the ways they can be used for management accounting purposes and the resulting advantages and disadvantages. It is assumed that students are familiar with the more common terms used in data processing; for example, hardware, software, files, VDU, disk storage, terminal, on-line, application packages, printers, program, and so on. Students unfamiliar with these terms or who wish to study computers and data processing in more detail are advised to consult a comprehensive book on the subject, for example Data Processing by Oliver and Chapman, D P Publications Ltd. Any question in a management accounting examination which involve computers are thought unlikely to require much detailed technical computer knowledge, rather it is expected that they will test understanding of the application of computers to various facets of management accounting.

WHAT ARE COMPUTERS USEFUL FOR MANAGEMENT ACCOUNTING?

3.   Computers can be valuable tools for management accounting purposes for the same reasons as they are for all other applications, namely, speed, accuracy, filing and retrieval abilities, calculating and decision making capabilities, input and output facilities.

These points are expanded below:

Speed

Relative to manual methods, all aspects of computer operations (except the initial manual input of data via the keyboard) take place at very high speeds. Whether the computer is calculating an overhead variance, making an entry on a job cost file, printing an actual/budget statement or carrying out some other task the computer does this in a minute fraction of the time it would take manually.

Accuracy

All computers incorporate inbuilt checking features which ensure for all practical purposes 100% accuracy in following a program. If a program has been thoroughly tested and produces the required output or performs the correct calculations, then this will be followed faithfully time after time after time.

On occasions computer systems do produce errors but investigations invariably show that these errors arise from such factors as errors contained in the data input or programming errors or an unforeseen combination of circumstances not allowed for in the program and not from computer malfunction.

Filing and retrieval abilities

Computer files, nowadays invariably maintained on some type of disk storage, and the associated software file handling systems, permit the rapid updating, amendment, cross-referencing and retrieval of huge volumes of data that would be virtually impossible using any manual system. Computer backing storage systems are becoming physically smaller, cheaper and permit faster access. These developments mean that accountants and managers can have more and more information readily available for instantaneous display on their terminal.

Calculating and decision making capability

Computer calculating speeds are measured in millionths of a second and are the heart of their power. In computer terms, the calculations required for management accounting purposes are very modest yet these same calculations done manually are tedious and time-consuming. Take for example the calculations required for apportioning various items of overhead expenditure over cost centres, which is a routine but necessary task. Each calculation is simple but the overall task, including cross and down totalling, can be lengthy when done manually, yet is ideally suited to the computer where it would be done virtually instantaneously.

Allied to the calculating power of the computer is its ability to test different values or conditions and depending on the results, take different actions. It is this ability which enables the computer to make decisions and makes it qualitatively different from other machines. The speed, calculating power and decision-making ability of the computer enables the accountant to extend the scope of his analysis beyond that which would be feasible manually, except for a special once-off exercise. As an example, manually-prepared variance statements typically highlight variances above a certain value (say, £1000) or those more than a given percentage (say ± 5%) away from standard. The computer could be programmed to do this and also to analyse the variance and its significance by statistical methods – including the calculation of the standard deviation – and, where a significant variance is detected, to retrieve the history of this variance for comparison and to ascertain trends. In short, a more detailed analysis could routinely be undertaken, where required, without extra effort on the part of the accountant who would know that all truly significant variances would be highlighted so leaving more time for any personal investigations felt necessary. This, incidentally, is the key to effective use of computers for management accounting (or any other) purposes. They should be used, where feasible for all forms of routine ledger keeping, calculating, searching, periodic statement/report production and so on in order that there is more time for activities requiring the human touch; for example interpretation of results, special investigations, planning, interviewing and so on.

Input and Output facilities

Computers can read and search files, print results or display information on VDU's at very high speeds. With modern software, report layouts can be altered at will, results can be displayed using a range of diagrammatic and graphical displays, often in full colour, and displays can be interrogated and manipulated by the user without leaving his desk. Taken together the various facilities provide a far more flexible and speedy service than would be possible using manual means.

MANAGEMENT ACCOUNTING AND MANAGEMENT INFORMATION SYSTEMS (MIS)

4.   Management accounting is only one part of the overall MIS of the organisation. Because of the integration of tasks and the need to use files of data in common for various purposes rarely is a management accounting application dealt with separately by the computer system.

Management Accounting information is usually produced in conjunction with, or as a by-product of, some other computer application. As an example, information on material usage and wastage is likely to be produced in conjunction with the main inventory control and re-ordering system. The material usage and wastage information would then be used as the basis of computer produced variance analysis and product costing information. The inter-relationship of management accounting and the rest of the organisation's information is receiving increasing recognition in examinations. For example the commentary on the new ACCA Cost and Management Accounting II syllabus states, "Students should be encouraged to see management accounting as part of an overall information system and not in isolation". Accordingly it is not sufficient merely to examine the role of computers for management accounting purposes only but to widen the study to include the role of computers in management information system (MIS) generally.

ARE COMPUTERS ESSENTIAL FOR MIS?

5.   The short answer to this question is, not essential but they can be very useful. The study of MIS is not about the use of computers, it is about the provision and use of information relevant to the user. Computers are one – albeit important – means of producing information and concentration on the means of producing information and concentration on the means of production rather than the needs of the user can lead to expensive mistakes. There is undoubtedly an important and growing role for computers in MIS but the technology must be used with discretion.

Computers are good at rapid and accurate calculations, manipulation, storage and retrieval but less good at unexpected or qualitative work or where genuine judgement is required. It has been suggested that computers can be used to best advantage for processing information which has the following characteristics:

  (a)   a number of interacting variables
  (b)   speed is an important factor
  (c)   there are reasonably accurate values
  (d)   accuracy of output is important
  (e)   operations are repetitive
  (f)   large amount of data exist

These characteristics can be related to the needs of the various management levels as shown in Figure 1.

The unshaded are of Figure 1 represents unstructured problems and decisions where human involvement is essential. The division between computer and human tasks is constantly changing. As software and hardware develops and organisations gain more skill in using computers, tasks previously requiring managerial expertise and judgement become worthwhile computer jobs.

An example is the now widespread use of 'credit scoring' in banks. An applicant for a loan fills in a detailed questionnaire and the answers are input into a computer. The program carries out a series of checks and tests and decides whether or not the loan should be granted. Previously all loan applications required a managerial decision which is now needed only for unusual requests, large loans or industrial applications.

Information Characteristics	Presence in Management Information		
	Operational Level	Tactical Level	Strategic Level
Interacting Variables	Frequent		Always
Speed Important	Usually		Rarely
Data Accuracy	High		Low
Output Accuracy	Always		Rarely
Repetition	Usually		Rarely
Data Volume	High		Low

Resulting Application of Computers

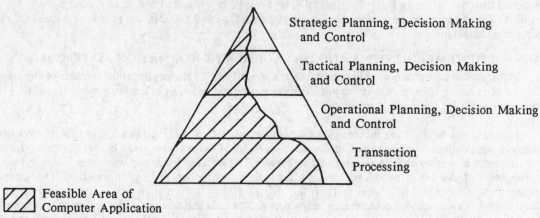

Strategic Planning, Decision Making and Control

Tactical Planning, Decision Making and Control

Operational Planning, Decision Making and Control

Transaction Processing

Feasible Area of Computer Application

Figure 1 FEASIBILITY OF COMPUTER APPLICATION BY MANAGEMENT LEVEL

COMPUTERS AND INFORMATION SYSTEMS

6.   Although the boundaries between them are blurred and there is substantial overlap it is possible to distinguish two major areas of application of computers in information systems. These are

- Data Processing (or Transaction Processing)
- Decision Support Systems (or End User Computing)

These categories are shown in Figure 2 and developed in the paragraphs which follow.

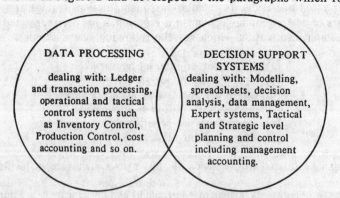

DATA PROCESSING

dealing with: Ledger and transaction processing, operational and tactical control systems such as Inventory Control, Production Control, cost accounting and so on.

DECISION SUPPORT SYSTEMS

dealing with: Modelling, spreadsheets, decision analysis, data management, Expert systems, Tactical and Strategic level planning and control including management accounting.

Figure 2 COMPUTERS AND INFORMATION SYSTEMS

DATA PROCESSING SYSTEMS

7.   These systems perform the essential role of collecting and processing the daily transactions of the organisation, hence the alternative term, transaction processing. Typically these include: all forms of ledger keeping, accounting receivable and payable, invoicing, credit control, rate demands, stock movements and so on.

These types of systems were the first to harness the power of the computer and originally were based on centralised mainframe computers. In many cases this still applies, especially for large volume repetitive jobs, but the availability of micro and mini computers has made distributed data processing feasible and popular. Distributed data processing has many variations but in essence means that data handling and processing are carried out at or near the point of use rather than in one centralised location.

Transaction processing is substantially more significant in terms of processing time, volume of input and output than say, information production for tactical and strategic planning. Transaction processing is essential to keep the operations of the organisation running smoothly and provides the base for all other internal information support. This is shown in Figure 3.

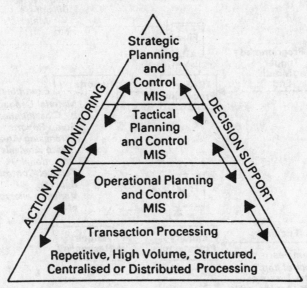

Figure 3 TRANSACTION PROCESSING AS A BASE FOR MIS

CHARACTERISTICS OF DATA PROCESSING SYSTEMS

8.   These systems are 'pre-specified'; that is their functions, decision rules and output formats cannot usually be changed by the end user. These systems are related directly to the structure of the organisation's datas. Any change in the data they process or the functions they perform usually requires the intervention of information system specialists such as system analysts and programmers.

Some data processing systems have to cope with huge volumes and a wide range of data types and output formats. As an example consider the Electricity and Gas Board Billing and Payment Handling systems, the Clearing Bank's Current Accounting Systems, the Motor Policy handling systems of a large insurer and so on. The systems and programming work required for these systems represents a major investment. For example, the development of a large scale billing system for a public utility represents something like 100 man years of effort. Of course, data processing also takes place on a more modest scale and the ready availability of application packages - ie software to deal with a particular administrative or commercial task - means that small scale users have professionally written and tested programs to deal with their routine data processing. The better packages provide for some flexibility and the user can specify - within limits - variations in output formats, data types and decision rules.

SCOPE OF TRANSACTION PROCESSING

9.   Transaction processing is necessary to ensure that the day to day activities of the organisation are processed, recorded and acted upon. Files are maintained which provide both the current data for transactions; for example the amount invoiced and cash received during the month for statement preparation, and which also serve as a basis for operational and tactical control and for answering enquiries.

Transaction processing can be sub-divided into:

  (a)   Current activity processing
  (b)   Report processing
  (c)   Inquiry processing

Figure 4 shows in outline these sub-divisions with examples of the various processing types drawn from inventory and materials processing.

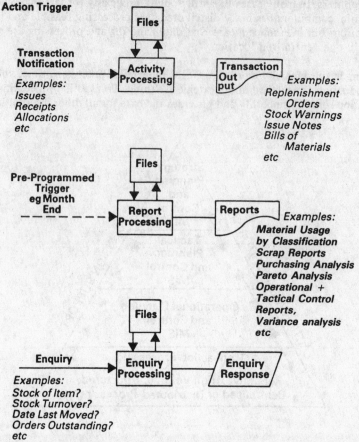

Figure 4 SUB-DIVISIONS OF TRANSACTION PROCESSING
(WITH INVENTORY CONTROL EXAMPLES)

A routine data processing system is not in itself an MIS because it does not support all the management functions of the organisation nor does it have the decision focus which is the primary objective of MIS. Nevertheless it should be apparent that routine transaction processing is essential for day-to-day activities and provides the indispensable foundation upon which the organisation's MIS is built. For example, there would be little point in developing a sophisticated flexible budgeting system complete with detailed variance analysis if the routine, but essential, cost analysis and recording system was not working perfectly.

DECISION SUPPORT SYSTEMS (DSS)

10.   DSS are alternatively termed end-user computing systems. Their objective is to support managers in their work, especially decision making.

DSS tend to be used in planning, modelling, analysing alternatives and decision making. They generally operate through terminals operated by the user who interacts with the computer system. Using a variety of tools and procedures the manager (ie the user) can develop his own systems to help perform his functions more effectively. It is this active involvement and the focus on decision making which distinguishes a DSS from a data processing system. The emphasis is on *support for decision making* not on *automated decision making* which is a feature of transaction processing.

DSS are especially useful for semi-structured problems where problem solving is improved by interaction between the manager and the computer system. The emphasis is on small, simple models which can easily be understood and used by the manager rather than complex integrated systems which need information specialists to operate them.

The main characteristics of DSS are:

(a)   The computer provides support but does not replace the manager's judgement nor does it provide pre-determined solutions.

(b) DSS are best suited to semi-structured problems where parts of the analysis can be computerised but the decision maker's judgement and insight is needed to control the process.

(c) Where effective problem solving is enhanced by interaction between the computer and the manager.

WHERE TO APPLY DSS

11. DSS are man/machine systems and are suitable for semi-structured problems. The problem must be important to the manager and the decision required must be a key one. In addition if an interactive computer-based system is to be used then some of the following criteria should be met.

(a) **There should be a large data base.**

A data base is an organised collection of structured data with a minimum duplication of data items. The data base is common to all users of the system but is independent of the programs which use the data. If the data base is too large for manual searching then a computer-supported approach may be worthwhile.

(b) **Large amount of computation or data manipulation.**

Where analysis of the problem requires considerable computation or data manipulation, computing power is likely to be beneficial.

(c) **Complex inter-relationships.**

Where there is a large data base or where there are numerous factors involved it is frequently difficult to assess all the possible inter-relationships without computer assistance.

(d) **Analysis by stages.**

Where the problem is an iterative one with stages for re-examination and re-assessment it becomes more difficult to deal with manually. The computer-based model can answer the question, 'What if?' quickly and effectively.

(e) **Judgement required.**

In complex situations judgement is required both to determine the problem and the solution. Unaided, no computer system can provide this.

(f) **Communication.**

Where several people are involved in the problem solving process, each contributing some special expertise, then the co-ordinating power of the computer can be of assistance.

It follows from the above criteria that DSS are inappropriate for unstructured problems and unnecessary for completely structured problems because these can be dealt with wholly by the computer and man/machine interaction is unnecessary.

In outline DSS require a database, the software to handle the database and decision support programs including, for example, modelling, spread sheet and analysis packages, expert systems and so on. The above elements of DSS are dealt with in the paragraphs which follow.

THE DATABASE CONCEPT

12. A database was defined earlier as a collection of structured data, with minimum duplication, which is common to all users of the system but is independent of programs which use the data. The database can grow and change and is built up stage by stage within the organisation. It will actually comprise several databases, each providing the anticipated information for several logically related management information systems where the data can be accessed, retrieved and modified with reasonable flexibility.

The data structures and relationships require highly technical software - known as the Data Base Management System (DBMS) - to deal with them. Fortunately the user is shielded, to a large extent, from the complexity and is able to access the data base with the minimum of technical knowledge.

Figure 5 shows the relationship between the database, transaction processing, decision support systems and the DBMS.

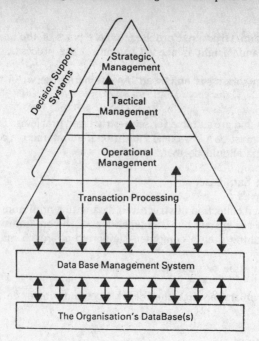

Figure 5 DATABASES AND DECISION SUPPORT SYSTEMS

The database concept allows data to be captured once at source and to be available for numerous applications. Redundancy and duplication are reduced and potentially there is more flexibility and an increase in data reliability, accuracy and consistency. It also means that the same data will support both transaction processing and serve as a reservoir for management use in decision support systems.

Where the only form of data storage possible was unrelated, unique files for each application, this engendered a narrow, parochial view of information. The reality is that management need information which crosses functions, applications and levels and the flexibility of databases and the linkages possible make the concept a powerful one and essential for decision support systems.

DATA BASE MANAGEMENT SYSTEMS (DBMS)

13. The DBMS is a complex software system which constructs, expands and maintains the database. It also provides the link or interface, between the user and the data in the base. Figure 6 provides a summary of the three main elements of DBMS – definition, processing and enquiry.

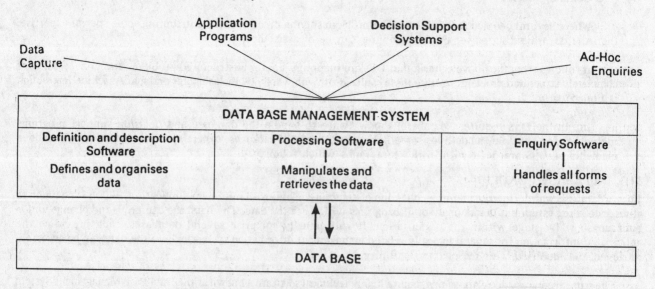

Figure 6 DATA BASE MANAGEMENT SYSTEMS

The three primary categories of DBMS are:

Relational.

Where each type of record is represented as existing in a table of file of like records. For example, there could be customer records, product records, order records and so on. These systems are relatively simple and are suitable for manipulation by non-data processing personnel (as in a DSS) but their technical efficiency may be poor.

Hierarchial.

This is a system having in-built linkages whereby there are 'owner' records which 'own' numerous 'member' records.

Network.

These are further developments of linkage systems with many more record types and linkages.

Both the linkage systems require the user to know what linkages have been established in order to know on what basis data can be retrieved. The linkage systems are technically more efficient but do require greater data processing knowledge so their use tends to be restricted to information specialists.

DECISION SUPPORT PACKAGES

14. The existence of the database and a DBMS to handle it means that the manager can interrogate and access a mass of data at will. He then needs to be able to use this data in exploring alternatives and making decisions. To do this there is an enormous range of packages available. These include packages for:

> (a) Modelling and simulation
> (b) Spreadsheets
> (c) Statistical analyses of all types
> (d) Forecasting
> (e) Non-Linear and Linear Programming
> (f) Regression analysis
> (g) Financial modelling
> (h) Sensitivity and risk analysis
> (i) Expert systems
>
> and so on.

It is clearly beyond the scope of this manual to describe all these types of packages in detail but three of the more relevant ones are briefly described below, namely, spreadsheets, expert systems and sensitivity analysis.

SPREADSHEET PACKAGES

15. A general outline of modelling and simulation has already been given together with an explanation of how modelling can help the manager and accountant in planning and decision making. One useful practical way of modelling is to use a spreadsheet package to show the results of different actions.

The basis of a spreadsheet package is an electronic worksheet whereby data can be stored and manipulated at will. The spreadsheet is a matrix of locations which can contain values, formulae and relationships. The key feature is that all elements in the matrix are changed automatically when one or more of the key assumptions are changed.

For example a series of interlocking departmental operating statements culminating in an overall projected profit and loss account may have been prepared on the spreadsheet. If one or more of the variables (rates of pay, output levels, sales, absorption rates and so on) needs to be altered then the new value needs only to be entered once and the whole of the matrix is recalculated virtually instantaneously with all relationships, sub-totals and totals automatically catered for. This facility allows a series of outcomes to be explored, providing answers to the 'what if' questions which are so essential to the manager. For example, what would be the effect on profit of a change in inflation rate/cost per unit/contribution margin/scrap rates or whatever factor need to be explored. Used in this way spreadsheet packages perform a modelling function and this facility is greatly expanded in the latest spreadsheet packages.

SPREADSHEETS AND BUDGETING

16. One of the important tasks of tactical level management is concerned with budgeting. Spreadsheets can be of great assistance in exploring the effect on a budget of different values and assumptions so that the manager can make more effective decisions. As one example, consider the Accountant dealing with cash budgeting.

Cash budgets are examples of routine but highly essential reports which need frequent updating to reflect current and forecast conditions, changes in credit behaviour, anticipated gains or expenditures and so on. Each period (weekly, monthly, quarterly, as required) changes and up-to-date information are input and, in combination with the brought forward file data, the cash budget will be automatically projected forward by the spreadsheet program with highlighted surpluses and/or deficiencies, balances carried forward from one period to another and all the usual contents of a cash budget. The budget could be shown in both an abbreviated and detailed format and could also be displayed in a graphical form.

Figure 7 shows the possible output of a Summary Cash Budget and a corresponding graphical display, the facility for which is increasingly being included in modern spreadsheet packages.

EXPERT SYSTEMS

17. At the present time, Expert Systems represent the most advanced stage of decision support systems. An Expert System is a computer system which embodies some of the experience and specialised knowledge of an expert or experts. An Expert System enables a non-expert to achieve comparable performance to an expert in the field. It uses a reasoning process which bears some resemblance to human thought.

The unique feature of an Expert System is the *knowledge base*, which is a network of rules which represents the human expertise. These rules and linkages are derived from discussions with experts and analysis of their decision making behaviour. Attempts are made to include the effects of uncertainty and judgement and clearly such an approach is likely to be costly and time consuming. Expert Systems are much more sophisticated and powerful than simply automating a typical structured decision but conversely, they are very much more difficult to implement.

Expert Systems have been developed in a number of fields of which the following are examples:

> Medical diagnosis
> Personal tax planning
> Product pricing
> Selection of selling methods
> Statutory Sick Pay Entitlement and Claims
> Credit approval in banking
> Air crew scheduling
> and so on.

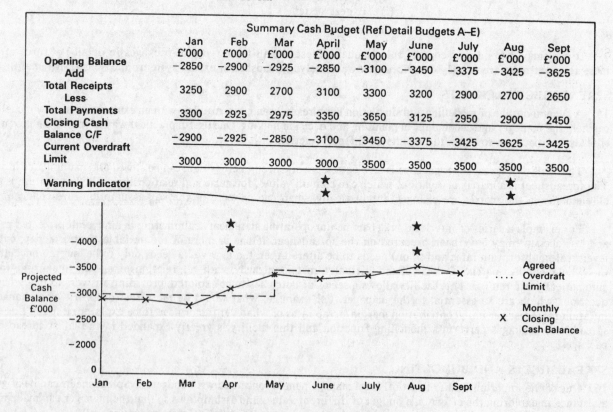

	Jan £'000	Feb £'000	Mar £'000	April £'000	May £'000	June £'000	July £'000	Aug £'000	Sept £'000
Summary Cash Budget (Ref Detail Budgets A–E)									
Opening Balance	−2850	−2900	−2925	−2850	−3100	−3450	−3375	−3425	−3625
Add									
Total Receipts	3250	2900	2700	3100	3300	3200	2900	2700	2650
Less									
Total Payments	3300	2925	2975	3350	3650	3125	2950	2900	2450
Closing Cash Balance C/F	−2900	−2925	−2850	−3100	−3450	−3375	−3425	−3625	−3425
Current Overdraft Limit	3000	3000	3000	3000	3500	3500	3500	3500	3500
Warning Indicator				★ ★				★ ★	

Figure 7 TABULAR AND GRAPHICAL CASH BUDGET

SENSITIVITY ANALYSIS

18. Dealing with uncertainty is an inescapable part of planning and decision-making. Accordingly the accountant must show the effects of uncertainty in the information provided to decision makers insofar as this is possible. It can be positively misleading to produce information for a decision which shows only a single value of profit or contribution or NPV when the factors which are involved in the decision - costs, sales expected, purchase prices and so on - cannot be forecast with certainty. Ideally the decision maker would like to know the expected result and how *sensitive* or *robust* is the solution. A robust solution is one which will still remain acceptable in spite of substantial variations in the factors involved whilst a sensitive solution is one that is vulnerable to minor variations in the factors which, in practise, is all too likely.

Sensitivity analysis is a practical way of assessing the degree of sensitivity of the solution for many types of decision for which the accountant provides information. The general procedure is simple; all the factors except one are held constant and the value of the one being studied is altered, increment by increment, in both an upwards and downwards direction. At each alteration the effect on the result (ie the profit, contribution, NPV or whatever) is noted. This process is then repeated for each of the factors in the problem and the sensitivity of the solution to changes in the values of each of the factors is thus identified. Although in principle a simple idea it can mean an enormous number of calculations hence the importance of computer assistance.

Many computer packages incorporate sensitivity analysis facilities and where these are not automatically provided a similar effect can be obtained by the multiple insertion of the input data suitably adjusted on each occasion. Typical of the areas where computer based sensitivity analysis will be found to be of value for management accounting purposes are:

> LP models
>   including   capital rationing
>   Product planning
>   Ingredient mix problems
> Investment appraisals
> Financial Modelling
> Budget planning
> Pricing models
> Decision analysis
> and so on.

SUMMARY

19. (a) Computers are useful for management accounting because of their speed, accuracy, filing and retrieval abilities, calculating and decision making capabilities.

(b) Management accounting is but one facet of the general information system of the organisation.

(c) Data processing, or transaction processing, deals with the routine ledger and transaction processing of the organisation and provides the base for the whole information system.

(d) Decision support systems support managers in their work especially decision making.

(e) DSS include; planning, modelling, simulation decision making.

(f) DSS are best for semi-structured problems where the solution is improved by interaction between the user and the computer system.

(g) DSS are best suited where there is a large data base, complex inter-relationships, step-by-step analysis and where judgement is necessary.

(h) Spreadsheets are valuable packages for accountants and can be used for numerous tasks including; cash budgeting, variance analysis, modelling.

(i) Expert systems incorporate a knowledge base which enables a non-expert to achieve comparable performance to an expert.

(j) Sensitivity analysis is a practical way of assessing the effects of uncertainty and, because of the repeated calculations, requires the assistance of a computer.

POINTS TO NOTE

20. (a) The declining real cost of computer systems makes their use cost-effective even for small, one-off jobs.

(b) Increasingly the decision regarding which computer system to purchase depends on the software support for the machine, especially, the availability of application packages.

(c) Problems can occur when using computers and the greatest care must be taken to obtain feedback from the users of the system, in order to overcome any difficulties which arise. Problems may include; use of generalised and inappropriate packages which do not deal adequately with specialised problems, over-abundant printouts which swamp managers with paper, delays in producing required results, antagonism from managers and staff used to manual systems, fear of the unknown, inadequate training, unexplained jargon and so on.

SELF REVIEW QUESTIONS

1. *Why are computers useful for management accounting? (3)*

2. *What is the relationship of management accounting to the information system of the firm? (4)*

3. *What characteristics of processing make it advisable to use computers? (5)*

4. *How do these characteristics of processing make it advisable to use computers? (5)*

5. *What is a data processing system? (7)*

6. *What is the scope of data processing? (9)*

7. *What is a decision support system? (10)*

8. *Where can a DSS be best applied? (11)*

9. *What is a Data Base? a Data Base Management System? (12)*

10. *Give examples of packages used in DSS. (14)*

11. *What is a spreadsheet package? (16)*

12. *Describe an Expert System. (17)*

13. *What is a sensitivity analysis and why is the use of a computer necessary? (18)*

EXAMINATION QUESTIONS WITH ANSWERS COMMENCING PAGE 368

A1. *Explain how the increasing use of computers can both:*

(a) provide a challenge to the practice of management accounting, and
(b) assist it.

Illustrate your answer with references to the planning and budgetary control processes or some alternative example of your choice.

ACCA, Management Accounting.

A2. *(a) It can be unrealistic and counterproductive to use deterministic models to analyse the financial aspect of systems and problem areas where there is considerable uncertainty. Sensitivity analysis can be used in conjunction with deterministic models but, to deal adequately with such situations, it may be necessary to use either (i) an analytical approach or (ii) simulation.*

Discuss the above using cost-volume-profit analysis to illustrate your answer.

(b) Explain the nature of computer spreadsheet packages that permit rapid calculations to be performed on tables of data and outline some of their uses in financial planning.

ACCA, Management Accounting.

A3. *(a) The manual for a computerised financial planning package includes sections on:*

(i) sensitivity analysis and
(ii) probabalistic simulation.

Describe the techniques that you might expect to be explained under each of these headings and discuss the relevance of these techniques to financial planning.

(b) Prepare a flow chart to explain the statement that 'budgeting is an iterative process'.

ACCA, Management Accounting.

**Solutions to
End of Chapter
Examination Questions**

Chapter 2

SOLUTION A1

(a) It is likely that the two bases of overhead recovery referred to are labour hours and machine hours.

The number of hours involved are as follows:

Product	Planned production p.a. '000s	Labour hours		Machine Hours	
		Per unit	Total (000's)	Per unit	Total (000's)
A	30	2	60	1	30
B	20	3	60	1	20
C	10	2	20	2	20
			140		70

∴ F.O.A.R. (on labour hours) = $\dfrac{£280,000}{140,000}$ = <u>£2 per hour</u>

F.O.A.R. (on machine hours) = $\dfrac{£280,000}{70,000}$ = <u>£4 per hour</u>

Cost Per unit using the Three Bases

	Product		
	A £	B £	C £
Direct Costing Basis, Variable Cost	2	4	3
Absorption Costing Basis, Variable Cost	2	4	3
Overheads Based on Labour Hours	4	6	4
Total	6	10	7
Absorption Costing Basis. Variable Cost	2	4	3
Overheads Based on Machine Hours	4	4	8
Total	6	8	11

The cost per unit of is used to calculate the profitability of each product and the total profit in each year as shown in the following statement.

Product Profitability Statement
(in £'000s)

	Year 1				Year 2			
	A	B	C	Total	A	B	C	Total
Absorption costing – labour hours recovery								
Sales	192	192	48	432	192	120	144	456
Costs	144	160	28	332	144	100	84	328
Profit	48	32	20	100	48	20	60	128
Absorption costing – machine hours recovery								
Sales	192	192	48	432	192	120	144	456
Costs	144	128	44	316	144	80	132	356
Profit	48	64	4	116	48	40	12	100
Direct costing								
Sales	192	192	48	432	192	120	144	456
Direct costs	48	64	12	124	48	40	36	124
	144	128	36	308	144	80	108	332
Fixed costs				280				280
Profit				£28				£52

(b)   The varying results shown reflect the anomalies in the accounting conventions used. This is particularly pronounced in this example as the overhead recovery is based entirely on fixed overheads which are written off in their entirety in the one period using direct or marginal costing but which are carried forward, to a greater or less extent, in the stock valuations using absorption costing.

None of the methods can be said to be wrong or right. All that can be said is that the different conventions produce different results. Any of the methods can be used for internal purposes but only the absorption costing methods are consistent with SSAP 9 .

(c)   The only change in expenditure from increasing production by 20% is the extra variable costs (assuming that such an increment does not change fixed costs).

Accordingly the extra expenditure is as follows:

Product	20% extra production units	Variable cost per unit	Extra costs
		£	£
A	6000	2	12,000
B	4000	4	16,000
C	2000	3	6,000
			£34,000

∴ Full year cost = £34,000 x 12% = £4,080

SOLUTION A2

(a)   By definition joint products are produced together and there is no means of determining the profit or loss of an individual joint product. The various methods used in cost accounting are conventions only and have no validity for any form of decision making. The 'loss' shown for Product Y in the question is due to the cost apportionment basis. Some other basis could equally have shown a profit.

(b) This is a valid decision making problem and the incremental costs after split off should be compared with the incremental revenues.

		Process 2	Process 3	Process 4
Output (litres)		50,000	30,000	20,000
		£	£	£
	Sales value after Processing	60,000	21,000	35,000
less	Sales value at split-off	40,000	9,000	26,000
	Incremental revenue	20,000	12,000	9,000
less	Incremental costs	13,333	9,000	14,000
	= Profit (Loss)	£6,667	£3,000	(£5,000)

Thus, on the basis of the figures Process 4 would appear to be unprofitable and Product Z should be sold at split-off point. This conclusion is only correct if the Processing costs of Process 4, £14,000, are variable costs and will cease if Process 4 is closed.

(c)

PROCESS 3

	Litres	£		Litres	£
*Opening W.I.P	1,000	350	Sales	30,000	21,000
Transfers from Process 1	30,000	6,000			
Processing exp.		9,000	Closing W.I.P	1,000	350
Profit to P & L a/c		6,000			
	31,000	21,350		31,000	21,350

PROCESS 4

	Litres	£		Litres	£
*Opening W.I.P.	2,000	2,433	Sales	20,000	35,000
Transfers from Process 1	20,000	17,333			
Processing exp.		14,000	Closing W.I.P.	2,000	2,433
Profit to P & L a/c		3,667			
	22,000	37,433		22,000	37,433

* Values adjusted in line with new cost apportionment basis.

(d)

PROCESS 1

	Litres	£			Litres	£
Opening W.I.P.	4,000	1,200	Transfers			
Material	99,000	9,900	X to Process 2		50,000	40,000
Processing exp.		39,500	Y to Process 3		30,000	9,000
			Z to Process 4		20,000	26,000
Profit to P & L		25,000	Closing W.I.P.		3,000	600
	103,000	75,600			103,000	75,600

PROCESS 4

	Litres	£		Litres	£
Opening W.I.P.	2,000	3,300	Sales	20,000	35,000
Transfer from Process 1	20,000	26,000	Loss to P & L		5,000
Process Exp.		14,000	Closing W.I.P.	2,000	3,300
	22,000	43,300		22,200	43,300

(e) As previously stated no form of joint cost apportionment has any validity for decision making. The main advantages of such apportionment is for stock valuation and for this purpose the apportionment based on sales value is likely to even out results so is probably to be preferred.

Using the sales value at split-off converts Process 1 into a profit centre as the transfer prices are based on a comparable outside value.

Chapter 3

SOLUTION A1

The main categories of fixed cost have been dealt with in the chapter and these could be reproduced in the first part of the question together with brief explanations.

The categories involved are:

(a) Time period classification
(b) Volume classification
(c) Joint classification
(d) Policy classification

The key feature of relevant costs for decision making is their avoidability, ie if a cost changes as a result of the decision it is avoidable and therefore relevant. If for a particular decision (eg an increase in output) an existing cost does not change it is fixed in relation to the particular decision and therefore not relevant. In the long run all costs are avoidable whatever their accounting classification. An important point to be emphasised is that it is the actual expected behaviour of the cost in relation to the decision being considered that is significant, and not the ostensible behaviour implied by the conventional accounting classification of a fixed cost.

Note: The relevance of particular costs for decision making is explored in more detail in Chapter 14.

Chapter 4

SOLUTION A1

Most of this question can be answered directly from the chapter (para 9) but the one all embracing characteristic of effective management information reports is that the reports must induce actions which produce sufficient benefits to outweigh the costs of preparation.

The desirable attributes (eg reality, relevance, accuracy, timeliness, understandability and so on) may to some extent conflict. For example accuracy may conflict with the need for speed of preparation; relevance may conflict with understandability where, say, relevant information on a particular decision involves the concept of opportunity cost which may not be understood by the recipient of the report.

Chapter 7

SOLUTION A1

(a)

INCREASE IN PROFIT (IGNORING FINANCING COSTS)

		Current Situation		Proposed		Increase
		£'000s		£'000s		£'000s
	Sales		2,400		3,960	1,560
less	Variable costs					
	Raw Materials	720		1,080		360
	Other	960	1,680	1,440	2,520	480	840
=	Contribution		720		1,440	720
less	Fixed Costs		600		600	-
	= PROFIT		120		840	720

∴ Increase in profit is £720,000

CONSEQUENT LONG-TERM WORKING CAPITAL REQUIREMENT

		£'000s	£'000s
Raw Materials	$\dfrac{1080}{12}$	90	
W.I.P.	$\dfrac{2050}{12}$	210	
Finished Goods	$\dfrac{2520}{12}$	210	
			510
Debtors	$\dfrac{3960}{360}$ x 70		770
			1280
less Creditors			90
			£1190

∴ Increase in working capital = £1,190 – 410 = £780
ie **£780,000**

(b)

CASH FORECAST
£'000's

	June	July	August	Sept	Oct	Nov	Dec
Opening Balance b/f	80	100	50	(200)	(330)	(368)	(398)
+ Receipt from sales							
Old credit terms	200	200					
New credit terms							
2 month's credit				120	132	132	198
3 month's credit					80	88	88
Total cash availability	280	300	50	(80)	(118)	(148)	(112)
- Expenditure							
Materials	60	90	90	90	90	90	90
Other v. costs	80	120	120	120	120	120	120
Fixed costs	40	40	40	40	40	40	40
Total Expenditure	180	250	250	250	250	250	250
= Closing balance b/f	100	50	(200)	(330)	(368)	(398)	(362)

(c) The volume and price increases have a positive effect on profits but at the expense of substantially increased working capital requirements and a considerable worsening of the cash position.

Care should be taken to apprise the company bankers of the situation (if necessary) and to assess the financing and contractual costs of covering the cash requirement.

SOLUTION A2

(a) This can be answered directly from the text. In most practical circumstances a single PBF is unrealistic. Where two or more binding constraints exist then LP can be used.

(b) Quantitative methods, properly used can be invaluable aids for the management accountant particularly for planning and decision making purposes, examples include:

– Regression analysis and statistical forecasting techniques.

– Inventory control models.

– Network analysis.

– Simulation and modelling.

Linear programming

The main problems in the application of these techniques are:

(a) Lack of familiarity and expertise by accountants and managers.

(b) Difficulties of obtaining relevant data for input into the models, eg stock holding costs for EOQ models, activity times and variabilities for network analysis, etc.

(c) Lack of access to suitable computer facilities and packages. This is likely to be less of a problem in the future.

SOLUTION A3

(a)   *Reconstructed budgets for January/February/March*

	Product 1		Product 2
Budgeted Sales (units)	30,000		57,000
Budgeted Production (units)	30,000		52,500
	£		£
Sales	450,000		1,026,000
Production Costs			
Direct Material	60,000		157,500
Direct Labour	30,000		105,000
Factory Overhead	210,000		532,500
	300,000		795,000
+ opening stock Finished Goods (8,000 Units)	80,000	(7,500 units)	105,000
	380,000		900,000
– closing stock Finished Goods (8,000 Units)	80,000	(3,000 units)	42,000
Manufacturing cost of sales	300,000		858,000
Manufacturing profit	150,000		168,000
Less Administration and selling costs	30,000		48,000
= Net Profit	120,000		120,000

151,500

(b)   *Budgets for both quarters with stocks valued at standard marginal cost*

	JANUARY-MARCH		APRIL-JUNE	
	Product 1	Product 2	Product 1	Product 2
Sales (units)	30,000	57,000	30,000	57,000
Production (units)	30,000	52,500	24,000	60,000
	£	£	£	£
Sales	450,000	1,026,000	450,000	1,026,000
Production Costs				
Direct Material	60,000	157,500	48,000	180,000
Direct Labour	30,000	105,000	24,000	120,000
Factory Overhead	210,000	532,500	204,000	540,000
	300,000	795,000	276,000	840,000
+ opening stock				
Finished goods	32,000	45,000	32,000	18,000
	332,000	840,000	308,000	858,000
- closing stock				
Finished goods	32,000	18,000	8,000	36,000
= Manufacturing costs	300,000	822,000	300,000	822,000
Manufacturing Profit	150,000	204,000	150,000	204,000
Admin & Selling costs	30,000	48,000	30,000	48,000
Net Profit	£120,000	£156,000	£120,000	£156,000

(c)   The differences arise simply because of the inclusion of fixed costs in stock valuations using absorption costing whereas in marginal costing all fixed costs are treated as period costs. Using marginal costing, profits vary directly with sales whereas with absorption costing profits vary as a function of sales and production.

SOLUTION A4

Redrafted Budget - Tomm Ltd

DEPARTMENT	CCI		PC2		PC3	
	20,000 Kg P12					
Output	40,000 Kg P13		40,000 P2		20,000 P3	
	£'000	£'000	£'000	£'000	£'000	£'000
Sales				1600		1600
Cost of goods						
Controllable Variable						
Raw Material	100		20		30	
Labour	120		150		110	
Processing Cost	120		20		5	
Total Controllable Variable	340		190		145	
Re-allocation of CCI	(340)		307	497	33	178
Contribution				1103		622
Fixed Cost-Controllable						
Admin. salaries	55		135		150	
Processing	25		90	225	130	280
	80					
Controllable Profit				878		342
Fixed Costs - Non Controllable						
Computer	10		8		2	
Overhead allocation	175		30		15	
	265		38		17	
Re-allocation of CCI	(265)		240	278	25	42
Revised budget profit				600		300

Notes and Workings
Apportionment of Computer costs

	CCI £'000	PC2 £'000	PC3 £'000
Separate Facilities	25	20	5
Net Savings (25 + 20 + 5 − 20) = 30			
apportioned 25:20:5	15	12	3
Net Cost	10	8	2

Apportionment of Joint Costs

	PC2	PC3
Sales Revenue	1600	800
Total Cost apportioned 2:1	1000	500
Separate Variable Costs	190	145
Separate Fixed Costs		
Admin. salaries	135	150
Processing Costs	90	130
Allocated Fixed costs		
Computer	8	2
General overhead	30	15
	453	442
Joint Cost apportionment		
CCI Variable	307	33
Fixed	240	25
	1000	500

SOLUTION A5

(a) Can be answered from the manual.

(b) The problems of R & D budgets are as follows:

1. No linkage with production or sales levels.
2. Usually determined by convention or policy essentially on an arbitrary basis.
3. Results difficult or impossible to measure.

The best system would be to have a budget or allocation for each current project and identify costs against the particular project. Periodically the R & D manager should have to report on progress, financial and otherwise, and relate this to the target dates and the budget. There is no complete answer to this very real practical problem.

Chapter 9

SOLUTION A1

(a) Budgets are a formalised system of quantified plans which have many objectives including those relating to behavioural factors such as goal congruence and motivation and those aimed at providing a simplified system of managerial control through budgetary reports.

To motivate staff the budgets should be accepted by them and should encourage them to act in ways which contribute to organisations objectives. The performance levels should be such that the staff are motivated to achieve the level set and research studies have shown that higher performance levels, if accepted, have a motivating influence.

From the managerial control viewpoint, attention is focused on the variances between budget and actual and such variances will have most meaning when the performance level is that which is realistically expected to be achieved. This performance level is not necessarily the level which will have the greatest motivational effect and as most budgeting and standard costing systems use only one level it is inevitable that the level selected will be a compromise.

(b) Three possible levels are:

Ideal or perfect levels. This level is that which assumes no waste, no mistakes and perfect efficiency. If such a level was made known, but not used for control, it might have some motivational purpose but if such a level was the only one used the continual production of adverse variances is likely to produce dysfunctional effects and will be of little value for control purposes.

Expected level of performance. This is the level of performance which appears to be most commonly used. it is the level which is expected to be achieved given high (but not impossible) levels of efficiency. Such a level should be seen as tough but realistic. This standard of performance has the advantage of producing meaningful variances but may not provide sufficient motivation.

Loose or slack standards. In general a loose standard would not be consciously set but it may arise through an error or through being out of date. Such a standard has no advantages and the obvious disadvantages of providing no motivation or control.

(c) If employees are involved then research evidence suggests that the budget levels are more likely to be accepted by them. However, Agyris has warned about pseudo-participation having a de-motivational effect so that it is important that if participation is to take place it is real participation.

If employees are involved and there is genuine participation it is likely that the levels of performance included in the budget may not be those that management would prefer and so the resulting variances will have less meaning and usefulness for control purposes.

SOLUTION A2

(a)   Variable: Fixed Cost Analysis Quarter IV

		Quarters I-III		Quarter IV	
		Fixed Cost	Variable/ Unit	Fixed Cost	Variable/ Unit
		£'000s	£	£'000s	£
	Quarter IV Calculations where x = Quarter I				
Material A	x + 20%		5		6
Material B			4		4
Labour	Fixed. x + 12½%	80	10	90	9
	Var. (x + 12½%) + 0.8				
Overheads	x + 20%	50	3	60	3
Depreciation		14		14	
Admin.					
Selling & Dist.	x + 20%	20	1		1

(b)   Flexible Budget - Production Costs
                              Quarter IV

	Production Level (units)			
	15000	18000	19000	21000
Costs £'000s				
Material A	90	108	114	126
Material B	60	72	76	84
Labour	225	252	261	*288
Factory Overheads	105	114	117	123
Depreciation	14	14	14	14
	494	560	582	635

*£90,000 + (21000 x £9) + (2000 x £4.50)

(c)   Profit Statement Quarter IV

Revenue & Costs £'000s	Activity Level (units)					
	15,000 (Low)		18,000 (Expected)		21,000 (High)	
Sales		600		720		840
less Production costs		494		560		635
		106		160		205
less Admin. costs	30		30		30	
S & D costs	39	69	42	72	45	75
= Profit		£37		£88		£130

Cash Flow Quarter IV
£'000s

	Activity					
	15000 units		18000 units		21000 units	
	£		£		£	
Cash Receipts						
From Q III Sales*		460		460		460
From Q IV Sales**		140		168		196
		600		628		656
Cash payments						
Production	480		546		621	
Admin.	30		30		30	
S & D	39	549	42	618	45	696
Net surplus or (Deficit)		51		10		(40)

*Cash from Q III Sales

			£
Month 7	30% of £200,000	=	60,000
8	100% of £200,000	=	200,000
9	100% of £200,000	=	200,000
			£460,000

**Cash from Q IV Sales
ie 70% of sales

		£
15,000 units = 70% x £200,000 =		140,000
18,000 units = 70% x £240,000 =		168,000
21,000 units = 70% x £280,000 =		196,000

(c) (ii)   Because of the accruals convention upon which accounting profits are calculated the profits show an immediate relationship to the increase in sales. Because of lags in receiving the cash from debtors and the need to pay for production and other costs when incurred any increase in production and sales is bound to lead to a deterioration in the cash position.

SOLUTION A3

(a) All terms are described in the manual except aspiration level which is described below:

Aspiration Level
This is the level of performance incorporated in a budget which the budget-holder perceives as a realistic standard against which to measure success or failure. A budget will not be accepted if it is thought to contain an unrealistic level of performance.

(b) This can be taken directly from the manual.

Chapter 10

SOLUTION A1

Preliminary data required for performance statement.

For actual production of 500 units the standard cost should be

	£
Direct labour 7000 hrs @ £2	14,000
Direct Materials	
Tfrs from A, 1500 kg @ £9	13,500
Usage of material X, 2000 Kg @ £5	10,000
Variable overheads 7000 hrs @ £1	7,000
Fixed Overheads	
Directly incurred Budget	1,200
Recovered from actual production	1,500
Actual expenditure	1,600
Allocated Budget	3,200
Recovered from production	4,000
Actual allocation	2,900

Dept B Performance Report

Total Cost Variance

(std cost of actual production – actual cost)
(500 x £10 – £59,000) = **£900 ADVERSE**

Accounted for by the following variances:

Variances directly attributable to Department B

	ADV £	FAV £
LABOUR		
Wage rate (6500 x £2 – £14000)	1000	
Efficiency (7000 – 6500)£2		1000
Overall labour variance	**NIL**	
MATERIALS		
Material X		
Price (1900 x £5 – 11,500)	2000	
usage (2000 x 1900)£5		500
Transferred from A		
Usage (1500 – 1400)£9		900
Overall material variance	**600 ADV**	
VARIABLE OVERHEADS		
Expenditure (6500 x £1 – £8000)	1500	
Efficiency (7000 – 6500)£1		500
Overall variable overhead variance	**£1000 ADV**	

FIXED OVERHEADS
Manufacturing overheads
Volume (500 x £3) – £1200   300
Expenditure £1200 – £1600   400
Allocated overheads
Volume (500 x £8) – £3200   800

           Overall fixed overhead variance   £700 FAV

∴ Total variance attributable to Department B's own operations = £900 ADV

Variances not directly attributable to Dept B

Materials transferred
Price (1400 x £9 – £21,000)   8,400
Allocated fixed overheads
  Expenditure £3200 – 2900)   300

           Overall variances not attributable   £8,100 ADV

           Overall cost variance =   £9,000 ADV
              made up of
              Controllable variances   £900 ADV
              Uncontrollable variances   £8100 ADV

               =   £9000 ADV

Note: It is assumed that Department B has control over all items except the material transferred and allocated fixed overheads.

(b)   On the basis of the information provided and the reasonable assumptions made, the Production Manager's comment is unjustified as 90% of total variance appears to be outside Dept. B's control. In general it is not useful to mix controllable and non controllable items and the standard costing system would be improved and department B's management given better motivation if the non controllable items were not included in the department's results.

SOLUTION A2

(a)   This can largely be answered from the text. Note that the overriding consideration is whether the expected benefits from the investigation are larger than the expected costs. Judgement is always involved; there is no objective answer.

(b)   Accumulated variances reflect the difference between actual and standard costs. At the end of the period it is normal to try to relate the standard costs to actual cost by apportioning the variances (where significant) to the cost of goods sold, finished goods, stock and W-I-P in the proportion of these categories at the period end.

Where the variances are insignificant they are usually written off in the period end operating statement as part of the cost of goods sold.

Chapter 11

SOLUTION A1

(a) Traditional variances
Operating contribution variance
= Standard contribution on actual sales - actual contribution
= (£26 x 1000) - (£26 x 1000) = **NIL**

which can be analysed as follows:

Variances	FAV £	ADV £
Labour rate (£6 - £4) x 5800		11,600
Labour efficiency (6000 - 5800) x £4	800	
Material price (£9 - £5) x 10,800		43,200
Material usage (10,800 - 10,000) x £5		4,000
Sales Price (£158 - 100) x 1000	58,000	
	58,800	58,800

(b) Comparison of actual position and the original and revised budgets.

	Sales		Labour		Material A		Material B	
	Qty	Price £	Qty	Rate £	Qty	Price £	Qty	Price £
Original 'ex-ante' budget	1000	100	6000	4	10000	5	10000	6
Revised 'ex-post' budget	1000	165	6000	6.25	10000	8.50	10000	7
Actual results	1000	158	5800	6	10800	0	-	-

Planning and operational variances for year

		£
Original budgeted contribution		26,000
Planning variances		

See notes

		£	
1.	Sales price	65,000 FAV	
2.	Labour rate	13,500 ADV	
3.	Material price	20,000 ADV	
3.	Material price	15,000 ADV	16,500 FAV
	= Revised budgeted contribution		42,500
4.	Labour rate	1,450 FAV	
5.	Labour efficiency	1,250 FAV	
6.	Material price	5,400 ADV	
7.	Material usage	6,800 ADV	
8.	Sales price	7,000 ADV	16,500 ADV
	= Actual contribution		£26,000

Notes
1. Sales price (£165 - 100) x 100 = £65,000 FAV uncontrollable.
2. Labour rate (£6.25 - £4) x 6000 = £13,500 ADV uncontrollable.
3. Material price (£7 - £5) x 10,000 = £20,000 ADV uncontrollable.
    Material price (£8.50 - £7) x 10,000 = £15,000 ADV. This part of the variance was avoidable.
4. Labour rate (£6.25 - 6.00) x 5800 = £1,450 FAV controllable.
5. Labour efficiency (6000 - 5800) x £6.25 = £1,250 FAV controllable.
6. Material price (£9 - £8.50) x 10,800 = £5,400 ADV controllable.
7. Material usage (10800 - 10000) x £8.50 = £6,800 controllable.
8. Sales price (£165 - 158) x 1000 = £7,000 ADV controllable.

(c)   Comparison of material variances.

	Traditional £	Planning/Operational £
Uncontrollable planning variances		20,000 ADV
Avoidable planning variances		15,000 ADV
Total planning variance		35,000 ADV
Price variances	43,200 ADV	5,400 ADV
Usage variances	4,000 ADV	6,800 ADV
	£47,200 ADV	£47,200 ADV

The advantages and disadvantages can be taken from the chapter.

SOLUTION A2

The meanings of the two terms can be taken from the text.

Applications of the two techniques could include:

(i)   The use of zero based budgeting for service activities particularly those of an administrative nature, eg personnel, management accounting, public relations.

(ii)   Cost reduction programmes using O & M, work study and other techniques could be applied to any area but especially areas where costs are rising faster than activity levels or inflation.

To gain most benefit it is preferable that the techniques are used systematically perhaps choosing areas or functions in rotation.

There are various difficulties in their application. These include:

(a)   Difficulty of making long term cost reductions which are not detrimental to operations. Short term cost savings are relatively easily made but may be counter-productive, eg skimping on maintenance.

(b)   At some stage or other in the process there are subjective elements and value judgements, eg what is the 'worth' of creating a favourable image of the organisation in the eyes of the community?

Chapter 12

SOLUTION A1

(a)   (i)   The first step is to calculate any variances arising from the period's operations.

Total Sales (as given)	72,000 units		
Total production (as given)	112,000 units		
Actual labour costs			£
Jan, Feb, Mar, minimum applies (3 x 75,000)	=		225,000
April	=		107,500
May	=		115,000
June	=		107,500
July	=		100,000
			£655,000

Variances for period		£
Labour rate (112,000 x £5) – £655,000	=	95,000 ADV
Fixed overhead		
Directly incurred		
£(12,000 x 7) – (112,000 x 60p)	=	16,800 ADV
Allocated		
£(28000 x 7) – (112,000 x £1.4)	=	39,200 ADV
Total Fixed overhead variance		£56,000

The above information can be used to prepare a conventional operating statement thus:

Operating Statement for period Jan – July

			£
	Sales (72,000 @ £20)		1,440,000
less	Standard cost of sales (72,000 x £16)		1,152,000
	= Standard profit		288,000
less	Production variances		
	Labour	£95,000	
	Fixed overheads	56,000	151,000
	= Profit from production		137,000
less	Delivery costs		
	Fixed	£60,000	
	Variable (72,000 x £2)	144,000	204,000
	= Profit (loss) from trading		(67,000)
less	Administration overheads 7 x £25,000		175,000
	= Net profit (loss)		(£242,000)

(ii)

Incremental Benefit to Purcell Ltd

	£	£
Departmental loss as calculated		(242,000)
Add back items which are not incremental expenses		
to Purcell as a whole		
Delivery standing charges (6 x £8000)	48,000	
Fixed overheads (72,000 x £1.4)	100,800	
Fixed overheads variance (ie allocated)	39,200	
Allocated Admin. costs (£25,000 x 7)	175,000	363,000
∴ Incremental benefit to Purcell =		£121,000

Note, however, that the incremental **accounting profit** for Purcell as a whole will not be just £121,000 higher but will be £121,000 + £56,000 = £177,000 higher. This is because £1.4/unit, the allocated fixed overheads, will be carried forward to the next period contained within the stock valuation of the 40,000 units closing stock. This would not be the case if stocks were valued at standard marginal cost.

(b)

Cash Balance End of July

	£
Inflows	
Sales income	
February	80,000
March	120,000
April (£200,000 x 90%)	180,000
May (£280,000 x 60%)	168,000
	548,000

Outflows	£	
Labour	655,000	
Materials (120,000 x £7)	784,000	
Delivery costs (6 @ £2000 + 7200 @ £2)	156,000	
Variable Overheads	224,000	
Fixed Overheads	70,000	1,889,000

	£
	1,341,000 deficit

∴ Contrary to the hope of the Managing Director the proposed expansion will not provide any cash resources and will need considerable financing.

SOLUTION A2

(a) In general cost apportionment causes difficulties and is likely to show misleading results. The amount of costs apportioned depends on the methods used for apportionment and not on operational realities or efficiencies. Apportioned costs cannot have any motivational advantages and may act as a disincentive. These general points apply to each of the four purposes listed.

(b) In this context the theory of Games could encourage sections of the firm to achieve optimum collaboration and to avoid sub-optimality. This could be appropriate for, say, a central advertising campaign which might be cheaper or more effective than individual departmental campaigns. The savings would be shared among participants in such a way that each department would be satisfied, yet the overall organisation would achieve optimality. However, it is unlikely that the perfect knowledge of outcomes, probabilities and so on assumed in Game Theory would be available in practice.

SOLUTION A3

(a) Cost Estimated based on Opportunity Costs.

See Notes		£
	Direct material and components	
1	A: 2000 units at £20/unit	40,000
2	B: 200 units at £20/unit	4,000
	Other materials	12,500
3	Direct Labour	–
	Overheads	
4	Dept P. 200 hours @ £30/hour	6000
5	Dept Q. 400 hours @ £8	3,200
6	Estimating Department charges	–
7	Planning Department charges	–
		65,700

Notes

1. The opportunity cost is the replacement cost not the historical cost.

2. The opportunity cost is the price of the regularly used material for which B can be substituted.

3. The labour will be paid anyway so the opportunity cost is zero.

4. The use of Dept. P's processing time will preclude outside sales at £30 per hour.

5. Of Dept. Q's costs only £8 per hour are incremental.

6. All these costs are sunk costs and not relevant.

7. As there is 'surplus capacity' a reasonable assumption is that the Planning department's costs are fixed and will not alter.

(b) The relevance of opportunity cost can be taken directly from the chapter. The major practical problem is to ascertain the real opportunity costs as rarely will conventionally recorded costs be true opportunity costs. In the context of the question where it is assumed that selling prices will be set at opportunity cost plus a margin such selling prices may well show a paper loss if calculated by the accounting conventions depicted in the cost estimate in the question.

(c) This part of the question can be taken directly from the chapter.

SOLUTION A4

(a) *Cost Estimate Using Opportunity Costs*
Note

	Direct Material	**£**
1.	material X (Resale value)	20,000
2.	Material Y (Replacement cost)	13,000
3.	Bought in (estimated)	12,000
	Direct Labour	
4.	Skilled Staff	
	Variable Overhead (2720 x £2)	5,440
5.	Trainees	
	Variable Overhead (1250 @ 80p)	1,000
6.	Curing Press (Rental foregone)	2,000
7.	Sub-contract (estimated)	20,000
8.	Supervisory Staff (overtime)	1,000
9.	Estimating (sunk cost)	-
10.	Admin. (Fixed)	-
		75,640

All other labour costs will be paid whether or not contract is accepted so are not relevant.

(b) (i) Although not always easy to identify opportunity costs are the correct ones to use for decision making. Where common resources can be used for a variety of alternatives then ranking by, say contribution, will produce the correct decision without explicitly identifying opportunity costs. Where alternatives do not use common resources then opportunity costs should be identified.

(ii) Opportunity costs are not recorded in any accounting system and change from decision to decision. Cost control entails the comparison of actual and budget both of which are recorded. It would be infeasible to use opportunity costs for cost control.

SOLUTION A5

(a) Can be largely taken from the chapter. Note that ranking of all combinations of alternatives is sometimes a lengthy and expensive process. In principle the identification of opportunity costs is an essential part of decision making.

(b) Yes, fixed costs, as conventionally classified by accountants, can be relevant for decision making if they are avoidable. Sunk costs are irrelevant because they have already been spent and are therefore unalterable. If a cost is controllable or avoidable *in the future* then it is relevant for decision making however it is classified by accounting convention.

Chapter 13

SOLUTION A1

Virtually all of the answer to this question can be taken from the chapter.

Particular points on the various parts of the question

(a) Where sales and production volumes differ the problem of stock valuation occurs. Where stocks are valued at marginal cost, and this is constant, then conventional C-V-P analysis can be used but where the stock valuation is different (eg full cost including fixed and variable costs) then accounting profit is related to two factors, sales and production volumes, so that C-V-P analysis cannot be used.

(b) This is dealt with in the chapter especially in the section dealing with the Economists c.f. Accountant's view.

(c) Conventional C-V-P analysis assumes either a single product or a constant product mix or a constant mark up on variable cost. Accordingly basic C-V-P analysis cannot generally be used where the product mix changes. In such cases a more detailed, numeric analysis of each product, its C/S ratio and sales volume is necessary.

(d)　The conventional C-V-P model is deterministic and ignores risk and uncertainty. However it is feasible that instead of single values, bands or ranges could be used to represent the uncertainties and it is possible to extend C-V-P analysis in this way, but it obviously becomes somewhat cumbersome. There are various ways of showing the effects of risk and uncertainty ranging from simple methods such as expected value through statistical techniques based on the properties of distributions, to computer based simulation models.

In general C-V-P analysis has many limitations, as implied by the question, and it needs to be used with a full understanding of the somewhat sweeping assumptions upon which it is based.

Properly used, over operational ranges, it can provide useful insights.

SOLUTION A2

STATEMENT OF EXPECTED OUTCOMES
(all values in '000s)

Sales units	Sales £	Variable Costs £	Material Cost £	Fixed Cost £	Material Sales £	Profit £	P £	Expected Value £

Selling Price £15 – No materials contract

Sales units	Sales £	Variable Costs £	Material Cost £	Fixed Cost £	Material Sales £	Profit £	P £	Expected Value £
20	300	100	160	50	–	(10)	0.1	-1
30	450	150	240	50	–	10	0.6	6
40	600	200	320	50	–	30	0.3	9
								14

Selling Price £15 – Materials contract min. 40,000 Kg

Sales units	Sales £	Variable Costs £	Material Cost £	Fixed Cost £	Material Sales £	Profit £	P £	Expected Value £
20	300	100	150	50	–	0	0.1	0
30	450	150	225	50	–	25	0.6	15
40	600	200	300	50	–	50	0.3	15
								30

Selling Price £15 – Materials contract min. 60,000 Kg

Sales units	Sales £	Variable Costs £	Material Cost £	Fixed Cost £	Material Sales £	Profit £	P £	Expected Value £
20	300	100	210	50	40	(20)	0.2	-2
30	450	150	210	50	–	40	0.6	24
40	600	200	280	50	–	70	0.3	21
								43

Selling price £24 – No materials contract

Sales units	Sales £	Variable Costs £	Material Cost £	Fixed Cost £	Material Sales £	Profit £	P £	Expected Value £
8	192	40	64	160	–	-72	0.1	-7.2
16	384	80	128	160	–	16	0.3	4.8
20	480	100	160	160	–	60	0.3	18.0
24	576	120	192	160	–	104	0.3	31.2
								46.8

Selling Price £24 materials contract min. 40,000 Kg

Sales units	Sales £	Variable Costs £	Material Cost £	Fixed Cost £	Material Sales £	Profit £	P £	Expected Value £
8	192	40	150	160	48	-110	0.1	-11
16	384	80	150	160	12	6	0.3	1.8
20	480	100	150	160	–	70	0.3	21
24	576	120	180	160	–	116	0.3	34.8
								46.6

Selling Price £24 materials contract min. 60,000 Kg

Sales units	Sales £	Variable Costs £	Material Cost £	Fixed Cost £	Material Sales £	Profit £	P £	Expected Value £
8	192	40	210	160	88	-130	0.1	-13
16	384	80	210	160	56	-10	0.3	-3
20	480	100	210	160	40	50	0.3	15
24	576	120	210	160	18	104	0.3	31.2
								30.2

Note: The realisable values of the sales of excess material are calculated as follows:

	Less than 16,000 Kgs £	16,000 Kgs and above £
Sales Price	2.4	2.9
Less costs	0.9	0.9
= Realisable value Kg	£1.5	£2.0

(b) **Statement of 'Expected Values', 'Worst Outcomes' and 'Desirability'**

	Strategy		Expected Value £'000s	Worst Outcome £'000s	Desirability Factor (L + 3E)
	Price	Contract			
(i)	£15	None	14	–10	32
(ii)	£15	40,000 Kg	30	0	90
(iii)	£15	60,000 Kg	43	–20	109
(iv)	£24	None	46.8	–72	68.4
(v)	£24	40,000 Kg	46.6	–110	29.8
(vi)	£24	60,000 Kg	30.2	–130	–39.4

Best choices:

		'Expected Value'	Strategy (iv)
	Best	'Worst outcome'	Strategy (ii)
		Desirability factor	Strategy (iii)

(c) (i) Other relevant factors in making a decision are:

    (a) The accuracy of the forecasts and probabilities.
    (b) The relationship and interaction of the new product with existing products.
    (c) The ability and capacity of the factory.
    (d) The effect of the new product on the competition.

(ii) The various decision criteria cleverly illustrate the facets which may be important to a particular decision. The averaging process of expected value ignores the extreme values whilst the 'minimum worst outcome' (ie the minimax regret criterion) is a pessimistic measure which ignores the possibility of profit. The desirability formula is an attempt to combine the two attributes and whilst, of course, it can be criticised it is an attempt to make explicit the subjective nature of the decision making process.

SOLUTION A3

(a) The various limitations of breakeven charts can be taken directly from the manual.

(b) Typical of the violations of conventional assumptions which are likely and which could be incorporated are the following:

    (i) Curvi-linear variable cost functions.
    (ii) Curvi-linear revenue functions.
    (iii) Stepped fixed costs.
    (iv) Linear cost and revenues with differing slopes.
    (v) Multiple breakeven points.

SOLUTION A4

(a) A table of all possible results is required.

Demand £	P	Inflation Rate	P	Total Contribution £	Fixed Cost £	Profit (loss) £	Combined Probability
50,000	0.3	1%	0.1	30,300	40,060	(9760)	0.03
50,000	0.3	5%	0.5	31,500	40,300	(8800)	0.15
50,000	0.3	10%	0.4	33,000	40,600	(7600)	0.12
75,000	0.6	1%	0.1	45,450	40,060	5390	0.06
75,000	0.6	5%	0.5	47,250	40,300	6950	0.30
75,000	0.6	10%	0.4	49,500	40,600	8900	0.24
100,000	0.1	1%	0.1	60,600	40,060	20540	0.01
100,000	0.1	5%	0.5	63,000	40,300	22700	0.05
100,000	0.1	10%	0.4	66,000	40,600	25400	0.04
							1.00

$\therefore$ P ($\geqslant$ Break-even) = 1 − (0.03 + 0.15 + 0.12) = 70%
$\therefore$ P ($\geqslant$ £20,000 profit) = 0.01 + 0.05 + 0.04 = 0.1

(b) The analysis is oversimplified using discrete probabilities. Continuous probability distributions of demand and inflation sampled at random would produce a continuous probability distribution of profit and loss.

SOLUTION A5

(a) Can be answered directly from the chapter.

(b) As stated in the manual, this variance is simply a balancing value and has little or no practical significance.

Chapter 14

SOLUTION A1

(i) Cost per unit and 'cost plus' selling prices

	Labour Hour Based Absorption		Machine Hours Based Absorption	
	Product X £'000s	Product Y £'000s	Product X £'000s	Product Y £'000s
Direct Labour	200	280	200	280
Direct Materials	240	160	240	160
Directly attributable Fixed overheads	120	280	120	280
General Overheads*	240	480	640	80
Total Cost	800	1200	1200	800
Units produced	40,000	10,000	40,000	10,000
Cost per unit	£20	£120	£30	£80
Selling price (cost + 20%)	£24	£144	£36	£96

* The overhead absorption rate used is calculated as follows:

	Labour hours	Machine hours
Product X	40,000	160,000
Product Y	80,000	20,000
	120,000	180,000
Overheads	720,000	720,000
$\therefore$ F.O.A.R./hour	£6	£4

(ii) and (iii)

Closing Stock Values and Profit for First Year

	Labour Hour Based Absorption			Machine Hour Based Absorption		
	Product X	Product Y	Total	Product X	Product Y	Total
Cost/Unit (from (i))	£20	£120		£30	£80	
Price/Unit (from (i))	£24	£144		£36	£96	
∴ Sales Qty (000s)	36	7		18	Limited to 10 because of capacity	
	£'000s	£'000s	£'000s	£'000s	£'000s	£'000s
Sales	864	1008	1872	648	960	1608
Production Costs	800	1200	2000	1200	800	2000
less Closing Stock	80	360	440	660	0	660
= Cost of Sales	720	840	1560	540	800	1340
= Profit	144	168	312	108	160	268

(b) Differences in accounting conventions and the mechanical application of cost plus pricing together produce substantial differences in disclosed profits.

It will be seen that costs per unit and therefore prices, vary according to the volume of production and the method of overhead absorption.

This in turn affects sales volume and profit and it is clearly unsatisfactory that the arbitrary choice of the conventions to be adopted affect real results in this manner. This example clearly bring out the potential problems of cost plus pricing where demand and the reactions to price changes are not considered. It would be better for French to calculate the marginal cost of manufacture and, having regard to the demand schedule supplied and production capacity, set prices which maximise profit.

(c) Determination of optimum prices for X and Y in Year 1 where competitive prices in Year 2 are £30 for X and £130 for Y.

Because Year 2 factors are involved it is necessary to assess the relevant value of closing stock in Year 1. This value is not the conventional accounting valuation but the opportunity cost in the two circumstances specified.

Case (i) Year 2 demand below productive capacity
In such circumstances the only benefit arising is that any units carried forward will not have to be made in Year 2 thus saving their marginal costs of £11 and £44 respectively.

Case (ii) Year 2 demand in excess of production capacity
In such circumstances if units are not available, sales will be lost so that the benefits are the sales prices of £30 and £130 respectively.

It is declared policy to operate at maximum capacity in Year 1 (ie 40,000 X and 10,000 Y) which means that, with respect of this decision, all the costs of £2,000,000 are fixed so can be ignored. The only variables are the sales price and hence total revenue and the imputed opportunity costs of the closing stocks. Accordingly prices should be set which maximise the total of sales revenue + closing stock opportunity costs.

Product X – Year 1 prices (Production 40,000 units)

Selling Price Per Unit	Sales Quantity	Closing Stock Quantity	Sales Revenue	Case (i) Closing Stock Value @ £11	Case (i) Total Value	Case (ii) Closing Stock Value @ £30	Case (ii) Total Value
£			£'000s	£'000s	£'000s	£'000s	£'000s
24	36000	4000	864	44	908	120	984
30	32000	8000	960	88	*1048	240	1200
36	18000	22000	648	242	890	660	**1308
42	8000	32000	336	352	688	960	1296

* Optimum point for Case (i) ie £30 selling price
** Optimum point for CAse (ii) ie £36 selling price

Product Y Year 1 Prices (Production 10,000 units)

Selling Price Per Unit	Sales Quantity	Closing Stock Quantity	Sales Revenue	Case (i) Closing Stock Value @ £44	Case (i) Total Value	Case (ii) Closing Stock Value @ £130	Case (ii) Total Value
£			£'000s	£'000s	£'000s	£'000s	£'000s
96	10000	0	960	0	960	0	960
108	10000	0	1080	0	1080	0	1080
120	9000	1000	1080	44	1124	130	1210
132	8000	2000	1056	88	*1144	260	1316
144	7000	3000	1008	132	1140	390	1398
156	5000	5000	780	220	1000	650	**1430

* Optimum point for Case (i) ie £132 selling price
** Optimum point for Case (ii) ie £156 selling price

SOLUTION A2

(a) This can be taken directly from Chapter 2.

(b) Most of the argument can be taken from this chapter. Particular points to note are:

The cost figure produced using absorption costing includes all costs both fixed and variable which ensures that the recovery of all costs is considered in setting selling prices. By including a charge for the fixed resources used it can be argued that this is an attempt, albeit imperfect, to include the opportunity cost of finite, fixed resources.

On the other hand the cost figure produced is dependent on accounting conventions and can only be correct for one activity level and mix of products. To set prices, information is required on demand, the elasticity of demand, and the behaviour of costs in relation to changes in activity levels.

Chapter 16

SOLUTION A1

Tax effects Project 1

Year	1	2	3
	£'000	£'000	£'000
Incremental sales	840	1,840	2,176
Incremental op. costs	549	970	1,315
Taxable surplus	271	870	861
Tax @ 35%	95	304	301
Tax saving from incremental depreciation	175	131	98
Tax payable	(80)	173	203

Cash Flows Project 1

Year	1	2	3	4
	£'000	£'000	£'000	£'000
Cash flow (from above)	271	870	861	
Tax payable (from above)		80	(173)	(203)
Salvage value			750	
Balancing allowance effect				33
Net cash flow	271	950	1,438	(170)
PV @ 8%	251	814	1,142	(125)

∴ Project 1 NPV = £2,082,000 - 2,000,000 = £82,000

Tax Effects Project 2

Year	1	2	3
	£'000	£'000	£'000
Incremental sales	1,930	2,876	3,854
Incremental op. costs	1,380	1,820	2,160
Taxable surplus	550	1,056	1,694
Tax @ 35%	192	370	593
Tax saving from incremental depreciation	306	230	172
Tax payable	(114)	140	421

Cash Flows Project 2

Year	1	2	3	4
	£'000	£'000	£'000	£'000
Cash flows (from above)	550	1,056	1,694	
Tax payable (from above)		114	(140)	(421)
Salvage value			1,500	
Balancing allowance effect				(8)
Net cash flow	550	1,170	3,054	(429)
PV @ 8%	509	1,003	2,425	(315)
Total = £3,622				

∴ Project 2 NPV = 3,622,000 - 3,500,000 = £122,000

∴ Project 2 is the recommended project

Notes:

Balancing allowance cash flow effect

Project 1
(750 - (2,000 - 1,156)) @ 35%   =   33

Project 2
(1,500 - (3,500 - 2,032)) @ 35%   =   <u>8</u>

(b) Possible further information
  -    Any technical, social or other non-financial factors
  -    Accuracy/reliability of estimates
  -    Comparative riskiness of projects.

(c) New present value of Project 1

Year	1	2	3	4	5	
	271	950	1,438	77	(188)	(£'000)
PV @ 8%	251	814	1,142	57	(128)	

Total = 2,136

∴ Project 1 NPV = £2,136,000 - 2,000,000 = £136,000

∴ as Project 1 has the higher NPV it is now the preferred project.

Note

From the details given in the question Project 1 as shown above is the preferred project. However, if it was assumed that there were replacement type projects which would be repeated indefinitely then the correct comparison is between the annualised equivalents of the project, ie

Project 1 $\dfrac{136,000}{3.993}$ =   £34,060

Project 2 $\dfrac{122,000}{3.312}$ =   £36,836

Thus, given the assumption of indefinite repeatability, Project 2 would be chosen.

(d) Can be taken directly from the manual.

Chapter 17

SOLUTION A1

This should be recognised as a single period capital rationing problem where the projects are not mutually exclusive and, it must be assumed, not divisible.

The first step is to calculate the Project NPVs at 16%. As regular amounts are received yearly Table B (Annuity Factors) can be used. For guidance the EVPI for each project is calculated.

Project A

	£
PV of returns (72,400 x 3.685)	267,163
less investment	250,000
NPV =	17,163
EVPI =	0.069

Project B
PV of returns for 5 years commencing
after 1 year

= 30,00 x 3.274 x 0.862 =	84,666
less investment	70,000
NPV =	14,666
EVPI =	0.210

Project C

PV of returns (45000 x 2.246)	101,070
less investment	110,000
NPV =	-8,930
EVPI =	-0.08

Project D

PV of returns (57,000 x 4.344)	247,608
less investment	210,000
NPV =	37,608
EVPI =	0.179

Project E

PV of returns (70,000 x 2.798)	195,860
less investment	170,000
NPV =	25,860
EVPI =	0.152

Project F

PV of returns (36,000 x 4.039)	145,404
less investment	135,000
NPV =	£10,404
EVPI =	0.077

Project C does not meet the cost of capital and is therefore excluded.

The best combinations of projects needs to be found within the £600,000 capital limit. Guidance can be found by ranking in sequence of EVPI, ie

Project	EVPI	Cumulative Investment £	
B	0.210	70,000	
D	0.179	280,000	PORTFOLIO
E	0.152	450,000	OF
F	0.077	585,000	PROJECTS
A	0.069	835,000	

Thus it will be seen that, in this case, ranking by EVPI gives an optimal grouping producing a total NPV of £14,666 + 37,608 + 25,860 + 10,404 = **£88,538**

Note: Although in this example ranking by EVPI does produce the optimal solution it is NOT a generalised solution method for two constraint problems such as this, ie single period rationing and project indivisibility. For example if the amount of investment of F and A was reversed whilst keeping their EVPI's as calculated then the optimal solution would be BDEA, because of the capital restriction, which would not be in accordance with their EVPI's.

(b) There are many other factors to be considered in making any investment decision including:

(i) Project independence or interdependence.

(ii) Interaction of projects with existing operations.

(iii) Risk and uncertainty especially the aggregate portfolio risk.

(iv) Forecasting errors in such factors as incomes, wages, costs, inflation and so on.

(v) The timing or project commencements and incomes.

(vi) The future position regarding capital availability.

SOLUTION A2

Expected returns and risk

Project 1
Return % x Probability

Return*
Deviations x Probability

2	0.2	0.4	10.6 x 0.4	22.47
8	0.3	2.4	4.6 x 0.3	6.35
15	0.3	4.8	3.4 x 0.3	3.47
25	0.2	5.0	12.4 x 0.2	30.75
	Expected return	12.6%	Variance	63.04

*Estimated return – calculated expected return.

The corresponding results for the other projects are

	Expected return	Variance
Project 2	10.3%	11.42%
Project 3	9.7%	3.62%

These values are then used to find the average return and portfolio risk (σp) of all the combinations of projects, ie 1 and 2, 1 and 3, 2 and 3.

Combination Projects 1 and 2

$$\text{Average return} = \frac{12.6 + 10.3}{2} = 11.45\%$$

$$\sigma p = \sqrt{VaX^2 + Vb(1-X)^2 + 2X(1-X)COVab}$$

where a and b are projects in a two project portfolio (ie in this first combination projects 1 and 2)

σp	=	portfolio risk
Va	=	variance of project a
Vb	=	variance of project b
X	=	proportion of total investment invested in project a
COVab	=	covariance between projects a and b

For projects 1 and 2, covariance is:

Return deviations 1	x	Return deviations 2	x	Prob	=	Covariance
10.6	x	5.3	x	0.2	=	11.24
4.6	x	1.3	x	0.3	=	1.79
3.4	x	1.7	x	0.3	=	1.73
12.4	x	4.7	x	0.2	=	11.66
				= Covariance		26.42

$$\therefore \sigma p = \sqrt{63.04(0.5)^2 + 11.42(0.5)^2 + 2 \times 0.5 \times 0.5 \times 26.42}$$

$$= 5.64$$

Thus combination projects 1 and 2 has an average return of 11.45% and a risk factor (σp) of 5.64%. A similar process for the other combinations produces the summary below.

Project Combinations	Average Return	Risk
1 & 2	11.45	5.64
1 & 3	11.15	4.76
2 & 3	10	2.57

Thus 1 & 2 have the highest return but also the highest risk whilst 2 & 3 have a lower return but also a lower risk.

(b) The weaknesses are

- lack of reliable information

- the fact that only a limited number of combinations have been calculations, the relationships with other projects and existing operations are ignored.

(d) An alternative technique is the Capital Asset Pricing Model which is described in the chapter.

Chapter 18

SOLUTION A1

This can be answered directly from the chapter.

The various measures of profit should be defined and discussed and a detailed comparison made between ROCE and Residual Profit together with their strengths and weaknesses.

SOLUTION A2

Results for £30 transfer price

	A £'000	B £'000
Sales	3,000	1,250
Transfers	750	-
	3,750	1,250
Variable Costs	1,875	
Contribution	1,875	250
Fixed Costs	500	225
Profit	1,375	25
Divisional investment	6,625	1,250
Return on investment	20.75%	2%

It is apparent from the above that the £30 transfer price distorts the relative apparent position of the 2 divisions. Naturally it makes no difference to the overall real profitability of the company derived from outside sales.

The minimum transfer price that could be used is the marginal cost of Product I in Division A, ie £15. This would have the effect of transferring all the profit arising from internal transfers from Division A to Division B. This is shown below:

Results with £15 transfer price

	A £'000	B £'000
Sales	3,000	1,250
Transfers	375	-
	3,375	1,250
Variable costs	1,875	625
Contribution	1,500	625
Fixed costs	500	225
Profit	1,000	400
Investment	6,625	1,250
Return on investment	15%	32%

With the new branch office and a transfer price between the two extremes of £15 and £30, say £22.50, the position would be as follows:

	A	B
	£'000	£'000
Sales	3,000	1,500
Transfers	675	–
	3,675	1,500
Variable cost	1,950	975
Contribution	1,725	525
Fixed cost	500	275
	1,225	250
Investment	6,625	1,250
Return on investment	18¼%	20%

This transfer price helps to equalise the notional return for each division. This may have motivational effects but transfer prices are artificial concepts and care must be exercised to ensure that decisions are taken by each division which are in the best interest of the firm as a whole not just an individual division.

SOLUTION A3

X Y Division
Budgeted 1985 Income Statement

Notes			£
1.	External Sales		1,000,000
	Standard Cost of Sales	£	
2.	Direct Material	355,000	
3.	Direct Labour	105,000	
4.	Overheads	162,000	622,000
			378,000
5.	Selling and Distribution Expenses	28,000	
	Central Overhead	20,000	48,000
	Net Profit		330,000

$$\text{Budgeted rate of return} = \frac{330,000}{2,200,000} = 15\%$$

Notes

1. $\dfrac{100}{75} \times £750,000 = £1m$

2. $\dfrac{100}{110} \times (420,000 - 29,500) = £355,000$

3. $\dfrac{100}{110} \times (128,000 - 12,500) = £105,000$

4. $\dfrac{100}{110} \times (177,000 - 6,900 - 81,000) + 81,000 = £162,000$

Budget to Actual Profit Reconciliation

		£
Budgeted Profit		330,000
+ Volume Variance (≡ Fixed ohd carried forward in stock)		8,100
		338,100
Profit by other divisions on purchases from XY division	37,500	
less selling costs	7,000	30,500
Revised budget for actual sales/production		307,600
less unfavourable variances (itemised)		68,000
		239,600
add favourable spending variances		17,600
		257,200

$$\text{Actual rate of return} \quad \frac{257,200}{2,200,000} = 11.7\%$$

(b) ROI c.f. Residual Income. This can be taken from the manual.

SOLUTION A4

(a) In general whilst there are some theoretical arguments for the inclusion of interest in the conventional cost accounts this is never done on a routine basis. It would be impractical and expensive to try to include the effect of interest paid or imputed in normal cost accounts. If it was feasible it could be argued that the costs thus calculated would more nearly approach the economic concept of opportunity cost including the interest charge.

There are some circumstances where interest would appear in the accounts. For example; interest paid or received on a loan or lease, or as an agreed element in a cost plus contract.

(b) This is the arguments for and against Residual Income covered in the Chapter.

SOLUTION A5

This can be answered directly from the manual.

Chapter 19

SOLUTION A1

Analysis of profit shortfall of £12,000

Note				£
	Profit per planning budget			45,000
1	Less Sales Volume variances			4,000 ADV
				41,000
	Less Cost Variances			
2	Material	2,245	ADV	
3	Labour	925	ADV	
4	Variable Overheads	325	ADV	
5	Fixed Overheads	1,505	ADV	
6	Selling Overheads	3,000	ADV	8,000
		= Actual profit		£33,000

Notes:

1. External sales volume variance
   (actual - budget) x Std profit/unit.
   (10,000 - 12,000) x £4 = £8,000 ADV
   Internal sales volume variance
   (4,000 - 3,000) x £4 = 4,000 FAV = £4,000 ADV
   (The central charges, being notional, have been ignored).

2.   Material Variances.

Price

| Material A | 30,000m² x 0.01 | = | £300 FAV |
| Component B | 90,000 x 0.03 | = | £2,700 ADV |

Usage

Material A	2,000m² x 0.20	=	£400 ADV	
Component B	1,500 x 0.37	=	£555 FAV	
				£2,245 ADV

3.   Labour variances

Rate

| 4,250 hours @ 0.10 | = | £425 ADV | |

Efficiency

| 250 hours @ £2 | = | £500 ADV | £925 ADV |

4.   Variable overheads

Spending

| (4,250 x £3) – 12,325 | = | £425 FAV | |

Efficiency

| 250 hours @ £3 | = | £750 ADV | £325 ADV |

5.   Fixed Manufacturing Overheads

Spending

| 25,505 – (15,000 x £1.50) | = | £3,005 ADV | |

Volume

| 1,000 units @ £1.5 | = | £1,500 FAV | £1,505 ADV |

6.   Selling Overheads

Expenditure

| £13,000 – (9,600 + 10,000 x 0.20) | = | 1,400 ADV |

Volume (fixed portion only)

$$2,0000 \text{ units } x \ \frac{£9,600}{12,000} = \underline{1,600 \text{ ADV}} = \underline{£3,000 \text{ ADV}}$$

The usual reasons can be given for the variances. Note that the poor quality material although showing a favourable price variance apparently causes several unfavourable variances.

(b) It is administratively convenient to separate out price variances on purchase but this may give rise to unrealistic stock values and causes a mismatch between profits and activity, when actual and standard prices differ considerably.

(c) In conditions of perfect competition the market price is an ideal transfer price leading to goal congruence on the part of divisional management. In this example because of external transaction costs (the selling overheads) the transfer price has been reduced by £1, the average unit selling cost. However the actual marginal selling cost is on 20p per unit so that the Penbrock division will probably consider external sales to be more profitable than internal transfers. The position is more more complicated than indicated because, as pointed out in the manual, the organisational objectives will be maximised when the marginal cost is equal to the marginal revenue of the transferee division.

SOLUTION A2

(a) Without the discipline of a market price or revenue value there will always be problems of deciding upon a realistic performance indicator. Costs can usually be determined easily but the quality or effectiveness of the service can only be decided upon with difficulty. Users may be wasteful with a free service and the producers may be inefficient because of the lack of the yardstick of sales. There may be difficulties in determining a suitable cost unit but this is more related to the type of product or service than to its being free issue. A central computer service providing services free to various user departments would have difficulty in deciding upon a realistic and meaningful cost unit, because of the variety of work involved, but a central generating facility would use a unit of electricity as a cost unit. This would be unambiguous and simple.

(b) The main implication of contingency theories of management is that the accountant must be aware that there are no standard solutions to the problems of designing information systems. All systems must be designed to suit the individual organisation and even personalities.

SOLUTION A3

Division A
Contribution at alternative selling prices

Selling Price	£20	£30	£40
Variable costs	11	11	11
= Contribution/unit	9	19	29
Demand	15,000	10,000	5,000
Total contribution	£135,000	£190,000	£145,000

The above table shows the £30 price to be the most profitable and that cutting prices would not result in increased profits.

Division B
Contribution at alternative selling prices
(with existing transfer price)

Selling price	£80	£90	£100
Variable cost (incl transfer price)	68	68	68
= Contribution	12	22	32
Demand	7,200	5,000	2,800
Total contribution	£86,400	£110,000	£89,600

To maximise divisional profits the manager of B is using a price of £90 which is not optimal for the firm as a whole. Division A cannot sell any more externally without reducing profits so the product should be transferred to B at the marginal cost of £10. This would mean that Manager B would adjust his production and pricing policy so as to be optimal for both the division and the firm as a whole. This produces the following position.

Division B
Contribution at alternative selling prices
(with transfer price of £10)

Selling price	£80	£90	£100
Variable cost (incl transfer price)	49	49	49
= Contribution/unit	31	41	51
Demand	7,200	5,000	2,800
Total contribution	£223,200	£205,000	£142,800

Best price

Thus Division B should be earning £223,200 contribution but is operating with a selling price of £90 which produces a contribution of £205,000 for the firm as a whole (ie £95,000 for A and £110,000 for B). Thus the incorrect transfer price has reduced contribution by £18,200.

(b) A transfer price of £12 produces £2 per unit contribution for A and the following results for B.

Division B
Contribution at alternative selling prices

Selling price	£80	£90	£100
Variable cost (inc. £12 transfer price)	51	51	51
= Contribution/unit	29	39	49
Demand	7,200	5,000	2,800
Contribution	£208,800	£195,000	£137,200

The £80 selling price gives a contribution of £208,800 which is £98,800 (208,800 – 110,000) greater than the current figure.

Division A's profits include £14,400 (7,200 x £2) attributable to Internal Transfers which is £80,600 less than the current figure (£95,000 – 14,400). Thus the overall increase in company profits would be + £98,800 – £80,600 = £18,200.

Chapter 20

SOLUTION A1

(a) There are a number of problems with the existing costing system:

-   There is no distinction between fixed and variable costs in the absorption costing system used.

-   A plant wide absorption rate will mask genuine cost differences between the departments.

-   A labour hour rate is not likely to be so suitable for Dept X.

Profit on sales value is but one measure of profitability and it is incorrect to make judgements based on a single criterion (see the Ratio Pyramid for other useful measures).

(b) Improvements could include:

-   possible use of a marginal costing approach.

-   separate departmental absorption rates; one based on labour hours, one on machine hours.

-   clearly differentiated fixed and variable costs.

A profit centre approach would enable profitability of the two departments to be assessed provided that the problems associated with setting a suitable transfer price can be resolved.

Chapter 21

SOLUTION A1

There is little doubt that the growing use of computers and their dramatically reducing real cost will have significant impacts on the work of the management accountant and, of course, on other people in the organisation. Whilst the use of computers does not of itself alter the objectives and concepts of management accounting it is likely that the accountant's working methods and knowledge requirements will change considerably.

In the context of planning, computer assistance should enable many more options to be considered and revisions to be made much more frequently than is possible using manual methods. Relevant statistical aids, eg forecasting, simulation, uncertainty analysis, should be readily available so that there is the likelihood that planning will be carried out more systematically and will take account of more factors than previously possible. Alterations in the values of key factors (eg inflation and interest rates, material and labour costs, sales returns) can be input into the computer system and the effects noted and, where necessary, plans revised.

Typical of the challenges involved are the following:

(a) Gaining a good working knowledge of computers, data processing and systems analysis in order to extract maximum advantage from the use of the new technology.

(b) Understanding sufficient of appropriate statistical and operational research techniques to be able to know when their use will be most effective, how to present the right input data, and, most importantly, to be able to interpret the computer produced results.

(c) The management accountant must have sufficient knowledge and professionalism to resist the challenge of the new specialists associated with computers.

(d) The art of selectivity will become more challenging. Computers can produce large volumes of information which can swamp and mislead recipients. An important function will be to select but not censor.

(e) The management accountant will have to be aware of and deal with the behavioural problems which seem inevitably to be encountered when computer based systems are introduced.

Typical of the ways which computers may assist the planning tasks of the management accountant are the following:

(a) Access to a larger pool of data, ie the data base.
(b) Use of appropriate techniques already mentioned.
(c) Rapid revision of plans.
(d) Enables more experimentation with changes in key variables.
(e) Better co-ordination of plans and resources available.
(f) Automatic breakdown of plans and budgets into resource requirements.
(g) Better scheduling.

SOLUTION A2

(a) Sensitivity analysis is described in the manual and applied to cost/volume/profit analysis would involve the following.

1. Identify the factors which make up the problem and the elements contained in the factors, eg

Factor	Elements
Variable cost	Direct Material
	Direct Labour
	Variable overheads

2. Select one of the elements and alter its value in + and - increments.

3. Note the effect on the result of the problem.

4. Repeat steps 2 and 3 on all the elements.

Used in this way sensitivity analysis is a useful but limited technique as only one change is explored at a time and no probability is attached to any of the results.

With a computer based simulation exercise probability distributions would be specified for each of the factors, say variable cost, selling price, demand, fixed costs and so on. The computer would then select at random from each of the factors and produce an overall value for the total profit or contribution. This process would be repeated many times and a probability distribution built up of the required profit or contribution with an expected value (ie the mean) and the expected dispersion (ie the standard deviation).

Simulation enables a more realistic picture of likely outcomes to be obtained which reflects the underlying probabilities of the factors in the problem.

(b) Can be taken directly from the manual.

SOLUTION A3

(a) (i)   Sensitivity Analysis - this can be taken from the manual.

  (ii) Probabilistic Simulation.
        Simulation is the process of manipulating a model in order to observe the results obtained in differing conditions. In business and accounting this means inserting various input values and noting the effect on the result. Probabilistic Simulation enables the combined effect of a number of variables to be evaluated. The model needs to have probability distributions estimated or calculated for each of the relevant variables (sales, costs, demand, etc.) which are sampled in combinations using a random number generator. Each iteration of the simulation produces a value of the required output and repeated iterations enable a probability distribution of the output to be determined.

(b) The diagram of the budgetary process in Chapter 7 is a suitable basis for the flow chart required.

Diagram A3

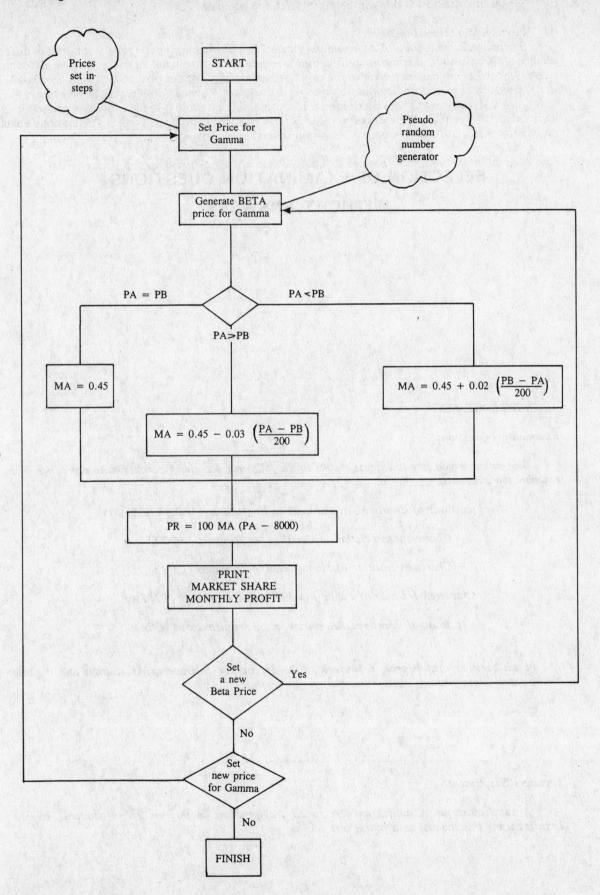

SELECTION OF EXAMINATION QUESTIONS
WITHOUT ANSWERS

ACKNOWLEDGEMENTS

Examination Questions

The author would like to express thanks to the following for giving permission to reproduce past examination questions:

Institute of Chartered Accountants in England and Wales (ICA)

Chartered Association of Certified Accountants (ACCA)

Chartered Institute of Management Accountants (CIMA)

Chartered Institute of Public Finance and Accountancy (CIPFA)

Institute of Chartered Secretaries and Administrators (ICSA)

Each question used is cross referenced to the appropriate Institute or Association and the title of the examination paper.

Lecturers Supplement

A supplement giving outline answers to all the questions in this section is available free to lecturers using this manual as a course text.

Chapter 2

EXAMINATION QUESTIONS WITHOUT ANSWERS

B1. *The following details are extracted from the books of the Alpha Construction Co Ltd in respect of two building contracts which they are currently undertaking.*

	X Development	Y Development
Value of Contract	£200,000	£100,000
Estimate period of contract	3 years	2 years
Date of Commencement	1.1.81	1.4.81
Retention	10%	15%
Balances b/fwd 1 April 1981	£	£
Cost of work not yet certified	7,000	
Plant on site at written down value	102,000	
Stock of materials on site	3,000	
Reserve of profit b/fwd	1,500	
Value of work certified to date	£38,000	
Less: Cash received	£34,200	
Retention money due from contractee	3,800	
Transactions during 1981-92:		
Materials delivered direct to site	23,860	12,270
Issues from stores	2,140	1,230
Plant sent to site	6,000	83,000
Wages	16,280	17,410
Overheads	8,400	8,090
Other expenses	2,320	2,000
Value of certificates issues	97,000	50,000
Cash received from contractee	87,300	41,000
Balances as at 31 March 1982 include:		
Cost of work not yet certified	8,000	3,000
Plant on site at written down value	73,000	65,000
Stock of materials on site	8,000	4,000

You are required to:

(a) prepare the contract account for the two contracts in columnar form as at 31 March 1982;

(b) show clearly your calculation of the profits to be taken in 1981/82;

(c) calculate the value of work in progress for inclusion in the Balance Sheet as at 31 March 1982 showing clearly the considerations you would have in mind when making such a calculation.

CIPFA, Management Accounting.

B2. *Your company produces specialised components to the specific requirements of its customers. A job costing system is in operation through which costs are allotted to cost centres and individual machine hour rates are then calculated and used for cost absorption purposes. A profit margin of 10 percent is added to the sum of all job costs but at the end of the year it has been found that the actual results show a profit-to-sales ratio of only two per cent. Write a report to the board explaining the investigations you propose to make and suggesting any procedures you consider desirable to monitor progress during the coming year.*

ICSA, Management Accounting.

B3. *An agricultural co-operative society, in addition to its warehouses and shops, operates fifty motor vans and lorries. At present all expenditure is accumulated for the entire fleet under the primary elements of cost.*

The managing director is concerned to find that the total expenditure on transport in the year ended 30th September, 1981 was 40% higher than in 1980. All other expenses of the society increased by about 18%. Total sales for 1981 were in line with those of 1980.

You are required to:

(a) state the reasons why the transport costs may have increased at a higher rate than other expenditure;

(b) outline a method by which the transport costs could be controlled; and

(c) provide a format for a monthly report on transport costs and productivity for an individual vehicle.

CIMA, Management Accounting 2.

B4. *An organisation has its own internal printing department. Initially the costs of this department were not charged to users. Three years ago the costs increased significantly when fast photocopying machines were introduced.*

In an effort to control the costs, management decided that the service request forms should be priced and the costs charged out to the five operating departments. This entailed the printing room staff recording the time taken to complete the job and details of the materials used. The costs are calculated in the accounting department. The user departments are coded on each slip and this is used to analyse costs by departments. The overall cost of the printing department staff and materials used is also calculated and used as a control check against the total of the individual items.

The work takes about 3 minutes for each service request form. Three accounting clerks are now used on the pricing and analysis. There are about 8,000 jobs a month averaging about £8 each. Of these 5% are recognised as major items and average about £46 each.

The management accountant believes that his manpower could be reduced by using a statistical cost allocation system. As his assistant you are required to prepare a memorandum for the operating department heads explaining:

(a) the basic idea of a statistical cost allocation;
(b) the way the statistical cost allocation would be undertaken;
(c) the degree of accuracy expected to be achieved, giving an example of a statistical cost allocation; and
(d) the savings in accounting manpower likely to be achieved if the statistical cost allocation were to be adopted.

CIMA, Management Accounting 2.

Chapter 3

EXAMINATION QUESTIONS WITHOUT ANSWERS

B1. *The A Division of SC Limited manufactures a single product which sells for £70 per unit. The following budgets have been prepared for the upper and lower levels of activity within which the division is likely to operate during the coming year:*

	Minimum level	Maximum level
Production (units)	11,000	22,000
	£	£
Manufacturing costs:		
Direct materials	264,000	528,000
Direct wages	209,000	418,000
Indirect wages	75,000	130,000
Maintenance and supplies	43,000	76,000
Depreciation	60,000	60,000
Sundry expenses	31,000	42,000
Selling and Distribution costs:		
Salaries and commissions	38,800	47,600
Advertising	32,000	54,000
Sundry expenses	19,000	30,000
Administration costs:		
Salaries	50,000	50,000
Sundry expenses	18,200	20,400

(a) Classify each of the cost items according to its character, ie variable, semi-variable and fixed, showing the basis of your classification in respect of semi-variable costs.

(b) Give calculations to show: (i) the break-even point for the Division in terms of units and sales value; (ii) the sales level and number of units to be sold in order to give a net profit before taxation of 5 per cent of sales.

(c) Show the additional sales value that would be required to justify expenditure of £5,000 per annum on additional clerical staff.

(d) Discuss the conditions that might cause cost behaviour patterns to vary from those which you have assumed in (a) above.

ICSA, Management Accounting.

B2. *Albatross Pty, the Australian subsidiary of a British packaging company, is preparing its budget for the year to 30th June 1080. In respect of fuel oil consumption it is desired to estimate an equation of the form* $y = a + bx$, *where 'y' is the total expense at an activity level 'x', 'a' is the fixed expense, and 'b' is the rate of variable cost.*

The following data relate to the year to 30th June 1979:

Year	Month	Machine Hours (000)	Fuel Oil Expense ($)	Year	Month	Machine Hours (000)	Fuel Oil Expenses ($)
1978	July	34	640	1979	January	26	500
	August	30	620		February	26	500
	September	34	620		March	31	530
	October	39	590		April	35	550
	November	42	500		May	43	580
	December	32	530		June	48	680

The annual total and monthly average figures for 1978/79 were as follows:

	Machine Hours (000)	Fuel Oil Expense ($)
Annual total	420	6,840
Monthly average	35	570

You are required to:

(a) estimate fixed and variable elements of fuel oil expense from the above data by both of the following methods:

   (i)   high and low points
   (ii) 'least squares' regression analysis

(b) compare briefly the methods used in (a) above in relation to the task of estimating fixed and variable elements of a semi-variable cost.

(c) accepting that the co-efficient of determination (r^2) *arising from the data given in the question is approximately 0.25, interpret the significance of this fact.*

ICA, Management Accounting.

Chapter 4

EXAMINATION QUESTIONS WITHOUT ANSWERS

B1. *You have recently been appointed the assistant management accountant of an organisation having middle management employees with various line and functional responsibilities.*

A considerable number of management accounting reports are issued but few of these are widely used by the executives. The first task you have been asked to undertaken, in your new position, is a review of these reports.

To assist in your review, you are required initially to prepare two lists indicating way in which generally:

(a) a report **format** *might be designed to have maximum impact, and*
(b) a report's **content** *might be presented to motivate the recipient to take effective action.*

CIMA, Management Accounting 2.

Chapter 7

EXAMINATION QUESTIONS WITHOUT ANSWERS

B1. *For a company making one product you are required to produce:*

(a) *the budgeted production requirement (in units) for each of the months of March, April and May;*
(b) *the budgeted purchased requirements of raw materials (in units) for each of the months of March and April;*
(c) *the budgeted profit and loss statement for April;*
(d) *the cash forecast for April.*

The following data are available as at 1st March:

1. *Budgeted Sales:*

	units
March	180,000
April	240,000
May	250,000
June	230,000

The selling price is £2 per unit.

   Sales are invoiced twice per month, in the middle of the month and on the last day of the month. Terms are 2% for 10 days and net 30 days. Sales are made evenly through the month and 50% of sales are paid within the discount period. The remaining amounts are paid within the 30-day period except for bad debts which average ½% of gross sales. Estimated cash discounts and bad debts are treated as deductions from sales in the company's profit and loss statements.

2. *Stocks of finished goods were 36,000 units on 1st March. The company's rule is that stock of finished goods at the end of each month should represent 20% of their budgeted sales for the following month. No work-in-progress is held.*

3. *Stocks of raw materials were 45,600 kilogrammes on 1st March. The company's rule is that, at the end of each month, a minimum of 40% of the following month's production requirements of raw materials should be in stock. Payment for raw materials are to be made in the month following purchase, and materials can only be bought in lots of 40,000 kilogrammes or multiples thereof.*

4. *The standard production cost of the product, based on a normal monthly production of 230,000 units, is:*

	Cost per unit £
Direct materials (¼ kilogramme per unit)	0.50
Direct wages	0.40
Variable overhead	0.20
Fixed overhead	0.10
Total	£1.20

   Fixed overhead includes £8,000 per month depreciation on production plant and machinery. Any volume variance is included in cost of sales.

5. *Production salaries and wages are paid during the month in which they are incurred.*

6. *Selling expenses are estimated at 10% of gross sales. Administration expenses are £60,000 per month of which £800 per month relates to depreciation of office equipment. Selling and administration expenses and all production overhead are paid in the month following that in which they are incurred.*

7. *The cash balance is expected to be £12,000 on 1st April.*

CIMA, Management Accounting 1.

B2. (a) *Explain the advantages and limitations of using flexible budgets in a manufacturing concern and comment upon the relevance of cost behaviour patterns in using this technique.*

(b) *The following table shows the budget for direct costs of a manufacturing company for an eight week period at various levels of activity.*

Units to be produced	11,000	12,000	13,000	14,000
Estimated costs	£	£	£	£
Labour	8,800	9,600	10,600	11,600
Materials	17,600	19,200	20,800	22,400

Notes:
- Variable overheads are estimated at 30% of direct costs.
- Fixed overheads are estimated at £1,500 per week.
- Labour costs increase by 25% for production levels in excess of 1,500 units per week.

The following actual information becomes available at the end of the period.

Production 12,400 units

Costs per unit:		£
Labour		0.80
Materials		1.55
Overheads	– Variable	0.71
	– Fixed	1.00

You are required to:

(i) produce a schedule for general management comparing actual costs incurred with the flexed budget, showing any variations'

(ii) comment briefly upon the manufacturing performance for the period.

CIPFA, Management Accounting.

B3. The Glenarm Carpet Co Ltd produces three grades of carpet, Standard, Super and De luxe. All grades are made from a special fibre imported directly from the sole supplier in the Far East. As a result of recent events, supplies of the fibre have been disrupted and it now seems likely that the company wil be unable to obtain more than half of its normal requirements in the coming year. The budget for the coming year had been prepared based on the following information provided by sales and production staff:

		Grade of Carpet			
		Standard	Super	De luxe	Total
Units sold (Estimate)		14,000	8,000	9,000	31,000
		£'000	£'000	£'000	£'000
Material		56	22	64	142
Wages		12	20	25	57
Overheads	– fixed	15	10	10	35
	– variable	10	11	7	28
Total Cost		93	63	106	262
Sales		120	80	138	338
Profit		£27	£17	£32	£76

(a) Advise the board on the best mix of products to market for the coming year in the light of the restricted availability of the special fibre. (Assuming no reduction in fixed costs and variable costs reduced in proportion to production level.)

(b) Prepare a revised budget for the coming year on the basis of the advice given above.

(c) Subsequently the company received an enquiry from a customer seeking 3,000 units of the De luxe grade carpet, for which the customer was willing to pay 25% more than the budget price. Advise the board on the course of action to be followed.

CIPFA, Management Accounting.

Chapter 8

EXAMINATION QUESTION WITHOUT ANSWER

B1. *The principles underlying managerial control systems such as budgetary control and stock control are conventionally identified with the principles upon which physical control systems are based, for example, a governor in an engine or a thermostat in a heating system. However, managerial control systems are so different from physical systems and there are so many operational difficulties that any similarity between the two types of system is very slight.*

You are required to:

(a) describe the control principles referred to in the first part of the statement;

(b) discuss whether or not you agree with the proposition in the second part of the statement.

CIMA, *Management Information Systems and Data Processing*

Chapter 9

EXAMINATION QUESTIONS WITHOUT ANSWERS

B1. *The trustees of a public hall have produced the followed budget for the year commencing 1st July 1981:*

	£'000
Income:	
Lettings at £250 a day	75
Franchise payment: bar/restaurant	10
car park	2
	87

	£'000	
Expenses:		
Administrative staff	10	
Operating staff	30	
Repairs and renewals	30	
Heating and lighting	8	
General expenses	2	
Maintenance reserve	5	
Financing charges	20	
		105
Loss		18

Letting reservations have been made as under:

	days
Exhibitions	75
Conference and meetings	105
Theatrical shows	60
Sporting events	60
	300

The 300 days is the maximum letting time available in the year.

Since preparing the budget, the treasurer to the trustees has approached the various organisations with hall reservations and all except the theatrical shows have now agreed to an increase of 10% in the letting fee. Also after negotiations, in addition to their franchise fees, the bar/restaurant operator has agreed to pay 1% of his gross takings and the car park operator a sliding scale fee as under:

Parking on any day	Extra fee per car pence
For the first 500 cars	Nil
For the next 500 cars	5
For the next 500 cars	6
For any additional cars	7

In the discussions, the theatrical show managers stated that they were near a point of financial balance and could not accept a higher charge. Also they considered there should be a differential charging system as their shows run for 6 days at a time and caused less work and expense other than bookings.

An investigation has shown the following facts to be relevant to the problem.

Administrative staff	50% full-time and 50% variable with attendances.
Operating staff	40% full-time and 60% variable with attendances.
Repairs and renewals	70% labour cost, of which 60% is variable with attendances; 30% material cost, all of which is fixed.
Heat and light	20% fixed and 80% variable.

All other expenses are fixed costs.

	Average attendance per day	Ratio cars to attendance	Average bar/ restaurant purchase per attendance/ day
			£
Exhibitions	4,000	0.4	0.30
Conferences and meetings	900	0.8	8.00
Theatrical shows	1,000	0.4	1.50
Sporting events	1,500	0.5	2.00

There is a clause in the trust deed requiring that lettings to any of the four groups should be within limits of 10% and 45% of the total days available. The contracts for the bar/restaurant and car park franchise are both in the fifth year of seven-year contracts at fixed amounts.

The relative usage of the variable elements of services provided is as follows:

	Per daily usage			
	Admin staff	Operating staff	Repairs & renewals	Heat and light
Exhibitions	5	5	3	7
Conferences and meetings	2	1	1	1
Theatrical shows	1	3	2.5	3
Sporting events	5	4	2	3.5

You are required, from the information given, to:

(a) calculate a revised budget for the year distinguishing between fixed and variable items;
(b) prepare a profitability statement for each of the four letting groups;
(c) calculating a differential daily letting fee for each group based on the revised budget;
(d) comment briefly on the assertion of the theatrical show managers that their letting fees should be the lowest;
(e) state the percentage of lettings to each group, within the limitations set, which would maximise profit for the year;
(f) indicate one aspect of the present financial arrangements which you believe requires further investigation giving reasons for your choice.

Work to nearest £100 in apportionments and to nearest £1 in daily rates.

CIMA Management Accounting 2.

B2. *The effective use of the control information provided by an organisation's accounting department might be reduced by the behaviour of its operating managers.*

> *(a) Explain briefly six motivations or attitudes that would result in less effective use of the control information.*
> *(b) Indicate very briefly what actions the accounting department might take to improve the situation.*

CIMA, Management Accounting 1.

B3. *The behavioural aspects of budgeting are as important as the accounting techniques – discuss.*

CIPFA, Management Accounting.

Chapter 10

EXAMINATION QUESTIONS WITHOUT ANSWERS

B1. *The Trucadero Motor Company produces identical lorries in two separate plants. The following information which relates to the body undersealing sections of the two plants is for the four week period ending 30 September 1981:*

> *(a) Common data relating to estimated standard performance etc for this period:*
>
> > *(i) Each lorry should be undersealed using 8 gallons of Type A material and 6 gallons of Type B material (the materials are not mixed before undersealing).*
> >
> > *(ii) The standard cost of Type A material is £3 per gallon and Type B material £4 per gallon. The materials are purchased through separate local companies in the areas of each plant.*
> >
> > *(iii) The company's standard performance for labour is that the undersealing of vehicles should involve 2 man hours per vehicle at an hourly rate of £4 inclusive.*
>
> *(b) the actual performance for the four week period was as follows:*

		Plant "Y"	Plant "Z"
Lorries undersealed		1,500	1,850
Underseal used	- Material A	12,500 galls	14,600 galls
	- Material B	9.500 galls	10,900 galls
Cost of underseal	- Material A	£37,250	£47,450
	- Material B	£36,860	£46,870
Labour hours worked		3,200	4,400
Labour costs		£12,640	£18,700

From the foregoing information:

> *(a) prepare a report for management showing the performance of the two undersealing sections against the standards laid down, identifying the variances from the standards.*
>
> *(b) comment on the possible causes for the variances and suggest possible action which may be necessary to improve the situation.*
>
> *(c) briefly outline the importance of careful monitoring in an efficient system of standard costing.*

CIPFA, Management Accounting.

B2. *(a) From three raw materials, (Gorgon, Camem and Stil) VLS manufactures a single cosmetic product called Eau de Vie. The standard mix of materials for one batch of output of Eau de Vie is as follows:*

				£
Gorgon	100 fl.oz. at	£15.00 per oz.	=	1,500
Camem	200 fl.oz. at	£7.15 per oz.	=	1,430
Stil	700 fl.oz. at	£0.10 per oz.	=	70
	1,000	£3.00		£3,000

Each batch should produce a standard output of Eau de Vie sufficient to fill five hundred bottles.

During June one hundred batches of materials were processed, producing enough Eau de Vie to fill forty-five thousand bottles. The actual consumption and cost of the materials were as follows:

				£
Gorgon	8,000 fl.oz. at	£19.00 per oz.	=	152,000
Camem	20,000 fl.oz. at	£6.85 per oz.	=	137,000
Stil	80,000 fl.oz. at	£0.10 per oz.	=	8,000
	108,000	£2.75		£297,000

Venuti, Lang and South are partners in VLS. Venuti has been working out the standard cost variances for materials in June. He has calculated inter alia that the total variance was £27,000 ADV, the mix variance was £29,000 FAV, and the yield variance was £30,000 ADV. However, he felt unsure of his methods of calculation, and asked Lang to make check calculations of the variances independently.

Lang agreed with Venuti's figures for the total cost and yield variances, but calculated the mix variance to be £53,000 FAV. South was therefore asked to check both sets of calculations, again working independently.

After a few minutes of work South said that he agreed that the total cost variance was £27,000 ADV, and that he agreed with Lang that the mix variance was £53,000 FAV; however, he calculated the yield variance to be £54,000 ADV.

You are required to calculate the total cost, price, quantity, mix and yield variances (including all workings) as they have probably been worked out by each of

(i) Lang and
(ii) South

(b) You are required to comment on the significance of mix and yield variances, using the figures from part (a) to illustrate your answer if you wish.

(c) In many process operations:

(i) price variances for materials are isolated when the materials are purchased and placed in inventory, and not at the time of usage, and

(ii) only the total batch input of materials is measured, any deviations from the standard mix being accidental and unmeasured.

Assume now that these conditions applied at VLS in June.

You are required to calculate the variance which would be measurable for the month of June, and to suggest how in practice the partners might seek to establish the cause of the variance.

ICA, Management Accounting.

B3. *A company has contracted to machine 20,000 castings in the year 1981. The machine shop budget which includes this work is based on operating for 50 weeks of 40 hours each. The normal standard for the company is set to allow a 90% labour utilisation. This particular job was estimated to need four ideal standard hours of labour at £3 per hour.*

As the work involves new technology the expected standard used in the estimate was based on normal standard but allowed additionally for 5% of finished castings to be rejected on final inspection. Of these 3% could be reworked in an average 20% of original machine time and would then be usable. The balance would be scrapped incurring a penalty of £6 per casting. Sufficient manpower was allowed to complete 400 castings per week on the basis of the expected standard.

The company operates a time recording system and the paid hours are obtained from the time clock records. In addition the machinists record the direct time spent on the machining operations on job cards. In the period since 1st January the paid hours have averaged 44 per week. The extra four hours are paid at a premium rate of time and one-half. The job cards showed an average of 32 hours per week on the direct machine operations. Of the initial output 7% have been rejected with 4% subsequently reworked, using an average 25% of original machine time each. No analysis is maintained of the time paid but not utilised on direct machining.

You are required from the information given:

A.   *to calculate:*

   (a)   the average manpower in the 1981 budget for this contract;

   (b)   for each good machined casting produced the number of direct labour hours needed and the cost incurred based on:
   (i)   normal standard,
   (ii)   expected standard, and
   (iii) current actual rate;

   (c)   the number of good machined castings which will be completed in the first 25 weeks if the current actual rate continues throughout;

   (d)   the average manpower needed in the second 25 weeks to complete the contract if the expected standard was achieved throughout that period;

   (e)   the additional cost incurred in 1981 on the contract, over that originally estimated, assuming that the first 25 weeks continue at the current actual rate, and that in the second 25 weeks the expected standard is achieved, but the hourly rate increases to £3.20.

B.   *to outline briefly a procedure you would advocate to analyse and control the difference between the paid hours and the direct labour hours utilised.*

CIMA, Management Accounting 2.

Chapter 11

EXAMINATION QUESTIONS WITHOUT ANSWERS

B1. *Explain:*

   (a) the problems concerning control of operations that a manufacturing company can be expected to experience in using a standard costing system during periods of rapid inflation;

   (b) three methods by which the company could try to overcome the problems to which you have referred in answer to (a) above, indicating the shortcomings of each method.

CIMA, Management Accounting 1.

B2. *A firm produces a plastic feedstock using a process form of manufacture. The firm operates in an industry where the market price fluctuates and the firm adjusts output levels, period by period, in an attempt to maximise profit which is its objective. Standard costing is used in the factory and the following information is available.*

Process 2 received input from process 1 and, after processing, transfers the output to finished goods. For a given period, the opening work-in-progress for process 2 was 600 barrels which had the following values:

	Value £	Percentage complete
Input material (from process 1)	3,000	100
Process 2 material introduced	6,000	50
Process 2 labour	1,800	30
Process 2 overhead	2,700	30
	£13,500	

During the period, 3,700 barrels were received from process 1 and at the end of the period, the closing work-in-progress was at the following stages of completion:

	Percentage completion
Input material	100
Process 2 material introduced	50
Process 2 labour	40
Process 2 overhead	40

The following standard variable costs have been established for process 2:

	Standard variable cost per barrel £
Input material *(standard cost process 1)*	5
Process 2 material	20
Labour	10
Overhead	15
	£50

During the period, actual costs for process 2 were

	£
Material	79,500
Labour	39,150
Overhead	60,200
	£178,850

In addition you are advised that the following theoretical functions have been derived:

Total cost (£) = 100,000 + 20 Q + 0.005 Q²
Price per barrel (£) = 76 - 0.002 Q

where Q represents the number of barrels.

You are required to

(a) determine the theoretical production level which will maximise profit;

(b) prepare the process 2 account assuming that the calculated production level is achieved;

(c) prepare the accounts for process 2 material, labour and overhead showing clearly the variance in each account.

CIMA, Management Accounting Techniques.

Chapter 12

EXAMINATION QUESTIONS WITHOUT ANSWERS

B1. *"Opportunity costs are not recorded in management accounts but they have an important bearing on decision making." Explain this statement and contrast opportunity cost concepts with incremental or marginal costing.*

ICSA, Management Accounting.

B2. *Butterfield Ltd manufactures a single brand of dog-food called 'Lots O'Grissle' (LOG). Sales have stabilised for several years at a level of £20 million per annum at current prices. This level is not expected to change in the foreseeable future (except as indicated below). It is well below the capacity of the plant. The managing director, Mr Rover, is considering how to stimulate growth in the company's turnover and profits. After rejecting all of the alternative possibilities that he can imagine, or that have been suggested to him, he is reviewing a proposal to introduce a new luxury dog-food product. It would be called 'Before Eight Mince' (BEM), and would have a recommended retail price of 50p per tin. It would require no new investment, and would incur no additional fixed costs.*

Mr Rover has decided that he will undertake this new development only if he can anticipate that it will at least break-even in the first year of operations.

(a) Mr Rover estimates that BEM has a 75% chance of gaining acceptance in the market-place. His best estimate is that if the product gains acceptance it will have sales in 1981 of £3.2 million at retail prices, giving a contribution of £1 million after meeting the variable costs of manufacture and distribution. If, on the other hand, the product fails to gain acceptance, sales in 1981 will, he thinks, be only £800,000 at retail prices, and for various reasons there would be a negative contribution of £400,000 in that year.

You are required to show whether, on the basis of these preliminary estimates, Mr Rover should give the BEM project further consideration.

(b) Mr Rover discusses the new project informally with his sales director, Mr Khoo Chee Khoo, who suggests that some of the sales achieved from the new product would cause lost sales of LOG. In terms of retail values he estimates the likelihood of this as follows:

There is a 50% chance that sales of LOG will fall by half of the sales of BEM.
There is a 25% chance that sales of LOG will fall by one-quarter of the sales of BEM.
There is a 25% chance that sales of LOG will fall by three-quarters of the sales of BEM.

The contribution margin ratio of LOG is 25% at all relevant levels of sales and output.

You are required to show whether, after accepting these further estimates, Mr Rover should give the BEM project further consideration.

(c) Mr Rover wonders also whether, before attempting to proceed any further, he should have some market research undertaken. He approaches Delphi Associates, a firm of market research consultants for whom he has a high regard. On previous occasions he has found them to be always right in their forecasts, and he considers that their advice will give him as near perfect information as it is possible to get. He decides to ask Delphi to advise him only on whether or not BEM will gain acceptance in the market-place in the sense in which he has defined it; he will back Mr Khoo Chee Khoo's judgements about the effects of the introduction of BEM on the sales of LOG. If Delphi advise him that the product will not be accepted he will not proceeds further. Delphi have told him that their fee for this work would be £100,000.

You are required to show whether Mr Rover should instruct Delphi Associates to carry out the market research proposals.

(d) Preliminary discussions with Delphi suggest that Delphi's forecast will not be entirely reliable. They believe that, if they indicate that BEM will gain acceptance, there is only a 90% chance that they will be right; and, if they indicate failure to gain acceptance, there is only a 70% chance that they will be right. This implies a 75% chance overall that Delphi will indicate acceptance, in line with Mr Rover's estimate.

You are required to show the maximum amount that Mr Rover should be prepared to pay Delphi to undertake the market research, given the new estimates of the reliability of their advice.

(e) You are required to outline briefly the strengths and limitations of your methods of analysis in (a) - (d) above.

ICA, Management Accounting.

B3. *For the past 20 years a charity organisation has held an annual dinner and dance with the primary intention of raising funds.*

This year there is concern that an economic recession may adversely affect both the number of persons attending the function and the advertising space that will be sold in the programme published for the occasion.

Based on past experience and current prices and quotations, it is expected that the following costs and revenues will apply for the function:

			£
Costs:	Dinner and Dance:	Hire of Premises	700
		Band and entertainers	2,800
		Raffle prizes	800
		Photographer	200
		Food at £12 per person (with a guarantee of 400 persons minimum)	
	Programme:	A fixed cost of £2,000, plus £5 per page	
Revenues:	Dinner and dance:	Price of tickets	£20 per person
		Average revenue from:	
		Raffle	£5 per person
		Photographs	£1 per person
	Programme:	Average revenue from advertising	£70 per page

A sub-committee, formed to examine more closely the likely outcome of the function, discovered the following from previous records and accounts:

No of tickets sold	No of past occasions
250 to 349	4
350 to 449	6
450 to 549	8
550 to 649	2
	20

No of programme pages sold	No of past occasions
24	4
32	8
40	6
48	2
	20

Several members of the sub-committee are in favour of using a market research consultant to carry out a quick enquiry into the likely number of tickets and the likely number of pages of advertising space that would be sold for this year's dinner dance.

You are required to:

(a) calculate the expected value of the profit to be earned from the dinner and dance this year;

(b) recommend, with relevant supporting financial and cost date, whether or not the charity should spend £500 on the market research enquiry and indicate the possible benefits the enquiry could provide.

NB: All workings for tickets should be in steps of 100 tickets and for advertising in steps of 8 pages.

CIMA, Management Accounting 1.

B4. *The Ruddle Co Ltd has planned to instal and, with effect from next April, commence operating sophisticated machinery for the production of a new product - product Zed. However the supplier of the machinery has just announced that delivery of the machinery will be delayed by six months and this will mean that Ruddle will not now be able to undertake production using that machinery until October.*

'The first six months of production' stated the commercial manager of Ruddle 'is particularly crucial as we have already contracted to supply several national supermarket groups with whatever quantities of Zed they require during that period at a price of £40 per unit. Their demand is, at this stage, uncertain but would have been well within the capacity of the permanent machinery we were to have installed. The best estimates of the total demand for the first period are thought to be:

Estimated demand – first 6 months

Quantity–Units	Probability
(000's)	
10	0.5
14	0.3
16	0.2

'Whatever the level of demand, we are going to meet it in full even if it means operating at a loss for the first half year. Therefore I suggest we consider the possibility of hiring equipment on which temporary production can take place.' Details of the only machines which could be hired are:

	Machine		
	A	*B*	*C*
Productive capacity per six month period – units	*10,000*	*12,000*	*16,000*
Variable production cost for each unit produced	*£6.5*	*£6*	*£5*
Other 'fixed' costs – total for six months	*£320,000*	*£350,000*	*£400,000*

In addition to the above costs there will be a variable material cost of £5 per unit. For purchases greater than 10,000 units a discount of 20% per unit will be given, but this only applies to the excess over 10,000 units.

Should production capacity be less than demand then Ruddle could subcontract production of up to 6,000 units but would be required to supply raw materials. Subcontracting costs are:

up to 4,000 units subcontracted – £30 per unit
any excess over 4,000 units subcontracted – £35 per unit.

These subcontracting costs relate only to the work carried out by the subcontractor and exclude the costs of raw materials.

The commercial manager makes the following further points 'Due to the lead time required for setting up production, the choice of which machine to hire must be made before the precise demand is known. However demand will be known in time for production to be scheduled so that an equal number of units can be produced each month. We will, of course, only produce sufficient to meet demand'.

We need to decide which machine to hire. However, I wonder whether it would be worthwhile seeking the assistance of a firm of market researchers? Their reputation suggests that they are very accurate and they may be able to inform us whether demand is to be 10, 14 or 16 thousand units'.

Required:

(a) For each of the three machines which could be hired show the possible monetary outcomes and, using expected values, advise Ruddle on its best course of action.

(b) (i) Calculate the maximum amount which it would be worthwhile to pay to the firm of market researchers to ascertain details of demand. (You are required to assume that the market researchers will produce an absolutely accurate forecast and that demand will be exactly equal to one of the three demand figures given.)

(ii) Comment on the view that as perfect information is never obtainable the calculation of the expected value of perfect information is not worthwhile. Briefly explain any uses such a calculation may have.

Ignore taxation and the time value of money.

ACCA, Management Accounting.

Chapter 13

EXAMINATION QUESTIONS WITHOUT ANSWERS

B1. *(a)* *A break-even chart is depicted below for Windhurst Ltd.*

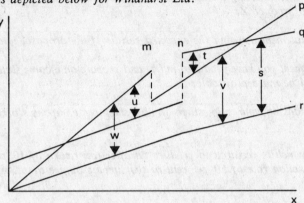

You are required:

(i) *to identify the components of the break-even chart labelled, p,q,r,s,t,u,v,w,x and y*

(ii) *to suggest what events are represented at the values of x which are labelled m and n on the chart*

(iii) *to assess the usefulness of break-even analysis to the senior management of a small company*

(b) *Hackett Ltd produces gudgeons and bludgeons. The company's budget for 1981 includes the following data:*

	Gudgeons	Bludgeons
Unit Selling price	£10	£5
Contribution margin ratio	40%	60%

The budget is designed to show a figure of profit or loss for each product, after apportioning joint fixed costs of £100,000 in proportion to the number of units of each product sold. For 1981 gudgeons are budgeted to show a profit of £14,000 and bludgeons a loss of £2,000. The number of units of each product sold is expected to be equal.

You are required to write a report to the managing director of Hackett Ltd advising him on the basis of the information given whether to implement any of the following three proposals:

(i) *to increase the price of bludgeons by 25% in the expectation that the price elasticity of demand over this range of prices will be unity*

(ii) *to make changes to the production process which would reduce the joint fixed costs by 12¼% and increase the variable costs of each product by 10%*

(iii) *to introduce both of the above changes*

ICA, Management Accounting.

B2. *CD Ltd manufactures three products, X, Y and Z. Standard selling prices and costs have been established for 1981 as follows:*

	Per unit		
	X	Y	Z
	£	£	£
Selling price	28	60	125
Direct materials	8	15	20
Direct wages	10	20	50
Variable overheads	5	10	25

Direct wages are paid at the rate of £2 per hour in each case. Fixed overheads are budgeted at £25,000 for the coming year.

In the short term the company cannot increase its direct labour force and as a result only 35,000 direct labour hours will be available in the coming year. The company has commitments to produce 500 units of each product.

It has been suggested that after meeting the minimum requirements for X, Y and Z, the balance of available direct labour hours should be used to produce Z:

(a) prepare an income statement showing the expected results if the proposal is adopted;

(b) comment on the statement you have produced in (a) and prepare an income statement for any alternative policy which you consider would be more profitable;

(c) basing your calculations on your suggestions in (b), show the company's break-even point in terms of units and sales value;

(d) show the sale value which is required to produce an after-tax return of 10 per cent on capital employed of £100,000, assuming a taxation rate of 50 per cent of the surplus before taxation.

ICSA, Management Accounting.

B3. *(a) XY Limited is to quote for contract No. 1701 to supply 10,000 units of a certain product to a large group with branches throughout the country.*

It knows that the group will accept the lowest bid and, from past experience and good intelligence within the industry, estimates the following probabilities of bids at various levels (in multiples of £5 only).

Price bid £	Probability of bids at that price
45	0.05
50	0.10
55	0.20
60	0.25
65	0.25
70	0.10
75	0.05
	1.00

XY Limited's out-of-pocket costs for these items are £32 per unit.

You are required to calculated the price XY Limited should bid for this contract if it wishes to obtain the contract and maximise its profit margin.

(b) In arriving at its out-of-pocket costs, XY Limited has estimated an amount per unit for servicing the items for one year as required by the terms of No. 1701 contract.

If it obtains the contract there are a number of ways in which it can satisfy this servicing requirement:

1. To sub-contract to AB Limited which is willing to undertake the work in all areas or any individual area and has quoted:

Area	No. of units to be serviced under the contract	Price quoted £
North	3,000	18,000
South	4,500	20,000
Midland	2,500	11,500

2. *For South area only, to sub-contract to CD Limited which has quoted £18,000 plus a charge for service calls above a certain level.*

These charges and the assessed probability of their occurrence are:

Calls made	CD Limited charge £	Probability of occurrence
750 or fewer	Nil	0.40
751 – 900	900	0.30
901 – 1,050	2,200	0.20
1,051 or more	3,500	0.10
		1.00

3. *For Midland area only, it can use its own organisation, but would need to take on extra staff.*

The cost of this staff and the probability of needing each level of extra staff are assessed as:

Cost of extra staff £	Probability of needing that level
4,500	0.20
7,000	0.35
11,000	0.45
	1.00

If sub-contractors are used, they will buy spares from XY Limited at an average price of £2 per unit to be serviced.

The out-of-pocket costs of these spares to XY Limited is £1.50 per unit.

You are required to calculate which combination of servicing arrangements will involve XY Limited in the minimum cost. (Assume that the quality of all servicing is comparable and acceptable).

CIMA Management Accounting 1.

B4. *L Johnson trades as a chandler at the Savoy Marina. His profit in this business during the year to 30th June 1981 was £12,000. Johnson also undertakes occasional contracts to build pleasure cruisers, and is considering the price at which to bid for the contract to build the* **Blue Blood** *for Mr B W Dunn, delivery to be in one year's time. He has no other contract in hand, or under consideration, for at least the next few months.*

Johnson expects that if he undertakes the contract he would devote one-quarter of his time to it. To facilitate this he would employ G Harrison, an unqualified practitioner, to undertake his bookkeeping and other paper-work, at a cost of £2,000.

He would also have to employ on the contract one supervisor at a cost of £11,000 and two craftsmen at a cost of £8,800 each; these costs include Johnson's normal apportionment of the fixed overheads of his business at the rate of 10% of labour cost.

During spells of bad weather one of the craftsmen could be employed for the equivalent of up to three months full-time during the winter in maintenance and painting work in the chandler's business. He would use materials costing £1,000. Johnson already has two inclusive quotations from jobbing builders for this maintenance and painting work, one for £2,500 and the other for £3,500, the work to start immediately.

The equipment which would be used on the **Blue Blood** *contract was bought nine years ago for £21,000. Depreciation has been written off on a straight-line basis, assuming a ten-year life and a scrap value of £1,000. The current replacement cost of similar new equipment is £60,000, and is expected to be £66,000 in one year's time. Johnson has recently been offered £6,000 for the equipment, and considers that in a year's time he would have little difficulty in obtaining £3,000 for it. The plant is useful to Johnson only for contract work.*

In order to build the **Blue Blood** *Johnson will need six types of materials, as follows:*

Material	No of units		Price per unit (£)		
Code	In stock	Needed for contract	Purchase price of stock items	Current purchase price	Current resale price
A	100	1,000	1.00	3.00	2.00
B	1,100	1,000	2.00	0.90	1.00
C	–	100	–	6.00	–
D	100	200	4.00	3.00	2.00
E	50,000	5,000	0.18	0.20	0.25
F	1,000	3,000	0.90	2.00	1.00

Materials B and E are sold regularly in the chandler's business. Material A could be sold to a local sculptor, if not used for the contract. Materials A and E can be used for other purposes, such as property maintenance. Johnson has no other use for materials D and F, the stocks of which are obsolete.

The **Blue Blood** *would be built in a yard held on a lease with four years remaining at a fixed annual rental of £5,000. It would occupy half of this yard, which is useful to Johnson only for contract work.*

Johnson anticipates that the direct expenses of the contract, other than those noted above, would be £6,500.

Johnson has recently been offered a one-year appointment at a fee of £15,000 to manage a boat-building firm on the Isle of Wight. If he accepted the offer he would be unable to take on the contract to build **Blue Blood**, *or any other contract. He would have to employ a manager to run the chandler's business at an annual cost (including fidelity insurance) of £10,000, and would incur additional living costs of £2,000.*

You are required:

(a) to calculate the price at which Johnson should be willing to take on the contract in order to break even, based exclusively on the information given above, and

(b) to set out any further considerations which you think that Johnson should take into account in setting the price at which he would tender for the contract.

Ignore taxation.

ICA, Management Accounting.

Chapter 14

EXAMINATION QUESTIONS WITHOUT ANSWERS

B1. *(a) Some businesses which supply two or more markets from a single source charge a higher price for sales to the home market than for export sales. They may justify this pricing policy by saying that they need to recover their research and development costs, plus production overheads, against home demand.*

You are required to explain briefly the rationale for such a differential pricing policy and to comment critically on it.

(b) The Jackass Motor Company of Ruritania has just developed a new motor car called the Midi which it is planning to launch in the near future. The home market in Ruritania is highly competitive, and prices are low by international standards. In contrast, the neighbouring country of Lusitania tends to have much higher car prices. These are largely the consequence of Lusitanian Government efforts to assist the relatively inefficient domestic motor industry in Lusitania. Government regulations have been imposed in both countries, for reasons of safety, which makes it impossible for anyone other than a motor manufacturer to import or export cars between the two markets. It would be quite possible therefore for Jackass to charge different prices in the two markets if it considered it profitable to do so. Market research has indicated that demand functions for the two countries are likely to be:

Ruritania: Price (£) = 4,940 − 0.05Q, and
Lusitania: Price (£) = 6,000 − 0.10Q

where Q represents monthly sales quantities.

Jackass's single plant is close to the border between the two countries, so that its costs are unaffected by any decision to switch car supplies from one market to the other. its total cost function for Midi production has been estimated as:

$$Total\ cost\ (£) = 50\ million + 2{,}000Q + 0.01Q^2$$

where Q again represents monthly quantities.

All Lusitanian sales prices have been converted back in Ruritanian pounds. The two countries have a fixed exchange rate, and Jackass's decisions will not be affected by taxation considerations. Jackass seeks to maximise its profits.

You are required to:

(i) calculate Jackass's monthly profit or loss if it confines its sales solely to its home market of Ruritania.

(ii) calculate the monthly profit or loss should it decide to sell in both Ruritania and Lusitania, and

(iii)   set out and explain the changes in both price and monthly quantity sold in Ruritania, and in total monthly profits or losses of Jackass, by comparing your answers to (i) and (ii) above.

ICA, Management Accounting.

B2. *(a) Outline the use and relevance of marginal costing in pricing decisions.*

(b) The L.C.D. Entertainment Group is about to launch a new product, which it is anticipated will have a fairly short selling life. They have carried out a thorough market survey and have produced the following assessment of the relationship between selling price and likely demand.

Price £	Quantity (units)
24	10,000
22	20,000
20	50,000
18	100,000
17	150,000
16	250,000
15	350,000

Plant capacity for this product is limited to 150,000 units. Fixed costs for the product ar projected at £400,000 and variable costs at £14.00 per unit.

(i)   Calculate the optimum price that will maximise income and the forecast profit at that level. discuss the viability of the product.

(ii)   It is estimated that the use of television in the advertising campaign will add £400,000 to fixed costs and lead to an alteration in the selling price/demand relationship to the following:

Price £	Quantity (units)
24	60,000
22	120,000
20	280,000
18	600,000
17	1,000,000
16	1,600,000

Determine whether or not the use of television would alter the conclusion you reached in (i) above on the viability of the product.

CIPFA, Management Accounting.

B3. *"In providing information to the product manager, the accountant must recognise that decision-making is essentially a process of choosing between competing alternatives, each with its own combination of income and costs; and that the relevant concepts to employ are future incremental costs and revenues and opportunity cost, not full cost which includes past or sunk costs." (Sizer, 1975)*

Descriptive studies of pricing decisions taken in practice have, on the other hand suggested that inclusion of overhead and joint cost allocations in unit product costs is widespread in connection with the provision of information for this class of decision. Furthermore these costs are essentially historic costs.

You are required to:

(a) explain the reasoning underlying the above quotation

(b) suggest reasons why overhead and joint cost allocation is nevertheless widely used in practice in connection with information for pricing decision, and

(c) set out your own views as to the balance of these arguments.

ICA, Management Accounting.

Chapter 15

EXAMINATION QUESTIONS WITHOUT ANSWERS

B1. *Riverside Processors plc recycles by-products from nearby industrial sites. It produces two products, Ackney and Boylle. The current level of production is 100 tonnes of each product per week but there remains some unused production capacity.*

Due to restrictions on the availability of an essential ingredient, Zalium, the maximum weekly output of Ackney is 150 tonnes. Furthermore the effluent from the production of Ackney is acid, but is neutralised by effluent from the production of Boylle; as a matter of policy, Riverside restricts the production of Ackney to not more than twice the production of Boylle.

The production process of each of the products requires heat, fuelled by gas. However, Riverside is restricted in the quantity of gas it can use, the maximum being 30,000 therms per week. The production of one tonne of either product requires 10 therms of gas. The production process of both Ackney and Boylle incorporates filtration, and the capacity of the filtration plant is limited to 1,750 labour hours per week in normal operation. The production of one tonne of Ackney requires 7 labour hours of filtration, and of one tonne of Boylle, 5 labour hours.

The company is test marketing a new product, Spotz; this requires neither additional process heat nor filtration, although it incorporates the scarce material, Zalium, which is also used in the production of Ackney. The following cost and revenue data are available concerning the three products (in £s per tonne):

	Ackney (actual)	Boylle (actual)	Spotz (estimated)
Variable cost:			
Input materials			
Zalium (one unit)	27	–	27
Other	10	48	25
Labour			
Filtration plant	28	20	1
Other	30	29	40
Process heat	20	20	–
Total variable costs	115	117	92
Selling price	171	137	130

The company's fixed costs £10,000 per week.

You are required

(a) assuming that the new product, Spotz, is not produced, to:

(i)   show the feasible outputs of Ackney and Boylle, and to calculate the optimal production plan for Riverside Processors plc

(ii) calculate the shadow prices of Zalium, filtration plant labour, and process heat for the optimal production plan which you have calculated in (i) above, and

(iii) calculate the maximum extra quantity of Zalium (in addition to the 150 units which are available at £27 per unit) which the company should be willing to buy if it could be imported at a price of £50 per unit and if filtration plant throughput cannot be increased, and

(b) assuming that the test marketing campaign for Spotz is successful in demonstrating a sufficient demand at the proposed selling price, and also assuming that no imported Zalium is obtainable, to:

(i)   calculate the shadow price of Zalium, and
(ii) calculate the optimum contribution which Riverside Processors plc can then earn

ICA, Management Accounting.

B2. *Brass Ltd produces two products, the Masso and the Russo. Budgeted data relating to these products on a unit basis for August 1980 are as follows:*

	Masso £	Russo £
Selling price	150	100
Materials	80	30
Salesmen's commission	30	20

Each unit of product incurs costs of machining and assembly. The total capacity available in August 1980 is budgeted to be 700 hours of machining and 1,000 hours of assembly, the cost of this capacity being fixed at £7,000 and £10,000 respectively for the month, whatever the level of usage made of it.

The number of hours required in each of these departments to complete one unit of output is as follows:

	Masso	Russo
Machining	1.0	2.0
Assembly	2.5	2.0

Under the terms of special controls recently introduced by the Government in accordance with EEC requirements, selling prices are fixed and the maximum permitted output of their product in August is 400 units (ie Brass Ltd may produce a maximum of 800 units of product). At the present controlled selling prices the demand for the products exceeds this considerably.

You are required:

(a) to calculate Brass Ltd's optimal production plan for August 1980, and the profit earned

(b) to calculate the value to Brass Ltd of an independent marginal increase in the available capacity for each of the machining and assembly, assuming that the capacity of the other department is not altered and the output maxima continue to apply, and

(c) to state the principal assumptions underlying your calculations in (a) and (b) above, and to assess their general significance.

ICA, Management Accounting.

Chapter 16

EXAMINATION QUESTIONS WITHOUT ANSWERS

B1. *Using the information given below:*

(a) Prepare tables showing the net present value of each project based on target rates of 6%; 9%; 12%; 15%.

(b) Plot the above results for the two projects on a single graph and read off the internal rate of return of each project.

(c) State a rate of return when project B is preferred to project A and suggest the reason for this.

	Project A	Project B
Initial investment	£100,000	£100,000
Net cash saving:		
Year 1	£5,000	£60,000
Year 2	£20,000	£40,000
Year 3	£100,000	£100,000
Year 4	£10,000	£5,000

Present value of £1

Rate	6%	9%	12%	15%
at end of Year 1	.94	.92	.89	.87
Year 2	.89	.84	.80	.76
Year 3	.84	.77	.71	.66
Year 4	.79	.71	.64	.57

CIPFA, Management Accounting.

B2. *(a)* *Annio Ltd is considering whether to invest in a new machine costing £60,000. The machine is expected to have a five year life, at the end of which time it will have a zero scrap value. Use of the machine will allow Annio Ltd to lay off immediately one supervisor currently earning £10,000 per annum, and to reduce its other overheads by £6,000 per annum at current prices. Annio Ltd expects to pay salary increases to all its supervisory labour in the future at an annual compound rate of 5%, and estimates that its bill for overheads will rise at an annual compound rate of 10%.*

Annio Ltd's financing policy is to maintain a constant debt/equity ratio, and as part of this overall policy the directors have decided to finance the cost of the machine either by negotiating a loan of £60,000, or by obtaining a lease for the life of the machine. The loan would run for five years and would incur annual interest payments of £9,258, which represent an effective after-tax interest rate of 8%. The lease would cost £15,000 per annum payable in advance.

Annio Ltd obtains corporation tax relief at 52% on its costs one year after they arise and expects such relief to continue indefinitely. A 100% first year tax allowance is available on this type of machine. Annio Ltd has a weighted average cost of capital, net of corporation tax, of 15% per annum.

Unless stated, you may assume that all cash flows arise on the last day of the year to which they relate.

You are required, as chief accountant, to prepare a report for the directors of Annio Ltd showing:

(i)   whether the investment in the machine is worthwhile
(ii) which financing alternative is to be preferred.

(b) You are required to explain the reasons for the recent growth in leasing as a method of financing new investment.

Ignore advance corporation tax.

ICA, Financial Management.

B3. *Due to the financial failure of an overseas competitor, a company sees the opportunity of taking up immediately a market for its product of 325,000 tonnes per annum which is forecast to rise at 9% per annum. Sales revenue is expected to be £8 per tonne ex plant.*

The company proposed to go into this market immediately and considers the methods of supply involving the import from elsewhere, the hiring of plant locally, and the construction of new plant.

Details are as follows:
- *Import from elsewhere*
  It could import up to a maximum of 500,000 tonnes per annum of the product at an average cost of £7.5 per tonne at the plant.

- *Hire of plant locally*
  It could hire plant capacity of 500,000 tonnes per annum at a nearby site. This is available immediately.

  The terms of the hiring are £1.2 per tonne of capacity for a minimum of 12 years, with the plant owner being responsible for any variable operating costs. Direct material costs of £6 per tonne would be payable by the company.

- *Construction of new plant*
  It could build a plant with an effective capacity of 500,000 tonnes per annum which will be completed in three years. In the meantime, requirements may be imported.

You are required, from the information given, to:

(a) *prepare a decision tree of the options open to the company;*

(b) *decide on a net present value (NPV) basis which option is the most attractive financially'*

(c) *calculate for the option chosen under (b) above:*

(i) *the discounted cash flow (DCF) rate; and*

(ii) *the accounting rate of return on capital employed (ROCE) for the years one to eight using a year-end net investment basis assuming no re-investment of funds; and*

(d) *comment briefly on the results.*

You may ignore the effects of taxation and inflation in your calculations.

CIMA, Management Accounting 2.

B3. *You have been appointed as chief management accountant of a well-established company with a brief to improve the quality of information supplied for management decision-making. As a first task you have decided to examine the system used for providing information for capital investment decision. You find that discounted cash flow techniques are used but in a mechanical fashion with no apparent understanding of the figures produced. The most recent example of an investment appraisal produced by the accounting department showed a positive Net Present Value of £35,000 for a five-year life project when discounted at 14% which you are informed 'was the rate charged on the bank loan raised to finance the investment'. You note that the appraisal did not include any consideration of the effects of inflation nor was there any form of risk analysis.*

You are required to:

(a) *explain the meaning of a positive Net Present Value of £35,000;*

(b) *comment on the appropriateness or otherwise of the discounting rate used;*

(c) *state whether you agree with the treatment of inflation and, if not, explain how you would deal with inflation in investment appraisals;*

(d) *explain what is meant by 'risk analysis' and describe ways this could be carried out in investment appraisals and what benefits (if any) this would bring.*

CIMA, Management Accounting Techniques.

Chapter 18

EXAMINATION QUESTIONS WITHOUT ANSWERS

B1. *A long-established, highly centralised, company has grown to the extent that its chief executive, despite having a good supporting team, is finding difficulty in keeping up with the many decisions of importance in the company.*

Consideration is therefore being given to re-organising the company into profit centres. These would be product divisions, headed by a divisional managing director, who would be responsible for all the division's activities relating to its products.

You are required to explain in outline:

(a) *the types of decision areas that should be transferred to the new divisional managing directors if such a re-organisation is to achieve its objectives;*

(b) *the types of decision areas that might reasonably be retained at company head office;*

(c) *the management accounting problems that might be expected to arise in introducing effective profit centre control.*

CIMA, Management Accounting 1.

B2. *A group wishes to evaluate two companies in the same industry on the basis of their return on capital employed.*

The following data are available on the two companies since their formation:

| £000 | Year | Additions to fixed assets | | Average working capital | Sales | Profits (after Depreci-ation) |
		Factory premises	Plant and machinery			
PQ Limited	1973	120 (a)	90 (a)	60	210	40
	1974	–	24	75	250	50
	1975	–	15	80	280	65
	1976	30	45	90	300	75
	1977	–	30	110	370	90
	1978	–	24	120	410	120
	1979	–	42	120	480	140
RS Limited	1976	–	300 (a)	140	430	85
	1977	–	45	145	580	105
	1978	–	30	150	680	130
	1979	–	60	160	770	170
		(a) = Initial purchase				

The following additional data are given:

1. *Charges for depreciation on plant and machinery are on the following bases:*

PQ Limited   *33⅓% on the reducing balance for three years with the remainder charged in the fourth year.*
RS Limited   *Straight line method over five years.*

All plant and machinery is disposed of at the end of its life at nil realisable value.

2. *The market value of PQ Limited's factory is estimated as having increased in value by 15% per annum.*

RS Limited uses rented factory space and is on an agreement to pay £40,000 per annum, rising by 25% after three years.

The group normally capitalises rented accommodation on the basis of a 12½% return.

3. *Both companies carried out an advertising campaign costing £30,000 in 1977.*

PQ Limited spread the cost over three years while RS Limited charged it all to the year in which the expenditure was incurred.

4. *The price level index for plant and machinery in this industry is as follows:*

End of year	Index
1972	90
1973	100
1974	115
1975	130
1976	150
1977	175
1978	200
1979	220

Assume that all purchases and additions were made at the beginning of the year.

You are required for the year 1979 to:

(a) (i) Calculate the return on capital employed (ROCE) for PQ Limited and for RS Limited based on book values.
(ii) Split these ROCE into their asset usage and sales profitability components.

(b) Calculate the ROCE for:
(i) PQ Limited after revision of its fixed asset values;
(ii) RS Limited after bringing its accounting treatment into line with that used by PQ Limited and/or that normally used by the group.

(c) Split (b)(i) and (b)(ii) above into their asset usage and sales profitability components.

(d) Comment briefly on the results shown by (b) and (c) above.

NB. All ROCE calculations are to be based on year-end values and all workings should be to the nearest £1,000.

CIMA, Management Accounting 1.

B3. *Minnow Limited has been formed with capital of £50,000 in cash to manufacture a new design of office cabinet. The firm will acquire a five-year lease of premises at an initial cost of £10,000 and a monthly rental of £300. Plant and equipment will be depreciated on a straight line basis over a ten-year period and vehicles over four years, no residual values being anticipated.*

A forecast of sales and production for the first year has been made as follows:

	Units	
	Production	Sales
1st quarter	400	300
2nd quarter	500	450
3rd quarter	600	600
4th quarter	750	750

An initial stock of materials and parts, sufficient for 300 units, will be required. The stock will be maintained at this level. Costs are estimated to be as follows:

	Per unit £
Direct wages	30
Materials and parts	25
Variable overheads	15

Fixed overheads (excluding depreciation, rent and amortisation of the lease) are budgeted to be £30,000 in the year.

The sales price will be £100 per unit.
Sales and production will be spread evenly over each quarter.
Stocks of finished goods will be valued at variable cost.
Debtors will be allowed one month's credit and creditors will allow two months.

Required:
(a) The budgeted quarterly trading results and balance sheets for the first year. Ignore taxation. State any assumptions made.

(b) Comment on the results with particular reference to profitability and return on capital.

(c) Explain and comment on any alternative basis for the valuation of finished goods.

ICSA, Management Accounting.

B4. *You have been asked to evaluate the performance of a department store in a retail group. The quality of the store's merchandise is fairly high and its image with its clientele is largely based on the interdependence of the merchandise in its different departments.*

The four departments are Garden Equipment (GE); Dining Furniture (DF); DIY Decorating Products (DIY); Crockery and Glassware (CG).

The following data have been prepared by the store accountant for the year ended 31 October 1987.

	Basis of apportionment	GE £000	DF £000	DIY £000	CG £000	Total £000
Sales	Actual	1,240	900	600	560	3,300
Gross margin	Actual	440	450	200	280	1,370
Direct costs:						
Supervision	Actual	15	20	20	25	80
Sales staff	Actual	135	216	81	108	540
Advertising	Actual	12	6	8	14	40
		162	242	109	147	660
Gross contribution		278	208	91	133	710
Costs apportioned:						
Rent and rates	Floor space at £4 per sq ft	30	48	18	24	120
Heat and light	Weighted floor space	10	12	3	10	35
		40	60	21	34	155
Net contribution		238	148	70	99	555
Other overhead	Sales	83	60	40	37	220
Net profit before tax		155	88	30	62	335

A new managing director with retailing experience has been appointed from outside the group. He has said that he considers that a department should achieve a net profit before tax of at least 7.5% on sales and that he is prepared to close any department not meeting that criterion.

You are required to:

(a) (i) identify which department, if any qualify for closure under this criterion,
(ii) state whether or not you would recommend their closure, explaining the reasons for your recommendations.

(b) recommend briefly what changes management might consider to improve the store's total profitability;

(c) advise what other departmental data might be fairly easily provided that would enable more comprehensive recommendations to be made.

CIMA, Management Accounting – Decision Making.

Chapter 19

EXAMINATION QUESTIONS WITHOUT ANSWERS

B1. *White Division is an important supplier to Rose Division in a group in which divisions are operated as autonomous profit centres. The group has established the following rules for calculating transfer prices:*

1.   If the product is being sold to customers outside the group, the average price for the past six months is to be used as the transfer price.

2.   If the product is not sold to outside customers, the transfer price to be used is the standard variable cost plus fixed overhead at minimum budgeted volume plus a 10% profit margin on cost.

The following data are available regarding each division.

White Division

   This division produces three products: A, B and C whose variable manufacturing costs per unit and apportioned fixed costs per annum are:

	A	B	C
	£	£	£
Variable manufacturing cost, per unit	6	13	18
Fixed cost, per annum	75,000	105,000	180,000

   The direct labour hour content of each of these products is 3 direct labour hours per unit, but the materials used are different. The production capacity of the factory is 180,000 direct labour hours and it is a requirement that at least 45,000 direct labour hours be used on each product. The remaining capacity can be used for any combination of the three products.

   The division has been selling 40% of its output of product A to customers outside the group and the average price over the past 6 months has been £13 per unit. Product A has also been sold to Rose Division as has all White Division's output of products B and C.

Rose Division

   This division produces three products: Theta, Sigma and Omega which use products A, B and C from White Division as follows:

Rose Division's product	Number of units of White Division's product used:		
one unit of Theta uses	5	5	–
one unit of Sigma uses	3	5	2
one unit of Omega uses	2	–	8

   The unit selling prices of this division's products, their other unit variable costs (ie excluding those from White Division) and apportioned fixed costs per annum are:

	Theta	Sigma	Omega
	£	£	£
Selling price, per unit	280	295	340
Other variable costs, per unit	30	25	45
Fixed costs, per annum	60,000	90,000	120,000

   Rose Division has no difficulty in making sales at the above prices and it must sell at least 1,500 per annum of each product. However, because product A is being sold by White Division to customers outside the group, Rose Division has complained that they are operating considerably below capacity.

   The group planning executive has therefore intervened and instructed White Division to stop selling outside the group.

A. You are required, on the basis that all White Division's production must be sold exclusively to Rose Division,

   (a) as general manager of White Division, to:

      (i)   state what production pattern you would adopt in your sales to Rose Division;
      (ii) calculate what profit per annum would be earned from those sales.

(b) *as general manager of Rose Division, to:*

    (i) *state what quantities of products A, B and C you would order from White Division;*
    (ii) *calculate what profit per annum would be earned from your sales.*

(c) *as group planning executive, to:*

    (i) *state what production pattern you would recommend to maximise group profit;*
    (ii) *calculate what profit per annum would be earned from that pattern.*

B. *The production engineers of White Division discover a method of increasing the capacity of the factory beyond the present limits of 180,000 direct labour hours but additional costs would be incurred as follows:*

Increase in capacity
  (in thousands of direct labour hours)   *9:18 27: 36*
Total additional cost, per annum (£000)   *15:55:125:210*

Increases can only be made in steps of 9,000 direct labour hours to be spread evenly over all three products and the maximum increase is 36,000 direct labour hours.

Assuming that:
(i) *all other data are as given earlier; and*
(ii) *the increase must be divided equally among Theta, Sigma and Omega;*

you are required, as group planning executive, to calculate what increased production, if any, would optimise group profit.

CIMA, Management Accounting 1.

B2. *B Limited, producing a range of minerals, is organised into two trading groups: one handles wholesale business and the other sales to retailers.*

One of its products is a moulding clay. The wholesale group extracts the clay and sells it to external wholesale customers as well as to the retail group. The production capacity is 2,000 tonnes per month but at present sales are limited to 1,000 tonnes wholesale and 600 tonnes retail.

The transfer price was agreed at £200 per tonne in line with the external wholesale trade price at the 1st July which was the beginning of the budget year. As from 1st December, however, competitive pressure has forced the wholesale trade price down to £180 per tonne. The members of the retail group contend that the transfer price to them should be the same as for outside customers. The wholesale group refute the argument on the basis that the original budget established the price for the whole budget year.

The retail group produces 100 bags of refined clay from each tonne of moulding clay which it sells at £400 a bag. It would sell a further 40,000 bags if the retail price were reduced to £3.20 a bag.

Other data relevant to the operations are:

	Wholesale group *£*	*Retail group* *£*
Variable cost per tonne	70	60
Fixed cost per month	100,000	40,000

You are required to:
(a) *prepare estimated profit statements for the month of December for each group and for B Limited as a whole based on transfer prices of £200 per tonne and of £180 per tonne when producing at:*

    (i) *80% capacity; and*
    (ii) *100% capacity utilising the extra sales to supply the retail trade;*

(b) *comment on the results achieved under (a) and the effect of the change in the transfer price; and*

(c) *propose an alternative transfer price for the retail sales which would provide greater incentive for increasing sales, detailing any problems that might be encountered.*

CIMA Management Accounting 2.

Chapter 20

EXAMINATION QUESTION WITHOUT ANSWER

B1. *AB Limited had the following abridged results for the year ended 30th November 1979:*

	£	£
Sales		500,000
Cost of goods sold		350,000
Gross profit		150,000
Overheads	80,000	
Depreciation	20,000	
		100,000
Net Profit before taxation		50,000
Taxation		25,000
Net Profit after taxation		25,000
Dividends		10,000
Profit retained		£15,000

Balance Sheet as at 30th November 1979

	£	£
Fixed Assets:		
Plant and equipment at cost		250,000
Less depreciation		90,000
		160,000
Current assets:		
Stock	30,000	
Debtors	100,000	
Bank	40,000	
	170,000	
Less Current liabilities:		
Sundry Creditors	45,000	
Taxation	25,000	
Dividends	10,000	
	80,000	90,000
		£250,000
Represented by:		
£1 ordinary shares		150,000
Reserves		100,000
		£250,000

The company is considering the introduction of a new product line. It is estimated that total sales in the coming year, including sales of the new product, would be £657,500 and cost of sales £460,000. Overheads would increase by £14,500. New plant would be purchased at a cost of £60,000 which would be depreciated over a five year period by the sum-of-the-years' digits method. Depreciation on existing plant would remain at £20,000 for the year. Taxation is expected to be at the rate of 50 per cent of net profit. A profit-sharing scheme is to be introduced for management whereby the staff concerned would participate in a bonus of 5 per cent of net profit before tax but after deduction of the bonus.

To finance part of the cost of new plant a right issue of 20,000 £1 Ordinary shares at par would be made. Dividends would be at the rate of 10p per share including the new shares.

The expected current assets and liabilities at 30th November 1980 are as follows:

	£
Stock	37,000
Debtors	101,500
Bank	66,000
Creditors (excluding taxation,	
profit bonus and dividends)	51,500

You are required to:

(a) prepare the budgeted income statement for the year to 30th November 1980 and a balance sheet at that date;
(b) write a short report to the board reviewing the projected results and introducing such measures of performance that you think appropriate.

ICSA, Management Accounting.

Chapter 21

EXAMINATION QUESTIONS WITHOUT ANSWERS

B1. *It is conventionally assumed that there are three levels in the organisation at which decision-making takes place.*

You are required to:

(a) define briefly the three levels;

(b) describe the characteristics of decision-making at the different levels;

(c) give an example, for each level, of the type of assistance or information a computer-based management information system could supply to aid decision-making.

CIMA, Management Information Systems and Data Processing.

B2. *Information in an accounting system may be considered under the three headings: past, present and future (or record keeping, management information and forecasting.*

Using a sales accounting system for illustration give practical examples of the three types of information and describe some of the difficulties each presents in systems design.

ACCA, Systems Analysis & Design.

Table A

PRESENT VALUE FACTORS: PRESENT VALUE OF £1 $(1 + r)^{-n}$

DISCOUNT RATES (r)%

Periods (n)	1%	2%	4%	6%	8%	10%	12%	14%	15%	16%	18%	20%	22%	24%	25%	26%	28%	30%
1	0.990	0.980	0.962	0.943	0.926	0.909	0.893	0.877	0.870	0.862	0.847	0.833	0.820	0.806	0.800	0.794	0.781	0.769
2	0.980	0.961	0.925	0.890	0.857	0.826	0.797	0.769	0.756	0.743	0.718	0.694	0.672	0.650	0.640	0.630	0.610	0.592
3	0.971	0.942	0.889	0.840	0.794	0.751	0.712	0.675	0.658	0.641	0.609	0.579	0.551	0.524	0.512	0.500	0.477	0.455
4	0.961	0.924	0.855	0.792	0.735	0.683	0.636	0.592	0.572	0.552	0.516	0.482	0.451	0.423	0.410	0.397	0.373	0.350
5	0.951	0.906	0.822	0.747	0.681	0.621	0.567	0.519	0.497	0.476	0.437	0.402	0.370	0.341	0.328	0.315	0.291	0.269
6	0.942	0.888	0.790	0.705	0.630	0.564	0.507	0.456	0.432	0.410	0.370	0.335	0.303	0.275	0.262	0.250	0.227	0.207
7	0.933	0.871	0.760	0.665	0.583	0.513	0.452	0.400	0.376	0.354	0.314	0.279	0.249	0.222	0.210	0.198	0.178	0.159
8	0.923	0.853	0.731	0.627	0.540	0.467	0.404	0.351	0.327	0.305	0.266	0.233	0.204	0.179	0.168	0.157	0.139	0.123
9	0.914	0.837	0.703	0.592	0.500	0.424	0.361	0.308	0.284	0.263	0.225	0.194	0.167	0.144	0.134	0.125	0.108	0.094
10	0.905	0.820	0.676	0.558	0.463	0.386	0.322	0.270	0.247	0.227	0.191	0.162	0.137	0.116	0.107	0.099	0.085	0.075
11	0.896	0.804	0.650	0.527	0.429	0.350	0.287	0.237	0.215	0.195	0.162	0.135	0.112	0.094	0.086	0.079	0.066	0.056
12	0.887	0.788	0.625	0.497	0.397	0.319	0.257	0.208	0.187	0.168	0.137	0.112	0.092	0.076	0.069	0.062	0.052	0.043
13	0.879	0.773	0.601	0.469	0.368	0.290	0.229	0.182	0.163	0.145	0.116	0.093	0.075	0.061	0.055	0.050	0.040	0.033
14	0.870	0.758	0.577	0.442	0.340	0.263	0.205	0.160	0.141	0.125	0.099	0.078	0.062	0.049	0.044	0.039	0.032	0.025
15	0.861	0.743	0.555	0.417	0.315	0.239	0.183	0.140	0.123	0.108	0.084	0.065	0.051	0.040	0.035	0.031	0.025	0.020
16	0.853	0.728	0.534	0.394	0.292	0.218	0.163	0.123	0.107	0.093	0.071	0.054	0.042	0.032	0.028	0.025	0.019	0.015
17	0.844	0.714	0.513	0.371	0.270	0.198	0.146	0.108	0.093	0.080	0.060	0.045	0.034	0.026	0.023	0.020	0.015	0.012
18	0.836	0.700	0.494	0.350	0.250	0.180	0.130	0.095	0.081	0.069	0.051	0.038	0.028	0.021	0.018	0.016	0.012	0.009
19	0.828	0.686	0.475	0.331	0.232	0.164	0.116	0.083	0.070	0.060	0.043	0.031	0.023	0.017	0.014	0.012	0.009	0.007
20	0.820	0.675	0.456	0.312	0.215	0.149	0.104	0.073	0.061	0.051	0.037	0.026	0.019	0.014	0.012	0.010	0.007	0.005
21	0.811	0.660	0.439	0.294	0.199	0.135	0.093	0.064	0.053	0.044	0.031	0.022	0.015	0.011	0.009	0.008	0.006	0.004
22	0.803	0.647	0.422	0.278	0.184	0.123	0.083	0.056	0.046	0.038	0.026	0.018	0.013	0.009	0.007	0.006	0.004	0.003
23	0.795	0.634	0.406	0.262	0.170	0.112	0.074	0.049	0.040	0.033	0.022	0.015	0.010	0.007	0.006	0.005	0.003	0.002
24	0.788	0.622	0.390	0.247	0.158	0.102	0.066	0.043	0.035	0.028	0.019	0.013	0.008	0.006	0.005	0.004	0.003	0.002
25	0.780	0.610	0.375	0.233	0.146	0.092	0.059	0.038	0.030	0.024	0.016	0.010	0.007	0.005	0.004	0.003	0.002	0.001

Table B

PRESENT VALUE ANNUITY FACTORS: PRESENT VALUE OF £1

RECEIVED ANNUALLY FOR n YEARS $\left(\dfrac{1-(1+r)^{-n}}{r}\right)$

DISCOUNT RATES $(r)\%$

Years (n)	1%	2%	4%	6%	8%	10%	12%	14%	15%	16%	18%	20%	22%	24%	25%	26%	28%	30%
1	0.990	0.980	0.962	0.943	0.926	0.909	0.893	0.877	0.870	0.862	0.847	0.833	0.820	0.806	0.800	0.794	0.781	0.769
2	1.970	1.942	1.886	1.833	1.783	1.736	1.690	1.647	1.626	1.605	1.566	1.528	1.492	1.457	1.440	1.424	1.392	1.361
3	2.941	2.884	2.775	2.675	2.577	2.487	2.402	2.322	2.283	2.246	2.174	2.106	2.042	1.981	1.952	1.923	1.868	1.816
4	3.902	3.808	3.610	3.465	3.312	3.170	3.037	2.914	2.855	2.798	2.690	2.589	2.494	2.404	2.362	2.320	2.241	2.166
5	4.853	4.713	4.452	4.212	3.996	3.791	3.605	3.433	3.352	3.274	3.127	2.991	2.864	2.745	2.689	2.635	2.532	2.436
6	5.795	5.601	5.242	4.917	4.623	4.355	4.111	3.889	3.784	3.685	3.498	3.326	3.167	3.020	2.951	2.885	2.759	2.643
7	6.728	6.472	6.002	5.582	5.206	4.868	4.564	4.288	4.160	4.039	3.812	3.605	3.416	3.242	3.161	3.083	2.937	2.802
8	7.652	7.325	6.733	6.210	5.747	5.335	4.968	4.639	4.487	4.344	4.078	3.837	3.619	3.421	3.329	3.241	3.076	2.925
9	8.566	8.162	7.435	6.802	6.247	5.759	5.328	4.946	4.772	4.607	4.303	4.031	3.786	3.566	3.463	3.366	3.184	3.019
10	9.471	8.983	8.111	7.360	6.710	6.145	5.650	5.216	5.019	4.833	4.494	4.192	3.923	3.682	3.571	3.465	3.269	3.092
11	10.368	9.787	8.760	7.887	7.139	6.495	5.988	5.453	5.234	5.029	4.636	4.327	4.035	3.776	3.656	3.544	3.335	3.147
12	11.255	10.575	9.385	8.384	7.536	6.814	6.194	5.660	5.421	5.197	4.793	4.439	4.127	3.851	3.725	3.606	3.387	3.190
13	12.114	11.343	9.986	8.853	7.904	7.103	6.424	5.842	5.583	5.342	4.910	4.533	4.203	3.912	3.780	3.656	3.427	3.223
14	13.004	12.106	10.563	9.295	8.244	7.367	6.628	6.002	5.724	5.468	5.008	4.611	4.265	3.961	3.824	3.695	3.459	3.249
15	13.865	12.849	11.118	9.712	8.559	7.606	6.811	6.142	5.847	5.575	5.092	4.675	4.315	4.001	3.859	3.726	3.483	3.268
16	14.718	13.578	11.652	10.106	8.851	7.824	6.974	6.265	5.954	5.669	5.162	4.730	4.357	4.033	3.887	3.751	3.503	3.283
17	15.562	14.292	12.166	10.477	9.122	8.022	7.120	6.373	6.047	5.749	5.222	4.775	4.391	4.059	3.910	3.771	3.518	3.295
18	16.328	14.992	12.659	10.828	9.372	8.201	7.250	6.467	6.128	5.818	5.273	4.812	4.419	4.080	3.928	3.786	3.529	3.304
19	17.226	15.678	13.134	11.158	9.604	8.365	7.366	6.550	6.198	5.877	5.316	4.844	4.442	4.097	3.942	3.799	3.539	3.311
20	18.046	16.351	13.590	11.470	9.818	8.514	7.469	6.623	6.259	5.929	5.353	4.870	4.460	4.110	3.954	3.808	3.546	3.316
21	18.857	17.011	14.029	11.764	10.017	8.649	7.562	6.687	6.312	5.973	5.384	4.891	4.476	4.121	3.963	3.816	3.551	3.320
22	19.660	17.658	14.451	12.042	10.201	8.772	7.645	6.743	6.359	6.011	5.410	4.909	4.488	4.130	3.970	3.822	3.556	3.323
23	20.456	18.292	14.857	12.303	10.371	8.883	7.718	6.792	6.399	6.044	5.432	4.925	4.499	4.137	3.976	3.827	3.559	3.325
24	21.243	18.914	15.247	12.550	10.529	8.985	7.784	6.815	6.434	6.073	5.451	4.937	4.507	4.143	3.981	3.831	3.562	3.327
25	22.023	19.523	15.622	12.783	10.675	9.077	7.843	6.873	6.464	6.097	5.467	4.948	4.514	4.147	3.985	3.834	3.564	3.329

Table C Areas Under the Normal Curve   407

Table C

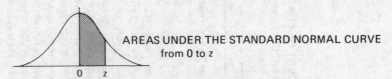

AREAS UNDER THE STANDARD NORMAL CURVE
from 0 to z

z	0	1	2	3	4	5	6	7	8	9
0.0	0.0000	0.0040	0.0080	0.0120	0.0160	0.0199	0.0239	0.0279	0.0319	0.0359
0.1	0.0398	0.0438	0.0478	0.0517	0.0557	0.0596	0.0636	0.0675	0.0714	0.0754
0.2	0.0793	0.0832	0.0871	0.0910	0.0948	0.0987	0.1026	0.1064	0.1103	0.1141
0.3	0.1179	0.1217	0.1255	0.1293	0.1331	0.1368	0.1406	0.1443	0.1480	0.1517
0.4	0.1554	0.1591	0.1628	0.1664	0.1700	0.1736	0.1772	0.1808	0.1844	0.1879
0.5	0.1915	0.1950	0.1985	0.2019	0.2054	0.2088	0.2123	0.2157	0.2190	0.2224
0.6	0.2258	0.2291	0.2324	0.2357	0.2389	0.2422	0.2454	0.2486	0.2518	0.2549
0.7	0.2580	0.2612	0.2642	0.2673	0.2704	0.2734	0.2764	0.2794	0.2823	0.2852
0.8	0.2881	0.2910	0.2939	0.2967	0.2996	0.3023	0.3051	0.3078	0.3106	0.3133
0.9	0.3159	0.3186	0.3212	0.3238	0.3264	0.3289	0.3315	0.3340	0.3365	0.3389
1.0	0.3413	0.3438	0.3461	0.3485	0.3508	0.3531	0.3554	0.3577	0.3599	0.3621
1.1	0.3643	0.3665	0.3686	0.3708	0.3729	0.3749	0.3770	0.3790	0.3810	0.3830
1.2	0.3849	0.3869	0.3888	0.3907	0.3925	0.3944	0.3962	0.3980	0.3997	0.4015
1.3	0.4032	0.4049	0.4066	0.4082	0.4099	0.4115	0.4131	0.4147	0.4162	0.4177
1.4	0.4192	0.4207	0.4222	0.4236	0.4251	0.4265	0.4279	0.4292	0.4306	0.4319
1.5	0.4332	0.4345	0.4357	0.4370	0.4382	0.4394	0.4406	0.4418	0.4429	0.4441
1.6	0.4452	0.4463	0.4474	0.4484	0.4495	0.4505	0.4515	0.4525	0.4535	0.4545
1.7	0.4554	0.4564	0.4573	0.4582	0.4591	0.4599	0.4608	0.4616	0.4625	0.4633
1.8	0.4641	0.4649	0.4656	0.4664	0.4671	0.4678	0.4686	0.4693	0.4699	0.4706
1.9	0.4713	0.4719	0.4726	0.4732	0.4738	0.4744	0.4750	0.4756	0.4762	0.4767
2.0	0.4772	0.4778	0.4783	0.4788	0.4793	0.4798	0.4803	0.4808	0.4812	0.4817
2.1	0.4821	0.4826	0.4830	0.4834	0.4838	0.4842	0.4846	0.4850	0.4854	0.4857
2.2	0.4861	0.4864	0.4868	0.4871	0.4875	0.4878	0.4881	0.4884	0.4887	0.4890
2.3	0.4893	0.4896	0.4898	0.4901	0.4904	0.4906	0.4909	0.4911	0.4913	0.4916
2.4	0.4918	0.4920	0.4922	0.4925	0.4927	0.4929	0.4931	0.4932	0.4934	0.4936
2.5	0.4938	0.4940	0.4941	0.4943	0.4945	0.4946	0.4948	0.4949	0.4951	0.4952
2.6	0.4953	0.4955	0.4956	0.4957	0.4959	0.4960	0.4961	0.4962	0.4963	0.4964
2.7	0.4965	0.4966	0.4967	0.4968	0.4969	0.4970	0.4971	0.4972	0.4973	0.4974
2.8	0.4974	0.4975	0.4976	0.4977	0.4977	0.4978	0.4979	0.4979	0.4980	0.4981
2.9	0.4981	0.4982	0.4982	0.4983	0.4984	0.4984	0.4985	0.4985	0.4986	0.4986
3.0	0.4987	0.4987	0.4987	0.4988	0.4988	0.4989	0.4989	0.4989	0.4990	0.4990
3.1	0.4990	0.4991	0.4991	0.4991	0.4992	0.4992	0.4992	0.4992	0.4993	0.4993
3.2	0.4993	0.4993	0.4994	0.4994	0.4994	0.4994	0.4994	0.4995	0.4995	0.4995
3.3	0.4995	0.4995	0.4995	0.4996	0.4996	0.4996	0.4996	0.4996	0.4996	0.4997
3.4	0.4997	0.4997	0.4997	0.4997	0.4997	0.4997	0.4997	0.4997	0.4997	0.4998
3.5	0.4998	0.4998	0.4998	0.4998	0.4998	0.4998	0.4998	0.4998	0.4998	0.4998
3.6	0.4998	0.4998	0.4999	0.4999	0.4999	0.4999	0.4999	0.4999	0.4999	0.4999
3.7	0.4999	0.4999	0.4999	0.4999	0.4999	0.4999	0.4999	0.4999	0.4999	0.4999
3.8	0.4999	0.4999	0.4999	0.4999	0.4999	0.4999	0.4999	0.4999	0.4999	0.4999
3.9	0.5000	0.5000	0.5000	0.5000	0.5000	0.5000	0.5000	0.5000	0.5000	0.5000

Table D

COMPOUND INTEREST. TABLE SHOWS AMOUNT OF £1 AT
COMPOUND INTEREST $(1 + r)^n$

INTEREST RATES (r)%

YEARS (n)	1	2	3	4	5	6	7	8	9	10	11	12	13	14	15	16	17	18	19	20	25	30
1	1.010	1.020	1.030	1.040	1.050	1.060	1.070	1.080	1.090	1.100	1.110	1.120	1.130	1.140	1.150	1.160	1.170	1.180	1.190	1.200	1.250	1.300
2	1.020	1.040	1.061	1.082	1.102	1.124	1.145	1.166	1.188	1.210	1.232	1.254	1.277	1.297	1.322	1.346	1.367	1.392	1.416	1.440	1.562	1.690
3	1.030	1.061	1.093	1.125	1.158	1.191	1.225	1.260	1.295	1.331	1.368	1.405	1.443	1.481	1.521	1.561	1.602	1.643	1.685	1.728	1.953	2.197
4	1.041	1.082	1.126	1.167	1.216	1.262	1.311	1.360	1.412	1.464	1.518	1.573	1.630	1.689	1.749	1.811	1.874	1.939	2.005	2.074	2.441	2.856
5	1.051	1.104	1.159	1.217	1.276	1.338	1.403	1.469	1.539	1.610	1.685	1.762	1.842	1.925	2.011	2.100	2.192	2.288	2.386	2.488	3.052	3.713
6	1.061	1.126	1.194	1.265	1.340	1.419	1.501	1.587	1.677	1.772	1.870	1.974	2.082	2.195	2.313	2.436	2.565	2.700	2.840	2.986	3.815	4.827
7	1.072	1.149	1.230	1.316	1.407	1.504	1.606	1.714	1.828	1.949	2.076	2.211	2.353	2.502	2.660	2.826	3.001	3.186	3.379	3.583	4.768	6.275
8	1.083	1.172	1.267	1.369	1.477	1.594	1.718	1.851	1.993	2.144	2.304	2.476	2.658	2.853	3.059	3.278	3.511	3.759	4.021	4.300	5.960	8.157
9	1.094	1.195	1.305	1.423	1.551	1.689	1.838	1.999	2.172	2.358	2.558	2.773	3.004	3.252	3.518	3.803	4.108	4.435	4.785	5.159	7.451	10.604
10	1.105	1.219	1.344	1.480	1.629	1.791	1.967	2.159	2.367	2.594	2.839	3.106	3.395	3.707	4.046	4.411	4.807	5.234	5.695	6.192	9.313	13.786
11	1.116	1.243	1.384	1.539	1.710	1.898	2.105	2.332	2.580	2.853	3.152	3.478	3.836	4.226	4.652	5.117	5.624	6.176	6.777	7.430	11.641	17.922
12	1.127	1.268	1.426	1.601	1.796	2.012	2.252	2.519	2.813	3.138	3.498	3.896	4.334	4.818	5.350	5.936	6.580	7.288	8.064	8.916	14.552	23.298
13	1.138	1.294	1.468	1.665	1.886	2.133	2.410	2.720	3.066	3.452	3.883	4.363	4.898	5.492	6.153	6.886	7.699	8.599	9.596	10.699	18.190	30.287
14	1.149	1.319	1.513	1.732	1.980	2.261	2.578	2.937	3.342	3.797	4.310	4.887	5.535	6.261	7.076	7.988	9.007	10.147	11.420	12.839	22.737	39.374
15	1.161	1.346	1.558	1.801	2.079	2.397	2.759	3.172	3.642	4.177	4.785	5.474	6.254	7.138	8.137	9.265	10.539	11.974	13.589	15.407	28.422	51.186
20	1.220	1.486	1.806	2.191	2.653	3.207	3.870	4.661	5.604	6.727	8.062	9.646	11.523	13.743	16.366	19.461	23.106	27.393	32.429	38.338	86.736	190.050
25	1.282	1.641	2.094	2.666	3.386	4.292	5.427	6.848	8.623	10.835	13.585	17.000	21.230	26.462	32.920	40.874	50.658	62.669	77.388	95.396	264.698	705.641

SECTION 3
THE REVISION SECTION

EXAMINATION TECHNIQUE

EXAMINER'S REPORTS

REVISION SUMMARIES BY TOPIC

**SELECTED QUESTIONS WITH COMMENTARY,
STEP BY STEP METHOD GUIDE AND ANSWERS**

MOCK EXAMINATIONS

ANSWERS TO MOCK EXAMINATIONS

1. EXAMINATION TECHNIQUE

INTRODUCTION

1.   If you are a genius and/or can calculate and reproduce facts and figures with the speed of a computer and/or know the examiner then there is no need for you to read this section. On the other hand if you do not fall into any of the above categories then you will stand more chance of passing your examinations first time if you study this section carefully and follow simple rules.

WELL BEFORE THE EXAMINATION

2.   No amount of examination room technique will enable you to pass unless you have prepared yourself thoroughly beforehand. The period of preparation may be years or months long. It is no use expecting to pass with a feverish last minute bout of revision.

By this stage you should have worked through all of Section 2 of the manual and you should be thoroughly familiar with the syllabus and the type of examination questions that have been set in the past.

By the end of your study and revision you should be able to answer **every** question in this manual.

IMMEDIATELY BEFORE THE EXAMINATION

3.   (a)   Make sure you know exact time, date and location of examination.
     (b)   Carefully check your travel arrangements. Leave yourself adequate time.
     (c)   Check over your examination equipment:
           Calculator? Spare battery? Pens? Slide rule? Tables? Watch? Sweets? Cigarettes? etc etc.
     (d)   Check your examination number.

IN THE EXAMINATION ROOM

4.   If you have followed the rules so far you are well prepared; you have all the equipment you need; you did not have to rush - YOU ARE CALM AND CONFIDENT.

Before you start writing:
(a)   Carefully read the whole examination paper including the rubric.
(b)   Decide what questions you are going to answer.
(c)   Decide the sequence you will tackle the questions. Generally, answer the easiest question first.
(d)   Decide the time allocation for each question. In general the time allocation should be in direct proportion to the marks for each question.
(e)   Read the questions you have decided to answer again. Do you know *exactly* what the examiner is asking?

Underline the key words in the question and keep these in our mind when answering.

EXAMINATION TECHNIQUE

5.   Dealing with the questions:

(a)   Make sure you plan each question first. Make a note of the main points or principles involved. If you are unable to finish the question you will gain some marks for these points.
(b)   Attempt all questions required and each part of each question.
(c)   Do not let your answer ramble on. Be as brief as possible consistent with covering all the points you know.
(d)   Follow a logical sequence in your answers.
(e)   Write neatly, underline headings and if the question asks for a particular sequence of answer then follow that sequence.
(f)   If diagrams, graphs or tables are required give them plenty of space, label them neatly and comprehensively, and give a key to symbols, lines etc, used. A simple clear diagram showing the main points can often gain a good proportion of the marks for a question.

When you have finished writing:
(a)   Check that you have followed the examination regulations regarding examination title, examination number, candidates number and sequence of answer sheet.
(b)   Make sure you include *all* the sheets you require to be marked.
(c)   If you have time carefully read each and every part of each answer and check each calculation.

General points:

    (a) Concentrate on answering the questions set not some related topic which you happen to know something about.

    (b) Do *not* leave the examination room early. Use every minute for checking and re-checking or adding points to questions answered.

    (c) Always attempt every question set and *every* part of each question.

EXAMINERS' REPORT

6.   After every examination an Examiner's Report is prepared and you are urged to obtain a copy and thoroughly digest the contents. Much useful advice is given not only about the detail of individual questions, but about the general approach to be adopted.

Ever since examination were invented examiners have complained, with justice about similar problems and deficiencies. The more common ones include:

    (a) failure to read the question;
    (b) failure to answer the question as set;
    (c) careless work, especially with calculations;
    (d) bad English;
    (e) poor writing;
    (f) poor charts/diagrams with no titles or keys;
    (g) rote learning rather than real understanding;
    (h) inadequate time planning resulting in the failure to answer all questions;
    (i) inclusion of irrelevant material;
    (j) failure to relate theory and practice.

You are **strongly advised** to note carefully the above list of common failings and to make sure that you are not guilty of any of them

Two recent examples of ACCA Examiners' Reports are reproduced below.

ACCA EXAMINER'S REPORT
PAPER 2.4 MANAGEMENT ACCOUNTING

    The paper contained a number of straightforward questions which enabled the well prepared candidate to obtain a high overall mark. Nevertheless, many candidates failed through poorly presented scripts and inadequate preparation. A large number of candidates were unable to gain marks even where parts of the question involved straightforward calculations rather than an evaluation of information. Many answers to essay questions in section B were too brief and/or consisted of general comment rather than focusing on the specific points raised in the question.

Question 1: was a straightforward exercise in the calculation of standard cost variances with the opportunity to comment briefly on their relevance. Material price variances calculated at the point of purchase or of issue were accepted as correct. Candidates lost marks by failing to prepare the reconciliation statement asked for in part (c) and by failing to make relevant comments in part (d).

Question 2: required candidates to assess how transfer prices would influence the transfer policy of intermediate and final divisions, and the effect of such policies on group profit. Many candidates produced unnecessarily long answers, with a large number of figures which did not arrive at the correct solution. This demonstrates a lack of ability to abstract relevant data and to utilise it to arrive at required decisions.

Question 3: required candidates to select relevant costs in order to arrive at a make or buy decision for each component and product. Many candidates failed to gain marks by not stating clearly the range of assumptions which had been made so that the make or buy decisions could be taken as accurate. In part (b) of the question many candidates failed to recognise the limiting factor situation or to rank correctly the components/products which should be produced with the limited resources in order to maximise profit.

Question 4: part (a) required candidates to prepare a tabulation of costs and profits, both per unit and in total, at various activity levels; part (b) required a calculation of the expected profit for the year; and part (c) required candidates to consider the implications for the customer if they accepted the proposed contract. In part (a), many candidates wasted time by attempting to analyse the semi-variable costs into fixed and variable elements. They lost marks by failing to give unit data as required. In part (b), many candidates arrived at the correct solution, some by preparing a joint probability distribution analysis as the basis of their answer. Others, however, seemed to have no knowledge of how to arrive at the expected value figure. In part (c), many candidates lost marks by failing to discuss adequately the implications for the customer.

Question 5: part (a) tested candidates' understanding of various costs; part (b) required them to evaluate the main effects of price level changes in the use of accounting information in the decision-making process. In meaning of the terms given. In their answers to part (b), many candidates commented on company pricing policies rather than on the impact of price level changes on the use of accounting information in decision-making.

Question 6: part (a) tested candidates' awareness of the factors in the relevant costs approach to decision-making; and part (b) asked them to explain the alternative methods of accounting for normal and abnormal spoilage in process costing. In part (a), candidates although they itemised some factors which might distinguish between relevant and non-relevant costs, failed to gain marks by not discussing the decision-making implications. In part (b) many answers consisted of brief comments on possible treatment of normal and abnormal losses with no attempt to explain the accounting treatment in an adequate manner.

Question 7: required candidates to explain the specific roles of planning, motivation and evaluation in a system of budgetary control, and to describe five areas in which the use of mathematical modelling with computers might benefit management accounting. Candidates, generally, answered part (a) well, but in part (b) many simply listed the names of some mathematical modelling techniques without attempting to explain how the use of computers could assist the management accountant to use such techniques in a range of planning, control and decision-making situations.

EXAMINER'S REPORT PAPER 2.4 MANAGEMENT ACCOUNTING

The paper was divided into two sections. Section A, the 'quantitative' part of the paper, was less well done than section B, the 'discursive' part. Many candidates seem happier to write about management accounting principles than to apply these principles/ At each examination the most common mistake in section A is a failure to identify relevant costs and benefits.

Question 1 was designed to test candidates' understanding of standard absorption costing and their ability to calculate and interpret a range of variances including direct material mix and yield variances, direct labour mix and productivity variances and sales variances. The question was relatively well answered but common mistakes and areas of difficulty were:

(a)   failure to recognise that cost variances relate to the actual (not the budgeted) level of production;
(b)   inability to calculate some of the variances, notably mix, yield and productivity cost;
(c)   calculation of the sales volume variance using standard contribution rather than actual standard profit – this makes it difficult to reconcile budgeted and actual profit in a full costing system;
(d)   uncertain appreciation of the usefulness of particular variances, particularly the mix, yield and productivity cost variances and the sales variances.

Question 2 sought to test candidates' ability to identify relevant costs in decision-making, specifically for pricing decisions and the choice of the best type of raw material. There were some good answers and those candidates who recognised that economic theory could be used to determine the optimal level of output (where marginal cost equalled marginal revenue) are to be commended. The overall standard, however, was disappointing for the following reasons:

(a)   a surprising number of candidates experienced difficulty in calculating the cost of wastage because this was expressed as a percentage of completed output;
(b)   many failed to recognise the dangers of using full cost figures for decision-making purposes;
(c)   there were few attempts to investigate the sensitivity of the solution to errors in the estimates;
(d)   many could not provide an appropriate cost-volume-profit graph.

Question 3 sought to test candidates understanding of joint cost apportionment and their ability to draft a statement which incorporated apportionments of budgeted figures. Few realised that the requirement that the budgeted profit rate should be the same for both profit centres could be met by inserting the cost allocations as balancing figures in the budgets. The layout of answers was often poor and a failure to observe the requirements of the question was not uncommon.

Question 4 sought to test candidates' understanding of transfer pricing principles. The standard of the answers was relatively satisfactory. A common mistake was a failure to recognise that, since division A has spare capacity, there is no contribution foregone when goods are transferred to division B and that the opportunity cost of such transfers is, therefore, the variable cost. The evaluation of the proposal to open a new branch caused difficulty for some candidates who did not focus on the additional cost benefits of such a decision.

Question 5 was straightforward and was designed to test candidates' understanding of some technical terms used in budgeting. In general the standard of answers was good.

Question 6, part (a) sought to test candidates' understanding of sensitivity analysis and Monte Carlo simulation in financial modelling. the standard of answers was reasonably good for this part. Part (b) was designed to test candidates' understanding of the iterative nature of the budget preparation process. This was not answered well.

Question 7 sought to examine candidates' ability to relate their knowledge of management accounting principles (a) to an important area of economic activity and (b) to a (relatively) new development in organisation theory. This was the least popular question and it seems that these topics may be omitted from many courses. Few candidates were able to discuss the difficulties of determining performance indicators for organisations which provide a free service and even fewer were aware of contingency theory.

REVISION SUMMARIES
BY TOPIC

INTRODUCTION TO MANAGEMENT ACCOUNTING (covering chapter 1)
Essential Knowledge

1. At the end of your studies you should be able to:
    (a) Define and explain the objectives of management accounting.
    (b) Know why the management accountant is concerned with the future rather than the past.
    (c) Understand the distinction between accounting conventions and economic reality.
    (d) Define goal congruence and understand the importance of the behavioural aspects of management accounting.
    (e) Understand that uncertainty has a profound influence on all aspects of management accounting.
    (f) Understand the central importance of decision-making to all aspects of management and management accounting.

COST ACCOUNTING AND COST ASCERTAINMENT (covering chapter 2)
Essential Knowledge

2. At the end of your studies your studies you should be able to:
    (a) Define cost accounting.
    (b) Give examples, from a range of organisations of the types of information provided by a costing system and be aware of how management uses this information.
    (c) Distinguish between costing, management accounting and financial accounting.
    (d) Define and exemplify cost and cost unit and be able to give examples of each.
    (e) Distinguish between direct and indirect costs and understand the build up of prime cost.
    (f) Define and exemplify conversion cost and added value.
    (g) Distinguish between cost allocation and cost apportionment and illustrate how typical costs are apportioned.
    (h) Explain the process of overhead absorption and be able to understand why it is necessary.
    (i) Understand how the alternative approaches could be applied in the routine cost accounting of the firm and the implications of SSAP 9.
    (j) Explain and use the main issue pricing systems; LIFO, FIFO, average price, standard price.
    (k) Deal with the costing problems caused by service cost centres, including the problems of reciprocal servicing.
    (l) Calculate product costs using all the types of costing methods; job and batch costing, contract costing, process costing.
    (m) Understand that much information produced by the cost accounting system of the firm is based on convention only and accordingly its use for management accounting purposes is limited.

COST BEHAVIOUR (covering chapter 3)
Essential Knowledge

3. At the end of your studies you should be able to:
    (a) Distinguish between fixed and variable costs and understand the typical assumptions on which these classifications are based.
    (b) Understand the problems associated with conventional cost classifications.
    (c) Define and give examples of, linear and non-linear variable costs, fixed costs, semi-variable costs, step costs.
    (d) Define the threee broad approaches to cost forecasting.
    (e) Explain the problems of using historical data for forecasting.
    (f) Define and use the 'high low' technique and understand its limitations.
    (g) Draw and interpret a scattergraph.
    (h) Explain the least squares method of regression analysis.
    (i) Remember and use the Normal Equations.
    (j) Extrapolate and interpolate using a calculated regression line.
    (k) Test for correlation using a t-test.
    (l) Calculate and interpret the coefficient of determination (r^2) for the regression line.
    (m) Explain why multiple linear regression is sometimes required.
    (n) Define the learning curve and know the formula.
    (o) Calculate b, the learning coefficient.

ESSENTIAL FORMULAE

1. Parabola (used for curvi-linear functions)

    $$y = bx + cx^2 + dx^3 + \ldots + px^n$$

    where b, c, d, . . ., p are the constants and x is the level of activity.

2. High-low method:

    $$\text{Variable cost per unit} \quad = \quad \frac{\text{Highest cost - lowest cost}}{\text{Highest activity level - lowest activity level}}$$

3. Least square normal equations:

    $$\Sigma y = an + b\Sigma x$$
    $$\Sigma xy = a\Sigma x + b\Sigma x^2$$

4. Least squares transposed normal equations:

    $$a = \frac{\Sigma y \Sigma x^2 - \Sigma x \Sigma xy}{n(\Sigma x^2) - (\Sigma x)^2}$$

    $$b = \frac{n\Sigma xy - \Sigma x \Sigma y}{n(\Sigma x^2) - (\Sigma x)^2}$$

5. Correlation coefficient r:

    $$r = \frac{n\Sigma xy - \Sigma x \Sigma y}{\sqrt{[n\Sigma x^2 - (\Sigma x)^2][n\Sigma y^2 - (\Sigma y)^2]}}$$

6. Learning curve

    $$y = ax^b$$

    where y = average labour hours per unit
    a = hours for first unit
    x = cumulative number of units
    b = learning coefficient

    $$b = \frac{\log (1 - \text{proportionate decrease})}{\log 2}$$

INFORMATION CHARACTERISTICS (covering chapter 4)
Essential Knowledge

4. At the end of your studies you should be able to:
    (a) Distinguish between data and information.
    (b) Know the attributes or relevant information.
    (c) Understand the parts of a typical communications system.
    (d) Understand the relationship between the costs and value of information.

PLANNING (covering chapters 5 and 6)
Essential Knowledge

5. At the end of your studies you should be able to:
    (a) Define a system and understand the system's approach.
    (b) Define sub-optimisation and know how it can be avoided.
    (c) Understand the relationship between planning and control.
    (d) Define planning and know the connection between long term and short term planning.
    (e) Explain corporate planning and to be able to state the various stages in developing a corporate plan.
    (f) Give examples of the areas in which objectives should be set for the organisation.
    (g) Explain planning gaps and gap analysis.
    (h) Describe the advantages and disadvantages of corporate planning.

(i) Understand the relationship between corporate planning and budgeting.

(j) Describe, in outline, the role of computers in corporate planning.

BUDGETING (covering chapter 7)
Essential Knowledge

6. At the end of your studies you should be able to:

(a) Understand the relationship between budgeting and corporate planning.

(b) Describe the benefits of a comprehensive budgeting system.

(c) Give the conditions necessary for budgeting to be successful.

(d) Define, and give examples of, a principal budget factor.

(e) Outline the stages in developing a budget.

(f) Give the content of a typical budget manual.

(g) Show, in a diagrammatic form, the relationship of budgets found in a typical firm.

(h) Understand what is meant by 'incremental' budgeting and to be able to discuss its shortcomings.

(i) Draw up a cash budget,

(j) Define rolling budgets.

(k) Distinguish between fixed and flexible budgets.

(l) Discuss the problems in developing and using flexible budgets.

(m) Distinguish between the level of activity and level of attainment.

(n) Define and discuss budgeting slack.

(o) Discuss the problem of dealing with uncertainty in the budgeting process.

(p) Define and discuss the advantages and disadvantages of zero-base budgeting.

(q) Explain the Program Planning and Budgeting System.

(r) Understand the relationship between budgetary planning and budgetary control.

CONTROL CONCEPTS (covering chapter 8)
Essential Knowledge

7. At the end of your studies you should be able to:

(a) Define control and understand the various types of control systems found in management accounting.

(b) Give the elements found in the control cycle.

(c) Define and give examples of feedback, both single loop and double loop.

(d) Define feed forward.

(e) Understand the purpose of negative feedback, both single loop and double loop.

(f) Distinguish between closed loop and open loop control systems.

(g) Understand why the timing of control action is so important.

(h) Realise the importance of the Law of Requisite Variety and its practical application.

(i) Define Pareto Analysis and give examples of its application.

BUDGETARY CONTROL (covering chapter 9)
Essential Knowledge

8. At the end of your studies you should be able to:

(a) Define budgetary control and relate it to the control cycle.

(b) Understand the importance of the flexible budgets for control purposes.

(c) Understand the relationship of budgetary control to the hierarchy of the organisation.

(d) Design an effective budgetary control report.

(e) Recognise and describe a significant variance.

(f) Set control limits for a budget allowance using statistical methods.

(g) Understand the importance of the behavioural aspects of budgeting.

(h) Discuss goal congruence in relation to budgeting.

(i) Understand how budgeting can improve motivation.

(j) Understand how dysfunctional behaviour can arise from poorly conceived budgeting systems.

(k) Give the benefits and problems of budgeting.

(l) Distinguish clearly between the activity level incorporated in a budget and the aspiration levels of the participants.

(m) Understand the place of budgeting in the information system of the organisation.

STANDARD COSTING (covering chapters 10 and 11)
Essential Knowledge

9. At the end of your studies you should be able to:
    (a) Define standard costing and explain its benefits.
    (b) Describe the types of standard and their possible uses.
    (c) Relate standards and budgets.
    (d) Know how to set standards for labour, materials and overheads.
    (e) Prepare a standard product cost.
    (f) Understand the importance of behavioural factors in standard costing.
    (g) Understand the purposes of variance analysis and how it can be a useful process.
    (h) Construct a chart of commonly encountered variances.
    (i) Calculate the basic labour and material variances.
    (j) Understand the basis of overhead variance analysis and especially the part played by overhead absorption rates and standard hours produced.
    (k) Calculate both variable and fixed overhead variances.
    (l) Calculate total overhead variances.
    (m) Understand the deficiencies of overhead variance analysis.
    (n) Calculate the activity, capacity and efficiency ratios.
    (o) Calculate the mix and yield variances.
    (p) Understand the deficiencies of traditionally calculated mix and yield variances.
    (q) Calculate the sales margin variances.
    (r) Understand the difference between standard costing based on total costs and that based on marginal costs.
    (s) Understand the concept of planning and operational variances.
    (t) Calculate planning and operational variances for labour and materials.
    (u) Discuss the advantages and disadvantages of standard costing.
    (v) Understand the principles of cost reduction and of the techniques used, ie variety reduction, value analysis, work-study and O & M.

ESSENTIAL FORMULAE

(a) Material variances

Actual purchase quantity x actual price (ie total purchase cost)
minus
actual purchase quantity x standard price
— Price variance

Actual quantity used for actual production x standard price
minus
Standard quantity for actual production x standard price
— Usage variance

⎫ Total direct materials cost variance

(b) Labour variances

Actual labour hours x actual rate (ie total labour cost)
minus
Actual labour hours x standard rate
— Rate variance

Actual labour hours x standard rate
minus
Standard labour hours x standard rate
— Efficiency variance

⎫ Total direct wages variance

(c) Variable overhead variances

Actual variable overheads
minus
Actual labour hours x VOAR
— Variable overhead expenditure variance

Actual labour hours x VOAR
minus
Standard hours of production x VOAR
— Variable overhead efficiency variance

⎫ Total variable overhead variance

(d) Fixed overhead variances

Actual expenditure on fixed overheads
minus
Budgeted fixed overheads } Fixed overhead expenditure variance
} Fixed overhead variance

Capacity variance } Fixed overhead variance volume

Actual labour hours x FOAR
minus
Standard hours of production x FOAR } Efficiency variance

(e) Total overhead variances

Actual total overheads
minus
Budgeted total overheads } Expenditure variance
} Total overhead variance

minus
Actual hours x OAR
minus
Standards hours x OAR } Volume variance

} Efficiency variance

(f) Material variances (including mix and yield)

Actual usage
Actual mix
Actual price

Actual usage
Actual mix
STANDARD PRICE } Direct materials price variance
} Direct materials cost variance

Mixture variance

Actual usage
STANDARD MIX
STANDARD PRICE } Usage variance

Yield variance

STANDARD USAGE
STANDARD MIX
STANDARD PRICE

(g) Sales margin variances

Actual units @ actual mix @ actual margin
minus
Actual units @ actual mix @ STANDARD MARGIN } Sales margin Price variance
} Total sales margin variance

minus
Actual units @ STANDARD MIX @ STANDARD MARGIN } Sales margin Mix variance
} Sales margin quantity variance

minus
STANDARD UNITS @
STANDARD MIX @
STANDARD MARGIN } Sales margin Volume variance

DECISION-MAKING (covering chapter 12)
Essential Knowledge

10. At the end of your studies you should be able to:
    (a) Understand that decision-making is the choice between future, uncertain alternatives and that only future costs and revenues are relevant.
    (b) Give the stages in the decision process.
    (c) Distinguish between *programmed* and *non-programmed* decisions.
    (d) Give the characteristics of relevant costs and revenues.
    (e) Define, and understand the importance of, opportunity costs in decision-making.
    (f) Calculate expected value.
    (g) Give the advantages and disadvantages of expected value.
    (h) Calculate expected value.
    (i) Explain the maximin, maximax and minimax regret rules.
    (j) Understand the relationship between opportunity loss and expected value.
    (k) Explain and draw a decision tree.
    (l) Understand the forward pass and the backward pass.

ESSENTIAL FORMULAE

Expected value = probability of outcome x value of outcome.

MARGINAL COSTING AND CVP ANALYSIS (covering chapter 13)
Essential Knowledge

11. At the end of your studies you should be able to:
    (a) Define marginal costing and know where it can be applied.
    (b) Compare and contrast the accountants and economists view on marginal cost.
    (c) Explain, and give examples of, key factors.
    (d) Give the basic decision rule used when there is a key factor and understand what conditions are necessary for the rule to be useful.
    (e) What are the steps in analysing a problem where marginal costing is to be applied.
    (f) Give examples of typical decisions for which marginal costing can be applied.
    (g) Define differential costing and understand where its use is necessary.
    (h) Give the assumptions on which CVP analysis is based.
    (i) Derive or remember the main CVP analysis formulae.
    (j) Draw traditional and contribution break-even charts.
    (k) Draw single and multi-product profit charts.
    (l) Adjust the charts to allow for changes in fixed costs, contributions and so on.
    (m) Understand the limitations of break-even and profit charts.
    (n) Draw alternative forms of charts with non-linear and stepped functions.
    (o) Compare the accountants and economists view on CVP analysis.
    (p) Understand why there are two break-even points on the economists' break-even chart.
    (q) Understand how differentiation can be used to optimise the level of activity of the firm.

ESSENTIAL FORMULAE

(a) Break-even-point (in units) = $\dfrac{\text{Fixed costs}}{\text{Contribution/unit}}$

(b) Break-even-point = $\dfrac{\text{Fixed costs}}{\text{Contribution/unit}}$ x Sales price/unit
    (£ sales)

    or fixed costs x $\dfrac{1}{\text{C/S ratio}}$

(c) C/S ratio = $\dfrac{\text{Contribution/unit}}{\text{Sales price per unit}}$ x 100

(d) Level of sales to result
    in target profit (in units) = $\dfrac{\text{Fixed cost + target profit}}{\text{Contribution/unit}}$

(e) Level of sales to result
in target profit after tax
(in units)

$$= \frac{\text{Fixed cost} + \left(\dfrac{\text{target profit}}{1 - \text{tax rate}}\right)}{\text{Contribution/unit}}$$

Level of sales to result
in target profit (£ sales)

$$= \frac{\text{Fixed costs x sales value}}{\text{Contribution}}$$

Note: The above formulae relate to a single product firm or one with an unvarying mix of sales. With a multi product firm it is possible to calculate the break-even point as follows

Break-even point
(£ sales)

$$= \frac{\text{Fixed Costs x Sales Value}}{\text{Contribution}}$$

PRICING DECISIONS (covering chapter 14)
Essential knowledge

12. At the end of your studies you should be able to:
    (a) Explain the factors which may need to be considered in a pricing decisions.
    (b) Know the micro-economic theory relating to pricing where there is imperfect competition.
    (c) Derive marginal revenue and marginal cost given the total revenue and total cost functions.
    (d) Understand price elasticity and remember the formula for the price elasticity of demand.
    (e) Understand the meaning of cross elasticity of demand and income elasticity of demand.
    (f) Explain the limitations of marginal analysis.
    (g) Understand the background to cost based pricing and what is meant by full cost pricing.
    (h) Explain rate of return pricing.
    (i) Criticise cost-plus systems and understand why they are widely used in practice.
    (j) Know how demand can be influenced other than by price changes.

ESSENTIAL FORMULAE
Profit maximising price with imperfect competition is when MR = MC.
Where MR = marginal revenue and MC = marginal cost.

Price elasticity of demand

$$= \frac{\text{\% change in quantity of demanded}}{\text{\% change in price}}$$

Cross elasticity of demand

$$= \frac{\text{\% change in quantity of X demanded}}{\text{\% change in price of Y}}$$

Percentage mark up on cost

$$= \frac{\text{Capital employed}}{\text{Total annual costs}} \quad \text{x} \quad \text{planned rate of return on capital employed}$$

LINEAR PROGRAMMING (covering chapter 15)
Essential knowledge

13. At the end of your studies you should be able to:
    (a) Define LP and give the conditions necessary to be able to use the technique.
    (b) Express the problem in the standard LP manner.
    (c) Explain; objective function, decision variables, constraints.
    (d) Understand the circumstances in which LP problems can be solved graphically.
    (e) Draw a graph of a LP problem and find the solution point.
    (f) Understand how to set up the initial tableau to be used in the simplex method.
    (g) Know the purpose of slack variables.
    (h) Interpret every aspect of the final simplex tableau.
    (i) Understand the meaning and usefulness of shadow prices.
    (j) Calculate the shadow price when the LP problem has been solved graphically.
    (k) Understand the importance of sensitivity analysis and how to carry it out.
    (l) Explain the limitations of LP.

INVESTMENT APPRAISAL (covering chapters 16 & 17)

14. At the end of your studies you should be able to:
    (a) Explain the three factors on which a decision to invest is based.
    (b) Define and know the disadvantages of the traditional investment appraisal techniques.
    (c) Understand the importance of cash flows and their timing to DCF.
    (d) Give the assumptions contained in basic DCF appraisal.
    (e) Calculate the NPV of any cash flows and understand its meaning.
    (f) Define and calculate the IRR.
    (g) Compare the features of NPV and IRR especially relating to the choice between mutually exclusive projects.
    (h) Explain the multiple rate problem and how it occurs.
    (i) Calculate the profitability index.
    (j) Understand the problems involved with finding the firm's cost of capital.
    (k) Define and calculate the weighted average cost of capital (WACC).
    (l) Explain the Gordon growth model of equity valuation.
    (m) Understand how gearing affects the WACC.
    (n) Contrast the Modigliani Miller traditional views on the effects of gearing.,
    (o) Explain the capital asset pricing model (CAPM) and understand the meaning of the beta coefficient.
    (p) Understand the effect of inflation on investment appraisal and be able to explain synchronised and differential inflation.
    (q) Distinguish between money and 'real' cash flows.
    (r) Deal with the main effects of taxation in investment appraisal.
    (s) Describe how uncertainty affects a project.
    (t) Explain how uncertainty affecting the individual project can be appraised.
    (u) Deal with the calculations of expected value in projects and extend this to discrete probabilistic analysis.
    (v) Explain and deal with continuous probabilistic analysis using statistical principles.
    (w) Undertake a sensitivity analysis of a project's cash flows.
    (x) Understand the portfolio effect of uncertainty.
    (y) Describe how the decision maker's attitude to risk affects his decision.
    (z) Describe capital rationing and distinguish between the hard and soft views.
    (aa) Decide between the projects where rationing exists for single and multi periods.

ESSENTIAL FORMULAE

Accounting rate of return $\quad = \dfrac{\text{Profit pa}}{\text{Investment}}$

$$\text{NPV} \quad = \quad \Sigma \ \frac{C_i}{(1 + r)^i}$$

where C is net cash flow in the period, i is the period number and r is the discount rate.

Profitability index $\quad = \dfrac{\text{NPV}}{\text{Initial investment}}$

Cost of perpetuity, $r = \dfrac{a}{v}$

where r = rate of interest, a = annual income, v = current market value.

Dividend valuation model:
- constant dividends to perpetuity

$$i = \frac{d}{v}$$

- with constant growth

$$i \quad = \quad \frac{d(1 + g)}{v} + g$$

$$\beta \quad = \quad \frac{\text{Covariance (Ra, Rm)}}{\text{Variance (Rm)}}$$

where Ra = expected return on security.
       Rm = expected return on a market portfolio.
       β = beta coefficient.

(see also appendix to chapter 16 for review of discounting formulae)

Real discount factor = $\dfrac{1 + \text{money discount factor}}{1 + \text{inflation rate}} + 1$

$$\sigma_{NPV} = \sqrt{\sum \frac{\sigma_i{}^2}{(1+r)^{i^2}}}$$

where σ_i is the standard deviation of the individual cash flows.

PERFORMANCE APPRAISAL (covering chapter 18)
Essential knowledge

15. At the end of your studies you should be able to:
    (a) Discuss the meaning of decentralisation and its objectives.
    (b) Understand the primary objectives of performance appraisal.
    (c) Distinguish between the types of responsibility centres.
    (d) Understand the various categories of profit used for performance appraisal: controllable profit, divisional profit, net profit, residual profit.
    (e) Define return on capital employed (ROCE) and understand the variants possible.
    (f) Understand the limitations of residual profit and ROCE.
    (g) Understand the imperfection which arise from using a single financial appraisal measure and what other appraisal could be used in addition.

TRANSFER PRICING (covering chapter 19)
Essential knowledge

16. At the end of your studies you should be able to:
    (a) Understand why transfer pricing is necessary and be able to discuss the three objectives which a transfer price should ideally fulfil.
    (b) Give the ideal transfer price according to economic theory, assuming a profit maximising objective.
    (c) Explain why it is difficult in practice to set the theoretically ideal transfer price.
    (d) Understand what is meant by market based transfer pricing.
    (e) Know the practical problems in applying market prices.
    (f) Explain the reasons why cost based transfer pricing is used and why standard costs are frequently used.
    (g) Define full cost transfer pricing and discuss its limitations.
    (h) Explain variable cost transfer pricing and its advantages and limitations especially for performance appraisal.
    (i) Discuss the reasons why a dual transfer price approach may be considered and the possible disadvantages.
    (j) Explain negotiated transfer prices and the difficulties which could arise from their use.

RATIO ANALYSIS (covering chapter 20)
Essential Knowledge

17. At the end of your studies you should be able to:
    (a) Explain the purpose of ratio analysis and the importance of trends and comparisons.
    (b) Understand the three broad categories into which ratios can be classified.
    (c) Construct a ratio pyramid culminating in the ROCE.
    (d) Discuss the various ways in which capital employed can be defined and the need to define profit appropriately.
    (e) Understand and define the supporting ratios relating to profit margins and asset turnover.
    (f) Discuss the importance of solvency ratios.
    (g) Calculate the major solvency ratios including; the current ratio, acid test, stock turnover, debtors collection period.
    (h) Understand and define the main investment ratios including; earnings per share, dividend yield and cover, PE ratio, earnings and dividend yield.
    (i) Describe how a Z score is derived.
    (j) Give the five key ratios developed by Altmann.
    (k) Discuss the features of value added statements.

ESSENTIAL FORMULAE

Return on capital employed $\quad = \quad \dfrac{\text{Operating profit}}{\text{Operating assets}}$

Asset turnover ratio $\quad = \quad \dfrac{\text{Sales}}{\text{Operating assets}}$

Profit margin ratio $\quad = \quad \dfrac{\text{Operating profit}}{\text{Sales}}$

Current ratio $\quad = \quad \dfrac{\text{Current assets}}{\text{Current liabilities}}$

Quick ratio $\quad = \quad \dfrac{\text{Current assets - stocks}}{\text{Current liabilities}}$

Stock turnover $\quad = \quad \dfrac{\text{Cost of goods sold in period}}{\text{Average stock held in period}}$

Collection period $\quad = \quad \dfrac{\text{Debtors}}{\text{Average daily credit sales}}$

Gearing ratio $\quad = \quad \dfrac{\text{Fixed interest capital}}{\text{Fixed interest capital + equity}}$

Earnings per share $\quad = \quad \dfrac{\text{Profits after tax less preference dividend}}{\text{Number of ordinary shares issued}}$

Dividend yield $\quad = \quad \dfrac{\text{Nominal share value x dividend \%}}{\text{Market price per share}}$

Price/earnings ratio $\quad = \quad \dfrac{\text{Market price per share}}{\text{Earnings per share}}$

Earnings yield $\quad = \quad \dfrac{\text{Earnings per share}}{\text{Market price per share}} \times 100\%$

MANAGEMENT ACCOUNTING AND COMPUTERS (covering chapter 21)

18. At the end of your studies you should be able to:

(a) Explain why computers can be useful for management accounting and other administrative tasks.

(b) Understand the relationship between management accounting and information systems in general.

(c) Give the characteristics of information for which computer processing is likely to be useful.

(d) Define and give the scope of data processing or transaction processing systems.

(e) Distinguish between current activity processing, report processing and inquiry processing.

(f) Understand the relationship between data processing systems and the organisations MIS.

(g) Define decision support systems (DSS) and give their characteristics.

(h) Understand a data base and the part played by the data base management system.

(i) Give examples of application packages that are commonly used in DSS.

(j) Describe spread sheets and give examples of their application.

(k) Define expert systems.

(l) Discuss the importance of sensitivity analysis to the management accountant.

SPECIAL REVISION
QUESTIONS

The following questions have been specially selected from past ACCA question papers either because they illustrate important principles or because they cover areas which experience shows that students find difficult.

Each question has a commentary, a step by step method guide and a fully annotated answer. These questions will be found to be of most value if you make an attempt at the question yourself then work carefully through the solutions given noting particularly the step by step approach which will assist you when dealing with similar questions in the future.

1. Bamfram plc is a well established manufacturer of a specialised product, a Wallop, which has the following specifications for production:

Components	Standard quantity	Standard price
		£
WALS	15	60
LOPS	8	75

The standard direct labour hours to produce a Wallop at the standard wage rate of £10.50 per hour has been established at 60 hours per Wallop.

The annual fixed overhead budget is divided into calendar months with equal production per month. The budgeted output of 2,400 Wallops pa.

Mr Jones, a marketing person, is now the managing director of Bamfram plc and must report to the board of directors later this day and seeks your advice in respect of the following operating information for the month of May:

	£	£
Sales		504,000
Cost of sales:		
Direct materials	281,520	
Direct labour	112,320	
	393,840	
Fixed production overheads	42,600	
		436,440
Gross profit		67,560
Administration expenses		11,150
Selling and distribution expenses		17,290
Net profit		39,210

The sales manager informs Mr Jones that despite adverse trading conditions his sale staff have been able to sell 180 Wallops at the expected standard selling price.

The production manager along with the purchasing department manager are also pleased that prices for components have been stable for the whole of the current year and they are able to provide the following information.

Stocks for May are as follows:

	1 May	31 May
Component WALS	600	750
Component LOPS	920	450

The actual number of direct labour hours worked in May was 11,700; considerably less than the production manager had been budgeted. Further the purchasing manager advised that WALS had cost £171,000 at a price of £57 per unit in the month of May and 1,000 LOPS had been acquired for £81,000.

Mr Jones eager to please the board of directors, requests you, as the newly appointed management accountant, to prepare appropriate statements to highlight the following information which is to be presented to the board.

(a) The standard product cost of a Wallop.   (3 marks)

(b) (i)   The direct material variances for both price and usage for each component used in the month of May assuming that prices were stable throughout the relevant period.
     (ii) The direct labour efficiency and wage rate variances for the month of May.
     (iii) The fixed production overhead expenditure and volume variances.

Note: you may assume that during the month of May there is no change in the level of finished goods stocks.
                                                                                   (10 marks)
(c) A detailed reconciliation statement of the standard gross profit with the actual gross profit for the month of May.   (4 marks)

(d) Draft a brief report for Mr Jones that he could present to the board of directors on the usefulness, or otherwise, of the statement you have prepared in your answer to (c) above.   (5 marks)

Commentary

A comprehensive standard costing question commencing with the calculation of the standard product cost through detailed variance calculation to the reconciliation of actual and standard profit. The answer provides alternative price variances, one based on purchase and the one based on usage.

Step-by-step method guide

Step 1: Calculate the standard product cost based on an output level of 2400.

Step 2: Calculate the material, labour and overhead variances.

Step 3: Reconcile the actual and standard profits.

Step 4: Draft a report on usefulness of reconciliation statement.

Step 1

(a) Standard product cost

Direct materials			*Standard cost*
			£
WALS	15 @ £60		900
LOPS	8 @ £75		600
			1,500
Direct labour			
	60 hours @ £10.50		630
Standard prime cost			2,130
Fixed overheads	504,000 ÷ 2,400		210
	= Product cost		£2,340

Step 2

(b) Price variances (based on purchases)

WALS
(SP–AP) x purchases
(60–57) x 3,000   = £9,000 FAV
LOPS
(75–81) X 100   = £6,000 ADV
Total   £3,000 FAV

Note: If the materials variance is based on usage not purchases the variances become:

WALS
(60–57) x 2,850   = £8,550 FAV
LOPS
(75–81) x 1,470   = £8,820 ADV
    £270 ADV

The usage figures are calculated below:

(i) Materials usage variance

		Units
WALS	Opening stock	600
	Purchases	3,000
		3,600
	Less closing stock	750
	= usage	2,850

∴ variance = (2,850 – (180 x 15)) x £60 = £9,000 ADV

LOPS	Opening stock	920
	Purchases	1,000
		1,920
	Less closing stock	450
		1,470

∴ variance = (1,470 – (180 x 8)) x £75 = £ 2,250 ADV
Total   £11,250 ADV

(ii)   Labour rate variance

$$(SR-AR) \times \text{hours worked}$$
$$(£10.50 - \frac{112,320}{11,700}) \times 11,700 = £10,530 \text{ FAV}$$

Efficiency variance

$$(SH-AH) \times \text{standard rate}$$

$$(180 \times 60 - 11,700) \times 10.50 = £9,450 \text{ ADV}$$

Total labour variance   £1,080 FAV

(iii)   Fixed overhead expenditure variance

$$\text{Budget} - \text{Actual}$$
$$£504,000 \div 12 - 42,600 = £600 \text{ ADV}$$

Volume variance

$$(\text{Budgeted} - \text{Actual volume}) \times OAR$$
$$(200 - 180) \times \frac{42,000}{200} = £4,200 \text{ ADV}$$

Step 3

(c)   Profit reconciliation

	ADV	FAV	£
Sales at standard (180 @ £2,800)			504,000
Less standard cost (180 @ £2,340)			421,200
Standard gross profit			82,800
Variances (from above)			
Materials			
Price	270		
Usage	11,250		
Wages			
Rate		10,530	
Efficiency	9,450		
Overheads			
Expenditure	600		
Volume	4,200		
	25,770	10,530	= 15,240 ADV
Actual gross profit			£67,560

Note

If the profit statement had been derived from opening and closing stock figures then the price variance based on purchases would have been used.

Step 4

(d)   The report should contain an analysis of the causes and significance of the several variances and of the trend in the variances compared with previous months. All these matters can be taken from the manual.

2. (a) A manufacturer has three products, A, B, and C. Currently sales, cost and selling price details and processing time requirements are as follows:

	Product A	Product B	Product C
Annual sales (units)	6,000	6,000	750
Selling price	£20.00	£13.00	£39.00
Unit cost	£18.00	£24.00	£30.00
Processing time required per unit	1 hour	1 hour	2 hours

The firm is working at full capacity (13,500 processing hours per year). Fixed manufacturing overheads are absorbed into unit costs by a charge of 200% of variable cost. This procedure fully absorbs the fixed manufacturing overhead.

Assuming that:

(i) processing time can be switched from one product line to another;
(ii) the demand at current selling price is:

	Product A	Product B	Product C
	11,000	8,000	2,000

and

(iii) the selling prices are not to be altered.

You are required to calculate the best programme for the next operating period and to indicate the increase in net profit that this should yield. In addition identify the shadow price of a processing hour. (11 marks)

(b) A review of the selling prices is in progress and it has been estimated that for each product, an increase in the selling price would result in a fall in demand at the rate of 2,000 units for an increase of £1 and similarly, that a decrease of £1 would increase demand by 2,000 units. Specifically the following price/demand relationships would apply.

Product A		Product B		Product C	
Selling price £	Estimated demand	Selling price £	Estimated demand	Selling price £	Estimated demand
24.50	2,000	34.00	2,000	39.00	2,000
23.50	4,000	33.00	4,000	38.00	4,000
22.50	6,000	32.00	6,000	37.00	6,000
21.50	8,000	31.00	8,000	36.00	8,000
20.50	10,000	30.00	10,000	35.00	10,000
19.50	12,000	29.00	12,000	34.00	12,000
18.50	14,000	28.00	14,000	33.00	14,000

From this information you are required to calculate the best selling prices, the revised best production plan *and* the net profit that this plan should produce. (11 marks)

COMMENTARY

This question uses the principle of maximising contribution per unit of the limiting factor and how to calculate the shadow price of a unit of the scarce resource. The second part requires the identification of the marginal contribution based on the given price/demand schedule. A practical question with a considerable amount of calculation.

STEP-BY-STEP METHOD GUIDE

Step 1: Calculate the unit contribution for the products and the contribution per processing hour.

Step 2: Rank the products in order of contribution per processing hour and calculate the best programme.

Step 3: Compare return from optimal plan to the existing programme and calculate the shadow price.

Step 4: Calculate the marginal contribution per product for 2,000 hour increments using the price/demand schedule.

Step 5: Allocate the total processing hours according to the marginal contributions and calculate the final net profit.

Step 1

The best programme would be that which maximised contribution per unit of the limiting resource, processing hours.

	A	B	C
	£	£	£
Unit cost	18	24	30
Fixed overhead	12	16	20
Variable cost	6	8	10
Selling price	20	31	39
Contribution	14	23	29
Contribution/hour	14	23	14.50

Step 2

∴ ranking B C A

The best programme is thus:

			£
B	8,000 units using 8,000 hours : contribution		184,000
C	2,000 units using 4,000 hours : contribution		58,000
A	1,500 units using 1,500 hours : contribution		21,000
			£263,000

Step 3

This compares with the existing programme with a contribution as follows:

		£
A	6,000 @ £14	84,000
B	6,000 @ £23	138,000
C	750 @ £29	21,750
		243,750

Thus as all the fixed overhead is already absorbed the new programme provides an extra £19,250 profit.
As the optimal plan produces B and C up to the demand maxima the next processing hour would have to be used for product A giving a contribution of £14 per hour which is the shadow price.

Step 4

Processing hours remain the limiting factor so the following table shows the marginal contribution by using 2,000 hour increments which give 2,000, 2,000 and 1,000 unit increments for A, B and C respectively.

Hours	A Total Contribution	A Marginal Contribution	B Total Contribution	B Marginal Contribution	C Total Contribution	C Marginal Contribution
	£'000	£'000	£'000	£'000	£'000	£'000
2,000	37	37	52	52	29.5	29.5
4,000	70	33	100	48	58	28.5
6,000	99	29	144	44	85.5	27.5
10,000	145	21	220	36	137.5	25.5
12,000	162	17	252	32	162	24.5
14,000	175	13	280	28	185.5	23.5

Step 5

The total amount of 13,500 processing hours is then used increment by increment according to the marginal contribution from the table.

Processing hours		Product	Marginal contribution £
First	2,000	B	52,000
Next	2,000	B	48,000
	2,000	B	44,000
	2,000	B	40,000
	2,000	A	37,000
	2,000	B	36,000
Balance	1,500	A	24,250 *
	13,500		281,250

* 3,500 (23.50 – 6) – 37,000 = £24,250

This gives total production of 10,000 B and 3,500 A so the selling prices to achieve these values are £30 B and £23.50 A.

Net profit = contribution £281,250
Less fixed cost £183,000 *
£98,250

* from part (a)

	£
6,000 units of A absorbs	72,000
6,000 units of B absorbs	96,000
750 units of C absorbs	15,000
Total fixed overheads	£183,000

Note: Because a stepped rather than continuous function has been used the above solution is only approximate.

3. Simplo Ltd make and sell a single product. A standard marginal cost system is in operation. Feedback reporting takes planning and operational variances into consideration. It is implemented as follows:

(a) Permanent non-controllable changes from the original standard are incorporated into a revised standard.
(b) The budgeted effect of the standard revision is reported for each variance type.
(c) the sales volume variance is valued at the revised standard contribution and is analysed to show the gain or loss in contribution arising from a range of contributory factors.
(d) The remaining operational variances are then calculated.

Information relating to period 6 is as follows:

(i)   A summary of the operating statement for period 6 using the variance analysis approach detailed above shows:

	£
Original budgeted contribution	51,200
Budget revision variances (net)	13,120 (F)
Revised budget contribution	64,320
Sales volume variance	16,080 (F)
Revised standard contribution for sales achieved	80,400
Other variances (net)	8,200 (A)
Actual contribution	72,200

(F) = favourable, (A) = adverse.

(ii)   Original standard cost data per product unit:

	£	£
Selling price		100
Less: direct material 5 kilos at £10	50	
direct labour 3 hours at £6	18	
		68
Contribution		32

(iii) The current market price is £110 per unit. Simplo Ltd sold at £106 per unit in an attempt to stimulate demand.

(iv)   Actual direct material used was 12,060 kilos at £10 per kilo. Any related variances are due to operational problems.

(v)   The original standard wage rate excluded an increase of £0.60 per hour subsequently agreed with the trade unions. Simplo Ltd made a short term operational decision to employ a slightly lower grade of labour, who were paid £6.20 per hour. The total hours paid were 7,600. These included 200 hours of idle time, of which 40% was due to a machine breakdown and the remainder to a power failure.

(vi)   Budgeted production and sales quantity   1,600 units
       Actual sales quantity   2,000 units
       Actual production quantity   2,400 units

Required

(a) Prepare a single operating statement for period 6 which expands the summary statement shown in (i) above.

This single operating statement should clearly show:

(i)   the basis of calculation of the contribution figures for original budget, revised budget and revised standard for sales achieved;

(ii)   the analysis of the budget revision variance by variance type;

(iii) the analysis of the sales volume variance showing the quantity and value of the gain or loss arising from each of the following factors:

    Additional capacity available;
    Idle time;
    Stock increase not yet translated into sales;

(iv)   The analysis of the 'other variances' by variance type.   (16 marks)

(b) Prepare a brief report to the management of Simplo on the performance in period 6 making full use of the information contained in the operating statement prepared in (a). Your report should indicate the relevance of the analysis utilised in the operating statement. (6 marks)

COMMENTARY

An unusual variance analysis question incorporating sales variances and planning and operational variances. An important theme running through the question was the requirement to analyse the results in an informative a manner as possible. It was not sufficient to be able to reconcile the overall difference between budgeted and actual contribution. What was needed was relevant detail and comment.

STEP-BY-STEP METHOD GUIDE

Step 1: Calculate the details of revised contribution, the unit equivalents to the time gained and lost, and the detailed variances.

Step 2: Prepare a revised operating statement commencing with the original budgeted contribution, moving through the revised budgeted contribution to the actual contribution.

Step 3: Prepare a detailed report with cross reference to the revised operating statement.

Step 1

(a) *Preliminary calculations:*

(i) Revised contribution per unit

Selling price			£110
Less: Direct material		£50	
Direct labour (3 x £6.6)		19.8	69.8
Contribution			£ 40.20

(ii) Sales volume variance analysis:

Actual hours	7,600	
Budget hours (1,600 x 3)	4,800	
Extra capacity	2,800	(≡ 933.3 units)
Actual hours	7,600	
Idle time	200	(≡ 66.7 units)
Usable hours	7,400	
Standard hours produced (2,400 x 3)	7,200	
Productivity loss	200	(≡ 66.7 units)
Stock increase	400 units	

(iii) Sales price variance = 2,000 x (£106 - 100) - £8,000(A), policy.
(iv) Material usage variance = (2,400 x 5 - 12,060) x £10 = £600(A).
(v) Labour efficiency variance = (2,400 x 3 - 7,400) x £6.6 = £1,320(A)
(vi) Labour idle time variance = 200 hours x £6.6 = £1,320(A).
(vii) Wage rate variance = 7,600 hours x (£6.6 - £6.2) = £3,040(A) policy.

Step 2

New Operating statement period 6.

		£	£
Original contribution (16,00 x £32)			51,200

Planning variances

Sales price (1,600 x £10)	16,000 (F)	
Wage rate (1,600 x 3 x 60p)	2,880 (A)	13,120 (F)
Revised contribution (1,600 x £40.20)		64,320

Operational variances

Total sales volume variance (2,000 – 1,600 x £40.20)

Comprising		Units		
Extra capacity	+	933.3	@ £40.20 37,520 (F)	
Productivity loss	–	66.7	@ £40.20 2,680 (A)	
Idle time	–	66.7	@ £40.20 2,680 (A)	
Stock increase	–	400.0	@ £40.20 16,080 (A)	16,080 (F)

=	Revised standard contribution for actual Sales (2000 x £40.20)	80,400
	Other operational and policy variances	

Sales price (policy)	£8,000 (A)	
Material usage (op)	600 (A)	
Labour efficiency (op)	1,320 (A)	
Idle time (op)	1,320 (A)	
Wage rate (policy)	3,040 (F)	8,200 (A)
	= Actual contribution	72,200

Step 3

The key points in the report are as follows:

(i) The breakdown of the planning variances into sales price and wage rate shows the effect of the budget revisions, ie:

	Selling price	*Wage rate*
	£	£
Original standard	100	6
Revised standard	110	6.60
Difference	£ 10	0.60 loss

(ii) The overall sales volume variance of £16,080 (F) shows the net benefit of selling an extra 400 units at the revised contribution of £40.20 per unit. The breakdown of the variances shows how the overall variance could be analysed, ie 933 extra units came from the extra capacity, some were lost through the drop in productivity and idle time, 400 were placed in stock leaving a net 400 to be sold.

(iii) The other operational and policy variances are deemed to be controllable or temporary policy items so have not been included into the revised budget.

4. (a) CB Division of the Meldon Group manufacturers a single component which it sells externally and can also transfer to other divisions within the group.

CB Division has been set the performance target of a budgeted residual income of £300,000 for the coming financial year.

The following additional budgeted information relating to CD Division has been prepared for the coming financial year:

   (i)   maximum production/sales capacity: 120,000 components;
   (ii) sales to external customers: 80,000 components at £20 each;
   (iii) variable cost per components: £14;
   (iv) fixed costs directly attributable to the division: £60,000;
   (v)   capital employed: £1,600,000 with a cost of capital of 15%.

The XY Division of the Meldon Group has asked CB Division to quote a transfer price for 40,000 components.

Calculate the transfer price per component which CB Division should quote to XY Division in order that its budgeted residual income target will be achieved.   (5 marks)

   (b) Explain why the transfer price calculated in (a) may lead to sub-optimal decision making from a group viewpoint.   (4 marks)

   (c) XY Division now establishes that it requires 50,000 components. External company L is willing to supply 50,000 components at £15.50 each but is not willing to quote for only part of the requirement of XY Division. External company M is willing to supply any number of components at £18 each.

For each of the cases below (taken separately), state the source or sources from which XY Division should purchase the components in order to maximise its own net profit and explain why the particular source or sources have been chosen, assuming that CB Division is willing to supply the components to XY Division:

   (i)   at an average price per component for the quantity required, such that the budget residual income of CB Division will still be achieved;
   (ii) at an average price per component which reflects the opportunity cost of components transferred;
   (iii) at prices per component which reflect the opportunity cost of *each* component.   (9 marks)

   (d) State which of the bases for transfer prices in (c) should lead to group profit maximisation and calculate the reduction in group profit which should arise from the operation of each of the other transfer price bases in comparison.   (4 marks)

COMMENTARY

A question on transfer pricing which requires knowledge of opportunity costs. Relatively little calculation is required but a clear understanding is required of transfer pricing principles and the effect these have on individual divisions and the group as a whole.

STEP-BY-STEP METHOD GUIDE

Because the question is divided into four sections which are further sub-divided it forms a natural series of steps providing it is answered in the sequence given in the question.

(a) Calculation of revenue required from transfers

	£
Variable costs (120,000 x £14)	1,680,000
Divisional fixed costs	60,000
Total costs	1,740,000
Imputed interest (15% of £1.6m)	240,000
Target residual interest	300,000
Total revenue requirements	2,280,000
Less: external sales (80,000 x £20)	1,600,000
Revenue required from transfers	680,000

$$\therefore \text{ transfer price/unit } = \frac{\text{Revenue required}}{\text{Units transferred}}$$

$$= \frac{680,000}{40,000} = \text{£17 per unit}$$

(b) The £17 transfer price calculated above is £3 more than the marginal cost of £14. If XY are forced to buy internally at the transfer price of £17 then this will be sub-optimal for the group if XY could buy externally at below £14 per unit. The problem with a transfer price above marginal cost is that the receiving departments may think that an external price *below* the transfer price, but *above* group marginal cost, is worthwhile. For example, if XY bought external at £16 the group would spend an extra £2 per unit.

(c) **Note:** Although not stated in this part it is assumed that CB has the same budget as in part (a).

    (i)   Average price per component:

Achieving target residual income

40,000 units	@£17	680,000
10,000 units	@£20	200,000
50,000		880,000

$$\therefore \text{ average price } = \frac{\text{£880,000}}{50,000} = \text{£17.6}$$

XY Division, quoted an average price of £17.6, will choose external company L as the cheapest source at £15.50 per unit.

$$\therefore \text{ cost to group} = 50,000 \times \text{£15.50} = \text{£775,000}$$

    (ii)   Reflecting the average opportunity cost:

	£
40,000 units @ variable cost of £14	560,000
10,000 @ sales foregone of £20	200,000
	760,000

$$\therefore \text{ average price} = \frac{760,000}{50,000} = \text{£15.2}$$

Thus XY will choose to buy from CB because the average price of £15.20 is lower than the external prices quoted by L and M.

Note: It should be understood that XY is deemed to know *only* the average price of £15.20 from CB not how it was made up.

    (iii)   Reflecting the individual opportunity costs:

CB will quote as follows:

        First 40,000 at £14
        Next 10,000 at £20.

Thus XY will choose 40,000 from CB at £14 and 10,000 at £18 from M.
Total cost to group = £(40,000 × 14) + (10,000 × 18) = £740,000

(d) Group profit is maximised in (ii) above, ie a total cost of £740,000.

The profit reductions would be:

Option (i) total cost £775,000
Therefore reduction in profit = £775,000 − 740,000 = £35,000
Option (ii) total cost £760,000
Therefore reduction in profit £760,000 − 740,000 = £20,000
The maximum profit position can only be obtained when there is full flow of information from CB to XY.

5. Stobo plc must decide whether to produce and sell either product X or product Y in the coming period.

The estimated demand probabilities for the period and the selling prices which have been set are as follows:

	Product X		Product Y	
Selling price per unit	£75		£150	
Sales (units)	5,600	1,400	3,200	1,600
Probability	0.6	0.4	0.3	0.7

The average direct material cost per product unit is expected to vary according to quantity purchased as follows:

Product X		Product B	
Units purchased Up to	Average material cost per unit £	Units purchased Up to	Average material cost per unit £
1,000	6.50	1,000	33
2,000	6.00	2,000	30
3,000	5.50	3,000	28
4,000	5.00	4,000	26
5,000	4.75		
6,000	4.50		

Each product would pass through two departments – making and finishing – where the maximum available labour hours are sufficient for all possible quantities. It may be assumed that labour hours which are paid for are balanced by natural wastage, so that labour hours which are surplus to actual production requirements do not need to be paid for.

The labour operations are subject to a learning curve effect of 80% for product X and 90% for product Y which would apply in both the making and finishing departments.

Initial batch sizes will be 700 units for product X and 800 units for product Y. For these sizes, the hours required per product unit are as follows:

	Product X hours per unit	Product Y hours per unit
Making department	4	5
Finishing department	3	4

Wages are paid at £4 per hour in the making department and £3.75 per hour in the finishing department.

Variable overheads would be incurred at 200% on productive wage costs for the making department and 250% on productive wage costs for the finishing department.

Company fixed overheads are normally apportioned to products as a percentage of sales revenue. During the coming period, when total sales revenue of Stobo plc is estimated at £12,000,000, the overheads have been budgeted at 17.5% of sales revenue. The fixed overheads which would be avoidable if products X and Y were not produced are as follows:

Product X	£36,000
Product Y	£5,000

Production would be adjusted to equate with sales in the period and the purchase of raw material would be matched with production requirements.

Required

(a) Showing all relevant calculations, explain which product Stobo plc should produce and sell.   (15 marks)
(b) Showing all relevant calculations, explain how the choice of product might be affected if the maximum available hours must be retained and paid for in the making and finishing departments but all other conditions are as above.   (7 marks)

COMMENTARY

This is an involved question which combines several aspects of management accounting; relevant cost identification, contribution calculations, learning curves and expected value calculations. Because it spans several parts of the syllabus there are no standard techniques available for its solution. What is required is a thorough grasp of basic principles and the ability to apply them in unusual questions.

STEP-BY-STEP METHOD GUIDE

(a) Step 1: Calculate the individual components of cost taking account of variable material costs and learning effects on wages.

Step 2: Calculate the four profit possibilities using costs in step 1.

Step 3: Weight the profits by the possibilities of the sales and find the expected value. Choose the option with the highest expected value.

(b) Step 4: Add back the wages cost to the original contributions because wages are now a fixed cost.

Step 5: Calculate the new expected value and choose option with the highest.

(a) Step 1
Preliminary calculations for cost elements.

Material costs: These are derived from the table given in the question, eg sales of X of 5,600 units gives a purchase quantity of up to 6,000 with a price of £4.50 unit.

Wages cost: The learning curve effect means that as the cumulative production doubles the labour time falls by the given percentage (80% for X and 90% Y). As an example, the full calculations for the making department are as follows:

Product X		Product Y	
Cumulative production	Hours/Unit	Cumulative production	Hours/unit
700 units	= 4	800 units	= 5
1,400 units	4 x 0.8 = 3.2	1,600 units	5 x 0.9 = 4.5
2,800 units	3.2 x 0.8 = 2.56	3,200 units	4.5 x 0.9 = 4.05
5,600 units	2.56 x 0.8 = 2.048		

The calculated hours per unit are multiplied by £4 and £3.75 per hour, respectively.

Variable overheads: The given percentages are applied to the wage cost (based on the learning effect calculations). As an example the variable overhead calculations for product Y in the making department are shown below:

		Product Y - making department			
Production	Hours/unit	Wages cost		Variable overheads	
1,600 units	4.5	4.5 x £4 = £18		£18 x 200% = £36	
3,200 units	4.05	4.05 x £4 = £16.20		£16.20 x 200% = £32.40	

Fixed overheads: For any form of decision-making it is only the costs which could change which are relevant. Thus in this example, the *avoidable* fixed costs are the only ones which are relevant.

Based on the detailed cost calculations described above the expected profit summary can be produced.

Step 2

	Product X		Expected profit summary	Product Y
Sales level (units)	5,600	1,400	3,200	1,600
	£	£	£	£
Selling price	75.00	75.00	150.00	150.00
Variable costs:				
Material	4.50	6.00	26.00	30.00
Wages: Making	8.192	12.80	16.20	18.00
Finishing	5.76	9.00	12.15	13.50
Overheads: Making	16.384	25.60	32.40	36.00
Finishing	14.40	22.50	30.375	33.75
Total variable costs	49.236	75.90	117.125	131.25
Contribution/unit	25.764	(0.90)	32.875	18.75
Total contribution	144,278	(1,260)	105,200	30,000
less avoidable FC	36,000	36,000	5,000	5,000
Profit (loss)	108,278	(37,260)	100,200	25,000

Step 3
EXPECTED VALUES

$$\text{Product X} = (108,278 \times 0.6) + (-37,260 \times 0.4) = £50,063$$
$$\text{Product Y} = (100,200 \times 0.3) + (25,000 \times 0.7) = £47,560$$

∴ on the basis of expected values, product X would be chosen. EV assumes risk neutrality and if risk aversion was considered then product Y would probably be chosen because the 'worst' outcome is £25,000 profit with a probability of 0.7 and product X has a 0.4 probability of a £37,260 loss.

(b) Step 4

Direct labour is now treated as a fixed cost so the amount of labour in part (a) can be added back to arrive at a revised contribution figure.

Revised profit summary

	Product X			Product Y	
Sales units	5,600	1,400		3,200	1,600
£	£	£		£	
Original contribution	25.764	(0.90)		32.875	18.75
Add back					
Wages: Making	8.192	12.80		16.20	18.00
Finishing	5.76	9.00		12.15	13.50
Revised contribution	39.716	20.90		61.225	50.525
Total contribution	£222,410	29,260		195,920	80,400
less: Avoidable FC	36,000	36,000		5,000	5,000
Profit (loss)	£186,410	(6,740		190,920	75,400

Step 5
EXPECTED VALUE

$$\text{Product X} = (186,410 \times 0.6) - (6,740 \times 0.4) = \underline{£109,150}$$
$$\text{Product Y} = (190,920 \times 0.3) + (75,400 \times 0.7) = \underline{£110,055}$$

∴ on the basis of EV product Y would (narrowly) be chosen.

MOCK EXAMINATION PAPERS

The following examination papers are made up from past ACCA examination questions and are representative of a typical professional examination.

You should attempt these papers under simulated examination conditions, ie without books or notes and within the time allowance, before referring to the suggested answers. You should attempt to mark your answers by reference to the answers supplied (or better still get a fellow student to do this for you) and adopt a hard line with your own work, ie give no marks unless they are genuinely earned.

ACCA MOCK EXAMINATION NO 1

Time allowed: 3 hours
Attempt all questions

Note: To obtain the maximum benefit from this examination you should work under *strict examination conditions*, ie keep to the time allowed, do not refer to notes or books, do not talk to other students - remember, if you cheat, you are cheating yourself.

1. *A company has two machines – A and B each of which may be used to produce products X and Y. The products are fabric, made in a number of widths by passing untreated fabric across one of the machines and then adding a colour dye.*

Budget/forecast data for 1988 are as follows:

(a) *Stocks at 1 January 1988:*
   Product X   30,000 metres at 120 cm width
   Product Y   5,000 metres at 200 cm width
   Untreated fabric   25,000 sq metres
   Fabric dye   25 kilos

(b) *The closing stock of untreated fabric is budgeted at 10% of the required input to production during 1988. No closing stocks of X and Y are budgeted.*

(c) *Fabric yield is budgeted at 90% of input for machine A and 80% of input for machine B, due to processing losses.*

(d) *Fabric dye is used at the rate of 1 kilo per 500 square metres of output for both products X and Y. The maximum quantity available from suppliers during 1988 is 520 kilos. If there is insufficient dye to meet production requirements, the output of the narrowest product would be reduced as required.*

(e) *The budgeted rates of good output for machines A and B are the same and vary with the width of products according to the following table:*

Product width (cm)	Good output per machine hour (metres)
100	120
120	100
140	90
160	80
180	70
200	50
240	40

(f) *The maximum output width of product from each machine is machine A; 140 cm, machine B 240 cm.*

It is company policy not to use Machine B for product widths less than 125 cm.

(g) *Each machine is manned for 35 hours per week for 46 weeks in the year. Part of this is budgeted to be lost as idle time as follows, machine A: 20% of manned hours; machine B: 30% of manned hours. This idel time does not include any idle time caused by a shortage of fabric dye.*

(h) *The sales forecast for 1988 is as follows:*

   Product X   90,000 metres at 120 cm width
                    70,000 metres at 160 cm width
   Product Y   30,000 metres at 200 cm width
                    100,000 metres at 100 cm width

(i) *If production capacity is not sufficient to allow the sales forecast to be achieved the budgets for production on each machine will be set by limiting the quantity of the narrowest product on that machine.*

Required:

(i)   *Prepare budgets for 1988 analysed by product type and width for (i) production quantities and (ii) sales quantities. The budgets should make maximum use of the available resources.*   (8 marks)

(ii) *Prepare a purchases budget for untreated fabric. Express the budget in terms of square metres purchased.*   (6 marks)

(iii) *Suggest ways in which the company might attempt to overcome any inability to meet the sales forecast. Comment on any problems likely to arise in the implementation of each of these ways.*   (8 marks)

                                                                                                              (22 marks)

2.   Two of the divisions of Sanco Ltd are the Intermediate division and the Final division. The Intermediate division produces three products A, B and C. The products are sold to overseas specialist producers as well as to the Final division at the same prices. The Final division uses products A, B and C in the manufacture of products X, Y and Z respectively.

Recently the Final division has been forced to work below capacity because of difficulties in obtaining sufficient supplies of products A, B and C. Consequently the Intermediate division has been instructed by the board of directors to sell all its products to the final division.

The price and cost data is as follows:

Intermediate division

Product	A	A	BC
		£	££
Transfer price	20	20	30
Variable manufacturing cost per unit	7	12	10
Fixed costs	50,000	100,000	75,000

The Intermediate division has a maximum monthly capacity of 50,000 units. The processing constraints are such that capacity production can only be maintained by producing at least 10,000 units of each product. The remaining capacity can be used to produce 20,000 units of any combination of the three products.

Final division

Product	X	Y	Z
	£	£	£
Final selling price	56	60	60
Variable cost per unit:			
Internal purchase	20	20	30
Processing in Final division	10	10	16
Fixed costs	100,000	100,000	200,000

The Final division has sufficient capacity to produce up to 20,000 units more than it is now producing, but because of the lack of products A, B and C, is limiting production. Further the Final division is able to sell all the products that it can produce at the final selling prices.

You are required to:

(a) *From the viewpoint of the Intermediate division, compute the products and quantities which would maximise its divisional profits and to calculate the total company profit, given that all Intermediate's production is transferred internally.*   (4 marks)

(b) *From the viewpoint of the Final division, compute the products and quantities purchased from the Intermediate division which would maximise its divisional profits and indicate the effect on the total company profits.*   (4 marks)

(c) *Compute the product mix which would maximise the total company profits assuming all transfers were internal.*   (4 marks)

(d) *If there were no transactions costs involved for either division in buying or selling A, B or C outside the company, what, if anything, is lost by the policy of internal transfers only?*   (4 marks)

(e) *Discuss the effectiveness or otherwise of the transfer pricing system currently used at Sanco Limited.*   (6 marks)

                                                                                                              (22 marks)

3.   Seeprint Limited is negotiating an initial one year contract with an important customer for the supply of a specialised printed colour catalogue at a fixed contract price of £16 per catalogue. Seeprint's normal capacity for producing such catalogues is 50,000 per annum.

Last year Seeprint Limited earned £11,000 profit per month from a number of small accounts requiring specialised colour catalogues. If the contract under negotiation is not undertaken, then a similar profit might be obtained from these customers next year, but if it is undertaken, there will be no profit from such customers,

The estimated costs of producing colour catalogues of a specialised nature are given below:

The costs below are considered certain with the exception of the direct materials price.

Cost data:

Variable costs per catalogue	£
Direct materials	4.50
Direct wages	3.00
Direct expenses	1.30

Semi-variable costs

	Output levels (capacity utilisation)		
	80%	100%	120
	£	£	£
Indirect materials	46,800	47,000	74,400
Indirect wages	51,200	55,000	72,000
Indirect expenses	6,000	8,000	9,600

Estimated fixed costs per annum:

Depreciation of specialist equipment	£8,000
Supervisory and management salaries	£20,000
Other fixed costs allocated to specialist colour catalogues production	£32,000

You are required to:

(a) Tabulate the costs and profits per unit and in total and the annual profits, assuming that the contract orders in the year are: (i) 40,000, (ii) 50,000 and (iii) 60,000 catalogues, at a direct material cost of £4.50 per catalogue. Comment on the tabulation you have prepared.   (10 marks)

(b) Calculate the expected profit for the year if it is assumed that the probability of the total order is:

  0.4 for 40,000 catalogues
  0.5 for 50,000 catalogues
  0.1 for 60,000 catalogues

  and that the probability of direct material cost is:

  0.5 at £4.50 per catalogue
  0.3 at £5.00 per catalogue
  0.2 at £5.50 per catalogue.   (6 marks)

(c) Discuss the implications for Seeprint Limited of the acceptance or otherwise of the contract with the important customer.   (6 marks)
          (22 marks)

4.   (a) When considering the way in which service department costs should be controlled, the management accountant must consider a range of aims.

  Identify and comment briefly on **three** such aims.   (9 marks)

(b) A charge may be made to user departments for the provision of a service by a service department, using any of the following charge bases:

     (i)   total actual cost;
     (ii)   standard absorption cost;
     (iii) variable cost;
     (iv) opportunity cost;
     (v)   no charge.

For any four of the above bases, comment on the circumstances in which their use might be appropriate and describe problems associated with their use.   (8 marks)

                                                                   (17 marks)

5.   (a) 'Excessive reliance on budgetary control of business and management performance may have dysfunctional consequences.'

       Comment on the relevance of the above statement in relation to each of the following:

       (i)   budgetary slack;
       (ii)   budget standard setting;
       (iii) short-term versus long-term objectives.   (9 marks)

   (b) *Itemise and comment on the physical and behavioural costs and benefits which could arise from the operation of a standard cost system.*   (8 marks)

                                                                   (17 marks)

ACCA MOCK EXAMINATION NO 2

Time allowed: 3 hours
Attempt all questions

Note: To obtain the maximum benefit from this examination you should work under *strict examination conditions*, ie keep to the time allowed, do not refer to notes or books, do not talk to other students - remember, if you cheat, you are cheating yourself.

1. *The budgeted income statement for one of the products of Derwen plc for the month of May 1986 was as follows:*

Budgeted income statement – May 1986

	£	£	£
Sales revenue			
10,000 units at £5			50,000
Production costs			
Budgeted production 10,000 units			
Direct materials:			
Material A 5,000 kg at £0.30	1,500		
Material B 2,600 kg at £0.70	3,500		
		5,000	
Direct labour:			
Skilled 4,500 hours at £3.00	13,500		
Semi-skilled 2,600 hours at £2.50	6,500		
		20,000	
Overhead cost:			
Fixed			10,000
Variable 10,000 units at £0.50		5,000	
		40,000	
Add Opening stock			
1,000 units at £4			4,000
		44,000	
Deduct Closing stock			
1,000 units at £4		4,000	
Cost of goods sold			40,000
	Budgeted profit		10,000

During May 1986 production and sales were both above budget and the following income statement was prepared:

Income statement – May 1986

	£	£	£
Sales revenue			
7,000 units at £5			35,000
4,000 units at £4.75			19,000
			54,000
Production costs			
Actual production 12,000 units			
Direct materials:			
Material A 8,000 kg at £0.20	1,600		
Material B 5,000 kgs at £0.80	4,000		
		5,600	
Direct labour:			
Skilled 6,000 hours at £2.95	17,700		
Semi-skilled 3,150 hours at £2.60	8,190		
		25,890	
Overhead cost:			
Fixed		9,010	
Variable 12,000 units at £0.625		7,500	
		48,000	
Add Opening stock			
1,000 units at £4		4,000	
		52,000	
Deduct Closing stock		8,000	
Cost of goods sold			44,000
	'Actual profit'		10,000

In the above statement stock is valued at the standard cost of £4 per unit.

Required
There is general satisfaction because the budgeted profit level has been achieved but you have been asked to prepare a standard costing statement analysing the differences between the budget and the actual performance. In your analysis, include calculations of the sales volume and sales price variances and the following cost variances: direct material price, mix, yield and usage variances; direct labour rate, mix, productivity and efficiency variances; and overhead spending and volume variances.   *(17 marks)*
                                                                                          (22 marks)

Provide a commentary on the variances and give your views on their usefulness.   *(5 marks)*

2.   *In the last quarter of 1985/6 it is estimated that YNQ will have produced and sold 20,000 units of their main product by the end of the year. At this level of activity it is estimated that the average unit cost will be:*

		£
Direct material		30
Direct labour		10
Overhead:	Fixed	10
	Variable	10
		60

This is in line with the standards set at the start of the year. The management accountant of YNQ is now preparing the budget for 1986/7. He has incorporated into his preliminary calculations the following expected cost increases:

	%
Raw material: price increase of	20
Direct labour: wage rate increase of	5
Variable overhead: increase of	5
Fixed overhead: increase of	25

The production manager believes that if a cheaper grade of raw material were to be used, this would enable the direct material cost per unit to be kept to £31.25 for 1986/7. The cheaper material would, however, lead to a reject rate estimated at 5% of the completed output and it would be necessary to introduce an inspection stage at the end of the manufacturing process to identify the faulty items. The cost of this inspection process would be £40,000 per year (including £10,000 allocation of existing factory overhead).

Established practice has been to reconsider the product's selling price at the time the budget is being prepared. The selling price is normally determined by adding a mark-up of 50% to unit cost. On this basis the product's selling price for 1985/86 has been £90 but the sales manager is worried about the implications of continuing the cost plus 50% rule for 1986/7. He estimates that demand for the product varies with price as follows:

Price:	£80	£84	£88	£90	£92	£96	£100
Demand ('000)	25	23	21	20	19	17	15

(a) You are required to decide whether YNQ should use the regular or the cheaper grade of material and to calculate the best price for the product, the optimal level of production and the profit that this should yield. Comment briefly on the sensitivity of the solution to possible errors in the estimates.   *(14 marks)*

(b) Indicate how one might obtain the answer to part (a) from an appropriately designed cost-volume-profit graph. You should design such a graph as part of your answer but the graph need not be drawn to scale providing that it demonstrates the main features of the approach that you would use.   *(8 marks)*
                                                                                          (22 marks)

3.   *The management of Alliance Engineering & Manufacturing Company Limited produce a range of components and products. They are considering next year's production, purchases and sales budgets. Shown below are the budgeted total unit costs for two of the components and two of the products manufactured by the company.*

	Component 12	Component 14	Product VW	Product XY
	£ per unit	£ per unit	£ per unit	£ per unit
Direct material	18	26	12	28
Direct labour	16	4	12	24
Variable overhead	8	2	6	12
Fixed overhead	20	5	15	30
	62	37	45	94

Components 12 and 14 are incorporated into other products manufactured and sold by the company, but they are not incorporated into the two products shown above.

It is possible to purchase components 12 and 14 from other companies for £60 per unit and £30 per unit respectively.

The current selling prices of products VW and XY are £33 and £85 respectively.

Your are required to:

(a) Evaluate, clearly indicating all the assumptions you make as to whether it would be profitable in the year ahead for the company to:

(i) purchase either of the components;
(ii) sell either of the above products. *(12 marks)*

(b) Prepare statements for management with supporting explanations as to how the following additional information would affect your evaluation in (a) above if next year's production requirements for the two components are 7,000 units of component 12 and 6,000 units of component 14 and the budgeted sales for the two products VW and XY are 5,000 units and 4,000 units respectively when a special machine, a MAC, is required.

The MAC machine is needed exclusively for these two components and two products because of specific customer requirements but for technical reasons the machine can only be used for a maximum of 80,000 hours in the year.

The budgeted MAC usage for any one year is 80,000 hours and requirements per unit for the various items are as follows:

Component 12	8 machine hours
Component 14	2 machine hours
Product VW	6 machine hours
Product XY	12 machine hours

The operating costs of the MAC machine have been included in the unit costs shown in (a) above.

(10 marks)
(22 marks)

4. (a) Write brief notes on your understanding of the following:

(i) absorption costs;
(ii) discretionary costs;
(iii) average variable costs.*(9 marks)*

(b) Price level changes have made it necessary for companies to formalise within their management accounting systems methods to enable them to cope with such movements.

Evaluate briefly the main effects that price level changes have in the use of accounting information in the decision-making process. *(8 marks)*
(17 marks)

5. (a) Explain the specific roles of planning, motivation and evaluation in a system of budgetary control.
(7 marks)

(b) 'Developments in information technology have significant effects on the accountant use of mathematical modelling',

Describe five areas in which the use of mathematical modelling using computers might benefit management accounting. *(10 marks)*
(17 marks)

ACCA MOCK EXAMINATIONS
COMMENTARY
ANSWERS

COMMENTARY ON MOCK EXAMINATION NO 1

The five questions were selected from recent ACCA examinations and the mix of topics is broadly representative of typical examinations. It will be realised that no one examination can cover *all* the topics in the syllabus so that if you found that these particular topics suited you make sure that it was because you were fully prepared across the *whole* syllabus and not merely lucky.

The topics covered included:

Production budgets - quantity and financial
Transfer pricing
Expected profit
Discussion on service department costs and charging
Discussion on behavioural aspects of budgeting.

It will be seen that the paper included a mix of numeric and discussion questions which again is typical. Do not neglect parts of questions which require some comment on the data provided in the question or on the calculations you have made. Although there appears to be only a few marks involved - for example 1(c) is worth 8 marks - these marks can often be picked up fairly easily.

In general, remember that the first few marks of a question are the easiest to obtain. It is invariably true that you can obtain five marks more readily from a new question rather than attempting to improve your mark from 15 to a maximum of 20 for a question upon which you have already spent a considerable time. This point should be kept in mind if you find yourself pressed for time with a question yet unattempted. It is hoped however, that you do not find yourself in this situation because, as a well prepared student, you should have planned the time you spend on each question.

It is always good examination practice to give relevant examples from your own experience wherever the question is appropriate. Remember though, that this only works if the experience you can relate is truly relevant to the exact requirements of the question.

The shotgun approach, whereby everything is thrown into an answer regardless of its relevance cannot be recommended. It is worth stressing yet again the most frequent comment made in examiners' reports, ie candidates do not answer the questions set!

A final comment regarding your answers to cost and management accounting (and other examinations) is to pay attention to the standard of English, the layout of answers - particularly where tables, accounts or reports are required - and to make sure that your writing is legible.

1. (a)

Preliminary calculations

	Machine A		Machine B	
Manned hours	1,610		1,610	
Less Idle time	322	(20%)	483	(30%)
Productive hours	1,288		1,127	

The opening stocks will be used first and then the productive hours will be used thus:

	A (hours)	B (hours)
Product Y (25,000 m @ 200 cm)		500
Product X (50,160 m @ 160 cm)		627
Product X (60,000 m @ 120 cm)	600	
Product Y (82,560 m @ 100 cm)	688	
= Productive hours	1,288	1,127

This production totals 284,816 square metres but the available 545 kilos of dye can dye 272,500 square metres only. This leaves a shortfall of (284,816 - 272,500) 12,316 square metres which limits production of the narrowest width, ie 100 cm by 12,316 m.

The budgets are thus:

	Production	Sales
X (at 160 cm)	50,160 m	50,160 m
X (at 120 cm)	60,000 m	90,000 m
Y (at 200 cm)	25,000 m	30,000 m
Y (at 100 cm)	70,244 m	70,244 m

(b)

	Purchase budget (square metres)		
	Machine A	Machine B	
Output:			
Product Y		50,000	
Product X		80,256	
Product X	72,000		
Product Y	70,244		
	142,244	130,256	
Process loss	10%	20%	Total
Input area	158,049	162,820	320,869
		+ closing stock (10%)	32,087
			352,956
		− Opening stock	25,000
		= Purchases budget	327,956

(c)   Possible ways of meeting forecast:

(i)   obtain more dye or get better usage from existing quantities;
(ii)   reduce idle time;
(iii) increase machine capacity by overtime working;
(iv)   sub-contract machining or dyeing.

2.   (a)

	Intermediate division			
Products	A	B	C	Total
Minimum production	10,000	10,000	10,000	
	£	£	£	£
Contribution/unit	13	8	20	
Total contribution	130,000	80,000	200,000	410,000
Plus contribution from best product, ie C				
Surplus capacity:				
20,000 x £20				400,000
				810,000

	Final division			
	X	Y	Z	
Units	10,000	10,000	10,000	
	£	£	£	
Contribution/unit	26	30	14	
Total contribution	260,000	300,000	420,000	980,000
			Total contribution	1,790,000
			Less fixed costs	625,000
			Company profit	£1,165,000

(b)   *Final division viewpoint*

From (a) it will be seen that Y produces the largest contribution so that above the specified minima the surplus capacity should be used to produce Y.

	X	Y	Z	
Production	10,000	10,000 + 20,000	10,000	
	£	£	£	£
Contribution/unit	26	30	14	
Total contribution	260,000	900,000	140,000	1,300,000
Plus contribution from intermediate division	A	B	C	
Product	10,000	30,000	10,000	
	£	£	£	
Contribution/unit	13	8	20	
Total contribution	130,000	240,000	200,000	570,000
		Total company contribution		1,870,000
		Less fixed costs		625,000
		Profit		£1,245,000

(c) *Product mix to maximise company profits*

Contributions:	A= £13	B = £8	C = £20
	X= £26	Y = £30	Z = £14
Total	£39	£38	£34

Units to maximise contribution:

	30,000	10,000	10,000	£
Contribution	£1,170,000	380,000	340,000	1,890,000
			Less fixed costs	625,000
			Total profit	£1,265,000

Thus A and X are most profitable.

(d) For Intermediate the most profitable plan is shown in (a), ie 10,000. A, 10,000, B and 30,000 C selling 20,000 C outside.

£

Divisional contribution 810,000

For the final the best plan is (b) above, ie sell 10,000 X, 30,000 Y and 10,000 Z and buy 20,000 B outside.

Divisional contribution	1,300,000
Company contribution	2,110,000
Less fixed costs	625,000
Total profit	1,485,000

Thus the profit of £1,485,000 should be compared with the profit of £1,265,000 in (c) showing that there is a (1.485 m - 1.265 m) £120,000 loss from an internal transfer policy.

(e) This can be taken from the manual. Main points are: conflict of divisional and corporate goals, need to ensure goal congruence, encourage initiative, fair assessment of profits especially where pay is related to performance.

3. (a)

Cost/profit statement

	80%		100%		120%	
Output level	40,000		50,000		60,000	
Quantities	*Total*	*Unit*	*Total*	*Unit*	*Total*	*Unit*
	£	£	£	£	£	£
Variable costs:						
Direct materials	180,000	4.50	225,000	4.50	270,000	4.50
Direct wages	120,000	3.00	150,000	3.00	180,000	3.00
Direct expenses	52,000	1.30	65,0000	1.30	78,000	1.30
	352,000	8.80	440,000	8.80	528,000	8.80
Semi-variable costs:						
Indirect materials	46,800	1.17	47,000	0.94	74,400	1.24
Indirect wages	51,200	1.28	55,000	1.10	72,000	1.20
Indirect expenses	6,000	0.15	8,000	0.16	9,600	0.16
	456,000	11.40	550,000	11.00	684,000	11.40
Fixed costs	60,000	1.50	60,000	1.20	60,000	1.00
Total costs	516,000	12.90	610,000	12.20	744,000	12.40
Sales price of £16 per unit	640,000	16.00	800,000	16.00	960,000	16.00
Profit	124,000	3.10	190,000	3.80	216,000	3.60

Comments

(i) The 80% level for the contract would not be worthwhile as it is less than the amount earned from existing small contracts.

(ii) The greatest profit per unit is at the normal 100% level due to the semi-variable costs being lowest at that point.

(b)   *Expected material cost*

$(0.5 \times 4.50) + (0.3 \times 5) + (0.2 \times £5.50) = £4.85$

It will be noted that this is $(£4.85 - £4.50)$ 35p more than the original price.

Expected profit calculations:

Contract size	Original profit £	–	Extra material cost £	=	New profit £
40,000	124,000	–	(40,000 x 0.35)	=	110,000
50,000	190,000	–	(50,000 x 0.35)	=	172,500
60,000	216,000	–	(60,000 x 0.35)	=	195,000

Expected profit = $(0.4 \times 110,000) + (0.5 \times 172,500) + (0.1 \times 195,000) = £149,750$

4.   (a)   Typical of the aims are:

(i)   Is the service department providing the service as effectively as possible?
(ii)   Do user departments use the service provided in the most economical way?
(iii) Does the pricing system used to charge out the service encourage efficiency both in the department providing the service and the user?

If the cost are too high either because of excessive and unnecessary usage or poor management in the service department then product cost will increase and profits lost.

A poor standard of service may cause hold-ups and inefficiencies which, apart from increasing costs, will have adverse motivational effects.

The call on the service is likely to be influenced by the charging system used. Too cheap and the user departments may use the service wastefully; too dear (eg, at full cost) and the service department will have little incentive to control their costs.

(b)   Charging bases.

(i)   **Total actual cost.** This would mean all costs are passed to the user department which may cause wastefulness in control of the service department.

(ii)   **Standard absorption cost.** This charge reflects the planned level of activity and efficiency. It provides a measure of control in the service department through variance analysis. Also a standard cost enables the user departments to plan their own costs more effectively.

(iii) **Variable cost.** This avoids the arbitrary process of absorbing fixed costs into cost units and retains the fixed costs in the service department where they are incurred. A low (ie variable only) charge may encourage wasteful usage.

(iv)   **Opportunity cost.** This would be presumably set at the level at which the service could be obtained externally. Theoretically this could lead to more informed decision making by the user departments but there is the very real problem of determining a realistic opportunity cost in all but the simplest cases.

(v)   **No charge.** This could lead to excessive and wasteful use of the service but may be useful where management wish to stimulate demand for a given service.

5.   (a)   (i)   **Budget slack.** Slack represents inefficiency and is sub-optimal for the company as a whole. To an extent a zero-based approach can improve the problem. It usually results from the budget bargaining process where there is poor information and/or strong personalities in the system.

(ii)   **Budget standard setting.** The standard of performance included in the budgets has an important behavioural effect on those concerned. Management are concerned about the level set which can adversely or favourably influence the way their performance is viewed.

(iii) **Short-term v long-term objectives.** Budgeting is a short-term process and sole reliance on budgeting (rather than long-range or corporate planning) will tend to emphasise short-term factors, eg cost levels, to the detriment of long-term factors such as market share, the environment, product quality, research and development, staff training and so on.

(b) This can be taken from the manual.

COMMENTARY ON MOCK EXAMINATION NO 2

General comments on the recommended approach to examinations have been given in the commentary to Mock Examination No 1 and these repay close study.

The topics covered in this paper included:

Variance analysis
Material selection and sensitivity analysis
Purchase and sales budgets
Discussion on cost types and inflation
Discussion on budgeting and mathematical modelling.

1.

Budget – actual analysis

		£	£
Budgeted profit			10,000
Plus sales volume variance		1,000	
Less sales price Var. (4,000 @ 25p)		1,000	
			10,000

Cost variances		£+	£-
Price	A 8,000 (0.3 - 0.2)	800	
	B 5,000 (0.7 - 0.8)		500
Mix	A (6,500 - 8,000) 0.3		450
	B (6,500 - 5,000) 0.7	1,050	
Yield	A (6,000 - 6,500) 0.3		150
	B (6,000 - 6,500) 0.7		350

Direct labour

Rate			
Skilled	6,000 (3 - 2.9)	300	
Unskilled	3,150 (2.5 - 2.6)		315
Mix			
Skilled	(5,799 - 6,000) 3		603
Unskilled	(3,351 - 3,150) 2.5	503	
Productivity			
Skilled	(5,400 - 5,799) 3		1,197
Unskilled	(3,120 - 3,351) 2.5		578

Overheads

Fixed spending (10,000 - 9,010)	990	
Volume 2,000 x £1	2,000	
Variable 12,000 (0.5 - 0.625)		1,500
	5,643	5,643

Actual profit   £10,000

Notes: The usage variances comprise the mix and yield variances:

A = £450 + £150 = £600 ADV
B = £1,050 - £350 = £700 FAV

The efficiency variance are the total of the mix and productivity variances:

Skilled   = £603 + 1,197 = £1,800 ADV
Unskilled   = £503 - £578   = £75 ADV

Most general points regarding variances can be taken from the manual. Special note should be made about the uninformative nature of mix and yield variances for each type of input. It is the *overall* effect on costs which is important. Similar remarks apply to the mix and productivity labour variances.

2.

Unit variable cost 1986/7

	Regular £	Cheaper £
Material	36.00	31.25
Labour	10.50	10.50
Variable overhead	10.50	10.50
	57.00	52.25
Wastage 52.25 x $\frac{5}{95}$		2.75
	£57.00	£55.00

Contribution/profit statements
Regular material

Price	£80	£84	£88	£90	£92	£96	£100
Demand ('000)	25	23	21	20	19	17	15
Revenue (£'000)	2,000	1,932	1,848	1,800	1,748	1,632	1,500
Var costs (£'000)	1,425	1,311	1,197	1,140	1,083	969	855
Contribution	575	621	651	660	665	663	645

Cheaper material

Revenue	2,000	1,932	1,848	1,800	1,748	1,632	1,500
Variable cost	1,375	1,265	1,155	1,100	1,045	935	825
Contribution	625	667	693	700	703	697	675
Extra overhead	30	30	30	30	30	30	30
Profit	595	637	663	670	673	667	645

This indicates that at all levels the cheaper grade material produces greater profits except at the 15,000 level. Thus the optimum solution is a price of £92 giving a demand of 19,000 units using the cheaper material. This solution will yield a profit of £673,000 - 1.25 (200,000) = £423,000 before making the £10,000 charge for existing overheads.

The solution will alter with relatively minor errors in the forecasts. For example, a 1% charge in the reject rate for the cheaper material would cause the regular to be worthwhile. Also if the demand figures altered slightly for the various prices the optimal policy would change as will be seen from the analysis above, the choice of a price in the £90 - £96 range has only a small effect on profit.

(b) See graph

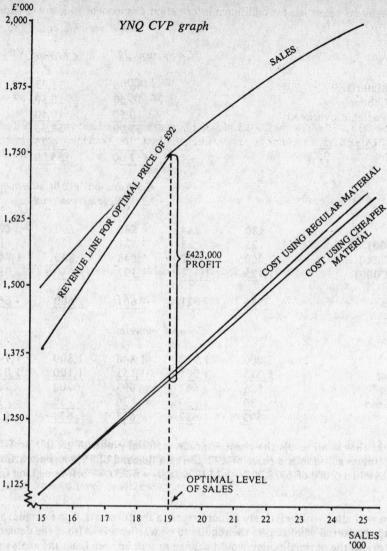

£'000

YNQ CVP graph

2,000

1,875

1,750

REVENUE LINE FOR OPTIMAL PRICE OF £92

SALES

£423,000
PROFIT

COST USING REGULAR MATERIAL

COST USING CHEAPER MATERIAL

1,625

1,500

1,375

1,250

OPTIMAL LEVEL
OF SALES

1,125

15   16   17   18   19   20   21   22   23   24   25

SALES
'000

3.   (a) *Contribution statement:*

	Component 12	Component 14	Product VW	Product XY
	£	£	£	£
Variable cost	42	32	30	64
Purchase price	60	30	–	–
Selling price	–	–	33	85
Saving (loss)	18	(2)	–	–
Contribution			3	21

Conclusions – make component 12, buy component 14, produce and sell VW and XY but where possible concentrate on XY.

Assumptions:

(i)   that fixed costs will not alter and variable cost are truly variable;

(ii)   that buying in component 14 will not cause any additional costs for inspection etc, or any labour problem;

(iii) that there are no other more profitable products which might be displaced.

(b) The statements below use the additional information. Component 14 is not considered because it will always be bought in.

MAC requirements:	Component 12	Product VW	Product XY
Production required	7,000	5,000	4,000
M/C time (hours)	56,000	30,000	48,000

Thus (56,000 + 30,000 + 48,000) 134,000 hours are required but only 80,000 available so there is a shortfall so that MAC hours are a *limiting factor*. Thus the best plan would be to rank in order of contribution per MAC hour thus:

	Component 12	Product VX	Product XY
	£	£	£
Savings/contribution	18	3	21
MAC hours	8	6	12
£/hour	£ 2.25	£0.50	£1.75
Ranking	1	3	2

Thus produce all component 12 and use the balance of hours for XY.

Component 12 = 7,000 x 8 = 56,000 hours used so that 24,000 hours remain. At 12 hours per unit of XY, 2,000 units can be made and sold.

Summary

7,000 component 12
2,000 product XY

4. (a) (i) **Absorption costs** - this can be taken directly from the manual.

   (ii) **Discretionary costs** - these are any type of costs about which there is management discretion. Examples include; research and development, advertising and so on. Unlike, say, power costs, which have a direct relationship with production levels, discretionary costs do not have a direct link. This means that there is no easy way to determine what the level should be or whether the expenditure is worthwhile.

   (iii) **Average variable costs** - (also known as marginal costs) these can be taken directly from the manual.

5. (a) Can be taken directly from the manual.

   (b) Virtually any area of management accounting could benefit from computer based mathematical modelling.

   Specific examples include:

   (i)   cash forecasting using spread sheets;
   (ii) budget analysis using different cost/value/inflation etc, figures;
   (iii) all forms of decision-making using cost/volume/profit analysis;
   (iv) production planning using optimising LP models;
   (v)   forecasting using statistical techniques.

   In all cases the use of the computer enables many more options to be explored, sensitivity analysis to be carried out and more realistic non-linear relationships to be explored.

458

Index

NOTES

NOTES

NOTES

NOTES

NOTES

NOTES

NOTES

NOTES

NOTES

NOTES

NOTES

NOTES

NOTES

NOTES

NOTES